Modern Derivatives Pricing and Credit Exposure Analysis

Modern Derivatives Pricing and Credit Exposure Analysis

Theory and Practice of CSA and XVA Pricing, Exposure Simulation and Backtesting

Roland Lichters, Roland Stamm, Donal Gallagher

palgrave
macmillan

First published 2015 by
PALGRAVE MACMILLAN

Palgrave Macmillan in the UK is an imprint of Macmillan Publishers Limited, registered in England, company number 785998, of Houndmills, Basingstoke, Hampshire RG21 6XS.

Palgrave Macmillan in the US is a division of St Martin's Press LLC, 175 Fifth Avenue, New York, NY 10010.

Palgrave Macmillan is the global academic imprint of the above companies and has companies and representatives throughout the world.

Palgrave® and Macmillan® are registered trademarks in the United States, the United Kingdom, Europe and other countries

ISBN: 978–1–137–49483–2

This book is printed on paper suitable for recycling and made from fully managed and sustained forest sources. Logging, pulping and manufacturing processes are expected to conform to the environmental regulations of the country of origin.

A catalogue record for this book is available from the British Library.

A catalog record for this book is available from the Library of Congress.

To our families

Contents

List of Figures

List of Tables

Preface

The past ten years have seen an incredible change in the pricing of derivatives, a change which has not ended yet. One major driver for the change was the credit crisis which started in 2007 with the near bankruptcy of Bear Stearns, reached a first climax with the implosion of the US housing market and the banking world's downfall, and then turned into a sovereign debt crisis in Europe. While the worst seems to be over, the situation is far from normal: Central banks around the globe have injected highly material amounts of cash into a system which is still struggling to find its way back to growth and prosperity. The spectre of developed country sovereign default has become an ever present and unwelcome guest. As with many other crises, people learnt from this one that they had made serious mistakes in pricing OTC derivatives: Neglecting the credit risk and funding led to mispricing. The second major driver, which was itself triggered by the banks' heavy losses and the near-death experience of the entire financial system, is *regulation*. Banks are or soon will be forced to standardize derivatives more, clearing them through a Central Counterparty (CCP) whenever possible, thus increasing the transparency and, supposedly, robustness of the derivatives markets. Derivatives that are not cleared are penalized by increased capital requirements. Dealers are therefore caught in a bind: They either face increased funding costs due to the initial margin that has to be posted to the CCP, or higher capital costs if they trade over the counter.

A time-travelling expert for financial derivatives pricing from the year 2005 who ended up in 2015 would rub her eyes in disbelief at what has happened since then:

- The understanding of what the risk-free rate should be has changed completely. The tenor basis spread, which was a rather esoteric area of research, has turned into a new risk factor with the bankruptcy of a LIBOR bank.
- The counterparty credit risk of derivatives, which was noted but viewed to be of little relevance by the majority of banks, became a major driver of losses during the crisis and has found its way into new regulation and accounting standards in the form of value adjustments and additional capital charges.
- Features of a collateral agreement such as options regarding what collateral to post and in which currency, thresholds and minimum transfer amounts, call frequency, independent amounts, etc. have an impact on the valuation of derivatives. First of all, they turn a portfolio of individually priced trades into a bulk that has to be valued as one. Second, they make the valuation of such a portfolio unique.

- With the implosion of the repo market in the aftermath of Lehman's default came the realization that funding is not for free, and that hedging creates funding costs. The regulators enforce or strongly incentivize the usage of central clearing wherever possible. Initial margins, which are mandatory when dealing with central counterparties, hit both sides of a trade, increasing the funding requirements for hedges even further. These funding costs result in more value adjustments.
- The higher capital requirements and additional charges lead to extra costs for derivatives trading which make yet another value adjustment necessary.

As a consequence, a bank running a large book of derivatives has to be able to compute all these value adjustments – which are usually summarized under the acronym *XVA* – by simulating a large number of risk factors over a large time horizon in order to compute exposures, funding costs and capital charges for a portfolio. Capital for market risk is based on value-at-risk-like numbers, as is the initial margin; it is thus clear that on top of exposure at each time point on each simulation path, one has to compute risk numbers as well. As if that was not enough, it is also more and more important to compute the sensitivities of the adjustments to the input parameters.

The challenge in this computation is to control the following aspects:

1. Accuracy: Of course we want the numbers to be as accurate as necessary. That means that we need models that are complex enough to give good prices for time zero pricing. The accuracy is naturally limited by the uncertainties in the parameters that are fed into the models; see point 4 below.
2. Speed: Depending on the usage of the results – monthly accounting numbers, night batch for risk reporting, or near-time pricing for trading decisions – it is important that the calculations are done with the best possible performance. This need for speed obviously clashes with the requirement for accuracy.
3. Consistency: At least for internal models, the regulator has to approve the models used for exposure calculation, which means they also have to pass backtesting.
4. Uncertainty: Many of the input parameters, like future funding costs, funding strategies and capital requirements, are unknown at the time of pricing. Different assumptions can lead to largely different adjustment values. Key inputs such as probability of default and loss given defaults (or CDS spreads and recovery rates) may not be available for all derivative counterparties so that one has to resort to proxies ("similar" names) or historical estimates. This significant uncertainty puts the accuracy of pricing models for XVA into perspective and might justify relatively basic pricing approaches.
5. Model Risk: A sizeable derivatives portfolio contains a significant number of risk factors which, contrary to single trade pricing, have to be simulated in a simultaneous risk factor evolution, whose calibration is a numerical challenge.

The time horizon of the exposure calculation for a typical portfolio is measured in decades, sometimes as far as 50 years or more. The model risk inherent in each individual risk factor's evolution model accumulates at the portfolio level. Choosing simpler models to gain performance adds to that.

The aim of this book is to address the first three points in as much detail as possible. We present at least one model for each asset class – interest rates, foreign exchange, inflation, credit, equity and commodity – which satisfies the requirement for (reasonable) accuracy and yet allows for a well-performing implementation. For credit and inflation we present alternative models and discuss the advantages of each over the others. To boost performance further, we explain different approaches to prevent simulations or complex grid calculations embedded into the risk factor simulation (American Monte Carlo) or brute force computations of sensitivities by shifting each input risk factor individually (Algorithmic Differentiation). We also explain how to bridge the gap between risk-neutral pricing and real-world backtesting.

While it is impossible to get rid of the uncertainty and model risk inherent in long-term exposure simulations and XVA computations, we want to enable the reader to fully comprehend the assumptions and choices behind the models and the calculation approaches, so he or she can make an informed decision as to model choice, implementation and calibration.

The subject of this book makes it necessary to use mathematics extensively – never trust people who say they have a simple solution for a complex problem. We have put some background material into the large Appendix, but this is not a book from which to learn financial mathematics from scratch. For an introduction into the field of stochastic calculus we recommend the text book by Steven Shreve [136]; for an overview of the vast landscape of interest rate, foreign exchange, inflation and credit models, their calibration and the pricing of various financial products, see, for example, Brigo & Mercurio's text book [33], Hunt & Kennedy [91], or the comprehensive treatise on interest rate modelling by Andersen and Piterbarg [8] – to name a few, all important training grounds and sources of inspiration for the authors. Regarding the Monte Carlo simulation techniques we present here (and which we have used extensively in our professional life), we refer the reader to the texts by Glassermann [70] and Jaeckel [95]. This book can be seen as a sequel to the book [107] by Kenyon & Stamm, which gave an overview of many of the topics we present here. Nevertheless, this text is far more detailed as to the risk factor modelling, and of course includes the significant advances that derivatives pricing has seen over the past three years.

The book is organized in five parts. The first part, Discounting, describes the basis for the pricing of all financial instruments: How to compute the value of future cash flows, that is discounting. After a brief review of pre-crisis pricing, we explain the pricing under a central clearing regime (aka OIS discounting), for full collateralization in a currency that is different from the trade currency (which we refer to as *global discounting*), and finally for collateral agreements that contain certain options (aka CSA discounting). The final Chapter 6 in Part I describes how Fair Value Hedge Accounting under IFRS may be handled in a multi-curve world.

In Part II, Credit and Debit Value Adjustment, we lay the foundations for understanding CVA and DVA. After the basic definitions we present examples of CVA for single, uncollateralized trades.

The third part, Risk Factor Evolution, is the largest and at the same time the most technical part of the book. It contains one chapter per asset class which describes in great detail how to model the risk factors for the purpose of exposure calculation. While there are many instances where we combine the respective asset class with interest rate and FX modelling, this part is still mostly devoted to the individual asset classes.

Part IV on XVA starts with a description of a framework that comprises all the various asset classes together. It then investigates the impact of netting and collateral on the exposure simulation. Chapter 18 then introduces American Monte Carlo, and Chapter 19 Algorithmic Differentiation. The final two chapters are devoted to the funding value adjustment (FVA) and the capital value adjustment (KVA) mentioned before.

The last part, Credit Risk, looks at the "classic" credit risk rather than the pricing component linked to counterparty credit risk that is CVA. This notion of credit risk deserves special attention because of the key role it plays for the regulators. One of the great challenges in this area is the combination of market-conforming pricing and the correctness of risk factor predictions. We look at credit portfolio products in Chapter 23, since products such as Asset Backed Securities (ABS) and Collateralized Loan Obligations (CLO) are enjoying greater popularity again after an extended pause following the 2008 events. We then move on to the Basel regulations regarding capital for derivatives in Chapter 24, and close with Chapter 25 on backtesting.

Acknowledgements

This book would not have been possible without the contributions of the Quaternion team over the past five years – Sarp Kaya Acar, Francis Duffy, Paul Giltinan, Michael McCarthy, Niall O'Sullivan, Gearoid Ryan, Henning Segger and Markus Trahe – in working out the theoretical foundations as well as implementing and testing many of the models and methods presented in this book.

We are also grateful for valuable comments on the manuscript by Peter Caspers, Marcus R. W. Martin and Norbert Patzschke.

Furthermore, we would like to thank the administrators, authors, contributors and sponsors of QuantLib, the free/open-source library for quantitative finance [2], for almost 15 years of continuous effort put into the development and support of this invaluable financial modelling toolbox. We could not have built the software which produced the examples shown in this text without QuantLib at its core.

And finally, without the appreciation and support of our families we would simply not have been able to mobilize the time for putting together this text.

List of Abbreviations and Symbols

$\mathbb{1}_{\{\tau \in M\}}$	Indicator function, $= 1$ if $\tau(\omega) \in M$, 0 else
$\lambda(t)$	Default intensity (hazard rate) process
τ	Stopping or default time
X^+	Positive value of X: $X^+ = \max(X, 0) = X - X^-$
X^-	Negative value of X: $X^- = \min(X, 0) = X - X^+$
ABS	Asset-Backed Security
BK	Black-Karasinski
CDO	Collateralized Debt Obligation
CDS	Credit Default Swap
CIR	Cox-Ingersoll-Ross
CLO	Collateralized Loan Obligation
JCIR	Cox-Ingersoll-Ross with Jumps
LGD	Loss Given Default
PD	Probability of Default
PK	Peng-Kou
DK	Dodgson-Kainth
HW	Hull-White
JY	Jarrow-Yildirim
LGM	Linear Gauss-Markov
LMM	LIBOR Market Model

$\delta(s, t)$	The length of the time period between s and t in years
δ_i	The length of period i (usually from t_{i-1} to t_i) in years
$r(t), r_t$	The risk-free interest rate at time 0 for maturity t
$R(t, T)$	The stochastic interest rate at time t for maturity $T > t$
$r^s(t), r^s_t$	The stochastic short rate at time t
$B(t), B_t$	The bank account process
$df(t), df_t$	The deterministic discount factor at time 0 for maturity t
$D(t, T)$	The stochastic discount factor at time t for maturity $T > t$
$P(t, T)$	The price of a zero bond with maturity $T > t$ as seen at time t
$f^\delta(t; S, T)$	The forward rate for the period from S to T, as seen at time t, for tenor δ
AAD	Adjoint Algorithmic Differentiation

AD	Automatic Differentiation or Algorithmic Differentiation
AfS	Assets for Sale
AMC	American Monte Carlo
ATM	At-the-Money
CCP	Central Counterparty (aka Clearing House)
CCR	Counterparty Credit Risk
CEM	Current Exposure Method
CPI	Consumer Price Index
CRD IV	Fourth Capital Requirements Directive
CRR	Capital Requirements Regulation
CSA	Credit Support Annex
DRV	Deutscher Rahmenvertrag (German CSA variant)
EAD	Exposure at Default
EE	Expected Exposure
EEE	Effective Expected Exposure
EEPE	Effective Expected Positive Exposure
ENE	Expected Negative Exposure
EPE	Effective Positive Exposure
FRA	Forward Rate Agreement
FRN	Floating Rate Note
FVHA	Fair Value Hedge Accounting
GBM	Geometric Brownian Motion
IMM	Internal Model Method
ISDA	International Swaps and Derivatives Association
ITM	In-the-Money
LGD	Loss Given Default
LPI	Limited Price Indexation
MC	Monte Carlo
NPV	Net Present Value
OCI	Other Comprehensive Income
OIS	Overnight-Indexed Swap
OTM	Out of the Money
PD	Probability of Default
PDE	Partial Differential Equation
PFE	Potential Future exposure
RFE	Risk Factor Evolution
SA-CCR	Standard Approach for Counterparty Credit Risk
SDE	Stochastic Differential Equation
VaR	Value at Risk
WWR	Wrong-Way Risk
YoYIIC	Year-on-Year Inflation-Indexed Cap

YoYIIS	Year-on-Year Inflation-Indexed Swap
ZCIIB	Zero Coupon Inflation-Indexed Bond
ZCIIC	Zero Coupon Inflation-Indexed Cap
ZCIIS	Zero Coupon Inflation-Indexed Swap

$\mathbb{P}$	Arbitrary probability measure, often the real-world measure
$\mathbb{E}$	Expectation under $\mathbb{P}$
$\mathbb{V}$	Variance under $\mathbb{P}$
$\mathbb{E}(\cdot, \mathcal{F}_t), \mathbb{E}_t$	Expectation conditional on $\mathcal{F}_t$
$\mathbb{Q}^N$	Risk-neutral measure associated with numeraire N
$\mathbb{E}^N$	Expectation under $\mathbb{Q}^N$
$\mathcal{F}_t$	Filtration containing market information excluding defaults
$\mathcal{G}_t$	Filtration containing market information including defaults
PIT	Probability Integral Transform
$W(t), W_t$	Standard Wiener process (Brownian Motion) at time t, adapted to $\mathcal{F}_t$
$W^{\mathbb{Q}}(t), W_t^{\mathbb{Q}}$	Standard Wiener process at time t under measure $\mathbb{Q}$
$W^N(t), W_t^N$	Standard Wiener process at time t under measure $\mathbb{Q}^N$ associated with numeraire N
AVA	Additional Value Adjustment
CVA	Credit Value Adjustment
DVA	Debit Value Adjustment
FBA	Funding Benefit Adjustment
FCA	Funding Cost Adjustment
FVA	Funding Value Adjustment
KVA	Capital Value Adjustment
MPR	Margin Period of Risk
MTA	Minimum Transfer Amount
MVA	Margin Value Adjustment
TVA	Tax Value Adjustment
XVA	One of many Value Adjustments (CVA, DVA, FVA, MVA, KVA, TVA...)

I | Discounting

1 Discounting Before the Crisis

1.1 The risk-free rate

The main ingredient for pricing is the zero curve $r(t)$ which assigns an interest rate to any given maturity $t > 0$. It tells us what the value of 1 currency unit will be at time t if invested at the risk-free rate. For most theoretical applications, the zero rate is expressed as *continuously compounding*, so the value at time t will be given by

$$V(t) = \exp(r(t)t).$$

Other conventions are also common. Linear compounding is typically used for short-term interest (less than one year):

$$V(t) = 1 + t\,r(t).$$

Simple compounding takes interest on interest into account, in particular for maturities beyond one year:

$$V(t) = (1 + r(t))^t.$$

Conversely, today's value of one currency unit paid in t years is given by

$$P(0,t) = \exp(-r(t)t).$$

$P(0,t)$ is the price of a risk-free zero bond with maturity t, as seen today (at time 0). It is also referred to as the (deterministic) discount factor for time t, df_t.

This immediately raises the question: What is the risk-free rate, which is the compensation to lenders for not using their money for consumption immediately? The person or institution making the promise of paying back the money would have to be seen as non-defaultable, no matter what happens. Obviously, such an entity does not exist, so people use proxies like certain highly rated governments or supra-national institutions. Before the near-default of Bear Stearns, people viewed banks that were rated AA or higher as virtually default-free, and therefore used the LIBOR rate as proxies for the risk-free rate.

1.2 Pricing linear instruments

1.2.1 Forward rate agreements

The most important building block in interest rate modelling is the forward rate agreement, or FRA for short. This is a contract by which two parties agree today (at $t = 0$) on an interest rate $f(0;t_1,t_2)$ to be paid in t_2 for a loan spanning a future period t_1 to t_2. If the market (i.e. LIBOR) rate $L(t_1,t_2)$ which is fixed in t_1 for that period exceeds $f(0;t_1,t_2)$, the payer of the rate has made a profit. Otherwise, the receiver gains more than the market rate.

Market practice is that the payment is actually paid in t_1 by computing the cash flow in t_2 and discounting it to t_1 with the fixed LIBOR rate. For pricing purposes, this is virtually irrelevant (see [117]), so we ignore this distinction.

Pricing this correctly is obviously equivalent to predicting the LIBOR rate in a market-accepted manner.

What rate can we expect in three months' time if we want to borrow money for six months at that time? Calculate the forward rate of a 3M into 9M FRA as follows:

- Borrow $df_{0.25} = P(0,0.25)$ units for three months at the risk-free three-month rate
- Invest the money for nine months at the risk-free rate for nine months
- Borrow 1 unit in an FRA in three months (maturing six months later) to pay back the loan with interest
- After another six months, pay back the loan with the $df_{0.25}/df_{0.75}$ from the investment
- By the no-arbitrage principle, the combination has to be worth 0. The forward rate therefore has to be

$$f(0;0.25,0.75) = \frac{df_{0.25} - df_{0.75}}{df_{0.75} \times 0.5}.$$

Note that, in general, the period lengths are not exactly a quarter or half a year but rather depend on the day count fraction of the rates used. In Euroland, this would be ACT/360, for example.

In Figure 1.1, we must have (assuming linear compounding, as is the market custom for periods of less than one year)

$$1 + r(t_0;t_2)\delta_{0,2} = (1 + r(t_0;t_1)\delta_1) \times (1 + f(t_0;t_1,t_2)\delta_2).$$

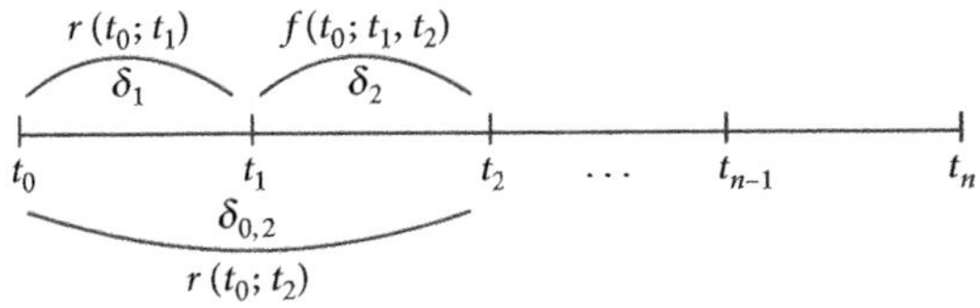

Figure 1.1 Replication of the forward rate

In other words

$$\begin{aligned} f(t_0; t_1, t_2) &= \frac{1}{\delta_2}\left(\frac{1 + r(t_0; t_2)\delta_{0,2}}{1 + r(t_0; t_1)\delta_1} - 1\right) \\ &= \frac{1}{\delta_2}\left(\frac{df_{t_1}}{df_{t_2}} - 1\right). \end{aligned}$$

In general, the forward rate for time t (in years from today) for a period of δ (in years) is given by

$$f(t, t+\delta) = \frac{df_t - df_{t+\delta}}{df_{t+\delta} \times \delta} = \frac{1}{\delta}\left(\frac{df_t}{df_{t+\delta}} - 1\right). \tag{1.1}$$

The present value of the forward rate paid on a notional of 1 unit is therefore

$$f(t, t+\delta) \times df_{t+\delta} \times \delta = df_t - df_{t+\delta}. \tag{1.2}$$

Note that this is true because we use the same discount factors in the forward rate replication as when discounting cash flows. The main assumption in this replication argument is that I (at least a bank) can borrow and lend arbitrary amounts at the risk-free (LIBOR) rate.

We can take a look at what happens if we let δ approach 0 in formula (1.1), under the assumption that the discount curve is differentiable:

$$\begin{aligned} f(t) &:= \lim_{\delta \to 0} f(t, t+\delta) \\ &= \lim_{\delta \to 0} \frac{df_t - df_{t+\delta}}{df_{t+\delta} \times \delta} \\ &= -\frac{1}{df_t}\frac{\partial df_t}{\partial t} \\ &= -\frac{\partial \ln(df_t)}{\partial t}, \end{aligned} \tag{1.3}$$

which also implies that

$$df_t = \exp\left(-\int_0^t f(s)\,ds\right). \tag{1.4}$$

Forward rates are used as expected values for the LIBOR fixing for a future time period. Most importantly, this is done in interest rate swaps.

1.2.2 Interest rate swaps

An interest rate swap, or swap for short, is a contract by which two parties agree to exchange interest payments on a predetermined notional on a regular basis. One party pays the fixed rate with the frequency which is standard in the chosen currency. For EUR, for instance, this is annually; for USD, on the other hand, this is semi-annually. The other party pays a floating rate linked to LIBOR of some given frequency (1, 3, 6 or 12 months), possibly with a spread. There is also a standard frequency for floating legs in most currencies: in EUR, this is six months, and in USD, it is three months, for instance.

At inception, the value of a receiver swap (i.e. from the perspective of the party receiving fixed interest) with notional 1 is therefore given by[1]

$$\begin{aligned} PV = &\ \overbrace{c\sum_{i=1}^{n}\delta_i df_i}^{\text{fixed leg value}} - \overbrace{\sum_{i=1}^{n} f(t_{i-1},t_i)\delta_i df_i}^{\text{floating leg value}} \\ &= c\sum_{i=1}^{n}\delta_i df_i - \sum_{i=1}^{n}(df_i - df_{i-1}) \qquad (1.5) \\ &= c\sum_{i=1}^{n}\delta_i df_i - (df_0 - df_n), \qquad (1.6) \end{aligned}$$

where c is the fixed coupon and t_0 is the spot date. In most currencies, there is a spot lag of two days. The equality in (1.5) assumes that on the float leg, the end date of an interest period is also the start date of the next period.

Formula (1.6) is valid regardless of the payment frequency of the floating leg (or the fixed leg, for that matter). The *par rate* is the one that makes $PV = 0$, i.e.

$$c_0 = \frac{df_0 - df_n}{\sum_{i=1}^{n}\delta_i df_i}. \tag{1.7}$$

[1] This swap is assumed to have no spread on the floating leg, because we want to derive the fair fixed swap rate for a trade that pays LIBOR flat. It is very easy to include the spread in the valuation formula.

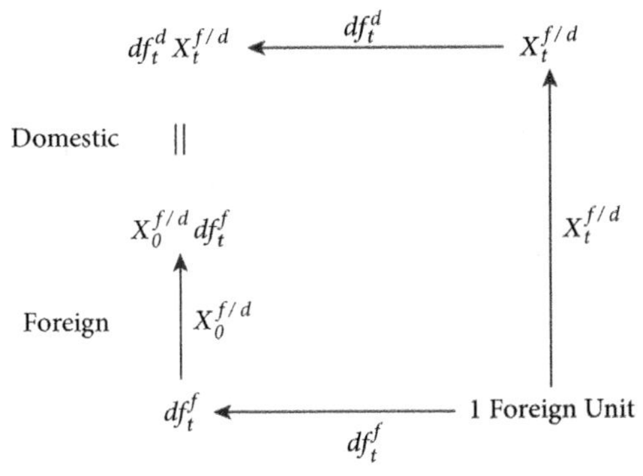

Figure 1.2 The equivalence of discount first, convert after and convert first, discount after is proven by using the no-arbitrage principle

The term $A = \sum \delta_i df_i$ is called the *annuity*[2] of the (fixed leg of the) swap.

1.2.3 FX forwards

In an FX forward, two parties agree to exchange two amounts in two different currencies at a future point in time. FX forward rates are quoted for many currency pairs for as long as ten years maturity. They are usually quoted in *points* that have to be added to the FX spot rate X_0 to get the forward rate X_t for time t.

Figure 1.2 shows us that there are two equivalent ways to price the payment of one foreign currency unit at a future date as of today. That is, we have (d = domestic, f = foreign currency)

$$df_t^f X_0^{f/d} = X_t^{f/d} df_t^d \text{ or } X_t^{f/d} = \frac{df_t^f}{df_t^d} X_0^{f/d}. \tag{1.8}$$

However, this was not exactly true even before the crisis, because even then there was a (small) basis between some currency pairs.

1.2.4 Tenor basis swaps

In a *tenor basis swap*, two parties exchange LIBOR rates, but with different frequencies, e.g. three-month vs six-month LIBOR. From formula (1.6), we see that both legs of such a swap are worth the same at each common reset date, namely

$$PV = df_0 - df_T,$$

[2] It is also sometimes referred to as the basis point value, BPV or PVBP.

where t_0 is the spot date, and T is the final maturity. Therefore, the value of such a swap is 0 at each common reset date. Even before the crisis, there used to be a spread quoted on the leg with the shorter tenor, but this was so small as to be negligible.

1.2.5 Cross-currency basis swaps

In a *cross-currency basis swap*, two parties exchange LIBOR rates, but in different currencies, e.g. 3m USD LIBOR vs 3m EURIBOR. In contrast to single-currency trades, there is a notional exchange at the beginning and the end of the swap. The notional values are chosen such that they reflect the prevailing spot FX rate $X_0^{f/d}$, i.e. $N_d = X_0^{f/d} N_f$. At every fixing date, such a swap should be worth 0, because each leg is worth $N_f(df_0^f - df_T^f + df_T^f) = df_0^f N_f$ in each currency x.

Even before the crisis, there had always been a small cross-currency basis spread on one of the legs for some currency pairs, but these spreads were ignored by many for pricing. For an early exposition on the topic, see for instance [30].

1.3 Curve building

To build a curve from market quotes, we need two or three segments. The first segment consists of money market cash rates, e.g. overnight, tom/next, 1M, 3M, 6M, 9M and 12M. The overnight rate r_{ON} gives us the discount factor to tomorrow:

$$df_{ON} = \frac{1}{1 + r_{ON}\delta_{ON}},$$

where δ_{ON} is the length of the overnight period in years. The tom/next rate r_{TN} gives us the discount factor for the next day:

$$df_{TN} = \frac{df_{ON}}{1 + r_{TN}\delta_{TN}}.$$

All the other money market rates are linearly compounding spot rates, so we have for the period starting in spot and ending in x months:

$$df_{xM} = \frac{df_{TN}}{1 + r_{xM}\delta_{xM}}.$$

We ignore the difference between futures and forwards here. We can use (1.1) to extract discount factors from futures or forward rates by choosing an end date beyond our existing curve. Assume for instance that we already have a 12-month point and want to infer a 15-month point. We use either a three-month forward starting in 12 months or a three-month future expiring in 12 months if that is available. Then we can shuffle the pieces in (1.1) around to get

$$df_{15M} = \frac{df_{12M}}{f\delta_{12M,15M} + 1}.$$

Equation (1.7) can now be used to extend the curve further using quoted swap rates. Note that from here on we need to take the interpolation of the discount curve into account (though possibly earlier), because unless we use the same period length for the fixed as for the floating side, the forward rates needed on the floating side will have gaps.

In the pre-crisis setting we do not have to think about the tenor of the involved instruments: we can use three-month futures, six-month swaps, 12-month cash, etc.

1.4 Pricing non-linear instruments

In the pre-crisis world, all we needed for risk-neutral pricing was the (stochastic) risk-free short rate r_t for $t > 0$ and its derivatives: the bank account $B(t)$, the discount factor $D(t,T)$ and the zero bond prices $P(t,T)$; see Appendix A.

1.4.1 Caps and floors

An *interest rate cap* is a series of call options on a number of consecutive LIBOR fixing periods. In other words, for periods $[t_{i-1}, t_i], i = 1, \dots, n$, the payoff in period $[t_{i-1}, t_i]$ (a *caplet*) is given by

$$(L(t_{i-1}, t_i) - K)^+ N = \max(0, L(t_{i-1}, t_i) - K)N,$$

where N is the notional, $L(t_{i-1}, t_i)$ is the LIBOR fixing for the period, and K is the *strike* of the option. An *interest rate floor* is the corresponding put option with payoffs $(K - L(t_{i-1}, t_i))^+ N$ (the *floorlets*).

A cap's strike is said to be *at-the-money* (ATM) if it has the same value as the floor with the same strike and periods (so the floor's strike is also ATM). A long cap and a short floor with the same strike and maturity add to a swap with the same payment frequency on the fixed and the floating leg, so the ATM rate is the fair swap rate in the pre-crisis pricing, because the payment frequency used to be irrelevant for pricing.

Because either $L(t_{i-1}, t_i) - K \geq 0$ or $K - L(t_{i-1}, t_i) > 0$, we have the *put-call parity*

$$\text{long cap} + \text{short floor} = \text{payer swap},$$

where all three trades have the same strike K and the same periods. Note, however, that the swap appearing in the put-call parity has the same payment frequency and day count rules for the fixed and the floating side.

The present value of the ith caplet is $V = \mathbb{E}(N \max(0, L(t_{i-1}, t_i) - K)\, D(0, t_i))$, where $D(0, t_i) = B(0)/B(t_i)$ is the stochastic discount factor, and expectation is taken with respect to the risk-neutral measure associated with the bank account. Choosing the zero bond $P(0, t_i$ with maturity t_i as a numeraire, we get from the change-of-numeraire technique (FACT 2 in Appendix A)

$$
\begin{aligned}
V &= \mathbb{E}\left(N \max(0, L(t_{i-1}, t_i) - K)\, \frac{B(0)}{B(t_i)}\right) \\
&= N\mathbb{E}^{t_i}\left(\max(0, L(t_{i-1}, t_i) - K)\, \frac{P(0, t_i)}{P(t_i, t_i)}\right) \\
&= N\, P(0, t_i)\, \mathbb{E}^{t_i}(\max(0, L(t_{i-1}, t_i) - K)) \\
&= N\, P(0, t_i)\, \mathbb{E}^{t_i}(\mathbb{E}^{t_i}(\max(0, L(t_{i-1}, t_i) - K) \mid \mathcal{F}_{t_{i-1}})) \\
&= N\, P(0, t_i)\, \mathbb{E}^{t_i}(\max(0, \mathbb{E}^{t_i}(L(t_{i-1}, t_i) \mid \mathcal{F}_{t_{i-1}}) - K)) \\
&= N\, P(0, t_i)\, \mathbb{E}^{t_i}\left(\max\left(0, \frac{1}{\delta_{i,i-1}} \cdot \frac{P(0, t_{i-1}) - P(0, t_i)}{P(0, t_i)} - K\right)\right)
\end{aligned}
$$

where $\mathbb{E}^{t_i}$ is expectation taken with respect to the t_i-forward measure. Now the quotient $(P(0, t_{i-1}) - P(0, t_i))/P(0, t_i)$ is a martingale, because it is the quotient of the tradeable asset $P(0, t_{i-1}) - P(0, t_i)$ and the numeraire; see FACT 1 in Appendix A. A standard choice for the stochastic process driving the forward rate is a geometric Brownian Motion (GBM), because it is very easily tractable and does not allow negative rates. Of course, nowadays negative rates are a common phenomenon in several major currencies, so the choice of process has to be reviewed in that case.

Under the assumption that the forward rate follows a GBM under the t_i-forward measure, we can easily compute the present value using the Black76 formula (C.3): Let δ_i be the length of the period from t_{i-1} to t_i in years, df_i the discount factor for maturity t_i, $f(t_{i-1}, t_i)$ the projected LIBOR rate for period i, and σ the quoted market volatility for the cap. Then the present value of the cap is given by

$$
PV_C = N \sum_{i=1}^{n} \mathrm{Black}(1, f(t_{i-1}, t_i), K, \sigma\sqrt{t_{i-1}}) \cdot \delta_i \cdot df_i.
$$

The present value PV_F of the floor is the same, except that $\omega = -1$ in (C.3) in this case.

It should be noted that the pricing formula ignores the short fixing lag (usually two days) between the date of the fixing and the start of the actual interest period.

1.4.2 Swaptions

A *European swaption* gives the owner the right to enter into a swap at one specific time in the future. It is a payer resp. receiver swaption if the owner can enter into a swap paying resp. receiving the strike K. The strike is at-the-money if it is the forward swap rate for the expiry date.

If the option has physical delivery, the owner of the swaption receives a swap with present value $NPV^+(t_e; t_0, t_n)$ at expiry time t_e, because it is only exercised if the payoff is positive, and the swaption price at time $t < t_e$ is

$$\text{Swaption}(t; t_0, t_n) = \mathbb{E}_t^Q[D(t, t_e) \cdot NPV^+(t_e; t_0, t_n)]$$

The expectation under the risk-neutral (bank account) measure above uses the bank account numeraire

$$B(t) = e^{-\int_0^t r(s)\,ds}$$

where $r(t)$ denotes the short rate process (which we do not need to specify at this stage). The inverse of the bank account is the stochastic discount factor $D(0, t) = 1/B(t)$. The discount factor $D(t, t_e)$ used in the expectation above means discounting from t_e to $t < t_e$, i.e. $D(t, t_e) = B(t)/B(t_e)$. In terms of the risk-neutral measure, the expectation can be written (see Appendix A)

$$\text{Swaption}(t; t_0, t_n) = B(t)\,\mathbb{E}_t^B\left[\frac{NPV^+(t_e; t_0, t_n)}{B(t_e)}\right]$$

Since prices are invariant under change of numeraire (FACT 2 in Appendix A), we can replace B in the above expression for some other numeraire A,

$$\text{Swaption}(t; t_0, t_n) = A(t)\,\mathbb{E}_t^A\left[\frac{NPV^+(t_e; t_0, t_n)}{A(t_e)}\right].$$

What is a good choice here? Inspecting the concrete payoff $NPV^+(t_e; t_0, t_n) = \omega\, N\, A(t_e; t_0, t_n)\,(c(t_e; t_0, t_n) - K)^+$, choosing the annuity $A = A(t_e; t_0, t_n)$, leads to a convenient cancellation of terms in the enumerator and denominator appearing in the expectation under this annuity measure. Thus we arrive at

$$\text{Swaption}(t; t_0, t_n) = N \cdot A(t; t_0, t_n) \cdot \mathbb{E}_t^A[(\omega\,(c(t_e; t_0, t_n) - K))^+].$$

How does this help? The expectation's argument is simpler now: there is one stochastic quantity ($D(t, t_e)$) less to worry about. But the new numeraire has another advantage, looking at the swap rate

$$c(t_e; t_0, t_n) = \frac{P(t_e, t_0) - P(t_e, t_n)}{A(t_e; t_0, t_n)}.$$

Here is a second occurrence of the annuity numeraire in a denominator. FACT 1 in Appendix A tells us that relative asset prices are martingales under the measure associated with the numeraire. In fact both enumerator and denominator in the forward rate are tradeable assets, since they consist of zero bonds only. So the fact applies, and the relative asset price $F(t; t_0, t_n)$ is a martingale under the annuity measure. This means

$$c(t; t_0, t_n) = \mathbb{E}_t^A[F(t_e; t_0, t_n)], \qquad t < t_e$$

or, equivalently, the stochastic process of $F(t; t_0, t_n)$ has no drift. The martingale property is very helpful as it reduces the flexibility in choosing a process for $F(t; t_0, t_n)$. That is the final choice to make. With tractability in mind, as well as positivity of swap rates,[3] it is tempting to choose a simple model, namely a GBM, which means

$$dc(t; t_0, t_n) = \sigma\, c(t; t_0, t_n)\, dW^A(t),$$

and $c(t; t_0, t_n)$ has a log-normal distribution (probability density function) $\rho(\cdot)$, or equivalently, $\ln c(t; t_0, t_n)$ has a normal distribution with mean $\ln c(0; t_0, t_n)) - \sigma^2 t/2$ and variance $\sigma^2 t$. Knowing the p.d.f. of $F(t; t_0, t_n)$ allows us to solve

$$\mathbb{E}_t^A[(\omega\,(c(t_0; t_0, t_n) - K))^+] = \int_0^\infty [\omega\,(x - K)]^+\, \rho(x)\, dx$$

in closed form which leads to the Black76 swaption pricing formula (see Appendix C). This formula now expresses a swaption price in terms of a volatility quote (and a yield curve). It has been used by brokers and financial institutions for a long time as a quotation device for European swaptions.

If the option is delivered in cash, in the euro and sterling markets the owner of a payer swaption receives the cash flow $A'(t)(c_{t_0,t_n}(t) - K)^+$ at expiry time t, where $c_{t_0,t_n}(t)$ is the swap rate and

$$A'(t) = \sum_{i=1}^{n} \frac{\Delta}{(1 + c_{t_0,t_n}(t)\cdot\Delta)^i} = \frac{(1 + c_{t_0,t_n}(t)\cdot\Delta)^n - 1}{(1 + c_{t_0,t_n}(t)\cdot\Delta)^n \cdot c_{t_0,t_n}(t)}$$

is the annuity defined for cash settlement, as seen at expiry t. Δ is the (constant!) period length of the fixed leg in years. The reason for the simplified payoff formula

[3] As with the forward rates, swap rates can be negative in major currencies nowadays for several years to maturity.

is that it makes the payoff indisputable between the two parties; they do not have to argue about the discount curves they are using, etc. The swap rate used in the payoff is a fixing, like the one for LIBOR, and can therefore be readily retrieved from a market provider.

We see that the value of a cash-settled swaption differs from that of a physically settled one at expiry (and hence before as well); see also [33]. This does not yet consider the credit value adjustment for the swaption, which is fundamentally different for physical and cash settled swaptions, as we shall see in Chapter 11. Nevertheless, the Black76 formula is often employed to price cash settled swaptions as well.

2 What Changed with the Crisis

With the near-default of Bear Stearns in 2007, Equation (1.1) broke down, as Figure 2.1 shows: the curve starts to move away from 0 in early 2007 and jumps to 1.6% with Lehman's default. While the difference has reduced significantly, it cannot be assumed to be zero anymore. Therefore, the replication argument fails.

With the default of AA-rated banks came the realization that LIBOR rates contain credit risk: they are cash lending rates, based on the expectation of such banks. They therefore must contain a risk premium over collateralized lending rates.

Another change happened in the derivatives market. Since the crisis, derivatives traded between banks are *always* collateralized. While they are not default free, they are much closer to being that than unsecured loans.

It should therefore be clear why the replication argument underlying Equation (1.1) broke down: we mixed unsecured cash instruments with collateralized derivatives. These are now dealt with as two different classes of risk.

2.1 Basis products and spreads

2.1.1 Tenor basis swaps

We have already introduced tenor basis swaps in 1.2.4. They are quoted in the market as a spread.

- In the EUR market, the spread is the difference between par rates for two swaps with the two involved tenors. The par rate of the swap with the shorter tenor is subtracted from the other rate.
- In the USD market, the spread is the premium to be paid on the leg with the shorter tenor, for example on the three-month leg on a 3m/6m tenor swap.

What is the relation between the two concepts? Let c^{δ}, c^{Δ} be the par rates for tenor δ resp. Δ, and $s^{\Delta/\delta}$ the spread on the Δ leg of a Δ-δ basis swap which makes the swap fair. Then, assuming that the fixed sides of the IR swaps pay with the same

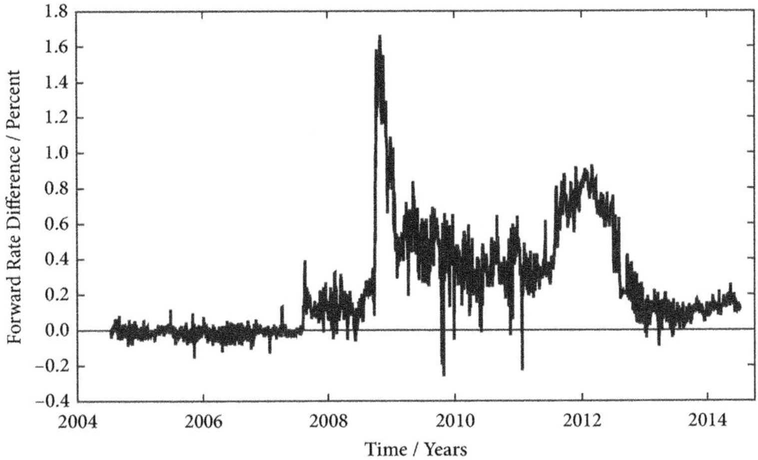

Figure 2.1 The difference between the replicated and the quoted FRA rate for 3m×3m month EURIBOR forwards from 2004 to 2014, in percentage points

frequency, we have by definition of the two spreads

$$
\begin{aligned}
(c^\delta - c^\Delta)A_{0,n}^{ON} &= \sum_{i=1}^{n_\delta} f_i^\delta \delta_i df_{t_i}^{ON} - \sum_{j=1}^{n_\Delta} f_j^\Delta \Delta_j df_{t'_j}^{ON} \\
&= \sum_{j=1}^{n_\Delta} (f_j^\Delta + s^{\Delta/\delta})\Delta_j df_{t'_j}^{ON} - \sum_{j=1}^{n_\Delta} f_j^\Delta \Delta_j df_{t'_j}^{ON} \\
&= s^{\Delta/\delta} A_{0,n_\Delta}^{ON,\Delta}. \qquad (2.1)
\end{aligned}
$$

In other words, the par rate differential and the floating spread differ by the quotient of two annuities: one with respect to the fixed side's pay frequency, the other with respect to the tenor Δ floating side's. This quotient is very close to 1, but does not match 1 exactly.

Regardless of the market, the spread is almost always positive, as the longer tenor fixings contain more credit and liquidity risk. However, there are abnormal situations where the spreads can be negative on single days; on the very few past occurrences, this was due to delayed communication by the central bank. It can happen, though, that the curve building algorithm and the assumptions and interpolations attached to it lead to negative basis spreads.

The discrepancy can already be observed on individual forward rates. Example (actual quotes from 11 December 2012):

- 1x4 FRA, starting 14 Jan 2013, maturing 15 Apr 2013, $\delta_{1,4} = 0.25278$: $r_{1,4} = 0.165\%$ (mid);

- 4x7 FRA, starting 15 Apr 2013, maturing 15 Jul 2013, $\delta_{4,7} = 0.25278$: $r_{4,7} = 0.126\%$ (mid);
- 1x7 FRA, starting 14 Jan 2013, maturing 15 Jul 2013, $\delta_{1,7} = 0.50556$: $r_{1,7} = 0.293\%$ (mid).

From the old replication argument, we would expect that

$$(1+\delta_{1,4}r_{1,4})(1+\delta_{4,7}r_{4,7}) = 1+\delta_{1,7}r_{1,7},$$

in other words that

$$r_{1,7} = \frac{(1+\delta_{1,4}r_{1,4})(1+\delta_{4,7}r_{4,7})-1}{\delta_{1,7}} = 0.146\%.$$

The difference to the quoted rate $r_{1,7}$ is 0.147% – more than the replicated value itself. We can view this as the short-term basis spread between three and six months. As a result, we see that we cannot project six-month forward rates from three-month instruments, either, and vice versa.

⇒ **We need a separate forward-generating curve (or projection curve) for each tenor (typically 1, 3, 6 and 12 months).** Such a curve must be built from instruments that have the same tenor and credit quality.

Fundamental Rules for Curve Building:

- No mixing of tenors
- No mixing of derivatives and cash instruments

The projected and the fixed cash flows are then discounted with the same risk-free discount curve, regardless from which instrument they come (as long as all instruments involved have the same credit quality).

Note that a fair swap is not a par swap anymore because the floating leg plus notional at maturity is not worth par anymore; the telescope trick we saw in Equation (1.6) does not work anymore. Nevertheless, the fair swap rates are still called par rates.

2.1.2 Cross-currency basis swaps

We have already introduced cross-currency basis swaps in 1.2.5. There are two major liquid markets for cross-currency swaps, namely USD and EUR. Cross-currency basis swaps are quoted in the market as a spread which is applied to the non-USD (resp. non-EUR) currency; exceptions are the USD-MXN and USD-CLP basis swaps. For some Eastern European currencies, there are only quotes for swaps against EUR available. To price a basis swap between two minor currencies (e.g. between JPY and GBP), one has to synthetically break it into two swaps, both against one of the major currencies.

Note that payment dates and period lengths can be slightly different from that of a single-currency swap in either currency because of the merged calendars that have to be used.

An important variance of the cross-currency swap pays notional adjustments at each fixing date to compensate the FX rate move since the last fixing. At the same time, the notional (and hence the interest) for the current period is adjusted accordingly. As an example, consider a USD-GBP cross-currency basis swap with a start notional of 100 million USD; let the exchange rate at inception be 0.75 GBP for 1 USD. At the end of the first period, assume that the rate has moved to 0.78 GBP per 1 USD. That means that the GBP leg has a notional of 78 million GBP now. The USD payer therefore pays 3 million GBP to the GBP payer. If the rate has moved to 0.72 GBP per 1 USD instead, the GBP payer pays 3 million GBP to the USD payer.

We shall see what impact this feature has on curve building in 4.1. It is also very important when calculating credit risk as it obviously significantly reduces the change in value due to FX moves. A swap with this feature is called rebalancing or mark-to-market.

2.2 Collateralization

After the crisis, derivatives trades between banks are almost always done under a collateral agreement. This is called a *Credit Support Annex* (CSA) to the ISDA contract. Its main features are:

- The values of all trades under the CSA are netted, i.e. positive and negative values are offsetting each other;
- The party that is out-of-the-money has to post collateral to the other party;
- The portfolio (and the collateral) is revalued and collateral adjusted on a regular basis.

There are many more details that can be defined in a CSA which we will discuss in 5.1.

Collateralization can significantly reduce credit risk but is not a panacea, as we shall see in Part IV.

Note that a netting agreement favours the derivatives counterparty over any other creditors for whom netting of assets and liabilities is usually not possible.

Now that we have seen all the changes in the market, we return to the question from the beginning of the chapter: what is the risk-free rate? We saw that LIBOR is not a good proxy anymore after Lehman defaulted. AA-rated banks *can* default, and LIBOR contains credit risk. Could we use the quotes from government bonds? This may be possible in some currencies, where the issuing government can directly influence the monetary policy of the central bank.[1] Certainly not in EUR – Eurozone governments *can* default, as the case of Greece has shown. In addition, the market for government bonds is distorted by tax issues, regulation and other factors; see for instance the market for German government bonds. Another problem with bonds is that there are no standard maturities available at all times, that is an issuance maturing in exactly 5 years, 10 years, 12 years and so on. On the other hand, there are often multiple issuances maturing on a given day, but they do not result in the same interest rate. The reason is that there is different demand for older vs new issuances and for higher vs lower coupons.

Another candidate for a risk-free rate might be the repo rate. This is an interest rate that is paid on a collateralized loan, and should therefore be very close to being risk-free. Unfortunately, the repo market is only liquid for maturities up to one year. For derivatives pricing, we need a curve that goes out to 30 years at least.

So here are our requirements. We have to derive the risk-free rate from a liquid market with many standardized and long-dated maturities. The instruments involved must have as little intrinsic credit risk as possible. The best candidate is the Overnight-Indexed Swap rate (OIS). This represents the average (fixed) rate that has to be paid in exchange for the daily overnight rate. Advantages are

- the EONIA rate is based on actual trades, not on estimated numbers like the LIBOR fixings;
- the overnight rate is as close to risk-free as possible for a cash rate because the counterparty can be changed on a daily basis;
- there is an active and liquid OIS market in several currencies, with instrument maturities of up to 30 years;
- the overnight rate is the interest paid on cash collateral.

The last point is often seen as the most important. We show below that it implies that the discount curve for collateralized derivatives has to be the collateral interest curve, that is the OIS curve. Here is a simple example first.

Consider a collateralized standard EUR swap whose last fixing on the floating leg (linked to six-month EURIBOR) has just happened:

- The fixed leg pays 5%;
- The last EURIBOR fixing was 0.952% p.a.;
- The six-month OIS rate is 0.483% p.a.;
- The notional of the swap is 100 million EUR.

[1] In most developed countries, this is formally forbidden. But let us be realistic about this: governments have always tried and will continue to try to bend the rules to their advantage.

Then the net payment due at the end of the period is $5 - 0.476 = 4.524$ million EUR, and the present value of the net payment is $4{,}524{,}000/(1 + 0.476\%) = 4{,}502{,}567.78$ EUR if we discount using the standard six-month curve. Given the six-month OIS rate is 0.483%, the expectation of the market is that the collateral of $4{,}502{,}567.78$ EUR will be worth $4{,}502{,}567.78 \cdot (1 + 0.483\%/2) = 4{,}513{,}441.48$ EUR in six months' time, which is more than 9,000 EUR less than the actual cash flow. If we discount the cash flow with the OIS rate, this discrepancy disappears.

The OIS and EURIBOR rates above are actual examples from the same day (7 April 2010). The difference between the two was even higher on some occasions during the credit crisis.

Now we formally show that the OIS rate is also the one that should be used for discounting collateralized cash flows. We closely follow Ametrano & Bianchetti [5]. There is a similar derivation in Piterbarg [125] which uses an additional repo rate. In the post-crisis world, we need for risk-neutral pricing:

- The funding rate $r_f(t)$ for $t > 0$;
- The collateral rate $r_c(t)$.

Both rates have associated bank accounts B_f resp. B_c and discount factors D_f resp. D_c.

Now assume we have a derivative $\Pi(t,X)$ on an additional risk factor $X(t)$ which follows the SDE

$$dX(t) = \mu(t,X)Xdt + \sigma(t,X)XdW(t), \qquad X(0) = X_0,$$

where $W(t)$ is a Brownian Motion under the real-world measure $\mathbb{P}$. We can change the measure such that

$$dX(t) = r_f(t)Xdt + \sigma(t,X)XdW^f(t), \qquad X(0) = X_0.$$

By Ito's formula, we get for the following SDE for Π:

$$d\Pi(t,X) = \left(\frac{\partial \Pi}{\partial t} + r_f X \frac{\partial \Pi}{\partial X} + \frac{\sigma^2 X^2}{2} \frac{\partial \Pi}{\partial X} \right) dt + \sigma X \frac{\partial \Pi}{\partial X} dW^f(t). \tag{2.2}$$

Under perfect collateralization, we must have $B_c(t) = \Pi(t,X)$, so the drift rate of $\Pi(t,X)$ must be

$$\mathbb{E}_t(d\Pi(t,X)) = r_c(t)B_c(t)dt = r_c(t)\Pi(t,X)dt. \tag{2.3}$$

Putting (2.2) and (2.3) together, we see that $\Pi(t,X)$ satisfies the PDE

$$\frac{\partial \Pi}{\partial t} + r_f(t)X(t)\frac{\partial \Pi}{\partial X} + \frac{1}{2}\sigma^2(t)X^2(t)\frac{\partial^2 \Pi}{\partial X^2} = r_c(t)\Pi.$$

The Feynman-Kac Theorem (see Appendix B) allows us to solve this PDE to give

$$\Pi(t,X) = \mathbb{E}^f(D_c(t,T)\Pi(T,X) \mid \mathcal{F}_t).$$

Note that the above argument only works for *perfect collateralization*, that is instantaneous, dispute-free posting of collateral. This is as good as true for CCP, but not for OTC derivatives, as we shall see in 5.1.

Hull and White argue in [90] that the correct discount curve is *always* the OIS curve regardless of the creditworthiness of the cash flow payer because risk-neutral pricing is always based on discounting with the risk-free rate. The creditworthiness and other considerations should be brought into the valuation as a value adjustment rather than changing the discount curve. They show that if CVA and DVA are computed correctly, the discount curve does not matter anyway. This view is also supported by the complications in considering CSA details (see 5.1) and capital cost in the valuation. A caveat would be that there are cases where the collateral receives the overnight rate minus a spread as interest, or where this interest is floored at zero, see Section 5.3. The bottom line is: the OIS curve is the correct risk-free curve but may have to be adjusted according to the details found in the collateral agreement.

3 Clearing House Pricing

3.1 Introduction of central counterparties

As a reaction to counterparty credit risk attached to uncollateralized derivatives and the non-transparency of the OTC derivatives markets, regulators decided to force banks to use central clearing with Central Counterparties (CCP) for derivatives trading (Dodd-Frank Act in the US, EMIR and CRR/CRD IV in Europe[1]) by introducing a penalizing CVA capital charge for non-cleared derivatives, see Section 24.7.

Aside from their contribution to increased transparency in the derivatives market, CCPs are supposed to reduce counterparty credit risk. However, they turn it into *liquidity risk* via their margin requirements.

A CCP has a number of *direct members*. These are the counterparties that deal with the CCP directly. The members contribute to the CCP's guarantee fund or default fund which is part of the defence against member or CCP default. In addition to that, the direct members usually agree to further funding if required. The maximum additional amount depends on the CCP. The guarantee fund contribution accrues interest at a sub-OIS rate.

Each direct member in turn can have an arbitrary number of clients who want to clear with the CCP through them. Any margin requirements are satisfied by the direct members who then in turn acquire the margin amounts from their clients.

Upon default of one of the members, the CCP will call the surviving members to recapitalize the guarantee fund. As a result, the members have a *credit exposure against each other member* which is not correlated with their trade exposure to them, and *over which they have no control.* In addition, members have a credit exposure against the CCP. These two residual sources of credit risk are recognized by the regulator and have to be capitalized, see Section 24.6.

3.2 Margin requirements

The CCP has two sources of risk for each member:

[1] At the time of writing, central clearing is still not mandatory for eligible derivatives. The current estimate for the enforcement of central clearing to start is the second quarter of 2016 or later.

- The exposure due to the current value of the portfolio with that member;
- The exposure due to potential adverse moves of the portfolio after the member defaults.

The current exposure is mitigated by the *Variation Margin* (VM). This is rebalanced at least once a day but more frequently up to three times a day. Rebalancing works similarly to collateralization for OTC derivatives, only faster, and there are no disputes.

Potential value losses after a member's default are mitigated by the *Initial Margin* (IM). This is calculated as either a Value-at-Risk (VaR) number or as Expected Shortfall (ES), based on a historical simulation. The time horizon of this risk number depends on the type of portfolio. The initial margin is updated on a regular basis so as to capture times of recent market stress.

Margins received usually accrue interest at the overnight rate, sometimes less a small spread. Margin reductions are posted back on the day they occur.

3.3 Building the OIS curve

The first curve that we have to construct is the discount curve, based on the risk-free rates. Where available, this is the Overnight-Indexed Swap (OIS) curve:

- EUR Euro Overnight Index Average = EONIA
- GBP Sterling Overnight Index Average = SONIA
- USD FedFunds
- JPY Mutan (sometimes Tokyo Overnight Average Rate TONAR)
- CHF Swiss Average Rate Overnight = SARON
- DKK DKKOIS
- AUD AONIA
- CAD CORRA
- HKD HONIX
- NZD NZIONA

In an OIS, two parties exchange a fixed coupon (paid annually for longer-dated swaps and as a single payment at maturity otherwise) against the daily fixed and compounded overnight rate. Daily compounding means that the rate paid at the end of period $i = 1, \ldots, n$ is given by

$$R_i = \frac{1}{\delta_i}\left[\prod_{k=1}^{n_i}(1 + F^{ON}(t_{i,k-1}, t_{i,k})\delta_{i,k}) - 1\right], \tag{3.1}$$

where

- δ_i is the length of period i in years using the OIS day count convention;
- n_i is the number of overnight fixings in period i;
- $F^{ON}(t_{i,k-1}, t_{i,k})$ is the kth overnight fixing in period i;
- $\delta_{i,k}$ is the length in years of the kth overnight period (mostly one day divided by the days in a year, but three on Fridays and up to 5 if there are holidays around a weekend).

In order to price an OIS, we need to project the fixings $F^{ON}(t_{i,k-1}, t_{i,k})$ and discount the resulting cash flows R_i to today. Note that the forward and discount curve tenor agree as both are based on the overnight frequency. Therefore, we can use formula (1.1) to project

$$F^{ON}(t_{i,k-1}, t_{i,k}) = \frac{1}{\delta_{i,k}} \left(\frac{df^{ON}_{i,k-1}}{df^{ON}_{i,k}} - 1 \right).$$

Thus we get in (3.1)

$$\begin{aligned} R_i &= \frac{1}{\delta_i} \left[\prod_{k=1}^{n_i} \frac{df^{ON}_{i,k-1}}{df^{ON}_{i,k}} - 1 \right] \\ &= \frac{1}{\delta_i} \left[\frac{df^{ON}_{i-1}}{df^{ON}_{i}} - 1 \right], \end{aligned}$$

which is just the forward expression from Equation (1.1) for the period t_{i-1} to t_i.

We would like to use the telescope sum to argue that the OIS floating leg's PV is

$$PV_{flt} = \sum_{i=1}^{n} R_i \delta_i df^{ON}_i = df^{ON}_0 - df^{ON}_n.$$

However, in most currencies, there is a payment lag between the last fixing and the payment date (for instance, two business days for EUR and USD, and one business day for GBP). This means that the actual present value of the floating leg is given by

$$PV_{flt} = \sum_{i=1}^{n} R_i \delta_i df^{ON}_{i,p},$$

where $df^{ON}_{i,p}$ is the discount factor for the payment date of the ith period. The very small convexity adjustment due to the payment lag can be ignored.

The fixed leg's PV is, as usual,

$$PV_{fix} = c\sum_{i=1}^{n} \delta_i df_{i,p}^{ON} = cA_{0,n}^{ON}.$$

For the (honest) par rate at inception we have

$$c_0 = \frac{PV_{flt}}{A_{0,n}^{ON}} = \left(\sum_{i=1}^{n}\left[\frac{df_{i-1}^{ON}}{df_i^{ON}} - 1\right] df_{i,p}\right) / A_{0,n}^{ON}. \tag{3.2}$$

For maturities below one year, we can thus use (3.2) directly to determine

$$df_1^{ON} = \frac{df_0^{ON}}{1 + c_0\delta_1}.$$

For maturities above one year, we can strip the OIS curve from OIS quotes using formula (3.2) similar to the single-curve world.

3.4 USD specialities

In the USD market, OIS swaps as described above – which pay the *geometric* average of the FedFunds rate vs fixed – are only liquidly quoted for maturities up to two to three years. Furthermore, for maturities beyond one year, the payment frequency is quarterly.

Beyond two to three years, the most liquid instruments are FedFunds weighted average vs LIBOR swaps. Here, the coupon paid for period i on the OIS leg is a spread (which is the quoted item) plus the *arithmetic* average

$$R_i^A = \sum_{k=1}^{n_i - 1} F^{ON}(t_{i,k-1}, t_{i,k})\delta_{i,k},$$

where δ_{i,n_i-1} is the length of the period from t_{i,n_i-2} to t_{i,n_i}, that is the fixing is frozen for the last two business days so as to make payment planning easier. Payment periods are quarterly rather than zero coupon or annually. That means that we have to solve

$$\sum_{i=1}^{N}(R_i^A + s_{t_N})\delta_i df_i^{ON} = \sum_{i=1}^{N} F_i^{3M}\delta_i df_i^{ON} = c_{t_N}^{3M} A_{t_N}^{ON}$$

for the df^{ON} appearing in the pricing *and* in the projection of the F^{ON} (and hence the R_i^A). In this equation, $c_{t_N}^{3M}$ is the par swap rate for a plain vanilla swap maturing in t_N. A simplifying assumption can help us reduce the complexity of the exercise. Note that $1 + x \approx e^x$ for very small x. For interest rates $F(t_{i,k-1}, t_{i,k})$ and periods mostly of length one to three days (i.e. $\delta_{i,k} \in [1/360, 1/120]$), we therefore have the following approximation for the compounded rate R_i^C:

$$\begin{aligned} R_i^C &= \frac{1}{\delta_i}\left[\prod_{k=1}^{n_i}(1 + F^{ON}(t_{i,k-1}, t_{i,k})\delta_{i,k}) - 1\right] \\ &\approx \frac{1}{\delta_i}\left[\exp\left(\sum_{k=1}^{n_i} F^{ON}(t_{i,k-1}, t_{i,k})\delta_{i,k}\right) - 1\right] \\ &= \frac{1}{\delta_i}\left[e^{R_i^A} - 1\right] \end{aligned}$$

or

$$R_i^A = \ln\left(1 + \delta_i R_i^C\right) = \ln\left(df_{i-1}^{ON}\right) - \ln\left(df_i^{ON}\right).$$

This approximation is actually quite good (less than half a basis point, see [139]) and only uses discount factors for quarterly dates, not daily ones.

3.5 Building the forward projection curves

Once the discount curve is available, we can use quoted forward and swap rates of the standard tenor to derive the forward projection curve. This is a zero curve whose sole purpose is to give forward rates according to formula (1.1) in a way that is compatible with the discount curve because the tenor of the forwards and the discount factors agree:

$$f^\delta(s, s+\delta) = \frac{df_s^\delta - df_{s+\delta}^\delta}{df_{s+\delta}^\delta \times \delta} = \frac{1}{\delta}\left(\frac{df_s^\delta}{df_{s+\delta}^\delta} - 1\right)$$

The forward projection curve can be interpreted as the risky discount curve attached to tenor δ default risk, and therefore yields the right forward for the cash LIBOR rate when using formula (1.1): replicated and replicating instruments have the same credit risk class. If available, we do the same for other tenors; if not, we use tenor basis swap spreads to derive the forward curve for other tenors, as we will describe below.

The short end of the curve (up to tenor δ) is usually built from cash rates. As these are not collateralized, they are fair if discounted at the tenor δ rate, so they directly give us the discount factor we need. Given a set of quoted forward rates for tenor δ and a δ discount factor for the forward's start date, we use formula (1.1) again to bootstrap the discount factor for the forward's maturity date:

$$df_{s+\delta}^{\delta} = \frac{df_s^{\delta}}{1+\delta f^{\delta}(s,s+\delta)}$$

Finally, we use the swap pricing formula to strip missing discount factors from the δ swap rate:

$$cA_{0,n}^{ON} = \sum_{i=1}^{n} f^{\delta}(t_{i-1},t_i)\delta_i df_i^{ON},$$

where $A_{0,n}^{ON}$ is the fixed side's annuity based on OIS discount factors which are all known.

As a result, we now have the discount curve, df_t^{ON}, and the forward-generating curve $f_t^{\Delta} = f^{\Delta}(t-\Delta,t)$ for the standard tenor Δ. If, for some non-standard tenor δ, we also have liquid market quotes for FRAs and swaps, we use them in the same fashion to construct the δ forward curve.

Next, assume that we only have basis swap spread quotes for tenor δ:

- If the spread is the difference of swap rates, compute the unknown ones from the standard tenor swap rates and the basis swap spread quotes, then build the curve as in the standard tenor case;
- Otherwise, convert the spread into a swap rate using formula (2.1):

$$c^{\delta} = c^{\Delta} - \frac{A_{0,n_{\Delta}}^{ON,\Delta}}{A_{0,n}^{ON}} s^{\delta/\Delta}$$

and proceed as before.

3.6 More USD specialities

Again, conventions for USD tenor basis swaps are slightly different from other currencies. For some tenor basis swaps, the shorter leg's fixings are compounded (before adding the spread), that is, the defining equation for the basis spread is given by (δ being the shorter tenor):

$$\sum_{i=1}^{n_{\Delta}} f_i^{\Delta}\Delta_i df_{t_i}^{ON} = \sum_{i=1}^{n_{\Delta}} \left(\left[\prod_{j=1}^{\Delta/\delta} (1+f_{i,j}^{\delta}\delta_{i,j}) - 1 \right] + s^{\delta/\Delta} \right) \Delta_i df_{t_i}^{ON}.$$

As in the OIS case, we can view the compounded δ-forward rates with tenor δ as the Δ-forward rate computed off the δ curve:

$$f_i^{\delta,\Delta} := \prod_{j=1}^{\Delta/\delta}(1 + f_{i,j}^{\delta}\delta_{i,j}) - 1 = \frac{df_{i-1}^{\delta}}{df_i^{\delta}} - 1.$$

This shows how important it is to understand the conventions of the instruments one is using.

3.7 Example: implying the par asset swap spread

In a par asset swap package, the buyer receives a bond paying a fixed coupon c and simultaneously enters into a swap paying c and receiving LIBOR plus a spread s, which is chosen such that the bond market price P^M plus the swap present value equal the notional (par):

$$\begin{aligned}
1 &= P^M - c\sum_{i=1}^{m}\delta_i\, df_{t_i}^{OIS} + \sum_{j=1}^{n}(f_j^{\Delta} + s)\,\Delta_j\, df_{T_j}^{OIS} \\
&= P^M - c\sum_{i=1}^{m}\delta_i\, df_{t_i}^{OIS} - df_{t_m}^{OIS} + \sum_{j=1}^{n}(f_j^{\Delta} + s)\,\Delta_j\, df_{T_j}^{OIS} + df_{T_n}^{OIS} \\
&= P^M - c\sum_{i=1}^{m}\delta_i\, df_{t_i}^{OIS} - df_{t_m}^{OIS} + 1 + (s - s^{\Delta}(T_0, T_n))\sum_{j=1}^{n}\Delta_j\, df_{T_j}^{OIS} \\
&= P^M - P^{RF} + 1 + (s - s^{\Delta}(T_0, T_n))\, A^{OIS,\Delta}(T_0, T_n)
\end{aligned}$$

which means that (P^{RF} being the risk-free bond price)

$$\begin{aligned}
s &= \frac{P^{RF} - P^M}{A^{OIS,\Delta}(T_0, T_n)} + s^{\Delta}(T_0, T_n) \\
&\approx c + s^{\Delta}(T_0, T_n) - \frac{P^M}{A^{OIS,\Delta}(T_0, T_n)}.
\end{aligned}$$

Note that we ignored the fixing of the current period and the settlement lag which is usually one to three business days. Before the emergence of the tenor basis, the spread $s^{\Delta}(T_0, T_n)$ was zero, so the asset swap spread was very intuitively given by the difference between the market and the risk-free price – the credit and liquidity premium of the bond – divided by the value of one basis point. For details, see [107]. With a tenor basis spread in place, we just have to add this spread between the tenor of the asset swap and the OIS discount curve.

Typically, the market still assumes LIBOR discounting for the risk-free price of the bond but OIS discounting for the swap, in which case we get

$$
\begin{aligned}
s &= \frac{P^{RF,OIS} - P^M}{A^{OIS,\Delta}(T_0,T_n)} + s^\Delta(T_0,T_n) \\
&= \frac{1}{A^{OIS,\Delta}(T_0,T_n)}\left(P^{RF,\Delta}\frac{A^{OIS,f}(T_0,T_n)}{A^{\Delta,f}(T_0,T_n)} - P^M\right) + s^\Delta(T_0,T_n).
\end{aligned}
$$

3.8 Interpolation

The market does not quote a continuous set of instruments, zero rates or discount factors. Only a limited number of maturities on any curve are quoted, and not all of those quotes are necessarily liquid. One therefore has to find ways to produce values between (interpolation) and beyond (extrapolation) the quoted values. Commonly used interpolation methods are:

- Linear interpolation on the zero curve:

$$r_t = r_1\frac{t_2-t}{t_2-t_1} + r_2\frac{t-t_1}{t_2-t_1};$$

- Loglinear on the discount curve:

$$df_t = \ln(df_1)\frac{t_2-t}{t_2-t_1} + \ln(df_2)\frac{t-t_1}{t_2-t_1},$$

  which amounts to

$$r_t = r_1\frac{t_1}{t}\frac{t_2-t}{t_2-t_1} + r_2\frac{t_2}{t}\frac{t-t_1}{t_2-t_1}$$

  if zero rates are continuously compounding;
- Monotonic cubic spline on the log discounts.

Cubic splines are piecewise polynomials of degree ≤ 3 with the following properties. Given a set of points $\{(t_i,r_i)|i=0,\ldots,n\}$ we want to find a function $S(t), t_0 \leq t \leq t_n$ such that $S(t_i)=r_i$, $S(t)$ is a polynomial of order ≤ 3 on each interval t_{i-1},t_i, and S is twice continuously differentiable everywhere. It is not difficult to find such a function for any given set of points. However, without further restrictions, the spline function may not behave as expected, for example it does not respect the monotonicity of the original data. Therefore, one has to use a method to enforce good behaviour. One of these methods is the so-called Hyman filter, see [92].

The two linear interpolation methods are very easy to implement, and fast. The zero curves behave very well, but the forwards show a sawtooth pattern. Cubic splines produce smoother forward curves because of their differentiability even at the given time points. Note that the spline method is a *global* interpolation scheme, that is adding a data point can change the interpolation function everywhere. For a comparison of the methods, see [5].

3.9 Pricing non-linear instruments

3.9.1 European swaptions

We saw in Section 1.4 that the classic Black76 formula (C.3) for pricing swaptions is derived as follows:

- Define the annuity factor of the underlying swap as the new numeraire
- Perform a change of measure from the risk-neutral measure to the annuity measure
- Under this annuity measure, the par swap rate, written as the quotient $(df_0 - df_n)/A_{t_0,t_n}$, is a martingale. If swap rates cannot be negative (which unfortunately they can), we can assume this martingale to be a geometric Brownian Motion
- Standard methods as described in Appendix C show that the swaption value is then given by formula (C.3).

The good news is that the same argument still works under OIS discounting, and we have (see, e.g., [117]):

$$PV = N \cdot \mathrm{Black}(\omega, c^{\delta}_{t_0,t_n}(0), K, \sigma\sqrt{t_0}) \cdot A^{ON}_{t_0,t_n}(0), \tag{3.3}$$

with the right definition of the forward swap rate:

$$c^{\delta}_{t_0,t_n}(0) = \frac{1}{A^{ON}_{t_0,t_n}(0)} \sum_{i=1}^{n} f^{\delta}(0; t_{i-1}, t_i) \cdot \delta_i \cdot df_i^{ON}.$$

But what volatilities do we use? In the past, there used to be only one tenor for which swaption volatilities were quoted, usually the standard tenor. Even though volatilities for non-standard tenors are quoted now, these quotes still assume that collateral and trade currency are the same.

The market makes the following standard assumption. The *normal volatility* does not depend on the tenor of the underlying swap, where the normal volatility is the one for which the normal Black76 formula (C.5) yields the same value as the standard Black76 formula (C.3) for the log-normal (quoted) volatility.

The following parameters in (C.5) depend on the tenor of the underlying swap: annuity $A^{\delta}_{t_0,t_n}(0)$, forward swap rate $c^{\delta}_{t_0,t_n}(0)$ and moneyness $a^{\delta} = c^{\delta}_{t_0,t_n}(0) - K$. If σ does not depend on the tenor, then we must have for different tenors δ and Δ

$$\begin{aligned}V^{\delta}(0;t_0,t_n,a^{\delta},\sigma(a^{\delta})) &= V^{\Delta}\left(0;t_0,t_n,a^{\delta},\sigma(a^{\delta})\right)\cdot\frac{A^{\delta}_{0,t_0,t_n}}{A^{\Delta}_{0,t_0,t_n}}\\ &= V^{\Delta}\left(0;t_0,t_n,a^{\Delta}+s^{\delta/\Delta}_{t_0,t_n},\sigma(a^{\Delta}+s^{\delta/\Delta}_{t_0,t_n})\right)\cdot\frac{A^{\delta}_{0,t_0,t_n}}{A^{\Delta}_{0,t_0,t_n}},\end{aligned}$$

where $s^{\delta/\Delta}_{t_0,t_n} = c^{\delta}_{t_0,t_n}(0) - c^{\Delta}_{t_0,t_n}(0)$, which is just the tenor basis spread. Now given a (log-normal) volatility cube for tenor Δ, we

- compute prices using the Black76 formula (C.3);
- imply normal volas using (C.5);
- shift the moneyness by the basis spread and compute prices for tenor δ using (C.5) again;
- imply log-normal volatilities using (C.3).

In the current market environment in Europe with its low interest rates even for very long maturities, options have to be priced with adjusted models. Either the rate process is assumed to be normal, that is rates can naturally become negative, or the log-normal Black model has to be replaced by a shifted log-normal model. It has become quite common that volatilities are quoted both for a normal and a lognormal Black76 formula.

3.9.2 Bermudan swaptions

Bermudan swaptions need a more sophisticated model. A Bermudan swaption gives the owner the right to enter into a swap on several predetermined dates.

The simplest model is to use a short-rate model for the involved risk factors. Several approaches are possible:

1. Model the discount curve stochastically, keep the tenor spread term structure constant when computing the forward projection curve. While this allows the usage of models that are very similar to the single-curve ones, this approach has an important issue. The main reason for getting the basis spread into the equation is that it is *not* constant. Nevertheless, this approach is widely used.
2. Model the two involved interest rate curves (three in foreign currencies) stochastically, see Section 7.2.1 in [107].
3. Model the discount curve and the tenor basis spread over it stochastically, see Section 7.2.2 in [107].
4. We present a version of the Linear Gauss-Markov (LGM) model that takes the tenor basis spread into account in Section 11.2.2.

There is not enough market data available to calibrate the models in approaches 2 and 3 above properly as one would need either OIS swaption volatilities or basis swaption volatilities. The necessary instruments are simply not quoted. It is therefore common market practice to choose the first approach above, that is keep the current basis spread term structure constant and model only one interest curve (either the forward or the discount curve) stochastically. Can the assumption of a static basis be justified?

Assume that the basis spread term structure and the zero curve are independent, and that we have a Δ-LIBOR vs fixed (with period length δ) swap starting in $t = t_0 = T_0$ in the future, with maturity $t_m = T_n$ and notional 1. We write

- $df^{\Delta}(t;s)$: discount factor for time s based on the LIBOR (forward-generating) curve, as seen at time t;
- $df^{OIS}(t;s)$: discount factor for time s based on the OIS curve, at t;
- the *tenor basis adjustment factor* as seen at time t

$$S^{\Delta}(t;s) = \frac{df^{OIS}(t;s)}{df^{\Delta}(t;s)}.$$

For a constant, continuously compounding basis spread $s_c^{\Delta}(t;t_0,t_m)$ we can write $S^{\Delta}(t;s) = e^{s_c^{\Delta}(t;t_0,t_m)\,s}$.

Then the (stochastic) time-t present value of the swap is given by:

$$PV(t) = c\sum_{i=1}^{m}\delta_i\, df^{OIS}(t;t_i) - \sum_{j=1}^{n} f^{\Delta}(t;T_{j-1},T_j)\,\Delta_j\, df^{OIS}(t;T_j).$$

Analysing the floating side we get

$$
\begin{aligned}
&\sum_{j=1}^{n} f^{\Delta}(t;T_{j-1},T_j)\,\Delta_j\, df^{OIS}(t;T_j)\\
&=\sum_{j=1}^{n} f^{\Delta}(t;T_{j-1},T_j)\,\Delta_j\, df^{\Delta}(t;T_j)\, S^{\Delta}(t;T_j)\\
&=\sum_{j=1}^{n} (df^{\Delta}(t;T_{j-1}) - df^{\Delta}(t;T_j))\, S^{\Delta}(t;T_j)\\
&=\sum_{j=1}^{n} (df^{OIS}(t;T_{j-1}) - df^{OIS}(t;T_j))\\
&\quad -\sum_{j=1}^{n} df^{\Delta}(t;T_{j-1})(S^{\Delta}(t;T_{j-1}) - S^{\Delta}(t;T_j))\\
&=1-df^{OIS}(t;T_n) - \sum_{j=1}^{n} df^{OIS}(t;T_{j-1})\left(1-\frac{S^{\Delta}(t;T_j)}{S^{\Delta}(t;T_{j-1})}\right)\\
&=1-df^{OIS}(t;T_n) - \sum_{j=1}^{n} df^{OIS}(t;T_j)\frac{df^{OIS}(t;T_{j-1})}{df^{OIS}(t;T_j)}\left(1-\frac{S^{\Delta}(t;T_j)}{S^{\Delta}(t;T_{j-1})}\right)\\
&=1-df^{OIS}(t;T_n) - \sum_{j=1}^{n} df^{OIS}(t;T_j)\left(\frac{df^{OIS}(t;T_{j-1})}{df^{OIS}(t;T_j)}-\frac{df^{\Delta}(t;T_{j-1})}{df^{\Delta}(t;T_j)}\right).
\end{aligned}
$$

Keeping the basis constant amounts to using a standard method from the LMM model called "freezing the forwards" (see, for instance, [33]) which only yields a good approximation if the volatility of the basis spread is much lower than that of the discount factors, which remains to be shown. Only then can the floating side's value be approximated by

$$1-df^{OIS}(t;T_n) - \sum_{j=1}^{n} df^{OIS}(t;T_j)\left(\frac{df^{OIS}(\mathbf{0};T_{j-1})}{df^{OIS}(\mathbf{0};T_j)}-\frac{df^{\Delta}(\mathbf{0};T_{j-1})}{df^{\Delta}(\mathbf{0};T_j)}\right).$$

The expression

$$\frac{df^{OIS}(t;T_{j-1})}{df^{OIS}(t;T_j)}-\frac{df^{\Delta}(t;T_{j-1})}{df^{\Delta}(t;T_j)} \tag{3.4}$$

is just the difference of the forward rates from the two discount curves, that is a basis spreadlet; the quoted (flat) basis spread is the weighted average of these period forward components, with weights

$$w_j := \frac{df^{OIS}(t; T_j)}{\sum_{k=1}^{n} df^{OIS}(t; T_k)}.$$

3.10 Not all currencies are equal

The above derivation of discount and forwarding curves gives a sound framework for pricing collateralized derivatives – as long as the required instruments are available. As an example that this is not always the case even in G20 countries we look at OIS Discounting in South Africa. The country is different from others in that there are exchange controls on the South African Rand (ZAR), meaning that there is a cap in place that limits the amount of ZAR that can be traded against foreign currencies per day. Furthermore, there is no local clearing house, which means that the international players that offer central clearing in South Africa – CME and LCH.ClearNet – require USD as collateral. This, together with the exchange restriction, puts a limit on the trading activities, even though the South African regulator has exempted margin payments in Rand and foreign currencies from the exchange restriction, see [143]. As there is no OIS market, it also means that there is no OIS data whatsoever available for ZAR yet. The derivation of a proxy for ZAR OIS is more complicated because the money market is different from currencies with an active LIBOR market:

- The standard ZAR money market rate is the Johannesburg Interbank *Agreed* Rate (JIBAR), calculated as an average of actual quoted *mid* rates from nine contributors (note the difference to other IBOR rates which are, by definition, *offer* rates).
- The standard ZAR overnight rate is the SAFEX ON (aka South African Rand Overnight Deposit Rate), an average of actual ON deposit rates paid by A1-rated local and F1-rated foreign banks where SAFEX places its daily margin proceeds – thus it contains a link to FX rates.
- Top 20 Call Rate: weighted average of the 20 highest rates paid by banks on deposits by non-banks.
- South African Benchmark Overnight Rate on Deposits (SABOR): seen as the benchmark for ON rates in the interbank market, however it contains an FX component as well.

According to the RISK magazine articles [116] and [24], the South African regulator has still not decided whether to require a local CCP or not. At the same time, it wants banks to abide by the Basel III rule of the CVA capital charge for uncleared trades. The local banks that dominate the derivatives market have signed on with international CCPs and are loath to bear the additional cost of a local CCP membership, which in their view offers little to no extra benefit due to lack of market depth and liquidity. At the time of writing, the debate between the South African regulator, local banks and international CCPs still continues, so it may still be a while before a ZAR OIS curve becomes available.

4 Global Discounting

4.1 Collateralization in a foreign currency

We saw before that the collateral determines the discount rate: a EUR swap which is cash-collateralized in EUR is priced using the EONIA curve.

What if it is collateralized in USD?

In the naive approach, we use the USD/EUR FX forwards from Equation (1.8)

$$X_t^{€/\$} = \frac{df_t^{€}}{df_t^{\$}} X_0^{€/\$} \tag{4.1}$$

to transform any EUR future cash flow into USD, and discount it using the USD OIS curve.

However, quoted FX forward rates are not replicated by Equation (4.1).

Since X_0, X_t and $df_t^{\$}$ are all quoted in the market (always assuming that collateral currency is USD), we see that *the EUR discount curve must be changed.* Therefore, we use (4.1) to *define* the EUR discount rates under USD collateral:

$$df_t^{€} = \frac{X_t^{€/\$}}{X_0^{€/\$}} df_t^{\$}. \tag{4.2}$$

One obstacle to proceeding like this is that, even in major currencies, FX forwards are only liquid for two to five years, quoted at most for ten years. Hence we need other liquid, long-dated market data to build a long curve, namely cross-currency basis swap spreads which are quoted for at least 30 years for many currencies against USD or EUR. In a Ccy/USD swap, the spread is in general on the non-USD leg (there are few exceptions like MXN and CLP, where the spread is on the USD leg). For some Eastern European currencies like HUF, there are only Ccy/EUR swaps, with the spread on the non-EUR leg.

Both legs usually pay 3M-IBOR interest quarterly (there are some exceptions like INR, CNY and NDS which are quoted 3M fixed vs 3M USD LIBOR). However, note that the payment dates may differ slightly from the standard one for either involved currency because the standard calendars of each IBOR are merged so as to ensure payments are possible in both currencies.

Of course, there are all sorts of cross-currency trades done over the counter, but only two variants of cross-currency basis swaps are quoted:

- Each leg has only one notional exchange at the beginning and the end of the trade.
- One notional is adjusted at the end of each period to reflect the current FX rate (rebalancing basis swap).

Note that the period lengths and payment dates of each float leg may differ slightly from the standard floating leg in a single-currency swap because calendars in the two currencies have to be merged.

We make two important general assumptions which are market standard:

1. FX products like FX forwards and cross-currency swaps have the same price *regardless of the collateral currency*;
2. Forward-generating curves are the same *regardless of the collateral currency*, only discounting curves change with collateral currency.

In both cases, curves are first stripped using the standard currency as collateral – in case 1 that is usually USD or EUR, in case 2 the currency in which the curve-building instruments are quoted, and then kept fixed when considering different collateral currencies.

4.2 Non-rebalancing cross-currency swaps

Given the three-month IBOR projection curve for both currencies, we can use Equation (4.2) both ways, for example to define a EUR discount curve for USD collateral and vice versa at the short end. Furthermore, we can easily strip the long end of a currency 1 discount curve for currency 2 collateral from the cross-currency basis spread. As an example, consider EUR and USD:

$$\begin{aligned}-df_0^{€} + \sum_{i=1}^{n}(f_i^{€3M} + s_{t_n}^{€/\$})\delta_i\, df_i^{€} + df_n^{€} &= -df_0^{\$} + \sum_{i=1}^{n} f_i^{\$3M}\delta_i\, df_i^{\$} + df_n^{\$} \\ &= -df_0^{\$} + c_m^{\$}\sum_{j=1}^{m}\delta_j'\, df_{t_j'}^{\$} + df_n^{\$}, \qquad (4.3)\end{aligned}$$

where the second equality uses the fact that the flat USD floating leg has the same value as a fixed leg paying the USD par swap rate c_m. As mentioned above, the payment dates of the USD floating leg may differ slightly from those of a single-currency USD LIBOR leg, but the resulting difference is usually ignored. Alternatively, because of assumption 2, we can compute the USD forwards from the three-month LIBOR curve over FedFunds and plug them into the first equation in (4.3) to get an exact match.

For currency pairs that do not include USD, we have to go through USD anyway unless the FX forwards and cross-currency basis swaps are quoted for the pair in question. As an example, we want to compute the JPY discount curve for derivatives that are collateralized in EUR. Both pairs are quoted against USD with a spread on the non-USD currency, which means that we have

$$-df_0^{\$} + \sum_{i=1}^{n} f_i^{\$3M} \delta_i \, df_i^{\$} + df_n^{\$} = -df_0^{€} + \sum_{i=1}^{n} (f_i^{€3M} + s_{t_n}^{€/\$}) \delta_i \, df_i^{€} + df_n^{€}$$

$$= -df_0^{¥} + \sum_{i=1}^{n} (f_i^{¥3M} + s_{t_n}^{¥/\$}) \delta_i \, df_i^{¥} + df_n^{¥}. \quad (4.4)$$

Note that to be precise, again the payment dates in (4.4) do not necessarily match because the EUR leg uses a merged calendar between London, New York and Target while the JPY leg uses a calendar based on London, New York and Tokio. Therefore, the δ_i appearing on the two non-USD legs in (4.4) are not the same, strictly speaking, and the equation is only an approximation.

Assumption 2 now tells us that we can use the three-month forwards for the JPY MUTAN and EUR EONIA curves, respectively, and EONIA discount factors for the EUR leg. Thus, we can imply the EUR-based JPY discount curve from (4.4).

4.3 Rebalancing cross-currency swaps

For rebalancing cross-currency swaps we use

$$N_i^C = N^{\$} X_i \text{ and } df_i^C = \frac{X_0}{X_i} df_i^{\$}.$$

Assume that we want to derive a discount curve for currency C which is used for USD-collateralized trades. Then we have to solve for df_i^C and/or X_i

$$N^{\$} \left[-df_0^{\$} + \sum_{i=1}^{n} f_i^{\$3M} \delta_i df_i^{\$} + df_n^{\$} \right]$$

$$= \frac{1}{X_0} \left[-N_0^C df_0^C + \sum_{i=1}^{n} \left(N_{i-1}^C (f_i^{C3M} + s_{t_n}^{C/\$}) \delta_i + (N_{i-1}^C - N_i^C) \right) df_i^C + N_n^C df_n^C \right]$$

$$
\begin{aligned}
&= \frac{N^\$}{X_0} \sum_{i=1}^{n} (f_i^{C3M} + s_{t_n}^{C/\$}) X_{i-1} \delta_i \, df_i^C + X_{i-1}(df_i^C - df_{i-1}^C) \\
&= N^\$ \sum_{i=1}^{n} (f_i^{C3M} + s_{t_n}^{C/\$}) \frac{X_{i-1}}{X_i} \delta_i \, df_i^\$ + \frac{X_{i-1}}{X_i} df_i^\$ - df_{i-1}^\$ \\
&= N^\$ \sum_{i=1}^{n} \left(1 + (f_i^{C3M} + s_{t_n}^{C/\$})\delta_i\right) \frac{X_{i-1}}{X_i} df_i^\$ - df_{i-1}^\$.
\end{aligned}
$$

As a result, we have the equation

$$
\begin{aligned}
\sum_{i=1}^{n} \left(1 + f_i^{\$3M}\delta_i\right) df_i^\$ &= \sum_{i=1}^{n} \left(1 + (f_i^{C3M} + s_{t_n}^{C/\$})\delta_i\right) \frac{X_{i-1}}{X_i} df_i^\$ \\
&= \sum_{i=1}^{n} \left(1 + (f_i^{C3M} + s_{t_n}^{C/\$})\delta_i\right) \frac{df_i^C}{df_{i-1}^C} df_{i-1}^\$ \qquad (4.5)
\end{aligned}
$$

where everything but df_i^C for $i = n - 4k + 1, \ldots, n$ is known ($k = 1$ for shorter maturities, can be 5 or 10 for longer ones).

It is important to note that swap rates in a non-CSA currency will be (slightly) different for each collateral currency. The discrepancy from the quoted swap rates for the currency in question depends – among other things – on the maturity of the swap. We give an example below. First, cross-currency basis spreads as of 30 September 2014 are shown in Table 4.1 for three-month USD LIBOR vs 3M IBOR for EUR, GBP, CHF and JPY. Secondly, Table 4.2 shows the three-month EURIBOR swap rates. Finally, Table 4.3 and Figure 4.1 show the resulting differences in the swap rates.

Table 4.1 Cross-currency spreads for 3M USD LIBOR vs 3M IBOR in another currency as of 30 September 2014

Years	EUR	GBP	CHF	JPY
1	−0.0014	−0.000025	−0.001525	−0.0026
2	−0.001475	−0.000025	−0.0017	−0.00325
3	−0.00145	−0.000125	−0.00185	−0.00385
4	−0.001425	−0.000225	−0.002025	−0.0044
5	−0.00133	−0.000275	−0.00218	−0.004875
7	−0.0012	−0.00043	−0.00258	−0.00545
10	−0.00093	−0.000675	−0.00288	−0.005675
15	−0.00065	−0.00105	−0.00288	−0.0056375
20	−0.000475	−0.0011	−0.0027	−0.0050375
30	−0.0004	−0.0007	−0.002125	−0.0040875

Table 4.2 3M EURIBOR swap rates as of 30 September 2014

Years	Rate
1	0.00074
2	0.00089
3	0.00136
4	0.00217
5	0.00327
6	0.00459
7	0.00605
8	0.00753
9	0.00893
10	0.01022
12	0.01242
15	0.01484
20	0.01712
25	0.01811
30	0.01854

Table 4.3 Differences from the 3M EURIBOR swap rates depending on the collateral currency as of 30 September 2014

Years	GBP	USD	CHF	JPY
2	−0.0001%	0.0000%	0.0001%	0.0000%
3	0.0000%	−0.0001%	0.0001%	0.0000%
4	0.0001%	−0.0001%	−0.0002%	−0.0003%
5	0.0003%	−0.0001%	−0.0008%	−0.0008%
6	0.0003%	0.0000%	−0.0018%	−0.0016%
7	0.0005%	0.0002%	−0.0031%	−0.0026%
8	0.0005%	0.0005%	−0.0046%	−0.0037%
9	0.0002%	0.0009%	−0.0063%	−0.0047%
10	0.0001%	0.0014%	−0.0079%	−0.0056%
11	−0.0001%	0.0019%	−0.0095%	−0.0064%
12	−0.0005%	0.0025%	−0.0110%	−0.0072%
13	−0.0009%	0.0031%	−0.0124%	−0.0078%
14	−0.0013%	0.0037%	−0.0137%	−0.0084%
15	−0.0016%	0.0043%	−0.0147%	−0.0089%
16	−0.0019%	0.0048%	−0.0157%	−0.0094%
17	−0.0022%	0.0053%	−0.0164%	−0.0097%
18	−0.0025%	0.0057%	−0.0171%	−0.0099%
19	−0.0027%	0.0061%	−0.0176%	−0.0099%
20	−0.0029%	0.0064%	−0.0179%	−0.0100%
21	−0.0031%	0.0066%	−0.0182%	−0.0100%
22	−0.0032%	0.0068%	−0.0183%	−0.0099%
23	−0.0033%	0.0069%	−0.0183%	−0.0098%
24	−0.0033%	0.0070%	−0.0182%	−0.0097%
25	−0.0033%	0.0070%	−0.0181%	−0.0095%
26	−0.0032%	0.0070%	−0.0180%	−0.0094%
27	−0.0032%	0.0069%	−0.0178%	−0.0092%
28	−0.0031%	0.0069%	−0.0175%	−0.0091%
29	−0.0031%	0.0068%	−0.0173%	−0.0089%
30	−0.0030%	0.0068%	−0.0171%	−0.0088%

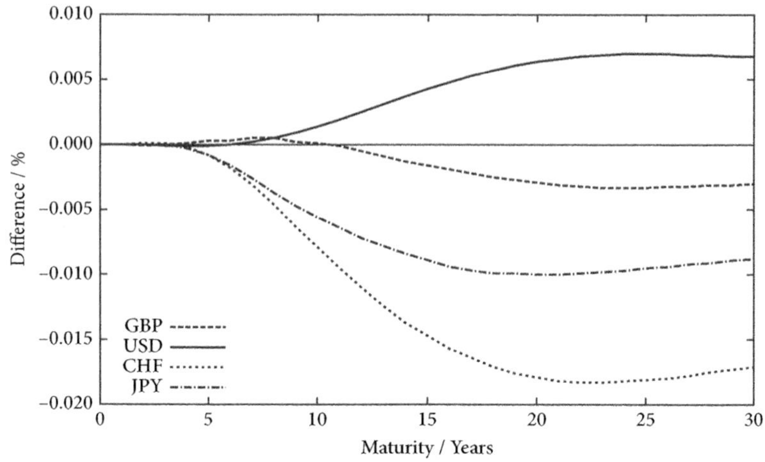

Figure 4.1 Differences from the 3M EURIBOR swap rates depending on the collateral currency as of 30 September 2014

To summarize we need

- One discount curve per currency which serves as the starting curve;
- One forward projection curve for every relevant tenor, per currency, based on the basic discount curve;
- One further discount curve for every combination of trade currency/collateral currency.

Each of these additional curves becomes a risk factor which has to be taken into account in risk calculations. Apart from the technical changes to the involved systems, the hardest part in a change project is to convince all departments that a single-currency derivatives trader can still be a cross-currency trader if the collateral currency is different from the trade currency. If a USD swap is collateralized in EUR, the main interest rate risk comes from the EONIA curve, not the FedFunds curve.

If non-linear products are affected, volatilities have to be recalculated as well. More complex products need new models which can cope with multiple curves. Other processes may be affected as well, for example Fair Value Hedge Accounting.

4.4 Examples: approximations of basis spreads

In this section we want to present some intuitive approximations for the curve construction. We closely follow the Bloomberg paper [28].

We take an abstract approach at pricing basis swaps and generating forwards here. Assume that we are given a discount curve $df^d(t), t \geq 0$, and a forward curve $f(t), t > 0$. As an example, the discount curve can be the one associated with currency 1, used for trades collateralized in currency 2. Another example is that it is simply the OIS curve in a given currency. Then we can define the annuity

$$A^f(t_n) = \sum_{i=1}^{n} \delta_i \, df_i,$$

where δ is the tenor of the forward rate f, the swap rate based on the forward curve

$$c^f(t_n) = \frac{\sum_{i=1}^{n} f(t_i)\,\delta_i\, df_i}{A^f(t_n)},$$

and the swap rate based on the discount curve

$$c^d(t_n) = \frac{1 - df_n}{A^f(t_n)}.$$

If we have a basis swap between two such set-ups, that is discount and forward curves 1 and 2, respectively, with a basis spread on leg 2, we can compute the present values of each leg as[1]

$$PV_1 = \sum_{i=1}^{n} f_1(t_i)\,\delta_i\, df_1(t_i) + df_1(t_n) = \left(c_1^f(t_n) - c_1^d(t_n)\right) A_1^f(t_n) + 1 \text{ and}$$

$$PV_2 = \sum_{j=1}^{n} \left(f_2(t_j') + s\right)\delta_i\, df_2(t_j') + df_2(t_n) = \left(c_2^f(t_n) - c_2^d(t_n) + s\right) A_2^f(t_n) + 1.$$

If the swap is fair, its total PV is 0, so

$$\left(c_1^f(t_n) - c_1^d(t_n)\right) A_1^f(t_n) = \left(c_2^f(t_n) - c_2^d(t_n) + s\right) A_2^f(t_n)$$

or

$$s = \left(c_1^f(t_n) - c_1^d(t_n)\right)\frac{A_1^f(t_n)}{A_2^f(t_n)} - \left(c_2^f(t_n) - c_2^d(t_n)\right). \tag{4.6}$$

[1] For tenor basis swaps, we artificially introduce the notional repayment at maturity, which has no influence on the present value of the overall swap; for cross-currency basis swaps, we assume constant notionals on both sides. In the latter case, we have converted any foreign currency amounts back into the other leg's currency, so we do not need to bother with any FX spot rates.

4.4.1 Tenor basis spreads

The first and easiest observation from (4.6) is that it recovers (2.1): in the case of a tenor basis spread, the discount curves df_1 and df_2 are the same because they are based on the same currency, and the forward curves f_1 and f_2 yield different swap rates, so we are left with

$$s = c_1^f(t_n)\frac{A_1^f(t_n)}{A_2^f(t_n)} - c_2^f(t_n),$$

which is just (2.1).

4.4.2 Flat cross-currency swaps

As a next application, assume we have a cross-currency swap without a spread, that is both sides pay LIBOR flat in their respective currencies. What is the present value of the swap if we discount each leg with its native OIS curve? Heuristically, we have a pricing gap of the OIS-δ spread on each leg, so we expect the pricing difference to be of the order of the difference of these spreads times the respective annuity factor. If we express the difference in terms of a spread $s^{LO,LO}$ which would make the swap fair, we see from (4.6) that

$$s^{LO,LO} = \left(c_1^L(t_n) - c_1^O(t_n)\right)\frac{A_1(t_n)}{A_2(t_n)} - \left(c_2^L(t_n) - c_2^O(t_n)\right)$$

as expected, bearing in mind that in this case $c_i^L(t_n) - c_i^O(t_n)$ is the OIS-δ spread s_i^{LO} in currency i. The annuity quotient is very close to 1, so we get a good approximation

$$s^{LO,LO} \approx s_1^{LO} - s_2^{LO}. \tag{4.7}$$

4.4.3 OIS cross-currency basis spread

We now look at the situation where we have two OIS legs in a single currency, but one is discounted at OIS, the other at the rate implied from some foreign currency. That is, the forward curves are identical in this case, namely the one associated with forwards generated off the OIS curve, but the discount curves are df^{FX} and df^O for the FX-implied and the OIS-based rates, respectively. We compensate the price difference by a spread s^{FXO} on the FX-implied leg. The other leg, on which discounting and forward generation agree, is worth 1, so we have the equation

$$s^{FXO} = c^{FX} - c^O. \tag{4.8}$$

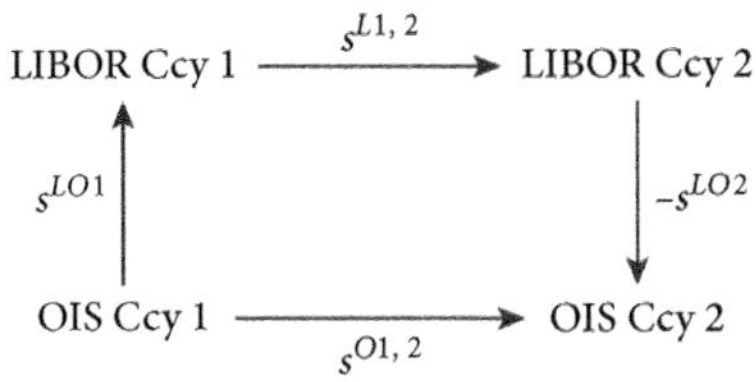

Figure 4.2 The approximate equivalence of $s^{L1,2}$ and $s^{LO,LO} + s^{O1,2}$

Given a "proper" OIS cross-currency swap between the collateral currency and a second currency, we have two OIS floating legs, where leg 2 contains the quoted OIS basis spread $s^{O1,2}$, and both legs are discounted with the discount curve induced by the collateral currency OIS curve. In other words, on leg 1 we use df_1^O, and on leg 2 we use df_2^{FX}. The forward curves are the ones associated with the OIS curves. Thus, leg 1 is worth 1, and we see that

$$s^{O1,2} = c_2^{FX} - c_2^O = s^{FXO}. \tag{4.9}$$

We can interpret this result by saying that the FX-implied discount curve is just the OIS curve plus the OIS basis spread.

4.4.4 LIBOR cross-currency basis spread

Finally, we approximate the quoted cross-currency basis spread $s^{L1,2}$ for LIBOR legs. Forward curves are the LIBOR curves in the two currencies; leg 1 is discounted with the OIS rate df_1^O of the collateral currency, while leg 2 is discounted using the FX-implied discount rate df_2^{FX}. We get from (4.6)

$$\begin{aligned} s^{L1,2} &\approx (c_1^L - c_1^O) - (c_2^L - c_2^{FX}) \\ &= s_1^{LO} - (c_2^L - c_2^O - s^{O1,2}) \\ &\approx s^{LO,LO} + s^{O1,2} \end{aligned} \tag{4.10}$$

Note that this means that the diagram in Figure 4.2 is approximately commutative.

5 CSA Discounting

5.1 ISDA agreements and CSA complexities

The International Swaps and Derivatives Association (ISDA) presented the so-called master agreement in 1987 (USD only), an updated version in 1992, and a further update in 2002. All of these master agreement types are still in use because many have not yet been updated. The master agreement allocates the financial risks in transactions between two counterparties without containing specific commercial information for individual trades, it just gives a framework for the portfolio of trades between the two signing parties. For instance, Section 5 of the master agreement defines "Events of Default" and "Termination Events", and Section 6 clarifies the conditions under which early termination of transactions is possible for one party if such events occur, including close-out and netting. Nowadays, the MA usually has a Credit Support Annex (CSA) which details the collateralization provisions:

- Which side has to post collateral (this can be restricted to either side, or both have to post collateral). Obviously, it makes a big difference if one party is exempt from posting collateral: It will have reduced counterparty credit risk itself, but its counterparty faces the full credit exposure. The collateral is intended to mitigate net or "netting set" exposures; i.e. it is held against the entire portfolio of OTC contracts covered by the ISDA agreement.
- Thresholds, (MTA) and collateral call frequency. The threshold gives a minimum level of net exposure that has to be reached so that collateral has to be posted. It can be different for the two parties involved, or be variable depending on each party's rating. In some cases, the threshold can also change deterministically over time. Evidently, the case where only one side has to post collateral can be represented by a threshold of infinite size.

  The MTA is the minimum extra amount by which the exposure has to increase since the last collateral call so that additional collateral has to be posted. The call frequency determines how often calls happen. Nowadays, most CSAs prescribe daily calls, but there are still many old CSAs in use which have weekly or even monthly call frequencies. The process of calling for additional collateral or for excess collateral to be returned is called *margining*. The difference amount that is posted either way is called the *variation margin*.

- Independent amounts: These are similar to the initial margin one has to post at a central counterparty, see Section 3.2. However, the basis for calculating the independent amount may vary significantly from one CSA to the other, from fixed amounts or fractions of notional to more sophisticated risk-related formulas. Furthermore, the posting of an independent amount is often only triggered by a downgrade trigger.
- Eligible collateral: Which currencies can be used if cash is posted. A lot of CSAs allow cash collateral in several different currencies. Which assets can be used as collateral in addition to cash: The CSA may contain a list of eligible assets with a predetermined haircut attached to each of them. The haircut is a percentage by which the market value of the collateral asset has to be reduced to give the collateral amount.
- Treatment of collateral by the receiving party: Can collateral be reused as collateral in other CSAs or repo transactions (rehypothecation) or not?

The curve building described so far assumes perfect collateralization with cash collateral posted in one single currency. In reality, CSAs have features that render the collateralization far from perfect, and therefore have an impact on the valuation. Note that at this point it becomes impossible to price an individual derivatives transaction; it is necessary to consider the whole portfolio that is governed by the CSA. This is a fact that will come up again and again when we introduce the various value adjustments.

Another remark to be made is that there is often an additional delay in the posting of collateral which is due to disputes which in particular occur for structured products. When the two counterparties cannot agree on the market value of one or more transactions that are governed by a CSA, they open discussions as to why they disagree. This may be caused by different market data sources or snapshot times, different pricing models or different estimates for model parameters such as volatilities, correlations or liquidity premia. If they cannot resolve their dispute, one of the parties is authorized by the CSA to go to the market and ask for a price from several market participants. The average of such indications then has to be used as the basis for the collateral call. Since this entire process can take quite some time, larger positions may meanwhile move adversely for one party, thus increasing the credit exposure. For trades with a CCP, disputes are not an issue as the CCP's collateral call cannot be disputed, and the products traded via CCPs are only vanilla anyway, leaving less room for price differences.

Even if the two counterparties agree on the collateral amount all the time, the actual replacement cost after the default of one side can be very different from the collateral received. Many counterparties of Lehman Brothers experienced this after its default in 2008, which sent the markets into turmoil, thus moving market values and liquidity premia significantly. The posted collateral was often not enough to compensate the replacement costs.

5.2 Currency options

The currency option is complicated enough but in addition depends on the jurisdiction:

- Under US law, collateral payer can decide to switch all collateral (posted and new) from one currency to another any day $\Rightarrow$ we can always expect the collateral currency as a whole to be optimal;
- Under British law, collateral payer can only decide to pay additional collateral in an eligible currency (switching the currency for posted collateral can be rejected) $\Rightarrow$ the collateral account may be fragmented into various bits in different currencies. This is sometimes referred to as the "Sticky Amount" version.

To illustrate the second possibility, assume that we have a trade under British law with a collateral currency option for GBP, EUR or USD. Counterparties A and B execute in t_0 at value V_0 (GBP), which is paid by B to A (transaction fee). At each time point t_i, we have

- Values V_i (in GBP),
- OIS rates $r_i^{GBP}, r_i^{USD}, r_i^{EUR}$ for the period t_i to t_{i+1},
- OIS cross-currency basis spreads $s_i^{GBPUSD}, s_i^{GBPEUR}$ (on the GBP leg) for the period t_i to t_{i+1},
- Exchange rates $FX_i^{GBPUSD}, FX_i^{GBPEUR}$ (expressing the value of 1 GBP in the other currency).

We want to understand the cash flows if A optimizes its collateral postings currency-wise. We assume the following scenarios:

- $r_0^{EUR} + s_0^{GBPEUR} > r_0^{GBP} > r_0^{USD} + s_0^{GBPUSD}$ and $V_1 > V_0$,
- $r_1^{GBP} > r_1^{EUR} + s_1^{GBPEUR} > r_1^{USD} + s_1^{GBPUSD}$ and $V_2 > V_1$,
- $r_2^{USD} + s_2^{GBPUSD} > r_2^{EUR} + s_2^{GBPEUR} > r_2^{GBP}$ and $V_3 = 0$.

In t_0, it is advantageous for A to post collateral in EUR because this will yield the highest interest on the collateral. So A

- Enters into an FX swap, swapping $FX_0 V_0$ EUR at r_0^{EUR} against V_0 GBP at $r_0^{GBP} + s_0^{GBPEUR}$ and
- Pays $FX_0 V_0$ EUR to B.

In t_1, it is better to pay collateral in GBP, so A

- Receives EUR interest $r_0^{EUR}\delta_0 FX_0^{GBPEUR} V_0$ from A;
- Returns $(1 + r_0^{EUR}\delta_0) FX_0^{GBPEUR} V_0$ EUR in the FX swap;
- Receives back $(1 + (r_0^{GBP} + s_0^{GBPEUR})\delta_0) V_0$ GBP from the FX swap;
- Rolls the FX swap, swapping $\frac{FX_0^{GBPEUR}}{FX_1^{GBPEUR}} V_0$ GBP at $r_1^{GBP} + s_1^{GBPEUR}$ against $FX_0^{GBPEUR} V_0$ EUR at r_1^{EUR} and
- Pays $V_1 - \frac{FX_0^{GBPEUR}}{FX_1^{GBPEUR}} V_0$ GBP as additional collateral to B.

In t_2, it is better to pay collateral in USD, so A

- Receives interest $r_1^{EUR}\delta_1 FX_0^{GBPEUR} V_0$ in EUR and $r_1^{GBP}\delta_1 \left(V_1 - \frac{FX_0^{GBPEUR}}{FX_1^{GBPEUR}} V_0 \right)$ in GBP from A,
- Returns $(1 + r_1^{EUR}\delta_1) FX_0^{GBPEUR} V_0$ in the FX swap,
- Receives back $(1 + (r_1^{GBP} + s_1^{GBPEUR})\delta_1) \frac{FX_0^{GBPEUR}}{FX_1^{GBPEUR}} V_0$ from the FX swap,
- Rolls the FX swap, swapping $\frac{FX_0^{GBPEUR}}{FX_2^{GBPEUR}} V_0$ GBP at $r_2^{GBP} + s_2^{GBPEUR}$ against $FX_0^{GBPEUR} V_0$ EUR at r_2^{EUR},
- Enters into a second FX swap, swapping $V_2 - V_1 - \frac{FX_0^{GBPEUR}}{FX_2^{GBPEUR}} V_0$ GBP at $r_2^{GBP} + s_2^{GBPUSD}$ against $FX_2^{GBPUSD} \left(V_2 - V_1 - \frac{FX_0^{GBPEUR}}{FX_2^{GBPEUR}} V_0 \right)$ USD at r_2^{USD},
- Pays $FX_2^{GBPUSD} \left(V_2 - V_1 - \frac{FX_0^{GBPEUR}}{FX_2^{GBPEUR}} V_0 \right)$ USD as additional collateral to B.

In t_3, everything is paid back with interest. Table 5.1 shows the cash flows resulting from these choices.

Smaller banks often ignore currency options. One simple approach is to use a blended discount curve which consists of the cheapest (lowest) parts of the spread-adjusted OIS discount curves of the involved currencies. However, this only applies to American law as it does not capture the collateral already posted in the British law case. It should be noted that this approach only yields the intrinsic

Table 5.1 The various different cash flows from the example of a collateral currency option in the text

Time	CP	GBP	EUR	USD
0	M	$-V_0$	$FX_0^{GE}V_0$	
	B		$-FX_0^{GE}V_0$	
1	M	$(1+(r_0^G+s_0^{GE})\delta_0)V_0$	$-(1+r_0^E\delta_0)FX_0^{GE}V_0$	
	M	$-\frac{FX_0^{GE}}{FX_1^{GE}}V_0$	$FX_0^{GE}V_0$	
	B	$-V_1+\frac{FX_0^{GE}}{FX_1^{GE}}V_0$	$r_0^E\delta_0 FX_0^{GE}V_0$	
2	M	$(1+(r_1^G+s_1^{GE})\delta_1)\frac{FX_0^{GE}}{FX_1^{GE}}V_0$	$-(1+r_1^E\delta_1)FX_0^{GE}V_0$	
	M	$-\frac{FX_0^{GE}}{FX_2^{GE}}V_0$	$FX_0^{GE}V_0$	
	M	$-V_2+V_1+\frac{FX_0^{GE}}{FX_2^{GE}}V_0$		$\left(V_2-V_1-\frac{FX_0^{GE}}{FX_2^{GE}}V_0\right)FX_2^{GU}$
	B	$r_1^G\delta_1\left(V_1-\frac{FX_0^{GE}}{FX_1^{GE}}V_0\right)$	$r_1^E\delta_1 FX_0^{GE}V_0$	$-\left(V_2-V_1-\frac{FX_0^{GE}}{FX_2^{GE}}V_0\right)FX_2^{GU}$
3	M	$(1+(r_2^G+s_2^{GE})\delta_2)\frac{FX_0^{GE}}{FX_2^{GE}}V_0$	$-(1+r_2^E\delta_2)FX_0^{GE}V_0$	
	M	$(1+(r_2^G+s_2^{GU})\delta_2)\times$ $\left(V_2-V_1-\frac{FX_0^{GE}}{FX_2^{GE}}V_0\right)$		$-(1+r_2^U\delta_2)\times$ $\left(V_2-V_1-\frac{FX_0^{GE}}{FX_2^{GE}}V_0\right)FX_2^{GU}$
	B	$(1+r_2^G\delta_2)\left(V_1-\frac{FX_0^{GE}}{FX_1^{GE}}V_0\right)$	$(1+r_2^E\delta_2)FX_0^{GE}V_0$	$(1+r_2^U\delta_2)\times$ $\left(V_2-V_1-\frac{FX_0^{GE}}{FX_2^{GE}}V_0\right)FX_2^{GU}$

value of the option as it ignores the stochasticity and variation of the spread curves over time. Because of the very bespoke nature of the resulting curve, more collateral disputes are likely, especially with counterparties using only one collateral currency (their funding currency). Note that there are still many banks that have not yet switched their entire derivatives portfolio to OIS discounting, let alone more sophisticated curves like the one discussed here. We discuss alternative approaches in Section 12.4.

There is no industry-wide standard for tackling this problem; most banks try to reduce their options by renegotiating their CSAs. However, if they are not capable of calculating the value of the currency option approximately correctly, they are not in a position to decide whether the fee offered or requested for dispensing with the option is adequate.

5.3 Negative overnight rates

Negative interest rates are not a new phenomenon. They occurred in Japanese yen in the 1990s, and during the eurozone credit crisis in Swiss francs. During that period, German government bonds with maturities up to two years also had negatives yields. Very recently, with the latest policy decisions of the ECB, the euro overnight rates became negative as well, with the EONIA forward curve showing negative values for a couple of years.

In addition, the interest which is accrued for posted collateral is often the overnight rate minus a spread. The view of many European banks seems to be that interest on posted collateral should never be negative, that is when O/N falls below zero, it is set to zero for collateral interest compounding purposes, even if this is not explicitly stated in the CSA. US-based banks, on the other hand, seem to be of the opinion that if rates are negative, the interest has to be paid by the poster of collateral, see Wood [144]. The issue is still undecided at the time of writing (April 2015); it should be monitored closely as it might have an impact on how discount curves are built, as we shall see. The ISDA publishes the list of parties adhering to its "ISDA 2014 Collateral Agreement Negative Interest Protocol" on the website https://www2.isda.org/functional-areas/protocol-management/protocol-adherence/18. More and more banks, including many European ones, are listed as adhering to the protocol there (27 new ones in April 2015 alone, all but one European).

For Central Counterparties (CCP), however, there is no floor in general (anymore), as the following example from LCH SwapClear Circular No. 136 shows:

> LCH.Clearnet Ltd pays interest on cash posted to cover Client initial margin requirements in its SwapClear service at a rate known as Client Deposit Rate (CDR). We publish a CDR in 3 currencies: USD, EUR & GBP. CDR is calculated by adjusting an external benchmark interest rate by a spread.
>
> As of 2 January 2015, we have amended SwapClear's CDRs as follows:
>
> - We have removed the floor that had previously applied in all 3 currencies, such that CDR may now become negative
> - In EUR, we have amended the spread to EONIA, from its prior level of −30 to an improved level of −15
> - In USD and GBP, there has been no change to the spread
>
> As a result, the new CDR rates are:

Currency	Benchmark	Spread as of 2 January 2015
EUR	EONIA	−15
USD	FedFunds	−5
GBP	SONIA	−10

There are still CSAs in place which explicitly state a floor at 0. What does this floor mean in terms of curve building and pricing?

As a first approach, we could take the floor into account when building the discount curve. Our argument from Section 2.2 that the collateral interest rate should be used for risk-neutral pricing still holds, so it is the floored overnight rate (with spread if applicable) that is the correct one. This means that we have to compute an expectation of the form

$$\mathbb{E}\left[\exp\left(-\int_0^T \max(r(t)-s,0)\,dt\right)\right] \tag{5.1}$$

under the bank account measure, where $r(t)$ is the overnight rate and s is the spread subtracted to compute the accrual rate and hence the risk-free discount curve. It is clear from this that we need to choose a model in order to compute this expectation.

Note, though, that discounting expected future cash flows with this adjusted discount curve does not give the correct results if the cash flows are not deterministic. If they depend on the discount factors (like, for instance, forward rates), it is necessary to compute them using the unadjusted overnight rates first and then apply the floor in the discounting. This means that even for a simple product like a swap, it is necessary to simulate the overnight rate just for pricing purposes.

We will revisit this topic in Section 11.3, after we have presented the necessary model descriptions.

Finally, we see that we need the volatilities of the overnight rate. These are not directly quoted in the market but can be derived from quoted swaption volatilities either by applying the move through the normal volatilities (which, almost by definition, is the natural view once interest rates have become negative) or by calibrating the model to quoted volatilities under the assumption of deterministic basis spreads; compare Sections 3.9.2 and 11.2.3.

5.4 Other assets as collateral

If bonds can be posted as collateral, the picture becomes even more complicated. Assume any eligible bond can be acquired in the repo market (i.e. accepted as collateral in a repo transaction) and rehypothecated. Given eligible bonds $i = 1,\ldots,n$ with given CSA haircuts H_i^{CSA}, repo market haircuts H_i^R and repo market rates r_i, the collateral poster could maximize the returns $R_i = \frac{1-H_i^{CSA}}{1-H_i^R} r_i$ and any cash rate to choose the cheapest to deliver collateral. However, this choice has to be readjusted dynamically. The option can be priced as in the currency option case above but only under independence and zero-switching-cost assumptions (which are both questionable). Under British law this is an even bigger challenge than under US law. Note also that this has to be done for every CSA separately.

We see that the question of rehypothecation already plays an important role in this case; it is even more important when we address the issue of funding costs related to derivatives and collateral cash flows in Chapter 20.

5.5 Thresholds and asymmetries

It is not clear how thresholds and asymmetries can be handled by changing the discount curve. It seems to be market consensus that the uncollateralized part of the portfolio should be discounted with the funding curve, and only the collateralized bit with the OIS/CSA curve – but how are we to determine which part of the portfolio causes a threshold breach? The portfolio value changes dynamically anyway, so how can a static curve capture the dynamics of future value changes in order to discount correctly the cash flows?

On the other hand, OIS *is* the risk-free rate and should be used for discounting for theoretical reasons, see Section 2.2. This then brings us into the realm of CVA and FVA: Discount using OIS (maybe bond-adjusted) curves, though consider the CSA details in the XVA simulation. As long as the CSAs are as diverse as they currently are, changing the discount curve is no panacea for pricing issues. XVA methods are needed instead.

5.6 Some thoughts on initial margin

Initial margin (IM) has to be posted by both parties of a derivatives transaction – actually, in a cleared transaction, there are *three* parties involved as the two trading parties end up with deals with the CCP. The individual impact depends on each party's portfolio with the CCP but it is clear that IM creates some cost for both parties. The IM liquidity has to be funded (usually at the unsecured level, but there may be cash or liquid assets available in the form of rehypothecable received collateral). Even though the risk for a single new trade is identical for all CCP members and sub-members, its marginal cost depends on the funding spread, the existing portfolio and the pool of eligible CCPs. It is not clear how this (idiosyncratic) cost should be captured in the discount curve. So even in the case of perfect collateralization, we see that the requirement of IM implies that a long-term portfolio simulation is needed to calculate the value correctly. The cost attached to IM is often called margin value adjustment (MVA) and will be discussed in more detail in Chapter 20.

6 Fair Value Hedge Accounting in a Multi-Curve World

6.1 Introduction

Fair Value Hedge Accounting (FVHA) is a tool for financial reporting that allows us to recognize gains and losses as well as revenues and expenses that come from a hedged item and a hedging instrument in the same accounting period. Its use and conditions are described in the International Accounting Standards (IAS 39, [93]) and the FAS 133 for the US. IAS 39 will be replaced by the International Financial Reporting Standard (IFRS) 9 [94] on 1 January 2018.

We only want to describe one particular aspect of FVHA here, namely the effect of applying the multi-curve pricing framework to instruments that are hedged by interest rate swaps, which includes structured payoffs that might be linked to other asset classes such as FX, inflation or equity. Discounting derivatives with an OIS curve changes the application of FVHA because the basis spread between the OIS and the forward projection causes P&L swings which are not hedged. Schubert [132] presents a way out of this dilemma by using the hedging cost approach which we will describe below, and a continual de-designation and re-designation of hedge relationships.

We do not give financial advice here. While we do know reference users that apply the method we describe below, any potential users should discuss the application with their auditors. They should be aware that not all auditors agree with Schubert's [132] way of including multi-curve pricing into FVHA.

For a thorough introduction to the topic in general, see for instance Ramirez [127]. We also do not discuss *Portfolio* FVHA here because the principle underlying it is the same, while the details of implementing it are a lot messier. And finally, we restrict ourselves to hedged items that are assets or liabilities and hedging instruments that are derivatives.

To cite Ramirez ([127], p. 8), "the aim of the fair value hedge is to offset in P&L the change in fair value of the hedged item with the change in fair value of the derivative." This is done to reduce P&L moves due to value changes in the hedging instrument, which usually is a derivative and therefore has to be recognized at fair value at all times, whereas the hedged item (also often referred to as the underlying) is often of the IFRS category Loans and Receivables (LaR) and is therefore recognized at amortized cost. Items in the category Available for Sale (AfS) are also eligible for FVHA. In such a situation, FVHA allows the user to show the value changes of the underlying and the hedging instruments in the P&L; the more effective the hedge, the less the P&L will move.

6.2 Hedge effectiveness

The effectiveness of the hedge relationship has to be measured regularly, and both in a prospective and a retrospective manner. This means that at hedge inception and on any reporting date, the reporting entity has to verify that the hedge will remain effective in the future, and that it has been effective over the last reporting period. The IAS 39 set a hard criterion for the effectiveness measure: If the hedged item's value has moved (retrospective) or is expected to move (prospective) by 100 currency units, the hedging instrument has to move or have moved by no less than 80 and no more than 125 units, but in the opposite direction. We denote the value change of the underlying by ΔU, and the value change of the hedging instrument by ΔH. It is very important to note that the differences are to be based on the moves *due to changes in the hedged risk factor(s)* only.

There are several methods that are allowed for measuring effectiveness; compare Ramirez [127]:

- The critical terms method, where all the terms of both the underlying and the derivative that are relevant to pricing have to match (these are notional amount, maturity, underlying of the derivative and hedged instrument, and zero start value of the derivative). This test can only be used prospectively. While it seems logical that a match of the relevant parameters should result in a good hedge, it is not considered sufficient by the standard.
- Scenario analysis: The hedged risk factors are stressed or simulated, and the resulting moves ΔU and ΔH have to lie within the prescribed relative range. Again, this can only be used for prospective testing. The drawback of this method is that the selection of scenarios is subjective.
- The ratio analysis or dollar offset method, where the quotient $-\Delta H/\Delta U$ of the actual moves over the reporting period has to lie within the range $[0.8, 1.25]$. This method only looks at the total move over the reporting period; it would not raise an alarm if the hedge went haywire in a sub-period.
- Regression analysis: In this retrospective test, the daily moves ΔU_i and ΔH_i, $i = 1, \ldots, n$ are examined in a regression analysis. If the regression line has a slope in the range of $[-1.25, -0.8]$, then the hedge is deemed effective. The regression analysis has the advantage that the correlation between the two data

sets $\{\Delta U_i \mid i = 1, \ldots, n\}$ and $\{\Delta H_i \mid i = 1, \ldots, n\}$ is investigated as well. An honest hedge relationship should show a correlation close to -1 as well as a regression in the prescribed range.

- Volatility risk reduction method: It is checked whether the reduction in volatility due to hedging is sufficiently high by looking at the ratio

$$\frac{\sqrt{Var(\Delta U_i + \Delta H_i)}}{\sqrt{Var(\Delta U_i)}}.$$

The drawback of this method is that the user has to make a connection between the volatility ratio threshold and the effectiveness range prescribed by IAS 39.

If a hedging relationship fails the effectiveness test at some point, it has to be broken up. As this is not a welcome result, users are interested in high effectiveness scores.

6.3 Single-curve valuation

When hedging a bond or loan with an interest rate swap, one can use the *hedging cost approach* as described in Schubert ([132], [133]). This means that we first have to define the risk that we want to hedge. As an example, assume we want to hedge the 6M-EURIBOR swap curve risk[1] contained within a fixed-rate bond paying interest in EUR. We then determine the hedged portion of the hedged item as the notional exchange plus the cash flow corresponding to the six-month par swap rate at inception of the hedge relationship. Since swap rates can be considered risk-free due to collateralization, the unhedged portion – the difference between the coupon of the bond and the risk-free coupon – is the credit spread[2] of the bond. In other words, at inception $t = 0$ of the hedge relationship, we have

$$c_B = c^{6M}(0) + s_{CR}(0),$$

where c_B is the bond coupon, c^{6M} is the fair six-month EURIBOR swap rate, and s_{CR} is the credit spread component of the coupon. The rate $c_{RE} := c^{6M}(0)$ (i.e. the hedged portion of the bond) is also referred to as the *risk-equivalent coupon*. The hedge would then be a par swap which pays the fair swap rate as of inception and receives six-month EURIBOR flat.

Figure 6.1 illustrates the notation of time points that we will use. Time t is the date at which the analysis is done. Un-primed times t_i indicate the period start

[1] This means the risk of price changes of the bond due to moves of the six-month swap curve.

[2] This is only true at inception. As interest rates move, the package of bond and swap will move away from par over time. This definition of credit spread is only one of many possible ones. It is usually referred to as the *yield spread* if the bond is worth par at inception.

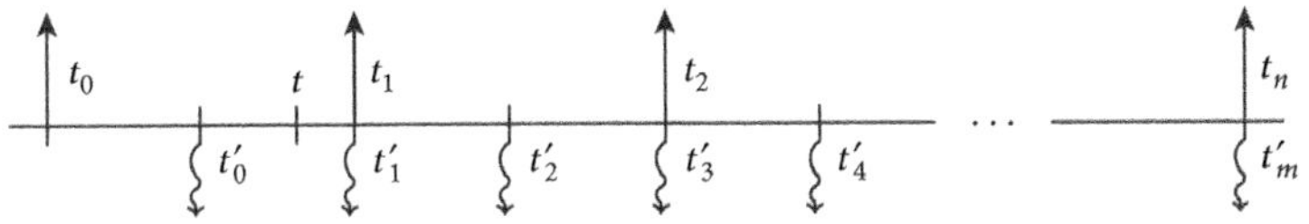

Figure 6.1 Fixed cash flows with annual periods vs semi-annual variable flows. The curly arrows depict the variable (stochastic) flows

and end dates of a fixed instrument like a bond or a fixed swap leg, while primed times t'_j indicate the period start and end dates for floating rate instruments. While the single-curve case would allow us to assume those dates to be the same, the distinction helps us to get the right understanding for the multi-curve setup, where the distinction is necessary. We further assume that payments always occur on a period end date, and that fixings happen on the period start date. In the most general case, t will be in the middle of a fixed and floating period, such that $t_0 \leq t'_0 \leq t < t'_1 \leq t_1$. The end dates of floating and fixed instruments will always be the same in our analysis (which is not a necessary condition for a hedge to be valid).

To ease notation, we define the usual annuity factors at time t:

$$A^{\delta}(t, t_n) = \sum_{i=1}^{m} \delta_{t'_{i-1}, t'_i}\, df_{t'_i}$$

for the floating rate side of the swap and

$$A^{f}(t, t_n) = \sum_{i=1}^{n} \delta_{t_{i-1}, t_i}\, df_i$$

for the fixed side of the swap (and the bond). We will also work with clean values a lot in this chapter, so for $t_0 \leq t'_0 \leq t < t'_1 \leq t_1$ we will need the *clean annuities*

$$\hat{A}^{\delta}(t, t_n) = A^{\delta}(t, t_n) - \delta_{t'_0, t}$$

for the floating rate side of the swap and

$$\hat{A}^{f}(t, t_n) = A^{f}(t, t_n) - \delta_{t_0, t}.$$

Very often, the underlying is hedged by an asset swap which exactly mirrors the bond coupon payments on one side and has variable payments of the type LIBOR plus asset swap spread, s. In this case, the hedged portion of the underlying is the bond coupon minus the spread on the floating leg of the swap, adjusted by the annuity quotient of the two legs, which amounts to the same type of definition of the risk-equivalent coupon: In both cases, the sum of the cash flows defined by the hedged portion of the underlying – the risk-equivalent coupons – and the derivative's cash flows add up to a floating rate note in terms of clean present values. Therefore, the following equality of clean PVs should be satisfied at all times t (the subscripts *FRN*, *DER* and *REB* standing for floating rate note, derivative and risk-equivalent bond, respectively):

$$CPV_{FRN}(t) = CPV_{DER}(t) + CPV_{REB}(t) \tag{6.1}$$

In the single-curve world, the value of an FRN is always 1 on a fixing date. In particular, we must have at inception $t = 0$

$$1 = CPV_{DER}(0) + c_{RE}A^f(0, t_n) + df_n, \tag{6.2}$$

where the clean (and dirty) present value of the derivative at inception is

$$CPV_{DER}(0) = -\underbrace{c_S A^f(0, t_n)}_{\text{fixed leg}} + \underbrace{1 - df_n + sA^\delta(0, t_n)}_{\text{floating leg}}, \tag{6.3}$$

with c_S the fixed rate and s the spread on the floating leg of the swap. This is the defining property of the hedge relationship under the hedging cost approach, which implies that

$$c_{RE} = c_S - s\frac{A^\delta(0, t_n)}{A^f(0, t_n)}, \tag{6.4}$$

as we claimed above. If $c_S = c_B$, then s will be the asset swap spread of the bond; if $s = 0$, then c_S must be the par swap rate ($PV = 0$).

Now, if we generalize (6.2) to the case where t is within a (floating) period, $t_0 \leq t'_0 \leq t < t'_1 \leq t_1$, then we see that in terms of clean values[3] we have

$$\begin{aligned} CPV_{DER}(t) + CPV_{REB}(t) = L(t'_0)\hat{A}^\delta(t'_0, t'_1) + df_{t'_1} - df_n + s\hat{A}^\delta(t, t_n) \\ - c_S\hat{A}^f(t, t_n) + c_{RE}\hat{A}^f(t, t_n) + df_n. \end{aligned}$$

[3] In (6.2) we did not care for the distinction between clean and dirty values because they are identical at inception.

$$
\begin{aligned}
&= L(t_0')\hat{A}^\delta(t_0', t_1') + df_{t_1'} + s\hat{A}^\delta(t, t_n) \\
&\quad - c_S\hat{A}^f(t, t_n) + c_S\hat{A}^f(t, t_n) - s\frac{A^\delta(0, t_n)}{A^f(0, t_n)}\hat{A}^f(t, t_n) \\
&= L(t_0')\hat{A}^\delta(t_0', t_1') + df_{t_1'} \\
&\quad + s\hat{A}^\delta(t, t_n)\left(1 - \frac{A^\delta(0, t_n)\hat{A}^f(t, t_n)}{A^f(0, t_n)\hat{A}^\delta(t, t_n)}\right),
\end{aligned}
$$

which is approximately the clean value of a floating rate note at time t, since the factor by which s is multiplied is negligible. From this, we see that for a precise match with a floating rate note, we would have to define a risk-equivalent coupon which depends on time t by

$$
c_{RE}(t) = c_S - s\frac{\hat{A}^\delta(t, t_n)}{\hat{A}^f(t, t_n)}. \tag{6.5}
$$

When we move on to the multi-curve world, that is exactly what we will do.

Hedge effectiveness is now measured between a synthetic bond paying the risk-equivalent coupon c_{RE} and the swap. All cash flows are discounted using the risk-free discount curve (six-month EURIBOR in our example). This is because we defined the hedged risk solely to be the six-month EURIBOR interest rate risk, so any value moves due to the credit spread are not booked through P&L but through Other Comprehensive Income (OCI).

As an alternative approach, we define the *risk-induced fair value* of the hedge package, and show that it gives equivalent results to the hedging cost approach.

Assume we are given an asset swap package of notional 1, consisting of a bond (an asset) paying a coupon c_B and a swap which pays a coupon c_S on the bond coupon payment dates, while receiving LIBOR plus a spread s. The package was done at par. Looking at the economic P&L of this hedge package, we have the following components:

- The bond's value move

$$
P(t) - 1 = c_B \sum_{i=1}^{n} \delta_{t_{i-1},t_i}\, df_i\, e^{-z(t)\,\delta_{t,t_i}} + df_n\, e^{-z(t)\,\delta_{t,t_n}} - 1
$$

  where $t_0 \leq t$ is the current period's start date;
- The swap fixed leg

$$
-\,c_S A^f(t_0, t_n);
$$

- The first floating period's coupon, which was fixed as $L(t'_0)$ on some date $t'_0 \leq t$

$$(L(t'_0) + s)\, A^{\delta}(t, t'_1);$$

- The yet unknown LIBOR rates of the float leg

$$\sum_{j=2}^{m} (f(t, t'_{j-1}, t'_j) + s)\, \delta_{t'_{j-1}, t'_j}\, df_{t'_j}.$$

Here, $z(t)$ is the zero credit spread of the bond as of the value date. We see that the present values of the bond and the swap do not add up to 1 even on a fixing date unless both $z(t)$ and s are zero, or their effects cancel out by chance. Between fixing dates, the fixing of the current floating period introduces additional ineffectiveness.

We then define the risk-induced fair value as the credit risk-free value of the bond, minus the unhedged credit spread components, namely

$$\begin{aligned} RIFV(t) &= \underbrace{c_B A^f(t_0, t_n) + df_n}_{\text{bond value}} - \underbrace{\Big((c_B - c_S) A^f(t_0, t_n) + s\, A^{\delta}(t'_0, t_n)\Big)}_{\text{credit spread components}} \\ &= c_S A^f(t_0, t_n) + df_n - s\, A^{\delta}(t'_0, t_n). \end{aligned} \tag{6.6}$$

Note that the annuities for the fixed and floating sides start at different past times t_0 resp. t'_0 in general because the period lengths of the two legs are usually different. Because of the potentially different start dates, we have to use clean values again, that is we have to subtract the accrued interest of each instrument. The *clean* risk-induced fair value is

$$\begin{aligned} CRIFV(t) &= c_S \hat{A}^f(t, t_n) + df_n - s\hat{A}^{\delta}(t, t_n), \\ &= \left(c_S - s\frac{A^{\delta}(0, t_n)}{A^f(0, t_n)}\right)\hat{A}^f(t, t_n) + df_n + s\left(\frac{A^{\delta}(0, t_n)\,\hat{A}^f(t, t_n)}{A^f(0, t_n)} - \hat{A}^{\delta}(t, t_n)\right) \\ &= CPV_{REB}(t) + s\hat{A}^{\delta}(t, t_n)\left(\frac{A^{\delta}(0, t_n)\hat{A}^f(t, t_n)}{A^f(0, t_n)\hat{A}^{\delta}(t, t_n)} - 1\right), \end{aligned}$$

an almost exact match.[4] Note, however, that the hedging instrument introduces a new risk which the bond does not have, namely the short-term interest rate risk that comes from the fixing of the current floating period; the hedge is only "perfect" on fixing dates. This (clean) fixing effect $L(t'_0)\, \hat{A}^{\delta}(t, t'_1)$ therefore represents an intrinsic

[4] If we had a dynamic risk-equivalent coupon as defined in (6.5), the match would be exact.

ineffectiveness of the hedge which has to go through the P&L. The user may decide to subtract this term in the definition of the risk-induced fair value,[5] which is what we will assume from now on. The reason will become clear in the next section when we define the RIFV in the multi-curve world.

As mentioned above, the credit spread risk of the bond has to be taken out of the effectiveness testing because it is not hedged. We therefore either only price the synthetic bond that pays the hedged-portion coupon – i.e. the par swap rate at inception – in the case where the swap's funding leg has no spread, and compare those price moves against the moves in fair value of the swap. In other words, we set the unhedged portion of the coupon to zero (or ignore it,[6] which amounts to the same thing). Alternatively, we price the bond as is but ignore the locked-in asset swap spread on the funding leg of the swap, and compare the value moves of those two instruments. This is what we do in the example above: We ensure effectiveness by setting both $z(t)$ and s to zero in order to calculate the risk-induced fair value. As a result, the only hedge ineffectiveness that remains in the example is the one coming from the first fixing. Of course, a hedge that is not exactly offsetting as in the example will show additional ineffectiveness, for instance if the payment dates of the swap fixed leg do not match the bond's exactly, maturities do not match, etc.

We do not have to restrict ourselves to plain vanilla fixed rate assets here. The same logic applies for assets with structured coupons, amortizers and even call or knockout features.

6.4 Multi-curve valuation

When moving from LIBOR to OIS discounting, we introduce a new risk factor into the value moves of a hedge relationship. At first sight, this risk factor is only relevant on the derivative side, because a fixed rate bond obviously has no basis risk. The value of the not yet fixed part of the floating leg of the hedging instrument is now given by[7]

$$\begin{aligned}&\sum_{j=2}^{m}(f^{LIBOR}(t,t'_{j-1},t'_j)+s)\,\delta_{t'_{j-1},t'_j}\,df^{OIS}_{t'_j}\\&\quad=\sum_{j=2}^{m}(f^{OIS}(t,t'_{j-1},t'_j)+s^{OIS/LIBOR}(t,t'_1,t_n)+s)\,\delta_{t'_{j-1},t'_j}\,df^{OIS}_{t'_j},\end{aligned}\qquad(6.7)$$

5 Provided that the auditor accepts that.
6 Only for measuring effectiveness.
7 Throughout this section, we assume a notional of 1.

where $s^{OIS/LIBOR}(t, t'_1, t_n)$ is the basis spread between OIS and LIBOR for the period $[t'_1, t_n]$. Unfortunately, we can neither collapse the LIBOR floating leg to $1 - df_n$ on a fixing date anymore, nor to $L(t'_0)\,\delta_{t'_0,t'_1}\,df_{t'_1} + df_{t'_1} - df_n$ for t between two fixing dates. However, this is still true for the OIS floating leg, because there the discount and forward curves are identical.

In total, we now have the following parts in the economic P&L to consider, where c_B is the bond's coupon, and c_S is the fixed rate paid on the hedging swap:

- The bond's value move

$$P(t) - 1 = c_B \sum_{i=1}^{n} \delta_{t_{i-1},t_i}\, df_i^{OIS}\, e^{-\tilde{z}(t)\,\delta_{t,t_i}} + df_n^{OIS}\, e^{-\tilde{z}(t)\,\delta_{t,t_n}} - 1$$

  with some OIS-adjusted zero credit spread[8] $\tilde{z}(t)$;
- The swap fixed leg

$$-\, c_S \sum_{i=1}^{n} \delta_{t_{i-1},t_i}\, df_i^{OIS};$$

- the first floating period's coupon

$$(L(t'_0) + s)\,\delta_{t'_0,t'_1}\, df_{t'_1}^{OIS};$$

- The yet unknown LIBOR rates of the float leg

$$\sum_{j=2}^{m} (f^{OIS}(t, t'_{j-1}, t'_j) + s)\,\delta_{t'_{j-1},t'_j}\, df_{t'_j}^{OIS};$$

- The basis spread value

$$s^{OIS/LIBOR}(t, t'_1, t'_n) \sum_{j=2}^{m} \delta_{t'_{j-1},t'_j}\, df_{t'_j}^{OIS}.$$

As in the single-curve case, we would like to reduce the hedge package to a plain vanilla floating rate. By paying the OIS rate now, we have chosen the OIS rate as the risk to be hedged. This is also the reason why we have used the OIS curve for discounting the underlying's cash flows. Discounting them with LIBOR while using OIS for the derivative would lead to inconsistencies which are difficult to

[8] If the hedged item is liquidly traded in the market, the market price $P(t)$ is quoted, and the spread $\tilde{z}(t)$ implied directly from it. If the underlying does not have a quoted price, the spread has to be estimated regardless of which discount curve we use.

justify.[9] Likewise, the risk-induced fair value calculation should lead to a similar result, namely that the remaining ineffectiveness is determined by a fixing of the current period. Heuristically (and economically), this should be the same as simply dropping the basis spread from the calculation of the risk-induced fair value, which we will define below. The value changes due to moves of the basis spread should go through OCI just as in the credit spread case.

If we want to replicate the strategy used in the single-curve case, we have to define the hedged portion. We set this to be the sum of the following two components:

- The OIS swap rate for the maturity of the underlying, to be fixed until maturity. This is because the hedged risk is the OIS interest rate and therefore completely analogous to the single-curve case.
- The OIS/LIBOR basis spread for the maturity of the underlying, which is *adjusted over time.*

At inception, it is the same as in the single-curve case by definition, but over time it will vary with the movement of the basis spread. A technical consequence is that the hedge relationship has to be continuously de-designated and re-designated because IAS 39 only knows static hedges. We now show how to determine the hedged portion for a plain vanilla asset at each re-designation time t.

To ease on notation, we drop all superscripts *OIS* to discount factors, bearing in mind that they are always based on OIS rates in this section. We then fix the time point t on which we do the valuation. This is in general not the start date of a fixed or floating period, so we also have two times, t_0 and t'_0, which are both $\leq t$ and denote the start date of the current fixed resp. floating period, respectively. Then we define

- the initial value PV_0 of the hedging instrument which is in general not 0;
- the annuity factors

$$A^{\delta}(t,t_n) = \sum_{i=1}^{n} \delta_{t'_{i-1},t'_i}\, df_{t'_i},$$

  where δ can be any of $1D, 1M, 3M, 6M, 12M$ or the frequency of the fixed leg of a swap which we denote by f.[10] The $1D$ tenor will always appear in conjunction with another tenor δ. It is to be understood that the payment frequency of the OIS floater then is δ as well. The starting point of the annuity t'_0 is defined as the last period start $\leq t$;

[9] Many FVHA users follow this approach anyway.

[10] This can be $12M$ in EUR or $6M$ in USD, for instance, but usually with a different basis, so the year fractions δ_{t_{i-1},t_i} will in general be different from those of a floating leg with the same frequency.

- the clean annuity factors

$$\hat{A}^{\delta}(t,t_n) = \sum_{i=1}^{n} \delta_{t'_{i-1},t'_i}\, df_{t'_i} - \delta_{t'_0,t};$$

- the dirty present value of a floating leg of the swap without a spread

$$\begin{aligned} F^{\delta}(t,t_n) &= L^{\delta}(t'_0)\,A^{\delta}(t'_0,t'_1) + \sum_{i=2}^{m} f^{\delta}(t,t'_{i-1},t'_i)\,\delta_{t'_{i-1},t'_i}\,df_{t'_i} \\ &= L^{\delta}(t'_0)\,A^{\delta}(t'_0,t'_1) + (df_{t'_1} - df_n) + s^{OIS/LIBOR} A^{\delta}(t'_1,t_n) \end{aligned}$$

  for $\delta = 1M, 3M, 6M, 12M$;
- the dirty PV of an OIS floater without a spread

$$\begin{aligned} F^{1D}(t,t_n) &= x(t'_0,t)\,y(t,t'_1)\,\delta_{t'_0,t'_1}\,df_{t'_1} + \sum_{i=2}^{n} f^{OIS,\delta}(t,t'_{i-1},t'_i)\,\delta_{t'_{i-1},t'_i}\,df_{t'_i} \\ &= x(t'_0,t)\,y(t,t'_1)\,\delta_{t'_0,t'_1}\,df_{t'_1} + df_{t'_1} - df_n, \end{aligned}$$

  where $x(t'_0,t)$ is the geometric average of the already fixed overnight rates up to time t, and $y(t,t'_1)$ is the geometric average of the overnight forward rates up to time t'_1. As for the annuities, the OIS floater always appears in the context of a δ-tenor floater, hence the period length δ;
- the clean present value of a floating leg of the swap without a spread

$$\begin{aligned} \hat{F}^{\delta}(t,t_n) &= L^{\delta}(t'_0)\,\hat{A}(t'_0,t'_1) + \sum_{i=2}^{m} f^{\delta}(t,t'_{i-1},t'_i)\,\delta_{t'_{i-1},t'_i}\,df_{t'_i} \\ &= L^{\delta}(t'_0)\,\hat{A}^{\delta}(t'_0,t'_1) + (df_{t'_1} - df_n) + s^{OIS/LIBOR} A^{\delta}(t'_1,t_n); \end{aligned}$$

- the clean present value of an OIS floater without a spread

$$\hat{F}^{1D}(t,t_n) = F^{1D}(t,t_n) - x(t'_0,t)\,\delta_{t'_0,t};$$

- the par swap rates

$$c^{\delta}(t,t_n) = \frac{\hat{F}^{\delta}(t,t_n)}{\hat{A}^{f}(t,t_n)}.$$

  If t falls on a date for which the (forward) swap rate is quoted, we will by construction replicate it exactly. Otherwise, we interpret the par rate defined as above as a "broken" period swap rate.

As in the single-curve case, we define the risk-induced fair value as the (risk-free) fair value of the bond minus any unhedged components. In the multi-curve world, the unhedged parts are the values of the locked-in credit spread, the combined tenor basis and fixing effect:[11]

$$
\begin{aligned}
RIFV(t) = {} & \underbrace{c_B A^f(t,t_n) + df_n}_{\text{bond value}} - \underbrace{\Big((c_B - c_S)A^f(t,t_n) + sA^\delta(t,t_n)\Big)}_{\text{credit spread components}} \\
& - \underbrace{(F^\delta(t,t_n) - F^{1D}(t,t_n))}_{\text{fixing and basis effect}}.
\end{aligned}
\tag{6.8}
$$

The clean risk-induced fair value is thus given by

$$
\begin{aligned}
CRIFV(t) = {} & c_B \hat{A}^f(t,t_n) + df_n - s\hat{A}^\delta(t,t_n) - (c_B - c_S)\hat{A}^f(t,t_n) \\
& - (\hat{F}^\delta(t,t_n) - \hat{F}^{1D}(t,t_n)).
\end{aligned}
\tag{6.9}
$$

We now set out to compute the time-dependent hedged portion – the risk-equivalent coupon – $c_{RE}(t)$ of the bond under the hedging cost approach. At any point in time $t \leq t_n$, the sum of the clean fair value $CPV_{DER}(t)$ of the swap and the clean fair value $CPV_{REB}(t)$ of the risk-equivalent bond must be the clean fair value of a risk-free OIS floating rate note with payment frequency δ, which means

$$
\begin{aligned}
\hat{F}^{1D}(t,t_n) + df_n &= CPV_{DER}(t) + CPV_{REB}(t) \\
&= \underbrace{\hat{F}^\delta(t,t_n) - c_S \hat{A}^f(t,t_n) + s\hat{A}^\delta(t,t_n)}_{\text{clean PV of the swap}} + \underbrace{c_{RE}(t)\hat{A}^f(t,t_n) + df_n}_{\text{clean PV of RE bond}}
\end{aligned}
\tag{6.10}
$$

by definition. We conclude that

$$
c_{RE}(t) = c_S - s\frac{\hat{A}^\delta(t,t_n)}{\hat{A}^f(t,t_n)} + \frac{\hat{F}^{1D}(t,t_n) - \hat{F}^\delta(t,t_n)}{\hat{A}^f(t,t_n)}. \tag{6.11}
$$

The risk-equivalent coupon is very similar to the one in the single-curve case (6.5); only the part $(\hat{F}^{1D}(t,t_n) - \hat{F}^\delta(t,t_n))/\hat{A}^f(t,t_n)$ is new. This is needed in order to get

[11] See the discussion on the fixing effect at the end of the previous section.

a consistent dynamic hedged portion. Note that on a fixing date,

$$\begin{aligned}\frac{\hat{F}^{1D}(t,t_n) - \hat{F}^{\delta}(t,t_n)}{\hat{A}^f(t,t_n)} &= \frac{F^{1D}(t,t_n) - F^{\delta}(t,t_n)}{A^f(t,t_n)} \\ &= c^{OIS}(t,t_n) - c^{\delta}(t,t_n),\end{aligned}$$

the basis spread between the OIS and the δ swap curve. Furthermore, we have at inception ($t = 0$)

$$CPV_{DER}(0) = (c^{\delta}(0,t_n) - c_S)\,A^f(0,t_n) + s\,A^{\delta}(0,t_n),$$

implying that

$$c_S = c^{\delta}(0,t_n) + s\frac{A^{\delta}(0,t_n)}{A^f(0,t_n)} - \frac{CPV_{DER}(0)}{A^f(0,t_n)}.$$

Plugging this into (6.11), we get

$$\begin{aligned}c_{RE}(t) &= c_S - s\frac{\hat{A}^{\delta}(t,t_n)}{\hat{A}^f(t,t_n)} + \frac{\hat{F}^{1D}(t,t_n) - \hat{F}^{\delta}(t,t_n)}{\hat{A}^f(t,t_n)} \\ &= c^{\delta}(0,t_n) + s\frac{A^{\delta}(0,t_n)}{A^f(0,t_n)} - \frac{CPV_{DER}(0)}{A^f(0,t_n)} \\ &\quad - s\frac{\hat{A}^{\delta}(t,t_n)}{\hat{A}^f(t,t_n)} + c^{OIS}(t,t_n) - c^{\delta}(t,t_n) \\ &= c^{OIS}(0,t_n) + \left[c^{\delta}(0,t_n) - c^{OIS}(0,t_n)\right] \\ &\quad - \left[c^{\delta}(t,t_n) - c^{OIS}(t,t_n)\right] \\ &\quad + s\left(\frac{A^{\delta}(0,t_n)}{A^f(0,t_n)} - \frac{\hat{A}^{\delta}(t,t_n)}{\hat{A}^f(t,t_n)}\right) - \frac{CPV_{DER}(0)}{A^f(0,t_n)}.\end{aligned}$$

The difference of the annuity quotients by which s is multiplied is very small. Thus, the risk-equivalent coupon at time t can approximately be interpreted as the fair OIS swap rate at inception plus the move in the OIS-δ-basis between inception and t, minus the present value of the derivative at inception expressed as a running spread. This last component is just the locked-in credit spread of the bond:

$$c^{\delta}(0,t_n) - c_S + s\frac{A^{\delta}(0,t_n)}{A^f(0,t_n)}.$$

The approach suggested by Schubert [132] is to use this definition for a hedge relationship that is theoretically de-designated and re-designated at each instant. In practice, this would only happen monthly or even quarterly, and the time effect for each period due to this discretization would have to be amortized until maturity. This is operationally challenging and complicates things unnecessarily. We want to show that the clean fair value CRE_t of the risk-equivalent bond is the same as the clean risk-induced fair value as defined in (6.9) at any time point t, because then we can use this much more practical approach to do the hedge effectiveness calculations.

The clean value of the risk-equivalent bond is

$$
\begin{aligned}
CPV_{REB}(t) &= c_{RE}\hat{A}^f(t,t_n) + df_n \\
&= \left(c_S - s\frac{\hat{A}^\delta(t,t_n)}{\hat{A}^f(t,t_n)} + \frac{\hat{F}^{1D}(t,t_n) - \hat{F}^\delta(t,t_n)}{\hat{A}^f(t,t_n)} \right) \hat{A}^f(t,t_n) + df_n \\
&= c_S\hat{A}^f(t,t_n) - s\hat{A}^\delta(t,t_n) - \hat{F}^\delta(t,t_n) + \hat{F}^{1D}(t,t_n) + df_n \\
&= c_B\hat{A}^f(t,t_n) + df_n - \left(s + (c_B - c_S)\frac{\hat{A}^f(t,t_n)}{\hat{A}^\delta(t,t_n)} \right) \hat{A}^\delta(t,t_n) \\
&\quad - \left(\hat{F}^\delta(t,t_n) - \hat{F}^{1D}(t,t_n) \right) \\
&= CRIFV(t)
\end{aligned}
$$

as desired. There is no leftover fixing effect as in the single-curve case because that is now contained in the component $(\hat{F}^{1D}(t,t_n) - \hat{F}^\delta(t,t_n))/\hat{A}^f(t,t_n)$ of the risk-equivalent coupon. Note that this makes total sense: Since we hedge the bond into an OIS floating rate note in the multi-curve case, the fixing effect reduces to the difference between the overnight fixing at time t and the forward overnight rate in t, which can be safely assumed to be 0.

This analysis shows that our intuition was right: When computing the hedge effectiveness, we have to take the value of the basis spread out of the calculation, just as we do with the locked-in margin and the credit spread in the single curve case.

Without going into further detail, it is worth noting that as long as the "non-bond" leg is a simple LIBOR leg, the same result can be proven for

- amortizing notionals (by replacing the annuity factors with the appropriate sums);
- step-up coupons or margins;

- structured coupons of any kind (the definition of the risk-equivalent coupon becomes a lot more complicated in this case, however);
- callable packages.

In all these cases, the strategy is the same: Reduce the risk-induced fair value by the present value of the basis spread, which is the difference between the derivative's value using the LIBOR forward curve on its funding leg and the value resulting from replacing the LIBOR forward curve with the discount (i.e. OIS) curve.

II Credit and Debit Value Adjustment

7 Introduction

The new curves introduced in Part I reflect the segmentation of the interbank derivatives market, in particular following the crisis after the default of Lehman Brothers in 2008. These new curves allow us to consistently price *perfectly collateralized* vanilla interest rate swaps, tenor basis swaps and cross-currency swaps. However, we have already seen in Section 5.1 that collateralization is very often far from being perfect, and that we cannot capture all sources of imperfection in the discount curve. We therefore have to ask ourselves, what do we do if collateral is not exchanged "continuously" or at least daily? What if collateral is posted only beyond certain thresholds, or asymmetrically (i.e. by one party)? What if collateral is posted with delay due to operational problems or disputes? It is clear that credit risk is not mitigated entirely in these cases, and the question is to which degree this imperfection affects a derivative's price. The amount by which the perfectly collateralized derivative price deviates from the credit risk-adjusted derivative price is the *Credit Value Adjustment* (CVA). This depends in principle on the CSA details and complexities as described in Section 5, and computing it for a large portfolio can be a serious computational challenge. Since 2013 this is a challenge faced by all organizations reporting under the *International Financial Reporting Standard* (IFRS) – which comprises e.g. all listed companies in Europe – with IFRS 13 taking effect: CVA has to be reflected in derivatives' valuations for accounting purposes. It is not solely for "internal information" anymore. This not only affects banks but also corporates, insurance companies and pension funds that use derivatives, and the subject has gained attention among audit firms, not least due to IFRS 13. At the time of writing, a major part of the industry is moving or has to move towards applying prudent CVA analytics regularly, at least to check CVA materiality.

This part of the book is devoted to introducing the models and methods that are typically applied to address this challenge, and the obstacles one might face. We start with a summary of fundamentals in Chapter 8. To make things more concrete, we then consider the relatively simple case of uncollateralized vanilla derivatives in Chapter 9, where we can hope for (semi-)analytic CVA formulas and simple reasonable approximations. Finally we move to the complex challenge of taking netting, collateral and deal ageing into account. This forces us to move to a Monte Carlo framework and to choose and implement a machinery for market evolution, portfolio pricing under market scenarios, portfolio evolution and collateral account tracking.

8 | Fundamentals

Consider a derivative contract such as an Interest Rate Swap, an FX Forward, a Credit Default Swap CDS, etc. Its *net present value* (NPV) can be positive and negative during its life. If our counterparty defaults while the NPV is positive, then we lose our claim, unfortunately. This is similar to the situation where we lend money to the counterparty, which we might lose in the case of its default. On the other hand, if the NPV is negative at default time, the contract is not just terminated but the counterparty's claim to us persists, and the counterparty's liquidator will request full compensation for it. It is centuries-old practice in the loan business to ask for an extra margin in order to compensate the lender for the *expected loss* based on the borrower's creditworthiness. The equivalent compensation in the derivatives context is CVA. If we denote the default risk-free value as *NPV* then we write the default-risky value

$$NPV^D = NPV - CVA$$

subtracting the CVA, that is defining it as the compensation to ask for.

This is the connection between NPV and CVA, assuming that only our counterparty can default (and not us). It is hence called the *unilateral* CVA. Likewise, our counterparty might come up with a similar adjustment assuming that only we can default. This adjustment is called the unilateral *Debit Value Adjustment* (DVA) which is positive from our perspective, and hence increases the risk-adjusted NPV.

It is tempting to combine the two into one in an attempt to make the adjustment business symmetric so that both parties can come up with a unique value:

$$NPV^D = NPV - CVA + DVA$$

However, this turns out not to be symmetric if we simply combine the two unilateral adjustments. The true *bilateral* CVA/DVA has to take first default effects into account, that is the CVA is reduced by the fact that we can default first and hence stop claiming, and likewise DVA is reduced. We will review the precise mathematical formulation next.

8.1 Unilateral CVA

Brigo and Mercurio [33], on pages 749–751, state the following unilateral CVA formula

$$CVA(t) = \mathbb{E}^{\mathbb{Q}}\left[\mathbb{1}_{t<\tau\leq T} \cdot LGD(\tau) \cdot D(t,\tau) \cdot NPV^{+}(\tau) \,|\, \mathcal{G}_t\right]. \tag{8.1}$$

For a formal derivation see the following subsection.

What does (8.1) mean? The CVA can be written as a price: CVA at time t (today) for some financial instrument or *netting set* is computed as a risk-neutral expectation ($\mathbb{E}^{\mathbb{Q}}$) of discounted (via the stochastic discount factor, $D(t,\tau)$) "payoff" $\mathbb{1}_{t<\tau\leq T} \cdot LGD(\tau) \cdot NPV^{+}(\tau)$. We can imagine the expectation taken over many hypothetical scenarios/evolutions of the "world" (market data such as interest rates, fx rates or CDS spreads, including information on our counterparty's default). The standard market *filtration* $\{\mathcal{F}_t\}$ would be used if default information was excluded. When including default information, we use the filtration $\mathcal{G}_t$ here.[1] Time τ is a random variable here denoting the time of counterparty default, and the indicator function $\mathbb{1}_{t<\tau\leq T}$ is equal to one in scenarios where τ falls into the remaining lifetime of the instrument (up to time T), and zero if default occurs later.

Let us assume a scenario under which counterparty default happens at time $\tau < T$. Our payoff is then the prevailing NPV of the instrument (if positive: $NPV^{+}(\tau)$), stochastic as well, multiplied by the *loss given default*[2] (LGD), which is less than one:[3] Part of the NPV^{+} may be recovered by the liquidator, and the payoff is limited to the part of NPV^{+} which cannot be recovered. If it were all recovered ($LGD = 0$) then our CVA would vanish. This payoff at default time τ is discounted from default time τ to today (time t), hence we multiply by the stochastic discount factor $D(t,\tau)$. Now we iterate over many possible scenarios and compute the average to obtain the CVA figure.

Throughout the text we will assume a hazard rate model, that is the probability of default in a very short period of time $[t, t + dt]$, given that no default occurred

[1] $\mathcal{G}_t$ is generated by $\mathcal{F}_t$ and the σ-algebra generated by the default time $\{\tau > t\}$, which contains the default information.

[2] Even the *LGD* at default time can be considered random, but we neglect that possibility for now.

[3] In the loan business, it can happen that the LGD is greater than one if the collateral comes with some nasty surprise like toxic waste underneath a building which has to be removed at great cost. We assume that something like this is not possible for derivatives. Note, however, that in the commercial real estate business derivatives transactions are often secured by the same collateral as their underlying loans.

up to time t, is given by

$$\mathbb{Q}(t \leq \tau < t + dt \,|\, \mathcal{G}_t) = \lambda(t)\, dt.$$

The function λ is called the *hazard rate.* We define the *cumulated default intensity* $\Lambda(t) := \int_0^t \lambda(s)ds$ and further assume that the stochastic variable $\Lambda(\tau)$ is exponentially distributed. Then it follows that the *survival probability* up to time t is given by

$$\mathbb{Q}(\tau > t) = \mathbb{E}^{\mathbb{Q}}\left[\mathbb{1}_{\tau > t}\right] = e^{-\Lambda(t)} = e^{-\int_0^t \lambda(s)ds}.$$

In the following we will rewrite (8.1) to make it somewhat more accessible for numerical calculations. Note that

$$\mathbb{1}_{t < \tau \leq T} = \sum_{i=1}^{n} \mathbb{1}_{t_{i-1} < \tau \leq t_i}, \qquad t_0 = t, \quad t_n = T$$

for any sequence of times t_i, because the sub-intervals are a pairwise disjoint covering of $[t, T]$. If we make this partition arbitrarily fine by taking the limit $n \to \infty$, and setting

$$X(t_{i-1}) := LGD(t_{i-1}) \cdot D(t, t_{i-1}) \cdot NPV^{+}(t_{i-1})$$

we can write (8.1) as

$$\begin{aligned}
CVA(t) &= \lim_{n\to\infty} \sum_{i=1}^{n} \mathbb{E}^{\mathbb{Q}}\left[\mathbb{1}_{t_{i-1} < \tau \leq t_i} \cdot X(t_{i-1}) \,|\, \mathcal{G}_t\right] \\
&= \frac{\mathbb{1}_{\tau > t}}{\mathbb{Q}(\tau > t|\mathcal{F}_t)} \lim_{n\to\infty} \sum_{i=1}^{n} \mathbb{E}^{\mathbb{Q}}\left[\mathbb{1}_{t_{i-1} < \tau \leq t_i} \cdot X(t_{i-1}) \,|\, \mathcal{F}_t\right] \\
&= \frac{\mathbb{1}_{\tau > t}}{\mathbb{Q}(\tau > t|\mathcal{F}_t)} \lim_{n\to\infty} \sum_{i=1}^{n} \mathbb{E}^{\mathbb{Q}}\left[(\mathbb{1}_{\tau > t_{i-1}} - \mathbb{1}_{\tau > t_i}) \cdot X(t_{i-1}) \,|\, \mathcal{F}_t\right]
\end{aligned}$$

where we have used the filtration switching formula [33] (p. 777) for the second equality. We can replace the indicator under the expectation by hazard rate integrals,[4]

$$\mathbb{E}^{\mathbb{Q}}[\mathbb{1}_{\tau>t_i}\,|\,\mathcal{F}_t] = \mathbb{E}^{\mathbb{Q}}\left[e^{-\int_0^{t_i}\lambda(s)\,ds}\,\middle|\,\mathcal{F}_t\right]$$

$$\mathbb{E}^{\mathbb{Q}}[\mathbb{1}_{\tau>t_i}X(t_{i-1})\,|\,\mathcal{F}_t] = \mathbb{E}^{\mathbb{Q}}\left[e^{-\int_0^{t_i}\lambda(s)\,ds}X(t_{i-1})\,\middle|\,\mathcal{F}_t\right]$$

$$\mathbb{E}^{\mathbb{Q}}[\mathbb{1}_{\tau>t_i}X(t_i)\,|\,\mathcal{F}_t] = \mathbb{E}^{\mathbb{Q}}\left[e^{-\int_0^{t_i}\lambda(s)\,ds}X(t_i)\,\middle|\,\mathcal{F}_t\right]$$

so that

$$\begin{aligned} CVA(t) &= \frac{\mathbb{1}_{\tau>t}}{\mathbb{Q}(\tau>t|\mathcal{F}_t)}\lim_{n\to\infty}\sum_{i=1}^{n}\mathbb{E}^{\mathbb{Q}}\left[\left(e^{-\int_0^{t_{i-1}}\lambda(s)\,ds} - e^{-\int_0^{t_i}\lambda(s)\,ds}\right)\cdot X(t_{i-1})\,|\,\mathcal{F}_t\right] \\ &= \mathbb{1}_{\tau>t}\lim_{n\to\infty}\sum_{i=1}^{n}\mathbb{E}^{\mathbb{Q}}\left[\left(e^{-\int_t^{t_{i-1}}\lambda(s)\,ds} - e^{-\int_t^{t_i}\lambda(s)\,ds}\right)\cdot X(t_{i-1})\,|\,\mathcal{F}_t\right] \end{aligned}$$

using $Q(\tau > t|\mathcal{F}_t) = \exp(-\int_0^t \lambda(s)\,ds)$ in the second step. We can finally approximate this Riemann-Stieltjes integral (infinite sum) using a finite sum over time intervals $\Delta t = t_i - t_{i-1}$, where we can choose a point $\bar{t}_i \in [t_{i-1}, t_i]$ for the evaluation of $X(\bar{t}_i)$:[5]

$$\text{U-CVA}(t) \approx \mathbb{1}_{\tau>t}\sum_{i=1}^{n}\mathbb{E}^{\mathbb{Q}}\left[(S(t,t_{i-1}) - S(t,t_i))\cdot X(\bar{t}_i)\,|\,\mathcal{F}_t\right] \tag{8.2}$$

with $S(t,t_i) := \exp\left(-\int_t^{t_i}\lambda(s)\,ds\right)$. Depending on the choice of $\bar{t}_i$ as the beginning respectively the end of the time interval, we will distinguish – following [33] – “anticipated” respectively “postponed” approximations to the CVA.

Proof of (8.1)

This subsection is for readers who prefer a formal justification of our starting point in this section, the unilateral CVA formula (8.1). We follow Brigo and Mercurio [33], p. 749, and consider a defaultable claim's (discounted) payoff $\Pi^D(t)$ at time t:

$$\Pi^D(t) = \mathbb{1}_{\{\tau>T\}}C(t,T) + \mathbb{1}_{\{t<\tau\le T\}}[C(t,\tau) + D(t,\tau)(R(V(\tau))^+ - (-V(\tau))^+)]$$

4 This is possible for the expectations containing $X(t_i)$ and $X(t_{i-1})$ since these are both $\mathcal{F}_{t_i}$-measurable; apply the tower law of conditional expectations.

5 We choose $\bar{t}_i$ typically at the beginning or the end of the interval $[t_{i-1}, t_i]$

with

$C(s,t)$	cash flows in $[s,t]$ discounted back to time s; s or t can also be τ
$D(t,\tau)$	stochastic discount factor for time τ
$V(\tau)$	value of outstanding flows at default $\mathbb{E}[C(\tau,T)\,|\,\mathcal{G}_\tau]$
R	recovery rate $R = 1 - LGD$

If default occurs after the final maturity of the contract, our payoff is just the sum of contractual cash flows between time t and T discounted back to time t; we label that $C(t,T)$. If default occurs at time τ before maturity, payoff is the sum of three terms

- the discounted sum of flows up to default time τ, $C(t,\tau)$;
- recovery on the defaulted value of future flows, discounted back to time t, that is $D(t,\tau)(R(V(\tau))^+$;
- our continued liability to the counterparty if the value of future flows is out-of-the-money at default, that is $-(-V(\tau))^+$.

This is summed into payoff $\Pi^D(t)$ above. We rearrange its terms now step by step:

$$
\begin{aligned}
\Pi^D(t) &= \mathbb{1}_{\{\tau>T\}}C(t,T)\\
&\quad + \mathbb{1}_{\{t<\tau\leq T\}}[C(t,\tau)+D(t,\tau)(R(V(\tau))^+ - (-V(\tau))^+)]\\
&= \mathbb{1}_{\{\tau>T\}}C(t,T) + \mathbb{1}_{\{\tau\leq T\}}C(t,T)\\
&\quad + \mathbb{1}_{\{t<\tau\leq T\}}\left[C(t,\tau) - C(t,T) + D(t,\tau)(R(V(\tau))^+ - (-V(\tau))^+)\right]\\
&= C(t,T)\\
&\quad + \mathbb{1}_{\{t<\tau\leq T\}}\left[D(t,\tau)(-C(\tau,T) + R(V(\tau))^+ - (-V(\tau))^+)\right]\\
&= C(t,T)\\
&\quad + \mathbb{1}_{\{t<\tau\leq T\}}\left[D(t,\tau)(-C(\tau,T) + (R-1)\,(V(\tau))^+ + V(\tau))\right]\\
&= C(t,T)\\
&\quad + \mathbb{1}_{\{t<\tau\leq T\}}\left[D(t,\tau)\,(V(\tau) - C(\tau,T)) - LGD\cdot D(t,\tau)\cdot V^+(\tau)\right]
\end{aligned}
$$

And now we price the discounted payoff as usual by taking the expectation of Π^D:

$$
\begin{aligned}
\mathbb{E}\left[\Pi^D(t)\,|\,\mathcal{G}_t\right] = \mathbb{E}\,[C(t,T)\,|\,\mathcal{G}_t]&\\
+\mathbb{E}\left[\mathbb{1}_{t<\tau\leq T}\,D(t,\tau)\,(V(\tau) - C(\tau,T))\,|\,\mathcal{G}_t\right]&\\
-\mathbb{E}\left[LGD\cdot D(t,\tau)\cdot V^+(\tau)\,|\,\mathcal{G}_t\right].&
\end{aligned}
$$

The first term is just the non-defaultable price $\mathbb{E}\left[\Pi(t)\,|\,\mathcal{G}_t\right]$. The second term vanishes due to the tower property of conditional expectations, and the third term is our CVA adjustment (8.1).

8.2 Bilateral CVA

Bilateral CVA can be written as the difference of a CVA and DVA term

$$\text{B-CVA}(t) = CVA(t) - DVA(t)$$

where the CVA part is predominantly driven by the counterparty's default and DVA by ours. Recall the unilateral case where we have

$$\text{U-CVA}(t) = \mathbb{E}^{\mathbb{Q}}\left[\mathbb{1}_{t<\tau_2\leq T}\cdot LGD_2(\tau_2)\cdot D(t,\tau_2)\cdot NPV^{+}(\tau_2)\,|\,\mathcal{G}_t\right]$$

where index 2 denotes the counterparty's default time and LGD, and accordingly, the unilateral DVA is

$$\text{U-DVA}(t) = \mathbb{E}^{\mathbb{Q}}\left[\mathbb{1}_{t<\tau_1\leq T}\cdot LGD_1(\tau_1)\cdot D(t,\tau_1)\cdot (-NPV(\tau_1))^{+}\,|\,\mathcal{G}_t\right]$$

with index 1 denoting our own default time and LGD ("our DVA is their CVA"). If both parties can default then we have to amend the expectations and take the order of defaults into account: If we default first, then the counterparty's later default does not count anymore, that is this scenario does not contribute to the CVA expectation, and vice versa. CVA and DVA components are therefore modified as follows

$$\begin{aligned} \text{B-CVA}(t) &= CVA(t) - DVA(t) \qquad (8.3)\\ CVA(t) &= \mathbb{E}^{\mathbb{Q}}\left[\mathbb{1}_{t<\tau_2\leq T}\cdot \mathbb{1}_{\tau_2<\tau_1}\cdot LGD_2(\tau_2)\cdot D(t,\tau_2)\cdot NPV^{+}(\tau_2)\,|\,\mathcal{G}_t\right]\\ DVA(t) &= \mathbb{E}^{\mathbb{Q}}\left[\mathbb{1}_{t<\tau_1\leq T}\cdot \mathbb{1}_{\tau_1<\tau_2}\cdot LGD_1(\tau_1)\cdot D(t,\tau_1)\cdot (-NPV(\tau_1))^{+}\,|\,\mathcal{G}_t\right] \end{aligned}$$

in line with e.g. Brigo, Pallavicini and Papatheodorou in [35].

How do we deal with these products of indicator functions? Let us consider the CVA expectation and recall from the previous section that

$$\mathbb{1}_{t<\tau\leq T} = \sum_{i=1}^{n} \mathbb{1}_{t_{i-1}<\tau\leq t_i}, \qquad t_0 = t, \quad t_n = T$$

for any sequence of times t_i. Applying this kind of decomposition (in the limit $n \to \infty$) to the product of indicator functions, we have

$$\mathbb{1}_{t<\tau_2\le T} \cdot \mathbb{1}_{\tau_2<\tau_1} = \sum_{i=1}^{n} \mathbb{1}_{t_{i-1}<\tau_2\le t_i} \cdot \mathbb{1}_{\tau_1>t_i}.$$

We now insert this into our CVA expectation

$$\begin{aligned}
CVA(t) &= \mathbb{E}^{\mathbb{Q}}\left[\mathbb{1}_{t<\tau_2<T} \cdot \mathbb{1}_{\tau_2<\tau_1} \cdot X(t,\tau_2) \,|\, \mathcal{G}_t\right] \\
&= \lim_{n\to\infty} \mathbb{E}^{\mathbb{Q}}\left[\sum_{i=1}^{n} \mathbb{1}_{t_{i-1}<\tau_2\le t_i} \cdot \mathbb{1}_{\tau_1>t_i} \cdot X(t,t_{i-1}) \,|\, \mathcal{G}_t\right] \\
&= \lim_{n\to\infty} \sum_{i=1}^{n} \mathbb{E}^{\mathbb{Q}}\left[\left(\mathbb{1}_{\tau_2>t_{i-1}} - \mathbb{1}_{\tau_2>t_i}\right) \cdot \mathbb{1}_{\tau_1>t_i} \cdot X(t,t_{i-1}) \,|\, \mathcal{G}_t\right]
\end{aligned}$$

where

$$X(t,s) = LGD_2(\tau) \cdot D(t,s) \cdot NPV^{+}(\tau)$$

and switch filtration to $\mathcal{F}_t$:

$$\begin{aligned}
CVA(t) =& \frac{\mathbb{1}_{\tau_1>t}}{\mathbb{Q}(\tau_1 > t|\mathcal{F}_t)} \frac{\mathbb{1}_{\tau_2>t}}{\mathbb{Q}(\tau_2 > t|\mathcal{F}_t)} \\
& \times \lim_{n\to\infty} \sum_{i=1}^{n} \mathbb{E}^{\mathbb{Q}}\left[\left(\mathbb{1}_{\tau_2>t_{i-1}} - \mathbb{1}_{\tau_2>t_i}\right) \cdot \mathbb{1}_{\tau_1>t_i} \cdot X(t,t_{i-1}) \,|\, \mathcal{F}_t\right]
\end{aligned}$$

With the same arguments as in the previous section we can replace indicator functions by hazard rate functions to get

$$CVA(t) = \mathbb{1}_{\tau_1>t}\mathbb{1}_{\tau_2>t} \lim_{n\to\infty} \sum_{i=1}^{n} \mathbb{E}^{\mathbb{Q}}\left[PD_2(t,t_{i-1},t_i) \cdot S_1(t,t_i) \cdot X(t,t_{i-1}) \,|\, \mathcal{F}_t\right]$$

where

$$\begin{aligned}
S_{1,2}(t,T) &= e^{-\int_t^T \lambda_{1,2}(s)\,ds} \\
PD_{1,2}(t,t_{i-1},t_i) &= S_{1,2}(t,t_{i-1}) - S_{1,2}(t,t_i).
\end{aligned}$$

Similarly we obtain the expression for the DVA component

$$DVA(t) = \mathbb{1}_{\tau_1>t}\mathbb{1}_{\tau_2>t} \lim_{n\to\infty} \sum_{i=1}^{n} \mathbb{E}^{\mathbb{Q}}\left[PD_1(t,t_{i-1},t_i)\cdot S_2(t,t_i)\cdot Y(t,t_{i-1})\,|\,\mathcal{F}_t\right]$$

$$Y(t,s) = LGD_1(\tau)\cdot D(t,s)\cdot(-NPV(\tau))^+.$$

Relaxing the limit and evaluating the expressions on a finite time grid then yields an approximation of the true bilateral CVA:

$$\text{B-CVA}(t) = CVA(t) - DVA(t) \tag{8.4}$$

$$CVA(t) \approx \mathbb{1}_{\tau_1>t}\mathbb{1}_{\tau_2>t} \sum_{i=1}^{n} \mathbb{E}^{\mathbb{Q}}\left[PD_2(t,t_{i-1},t_i)\cdot S_1(t,t_i)\cdot X(t,\bar{t}_i)\,|\,\mathcal{F}_t\right]$$

$$DVA(t) \approx \mathbb{1}_{\tau_1>t}\mathbb{1}_{\tau_2>t} \sum_{i=1}^{n} \mathbb{E}^{\mathbb{Q}}\left[PD_1(t,t_{i-1},t_i)\cdot S_2(t,t_i)\cdot Y(t,\bar{t}_i)\,|\,\mathcal{F}_t\right]$$

with $\bar{t}_i$ again chosen in the interval $[t_{i-1},t_i]$.

In the next section we continue with evaluating (8.2) and (8.4) for particularly simple cases.

9 Single Trade CVA

It is certainly important to capture the CVA of collateralized portfolios, because the portfolio size can lead to a significant number. As discussed in Chapter 7, such an analysis can only be done by simulating the whole portfolio including collateral development and deal ageing. Uncollateralized portfolios may be smaller nowadays, but the CVA impact per trade is obviously more pronounced. We therefore start by delving into actual CVA calculations for the latter, simpler case and look into CVA for a few vanilla derivative products.

Simplifications

We start with a few simplifying assumptions:

- Unilateral case: only the counterparty can default
- The counterparty's hazard rate process $\lambda(t)$ is independent of the market factors which drive the instrument's value
- The counterparty's LGD is constant
- No collateral is posted

What does this mean for the unilateral CVA formula (8.2)? The LGD can be taken out of the expectation as a factor in front of the sum. Moreover, the expectation simplifies into a product of expectations[1]

$$\mathbb{E}_t^{\mathbb{Q}}\left[S(t,t_{i-1}) - S(t,t_i)\right] \times \mathbb{E}_t^{\mathbb{Q}}\left[D(t,\bar{t}_i)\cdot NPV^+(\bar{t}_i)\right].$$

The first factor then by definition reduces to the difference of market survival probability curves[2] since

$$S^M(t,T) = \mathbb{E}_t^{\mathbb{Q}}\left[S(t,T)\right] = \mathbb{E}_t^{\mathbb{Q}}\left[e^{-\int_t^T \lambda(s)\,ds}\right],$$

[1] Note that we will abbreviate expectations $\mathbb{E}^{\mathbb{Q}}[\ldots|\mathcal{F}_t] = \mathbb{E}_t^{\mathbb{Q}}[\ldots]$ from now on.
[2] For example bootstrapped from CDS quotes.

so that

$$\text{U-CVA}(t) = \mathbb{1}_{\tau>t}\, LGD \sum_{i=1}^{n} \left[S^M(t,t_{i-1}) - S^M(t,t_i) \right] \times \mathbb{E}_t^{\mathbb{Q}} \left[D(t,\bar{t}_i) \cdot NPV^+(\bar{t}_i) \right]. \tag{9.1}$$

Assuming that the market default curve is given,[3] we are left with the evaluation of expectations

$$\mathbb{E}_t^{\mathbb{Q}} \left[D(t,t_i) \cdot NPV^+(t_i) \right].$$

These, however, are nothing but European option prices on the underlying derivative with expiry in time t_i (and physical settlement). Depending on the complexity of the underlying derivative this can be a straightforward analytical calculation or a challenging numerical task.

9.1 Interest rate swap

Our first example is a vanilla interest rate swap, following the track of Soerensen & Bollier [138] and Brigo & Mercurio [33].

The swap has constant notional N, pays a fixed rate K and receives vanilla floating interest without spread. We assume single-curve pricing,[4] that is the discount and forward curves agree. This means that we can write the value of the swap starting at time t_j as

$$NPV(t;t_j,t_n) = \omega\, N \left[P(t,t_j) - P(t,t_n) - K \sum_{i=j+1}^{n} \delta(t_{i-1},t_i)\, P(t,t_i) \right] \tag{9.2}$$

using the telescoping property on the single-curve floating leg. $\delta(t_{i-1},t_i)$ is the year fraction for period $[t_{i-1},t_i]$, and $\omega = \pm 1$ switches between the payer and receiver swaps. For $t=0$, $NPV(0)$ is today's swap value, and $P(0,t_i)$ is simply today's discount curve (zero bonds) for a cash flow at time t_i. For a future time t, this present value $NPV(t)$ is stochastic, and $P(t,t_i)$ is the stochastic zero bond price which is defined as a conditional expectation of the stochastic discount factor

[3] Finding CDS quotes or appropriate proxies for relevant counterparties can turn out to be a major issue in CVA calculation. Here we assume these are given, and we focus on the problem of computing the expectations.

[4] We will later move to multi-curve pricing as well.

$D(t, t_i)$ in the risk-neutral measure:

$$P(t, t_i) = \mathbb{E}_t^{\mathbb{Q}}[D(t, t_i)]$$

Its concrete form depends on the model and measure we choose. We come back to this in the next section. Here we can take a short cut as follows. We first write the future swap price in the form

$$NPV(t; t_j, t_n) = \omega N A(t; t_j, t_n) \left(c(t; t_j, t_n) - K\right)$$

with fixed leg annuity

$$A(t; t_j, t_n) = \sum_{i=j+1}^{n} \delta(t_{i-1}, t_i) P(t, t_i) \tag{9.3}$$

and fair swap rate

$$c(t; t_j, t_n) = (P(t, t_j) - P(t, t_n))/A(t; t_j, t_n). \tag{9.4}$$

A European swaption (option on such an underlying swap) with expiry on reset date t_j and *physical settlement* has the payoff $\text{Swaption}(t_j; t_j, t_n) = NPV^+(t_j; t_j, t_n)$ at expiry, and the swaption price at time $t < t_j$ is

$$\text{Swaption}(t; t_j, t_n) = \mathbb{E}_t^{\mathbb{Q}}[D(t, t_j) \cdot NPV^+(t_j; t_j, t_n)],$$

where the expectation is computed in the risk-neutral measure. Moving to the annuity measure and assuming *geometric Brownian Motion* (GBM) with volatility $\sigma(t)$ for the forward swap rate leads to the usual Black76 formula for swaptions (see Section 1.4.2 and Appendix C)

$$\text{Swaption}(t; t_j, t_n) = N A(t; t_j, t_n) \,\text{Black}\left(\omega, c(t; t_j, t_n), K, \int_t^{t_j} \sigma^2(s)\, ds\right). \tag{9.5}$$

Equipped with the swaption pricing formula (9.5), we can now go ahead and compute the unilateral CVA as shown in (9.1). The question now is which discretization of the time axis to choose. It is tempting to pick the swap's fixed leg's reset times, so that the expectation above represents a vanilla swaption price so as to avoid exercise in the middle of an interest period:

$$\text{U-CVA}(t) = \mathbb{1}_{\tau > t}\, LGD \sum_{i=1}^{n} \left[S^M(t, t_{i-1}) - S^M(t, t_i)\right], \times \text{Swaption}(t; t_j, t_n) \tag{9.6}$$

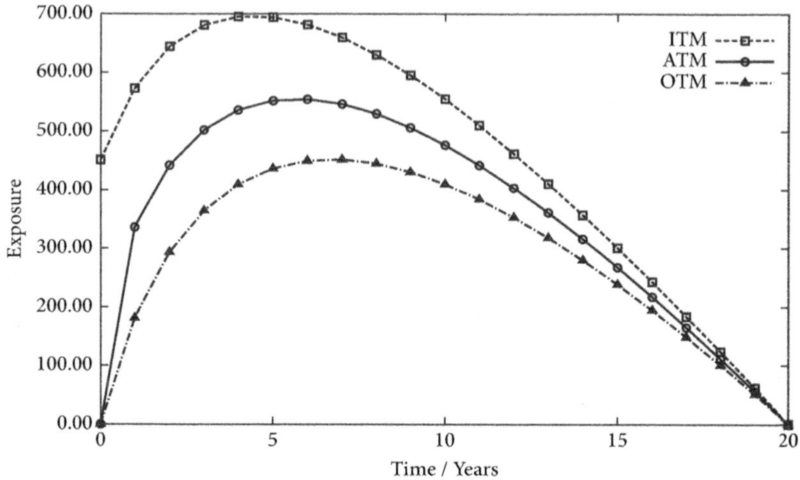

Figure 9.1 Vanilla swap exposure as given by Equation (9.5) as a function of time for payer swaps that are in-the-money (swap rate 0.9 times fair rate), at-the-money and out-of-the-money (swap rate 1.1 times fair rate), notional 10,000, maturity 20 years, volatility 20%. Exposure is evaluated at the fixed leg's interest period start and end dates

with summation index running up to the underlying swap's maturity t_n and $j=i-1$ (resp. $j=i$) for the anticipated (resp. postponed) CVA approximation. We will come back to the discretization and the importance of intra-period sampling later on. Figure 9.1 shows typical swap exposure evolutions, that is Swaption$(0;t_j,t_n)$ as a function of time (swaption exercise) t_j.

9.1.1 Exercise within interest periods

The swaption pricing formula (9.5) needs to be modified if we want to evaluate the exposure at an "exercise" date that does not match coinciding fixed and floating reset dates (which is the general case in the CVA formula (9.6)). This is particularly important when the payment frequencies on the swap's fixed and floating leg differ as in Figure 9.2 (as they generally do), because this leads to intra-period jumps in the exposure evolution when we pass payment times. The exposure graphs in Figure 9.1 show the exposure just at the dates where both the fixed and floating legs pay interest.

We start with refining the swap payoff (9.2) for this more general case:[5]

$$NPV(t;t_j,t_n) = \omega N \left[\Pi_{flo}(t) - \Pi_{fix}(t)\right]$$

[5] Assume, for instance, that $t_{k+1} < t < t_{k+2}$ in Figure 9.2.

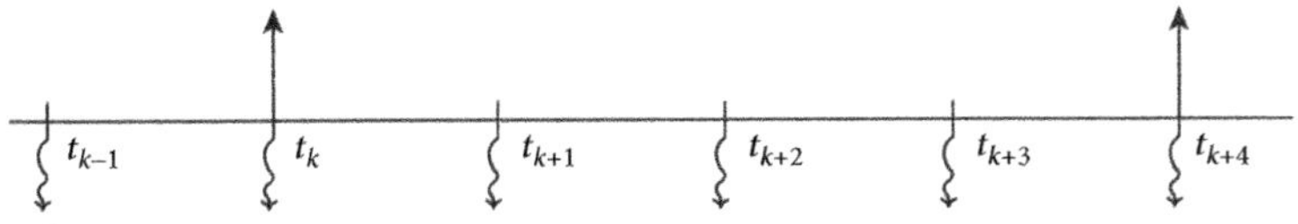

Figure 9.2 Cash flows on a swap with annual fixed flows vs quarterly variable flows. The curly arrows depict the variable (stochastic) flows

The "exercise" time t is in the first fixed interest period $[t_j, t_{j+1}]$, the first fixed payment at t_{j+1} is still outstanding, so that the fixed leg payoff is unchanged,

$$\Pi_{fix}(t) = N\,K \sum_{i=j+1}^{n} \delta(t_{i-1}, t_i)\, P(t, t_i) = N\,K\,A_{jn}(t).$$

On the floating leg (still without spread) we now separate the current coupon period around time t (which is fixed before time t). If we denote the current floating period's start and end date t_s and t_e (with $t_s < t < t_e$) we can write the floating leg payoff

$$\Pi_{flo}(t) = N\,C(t) + N\,(P(t, t_e) - P(t, t_n)), \quad C(t) = \mathrm{Ibor}(t_s)\,\delta_{flo}\,P(t, t_e)$$

where $\mathrm{Ibor}(t)$ stands for the floating index fixing at time t_s (also stochastic, but known at time $t > t_s$). Moreover we separate the value of accrued interest at time t on fixed and floating leg

$$\mathrm{Acc}_{fix}(t) = \delta_{fix}\,\frac{t - t_j}{t_{j+1} - t_j}$$
$$\mathrm{Acc}_{flo}(t) = \delta_{flo}\,\frac{t - t_s}{t_e - t_s}$$

and define the *clean annuity*

$$\widetilde{A}_{jn}(t) = A_{jn}(t) - \mathrm{Acc}_{fix}(t)$$

which represents the remaining swap length from time t to t_n. Our swap payoff can hence be written

$$NPV(t; t_j, t_n) = \omega\,N\left[\Pi_{flo}(t) - K\,\widetilde{A}_{jn}(t) - K\,\mathrm{Acc}_{fix}(t)\right]$$

$$= \omega N \widetilde{A}_{jn}(t) \left[\frac{\Pi_{flo}(t) - \text{Ibor}(t_s)\,\text{Acc}_{flo}(t)}{\widetilde{A}_{jn}(t)} - \left(K + \frac{K\,\text{Acc}_{fix}(t) - \text{Ibor}(t_s)\,\text{Acc}_{flo}(t)}{\widetilde{A}_{jn}(t)} \right) \right]$$

$$= \omega N \widetilde{A}_{jn}(t) \left[\widetilde{F}(t) - \widetilde{K} \right]$$

with modified strike

$$\widetilde{K} = K + \frac{K\,\text{Acc}_{fix}(t) - \text{Ibor}(t_s)\,\text{Acc}_{flo}(t)}{\widetilde{A}_{jn}(t)}$$

and forward swap rate for period (t, t_n)

$$\widetilde{F}(t) = \frac{\Pi_{flo}(t) - \text{Ibor}(t_s)\,\text{Acc}_{flo}(t)}{\widetilde{A}_{jn}(t)} \approx \frac{1 - P(t, t_n)}{\widetilde{A}_{jn}(t)}$$

If we now simplify $\widetilde{K}$ by replacing the stochastic $P(t, T)$ by forward zero bonds $P(0, T)/P(0, t)$ and the index fixing $\text{Ibor}(t_s)$ by its forward rate as of today for period (t_s, t_e), then we can again apply the Black76 swaption pricing formula with clean annuity and strike to get an approximate swaption price with intra-period exercise. Figure 9.3 shows a typical exposure evolution for a swap with different fixed and floating payment frequencies.

9.1.2 Amortizing swap

The swap with changing notional (amortizing or accreting) is another useful example that can still be priced in a generalized Black model framework. The approach is outlined in [97], page 304, example 2. The basic idea is valuing the instrument as an option on the exchange of two assets which are the legs of the underlying swap. Jamshidian covers the case of constant fixed rate, zero spread and assumes identical payment frequencies on the fixed and floating legs. The following is a slight generalization of his approach. We assume that the notional on both the fixed and float legs changes in parallel, that is the minimum period between changes is given by the leg with the longer interest period. As before, the floating leg is vanilla, that is fixed in advance, and the index tenor corresponds with the leg's period.

Let Π_{flo} and Π_{fix} denote the fair value of the floating and fixed legs, respectively, once more using the single-curve approach. Let the floating leg have n periods with notional $N_{i-1}, i = 1, \ldots, n+1$ the notional of the i-th period between t_{i-1} and t_i, $N_n = 0$, $P_i = P(t_i)$, $\delta_i = \delta(t_{i-1}, t_i)$ the floating leg year fraction between

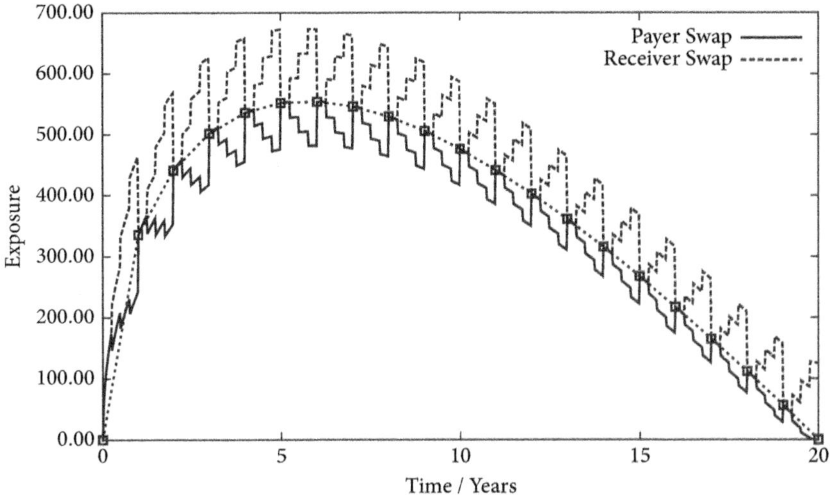

Figure 9.3 Vanilla swap exposure as a function of time for an at-the-money payer and receiver swap with annual fixed frequency and quarterly floating frequency; other parameters as in 9.1; squared symbols follow the at-the-money curve from Figure 9.1. This shows that the CVA for the at-the-money payer and receiver swaps will differ due to the different pay and receive leg frequencies

dates t_{i-1} and t_i, F_i the forward rate fixed at time t_{i-1} and paid at t_i, s_i the floating spread that applies to period (t_{i-1}, t_i), n' the number of fixed periods, N'_{i-1} the fixed leg notional amount in period (t'_{i-1}, t'_i), r_i the fixed rate that applies to period (t'_{i-1}, t'_i), δ'_i the fixed leg year fraction between dates t'_{i-1} and t'_i, and $P'_i = P(t'_i)$. Note that we explicitly allow the spread on the floating leg and the fixed rate to change at the beginning or end of each period as well. With these definitions, we have

$$\begin{aligned}
\Pi_{flo} &= \sum_{i=1}^{n} N_{i-1}\,(F(t_{i-1}, t_i) + s_i)\,\delta_i\,P_i \\
&= \sum_{i=1}^{n} N_{i-1}\,(P_{i-1} - P_i) + \sum_{i=1}^{n} N_{i-1}\,s_i\,\delta_i\,P_i \\
&= \sum_{i=1}^{n} \underbrace{(N_{i-1} - N_i)(P_0 - P_i)}_{(\text{note } \sum_{i=1}^{n} N_{i-1} - N_i = N_0)} + \sum_{i=1}^{n} N_{i-1}\,s_i\,\delta_i\,P_i, \\
\Pi_{fix} &= \sum_{i=1}^{n'} N'_{i-1}\,r_i\,\delta'_i\,P'_i.
\end{aligned}$$

We now define the spread present value *SPV*, fixed *BPS*, and strike K as

$$SPV := \sum_{i=1}^{n} N_{i-1}\, s_i\, \delta_i\, P_i \tag{9.7}$$

$$BPS := \sum_{i=1}^{n'} N'_{i-1}\, \delta'_i\, P'_i := Y \tag{9.8}$$

$$K := \frac{\Pi_{fix} - SPV}{BPS} \tag{9.9}$$

$$X := \Pi_{flo} - SPV = \sum_{i=1}^{n} (N_{i-1} - N_i)(P_0 - P_i). \tag{9.10}$$

If the notional, spread and fixed rate were constant, *BPS* would just be $N \times$ annuity, X would be the pure floating leg $N \times (P_0 - P_n)$, and K would be the locked-in swap rate, where the spread was reformulated as a part of the fixed coupon. Now the swap present value can be written as

$$\begin{aligned}\Pi_{Swap} &= \Pi_{flo} - \Pi_{fix} \\ &= X + SPV - \Pi_{fix} \\ &= X - K\, Y.\end{aligned} \tag{9.11}$$

A swap with exchange of assets X against $K\,Y$ is therefore equivalent to the original swap in the sense that their current values agree. This does not hold for future values if the spreads s_i are non-zero or fixed rates r_j vary – the strike K is then a function of time.

The European option on the swap is now treated as an option on the exchange of two assets with payoff $[\omega\,(X_T - K\,Y_T)]^+ = Y_T\,[\omega\,(X_T/Y_T - K)]^+$ at maturity T where $\omega = \pm 1$ for a call or fixed payer (put or fixed receiver). In the annuity measure (associated with numeraire Y, i.e. including the changing notional), the option price Π is given by

$$\Pi_{Swaption} = Y_0\, \mathbb{E}^Y\{[\omega\,(X_T/Y_T - K)]^+\}. \tag{9.12}$$

The forward yield $S = X_T/Y_T$ is a quotient of a tradable asset and the numeraire and hence a martingale under this annuity measure. Now the key assumption is that S can be modelled as a drift-free log-normal variable so that we can apply the Black76 formula (C.3) to evaluate the expectation (9.12).

The remaining task is to determine the volatility σ of variable S, which we do as follows. From Equations (9.8) and (9.10) we infer that one can write the yield!forwardforward yield S as a linear combination of simple yield!swapswap yields S_i:

$$S = \frac{X}{Y} = \sum_{i=1}^{n} w_i S_i, \quad S_i = \frac{P_0 - P_i}{\sum\limits_{t_0 < t'_k \le t_i} \delta'_k P'_k}, \quad w_i = \frac{1}{Y}(N_{i-1} - N_i) \sum_{t_0 < t'_k \le t_i} \delta'_k P'_k.$$

Note that the denominator in the expression for S_i represents the annuity of a standard swap based on conventional payment frequency and day count fraction. The variance of S can therefore be written

$$\langle S^2 \rangle_t = \sum_{i=1}^{n}\sum_{j=1}^{n} \langle w_i S_i w_j S_j \rangle_t \approx \sum_{i=1}^{n}\sum_{j=1}^{n} w_i w_j \langle S_i S_j \rangle_t$$

where in the second step we have frozen the weights w_i (since annuities have little sensitivity to rate changes). Since S and S_i are log-normal variables,

$$\langle S^2 \rangle_t = S^2 \left(e^{\langle (ln\, S)^2 \rangle_t} - 1 \right) = S^2 \left(e^{\sigma^2 t} - 1 \right)$$

$$\langle S_i S_j \rangle_t = S_i S_j \left(e^{\langle ln\, S_i \, ln\, S_j \rangle_t} - 1 \right) = S_i S_j \left(e^{\rho_{ij} \sigma_i \sigma_j t} - 1 \right)$$

where σ and σ_i are the annualized percentage volatilities of the log-normal variables, and time t is measured in years. These relations are solved to yield

$$\sigma^2 t = \ln \left(1 + \sum_{i=1}^{n}\sum_{j=1}^{n} w_i w_j \frac{S_i S_j}{S^2} \left(e^{\rho_{ij} \sigma_i \sigma_j t} - 1 \right) \right) \tag{9.13}$$

where t is the time to expiry. Knowing the forward yield S, its volatility σ, strike K and time to expiry t, one can now apply the Black formula (C.3) to evaluate expectation (9.12).

9.1.3 A simple swap CVA model

In this section we derive closed-form (analytical) approximations to the vanilla swap CVA allowing rapid evaluation. We start from the discrete formula (9.6) and choose an arbitrarily fine discretization to arrive at the continuous formula[6]

$$\text{U-CVA}(0) = LGD \int_0^T \text{Swaption}(0; t, T) \cdot \rho(t)\, dt, \tag{9.14}$$

[6] And we assume that the counterparty has not defaulted before $t = 0$, so that $\mathbb{1}_{\tau > 0} = 1$.

with the swaption price from (9.5) and default density $\rho(t) = -\frac{\partial}{\partial t} S(t)$ (where $S(t)$ is the survival probability up to time t). We further make the following simplifying assumptions:

- Flat hazard rate curve λ, the default density is then given by $\rho(t) = \lambda\, e^{-\lambda t}$;
- Flat zero curve z, discount factors are given by $P(t) = e^{-zt}$;
- Flat swaption volatility structure $\sigma(t, T) \equiv \sigma$;
- Swaps are "vanilla", i.e. have constant notional and exchange fixed vs vanilla floating payments with the same payment frequency δ, and period lengths are also constant.

We can then write the annuity (9.3) in closed form

$$A(0; t, T) = \delta\, \frac{e^{-zt} - e^{-zT}}{e^{z\delta} - 1} = A_0\, \frac{e^{-zt} - e^{-zT}}{1 - e^{-zT}}, \qquad A_0 = A(0; 0, T), \tag{9.15}$$

and the fair forward swap rate reads

$$K(0; t, T) = \frac{e^{z\delta} - 1}{\delta}. \tag{9.16}$$

In-the-money

For a swaption that is deeply in or out-of-the-money, that is $|F(0; t, T) - K| \gg 0$, the swaption value (9.5) simplifies to its intrinsic value

$$\text{Swaption}_{\text{intr}}(0, t, T) = \begin{cases} N\, A(0; t, T)\, \omega\, (F(0; t, T) - K) & ;\, \omega\, (F(0; t, T) - K) > 0 \\ 0 & ;\, \text{otherwise.} \end{cases}$$

The approximate CVA formula then follows by integrating (9.14) over exercise time t,

$$\text{U-CVA}^{ITM} = LGD \cdot S_0 \cdot I_1(z, \lambda, T) \tag{9.17}$$

with

$$S_0 = N\, A_0\, \omega\, (F(0; 0, T) - K)$$

$$I_1(z, \lambda, T) = \lambda \int_0^T \frac{e^{-zt} - e^{-zT}}{1 - e^{-zT}}\, e^{-\lambda t}\, dt \;=\; 1 - \frac{z}{z + \lambda}\, \frac{1 - e^{-(z+\lambda)T}}{1 - e^{-zT}}.$$

Expanding to first order in $\lambda T < 1$ and $zT < 1$ we obtain the following approximation which is a simple upper bound to (9.17) for $S_0 > 0$,

$$\text{U-CVA}^{ITM} = LGD\, \lambda\, S_0\, \frac{T}{2} + O(\lambda^2 T^2).$$

Note that $LGD \cdot \lambda$ is equal to the CDS spread (flat curve assumptions, first order approximation in λ), and that S_0 is the present value of the swap.

At-the-money

We next consider the at-the-money case, $F(0;0,T) = K$ and $S_0 = 0$. Then

$$\begin{aligned}\text{Swaption}(0;t,T) &= N\,A(0;t,T))\,\omega K\left\{2\,\Phi\left(\omega\frac{\sigma\sqrt{t}}{2}\right)-1\right\}\\ &= N\,A(0;t,T)\,K\sigma\sqrt{\frac{t}{2\pi}}+O(\sigma^2 T).\end{aligned}$$

The approximate CVA formula is then (dropping $O(\sigma^2 T)$ terms)

$$\text{U-CVA}^{ATM} = \frac{1}{\sqrt{2\pi}}N\,A_0\,LGD\,K\sigma\,I_2(z,\lambda,T) \tag{9.18}$$

$$\begin{aligned}I_2(z,\lambda,T) &= \lambda\int_0^T\frac{e^{-zt}-e^{-zT}}{1-e^{-zT}}\sqrt{t}\,e^{-\lambda t}\,dt\\ &= \frac{\lambda}{1-e^{-zT}}\left\{\frac{\gamma\left(\frac{3}{2},(\lambda+z)\,T\right)}{(z+\lambda)^{3/2}}-\frac{e^{-zT}\gamma\left(\frac{3}{2},\lambda\,T\right)}{\lambda^{3/2}}\right\}\end{aligned}$$

where $\gamma\,(s,x)$ is the incomplete gamma function.[7]

Near the money

We now develop an expansion in a moneyness parameter that yields a CVA approximation that extends (9.18) into the vicinity of the ATM case. We start as before with (9.5):

$$\text{Swaption}(0;t,T) = N\,A(0;t,T)\,\omega\,\{F(0;t,T)\,\Phi(\omega\,d_+)-K\,\Phi(\omega\,d_-)\},$$

and introduce a *moneyness* parameter, δ, given by

$$F(0;t,T) = K(1+\delta).$$

The moneyness δ measures how far the current fair rate is from the strike rate of the swaption in relative terms. We can express the swaption price in terms of δ as

$$\text{Swaption}(0;t,T) = N\,A(0;t,T)\,\omega\,\{K\,(\Phi(\omega\,d_+)-\Phi(\omega\,d_-))+\delta K\,\Phi(\omega\,d_+)\}$$

[7] The incomplete gamma function $\gamma\,(s,x) = \int_0^x t^{s-1}\,e^{-t}\,dt$, can be constructed from $\Gamma(s) = \gamma\,(s,\infty)$ and the cumulative gamma distribution $F(x;k,\theta)$ via $\gamma\,(s,x) = \Gamma(s)\cdot F(x;s,1)$. $\Gamma(s)$ is available in Excel as `EXP(GAMMALN(s))`, the cumulative gamma distribution $F(x,s,1)$ as `GAMMADIST(x, s, 1, 1)`.

Recalling that

$$d_{\pm} = \frac{\ln(F(0;t,T)/K)}{\sigma\sqrt{t}} \pm \frac{1}{2}\sigma\sqrt{t}$$

and keeping first order terms in δ we see that

$$\begin{aligned} d_{\pm} &= \frac{\delta}{\sigma\sqrt{t}} \pm \frac{1}{2}\sigma\sqrt{2\pi t} + O(\delta^2) \\ &= \sigma\sqrt{t}\left(\frac{\delta}{\sigma^2 t} \pm \frac{1}{2}\right) \end{aligned}$$

There are two important timescales in this equation, depending on the dimensionless parameter

$$t' = \frac{\sigma^2 t}{\delta}.$$

The first timescale is $\sigma\sqrt{t}$ which is a small parameter over our range of interest. The second timescale is $\delta/\sigma^2 t$. This timescale is very short and can generally be ignored except in the neighbourhood of $t = 0$.

We can develop two asymptotically valid expansions for the swaptions, one valid for $t' \ll 1$ and one valid for $t' \gg 1$. We focus first on the long-time regime, $t' \gg 1$. We note that for most realistic swaps, $\sigma^2 t$ is a small number in any case, and we use this fact to derive further approximations.

Long-time regime

In this regime $\sigma^2 t \gg \delta$ and a function of $d_{\pm}$ can safely be expanded in a regular expansion around $\pm\sigma\sqrt{t}/2$. We find that

$$\Phi(\omega d_{\pm}) = \Phi\left(\pm\frac{1}{2}\omega\sigma\sqrt{t}\right) + \frac{\omega\delta}{\sigma\sqrt{2\pi\, t}}\exp\left(-\frac{\omega^2}{8\sigma^2 t}\right) + O(\delta^2),$$

and so we conclude that

$$\begin{aligned} \text{Swaption}(0;t,T) = N A(t)\,\omega K \Big\{&\Phi(\omega\sigma\sqrt{t}/2) - \Phi(-\omega\sigma\sqrt{t}/2)) \\ &+\delta\,\Phi(\omega\sigma\sqrt{t}/2)\Big\} + O(\delta^2) \end{aligned}$$

This expression is compact but does not lend itself to easy integration. In order to derive a simple CVA expression, we now proceed one step further by employing a regular expansion in powers of $\sigma\sqrt{t}$ to get an analytically integrable expression

$$\text{Swaption} = N\,A(0;t,T)\,K\left\{\frac{\omega\,\delta}{2} + \left(1+\frac{\delta}{2}\right)\sigma\sqrt{\frac{t}{2\pi}}\right\} + O(\delta^2). \tag{9.19}$$

We note that the limit of this expression is $NA(0)\,K\,\delta/2$ as $t \to 0$ which is *not* the correct limit for the swaption price (which is either 0 or $NA(0)K\delta$ depending on the moneyness). This is because this expansion breaks down for timescales on the order of δ/σ^2. However, the error that we make in employing expression (9.19) in an integral to compute the CVA is $O(\delta)$ over an interval of length $O(\delta/\sigma^2)$, and so the error we make is of order δ^2/σ^2. As long as δ is small relative to σ, expression 9.19 can therefore be considered a valid approximation under the integral.

We return now to compute the CVA. Using expression (9.19), we see that

$$\begin{aligned}\text{U-CVA}^{NTM} &= LGD\,\lambda\,N\,K\int_0^T\left\{\frac{\omega\,\delta}{2} + \left(1+\frac{\delta}{2}\right)\sigma\sqrt{\frac{t}{2\pi}}\right\}A(t)\;e^{-\lambda\,t}\,dt\\ &\quad + O(\delta^2,\delta^2/\sigma^2)\end{aligned}$$

As before this gives rise to the expression

$$\begin{aligned}\text{U-CVA}^{NTM} &= LGD\,N\,A_0\,K\,\frac{\omega\,\delta}{2}\cdot I_1(z,\lambda,T)\\ &\quad + LGD\,N\,A_0\,K\left(1+\frac{\delta}{2}\right)\frac{\sigma}{\sqrt{2\pi}}\cdot I_2(z,\lambda,T) + O(\delta^2,\delta^2/\sigma^2).\end{aligned} \tag{9.20}$$

Note that this agrees with U-CVA^{ATM} for $\delta = 0$, as expected, and that the first term equals $\text{U-CVA}^{ITM}/2$. Employing the small λ expansion we find

$$\text{U-CVA}^{NTM} = N\,A_0\,K\,LGD\,\lambda\left\{\frac{\omega\delta T}{2} + \left(1+\frac{\delta}{2}\right)\frac{\sigma\;T^{3/2}}{\sqrt{2\pi}}\right\} + O(\delta^2,\delta^2/\sigma^2,\lambda\,T).$$

Figures 9.4 and 9.5 compare the CVA approximations with the "exact" CVA from numerically integrating (9.14). These comparisons indicate that

$$\text{U-CVA} \approx \max\left[\text{U-CVA}^{ITM},\text{U-CVA}^{NTM},0\right] \tag{9.21}$$

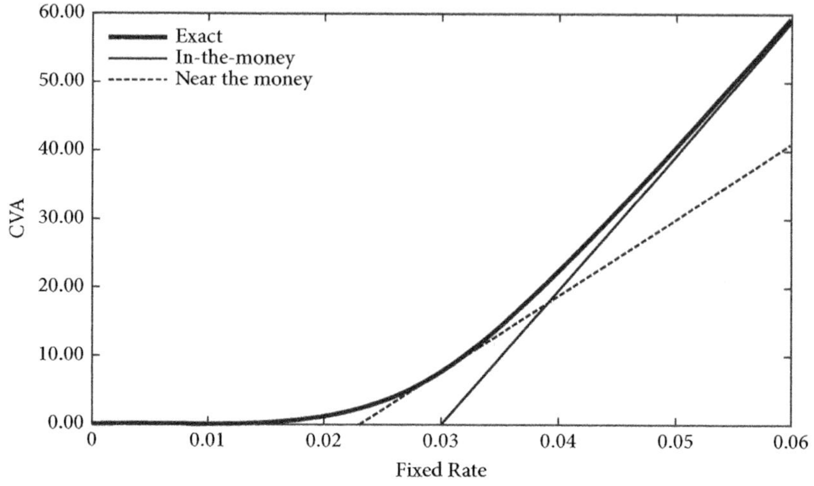

Figure 9.4 CVA approximations (9.17, 9.20) as a function of fixed rate K for a receiver swap with notional 10,000, time to maturity 10; fair swap rate 3%, volatility 20%, hazard rate 1%, LGD 50%

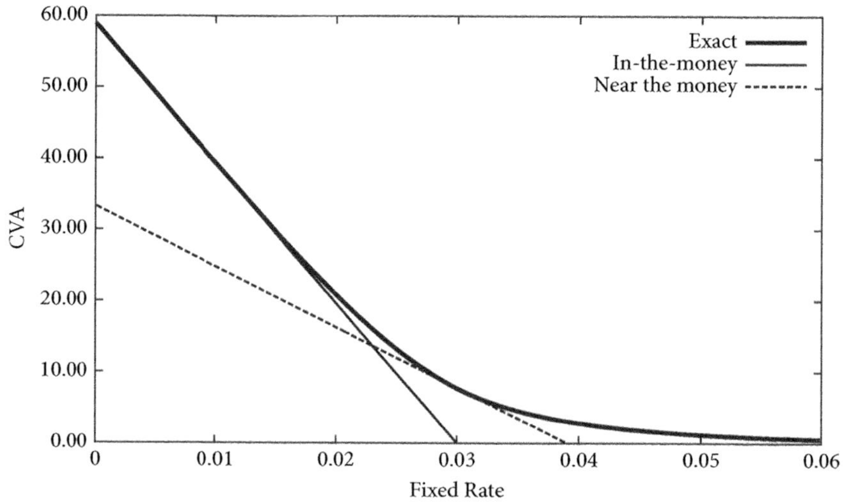

Figure 9.5 CVA approximations (9.17, 9.20) as a function of fixed rate K for a payer swap with notional 10,000, time to maturity 10; fair swap rate 3%, volatility 20%, hazard rate 1%, LGD 50%

is a reasonable approximation to the "exact"[8] CVA for a wide range of fixed rates K which can be easily implemented. Note that the absolute approximation errors

[8] Within the model assumptions: vanilla swap with flat yield curve, flat hazard rate curve, flat volatility structure.

are particularly large at the intersections of the U-CVA$^{NTM}(K)$ with $K = 0$ and U-CVA$^{ITM}(K)$, that is

$$\delta = \mp \frac{2\sigma\, I_2(z,\lambda,T)}{\omega\sqrt{2\pi}\, I_1(z,\lambda,T) \pm \sigma\, I_2(z,\lambda,T)}.$$

Summary

The CVA approximation (9.21) is useful to develop a qualitative understanding and to quickly estimate swap CVA, for example in a spreadsheet based on a few key inputs. The authors have indeed used the formula in early times to check CVA materiality for client derivatives portfolios (where each netting set only contained a small number of derivatives, without collateralization), as it is an improvement compared to the crude estimate of the unilateral U-CVA $\approx PD \times LGD \times NPV^+$ for each netting set. For actual single-trade CVA calculations one would rather apply (9.6) and use an appropriate swaption pricing method. Rather than drilling deeper into the pricing of interest rate swap variations, we now move on to a few more products that can be handled with little or moderate effort.

9.2 Cash-settled European options

The unilateral CVA for single *cash-settled European option* products is easily evaluated. We start again from (9.1). Option NPVs are either positive (if long) or negative (if short). Obviously, the CVA of a short option position vanishes. In the case of long positions, we can replace $NPV^+(\bar{t}_i) = NPV(\bar{t}_i)$. In other words, the unilateral CVA as of today assuming no default so far is

$$\text{U-CVA} = LGD \sum_{i=1}^{n} \left[S^M(0,t_{i-1}) - S^M(0,t_i) \right] \times \mathbb{E}_0^{\mathbb{Q}} \left[D(0,\bar{t}_i) \cdot NPV(\bar{t}_i) \right].$$

For *cash settled European options*, there is only a single flow at option expiry T. We can therefore truncate the sum at option expiry T as $NPV(t) = 0$ beyond that point. Moreover, the expectation $\mathbb{E}_0^{\mathbb{Q}}[\cdot]$ yields today's option price

$$\text{Option} = \mathbb{E}_0^{\mathbb{Q}} \left[D(0,\bar{t}_i) \cdot NPV(\bar{t}_i) \right]$$

for each (arbitrarily short) interval $[t_{i-1}, t_i]$, so that we can move the price in front of the sum and arrive at the simple result

$$\text{U-CVA} = LGD \cdot \left[1 - S^M(0,T) \right] \cdot \text{Option} \tag{9.22}$$

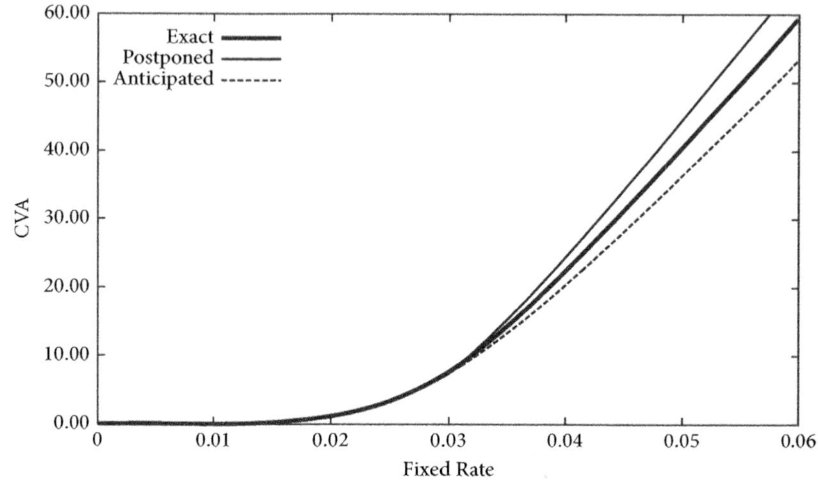

Figure 9.6 CVA as a function of fixed rate K for a receiver swap with notional 10,000, time to maturity 10; fair swap rate 3%, volatility 20%, hazard rate 1%, LGD 50%. This graph compares the "exact" CVA integral (9.14) to the "anticipated" and "postponed" discretizations where the exposure is evaluated at the beginning and the end of each time interval, respectively

where the term in brackets is the cumulative probability of counterparty default up to option expiry. This generally applies to cash settled European options such as swaptions, caplets and floorlets (hence also caps and floors, which are sums of caplets and floorlets), FX options, etc.

Under *physical settlement*, when cash flows can occur beyond expiry, the situation is more complex, and the simple formula (9.22) is not applicable. We will investigate such cases later on in this chapter.

9.3 FX forward

The payoff of an FX forward on its value date T is

$$NPV(T) = N_f \cdot \omega \cdot (X_{fd}(T) - K)$$

where N_f is the cash flow in foreign currency, $X_{fd}(T)$ is the foreign exchange rate at the value date for converting the foreign currency amount into domestic currency, and K is the strike FX rate which is agreed and fixed on the trade date. The FX forward's value at any earlier time $t < T$ is

$$NPV(t) = N_f \cdot \mathbb{E}_t^{\mathbb{Q}}\left[D(t,T) \cdot \omega \cdot (X_{fd}(T) - K)\right]$$

Moving to the T-forward measure (associated with the domestic discount bond with maturity T), we can write this as

$$NPV(t) = N_f \cdot P_d(t,T) \cdot \mathbb{E}_t^T \left[\omega \left(X_{fd}(T) - K\right)\right].$$

Now consider the FX forward rate

$$F(t,T) = X_{fd}(t) \frac{P_f(t,T)}{P_d(t,T)} \tag{9.23}$$

which agrees with the payoff's spot FX rate at time T, that is $F(T,T) = X_{fd}(T)$. Note that $F(t,T)$ is by definition a quotient of a tradable asset in domestic currency and the numeraire asset $P_d(t,T)$. From FACT 1 in Appendix A, we see that $F(t,T)$ is a martingale under the T-forward measure, that is

$$\mathbb{E}_t^T \left[X(T)\right] = \mathbb{E}_t^T \left[F(T,T)\right] = F(t,T).$$

We therefore have

$$\begin{aligned} NPV(t) &= N_f \, P_d(t,T) \, \omega \left(F(t,T) - K\right) \\ &= N_f \, \omega \left(X_{fd}(t) \, P_f(t,T) - K \, P_d(t,T)\right). \end{aligned}$$

For the simple unilateral CVA (9.1) we then need to evaluate expectations

$$\begin{aligned} \mathbb{E}_0^{\mathbb{Q}} \left[D(0,t) \, NPV^+(t)\right] &= P_d(0,t) \, \mathbb{E}_0^t \left[NPV^+(t)\right] \\ &= P_d(0,t) \, N_f \, \mathbb{E}_0^t \left[(\omega (F(t,T) - K))^+\right] \\ &= P_d(0,t) \, N_f \, \mathbb{E}_0^t \left[\left(\omega \left(X_{fd}(t) \, P_f(t,T) - K \, P_d(t,T)\right)\right)^+\right] \end{aligned} \tag{9.24}$$

Note that (9.24) is an option on the FX *forward* rate, not a vanilla FX option (on the FX spot rate). Generally this requires modelling of interest rates in both economies and the FX rate, that is at least three factors. We will come back to this general problem in Section 9.4 below. Here we keep it simple and assume deterministic rates.[9] If we now apply a *Garman-Kohlhagen* model for the FX rate involved, we arrive at a Black76 formula for the expectations (9.24):

[9] In that case we can take $P_f(t,T)$ out of the expectation and rewrite (9.24)

$$\mathbb{E}_0^{\mathbb{Q}} \left[D(0,t) \, NPV^+(t)\right] = P_d(0,t) \, P_f(t,T) \, N_f \, \mathbb{E}_0^t \left[\left(\omega \left(X_{fd}(t) - K'\right)^+\right]$$

with $K' = K \, P_d(t,T) / P_f(t,T)$ which has the form of a vanilla FX option price with strike K' and nominal $N_f \, P_f(t,T)$.

The Garman-Kohlhagen model [68] assumes that the spot FX rate X_{fd} (1 unit of foreign currency in domestic currency) follows Geometric Brownian Motion (GBM)

$$\frac{dX}{X} = \mu(t)\,dt + \sigma(t)\,dW$$

which is solved by

$$X(t) = X(0)\exp\left\{\int_0^t \left(\mu(s) - \frac{1}{2}\sigma^2(s)\right) ds + \int_0^t \sigma(s)\,dW(s)\right\}.$$

The model's drift is calibrated such that the expected future spot rate

$$\mathbb{E}[X(T)] = X(0)\exp\left(\int_0^T \mu(s)\,ds\right)$$

agrees with today's fair FX forward rate for exchange at time T

$$F(0,T) = X(0)\frac{P_f(0,T)}{P_d(0,T)} \quad \Rightarrow \quad \int_0^T \mu(s)\,ds = \ln\frac{P_f(T)}{P_d(T)}.$$

This also means that the FX forward rate $F(t,T)$ in (9.23) follows drift-free GBM

$$dF(t,T) = \sigma(t)\,F(t,T)\,dW.$$

Expectation (9.24) therefore directly leads to a Black76 formula (see Appendix C)

$$\mathbb{E}_0^{\mathbb{Q}}\left[D(0,t)\,NPV^+(t)\right] = P_d(0,t)\,N_f\,\text{Black}\left(\omega, F(0,t), K, \int_0^t \sigma^2(s)\,ds\right). \qquad (9.25)$$

which makes the calculation of single-trade CVA for FX forwards about as simple as for cash-settled European options and interest rate swaps. Figure 9.7 shows typical evolutions of FX forward exposure (9.25).

9.4 Cross-currency swap

The last single trade CVA case we will investigate here is the *cross-currency interest rate swap* (CCS). A CCS exchanges fixed interest payments in one currency for floating payments in another currency with notional exchanges on the start and maturity dates. A *cross-currency basis swap* (CCBS) exchanges floating rate payments in different currencies. Like FX forwards, CCS are sensitive to interest and FX rates, but are typically longer term. The NPV of a CCS with constant

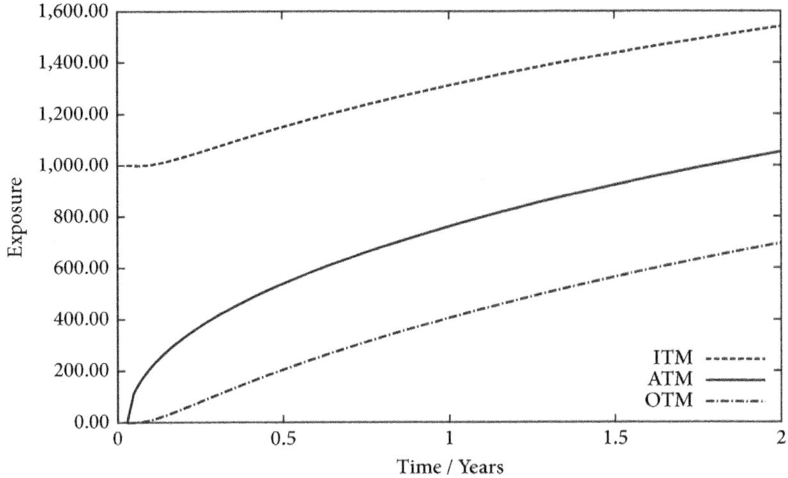

Figure 9.7 Exposure evolution (9.25) as a function of time for in-the-money (strike at 0.9 times forward), at-the-money and out-of-the-money (strike at 1.1 times forward) FX forwards, notional 10000, maturity two years, volatility 20%

notional $N_d = K\,N_f$ can be written as the exchange of the assets denominated in two currencies

$$NPV(t) = N_f\,\omega\,\left(X_{df}(t)\,\Pi_f(t,t) - K\,\Pi_d(t,t)\right)$$

where $\Pi_{d,f}(t,t')$ denote the time-t values, in respective currencies, of the foreign and domestic (fixed or floating) legs with cash flows beyond time t', and $X_{df}(t)$ is the exchange rate, as before. Note that the legs contain final notional exchanges in the CCS case, that is a fixed leg has the form

$$\Pi(t,t') = N\,c\sum_{t_i>t'}\delta(t_{i-1},t_i)\,P(t,t_i) + N\,P(t,t_{end}).$$

We can derive a Black pricing formula for the cross-currency swaption, needed for the simple unilateral CVA (9.1), as follows

$$\begin{aligned}\text{CCSwaption} &= \mathbb{E}_0^{\mathbb{Q}}\left[D(0,t)\,NPV^+(t)\right]\\ &= N_f\,B(0)\,\mathbb{E}_0^{\mathbb{Q}}\left[\left(\omega\,\frac{X(t)\Pi_f(t,t) - K\,\Pi_d(t,t)}{B(t)}\right)^+\right]\end{aligned}$$

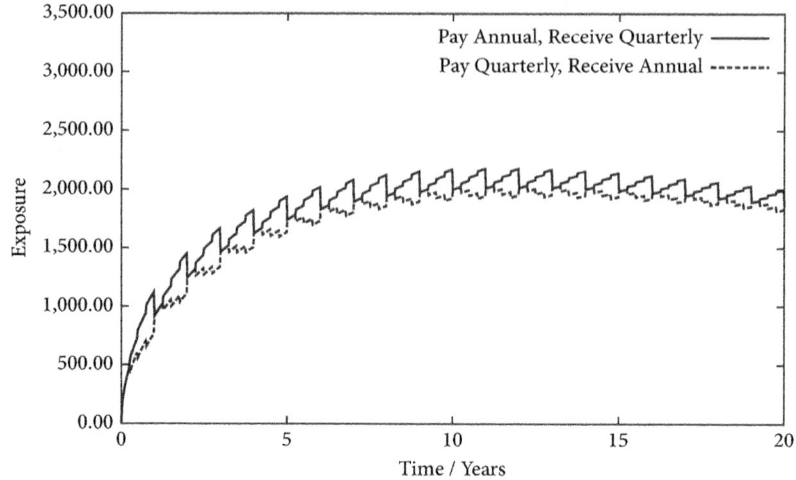

Figure 9.8 Exposure evolution (9.26) as a function of time for at-the-money cross currency swaps with 20-year maturity exchanging fixed payments on both legs, foreign notional 10000, domestic notional 12000, FX spot rate 1.2, flat foreign and domestic yield curve at same (zero rate) level 4%, Black volatility 20%

$$= N_f\,\Pi_d(0,t)\,\mathbb{E}_0^{\Pi_d}\left[\left(\omega\left(X(t)\frac{\Pi_f(t,t)}{\Pi_d(t,t)}-K\right)\right)^+\right]$$

$$= N_f\,\Pi_d(0,t)\,\text{Black}\left(\omega, X(0)\frac{\Pi_f(0,t)}{\Pi_d(0,t)}, K, \int_0^t \sigma^2(s)\,ds\right) \qquad (9.26)$$

Here we switched to the measure associated with the domestic leg (a tradable asset). Again, $X(t)\,\Pi_f(t,t)/\Pi_d(t,t)$ is a martingale under this measure, and we made the assumption that this quantity follows GBM with volatility $\sigma(t)$. We can use this to draw a qualitative picture of the cross-currency swap exposure evolution, see Figures 9.8 and 9.9, which combines – not surprisingly – the features of a single currency swap and FX forward exposures.

The problem with (9.26) is how to calibrate $\sigma(t)$ in the absence of quoted cross-currency swaptions. To overcome this, one has to model both interest rate curves and the FX rate explicitly in at least a three-factor model setting which can be calibrated for example to quoted FX options and swaptions. The model presented in the following is an established, still relatively simple, choice.

Cross-currency Hull-White model

The *Cross-Currency Hull-White* model is a coupled interest rate and FX model for pricing instruments depending on interest rates in two economies and the exchange

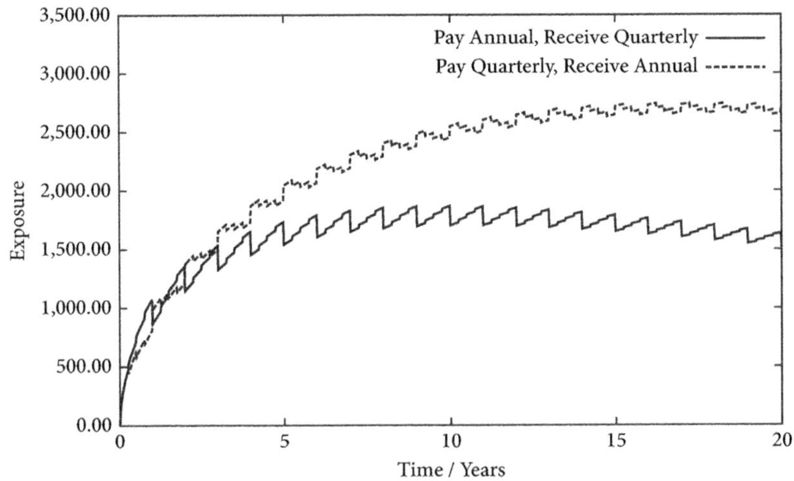

Figure 9.9 Exposure evolution (9.26) as a function of time for cross-currency swaps as in Figure 9.8, but with flat foreign and domestic yield curve at 4% and 3% zero rate levels, respectively. The swaps are at-the-money initially and move in and out-of-the-money, respectively, over time

rate between the two. References to the model can be traced back to work by Babbs in 1994 [14, 57, 123, 124].

In the domestic spot (bank account) measure, the model's SDE reads

$$
\begin{aligned}
\frac{dx}{x} &= \left[r_d(t) - r_f(t)\right] dt + \sigma_x \, dW_x \\
dr_d &= \lambda_d \left[\theta_d(t) - r_d(t)\right] dt + \sigma_d \, dW_d \\
dr_f &= \lambda_f \left[\theta_f(t) - r_f(t)\right] dt - \rho_{xf}\sigma_x\sigma_f \, dt + \sigma_f \, dW_f \\
dW_x \, dW_d &= \rho_{xd} \, dt \\
dW_x \, dW_f &= \rho_{xf} \, dt \\
dW_d \, dW_f &= \rho_{df} \, dt
\end{aligned}
$$

In the literature one also finds the equivalent formulation in terms of zero bond price processes. The model has been popular in the market for pricing long-dated *Power Reverse Dual Currency* trades [137]. More recent research [124, 55] deals with local volatility extensions of the model to take FX skew into account.

Note:

- The FX process is – as in the Garman-Kohlhagen model – log-normal, however it is now driven by the stochastic short rate differential between the two economies
- Interest rates are driven by one-factor Hull-White processes [85] in each economy
- Drift term $-\rho_{xf}\sigma_x\sigma_f\,dt$ in the foreign short rate process is due to the change of measure to the *domestic* spot (bank account) measure.
- We consider the simplest Hull–White model flavour here with constant parameters; generalization to time-dependent volatility is straightforward.

The model has an analytical solution in terms of the joint (mutivariate normal) density of the three variables $\ln x$, r_d and r_f for any given time t. This fact allows for efficient pricing routines. Model details including specification of the joint density and model calibration are discussed in Appendix D.3.

Cross-currency Swaption with cross-currency Hull-White

In this case it is convenient to compute the expectations (cross-currency swaption prices) in the t-forward measure

$$\begin{aligned}
\text{CCSwaption} &= \mathbb{E}_0^{\mathbb{Q}}\left[D(0,t)\,NPV^+(t)\right] \\
&= P_d(0,t)\,\mathbb{E}_0^t\left[NPV^+(t)\right] \\
&= N_f\,P_d(0,t)\,\mathbb{E}_0^t\left[\left(\omega\left(X(t)\,\Pi_f(0,t)-K\,\Pi_d(0,t)\right)\right)^+\right].
\end{aligned}$$

The payoff is a function of all three variables $\ln x$, r_d and r_f (we will refer to them as z_1, z_2 and z_3 in the following). As we know the multivariate normal joint density $\Phi(z,t)$ for any time t (see Appendix D.3), we can write the expectation as a triple integral

$$\text{CCSwaption} = N_f\,P_d(0,t)\iiint\left[\omega\left(X(t)\Pi_f(t)-K\Pi_d(t)\right)\right]^+\Phi(z,t)\,dz_1\,dz_2dz_3.$$

Computing such a triple integral numerically is computationally quite expensive, but we want to keep efforts low as we need many evaluations for CVA as in (9.1). Fortunately, we can solve one of the integrals analytically. Let us choose to do the z_1-integral analytically that allows a closed-form solution, conditional on (z_2, z_3), which is then integrated numerically:

$$\Pi = \iint \Pi(z_2, z_3)\, \Phi(z_2, z_3)\, dz_2\, dz_3 \tag{9.27}$$

$$\Pi(z_2, z_3) = N_f P_d(0, T) \int_{-\infty}^{\infty} \left[\omega \left(e^{z_1} \Pi_f(z_3) - K \Pi_d(z_2)\right)\right]^+ \Phi_{z_2, z_3}(z_1)\, dz_1$$

$$= N_f P_d(0, T) \Pi_f(z_3) \left\{ e^{\mu'_x + \Sigma'^2_x/2} N(\omega\, d'_1) - K' N(\omega\, d'_2) \right)$$

$$K' = K \frac{\Pi_d(z_2)}{\Pi_f(z_3)}$$

$$d'_1 = \frac{\ln \frac{1}{K'} + \mu'_x}{\Sigma'_x} + \Sigma'_x$$

$$d'_2 = d'_1 - \Sigma'_x$$

where μ'_x and Σ'_x are modified drift and variance due to conditioning on two variables, see Appendix D.3. The numerical double integral can be computed efficiently with two-dimensional Gauss-Hermite integration [96]. In the case of a fixed/floating swap with zero floating spread the two-dimensional numerical integration can even be replaced by a one-dimensional numerical integration with conditioning on one variable for the modified mean and variance in the closed-form inner solution.

Because of this semi-analytical approach, which reduces the integration to 1d and 2d, respectively, this pricing method is still quite efficient.

9.5 Rebalancing cross-currency swap

As of today, CCS are typically of the *rebalancing* or *mark-to-market* type: the notional on one of the legs is adjusted at the end of each interest period to the prevailing FX rate at that time, giving rise to additional interim cash flows to exchange the notional difference. The effect of this feature is that the rebalancing CCS exposure does not build up as in Figures 9.8 and 9.9; the FX exposure can only build up over a single period rather than the entire life of the swap. The rebalancing CCS exposure is therefore similar to single currency interest rate swap exposure evolution. We will compare the exposures of "conventional" and rebalancing CCS later on in Section 12.5 using a Monte Carlo simulation framework for CVA analysis which we will develop in the following part.

III Risk Factor Evolution

10 Introduction – A Monte Carlo Framework

The semi-analytical single-trade CVA calculations of the previous chapters are computationally very efficient, especially when closed-form option pricing formulas are available. However, when we need to compute CVA for a *netting set* of derivatives – which is the more common case – this option pricing approach quickly reaches its limits:

- We would need to come up with an option pricing formula for varying underlying derivative portfolios. While this may still be possible for sufficiently simple portolios, each portfolio/trade combination represents a new problem which requires customization, mapping or development efforts.
- When the portfolio is complex and contains structured products, closed-form option pricers are not available anymore, and we would have to resort to numerical techniques for the option price in each case.
- When the portfolio is *collateralized*, and CSA details have to be taken into account, semi-analytical approaches are not feasible anymore.

What we need is a generic approach that

- solves the netting problem without bespoke mapping/customization,
- covers a wide range of products and asset classes,
- can handle collateral in a straightforward fashion,
- can also tackle more general CVA/DVA tasks: when independence of hazard rates and other market drivers is not justified, both parties' default risk has to be taken into account, that is when we need to address (8.2) and (8.4) without the simplifications of Chapter 9.

This can be achieved with a Monte Carlo simulation framework which evaluates the expectations in (8.4), repeated here for $t = 0$,

$$\begin{aligned} \text{B-CVA} = & \sum_{i=1}^{n} \mathbb{E}_0^{\mathbb{Q}} \left[PD_2(t_{i-1}, t_i) \cdot S_1(t_i) \cdot LGD_2(\bar{t}_i) \cdot D(\bar{t}_i) \cdot NPV^+(\bar{t}_i) \right] \\ & - \sum_{i=1}^{n} \mathbb{E}_0^{\mathbb{Q}} \left[PD_1(t_{i-1}, t_i) \cdot S_2(t_i) \cdot LGD_1(\bar{t}_i) \cdot D(\bar{t}_i) \cdot (-NPV(\bar{t}_i))^+ \right], \end{aligned} \tag{8.4}$$

for any netting set numerically. All the terms in both expectations are potentially stochastic and correlated with each other – default/survival probabilities, loss given default, discount factors and the contributions to the netting set's NPV, including the collateral account balance.

The Monte Carlo simulation we envisage has to generate paths (through time) of the "drivers" of all these quantities, including

- interest rates
- foreign exchange rates
- consumer price indices and real rates
- hazard rates and recovery rates
- equity prices
- commodity (futures) prices

in order to cover a wide range of asset classes. On each path we then evaluate the portfolio through time – a lot of instruments at many future points in time. Repeating this for a large number of paths yields the famous "cube" of NPVs. Its production is computationally expensive,[1] but this should be viewed as the price for a flexible framework. To keep computational efforts manageable, it is key to keep market scenario generation and especially individual trade pricing efficient. Our desired exposures and CVAs (as well as other numbers to be discussed later) result from relatively straightforward aggregation and transformation of the large amount of "cube" data.[2]

With performance in mind, our aim is to develop a comprehensive model (covering all asset classes) which is accurate enough for the purpose at hand, yet still simple and analytically tractable (with few exceptions). We will therefore also restrict ourselves here to models with minimal numbers of factors (usually one, at most two, per risk class).

In the next sections we will build the Monte Carlo framework step by step, starting with a model for interest rate evolution, then adding foreign exchange rates, inflation, credit, and finally equity and commodity. The framework consists of the stochastic differential equations for the market drivers combined with pricing methods for market-quoted instruments to allow model calibration.

[1] Typical dimensions are 10,000 trades, 120 evaluation dates in quarterly steps over 30 years, 10,000 paths/samples, so that the cube contains 12 billion NPVs. If a single trade pricing takes on average 50 microseconds on a single core, this means about 170 CPU hours on a single core machine or 2.5 hours on 64 cores.

[2] To do this aggregation quickly and in flexible subsets of the portfolio is in itself a technical challenge.

11 Interest Rates

We are going to use a single-factor interest rate model, the Linear Gauss Markov model (LGM) which has been propagated by Patrick Hagan [77], see also Hagan and Woodward's 1999 paper [81] and Andersen's and Piterbarg's summary of the model in [8]. The LGM model is closely related to the one-factor Hull-White model with time-dependent parameters. It is formulated in an unusual measure (none of the bank account, forward or annuity measures we have seen before). This makes it particularly tractable, as we will show for a few examples below. A step-by-step derivation of the LGM model from the one-factor Hull-White model is provided in Appendix E.

11.1 Linear Gauss Markov model

Quoting Hagan [77], a "modern interest rate model consists of three parts: a numeraire, a set of random evolution equations in the risk neutral world, and the Martingale pricing formula". Here is what this means in the LGM case:

1. The LGM numeraire is given by

$$N(t) = \frac{1}{P(0,t)} \exp\left\{ H_t z_t + \frac{1}{2} H_t^2 \zeta_t \right\} \tag{11.1}$$

   where $P(0,t)$ is today's zero bond for maturity t and H_t is a time-dependent model parameter (related to the Hull-White mean reversion speed).
2. z_t is the normally distributed model "factor" with zero mean and variance ζ_t,

$$dz_t = \alpha_t\, dW_t, \qquad z_0 = 0, \qquad \zeta_t = \int_0^t \alpha_s^2\, ds.$$

3. Finally, the martingale pricing formula is

$$\frac{V(t)}{N(t)} = \mathbb{E}_t^N \left[\frac{V(T))}{N(T)} \right].$$

We can write the reduced values $\widetilde{V}(t) = V(t)/N(t)$ in terms of the Gaussian transition density of $z_T - z_t$ as follows:

$$\widetilde{V}(t, z_t) = \frac{1}{\sqrt{2\pi\,\Delta\zeta}} \int_{-\infty}^{\infty} e^{-(z_T - z_t)^2/2\Delta\zeta}\, \widetilde{V}(T, z_T)\, dz_T \tag{11.2}$$

where $\Delta\zeta = \zeta(T) - \zeta(t)$.

Applying (11.2) to the zero bond payoff $V(T) = 1$, we arrive at the closed-form expression for the reduced stochastic zero bond price:

$$\widetilde{P}(t, T, z_t) = \frac{P(t, T, z_t)}{N(t)} = P(0, T)\, \exp\left\{ -H_T\, z_t - \frac{1}{2} H_T^2\, \zeta_t \right\}, \tag{11.3}$$

and multiplying it by (11.1), we see that the zero bond price is

$$P(t, T, z_t) = \frac{P(0, T)}{P(0, t)}\, \exp\left\{ -(H_T - H_t)\, z_t - \frac{1}{2}\left(H_T^2 - H_t^2\right) \zeta_t \right\}. \tag{11.4}$$

This shows that the instantaneous forward rate $f(t, T)$ and short rate r are given by

$$f(t, T) = -\frac{\partial \ln P(t, T)}{\partial T} = f(0, T) + z(t)\, H'(T) + \zeta(t)\, H'(T) H(T) \tag{11.5}$$

$$r(t) = f(t, t) = f(0, t) + z(t)\, H'(t) + \zeta(t)\, H'(t) H(t). \tag{11.6}$$

Pricing in LGM is a series of applications of the numeraire (11.1), the reduced zero bond (11.3) and the rollback by convolution (11.2). Note that the model is "by construction" calibrated to today's yield term structure, $P(0, T, z_0) = P(0, T)$.

The advantage of the LGM model (compared to the Hull-White model in the bank account measure) is the fact that both the numeraire (11.1) and the reduced zero bond price (11.3) are driven by the same single factor $z(t)$. This facilitates analytical pricing (see next section for the zero bond option example), but also numerical implementations (e.g. Bermudan swaption pricing) and the implementation of Monte Carlo schemes.

11.1.1 Multiple curves

What yield term structure are we referring to? Our aim is to value derivatives, starting with interest rate derivatives, interest rate swaps in the simplest case. But as we have elaborated in Part I, the times of single "swap curves" per currency are over, and we have to deal – per currency – with one curve for discounting and various forward curves depending on tenor or fixing frequency. Does this make the simple one-factor LGM obsolete? Not necessarily, as we can assume that all these curves are in fact driven by a single common factor z_t per currency. For each currency, we pick one numeraire, associated with the discount curve $P_d(0,T)$,

$$N(t) = \frac{1}{P_d(0,t)} \exp\left\{ H_t\, z_t + \frac{1}{2} H_t^2\, \zeta_t \right\},$$

and we have a bunch of yield curves

$$\widetilde{P}_c(t,T,z_t) = P_c(0,T)\, \exp\left\{ -H_T\, z_t - \frac{1}{2} H_T^2 \zeta_t \right\}$$

where $c \in \{d, f_1, f_2, \ldots\}$ denotes either the discount or one of the various forward curves. We can express "forward" curve zero bonds in terms of "discount curve" zero bonds as

$$P_f(t,T,z_t) = \frac{P_f(t,T,0)}{P_d(t,T,0)}\, P_d(t,T,z_t).$$

The instantaneous forward rates associated with each curve are

$$F_c(t,T) = -\frac{\partial \ln P_c(t,T)}{\partial T} = F_c(0,T) + \dot{H}(T) \cdot z(t) + \dot{H}(T)\, H(T)\, \zeta(t). \qquad (11.7)$$

where the dot in $\dot{H}(T)$ denotes differentiation with respect to time T. This shows that the forward curves move in parallel with a deterministic spread between them.

11.1.2 Invariances

Hagan [77] pointed out that his model has two invariances, that is parameter transformations that leave prices unchanged:

1. $H(t) \to H(t) + C$
2. $H(t) \to K\, H(t)$ and $\zeta(t) \to \zeta(t)/K^2$, $\alpha(t) \to \alpha(t)/K$

The second invariance is obvious from inspecting the numeraire (11.1) and the stochastic zero bond price (11.4) – the terms $H(T)\, z(t)$ and $H^2(T)\,\zeta(t)$ remain unchanged under parameter change 2. The same holds for any function of these. Hence this is a "true" invariance of the model.

The first "invariance" is less obvious, as a shift applied to $H(t)$ does change the numeraire and stochastic zero bond. So what does invariance mean in this case? The parameter shift of the first type is in fact a change of measure, and a change of measure leaves prices (expectations) unchanged. We use the change of numeraire toolkit from Appendix A to show this. Consider a drift $C\alpha^2(t)\, dt$, that is the model SDE is changed to

$$dz = C\alpha^2(t)\, dt + \underbrace{\alpha(t)\, d\widetilde{W}}_{=d\tilde{z}} = \alpha(t)\, \underbrace{(d\widetilde{W} + C\alpha(t)\, dt)}_{=dW}$$

under the new measure. The Radon-Nikodym derivative for the change of measure (indicated by $\widetilde{W}$), based on drift $\theta(t) = -C\alpha(t)$, is then

$$
\begin{aligned}
Z(t) &= \exp\left(-\int_0^t \theta(s)\,dW(s) - \frac{1}{2}\int_0^t \theta^2(s)\,ds\right) \\
&= \exp\left(C\int_0^t \alpha(s)\,dW(s) - \frac{1}{2}C^2\int_0^t \alpha^2(s)\,ds\right) \\
&= \exp\left(C\,z(t) - \frac{1}{2}C^2\,\zeta(t)\right).
\end{aligned}
$$

The new numeraire is then

$$
\begin{aligned}
\widetilde{N}(t) &= N(t)\,Z(t) \\
&= \frac{1}{P(0,t)}\exp\left(H(t)\,z(t) + \frac{1}{2}H^2(t)\zeta(t) + C\,z(t) - \frac{1}{2}C^2\zeta(t)\right) \\
&= \frac{1}{P(0,t)}\exp\left((H(t)+C)\,z(t) + \frac{1}{2}\left(H^2(t) - C^2\right)\zeta(t)\right) \\
&= \frac{1}{P(0,t)}\exp\left((H(t)+C)\,(\tilde{z}(t) + C\zeta(t)) + \frac{1}{2}\left(H^2(t) - C^2\right)\zeta(t)\right) \\
&= \frac{1}{P(0,t)}\exp\left((H(t)+C)\,\tilde{z}(t) + \frac{1}{2}(H(t)+C)^2\zeta(t)\right).
\end{aligned}
$$

So the change of measure generated by drift $\theta(t) = -C\alpha^2(t)$ leads to a numeraire which is of the LGM form (11.1) again, but shifted to $H(t)+C$. This explains the LGM model invariance of the first type.

11.1.3 Relation to the Hull-White model in *T*-forward measure

If we choose a shift $C = -H(T)$ with $T > t$, then we obtain the numeraire

$$
\widetilde{N}(t) = \frac{1}{P(0,t)}\exp\left(-(H(T)-H(t))\,\tilde{z}(t) + \frac{1}{2}(H(T)-H(t))^2\zeta(t)\right)
$$

which has the form of the numeraire of the Hull-White model in the T-forward measure, see Appendix D.2. Therefore one might say that the latter is contained in LGM with "invariance" 1.

When we use a zero bond with maturity T as a numeraire asset, then it seems obvious to restrict time t to less than the bond maturity T. In the LGM model with the particular choice $C = -H(T)$, however, we arrive at this numeraire form without explicitly selecting a T-maturity bond as numeraire asset, and hence we are free to consider times $t > T$. It just happens that the variance term in the numeraire's exponent has a root at time $t = T$.

Let us review the short rate expression (11.6) when we apply a constant shift $C = -H(T)$ to $H(t)$:

$$r(t) = f(0,t) + z(t)\,H'(t) + \zeta(t)\,H'(t)\,(H(t) - H(T)).$$

The convexity term's root at $t = T$ means that $r(T) = f(0,T) + \tilde{z}(T)\,H'(T)$. Since $\mathbb{E}^{\tilde{N}}[\tilde{z}] = 0$ the short rate's expectation at the horizon T matches the instantaneous forward curve $f(0,T)$, as expected in the T-forward measure.

The freedom to apply any constant shift to $H(t)$ turns out to be useful for controlling Monte Carlo simulation error. We come back to this in Section 16.4.

So what *is* the LGM numeraire?

We have seen that both numeraire (11.1) and zero bond (11.4) are driven by the same random variable.[1] This means that one can view the LGM numeraire as a function (i.e. derivative) of any zero bond $P(t,T)$ with maturity $T > t$. Some algebra eliminating z_t from (11.1) leads to the explicit function

$$N(t) = \frac{1}{P(0,t)} \left[\frac{P(0,T)}{P(0,t)} \frac{1}{P(t,T)} \right]^{\frac{H_t}{H_T - H_t}} e^{-\frac{1}{2} H_T H_t \zeta_t}. \tag{11.8}$$

This makes $N(t)$ a perfectly valid numeraire, quoting Shreve [136]: "The asset we take as numeraire could be one of the primary assets ... or it could be a derivative asset".

To put it differently, we start from the SDEs of numeraire and zero bond in the bank account measure:

$$\frac{dN_t}{N_t} = \frac{dB_t}{B_t} + H_t\,\alpha_t\,dW_t$$

[1] This is also true under the bank account measure, see Appendix E, from which we extract

$$N(t) = \frac{1}{P(0,t)} \exp\left(H_t \int_0^t \alpha_s\,dW_s + \frac{1}{2} \int_0^t [(H_t - H_s)^2 - H_s^2]\,\alpha_s^2\,ds \right)$$

$$P(t,T) = \frac{P(0,T)}{P(0,t)} \exp\left(-(H_T - H_t) \int_0^t \alpha_s\,dW_s - \frac{1}{2} \int_0^t [(H_T - H_s)^2 - (H_t - H_s)^2]\,\alpha_s^2\,ds \right)$$

and stochastic zero bond

$$\frac{dP_{tT}}{P_{tT}} = r\,dt - \alpha_t\,(H_T - H_t)\,dW_t.$$

Now we can eliminate dW_t from the former and express dN/N in terms of differentials of "primary" assets B_t and P_{tT}:

$$\frac{dN_t}{N_t} = a_{tT}\cdot\frac{dB_t}{B_t} + (1-a_{tT})\cdot\frac{dP_{tT}}{P_{tT}}, \qquad a_{tT} = \frac{H_T}{H_T - H_t}.$$

11.2 Products

11.2.1 Zero bond option

A key component for calibrating the model to option products is the zero bond option. Its pricing in LGM is quite straight forward. In this respect LGM is comparable to the Hull-White model in the T-forward measure where T coincides with option expiry. The pricing formula for a call is

$$\begin{aligned}
\Pi &= \mathbb{E}^N\left[\frac{(P(t,T)-K)^+}{N(t)}\right]\\
&= \frac{1}{\sqrt{2\pi\,\zeta_t}}\int_{-\infty}^{\infty} e^{-\frac{z^2}{2\zeta_t}}\left(P(0,T)\,e^{-H_T z_t - \frac{1}{2}H_T^2\zeta_t} - P(0,t)\,K\,e^{-H_t z_t - \frac{1}{2}H_t^2\zeta_t}\right)^+ dz\\
&= \frac{1}{\sqrt{2\pi\,\zeta_t}}\int_{-\infty}^{\infty}\left(P(0,T)\,e^{-\frac{(z+H_T\zeta_t)^2}{2\zeta_t}} - P(0,t)\,K\,e^{-\frac{(z+H_t\zeta_t)^2}{2\zeta_t}}\right)^+ dz\\
&= \frac{1}{\sqrt{2\pi\,\zeta_t}}\int_{-\infty}^{\infty}\left(P(0,T)\,e^{-\frac{(z+[H_T-H_t]\zeta_t)^2}{2\zeta_t}} - P(0,t)\,K\,e^{-\frac{z^2}{2\zeta_t}}\right)^+ dz\\
&= P(0,T)\,\frac{1}{\sqrt{2\pi}}\int_{-\infty}^{d_+} e^{-\frac{z^2}{2}}\,dz - P(0,t)\,K\,\frac{1}{\sqrt{2\pi}}\int_{-\infty}^{d_-} e^{-\frac{z^2}{2}}\,dz\\
&= P(0,T)\,\Phi(d_+) - P(0,t)\,K\,\Phi(d_-)
\end{aligned}$$

where

$$d_\pm = \frac{1}{\Sigma}\left(\ln\frac{P(0,T)}{K\,P(0,t)} \pm \frac{1}{2}\Sigma^2\right), \qquad \Sigma^2 = (H_T - H_t)^2\,\zeta_t$$

that is yet another Black76 price. Note the price invariance under parallel shifts of $H(t)$ and simultaneous scaling $K \cdot H(t)$ and $\zeta(t)/K^2$. This is also true for European swaption prices, as we will see now.

11.2.2 European swaption

As we elaborated in the first part of this book, the times of single "swap curves" per currency are over, and we have to take two curves into account when we talk about swap and swaption pricing. The market is still quoting European swaption prices in terms of Black (or sometimes normal Black) volatilities, and swaption pricing formula (3.3) converts between volatilities and prices when forward and discount curves differ, in particular when we discount using OIS curves. We can still use and calibrate our one-factor LGM model in this multi-curve world, if we assume that the basis spreads (OIS vs 3M Euribor, OIS vs 6M Euribor, etc.) are *deterministic*, so that our model factor is driving all of these curves.

To price the two-curve swaption, let us recall the two-curve swap price at time t conditional on z_t, where P_d resp. P_f stands for the discount factors from the discount resp. forward curve:

$$\Pi(t,z_t) = \omega \left(\sum_{j=1}^{m} \delta'_j (F_f(t,t'_{j-1},t'_j,z_t) + s_j)\, P_d(t,t'_j,z_t) - \sum_{i=1}^{n} r_i \delta_i\, P_d(t,t_i,z_t) \right)$$

where

$$\begin{aligned}
&F_f(t,S,T,z_t)\, P_d(t,T,z_t)\,\delta \\
&= \left(\frac{P_f(t,S,z_t)}{P_f(t,T,z_t)} - 1 \right) P_d(t,T,z_t) \qquad (11.9)\\
&= \left(\frac{P_d(t,S,z_t)}{P_d(t,T,z_t)} \frac{P_f(0,S)}{P_d(0,S)} \frac{P_d(0,T)}{P_f(0,T)} - 1 \right) P_d(t,T,z_t)\\
&= P_d(t,S,z_t) \frac{P_f(0,S)}{P_d(0,S)} \frac{P_d(0,T)}{P_f(0,T)} - P_d(t,T,z_t)\\
&= P_d(t,S,z_t) - P_d(t,T,z_t) + \left(\frac{P_f(0,S)}{P_d(0,S)} \frac{P_d(0,T)}{P_f(0,T)} - 1 \right) P_d(t,S,z_t)\\
&= P_d(t,S,z_t) - P_d(t,T,z_t) + P_d(t,S) \frac{P_d(0,T)}{P_d(0,S)} \left(\frac{P_f(0,S)}{P_f(0,T)} - \frac{P_d(0,S)}{P_d(0,T)} \right)\\
&= P_d(t,S,z_t) - P_d(t,T,z_t) + P_d(t,S,z_t) \frac{P_d(0,T)}{P_d(0,S)}\, \delta A_{ST} \qquad (11.10)
\end{aligned}$$

with *deterministic* basis spreadlet[2]

$$A_{ST} = F_f(0,S,T) - F_d(0,S,T) = \frac{1}{\delta}\left(\frac{P_f(0,S)}{P_f(0,T)} - \frac{P_d(0,S)}{P_d(0,T)}\right).$$

It is tempting to argue that because we use the deterministic basis spreadlet A_{ST}, we might as well go all the way and use the approximation $P_d(0,S) \approx P_d(t,S,z_t)$, leading to the approximation

$$F_f(t,S,T,z_t)\,P_d(t,T,z_t)\,\delta = P_d(t,S,z_t) - P_d(t,T,z_t) + P_d(t,T,z_t)\,\delta\,A_{ST}, \quad (11.11)$$

as we could actually derive (11.11) much more quickly using first the definition of the stochastic basis spreadlet $A(t,S,T,z_t) = F_f(t,S,T,z_t) - F_d(t,S,T,z_t)$ and then arguing that it is deterministic. However, it is not really clear if the approximation is very good in every situation; see the discussion in Section 3.9.2.

Note that A_{ST} is discounted using the *initial* discount curves from T to $S < T$ and then *stochastically* back from S to $t < S$ so that we cannot combine the basis spreadlet with margin s_j (without approximation). This review simply shows that – as in the pre-crisis single-curve pricing – we can write the swap value as a linear combination of zero bonds

$$\Pi(t,z_t) = \omega\left(\sum_{j=0}^{m} c_j^{flo}\, P_d(t,t_j',z_t) - \sum_{i=1}^{n} c_i^{fix}\, P_d(t,t_i,z_t)\right) \quad (11.12)$$

For the typical example where floating payments are more frequent than fixed payments, Table 11.1 shows an excerpt of the cash flows. We now *roll the margin*

Table 11.1 "Cash flow" coefficients of the fixed and floating swap leg, with abbreviations $A_{i,j} = A_{t_i',t_j'}$

j	c_j^{flo}	i	c_i^{fix}
0	$1+\delta_1' \frac{P_d(0,t_1')}{P_d(0,t_0')} A_{0,1}$		
1	$\delta_1' s_1 + \delta_2' \frac{P_d(0,t_2')}{P_d(0,t_1')} A_{1,2}$		
2	$\delta_2' s_2 + \delta_3' \frac{P_d(0,t_3')}{P_d(0,t_2')} A_{2,3}$	1	$-k_1\,\delta_1$
3	$\delta_3' s_3 + \delta_4' \frac{P_d(0,t_4')}{P_d(0,t_3')} A_{3,4}$		
4	$\delta_4' s_4 + \delta_5' \frac{P_d(0,t_4')}{P_d(0,t_3')} A_{4,5}$	2	$-k_2\,\delta_2$
$\vdots$	$\vdots$	$\vdots$	$\vdots$
m	$-1+\delta_m s_m$	t_n	$-k_n\,\delta_n$

[2] We call it a spreadlet because it only spans one interest period and changes from one period to the next. The overall basis spread is the weighted average of the spreadlet over the life of the trade, see 3.4.

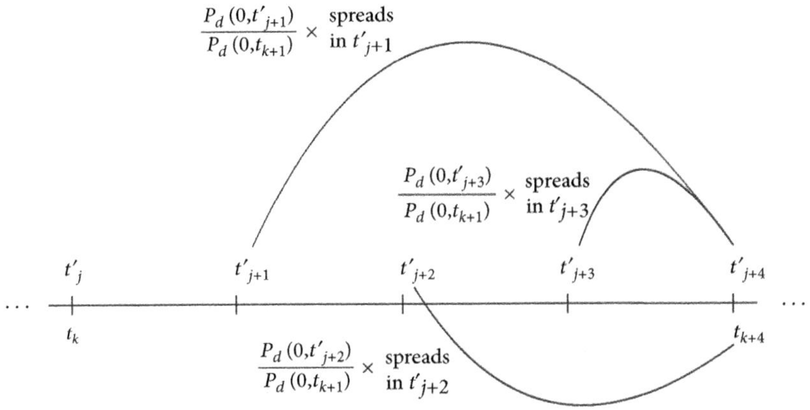

Figure 11.1 Mapping A: compounding the spread flows from the floating payment dates to the next fixed payment date using today's zero bond prices

and basis spread payments over to the fixed leg by compounding them at today's zero rate to the next fixing payment date, that is by mapping all spread flows to the fixed leg's grid including exercise time t_0. We refer to this approximation method as Mapping A, see Figure 11.1. From this we get a bond-like pricing formula of the form

$$\Pi(t, z_t) \approx \omega \sum_{k=0}^{n} c_k \, P_d(t, t_k, z_t) \tag{11.13}$$

with

$$c_0 = c_0^{flo}$$

$$c_1 = c_1^{fix} + c_1^{flo} \frac{P_d(0, t'_1)}{P_d(0, t_1)} + c_2^{flo} \frac{P_d(0, t'_2)}{P_d(0, t_1)}$$

$$c_2 = c_2^{fix} + c_3^{flo} \frac{P_d(0, t'_3)}{P_d(0, t_2)} + c_4^{flo} \frac{P_d(0, t'_4)}{P_d(0, t_2)}$$

$$\vdots$$

$$c_n = -1 + c_n^{fix} + c_m^{flo} \frac{P_d(0, t'_m)}{P_d(0, t_n)}$$

At $t = 0$, this yields the same value as the exact cash flow list, though it is indeed an approximation for $t > 0$.

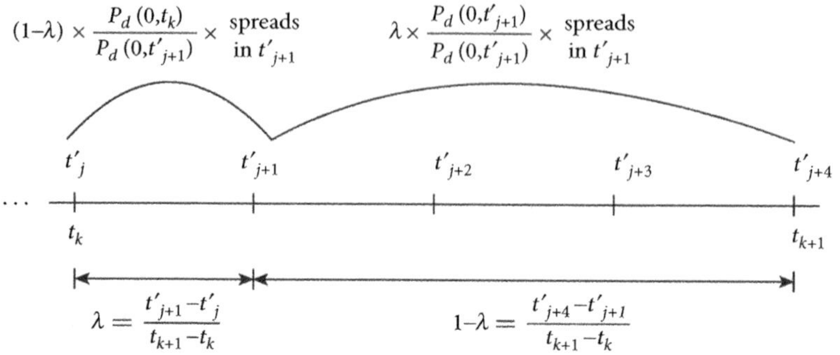

Figure 11.2 Mapping B: the spread flows are distributed to the two adjacent fixed payment dates using today's zero bond prices. Note that the discounted spreads use the inverse quotient from the compounded spreads (and, of course, a different index)

As an alternative approximation algorithm, we introduce Mapping B which assigns only a portion of a spread cash flow to the next fixed payment date, and the rest to the previous one. The portion is the distance of the spread payment date to the previous fixed payment date relative to the length of the fixed period it falls into. The closer the spread payment date to the next fixed payment date, the larger the part that is compounded forward; the rest is discounted back. This is depicted in Figure 11.2. We investigate the error introduced by these approximations below.

The price of a swaption with expiry $t = t_0$ is then

$$\Pi_{Swaption} = \mathbb{E}^N\left[\left(\frac{\Pi(t,z_t)}{N(t)}\right)^+\right] = \mathbb{E}^N\left[\left(\omega \sum_{k=0}^{n} c_k \widetilde{P}_d(t,t_k,z_t)\right)^+\right]. \quad (11.14)$$

To apply Jamshidian's trick as usual we first find the root z^* of

$$\sum_{k=0}^{n} c_k P_d(t,t_k,z^*) = 0 \quad (11.15)$$

and subtract the above equation (equal to zero) to write

$$\Pi_{Swaption} = \mathbb{E}^N\left[\left(\omega \sum_{k=1}^{n} c_k \left(\widetilde{P}_d(t,t_k,z_t) - \widetilde{P}_d(t,t_k,z^*)\right)\right)^+\right]$$

where the $k = 0$ term vanishes because $P_d(t,t,z_t) = P_d(t,t,z^*) = 1$. Since all coefficients c_k have the same sign[3] for $k > 0$ (this is why we collapsed all flows on

[3] Assuming that margins and basis spreads do not exceed fixed coupons.

fixed leg flows), we conclude

$$\Pi_{Swaption} = \sum_{k=1}^{n} |c_k| \cdot \mathbb{E}^N \left[\left(\mathrm{sgn}(c_k)\, \omega \left(\widetilde{P}_d(t, t_k, z_t) - \widetilde{P}_d(t, t_k, z^*) \right) \right)^+ \right] \tag{11.16}$$

which is a series of zero bond options with Black pricing formulas for strikes $K_k = P_d(t, t_k, z^*)$, see previous section. Apart from the root search (11.15) to find z^*, this is an analytic formula which gives us an efficient pricing method that can be used to quickly calibrate LGM to swaptions.

In summary, whenever the instrument flows can be rearranged into flows with the same signs, we can apply the decomposition (11.16). Otherwise we have to go back and evaluate (11.14), for example using a 1-d numerical integration or Monte Carlo sampling.

The error of rolling the spreads

In order to ensure good quality calibration when using the Jamshidian decomposition, we now investigate the approximation error of Mappings A and B in a simple setting. Note that in a two-curve pricing set-up, we have to approximate even for vanilla swaps with zero margin, so it is important to do this exercise. Let us consider a European swaption with expiry in five years from today, and an underlying swap with a ten-year term with four alternative floating leg reset frequencies – monthly, quarterly, semi-annual and annual (where only the middle two are relevant in real calibration scenarios). The "market" is represented by a flat zero curve for discounting at 2% (actual/actual) and a flat forward curve at 2.5%, 3% and 4%, respectively, with the same conventions as the discounting rate, that is quite an extreme basis spread. We assume fair swaps, that is the swap rate varies somewhat with the floating leg reset frequency as discussed in Chapter 3. Moreover, we assume that the swaption "market" (our single European swaption) is represented by a simple version of the LGM model expressed in terms of typical constant Hull-White mean reversion speed $\lambda = 0.03$ and volatility $\sigma = 0.01$. We now price the European swaption using the exact formula (11.14) with numerical integration, and the approximate formula (11.16) with Jamshidian decomposition. Table 11.2 shows the difference between exact and approximate price in upfront basis points of notional for forward rate at 2.5%, 3% and 4%, respectively.

The approximate prices using Mapping A are systematically lower than the exact ones, and the error grows with basis spread and with floating reset frequency due to the aggregation with *subsequent* grid dates only. This can be significantly improved by using Mapping B, which reduces the error to almost zero even in the case of large basis spread (2%) and high reset frequency (monthly).

Table 11.2 The error resulting from the two mappings and the Jamshidian decomposition, compared with the exact results, in upfront basis points of notional

Reset frequency	Mapping A			Mapping B		
	2.5%	3%	4%	2.5%	3%	4%
Annual	0.0	0.0	0.0	0.00	0.00	0.00
Semiannual	−0.7	−1.5	−2.9	0.01	0.01	0.02
Quarterly	−1.1	−2.2	−4.4	0.01	0.01	0.03
Monthly	−1.4	−2.7	−5.4	0.01	0.01	0.03

11.2.3 Bermudan swaption with deterministic basis

With Mapping B above we can accurately represent the two curve swaption with deterministic basis as a single-curve swaption with spread-adjusted fixed rates. The impact of OIS discounting on a Bermudan swaption is then due to two effects – the strike shift, and the use of European swaption volatility quotes that refer to OIS discounted swaptions. The LGM model is calibrated to prices/volatilities of the latter European swaptions. The pricing of the equivalent single curve Bermudan is then done by means of a backward induction scheme as explained in detail in Hagan's paper [78]. We also illustrate the backward induction scheme in Section 18.1 in comparison to the Longstaff-Schwartz method.

11.2.4 Stochastic basis

This section is a detour where we drop the assumption of deterministic basis for a moment. We start by considering two curves, $P_d(t,T,z_t^d)$ for discounting and $P_f(t,T,z_t^f)$ to compute stochastic Libor rates with tenor $\tau = T - S$

$$\mathrm{Libor}_{ST}(t,z_t^f) = \frac{1}{\delta_{ST}}\left(\frac{P_f(t,S,z_t^f)}{P_f(t,T,z_t^f)} - 1\right) \tag{11.17}$$

where the "forward" curve $P_f(t,T,z_t^f)$ is driven by an additional LGM factor z^f, not perfectly correlated with z^d which drives the discount curve. Note that the market forward curve $P_f(0,T)$ as well as z^f are tenor specific – $P_f(0,T)$ is bootstrapped from instruments with tenor $\tau = T - S$ only (including especially FRAs), and z^f applies to these tenor Libors only. z^d and z^f need to be modelled under the same measure, and we choose the measure associated with z^d, the discount curve's LGM numeraire. This means for z^f that it is – unlike z^d – not drift free. We can write this as

$$
\begin{aligned}
dz^f &= \alpha_t^f \, dW^f + \varphi(t)\, dt \\
dW^d \, dW^f &= \rho \, dt \\
P_f(t,T,z_t^f) &= \frac{P_f(0,T)}{P_f(0,t)} \exp\left\{-(H_T^f - H_t^f)\, z_t^f - \frac{1}{2}\left((H_T^f)^2 - (H_t^f)^2\right)\zeta_t^f\right\}
\end{aligned}
$$

To determine the drift $\varphi(t)$ we claim that

$$
\mathbb{E}^N\left[\text{Libor}_{ST}(t,z_t^f)\,\delta_{ST}\,\widetilde{P}_d(t,T,z_t^d)\right] = P_d(0,T)\left(\frac{P_f(0,S)}{P_f(0,T)} - 1\right)
$$

which is the current value of an FRA. This identity implicitly defines the drift. To work it out we need to compute the expectation on the left-hand side,

$$
\begin{aligned}
&\mathbb{E}^N\left[\text{Libor}_{ST}(t,z_t^f)\,\delta_{ST}\,\widetilde{P}_d(t,T,z_t)\right] \\
&= \mathbb{E}^N\left[\left(\frac{P_f(t,S,z_t)}{P_f(t,T,z_t)} - 1\right)\widetilde{P}_d(t,T,z_t)\right] \\
&= \mathbb{E}^N\Bigg[\left(\frac{P_f(0,S)}{P_f(0,T)} \times \exp\left\{-(H_S^f - H_T^f)\, z_t^f - \frac{1}{2}\left((H_S^f)^2 - (H_T^f)^2\right)\zeta_t^f\right\} - 1\right) \\
&\qquad\qquad \times P_d(0,T)\exp\left\{-H_T^d z_t^d - \frac{1}{2}(H_T^d)^2\zeta_t^d\right\}\Bigg] \\
&= P_d(0,T)\Bigg(\mathbb{E}^N\Bigg[\frac{P_f(0,S)}{P_f(0,T)}\exp\left\{-(H_S^f - H_T^f)\, z_t^f - H_T^d z_t^d\right\} \\
&\qquad\qquad \times \exp\left\{-\frac{1}{2}\left((H_S^f)^2 - (H_T^f)^2\right)\zeta_t^f - \frac{1}{2}(H_T^d)^2\zeta_t^d\right\}\Bigg] \\
&\qquad\qquad - \mathbb{E}^N\left[\exp\left\{-H_T^d z_t^d - \frac{1}{2}(H_T^d)^2\zeta_t^d\right\}\right] - 1\Bigg) \\
&= P_d(0,T)\Bigg(\frac{P_f(0,S)}{P_f(0,T)}\mathbb{E}^N\Bigg[\exp\left\{-(H_S^f - H_T^f)\, z_t^f - H_T^d z_t^d\right\} \\
&\qquad\qquad \times \exp\left\{-\frac{1}{2}\left((H_S^f)^2 - (H_T^f)^2\right)\zeta_t^f - \frac{1}{2}(H_T^d)^2\zeta_t^d\right\}\Bigg] - 1\Bigg)
\end{aligned}
$$

where we have used the fact that for a Gaussian random variable X the exponential expectation is $\mathbb{E}\left[\exp(X)\right] = \exp\left(\mathbb{E}[X] + \frac{1}{2}\mathbb{V}(X)\right)$. To recover the correct (quoted) FRA value we want the remaining expectation on the last line to collapse to unity as well. Thus we compute its value using the same fact about the normal distribution as above,

$$
\begin{aligned}
E = \mathbb{E}^N \Bigg[& \exp\Big\{ -(H_S^f - H_T^f)\, z_t^f - H_T^d z_t^d \Big\} \\
& \times \exp\Big\{ -\frac{1}{2}\Big((H_S^f)^2 - (H_T^f)^2\Big)\, \zeta_t^f - \frac{1}{2}(H_T^d)^2 \zeta_t^d \Big\}\Bigg] \\
= {} & \exp\Big\{ -(H_S^f - H_T^f) \int_0^t \varphi(s)\, ds + \frac{1}{2}(H_S^f - H_T^f)^2 \zeta_t^f + \frac{1}{2}(H_T^d)^2 \zeta_t^d \Big\} \\
& \times \exp\Big\{ +\rho (H_S^f - H_T^f)\, H_T^d \int_0^t \alpha_s^f \alpha_s^d\, ds - \frac{1}{2}\Big((H_S^f)^2 - (H_T^f)^2\Big)\, \zeta_t^f \Big\} \\
& \times \exp\Big\{ -\frac{1}{2}(H_T^d)^2 \zeta_t^d \Big\} \\
= {} & \exp\Big\{ (H_T^f - H_S^f) \int_0^t \varphi(s)\, ds + H_T^f (H_T^f - H_S^f)\zeta_t^f \Big\} \\
& \times \exp\Big\{ -\rho (H_T^f - H_S^f)\, H_T^d \int_0^t \alpha_s^f \alpha_s^d\, ds \Big\} \\
= {} & \exp\Big\{ (H_T^f - H_S^f) \int_0^t \Big(\varphi(s) + H_T^f (\alpha_s^f)^2 - \rho\, H_T^d \alpha_s^f \alpha_s^d\Big)\, ds \Big\}.
\end{aligned}
$$

This shows that we have to choose

$$
\varphi(t) = H_T^d \rho\, \alpha_t^f \alpha_t^d - H_T^f (\alpha_t^f)^2. \tag{11.18}
$$

Note the T-dependence, which means that each FRA maturity T has its own associated drift adjustment while all FRAs with the same tenor are driven by the same factor z^f in our simple model.[4] We can express this in terms of a drift-free Gaussian random variable z^f as follows,

$$
\text{Libor}_{ST}(t, z_t^f) = \frac{1}{\delta_{ST}} \left(\frac{P_f(0,S)}{P_f(0,T)}\, e^{(H_T - H_S)(z^f + \phi_T(t)) - \frac{1}{2}(H_S^2 - H_T^2)\zeta_t^f} - 1 \right) \tag{11.19}
$$

[4] At first glance it is surprising that the adjustment (11.18) does not explicitly depend on the FRA start time S as well. However, note that the market forward curve $P_f(0,\cdot)$ is built for a specific tenor $T-S$. If we want to model a different tenor Libor, we have to use a different forward curve as input.

with

$$\phi_T(t) = \int_0^t \varphi(s)\,ds = H_T^d \rho\, \zeta_t^{df} - H_T^f \zeta_t^f.$$

$$dz^f = \alpha_t^f\, dW^f$$

$$dW^d\, dW^f = \rho\, dt$$

We recover the deterministic spread case by assuming $z_t^f \equiv z_t^d$, which implies perfect correlation $\rho = 1$, as well as $H_t^f \equiv H_t^d$ and $\alpha_t^f \equiv \alpha_t^d$, so that the drift adjustment $\phi_T(t)$ vanishes in this case.

According to (11.7), instantaneous forward rates are normally distributed, and so is the instantaneous basis spread

$$\begin{aligned}\mathrm{BS}(t,T) &= F_f(t,T) - F_d(t,T)\\ &= F_f(0,T) - F_d(0,T) + \dot{H}_T^f z_t^f - \dot{H}_T^d z_t^d\\ &\quad + \dot{H}_T^f H_T^f \zeta_t^f - \dot{H}_T^d H_T^d \zeta_t^d + \dot{H}_T^f \phi_T(t)\end{aligned}$$

with mean and variance

$$\mathbb{E}[\mathrm{BS}(t,T)] = F_f(0,T) - F_d(0,T) + \dot{H}_T^f H_T^f \zeta_t^f - \dot{H}_T^d H_T^d \zeta_t^d + \dot{H}_T^f \phi_T(t)$$

$$\mathbb{V}[\mathrm{BS}(t,T)] = (\dot{H}_T^f)^2 \zeta_t^f + (\dot{H}_T^d)^2 \zeta_t^d - 2\rho\, \dot{H}_T^f \dot{H}_T^d \zeta_t^{df}$$

In a minimal parameterization with $H_t^f \equiv H_t^d$, $\alpha_t^f \equiv \alpha_t^d$ but $\rho \neq 1$ this reduces to

$$\mathbb{E}[\mathrm{BS}(t,T)] = F_f(0,T) - F_d(0,T) - \dot{H}_T^d H_T^d \zeta_t^d (1-\rho) \tag{11.20}$$

$$\mathbb{V}[\mathrm{BS}(t,T)] = 2\,(\dot{H}_T^d)^2 \zeta_t^d (1-\rho), \tag{11.21}$$

which describes how the basis spread variance increases with the deviation of correlation from unity.

Equipped with the LGM Libor rate in (11.19) we can now proceed and explore the impact of the stochastic basis on the pricing of Libor derivatives. To illustrate the principle, we consider two basic instruments here

- a single period ATM swap (FRA) exchanging one Libor payment for a fixed rate payment

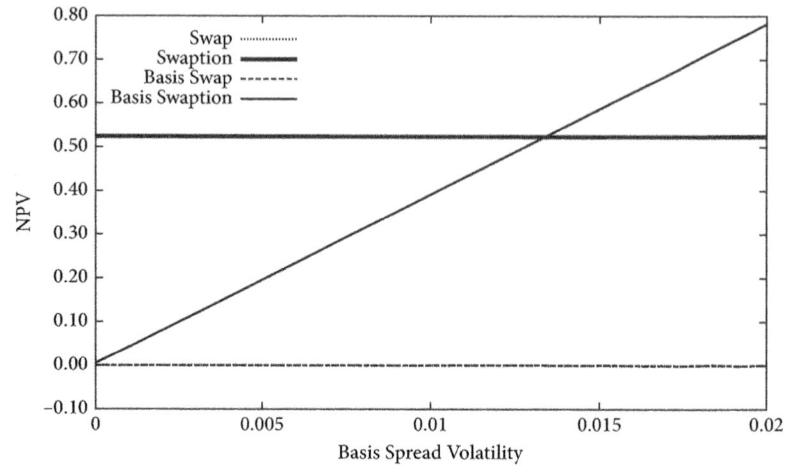

Figure 11.3 Impact of stochastic basis spread on the valuation of vanilla European swaption and basis swaption with single-period underlyings as described in the text. The variable on the horizontal axis is basis spread volatility, i.e. square root of (11.21). The simplified model parameters are zero rate for discounting at 2%, zero rate for forward projection at 3%, $\lambda = 0.03$ and $\sigma = 0.01$ for both discount and forward curve. This means that basis spread volatility is $\propto \sqrt{1-\rho}$ according to (11.21)

- a single period basis swap exchanging a single Libor payment for a single OIS-linked payment (an index linked to the discounting curve) fixed at period start only

and the associated European swaptions with exercise on period start. The future period starts at time $S = 2$ and ends at time $T = 3$. Both swaps are at-the-money, that is paying the fair rate and fair basis spread, respectively. Figure 11.3 shows the NPV dependencies on basis spread volatility in (11.21). As we vary $1 - \rho$ or basis spread volatility, we see no impact on the vanilla European swaption and a linear increase of the basis swaption value. If basis swaptions (Libor vs OIS) were quoted, they could therefore provide a simple and direct means to calibrate model parameter ρ.

Note that for a swaption with a usual basis swap as underlying that exchanges two Libor legs with different (non-OIS) tenors, we would need to consider three factors, z^d, z^{f_1} and z^{f_2}, and the essential pricing parameter would be the correlation between z^{f_1} and z^{f_2} in this case.

Semi-analytic pricing of European swaptions with stochastic basis

The examples in Figure 11.3 were evaluated with Monte Carlo sampling. This is quite easily implemented but inefficient. For the two-factor European swaption (vanilla or basis) we can come up with a more efficient semi-analytic pricing method as we will show in the following. Such a speed-up would be essential – for performance reasons – if we had to calibrate a two-factor model to such instruments regularly.

We start by considering the reduced value of a forward receiver swap at time t (conditional on z_t), where we pay a fixed rate R and receive Libor (11.19),

$$\widetilde{\Pi}_{RS}(t) = \sum_{i=1}^{n} \delta_i^{flt} \, \mathrm{Libor}_i(t) \, \widetilde{P}_d(t,t_i) - \sum_{j=1}^{m} \delta_j^{fix} \, R \widetilde{P}_d(t,t_j).$$

with short notation $\mathrm{Libor}_i(t) = \mathrm{Libor}_{t_{i-1},t_i}(t)$. The European swaption price is

$$\Pi = \mathbb{E}_0^N \left[\left(\omega \widetilde{\Pi}_{RS}(t)\right)^+ \right] = \int_{-\infty}^{\infty} \int_{-\infty}^{\infty} \left[\omega \widetilde{\Pi}_{RS}(t, z^d, z^f)\right]^+ \phi(t, z^d, z^f) \, dz^d \, dz^f$$

where $\phi(t,z^d,z^f)$ is the bivariate normal density of z^d and z^f. Using the Cholesky decomposition as in Jaeckel [96], we express $z^{d,f}$ in terms of independent standard normal variables u and v such that z^d depends on u only

$$z^f = \sqrt{\zeta_t^f} \left(\rho \, u + \sqrt{1-\rho^2} \, v\right), \qquad z^d = \sqrt{\zeta_t^d} \, u. \tag{11.22}$$

$\widetilde{P}_d(t,t_j)$ is hence also a function of u only, and $\mathrm{Libor}_{t_{i-1},t_i}(t)$ is a function of both u and v. Recall that z^f is drift-free as we have moved each Libor's drift into the Libor definition (11.19). We can now write the double integral explicitly using the independent new variables and choosing the u integration as outer integral

$$\Pi = \int_{-\infty}^{\infty} \left(\int_{-\infty}^{\infty} \left[\omega \widetilde{\Pi}_{RS}(t,u,v)\right]^+ \frac{1}{\sqrt{2\pi}} e^{-v^2/2} dv \right) \frac{1}{\sqrt{2\pi}} e^{-u^2/2} \, du. \tag{11.23}$$

Inspecting the Libor's definition (11.19) one sees that Libor is a monotonically increasing function of v. The inner integral in (11.23) therefore has a lower ($\omega = 1$) or upper ($\omega = -1$) cutoff at $v^*(u)$ given by

$$\widetilde{\Pi}_{RS}(t,u,v^*) = 0. \tag{11.24}$$

Once we have found $v^*(u)$ (by numerical search), we can therefore substitute

$$\sum_{j=1}^{m} \delta_j^{fix} \, R \widetilde{P}_d(t,t_j,u) = \sum_{i=1}^{n} \delta_i^{flt} \, \mathrm{Libor}_i(t,u,v^*) \, \widetilde{P}_d(t,t_i,u)$$

and write the receiver swap payoff

$$\widetilde{\Pi}_{RS}(t,u,v) = \sum_{i=1}^{n} \delta_i^{flt} \left(\mathrm{Libor}_i(t,u,v) - \mathrm{Libor}_i(t,u,v^*)\right) \widetilde{P}_d(t,t_i,u). \qquad (11.25)$$

Since $\mathrm{Libor}_i(t,u,v)$ is a monotonic function of v we can apply Jamshidian's trick as usual

$$\left[\omega\widetilde{\Pi}_{RS}(t,u,v)\right]^+ = \sum_{i=1}^{n} \delta_i^{flt} \left[\omega\left(\mathrm{Libor}_i(t,u,v) - \mathrm{Libor}_i(t,u,v^*)\right)\right]^+ \widetilde{P}_d(t,t_i,u).$$

Inserting the latter with the definition of $\mathrm{Libor}_i(t)$ (11.19)) and the decomposition (11.22) into (11.23) we arrive at the European swaption price

$$\Pi = \int_{-\infty}^{\infty} I(t,u) \frac{1}{\sqrt{2\pi}} e^{-u^2/2}\, du \qquad (11.26)$$

with

$$\begin{aligned}
I(t,u) &= \sum_{i=1}^{n} \widetilde{P}_d(t,t_i,u) \int_{-\infty}^{\infty} \left[\omega\left(A_i\, e^{B_i v} - C_i\right)\right]^+ \frac{1}{\sqrt{2\pi}} e^{-v^2/2}\, dv \\
A_i &= \frac{P_f(0,t_{i-1})}{P_f(0,t_i)}\, e^{(H_i^f - H_{i-1}^f)(\sqrt{\zeta_t^f}\,\rho\, u + \phi_i(t)) - \frac{1}{2}((H_i^f)^2 - (H_{i-1}^f)^2)\zeta_t^f} \\
B_i &= (H_i^f - H_{i-1}^f)\sqrt{\zeta_t^f}\,\sqrt{1-\rho^2} \\
C_i &= \frac{P_f(t,t_{i-1},u,v^*)}{P_f(t,t_i,u,v^*)}
\end{aligned}$$

The inner integral $I(t,u)$ can be solved in closed form (conditional on u),

$$I(t,u) = \omega \sum_{i=1}^{n} \left(A_i\, e^{B_i^2/2}\, \Phi(\omega(-v^* + B_i)) - C_i\, \Phi(-\omega\, v^*)\right) \widetilde{P}_d(t,t_i,u).$$

Note that – unlike the deterministic basis spread case – we did not make any approximations here as we did not have to roll the basis spread over to the fixed swap leg.

Finally, the remaining outer integral (11.26) has to be solved numerically, for example using Gauss-Hermite integration.

For semi-analytic pricing of a basis swaption (Libor vs OIS-linked), the procedure just described from (11.25) can be applied without changes. The different payoff only leads to a different root $v^*(u)$ in (11.24).

11.3 CSA discounting revisited

In Chapter 5 we saw that under the assumption of perfect cash collateral (continuous posting frequency, no threshold, etc.), and collateral compounding at the overnight rate (EONIA, FedFunds, SONIA, SARON, ...), we can justify the pricing of such collateralized vanilla products via OIS discounting – using a curve stripped from overnight-indexed swaps.

Among the complexities in CSAs there are a few that can be reflected accurately by a straight modification of the OIS discount curve (e.g. if the collateral rate is not O/N flat but O/N minus a spread). Other complexities such as non-zero thresholds or minimum transfer amounts can only be tackled properly by computing CVA/DVA price components added to/subtracted from the NPV based on OIS discounting, which is the main topic of this chapter.

In this section, however, we want to address one issue in more detail that we touched upon in Section 5.3: the problem of negative overnight rates in the EUR and CHF zone. We have to acknowledge that, at least currently, the market in Europe tends to *floor* the O/N rate at zero or to define the collateral rate as max(O/N, 0). How does this affect the discount curve for derivatives collateralized in this fashion?

For the following analysis we switch to the bank account measure and consider the Hull-White model with time-dependent parameters, see Appendix D. In summary:

The Hull-White model's short rate process

$$dr(t) = (\theta(t) - \lambda(t)\, r(t))\, dt + \sigma(t)\, dW(t)$$

is solved by the short rate

$$r(t) = \mu(t) + x(t)$$

where the Gaussian random variable

$$x(t) = e^{-\beta(t)} \int_0^t \alpha(s)\, dW(s), \qquad \alpha(t) = \sigma(t)\, e^{\beta(t)}, \quad \beta(t) = \int_0^t \lambda(s)\, ds$$

has zero mean and variance

$$\sigma_r^2(t) = \sigma_x^2(t) = e^{-2\beta(t)} \int_0^t \alpha^2(s)\, ds.$$

The deterministic drift is determined by today's yield curve, under the bank account measure

$$\mu(s) = f(0,t) + \frac{1}{2}\frac{\partial}{\partial t}\int_0^t (H(t) - H(s))^2\, \alpha^2(s)\, ds, \qquad H(t) = \int_0^t e^{-\beta(s)}\, ds.$$

where $f(0,t)$ is the instantaneous forward rate. Recall that for constant parameters

$$\sigma_x^2(t) = \frac{\sigma^2}{2\lambda}\left(1 - e^{-2\lambda t}\right)$$

$$\mu(t) = f(0,t) + \frac{\sigma^2}{2\lambda^2}\left(1 - e^{-\lambda t}\right)^2$$

Under the bank account measure, the zero bond price is given by

$$P(t,T) = \mathbb{E}_t\left[\exp\left(-\int_t^T r(s)\,ds\right)\right].$$

We assume here that the model represents the evolution of the OIS curve, with today's yield curve stripped from overnight index swaps and calibrated to European swaptions with 3M or 6M tenor, for example assuming a deterministic tenor basis between O/N and 3M/6M rates. Hence, the short rate $r(t)$ is the stochastic overnight rate, and $f(0,t)$ is the instantaneous forward curve implied from overnight index swaps.

If the collateral rate is now in fact defined as

$$c(t) = (r(t) - \Delta)^+,$$

then the associated discount curve as of today is given by

$$P_c(0,T) = \mathbb{E}\left[\exp\left(-\int_0^T (r(t) - \Delta)^+\,dt\right)\right]. \tag{11.27}$$

Unfortunately, we are not aware of a closed-form expression for such an expectation. It can be evaluated by Monte Carlo simulation, though, and we will do so now for a simple example to illustrate the effect. We consider a CSA in EUR with collateral spread $\Delta = -10$ bp – which is a reasonable spread in the market – and a collateral rate floored at zero. Figure 11.4 shows the EONIA (instantaneous forward) curve as of 30 September 2014 compared to the EONIA curve shifted by 10 bp down. The latter is negative up to a maturity of three years. In the zero order approximation (zero volatility of the EONIA curve, $x(t) = x(0) = 0$), the modified discount curve associated with the example CSA would simply be

$$P_c(0,T) = \exp\left(-\int_0^T (f(0,t) - \Delta)^+\,dt\right)$$

that is the curve which cuts the shifted EONIA forwards off at zero. To investigate the impact of volatility, we consider the simplified Hull-White model with constant

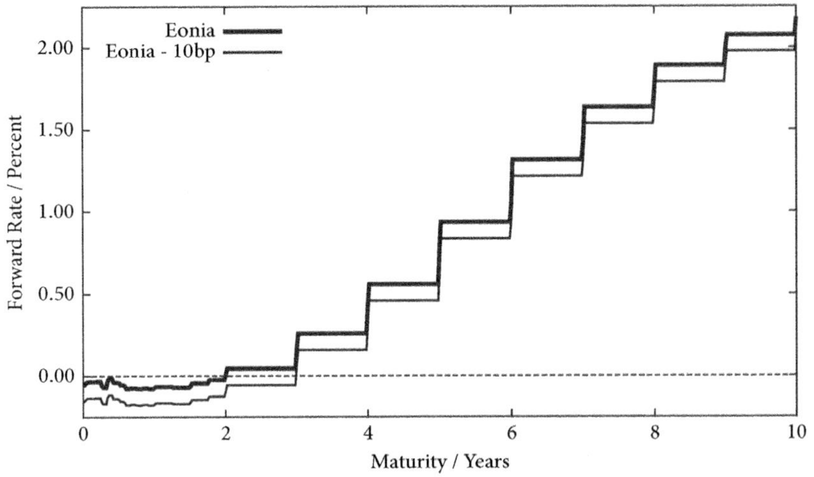

Figure 11.4 EONIA forward curve as of 30 September 2014 with negative rates up to two years. Under the CSA collateral is paid in EUR and based on EONIA – 10 bp

parameters $\lambda = 0.05$ and $\sigma = 0.004$ and compute the yield curve $P_c(0,T)$ as well as the "effective" forwards $f_c(0,T) = -\partial_T \ln P_c(0,T)$ by evaluating (11.27) using Monte Carlo paths of the short rate. The result is shown in Figure 11.5. The option's time value does not vanish anymore, hence the effective forward rate goes above zero even for very short maturities, and it approaches the "raw" shifted EONIA forward curve towards longer maturities.

Inspired by Antonov and Piterbarg [11], we now derive a semi-analytic approximation which we will then test with a Monte Carlo simulation. The approximation consists of moving the expectation into the exponential. We know that for a Gaussian random variable X the following holds

$$\mathbb{E}[\exp(X)] = \exp\left(\mathbb{E}[X] + \frac{1}{2}\mathbb{V}[X]\right) \approx \exp\left(\mathbb{E}[X]\right).$$

In the same spirit, we now try (although our argument of the exponential is *not* Gaussian due to the positive part operator)

$$P_c(0,T) \approx \exp\left(-\int_0^T \mathbb{E}\left[(r(t) - \Delta)^+\right] dt\right)$$

Since $r(t) - \Delta = x(t) + \mu(t) - \Delta$ has a normal distribution with mean $g(t) = \mu(t) - \Delta$ and variance $\sigma_x^2(t)$, we can compute the expectation in closed form using

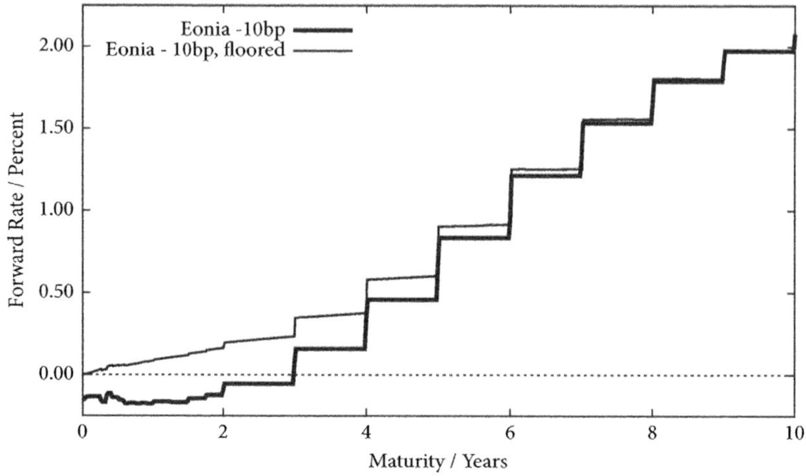

Figure 11.5 Shifted EONIA forward curve compared to the forward curve from (11.27) with collateral floor; Hull-White parameters are $\lambda = 0.05$ and $\sigma = 0.004$

the normal Black76 formula, see Appendix C:

$$\mathbb{E}[(x(t)+g(t))^+] = g(t)\,\Phi\left(\frac{g(t)}{\sigma_x(t)}\right) + \sigma_x(t)\,\phi\left(-\frac{g(t)}{\sigma_x(t)}\right),$$

so that

$$P_c(0,T) \approx \exp\left(-\int_0^T \left[g(t)\,\Phi\left(\frac{g(t)}{\sigma_x(t)}\right) + \sigma_x(t)\,\phi\left(-\frac{g(t)}{\sigma_x(t)}\right)\right] dt\right). \tag{11.28}$$

To check the approximation we compare (11.28) to the Monte Carlo evaluation with parameters in Figure 11.5. The comparison is shown in Figure 11.6 below.

The match is reasonably close for short maturities up to approximately 5Y, but the discrepancy gets more pronounced beyond 5Y and keeps growing with maturity. The deviation is simply the effect of ignoring the variance expression $\exp(\mathbb{V}[X]/2)$ above. Note that the volatility $\sigma = 0.004$ chosen in the example calculation is moderate, and realistic calibration would likely yield a volatility level of $\sigma \approx 0.01$. This will further increase the error of the first order approximation. If it is to be used in practice, the approximation therefore needs to be improved as suggested in [11].

The modified discount bond price formula (11.27) shows how the value of any fixed cash flow is affected by a floored collateral rate. To complete this section's detour, let us consider how the pricing of an interest rate swap would be affected,

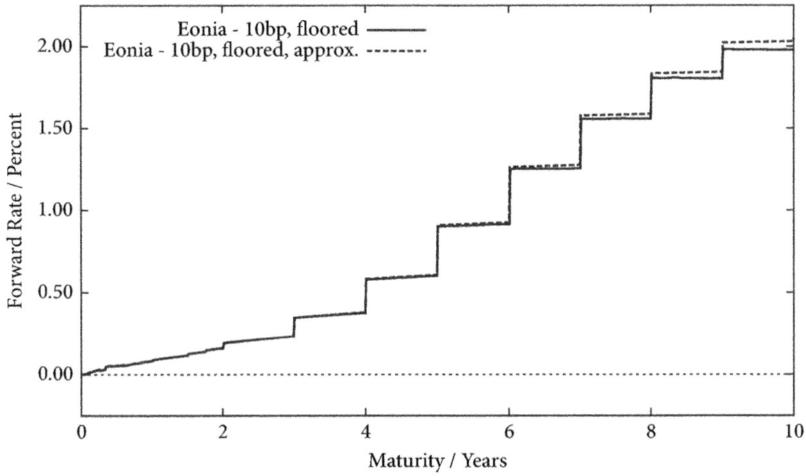

Figure 11.6 Comparison of the accurate Monte Carlo evaluation of the discount factor with Eonia floor (11.27) to the first order approximation (11.28)

that is the valuation of its floating leg. It is tempting to assume that we just need to replace the discount curve by (11.27) – as on the fixed leg – and keep the forward curve unchanged to come up with the revised floating leg value. To check this assumption, we compute the floating leg value

$$\Pi_{Float} = \mathbb{E}\left[\sum_{i=1}^{n} f(t_{i-1},t_i)\,\delta(t_{i-1},t_i)\,e^{-\int_0^{t_i} r^+(s)\,ds}\right]$$

with Monte Carlo simulation where the index fixing is given by the stochastic Hull-White discount bond and an appropriate deterministic basis spread s:

$$f(t,T) = \frac{1}{\delta(t,T)}\left(\frac{1}{P(t,T,r(t))} - 1\right) + s(t,T)$$

Table 11.3 shows the CSA floor impact on vanilla EUR Swaps with varying length, paying 4% fixed and receiving six-month Euribor. The full Monte Carlo evalution is shown in column "with floor", the approximate pricing with unchanged forward curve in column "approx". This shows that we do not capture the full impact of the CSA floor when we just exchange the discount curve. The error of 17 basis points upfront at 20 year maturity seems small but represents a significant fraction of the full CSA floor impact of 56 basis points. The two columns on the right-hand-side show the fair swap rates without CSA floor and with floor. The full floating leg

Table 11.3 CSA floor impact on vanilla swap prices in basis points of notional. The second column ("no floor") shows prices without CSA floor, the third column ("with floor") shows prices with CSA floor computed with full Monte Carlo evaluation of the floating leg, and the fifth column ("approx") shows prices we get when we price the swap with the revised discount curve only. The CSA floor terminates in all cases after year five, yield curve data is as of 30 June 2015, Hulll-White model parameters are $\lambda = 0.01$, $\sigma = 0.005$

Term	no floor	with floor	diff	approx	error	fair rate	with floor
2	−665.21	−663.02	2.19	−663.26	−0.24	0.6788 %	0.6803 %
3	−1135.64	−1129.83	5.81	−1130.54	−0.71	0.2196 %	0.2234 %
4	−1459.73	−1450.40	9.34	−1451.84	−1.44	0.3518 %	0.3560 %
5	−1743.69	−1730.53	13.16	−1732.88	−2.35	0.5062 %	0.5108 %
7	−2216.14	−2195.89	20.24	−2200.47	−4.58	0.8044 %	0.8100 %
10	−2757.42	−2728.46	28.96	−2735.91	−7.45	1.1664 %	1.1725 %
12	−3056.87	−3022.23	34.64	−3031.87	−9.64	1.3426 %	1.3493 %
15	−3485.65	−3442.96	42.69	−3455.76	−12.80	1.5143 %	1.5217 %
20	−4204.30	−4148.54	55.77	−4165.78	−17.24	1.6494 %	1.6575 %

evaluation also leads to a small shift in the fair rate on the order of one basis point for 20 year maturity.

We will revisit the CSA floor once more in Section 20.6 where we determine its impact on the value of interest paid/received on posted collateral.

11.4 Exposure evolution examples

Recall that the purpose of this chapter is to develop the interest rate modelling for the analysis of the evolution of exposures $\mathbb{E}[NPV^+(t)]$ of interest rate products through time, which is the key input into computing all sorts of value adjustments, most prominently CVA and DVA, but also FVA, KVA and others, which we shall introduce in Part I. The main device for this is the stochastic zero bond $P(t,T,z(t))$ where $z(t)$ follows the simple Gaussian process

$$dz(t) = \alpha(t)\,dW(t)$$

in the LGM measure, and we have seen all the ingredients for calibrating the model parameters $\alpha(t)$ and also $H(t)$ which affect $P(t,T,z(t))$. We can now generate *paths* of the Gaussian random variable $z(t)$, stepping over points in time t_i where we want to determine the expected exposure $\mathbb{E}[NPV^+(t_i)]$. At each point on this path we can then compute the stochastic zero bond $P(t_i,T,z(t_i))$ for any cash flow time T in the instrument we need to evaluate. For a vanilla interest rate swap this is all we need to price it. To be more precise, we also need a past index fixing if valuation time t is

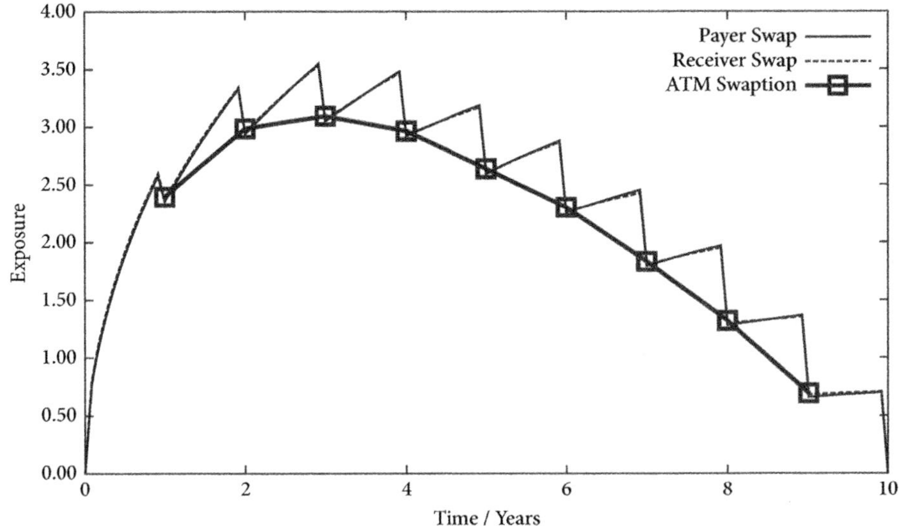

Figure 11.7 Single currency swap exposure evolution. Payment frequencies are annual on both fixed and floating legs. The swap is at-the-money, and the yield curve is flat. Note that the payer and receiver swap exposure graphs overlap

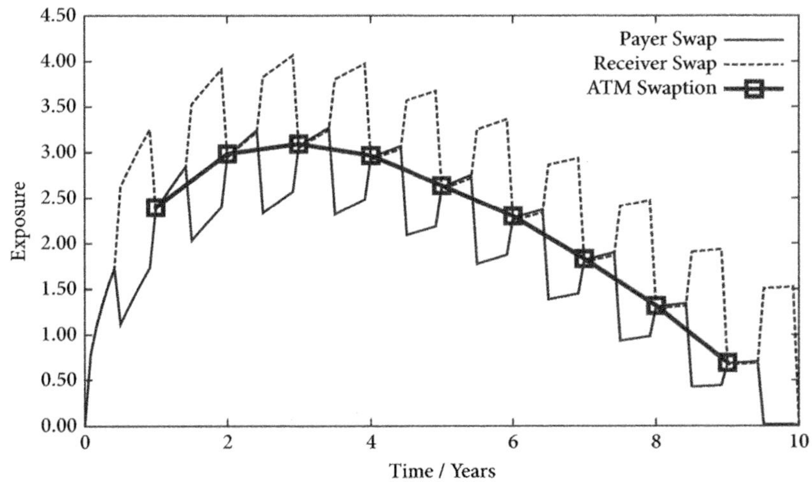

Figure 11.8 Single currency payer and receiver swap exposure evolution for annual fixed and semi-annual floating payments. The symbols denote analytical exposure values (swaption prices) at fixed period start dates

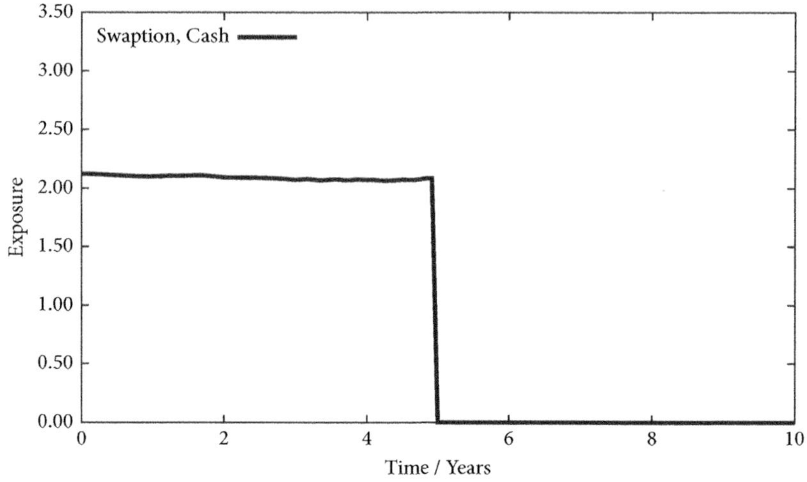

Figure 11.9 European swaption exposure, cash settlement, expiry in five years, swap term 5Y. Yield curve and swaption volatility structure are flat at 3% and 20%, respectively

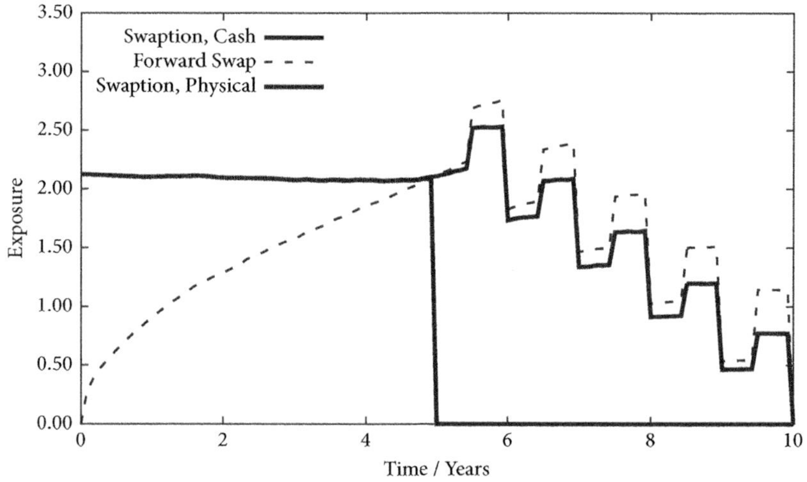

Figure 11.10 European swaption exposure with physical settlement, otherwise same parameters as in Figure 11.9

within an interest period of the trade. This has to be determined along the path as well and is a function of the stochastic zero bond at fixing time with maturity at the end of the current floating period. If we have to distinguish discount and forward curves, then both $P_d(t, T)$ and $P_f(t, T)$ are driven by the same random variable $z(t)$ assuming a deterministic *tenor* basis, see Section 11.1.1.

A single path of $z(t)$ therefore translates into a path of the swap value $NPV(t)$. Averaging the swap NPVs (after taking the positive part) over a large number of paths on a given valuation date then yields the desired exposure evolution. Figure 11.7 shows an example evolution for a 10Y swap with the same payment frequencies on the fixed and floating legs.

Figure 11.8 shows similar evolutions of 10y payer and receiver swaps but now with different payment frequencies on the fixed and floating legs. As the yield curve is chosen to be flat, exposures match at period start dates and agree at these points in time with analytical exposure calculations (i.e. European swaption prices).

Let us consider a European swaption with cash settlement now. A typical exposure evolution is shown in Figure 11.9. In this example we just evolve interest rates stochastically when we evaluate the swaption in the future, and we "move" the swaption volatility surface through time without amending it. Cash settlement means that the option value just collapses to zero when we pass the expiry date because the contract just ends with an exchange of cash at this time (or no exercise, in which case it is also worth zero beyond expiry). This is significantly different from the case of physical settlement, see Figure 11.10. If the physical swaption ends in-the-money at expiry, then it turns into the underlying swap; otherwise the contract just ends. We therefore see the same exposure evolution of cash and physically settled swaptions up to expiry, and a significant difference thereafter, where the physical swaption exposure has underlying swap exposure contributions from those scenarios where the underlying swap is in-the-money at expiry time. Figure 11.10 moreover shows the exposure evolution for the "standalone" forward starting swap. It is larger than the physical swaption exposure at all times beyond expiry, because the latter excludes scenarios where the swap has negative value at swaption expiry (the option expires worthless), yet the underlying swap assumes positive values beyond swaption expiry.

Further exposure evolution examples – for Bermudan swaptions with cash and physical settlement will be discussed in Part IV.

12 Foreign Exchange

This chapter is devoted to the extension of the framework to multiple economies or currencies. We start by putting a well known cross-currency model into the LGM setting in Section 12.1 and generalizing this to multiple currencies in Section 12.2. We will first assume that we can work with interest rate models in domestic and foreign currencies that are calibrated "in isolation". We will show then in Section 12.4 how the system is adjusted to take deterministic cross-currency basis into account so that the Monte Carlo framework prices single and cross-currency swaps in all currencies involved consistently.

12.1 Cross-currency LGM

We start this section off with the well-known Babbs cross-currency model [14, 57, 123, 124], formulated in the domestic bank account measure with interest rates modelled using single-factor Hull-White processes and the FX rate modelled as Geometric Brownian Motion with a drift given by the short rate differential:

$$\begin{aligned} dr_d &= \lambda_d\,[\theta_d(t) - r_d(t)]\; dt + \sigma_d\, dW_d^Q \\ dr_f &= \lambda_f\left[\theta_f(t) - r_f(t)\right]\, dt - \rho_{xf}\sigma_x\sigma_f\, dt + \sigma_f\, dW_f^Q \\ dx/x &= \left[r_d(t) - r_f(t)\right]\, dt + \sigma_x\, dW_x^Q \\ dW_a\, dW_b &= \rho_{ab}\, dt \quad \text{for} \quad a, b \in \{d, f, x\} \end{aligned}$$

Recall that the term $\rho_{xf}\sigma_x\sigma_f\, dt$ originates from switching the *foreign* interest rate process dr_f to the *domestic* bank account measure, indicated by exponent Q.

The goal of this section is to translate this model into the LGM setting we have chosen for interest rate modelling in this text. We will do this by slowly taking the reader through all the involved steps, thereby generalizing the derivation of LGM from Hull-White in Appendix E. The result is the following set of SDEs

$$dz_d = \alpha_d(t)\, dW_d^N, \tag{12.1a}$$

$$dz_f = \gamma_f(t)\, dt + \alpha_f(t)\, dW_f^N \tag{12.1b}$$

$$dx/x = \mu_x(t)\, dt + \sigma_x(t)\, dW_x^N \tag{12.1c}$$

$$dW_a\, dW_b = \rho_{ab}\, dt \quad \text{for} \quad a, b \in \{d, f, x\}$$

for the domestic and foreign LGM factors z_d and z_f, respectively. Exponent N indicates that we use the GM measure here associated with the LGM numeraire $N(t)$. Similar to Babbs's model, the drift term in the foreign LGM process is due to the change of measure to the *domestic LGM measure.* Our task is now to determine the drift terms $\gamma_f(t)$ and $\mu_x(t)$ such that the system of SDEs is free of arbitrage.

Recall the numeraire of the domestic LGM process

$$N_d(t) = \frac{1}{P_d(0,t)} \exp\left\{ H(t)\, z_d(t) + \frac{1}{2} H_d^2(t)\, \zeta_d(t) \right\}$$

For now we may assume that $P_d(0,t)$ is the yield curve associated with overnight index swaps in the domestic currency. Analogously to the domestic one, the foreign numeraire is given as follows

$$N_f(t) = \frac{1}{P_f(0,t)} \exp\left\{ H_f(t)\, z_f(t) + \frac{1}{2} H_f^2(t)\, \zeta_f(t) \right\}$$

By using Ito's lemma, the dynamics of the numeraire processes can be found as

$$\frac{dN_d(t)}{N_d(t)} = \left(r_d(t) + H_d^2(t)\alpha_d^2(t) \right) dt + H_d(t)\alpha_d(t)\, dW_d(t) \tag{12.2}$$

$$\frac{dN_f(t)}{N_f(t)} = \left(r_f(t) + H_f^2(t)\alpha_f^2(t) + H_f(t)\gamma_f(t) \right) dt + H_f(t)\alpha_f(t)\, dW_f(t) \tag{12.3}$$

Similarly, we find the SDE of the inverse numeraires,

$$d\left(\frac{1}{N_d(t)} \right) = \frac{1}{N_d(t)} \left[-r_d(t) dt - H_d(t)\alpha_d(t)\, dW_d(t) \right] \tag{12.4}$$

$$d\left(\frac{1}{N_f(t)} \right) = \frac{1}{N_f(t)} \left[-\left(r_f(t) + H_f(t)\gamma_f(t) \right) dt - H_f(t)\alpha_f(t)\, dW_f(t) \right] \tag{12.5}$$

Now, let us consider the foreign numeraire asset converted into domestic currency, $N_i(t)\,x_i(t)$. Its value in units of the domestic numeraire asset

$$Y(t) = \frac{N_f(t)\,x(t)}{N_d(t)}$$

is a martingale under the domestic LGM measure so that it is drift-free. Then,

$$\begin{aligned} dY(t) = {} & N_f(t)\,x(t)\,d\left(\frac{1}{N_d(t)}\right) + \frac{N_f(t)}{N_d(t)}\,dx(t) + \frac{x(t)}{N_d(t)}\,dN_f(t) \\ & + \frac{1}{N_d(t)}\,dN_f(t)\,dx(t) + N_f(t)\,d\left(\frac{1}{N_d(t)}\right)dx(t) \\ & + x(t)\,d\left(\frac{1}{N_d(t)}\right)dN_f(t), \end{aligned}$$

and substituting the dynamics (12.1c), (12.3) and (12.4):

$$\begin{aligned} dY(t) = Y(t)\Big[& \Big(r_f(t) - r_d(t) + H_f^2(t)\alpha_f^2(t) + \mu_x(t) + H_f(t)\,\gamma_f(t) \\ & + H_f(t)\,\alpha_f(t)\,\sigma_x\,\rho_{fx} - H_d(t)\,\alpha_d(t)\,\sigma_x\,\rho_{dx} \\ & - H_f(t)\,\alpha_f(t)\,H_d(t)\,\alpha_d(t)\,\rho_{df}\Big)\,dt \\ & - H_d(t)\,\alpha_d(t)\,dW_d(t) + H_d(t)\,\alpha_d(t)\,dW_f(t) + \sigma_x\,dW_x(t)\Big]. \end{aligned}$$

Since $Y(t)$ is a martingale under domestic LGM measure, the drift term vanishes, implying the dynamics of $Y(t)$

$$dY(t) = Y(t)\Big[-H_d(t)\,\alpha_d(t)\,dW_d(t) + H_f(t)\,\alpha_f(t)\,dW_f(t) + \sigma_x\,dW_x(t),\Big] \quad (12.6)$$

and the no-arbitrage drift $\mu_x(t)$ for the process $x(t)$ is given as follows

$$\begin{aligned} \mu_x(t) = {} & r_d(t) - r_f(t) - H_f^2(t)\,\alpha_f^2(t) \\ & - H_f(t)\,\alpha_f(t)\,\sigma_x\,\rho_{fx} + H_d(t)\,\alpha_d(t)\,\sigma_x\,\rho_{dx} + H_f(t)\,\alpha_f(t)\,H_d(t)\,\alpha_d(t)\,\rho_{df} \\ & - H_f(t)\,\gamma_f(t) \end{aligned} \quad (12.7)$$

Note that drift $\mu_x(t)$ depends on the quanto adjustment $\gamma_f(t)$. As a next step we will derive this quanto adjustment. In order to do so, let us consider the foreign bond converted into domestic currency, $P_f(t,T)\,x(t)$. Similarly, its value in units of the domestic numeraire asset

$$U(t) = \frac{P_f(t,T)\,x(t)}{N_d(t)}$$

is a martingale under the domestic LGM measure. $U(t)$ can be rewritten as follows:

$$U(t) = \widetilde{P}_f(t,T)\,\frac{N_f(t)\,x(t)}{N_d(t)} = \widetilde{P}_f(t,T)\,Y(t)$$

where $\widetilde{P}_f(t,T)$ is the reduced foreign bond value,

$$\widetilde{P}_f(t,T) = \frac{P_f(t,T)}{N_f(t)} = P_f(0,T)\,\exp\left\{-H_f(T)\,z_f(t) + \frac{1}{2}\,H_f^2(T)\,\zeta_f(t)\right\}.$$

Its dynamics are obtained by applying Ito's lemma:

$$\begin{aligned} d\widetilde{P}_f(t,T) &= -\widetilde{P}_f(t,T)\,H_f(T)\,dz_f(t) \\ &= -\widetilde{P}_f(t,T)\,H_f(T)\,\big(\gamma_f(t)\,dt + \alpha_f(t)\,dW_f(t)\big) \end{aligned} \tag{12.8}$$

Now

$$dU(t) = \widetilde{P}_f(t,T)\,dY(t) + Y(t)\,d\widetilde{P}_f(t,T) + d\widetilde{P}_f(t,T)\,dY(t),$$

and substituting the dynamics (12.6) and (12.8)

$$\begin{aligned} \frac{dU(t)}{U(t)} &= H_f(T)\Big(-\gamma_f(t) - H_f(t)\,\alpha_f^2(t) + H_d(t)\,\alpha_d(t)\,\alpha_f(t)\,\rho_{df} - \sigma_x(t)\,\alpha_f(t)\,\rho_{xf}\Big)\,dt \\ &\quad - H_d(t)\,\alpha_d(t)\,dW_d(t) - (H_f(T) - H_f(t))\alpha_f(t)\,dW_f(t) + \sigma_x(t)\,dW_x(t) \end{aligned} \tag{12.9}$$

Since $U(t)$ is a Martingale, the drift term $[\ldots]\,dt$ above must vanish. Therefore the no-arbitrage drift $\gamma\,(t)$ for the foreign process $z_f(t)$ is given by

$$\boxed{\gamma_f(t) = -H_f(t)\,\alpha_f^2(t) + H_d(t)\,\alpha_d(t)\,\alpha_f(t)\,\rho_{df} - \sigma_x(t)\,\alpha_f(t)\,\rho_{xf}} \tag{12.10}$$

Substituting the above equation in (12.7), we also obtain

$$\boxed{\mu_x(t) = r_d(t) - r_f(t) + H_d(t)\,\alpha_d(t)\,\sigma_x(t)\,\rho_{dx}} \tag{12.11}$$

Finally note that the expression for the foreign zero bond under the domestic LGM measure is

$$P_f(t,T) = \frac{P_f(0,T)}{P_f(0,t)}\,\exp\left\{-\big(H_f(t) - H_f(t)\big)\,z_f(t) - \frac{1}{2}\,\Big(H_f^2(t) - H_f^2(t)\Big)\,\zeta_f(t)\right\} \tag{12.12}$$

that is it has the same form as under the foreign LGM measure. See Appendix E.3 for a careful check.

12.2 Multi-currency LGM

The cross-currency LGM model is easily generalized to multiple currencies. For that purpose we identify a single *domestic* currency and its LGM process labelled z_0, and a set of n foreign currencies with associated LGM processes labelled z_i, $i=1,\ldots,n$. If we consider n foreign exchange rates for converting the foreign currencies into the single domestic currency by multiplication, x_i, $i=1,\ldots,n$, then the *multi-currency LGM* model is simply given by the system of SDEs

$$\begin{aligned} dz_0 &= \alpha_0\, dW_0^z \\ dz_i &= \gamma_i\, dt + \alpha_i\, dW_i^z, \qquad i>0 \\ \frac{dx_i}{x_i} &= \mu_i\, dt + \sigma_i\, dW_i^x, \qquad i>0 \end{aligned}$$

$$\begin{aligned} \gamma_i &= -\alpha_i^2\, H_i - \rho_{ii}^{zx}\, \sigma_i \alpha_i + \rho_{i0}^{zz}\, \alpha_i \alpha_0\, H_0 \\ \mu_i &= r_0 - r_i + \rho_{0i}^{zx}\, \alpha_0\, H_0\, \sigma_i \\ r_i &= f_i(0,t) + z_i(t)\, H_i'(t) + \zeta_i(t)\, H_i(t)\, H_i'(t), \quad \zeta_i(t) = \int_0^t \alpha_i^2(s)\, ds \end{aligned}$$

$$dW_i^a\, dW_j^b = \rho_{ij}^{ab}\, dt, \qquad a,b \in \{z,x\}$$

where $f_i(0,t)$ is the instantaneous forward curve in currency i.

The advantage of a model like this is its analytical tractability. The joint density of factors $z_i(t), \ln x_i(t)$ to any time horizon t is analytical, multivariate normal. It is fully determined by the expectations and covariances of the factors, and all moments can be computed in closed form or using numerical integration as we will show below. When the joint density for factor changes over any time horizon t is known, we can design a Monte Carlo scheme for evolving the factors efficiently and without time discretization error over large horizons: this only involves sampling random numbers from multivariate normal distributions.

Moreover, having evolved the factors to time horizon t, we can "span" stochastic domestic and foreign yield curves for any maturity $T > t$ using the analytic expressions (11.4) and (12.12). This has two advantages, the obvious first one is we do not need to evolve factors to final maturity which may save computational effort. The second advantage is a practical implementation aspect: suppose you have got a trusted software package which provides pricing (as of today) for a range of products. Being able to span yield curves (conditional on the state reached at time t), one can populate a hypothetical market at time t and – in principle – apply the same software package to price under such future markets. This means one may avoid re-implementing pricing methods for the purpose of future valuation in a

CVA context. This might save significant development and testing effort, that is time and money.

Such an approach has disadvantages as well, which we will discuss below in Section 16 , together with an elegant way to overcome an important performance bottleneck in relation to products with early exercise features.

To finish this IR/FX introduction, let us come back to the key ingredients for the "large-time step" propagation scheme, the factor expectations and covariances. To derive these, we start by stating the formal solution of the model SDE considering factor changes of a time interval (s,t):

$$
\begin{aligned}
\Delta z_0 &= \int_s^t \alpha_0(\tau)\, dW_0^z(\tau) \\
\Delta z_i &= \int_s^t \alpha_i(\tau)\, dW_i^z(\tau) + \int_s^t (-H_i \alpha_i^2 - \rho_{ii}^{zx}\, \alpha_i \sigma_i + \rho_{i0}^{zz}\, \alpha_i \alpha_0\, H_0)\, d\tau \\
\Delta \ln x_i &= \ln \frac{P_i(0,t)\; P_0(0,s)}{P_i(0,s)\; P_0(0,t)} - \frac{1}{2}\int_s^t \sigma_i^2\, d\tau + \int_s^t \zeta_0\, H_0\, H_0'\, d\tau - \int_s^t \zeta_i\, H_i\, H_i'\, d\tau \\
&\quad + \rho_{0i}^{zx} \int_s^t \alpha_0\, H_0\, \sigma_i\, d\tau - \int_s^t (H_i(t) - H_i(\tau))\, \gamma_i\, d\tau \\
&\quad + \int_s^t (H_0(t) - H_0(\tau))\, \alpha_0\, dW_0^z(\tau) + (H_0(t) - H_0(s))\, z_0(s) \\
&\quad - \int_s^t (H_i(t) - H_i(\tau))\, \alpha_i\, dW_i^z(\tau) - (H_i(t) - H_i(s))\, z_i(s) \\
&\quad + \int_s^t \sigma_i\, dW_i^x(\tau)
\end{aligned}
\tag{12.13}
$$

Based on these solutions we can compute conditional expectations of the factors, that is conditional on the initial factor values at time s:

$$
\begin{aligned}
\mathbb{E}_s[\Delta z_0] &= 0 \\
\mathbb{E}_s[\Delta z_i] &= \int_s^t \gamma_i\, d\tau \;=\; \int_s^t (-H_i \alpha_i^2 - \rho_{ii}^{zx}\, \alpha_i \sigma_i + \rho_{i0}^{zz}\, \alpha_i \alpha_0\, H_0)\, d\tau \\
\mathbb{E}_s[\Delta \ln x_i] &= \ln \frac{P_i(0,t)\; P_0(0,s)}{P_i(0,s)\; P_0(0,t)} \\
&\quad - \frac{1}{2}\int_s^t \sigma_i^2\, d\tau + \int_s^t \zeta_0\, H_0\, H_0'\, d\tau - \int_s^t \zeta_i\, H_i\, H_i'\, d\tau \\
&\quad + \rho_{0i}^{zx} \int_s^t \alpha_0\, H_0\, \sigma_i\, d\tau - \int_s^t (H_i(t) - H_i(\tau))\, \gamma_i\, d\tau \\
&\quad + (H_0(t) - H_0(s))\, z_0(s) - (H_i(t) - H_i(s))\, z_i(s)
\end{aligned}
\tag{12.14}
$$

where

$$\int_s^t \zeta_i H_i H_i' \, d\tau = \frac{1}{2}\left(H_i^2(t)\zeta_i(t) - H_i^2(s)\,\zeta_i(s) - \int_s^t H_i^2 \alpha_i^2 \, d\tau \right)$$

Likewise we arrive at the conditional covariances (assuming states at time s have been reached)

$$Cov[\Delta z_i, \Delta z_j] = \rho_{ij}^{zz} \int_s^t \alpha_i(\tau)\,\alpha_j(\tau)\,d\tau \tag{12.15}$$

$$\begin{aligned} Cov[\Delta z_i, \Delta \ln x_j] = &+\rho_{i0}^{zz} \int_s^t \alpha_i(\tau)\,(H_0(t) - H_0(\tau))\,\alpha_0(\tau)\,d\tau \\ &- \rho_{ij}^{zz} \int_s^t \alpha_i(\tau)\,(H_j(t) - H_j(\tau))\,\alpha_j(\tau)\,d\tau \\ &+ \rho_{ij}^{zx} \int_s^t \alpha_i(\tau)\,\sigma_j(\tau)\,d\tau \end{aligned} \tag{12.16}$$

and

$$\begin{aligned} Cov[\Delta \ln x_i, \Delta \ln x_j] = &+ \int_s^t (H_0(t) - H_0(\tau))^2\,\alpha_0^2(\tau)\,d\tau \\ &- \rho_{0j}^{zz} \int_s^t (H_0(t) - H_0(\tau))\,(H_j(t) - H_j(\tau))\,\alpha_0(\tau)\,\alpha_j(\tau)\,d\tau \\ &- \rho_{0i}^{zz} \int_s^t (H_0(t) - H_0(\tau))\,(H_i(t) - H_i(\tau))\,\alpha_0(\tau)\,\alpha_i(\tau)\,d\tau \\ &+ \rho_{0j}^{zx} \int_s^t (H_0(t) - H_0(\tau))\,\alpha_0(\tau)\,\sigma_j(\tau)\,d\tau \\ &+ \rho_{0i}^{zx} \int_s^t (H_0(t) - H_0(\tau))\,\alpha_0(\tau)\,\sigma_i(\tau)\,d\tau \\ &- \rho_{ij}^{zx} \int_s^t (H_i(t) - H_i(\tau))\,\alpha_i(\tau)\,\sigma_j(\tau)\,d\tau \\ &- \rho_{ji}^{zx} \int_s^t (H_j(t) - H_j(\tau))\,\alpha_j(\tau)\,\sigma_i(\tau)\,d\tau \\ &+ \rho_{ij}^{zz} \int_s^t (H_i(t) - H_i(\tau))\,(H_j(t) - H_j(\tau))\,\alpha_i(\tau)\,\alpha_j(\tau)\,d\tau \\ &+ \rho_{ij}^{xx} \int_s^t \sigma_i(\tau)\,\sigma_j(\tau)\,d\tau \end{aligned} \tag{12.17}$$

12.3 Calibration

12.3.1 Interest rate processes

Each interest rate component of the model can be calibrated as usual, for example to

- overnight index swaps for the discount curve
- interest rate swaps with tenor ∗M for the ∗M tenor forward curve
- European swaptions assuming OIS discounting and deterministic tenor basis as discussed in Section 11.1

This is clear for the domestic interest rate process, but applies to the foreign processes as well due to (12.12). Note that for the time being we ignore cross-currency basis spreads, but will incorporate them below in Section 12.4.

12.3.2 FX processes

The most basic instruments to calibrate an FX process are

- FX Forwards
- Vanilla European FX options

However, for now we assume that the fair FX forward rate K is correctly implied by the FX spot rate and the discount curves in the respective currencies,

$$K = x(0)\,\frac{P_f(0,T)}{P_d(0,T)}.$$

We will show in Section 12.4 how to ensure consistency with cross-currency basis. So the remaining task here is the calibration of FX options in order to fix the FX process's volatility function $\sigma_x(t)$. To do this we need to work out the pricing formula for a vanilla European FX option with expiry T in the model. In the N_0 measure it is

$$\Pi = \mathbb{E}^{N_0}\left[\left(\frac{\omega\,(x_i(T)-K)}{N_0(T)}\right)^+\right]$$

It is convenient to change to the T-forward measure for this calculation, using the domestic zero bond $P_0(t,T)$ as numeraire. Consider the forward FX rate

$$F_i(t,T) = \frac{P_i(t,T)}{P_0(t,T)}\,x_i(t) \quad \text{with} \quad F_i(T,T) = x(T),$$

so that

$$\Pi = P_0(0,T)\,\mathbb{E}^T\left[(\omega\,(F(T,T)-K))^+\right]$$

To compute the expectation we need to work out the distribution of $F_i(t,T)$ from its definition. Since F_i is a product of log-normal variables, F_i is log-normal too. Moreover, since $F_i(t,T)$ is a martingale under the T-forward measure, it is drift-free, and we can focus on collecting diffusion terms in the following. Recall

$$\frac{dx_i}{x_i} = (\dots)\,dt + \sigma_i\,dW_i^x$$
$$\frac{dP_i}{P_i} = (\dots)\,dt - (H_i(T) - H_i(t))\,\alpha_i(t)\,dW_i^z$$

Now compute the differential of $F_i(t,T)$, omitting all drift terms $(\dots)\,dt$:

$$\begin{aligned}\frac{dF_i}{F_i} &= \frac{dx_i}{x_i} + \frac{dP_i}{P_i} - \frac{dP_0}{P_0}\\ &= \sigma_i(t)\,dW_i^x - (H_i(T) - H_i(t))\,\alpha_i(t)\,dW_i^z + (H_0(T) - H_0(t))\,\alpha_0(t)\,dW_0^z\\ &= \widetilde{\sigma}_i\,d\widetilde{W}_i\end{aligned}$$

with overall volatility $\widetilde{\sigma}_i$ given by

$$\begin{aligned}\widetilde{\sigma}_i^2(t,T) &= (H_0(T) - H_0(t))^2\,\alpha_0^2(t) + (H_i(T) - H_i(t))^2\,\alpha_i^2(t) + \sigma_i^2(t)\\ &\quad - 2\,\rho_{0i}^{zz}\,(H_0(T) - H_0(t))\,(H_i(T) - H_i(t))\,\alpha_0(t)\,\alpha_i(t)\\ &\quad + 2\,\rho_{0i}^{zx}\,(H_0(T) - H_0(t))\,\alpha_0(t)\,\sigma_i(t)\\ &\quad - 2\,\rho_{ii}^{zx}\,(H_i(T) - H_i(t))\,\alpha_i(t)\,\sigma_i(t)\end{aligned} \tag{12.18}$$

The drift-free log-normal distribution of $F_i(t,T)$ now leads to the usual Black-like option pricing formula (for unit notional in foreign currency)

$$\Pi = \omega\,P_0(0,T)\,\{F_i(0,T)\,\Phi(\omega\,d_+) - K\,\Phi(\omega\,d_-)\}$$
$$d_\pm = \frac{1}{\Sigma_i\sqrt{T}}\ln\frac{F(0,T)}{K} \pm \frac{\Sigma_i\sqrt{T}}{2}$$
$$\Sigma_i^2 = \frac{1}{T}\int_0^T \widetilde{\sigma}_i^2(t,T)\,dt$$

where $\Sigma_i(T)$ is the Black FX volatility for expiry T. Note that

$$\Sigma_i^2 = \frac{1}{T}\,Var\left(\ln\frac{x_i(T)}{x_i(0)}\right) = \frac{1}{T}\,Var\,(\ln x_i(T)). \tag{12.19}$$

If all correlations are given (see also Section 12.3.3) and the LGM processes are calibrated (hence all $\alpha_i(t)$ and $H_i(t)$ are given), then we can use FX option quotes to "bootstrap" the remaining parameters $\sigma_i(t)$ in $Var[\ln x_i(T)]$.

We can write (12.18) in the following form

$$\widetilde{\sigma}^2(t,T) = a(t,T) + b(t,T) \cdot \sigma_x(t) + \sigma_x^2(t)$$

With $\sigma_x(t)$ piecewise constant between adjacent option expiries $T_1, T_2, T_3, \ldots$, the Black FX variance (12.19) can then be written

$$\Sigma_i^2(T_n) = \frac{1}{T_n} \int_0^{T_n} \widetilde{\sigma}_i^2(t, T_n)\, dt = A_n + \sum_{k=1}^{n} B_{nk}\, \sigma_k + \sum_{k=1}^{n} C_{nk}\, \sigma_k^2 \qquad (12.20)$$

where

$$A_n = \frac{1}{T_n} \int_0^{T_n} a(t, T_n)\, dt, \qquad B_{nk} = \frac{1}{T_n} \int_{T_{k-1}}^{T_k} b(t, T_n)\, dt, \qquad C_{nk} = \frac{T_k - T_{k-1}}{T_n}$$

Equation (12.20) can be solved iteratively for the piecewise constant segments σ_k of $\sigma_x(t)$.

So far we have not specified which market volatilities to calibrate to, that is which strike to choose. We are not restricted to at-the-money here, but we are limited to a *single strike* for each option expiry involved. To overcome this limitation and calibrate to the FX smile, one would have to extend the model for example to a local volatility flavour (see e.g. [124]). This, however, "damages" the analytical tractability of the overall model which we want to keep for the time being.

12.3.3 Correlations

The multi-currency LGM model comes with a bunch of correlations between the Wiener processes involved which need to be calibrated somehow. If we had market quotes for correlation-sensitive instruments (such as differential swaps) we could fix some of the correlations by actual calibration. As above, this would require expressing the instrument's value in terms of the multi-currency model parameters. In any case, for the remaining – if not all – correlation parameters, one usually resorts to historical estimates. Here we briefly show how this can be done in the context of the multi-currency LGM. We have to consider IR-IR, IR-FX and FX-FX correlations.

IR-IR case

Let us start with the IR-IR case and assume we will base the estimate on zero rates. The general approach is to compute *covariations* between model zero rates and match these with covariations computed from historical data, a common approach applied in Value at Risk model calibration to historical data. We consider the model implied covariation first and write down the model zero rate, continuously compounded, with tenor T which is by definition

$$Z(t,t+T) = -\frac{1}{T}\ln P(t,t+T) = Z(0,t+T) + \frac{1}{T}(H_{t+T} - H_t)\cdot z_t + \text{convexity}$$

The zero rate differential is then

$$dZ(t,t+T) = \frac{1}{T}(H(t+T) - H(t))\,dz(t) + \text{drift}$$

The essential part of the differential is the term containing $dz(t)$ so that we can be sloppy here with the remaining ones. For a parametrization with constant (time-independent) Hull-White λ this simplifies to

$$dZ(t,t+T) = \sigma(t)\,B(T)\,dW^z(t), \qquad B(T) = \frac{1-e^{-\lambda T}}{\lambda T}$$

The model covariation between two zero rates is then computed as

$$\begin{aligned} Cov_{ij}^{zz}(t,\Delta) &= \frac{1}{\Delta}\int_t^{t+\Delta} dZ_i(t,t+T)\cdot dZ_j(t,t+S) \\ &= \rho\,B_i(T)\,B_j(S)\,\frac{1}{\Delta}\int_t^{t+\Delta}\sigma_i^z(s)\,\sigma_j^z(s)\,ds, \qquad dW_i^z(t)\,dW_j^z(t) = \rho_{ij}^{zz}\,dt \end{aligned}$$

The normalized covariation is then

$$C_{ij}^{zz}(t,\Delta) = \frac{Cov_{ij}^{zz}(t,\Delta)}{\sqrt{Cov_{ii}^{zz}(t,\Delta)\cdot Cov_{jj}^{zz}(t,\Delta)}} = \rho_{ij}^{zz}\cdot f_{ij}^{zz}(t,\Delta),$$

where

$$f_{ij}^{zz}(t,\Delta) = \frac{\frac{1}{\Delta}\int_t^{t+\Delta}\sigma_i^z(s)\,\sigma_j^z(s)\,ds}{\sqrt{\frac{1}{\Delta}\int_t^{t+\Delta}(\sigma_i^z)^2(s)\,ds\cdot\frac{1}{\Delta}\int_t^{t+\Delta}(\sigma_j^z)^2(s)\,ds}}$$

This simplifies for constant, time-independent, σ_i^z and σ_j^z, since $f_{ij}^{zz}(t,\Delta) = 1$ in that case.[1] On the other hand, we can compute the historical estimate of zero rate

[1] When calibrating time-depending volatility functions, we see that $f_{ij}^{zz}(t,\Delta)$ is close to unity, typically larger than 0.99

covariation

$$\text{HistCov}_{ij}^{zz}(S,T) = \frac{1}{\Delta}\sum_{k=1}^{N}\big(Z_i(t_k,t_k+T) - Z_j(t_{k-1},t_{k-1}+T)\big)$$
$$\cdot\big(Z_j(t_k,t_k+S) - Z_j(t_{k-1},t_{k-1}+S)\big), \qquad t_N - t_0 = \Delta$$

with normalized historical estimate

$$\text{HC}_{ij}^{zz}(t,\Delta) = \frac{\text{HistCov}_{ij}^{zz}(t,\Delta)}{\sqrt{\text{HistCov}_{ii}^{zz}(t,\Delta)\cdot\text{HistCov}_{jj}^{zz}(t,\Delta)}}$$

In summary, to match model and historical covariation, we set the instantaneous model correlation to

$$\rho_{ij}^{zz} = \frac{\text{HC}_{ij}^{zz}(t,\Delta)}{f_{ij}^{zz}(t,\Delta)} \tag{12.21}$$

FX-FX case

Recall the FX process

$$dX(t)/X(t) = \sigma^x(t)\,dW^x + \text{drift}(t)$$

which yields the model covariation

$$Cov_{ij}^{xx}(t,\Delta) = \frac{1}{\Delta}\int_t^{t+\Delta}\frac{dX_i(s)}{X_i(s)}\cdot\frac{dX_j(s)}{X_j(s)} = \rho_{ij}^{xx}\frac{1}{\Delta}\int_t^{t+\Delta}\sigma_i^x(s)\,\sigma_j^x(s)\,ds,$$

normalized

$$C_{ij}^{xx}(t,\Delta) = \frac{Cov_{ij}^{xx}(t,\Delta)}{\sqrt{Cov_{ii}^{xx}(t,\Delta)\cdot Cov_{jj}^{xx}(t,\Delta)}} = \rho_{ij}^{xx}\cdot f_{ij}^{xx}(t,\Delta)$$

where

$$f_{ij}^{xx}(t,\Delta) = \frac{\frac{1}{\Delta}\int_t^{t+\Delta}\sigma_i^x(s)\,\sigma_j^x(s)\,ds}{\sqrt{\frac{1}{\Delta}\int_t^{t+\Delta}(\sigma_i^x(s))^2\,ds\cdot\frac{1}{\Delta}\int_t^{t+\Delta}(\sigma_j^x(s))^2\,ds}}$$

The associated historical covariation estimate is

$$\text{HisCov}_{ij}^{xx}(t,\Delta) = \frac{1}{\Delta}\sum_{k=1}^{N}\ln\frac{X_i(t_k)}{X_i(t_{k-1})}\cdot\ln\frac{X_j(t_k)}{X_j(t_{k-1})}, \qquad t_N - t_0 = \Delta,$$

or normalized

$$\mathrm{HC}_{ij}^{xx}(t,\Delta)=\frac{\mathrm{HistCov}_{ij}^{xx}(t,\Delta)}{\sqrt{\mathrm{HistCov}_{ii}^{xx}(t,\Delta)\cdot\mathrm{HistCov}_{jj}^{xx}(t,\Delta)}}$$

so that, to match model and historical covariation, we set the instantaneous model correlation to

$$\rho_{ij}^{xx}=\frac{\mathrm{HC}_{ij}^{xx}(t,\Delta)}{f_{ij}^{xx}(t,\Delta)} \tag{12.22}$$

IR-FX case

Finally, we get

$$Cov_{ij}^{xz}(t,\Delta)=\frac{1}{\Delta}\int_t^{t+\Delta}\frac{dX_i(s)}{X_i(s)}\cdot dZ_j(s,s+T)=\rho_{ij}^{xz}\,B(T)\,\frac{1}{\Delta}\int_t^{t+\Delta}\sigma_i^x(s)\,\sigma_j^z(s)\,ds,$$

normalized

$$C_{ij}^{xz}(t,T,\Delta)=\rho_{ij}^{xz}\cdot f_{ij}^{xz}(t,\Delta)$$

where

$$f_{ij}^{xz}(t,\Delta)=\frac{\frac{1}{\Delta}\int_t^{t+\Delta}\sigma_i^x(s)\,\sigma_j^z(s)\,ds}{\sqrt{\frac{1}{\Delta}\int_t^{t+\Delta}(\sigma_i^x(s))^2\,ds\cdot\frac{1}{\Delta}\int_t^{t+\Delta}(\sigma_j^z)^2(s)\,ds}},$$

historical covariation estimate

$$\mathrm{HistCov}_{ij}^{xz}(t,\Delta)=\frac{1}{\Delta}\sum_{k=1}^{N}\ln\frac{X_i(t_k)}{X_i(t_{k-1})}\cdot\big(Z_j(t_k,t_k+T)-Z_j(t_{k-1},t_{k-1}+T)\big),$$

normalized

$$\mathrm{HC}_{ij}^{xz}(t,\Delta)=\frac{\mathrm{HistCov}_{ij}^{xz}(t,\Delta)}{\sqrt{\mathrm{HistCov}_{jj}^{zz}(t,\Delta)\cdot\mathrm{HistCov}_{ii}^{xx}(t,\Delta)}},$$

so that

$$\rho_{ij}^{xz}=\frac{\mathrm{HC}_{ij}^{xz}(t,\Delta)}{f_{ij}^{xz}(t,\Delta)}. \tag{12.23}$$

12.4 Cross-currency basis

In the following we will assume that the cross-currency basis is deterministic. For this case we show here how to modify the multi-currency model to take a cross-currency basis into account. We consider two currencies here, domestic and foreign, the generalization to multiple foreign currencies is straightforward.

Suppose that we have calibrated the IR models for the domestic and foreign yield curves assuming collateral in the respective "local" currencies, that is with discounting in "local" OIS curves (EONIA, FedFunds, SONIA, SARON, etc.). We label the domestic discount curve in domestic collateral $P_{d,d}(t,T)$ and the foreign discount curve in foreign collateral $P_{f,f}(t,T)$. To switch the foreign discount curve to domestic collateralization we apply the deterministic cross-currency spread $q(t)$:

$$P_{f,d}(t,T) = P_{f,f}(t,T)\exp\left(-\int_t^T q(s)\,ds\right)$$

or

$$r_{f,d}(t) = r_{f,f}(t) + q(t)$$

where $r_{f,d}(t)$ is the foreign short rate under domestic collateral.

Recall that we can build today's foreign yield curve under domestic collateral using FX forwards and cross-currency basis swaps (see Section 4), so that we know $P_{f,d}(0,\cdot)$. This allows expressing the basis spread integral $\int_t^T q(s)\,ds$ in terms of today's $P_{f,d}(0,\cdot)$ curve:

$$P_{f,d}(t,T) = P_{f,f}(t,T)\,\frac{P_{f,d}(0,T)}{P_{f,d}(0,t)}\,\frac{P_{f,f}(0,t)}{P_{f,f}(0,T)}. \tag{12.24}$$

Likewise, we can switch the domestic yield curve model to foreign collateralization using today's domestic in foreign collateral $P_{d,f}(0,T)$:

$$P_{d,f}(t,T) = P_{d,d}(t,T)\,\frac{P_{d,f}(0,T)}{P_{d,f}(0,t)}\,\frac{P_{d,d}(0,t)}{P_{d,d}(0,T)}. \tag{12.25}$$

And finally, we can correct the FX rate process $x(t)$ by including the basis spread defined above in the interest rate differential

$$\begin{aligned}
\frac{dx(t)}{x(t)} &= (r_{d,d}(t) - r_{f,d}(t))\,dt + \sigma^x(t)\,dW^x(t)\\
&= (r_{d,d}(t) - r_{f,f}(t) - q(t))\,dt + \sigma^x(t)\,dW^x(t)\\
&= \frac{d\hat{x}(t)}{\hat{x}(t)} - q(t)\,dt
\end{aligned}$$

so that

$$x(t) = \hat{x}(t) \exp\left(-\int_0^t q(s)\, ds\right) = \hat{x}(t) \frac{P_{f,d}(0,t)}{P_{f,f}(0,t)}$$

where $\hat{x}(t)$ denotes the FX rate process without taking the cross-currency basis into account.

Stochastic cross-currency basis

Despite our assumption at the beginning of this section, the cross-currency basis is not deterministic. This became blatantly clear during the credit crisis, when basis spreads took off to previously inconceivable heights (or depths, as in the case of USD/EUR). Nevertheless, it is quite common in the market to make this assumption, in particular when building exposure models. The multitude of factors that have to be modelled and correlated with each other is already large enough without making basis spreads (cross-currency and tenor alike) stochastic. As we discussed in the Preface, something's gotta give – be it accuracy, model risk or speed. So for our main purpose in this text, a deterministic basis is acceptable.

There are instances, though, when it is important to include the stochasticity of the cross-currency basis. Most prominently this is the case for collateral agreements with an option on the collateral currency. As many banks try to standardize their CSAs, it is necessary to establish the value of such options. We have already discussed a simple method in Section 5.2, but applying that method precisely amounts to just calculating the intrinsic value of the option, and hence to ignoring the volatility of the spreads. There are more sophisticated ways to compute the option value, and they are actually very similar to what we did in Section 11.3. There, we explored the computation of discount factors like

$$P_c(0,T) = \mathbb{E}\left[\exp\left(-\int_0^T (r(t)-\Delta)^+\, dt\right)\right]. \tag{11.27'}$$

As Piterbarg shows in [125], the discount factor that has to be used for pricing a cash flow in domestic currency that is collateralized under a two-currency option is

$$P_d^f(0,T) = P_d(0,T)\mathbb{E}^{d,T}\left[\exp\left(-\int_0^T r_f(t) + s_{d,f}(t) - r_d(t)\, dt\right)\right], \tag{12.26}$$

where P_d^f is the discount factor including the option, P_d is the standard domestic discount factor, r_f is the foreign collateral short rate, r_d the domestic collateral short rate, $s_{d,f}$ the spread between the two, and expectation is taken under the domestic T-forward measure. We will switch from domestic to foreign collateral only if the quantity

$$q_{d,f}(t) := r_f(t) + s_{d,f}(t) - r_d(t) > 0,$$

that is when the return on foreign cash collateral is higher than the return on domestic cash collateral. We thus see that we have the same problem as in (11.27) if we assume $q_{d,f}(t)$ to be normally distributed, and we attack it by the same methods. That is, a massive improvement of the intrinsic value approach is to move the expectation inside the exponential function and the integral:

$$\mathbb{E}^{d,T}\left[\exp\left(-\int_0^T q_{d,f}(t)^+\,dt\right)\right] \approx \exp\left(-\int_0^T \mathbb{E}^{d,T}\left[s_{d,f}(t)^+\right]dt\right).$$

This result can be further improved by the second-order approximation described in Antonov & Piterbarg [11].

Note that it is important in this derivation that the CSA with the currency option is done under US law because only then can all of the collateral be switched to a different currency. Under British law, where only the outstanding collateral can be posted in any currency, there is no way to build a curve that captures the option.

12.5 Exposure evolution examples

To continue the series of examples we started in Section 11.4, let us take a look at a few additional elementary exposure evolution examples. Figure 12.1 shows the exposure evolution for three FX forwards which exchange EUR vs GBP amounts in ten years from today. The trade producing the solid line is at-the-money as of today, that is the rate of future amounts is in line with the fair FX forward rate. The upper and lower broken lines represent trades that are shifted 10% into and out-of-the-money, respectively. These exposure graphs – generated using indMonte Carlo simulation in the multi-currency LGM model – agree qualitatively with the analytical results in Section 9.3. Similarly, Figure 12.2 shows the evolutions of typical (long) FX options, as above comparing at-the-money to slightly in- and out-of-the-money cases. Under a risk-neutral measure we expect a perfectly flat FX option *expected exposure* evolution:

$$EE(t) = \mathbb{E}^N\left[\frac{NPV^+(t)}{N(t)}\right] = \mathbb{E}^N\left[\frac{NPV(t)}{N(t)}\right] = \mathbb{E}^N\left[\frac{\text{Payoff}(T)}{N(T)}\right] = NPV(0).$$

The long option NPV is always positive so that the positive part operator has no effect. Moreover there are no cash flows between today and option expiry T. Therefore, the martingale property of the expectation in the LGM measure of a tradable quantity "discounted" with the LGM numeraire $N(t)$ ensures that the expected exposure through time is constant and equal to today's option price. So what is the origin of the slight deviation in Figure 12.2 from the flat evolution? The answer lies in the valuation method we have chosen here for the FX option under

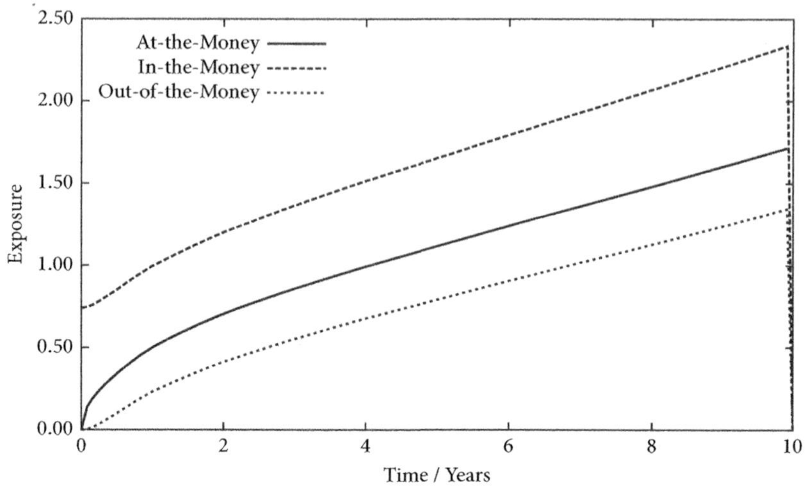

Figure 12.1 Exposure evolution for EUR/GBP FX forwards with (unusual) maturity in ten years, comparing three FX forwards which are at-the-money and 10% in- and out-of-the-money, respectively, at the start. The EUR and GBP yield curves are both kept flat at 3% so that the fair FX forward remains fixed through time, and we see the effect of widening of the FX spot rate distribution

future market scenarios: whereas we evolve the market using a multi-currency LGM model (which is perfectly calibrated to at-the-money FX options up to 10Y expiry), we price the option under future market scenarios using a Garman-Kohlhagen model[2] (introduced in Section 9.3) with an at-the-money volatility structure which is taken from time $t = 0$ and propagated through time without change. The entirely consistent alternative would be pricing the FX option in a cross-currency LGM model with the same calibration that is used for the market scenario evolution. This yields the expected perfectly flat exposure evolution. We will see a similar example of consistent option pricing under scenarios in Section 18.1.

Rebalancing cross currency swap

As a last example in this section we consider a rebalancing (resettable, mark-to-market) cross-currency swap. An example of this product exchanges fixed payments in a foreign currency (say GBP) for variable payments in a domestic currency (e.g. EUR). Let us imagine n quarterly payments on both legs and a valuation date within the first of these n periods. The key feature of a resettable swap is that the nominal amount on one of the legs (say EUR in this case) is adjusted on each interest period end date to match the other leg's constant notional if converted at the prevailing

[2] This means assuming geometric Brownian Motion for the spot FX rate with a deterministic drift given by the interest rate differential of the two currencies involved.

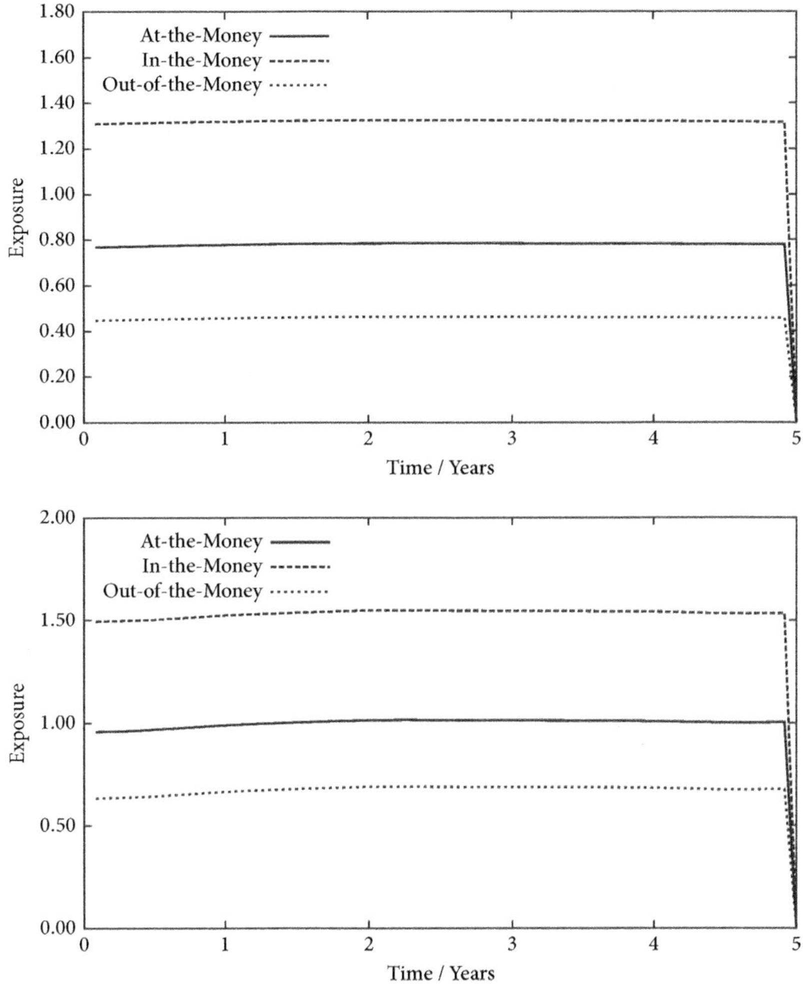

Figure 12.2 Typical FX option exposure evolution, the underlying is the EUR/GBP FX rate. The strikes are at-the-money and shifted slightly (10%) in- and out-of-the-money. Top: yield curve and FX volatility structure are flat at 3% and 10%, respectively. Bottom: flat yield curve, realistic ATM FX volatility structure ranging between 7% and 12%

FX rate. The notional change is associated then with a corresponding cash flow. Let us assume unit notional of the GBP leg and an FX quotation such that the EUR amount follows from multiplication with the FX rate $x(t)$. The fixed GBP leg is valued as usual in GBP and converted into EUR at the spot FX rate $x(t)$. The EUR leg's price consists of the value of notional flows due to FX rate change and final redemption $\Pi_{NTL}(t)$, as well as the value of interest rate flows Π_{INT} linked to 3m-Euribor based on the "current" EUR-equivalent nominal. We can write the value of nominal flows

$$\Pi_{NTL}(t) = \mathbb{E}_t^N \left[\sum_{i=1}^{n-1} \frac{x(t_{i-1}) - x(t_i)}{N(t_i)} + \frac{x(t_{n-1})}{N(t_n)} \right]$$

The interest payment value is

$$\Pi_{INT}(t) = \mathbb{E}_t^N \left[(L(t_0) + s_0)\, \delta_0 \frac{x(t_0)}{N(t_1)} + \sum_{i=1}^{n-1} (L(t_i) + s_i)\, \delta_i \frac{x(t_i)}{N(t_{i+1})} \right]$$

where we have separated the first term with the payment linked to the already fixed Euribor rate $L(t_0)$ at t_0. Now note that we can write the Euribor fixing $L(t_i)$ as

$$L(t_i)\, \delta_i = \frac{1}{P(t_i, t_{i+1})} - 1 + b_i\, \delta_i$$

where b_i is the tenor basis spread for period i and $P(t_i, t_{i-1})$ is the stochastic discount bond at time t_i for maturity t_{i+1} which is associated with the numeraire via

$$P(t_i, t_{i+1}) = \mathbb{E}_{t_i}^N \left[\frac{N(t_i)}{N(t_{i+1})} \right].$$

If we now plug the Euribor fixing $L(t_i)$ definition into $\Pi_{Int}(t)$ and compute the sum $\Pi(t) = \Pi_{Ntl}(t) + \Pi_{Int}(t)$, then we obtain

$$\Pi(t) = \mathbb{E}_t^N \left[\sum_{i=1}^{n-1} \frac{x(t_{i-1}) - x(t_i)}{N(t_i)} + \frac{x(t_{n-1})}{N(t_n)} \right]$$
$$+ \mathbb{E}_t^N \left[(L(t_0) + s_0)\, \delta_0 \frac{x(t_0)}{N(t_1)} + \sum_{i=1}^{n-1} \left(\frac{1}{P(t_i, t_{i+1})} - 1 + (b_i + s_i)\, \delta_i \right) \frac{x(t_i)}{N(t_{i+1})} \right]$$

taking out what is known and cancelling terms $x(t_{i-1})/N(t_i)$

$$\Pi(t) = \left[1 + (L(t_0) + s_0)\, \delta_0\right] x(t_0)\, \mathbb{E}_t^N \left[\frac{1}{N(t_1)} \right]$$
$$+ \mathbb{E}_t^N \left[\sum_{i=1}^{n-1} \left(\frac{1}{P(t_i, t_{i+1})} + (b_i + s_i)\, \delta_i \right) \frac{x(t_i)}{N(t_{i+1})} - \frac{x(t_i)}{N(t_i)} \right]$$

We can insert a nested expectation here conditional on information up to t_i

$$\mathbb{E}_{t_i}^N \left[\frac{1}{P(t_i, t_{i+1})} \frac{x(t_i)}{N(t_{i+1})} \right] = \frac{x(t_i)}{P(t_i, t_{i+1})} \mathbb{E}_{t_i}^N \left[\frac{1}{N(t_{i+1})} \right] = \frac{x(t_i)}{N(t_i)}$$

to see that we have a further cancellation and arrive at

$$\Pi(t) = \left[1 + (L(t_0) + s_0)\,\delta_0\right] x(t_0)\,\mathbb{E}_t^N\left[\frac{1}{N(t_1)}\right] + \sum_{i=1}^{n-1} (b_i + s_i)\,\delta_i\,\mathbb{E}_t^N\left[\frac{x(t_i)}{N(t_{i+1})}\right] \tag{12.27}$$

For a fixed leg with notional resetting feature, the interest flow value changes to

$$\Pi_{INT}(t) = \mathbb{E}_t^N\left[\sum_{i=1}^{n} c_i\,\delta_i\,\frac{x(t_{i-1})}{N(t_i)}\right],$$

and the total leg value including nominal exchanges is

$$\begin{aligned}\Pi(t) &= \mathbb{E}_t^N\left[\sum_{i=1}^{n-1}\frac{x(t_{i-1}) - x(t_i)}{N(t_i)} + \frac{x(t_{n-1})}{N(t_n)} + \sum_{i=1}^{n} c_i\,\delta_i\,\frac{x(t_{i-1})}{N(t_i)}\right] \\ &= \mathbb{E}_t^N\left[\sum_{i=1}^{n}(1 + c_i\delta_i)\frac{x(t_{i-1})}{N(t_i)} - \sum_{i=1}^{n-1}\frac{x(t_i)}{N(t_i)}\right].\end{aligned} \tag{12.28}$$

This leaves us with the following expectations to be computed

$$\mathbb{E}_t^N\left[\frac{x(S)}{N(T)}\right] = \mathbb{E}_t^N\left[\frac{x(S)}{N(S)}\,P(S,T)\right], \qquad S \le T$$

which simplifies in the S-forward measure to

$$P(t,S)\,\mathbb{E}_t^S\left[x(S)\,P(S,T)\right].$$

For $S = T$ it reduces to "FX Forward at time S times discount factor for maturity S". However, for $S < T$ this expectation is model dependent, and leads to the latter product with a multiplicative *quanto* adjustment that depends on FX and IR volatilities and correlations. For example, in the cross-currency LGM model introduced in this chapter this calculation can be done with the tools used throughout this text.

Figure 12.3 shows the exposure evolution of cross-currency interest rate swaps exchanging quarterly fixed payments in EUR for quarterly variable payments in GBP linked to the 3m GBP Libor index. The graphs show fixed (EUR) payer swaps, starting at-the-money at time zero. In the upper graph, the notional amounts remain constant throughout the trade's life. In the lower graph the cross-currency

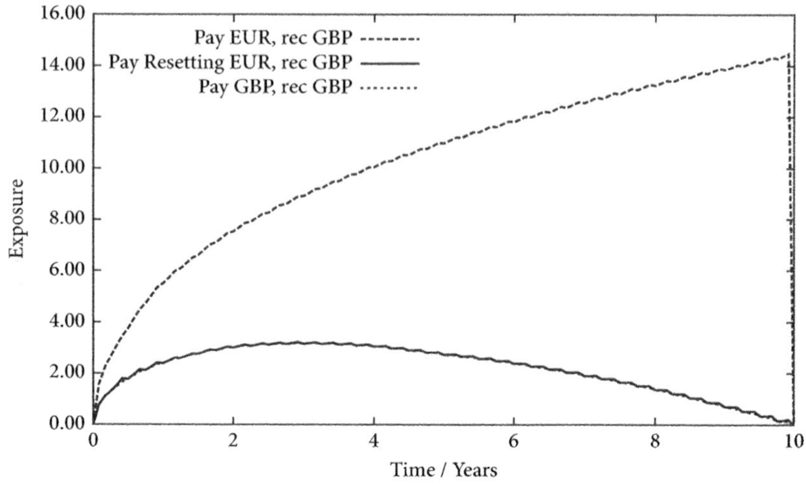

Figure 12.3 EUR/GBP cross-currency swaps exchanging quarterly fixed payments in EUR for quarterly 3m Libor payments in GBP. The trades start at-the-money. The upper graph shows a conventional cross-currency swap with fixed notionals on both legs, the lower graph is a resetting (mark-to-market) cross-currency swap where the EUR notional resets on each interest period start to the current value of the GBP notional in EUR

swap resets one of the notionals at each interest period end to the equivalent of the other leg's notional, since the latter avoids building up FX exposure over the lifetime of the trade. Its exposure evolution is barely distinguishable from a single currency (GBP vs GBP) interest rate swap, which is plotted here as well and almost matches the resetting swap's exposure profile because the FX exposure can build up only marginally over each quarterly period.

13 Inflation

To cover inflation-linked derivatives under CVA simulations we need to add an inflation model component to the multi-currency model introduced so far. In this section we present two alternative modelling approaches and formulate them with LGM as a nominal rate model in order to integrate inflation into the Monte Carlo framework. The first approach is the model by Jarrow and Yildirim [99]. The second one is the model introduced by Dodgson and Kainth [58]. But before we dive into these, let us review standard inflation-linked products which are traded in the market, and some of which we will eventually use to calibrate the models. For an overview of the inflation market, products and valuation methods refer to [108, 33].

13.1 Products

The most elementary inflation-linked product is the *Inflation-Indexed Bond.* The most important examples in terms of issuance volume are *Treasury Inflation-Protected Securities* (TIPS) in the US, inflation-indexed *Gilts* in the UK, French *OATi,* and inflation-indexed *Bund* and *Bobl* in Germany. The zero bond flavour has a single payment at maturity T which is the bond's face value *inflated* by the relative increase of a *Consumer Price Index* between issue and maturity date. We label the CPI as a function of time in short $I(t)$. The *Zero Coupon Inflation-Indexed Bond (ZCIIB)* payoff at time T for face value N is then

$$N \cdot \frac{I(T)}{I(T_0)}$$

where $I(T_0)$ stands for the relevant CPI fixing before issue date. The CPI is a relative price level for a representative basket of goods and services. Various CPIs are published depending on the region (US, UK, France, Germany, eurozone, etc.), the composition of the observed basket (including/excluding tobacco, etc.) and the averaging procedure used. Price indices are published monthly by the Bureau of Labor Statistics in the US (www.bls.gov), the Office for National Statistics in the UK (www.statistics.gov.uk), the Institut National de la Statistique et des

Etudes Economiques in France (www.insee.fr), or Eurostat for the eurozone. The *Zero Coupon Inflation-Indexed Swap (ZCIIS)*[1] is the simplest associated hedging instrument which exchanges an inflation-indexed payment

$$N\left(\frac{I(T)}{I(T_0)}-1\right)$$

for a fixed interest payment

$$N\left((1+r)^{T-T_0}-1\right).$$

Here and in the following, when we write the inflation index for some cash flow date or maturity T, then this refers to the inflation index fixing at an earlier time. For example, if T is in February 2015, then the relevant index fixing is typically as of November 2014 and published at the beginning of December 2014. This *observation lag* is typically two or three months (depending on the index) and ensures that the index fixing is available well before the related payoff. See [108] for a discussion of inflation lags.

ZCIISs are quoted in terms of the fair rate $r(T)$ for maturity T, which thus represents the expected (geometric) average inflation rate. ZCIIS quotes therefore allow extracting the term structure of market-implied CPI ratios $I(T)/I(T_0)$ in a direct way. The second important inflation swap variant is the *Year-on-Year Inflation-Indexed Swap (YoYIIS)*. This exchanges a series of annual inflation-indexed payments

$$N\left(\frac{I(T_i)}{I(T_{i-1})}-1\right)$$

for fixed interest payments. Associated with these basic payoffs there are two common option products traded in the market. The *Zero-Coupon Inflation-Index Cap/Floor (ZCIICF)* with individual caplet or floorlet payoff

$$N\left[\omega\left(\frac{I(T)}{I(T_0)}-K\right)\right]^+$$

and the *Year-on-Year Inflation-Index Cap/Floor (YoYIICF)* with caplet or floorlet payoff

$$N\left[\omega\left(\frac{I(T_i)}{I(T_{i-1})}-K\right)\right]^+.$$

[1] We follow the naming used in [33].

Among the derivatives mentioned above, only the ZCIIS can be priced in a model-independent way. The YoYIIS requires a model already, as well as, less surprisingly, the two option flavours.

13.2 Jarrow-Yildirim model

This popular model as published in [99] assumes that in addition to the conventional money market there is a market of instruments that generate "real" returns,[2] and the inflation index acts as an exchange rate between these two economies. In perfect analogy to Babbs's cross-currency model, the Jarrow-Yildirim (JY) model consists of two Hull-White processes to model the nominal and the so-called real rate, as well as a log-normal process for the inflation index itself:

$$\begin{aligned} dr_n(t) &= [\theta_n(t) - \lambda_n r_n(t)]\, dt + \sigma_n(t)\, dW_n(t) \\ dr_r(t) &= [\theta_r(t) - \lambda_r r_r(t) - \rho_{rI}\sigma_r(T)\sigma_I(t)]\, dt + \sigma_r(t)\, dW_r(t) \\ dI(t)/I(t) &= (r_n(t) - r_r(t))\, dt + \sigma_I(t)\, dW_I(t) \end{aligned}$$

where the indices n and r refer to the nominal and real rate, respectively, and where we use the bank account measure associated with the nominal rate. The nominal rate process establishes, as before, the stochastic nominal zero bond

$$P_n(t,T) = \mathbb{E}^{Q_n}\left[\exp\left(-\int_t^T r_n(s)\, ds\right)\right] = A_n(t,T)\, e^{-B(\lambda_n, T-t)\, r_n(t)},$$

where $B(\lambda, t) = (1 - \exp(-\lambda\, t))/\lambda$. And in perfect analogy to the cross-currency case (compare Appendix D.3), the real rate process establishes the real rate zero bond price

$$P_r(t,T) = \frac{1}{I(t)}\mathbb{E}^{Q_n}\left[\exp\left(-\int_t^T r_n(s)\, ds\right) \cdot I(T)\right] = A_r(t,T)\, e^{-B(\lambda_r, T-t)\, r_r(t)}.$$

Thus equipped, let us write down the price of the ZCIIS inflation leg (using the bank account measure) for unit notional at time $0 \leq t < T$,

$$\mathrm{ZCIIS}(t) = \mathbb{E}_t^{Q_n}\left[e^{-\int_t^T r_n(s)\, ds}\left(\frac{I(T)}{I(T_0)} - 1\right)\right] = \frac{I(t)}{I(T_0)} P_r(t,T) - P_n(t,T),$$

[2] That is, stripped of inflation effects.

and likewise the ZCIIB

$$\mathrm{ZCIIB}(t) = \mathbb{E}_t^{Q_n}\left[e^{-\int_t^T r_n(s)\,ds}\frac{I(T)}{I(T_0)}\right] = \frac{I(t)}{I(T_0)}\,P_r(t,T).$$

When we enter into a new ZCIIS at time t so that $T_0 = t$, then the fair ZCII Swap rate $r(t)$ at time t satisfies

$$P_r(t,T) - P_n(t,T) = \left((1+r(t))^{T-t} - 1\right) P_n(t,T) \tag{13.1}$$

or

$$r(t) = \left(\frac{P_r(t,T)}{P_n(t,T)}\right)^{\frac{1}{T-t}} - 1. \tag{13.2}$$

We could proceed in this fashion and work out the pricing formulas for the YoYIIS and the two caplet/floorlet flavours explicitly. But we stop here for now, because

1. we need to translate the JY model into the LGM context first (to be able to evolve the entire market in a common domestic LGM measure)
2. we will exploit the FX analogy to take shortcuts where possible.

Because of the FX analogy, we do not have to repeat the derivation here, but can state the result. The JY SDE in LGM form reads

$$dz_n(t) = \alpha_n(t)\,dW_n^N(t) \tag{13.3}$$

$$dz_r(t) = \gamma_r(t)\,dt + \alpha_r(t)\,dW_r^N(t) \tag{13.4}$$

$$dI(t)/I(t) = \mu_I(t)\,dt + \sigma_I(t)\,dW_I^N(t) \tag{13.5}$$

$$dW_a\,dW_b = \rho_{ab}\,dt \quad \text{for} \quad a,b \in \{n,r,I\}$$

with drift terms

$$\gamma_r(t) = -\alpha_r^2(t)\,H_r(t) - \rho_{rI}\,\sigma_I(t)\,\alpha_r(t) + \rho_{nr}\,\alpha_r(t)\,\alpha_n(t)\,H_n(t) \tag{13.6}$$

$$\mu_I(t) = r_n(t) - r_r(t) + \rho_{nI}\,\alpha_n(t)\,H_n(t)\,\sigma_I(t) \tag{13.7}$$

and nominal and real rate zero bonds

$$P_n(t,T) = \frac{P_n(0,T)}{P_n(0,t)} \exp\left(-[H_n(T) - H_n(t)]\, z_n(t) - \frac{1}{2}\left[H_n^2(T) - H_n^2(t)\right]\zeta_n(t)\right) \tag{13.8}$$

$$P_r(t,T) = \frac{P_r(0,T)}{P_r(0,t)} \exp\left(-[H_r(T) - H_r(t)]\, z_r(t) - \frac{1}{2}\left[H_r^2(T) - H_r^2(t)\right]\zeta_r(t)\right). \tag{13.9}$$

We can assume here that the nominal rate process is calibrated already. Moreover, the term structure of ZCIIS immediately determines $P_r(0,T)$ as a function of maturity T. We show next how to express the ZCII Caplet and YoYII Caplet prices in terms of model parameters, as we need to use their quotes to calibrate the remaining volatility functions of the model.

ZCII cap

We start with ZCII Caps/Floors here, because we can exploit the FX analogy and re-use previous results. Let us write the payoff

$$\mathrm{ZCIICF}(T) = N\left[\omega\left(\frac{I(T)}{I(T_0)} - K\right)\right]^+ = \widetilde{N}\left[\omega\left(I(T) - \widetilde{K}\right)\right]^+$$

where $\widetilde{N} = N/I(T_0)$ and $\widetilde{K} = K \cdot I(T_0)$, so that the caplet/floorlet price as of time $t < T$

$$\mathrm{ZCIICF}(t) = \widetilde{N}\,\mathbb{E}^N\left[\frac{1}{N(T)}\left[\omega(I(T) - \widetilde{K})\right]^+\right].$$

This is equivalent to an FX option price in the cross-currency LGM, and we can just copy the results from Section 12.3.2, replacing indices (foreign rate process to real rate process, FX rate to inflation index):

$$\mathrm{ZCIICF} = \widetilde{N}\,\omega\, P_n(0,T)\left(F_I(0,T)\,\Phi(\omega\, d_+) - \widetilde{K}\,\Phi(\omega\, d_-)\right)$$

$$d_\pm = \frac{1}{\Sigma_I}\ln\frac{F_I(0,T)}{\widetilde{K}} \pm \frac{\Sigma_I}{2}$$

$$\Sigma_I^2 = \int_0^T \widetilde{\sigma}_I^2(t,T)\,dt$$

with

$$
\begin{aligned}
F_I(t,T) &= I(t)\,\frac{P_r(t,T)}{P_n(t,T)} \\
\widetilde{\sigma}_I^2(t,T) &= (H_n(T)-H_n(t))^2\,\alpha_n^2(t) + (H_r(T)-H_r(t))^2\,\alpha_r^2(t) + \sigma_I^2(t) \\
&\quad -2\,\rho^{nr}\,(H_n(T)-H_n(t))\,(H_r(T)-H_r(t))\,\alpha_n(t)\,\alpha_r(t) \\
&\quad +2\,\rho^{nI}\,(H_n(T)-H_n(t))\,\alpha_n(t)\,\sigma_I(t) \\
&\quad -2\,\rho^{rI}\,(H_r(T)-H_r(t))\,\alpha_r(t)\,\sigma_I(t).
\end{aligned}
$$

For the YoYII Swap as well as the YoYII Caplet we are lacking similar equivalent products in the FX section, so we will derive pricing formulas for them in the following from scratch.

Put-Call parity

As usual, a long ZCII Cap and a short ZCII Floor with the same maturity T and strike K add up to a ZCII Swap, whose value is

$$
ZCIIS(T) = P_r(0,T) - K\,P_n(0,T).
$$

So given the cap $(C_{1,2})$ and floor prices $(F_{1,2})$ for two different strikes $K_{1,2}$ and the same maturity T, we have

$$
C_i - F_i = P_r(0,T) - K_i\,P_n(0,T), \qquad i=1,2,
$$

which implies

$$
P_n(0,T) = \frac{(C_2-F_2)-(C_1-F_1)}{K_1-K_2} \tag{13.10}
$$

and

$$
P_r(0,T) = \frac{K_1}{K_1-K_2}(C_2-F_2) - \frac{K_2}{K_1-K_2}(C_1-F_1). \tag{13.11}
$$

Note that the strikes K we use here are the compounded rates, that is they are of the form $K=(1+r)^T$.

As an example, we look at the ZCII Cap and Floor prices from 30 September 2014 in Tables 13.1 and 13.2. The resulting nominal and real zero bond prices, derived from different strike combinations, are shown in Tables 13.3 and 13.4.

Table 13.1 ZCII Cap prices as of 30 September 2015 in basis points

Mat	1%	2%	3%	4%
2	378.8	197.3	65.8	14.9
5	1014.1	568.7	218.8	59.1
7	1462.1	851.1	351.0	102.9
10	2166.0	1326.1	599.5	195.3
12	2636.1	1656.1	777.9	260.3
15	3372.9	2197.8	1087.5	374.3
20	4583.2	3131.0	1653.3	588.2
30	6747.1	4857.9	2700.6	922.5

Table 13.2 ZCII Floor prices as of 30 September 2015 in basis points

Mat	0%	1%	2%	3%
2	1.4	5.4	23.1	92.9
5	5.2	16.3	59.1	217.0
7	8.2	24.5	83.6	294.1
10	13.3	37.6	119.9	400.7
12	16.1	44.7	139.1	457.8
15	18.8	51.7	158.7	519.3
20	22.8	62.4	188.8	613.1
30	34.5	91.7	267.4	854.6

Table 13.3 The nominal discount factors P_n from the put-call parity using (13.10) for different strike pairs

Mat	1% vs 2%	2% vs 3%	1% vs 3%
2	0.98128	0.98195	0.98162
5	0.91990	0.92004	0.91997
7	0.87537	0.87525	0.87531
10	0.80631	0.80642	0.80637
12	0.75974	0.75984	0.75980
15	0.69340	0.69350	0.69345
20	0.59400	0.59407	0.59404
30	0.44549	0.44561	0.44556

YoYII swap

Consider the price of the ith YoYII Swaplet (with unit notional, inflation leg only) at time t:

$$\text{YoYIIS}(t) = \mathbb{E}^N \left[\frac{N(t)}{N(T_i)} \left(\frac{I(T_i)}{I(T_{i-1})} - 1 \right) \middle| \mathcal{F}_t \right]$$

Table 13.4 The real rate zero bond prices P_n from the put-call parity using (13.11) for different strike pairs

Mat	1% vs 2%	2% vs 3%	1% vs 3%
2	0.98128	0.98195	0.98162
2	1.03834	1.03904	1.03869
5	1.06661	1.06676	1.06668
7	1.08228	1.08214	1.08221
10	1.10351	1.10365	1.10358
12	1.11523	1.11537	1.11530
15	1.13714	1.13727	1.13720
20	1.17687	1.17698	1.17692
30	1.26599	1.26621	1.26608

$$
\begin{aligned}
&= \mathbb{E}^N\left[\frac{N(t)}{N(T_{i-1})}\,\mathbb{E}^N\left(\frac{N(T_{i-1})}{N(T_i)}\frac{I(T_i)}{I(T_{i-1})}\,\middle|\,\mathcal{F}_{T_{i-1}}\right)\middle|\,\mathcal{F}_t\right] \\
&\quad - \mathbb{E}^N\left[\frac{N(t)}{N(T_i)}\,\middle|\,\mathcal{F}_t\right] \\
&= \mathbb{E}^N\left[\frac{N(t)}{N(T_{i-1})}\,P_r(T_{i-1},T_i)\,\middle|\,\mathcal{F}_t\right] - P_n(t,T_i)
\end{aligned}
$$

where we have used the tower rule, or rule of iterated expectations to "roll back" to period start at time T_{i-1} in the first term. We now have to insert the expressions for numeraire and real rate zero bond and compute the remaining expectation. Setting $t=0$:

$$
\begin{aligned}
\mathbb{E}^N\left[\frac{P_r(S,T)}{N(S)}\right] &= P_n(0,S)\,\frac{P_r(0,T)}{P_r(0,S)}\,e^{-\frac{1}{2}H_n^2(S)\zeta_n(S)-\frac{1}{2}(H_r^2(T)-H_r^2(S))\zeta_r(S)} \\
&\quad\times \mathbb{E}^N\left[e^{-H_n(S)\,z_n(S)-(H_r(T)-H_r(S))\,z_r(S)}\right]
\end{aligned}
$$

Since z_n and z_r are Gaussian random variables, we can again apply the identity $\mathbb{E}(\exp(X)) = \exp(\mathbb{E}(X) + \mathbb{V}(X)/2)$ to arrive at

$$
\mathbb{E}^N\left[\frac{P_r(S,T)}{N(S)}\right] = P_n(0,S)\,\frac{P_r(0,T)}{P_r(0,S)}\,e^{C(S,T)}
$$

where

$$C(S,T) = (H_r(T) - H_r(S)) \cdot \left\{ \rho_{nr} H_n(S) \int_0^S \alpha_n(t)\alpha_r(t)\,dt \right. \\ \left. - H_r(S)\zeta_r(S) - \int_0^S \gamma_r(t)\,dt \right\} \tag{13.12}$$

Note that for $\rho_{nr} = \rho_{rI} = 0$, this *convexity adjustment* reduces to

$$C(S,T) = -(H_r(T) - H_r(S)) \cdot \int_0^S (H_r(S) - H_r(t))\,\alpha_r^2(t)\,dt.$$

In summary, the value of a YoYII Swaplet with unit notional (inflation leg only), start and end time $S < T$ is therefore given by

$$\text{YoYIIS} = P_n(0,S)\,\frac{P_r(0,T)}{P_r(0,S)}\,e^{C(S,T)} - P_n(0,T) \tag{13.13}$$

Having stripped the nominal and real rate term structures $P_n(0,t)$ and $P_r(0,t)$, one could then use YoYII Swaps to calibrate the real rate process volatility function. However, the following instrument is another candidate for this purpose.

YoYII caplet

The price of a YoYII Caplet/Floorlet with unit notional for period $[S,T]$ is

$$\text{YoYIICF} = \mathbb{E}^N\left[\frac{1}{N(T)}\left(\omega\left(\frac{I(T)}{I(S)} - K\right)\right)^+\right]$$

changing to the T-forward meaure

$$= P_n(0,T)\,\mathbb{E}^T\left[\left(\omega\left(\frac{I(T)}{I(S)} - K\right)\right)^+\right]$$

First note that $\ln I(T)/I(S)$ in the Jarrow-Yildirim model has a normal distribution. The expectation above will therefore lead to Black-like pricing formula. The key inputs are then mean m and variance v,

$$m = \mathbb{E}^T\left[\frac{I(T)}{I(S)}\right], \qquad v = \mathbb{V}\left[\ln\frac{I(T)}{I(S)}\right]$$

so that

$$\text{YoYIICF} = P_n(0,T)\,\omega\,[m\,\Phi(\omega\,d_+) - K\,\Phi(\omega\,d_-)]. \tag{13.14}$$

with

$$d_{\pm} = \frac{1}{\sqrt{v}} \ln \frac{m}{K} \pm \frac{1}{2}\sqrt{v}.$$

We have computed the mean m already in the previous section, which is essentially the first term of the YoYII Swaplet,

$$m = E^T\left[\frac{I(T)}{I(S)}\right] = \frac{1}{P_n(0,T)} E^N\left[\frac{P_r(S,T)}{N(S)}\right] = \frac{P_n(0,S)}{P_n(0,T)} \frac{P_r(0,T)}{P_r(0,S)} e^{C(S,T)}.$$

To determine the variance v, recall that it is measure-independent because any drift term from a change of measure does not add to the variance, so that we can use LGM measure expressions for this purpose. Using the FX analogy, we refer to Equation (12.13) which is the equivalent of $\ln(I(T)/I(S))$. To compute its variance we ignore all drift terms and focus on the Ito integral terms and the terms containing $z_n(S)$ and $z_r(S)$. The latter two terms were ignored in the *conditional* covariance calculation leading to (12.17), but are essential here. In terms of the inflation model parameters we therefore get:

$$\begin{aligned}
v &= \mathbb{V}\left[\ln \frac{I(T)}{I(S)}\right] \\
&= \int_S^T (H_n(T) - H_n(\tau))^2\,\alpha_n^2(\tau)\,d\tau + \int_S^T (H_r(T) - H_r(\tau))^2\,\alpha_r^2(\tau)\,d\tau \\
&\quad - 2\rho_{nr} \int_S^T (H_n(T) - H_n(\tau))\,(H_r(T) - H_r(\tau))\,\alpha_n(\tau)\,\alpha_r(\tau)\,d\tau \\
&\quad + 2\rho_{nI} \int_S^T (H_n(T) - H_n(\tau))\,\alpha_n(\tau)\,\sigma_I(\tau)\,d\tau \qquad (13.15) \\
&\quad - 2\rho_{rI} \int_S^T (H_r(T) - H_r(\tau))\,\alpha_r(\tau)\,\sigma_I(\tau)\,d\tau \\
&\quad + \int_S^T \sigma_I^2(\tau)\,d\tau + (H_n(T) - H_n(S))^2\,\zeta_n(S) + (H_r(T) - H_r(S))^2\,\zeta_r(S) \\
&\quad - 2\rho_{nr}\,(H_n(T) - H_n(S))\,(H_r(T) - H_r(S)) \int_0^S \alpha_n(\tau)\,\alpha_r(\tau)\,d\tau
\end{aligned}$$

which completes the YoYII Caplet pricing. Note the last three additional terms in comparison to the *conditional* variance (12.17) and in comparison to the ZCII Cap/Floor variance above. Moreover, note that we are integrating here from S to T and from 0 to S rather than from 0 to T.

We checked the ZCII cap/floor and YoYII caplet/floorlet pricing formulas derived here by comparison to Monte Carlo evaluation – generating Jarrow-Yildirim model paths with fine time discretization (100 time steps per year) and averaging the

Table 13.5 Pricing check for 6y maturity ZCII Cap and YOYII Caplet with unit notional and strikes 1.06 and 1.01, respectively. Model parameters: flat nominal term structure at continuously compounded zero rate of 4%, nominal LGM based on $\lambda_n = 0.03$ and $\sigma_n = 0.01$, real rate zero rate 3%, real rate LGM based on $\lambda_r = 0.035$ and $\sigma_r = 0.007$, CPI process volatility $\sigma_I = 0.03$, correlations $\rho_{nr} = 0.4$, $\rho_{nI} = 0.3$ and $\rho_{rI} = 0.5$

Product Type	Analytic	Monte Carlo
ZCII Swap (Inf. Leg)	0.048642	0.048686
ZCII Cap	0.035261	0.035223
YoYII Swaplet (Inf. Leg)	0.008111	0.008112
YoYII Caplet	0.011566	0.011496

discounted payoffs over a large number of samples (1 Mio). The relative price errors are of the order 0.1%, as expected for the number of Monte Carlo samples, see Table 13.5.

13.2.1 Calibration

We assume here that the nominal rate process is calibrated already. In the following we sketch a calibration strategy that we have seen working well in practice.

1. Imply real rate bond prices $P_r(0,T)$ from ZCII swaps
2. Calibrate the correlations ρ_{nr}, ρ_{nI}, ρ_{rI} from historical data; the real rate history for this purpose can be constructed from ZCII swap rates using $P_r(0,T) = P_n(0,T)\,(1 + r_{ZCIIS})^T$, i.e. in terms of continuously compounded zero rates[3] $z_{real} = z_{nominal} - z_{ZCIIS}$ for some common tenor T. The nominal rate – real rate correlation ρ_{nr} is typically high, above 90%.
3. Calibrate the real rate process ζ_r (based on constant HW σ) to historical real rate data
4. Calibrate the real rate process H_r (as a piecewise linear function of time) to ZCII Caps or Floors (depending on the portfolio, possibly at-the-money caps/floors)
5. Calibrate the CPI process σ_I (as a piecewise linear function of time) to YoYII Caps of Floors

Since $H_r(t)$ and $\sigma_I(t)$ affect both ZCII and YoYII floor prices, the calibration of σ_I in the last step affects the calibration quality of the previous step. For convergence one therefore needs to perform the last two steps either simultaneously or repeat these steps iteratively.

[3] With continuously compounded rates defined as $P_r(0,T) = \exp(-z_{real}\,T)$, $P_n(0,T) = \exp(-z_{nominal}\,T)$, $(1 + r_{ZCIIS})^T = \exp(z_{ZCIIS}\,T)$

Table 13.6 Jarrow-Yildrim model calibration using market data as of end January 2015. The ATM Cap prices are matched with the exception of the first Cap. YoY Caps are matched only approximately. Model parameters: $\rho_{nr} = 0.95$, $\rho_{nc} = 0.5$, $\rho_{rc} = 0.25$; $\alpha_r(t) = \sigma_r e^{\lambda_r t}$ with $\lambda_r = 0.03$ and $\sigma_r = 0.005$; $\sigma_C = 0.01$, $H_r(t)$ piecewise linear

Instrument	Strike	Term	Market Price	Model Price	Difference
CPI Cap	ATM	1Y	61.1	44.4	16.7
CPI Cap	ATM	2Y	83.3	83.3	0.01
CPI Cap	ATM	3Y	110.2	110.2	0.01
CPI Cap	ATM	5Y	212.0	212.0	0.02
CPI Cap	ATM	7Y	294.7	294.7	0.02
CPI Cap	ATM	12Y	579.8	579.7	0.04
CPI Cap	ATM	15Y	772.2	772.1	0.04
CPI Cap	ATM	20Y	1074.5	1074.5	−0.03
YOY Cap	ATM	1Y	45.9	44.0	1.8
YOY Cap	ATM	2Y	61.7	69.5	−7.7
YOY Cap	ATM	3Y	98.7	138.1	−39.4
YOY Cap	ATM	5Y	196.5	263.6	−67.1
YOY Cap	ATM	7Y	269.3	389.6	−120.3
YOY Cap	ATM	12Y	425.9	579.5	−153.6
YOY Cap	ATM	15Y	501.7	681.6	−179.9
YOY Cap	ATM	20Y	1058.9	1088.6	−29.7

This calibration does not guarantee a perfect match with the selected ZCII Caps/Floors and YoYII Caps/Floors. But we can typically achieve a good or perfect match with CPI Caps and an approximate match with YoYII Caps, see Table 13.6 for an example.

13.2.2 Foreign currency inflation

The JY inflation model (13.3–13.9) assumes a single currency economy so far. To fit this model into the cross-currency model setup, we need to consider a foreign currency version of the model that works with a selected *domestic* LGM numeraire in a currency which is different from the "home" currency of the inflation component. For example, we need to model UK or US inflation with a euro LGM numeraire. We know already how this affects the foreign currency nominal rate process (13.3). In this section we will work out the impact of using the domestic LGM numeraire on the foreign real rate and CPI process drifts in (13.4) and (13.5). To determine the amended two drift terms we analyse two martingales, both *foreign* inflation-linked assets divided by the domestic numeraire asset,

$$A(t) = \frac{N_r(t)\, I(t)\, x(t)}{N_n^d(t)} \qquad \text{and} \qquad B(t) = \frac{P_r(t,T)\, I(t)\, x(t)}{N_n^d(t)}$$

where $N_n^d(t)$ is the LGM numeraire of the domestic nominal rate process, $N_r(t)$ is the numeraire of the foreign real rate process, and $x(t)$ is the FX rate that converts from foreign into domestic currency. By claiming that their drift vanishes and following a similar analysis as in the IR/FX section we conclude that real rate and CPI drift terms change as follows:

$$\begin{aligned}\gamma_r(t) &= -\alpha_r^2(t)\, H_r(t) - \rho_{rI}\, \sigma_I(t)\, \alpha_r(t) + \rho_{nr}^d\, \alpha_r(t)\, \alpha_n^d(t)\, H_n^d(t) \\ &\quad - \sigma_x(t)\, \alpha_r(t) \rho_{xr} &(13.16)\\ \mu_I(t) &= r_n(t) - r_r(t) + \rho_{nI}^d\, \alpha_n^d(t)\, H_n^d(t)\, \sigma_I(t) \\ &\quad - \sigma_x(t)\, \sigma_I(t)\, \rho_{xI} &(13.17)\end{aligned}$$

Note the superscripts $\cdot^d$ which refer to domestic quantities here, for example ρ_{nI}^d is the correlation between the domestic nominal rate process and the inflation CPI process. Moreover, both drift terms have an additional *quanto* adjustment $\propto \sigma_x(t)$ now. We have checked the correctness of the amended drift terms (13.16, 13.17) by verifying

$$\mathbb{E}\,[A(t)] = A(0) \qquad \text{and} \qquad \mathbb{E}\,[B(t)] = B(0)$$

by Monte Carlo simulation.

13.3 Dodgson-Kainth model

The Dodgson-Kainth (DK) model was introduced in 2006 [58] and is a bit younger than Jarrow and Yildirim's approach. It is simpler in that it models inflation in terms of a single-factor Hull-White process for the *inflation short rate* $i(t)$,

$$di(t) = \lambda_I\, (\theta_I(t) - i(t))\, dt + \sigma_I\, dW_I^Q,$$

where the superscript Q indicates the measure associated with the nominal bank account. The inflation short rate is then linked to the CPI index $I(t)$ via

$$I(T) = I(t)\, \exp\left(\int_t^T i(s)\, ds\right)$$

which allows defining an inflation-linked zero bond

$$P_I(t,T) = \frac{1}{I(t)} \mathbb{E}_t^Q\left[e^{-\int_t^T r_n(s)\, ds}\, I(T)\right] = \mathbb{E}_t^Q\left[\exp\left(\int_t^T (i(s) - r_n(s))\, ds\right)\right]$$

where $r_n(t)$ denotes the nominal short rate. Note that this is the equivalent of Jarrow-Yildirim's real rate bond.[4] One can express the ZCII swap value in terms of $P_I(t,T)$ and $P_n(t,T)$ as

$$\mathrm{ZCIIS}(t) = \mathbb{E}_t^Q\left[e^{-\int_t^T r_n(s)\,ds}\left(\frac{I(T)}{I(T_0)}-1\right)\right] = \frac{I(t)}{I(T_0)}\,P_I(t,T) - P_n(t,T)$$

The fair ZCII swap rate $r(t)$ at time t (fixing $T_0 = t$) satisfies

$$P_I(t,T) - P_n(t,T) = \left((1+r(t))^{T-t} - 1\right) P_n(t,T)$$

or

$$r(t) = \left(\frac{P_I(t,T)}{P_n(t,T)}\right)^{\frac{1}{T-t}} - 1.$$

The ratio $P_I(t,T)/P_n(t,T)$ is not only key to the pricing of ZCII swaps but also of ZCII Caps/Floors, as we shall see below. Following [58], we therefore define the *forward* or *projected* price index

$$\hat{I}(t,T) = \frac{P_I(t,T)}{P_n(t,T)}$$

and use this abbreviation later on.

Like the JY model, the DK model therefore implies log-normal dynamics for the inflation index. However, it avoids the real rate process and comes with a reduced set of model parameters.

To integrate the DK model with our evolution model we have to put it into the LGM context, that is move the inflation rate process to the domestic LGM measure. The DK model including nominal rate process then reads (superscript N indicating the measure associated with the LGM numeraire)

$$dz_n = \alpha_n(t)\,dW_n^N(t) \tag{13.18}$$

$$di(t) = \lambda_I\,(\theta_I(t) - i(t))\,dt + \sigma_I(t)\,dW_I^N(t) + \gamma_I(t)\,dt \tag{13.19}$$

The $\gamma_I(t)$ drift term on the right-hand side reflects the change of measure to the LGM numeraire of the process. The formal solution of the inflation process's SDE

[4] And it differs from $P_I(t,T)$ in [58] by factor $1/I(t)$.

is given by

$$i(t) = \mu(t) + x(t)$$

$$x(t) = e^{-\lambda_I t} \int_0^t \alpha_I(u)\, dW_I(u), \qquad \alpha_I(u) = e^{\lambda_I u} \sigma_I(u),$$

where both drifts $\theta_I(t)$ and $\gamma_I(t)$ have been absorbed in $\mu(t)$. The precise dependence of $\mu(t)$ on the latter two functions is not relevant as $\mu(t)$ will subsequently be calibrated directly to market observables. For the steps below we will also need the following representation of the solution in terms of $x(t_0)$ at an earlier time $t_0 < t$:

$$x(t) = x(t_0)\, e^{-\lambda_I(t-t_0)} + e^{-\lambda_I t} \int_{t_0}^t \alpha_I(u)\, dW_I^N(u)$$

which suggests introducing $z_I(t) = e^{\lambda_I t} x(t)$ which satisfies

$$z_I(t) = z_I(t_0) + \int_{t_0}^t \alpha_I(u)\, dW_I^N(u).$$

We now want to compute the stochastic inflation-indexed bond price

$$P_I(t,T) = \frac{N(t)}{I(t)} \mathbb{E}_t^N\left[\frac{I(T)}{N(T)}\right] = N(t)\, \mathbb{E}_t^N\left[\frac{1}{N(T)}\, e^{\int_t^T i(s)\, ds}\right]. \tag{13.20}$$

Following the steps in Appendix F.1 we arrive at

$$P_I(t,T) = P_n(t,T) \exp\left((H_I(T) - H_I(t))\, z_I(t) + V(t,T) + \int_t^T \mu(s)\, ds \right) \tag{13.21}$$

with

$$\begin{aligned} V(t,T) = {} & \frac{1}{2} \int_t^T (H_I(T) - H_I(s))^2\, \alpha_I^2(s)\, ds \\ & - \rho^{nI} H_n(T) \int_t^T (H_I(T) - H_I(s))\, \alpha_n(s)\, \alpha_I(s)\, ds \end{aligned} \tag{13.22}$$

From the latter expression of $P_I(t,T)$ in (13.21) we can now eliminate the $\mu(s)$-dependence: we take the ratio of

$$P_I(0,T) = P_n(0,T)\, e^{V(0,T) + \int_0^T \mu(s)\, ds}$$

$$P_I(0,t) = P_n(0,t)\, e^{V(0,t) + \int_0^t \mu(s)\, ds}$$

and solve for the μ-integral:

$$e^{\int_t^T \mu(s)\,ds} = \frac{P_I(0,T)}{P_I(0,t)}\frac{P_n(0,t)}{P_n(0,T)}\,e^{V(0,t)-V(0,T)}.$$

This can be substituted in $P_I(t,T)$ to obtain the price of the inflation-linked zero bond:

$$P_I(t,T) = P_n(t,T)\,\frac{P_n(0,t)}{P_n(0,T)}\frac{P_I(0,T)}{P_I(0,t)}\,e^{+(H_I(T)-H_I(t))\,z_I(t)+\widetilde{V}(t,T)} \tag{13.23}$$

with

$$\widetilde{V}(t,T) = V(t,T) - V(0,T) + V(0,t) \tag{13.24}$$

The ratio $P_I(t,T)/N(t)$ needed in the following then reads

$$\begin{aligned}\frac{P_I(t,T)}{N(t)} &= \frac{P_n(t,T)}{N(t)}\frac{P_n(0,t)}{P_n(0,T)}\frac{P_I(0,T)}{P_I(0,t)}\,e^{+(H_I(T)-H_I(t))\,z_I(t)+\widetilde{V}(t,T)}\\ &= P_n(0,t)\,\frac{P_I(0,T)}{P_I(0,t)}\,e^{+(H_I(T)-H_I(t))\,z_I(t)-H_n(T)\,z_n(t)}\\ &\quad\times e^{\widetilde{V}(t,T)-\frac{1}{2}H_n^2(T)\zeta_n(t)}\end{aligned} \tag{13.25}$$

Finally, let us see whether we can express $I(t)$ in terms of the model "factor" $z_I(t)$. We compute

$$I(t) = I(0)\,e^{\int_0^t i(s)\,ds}$$

re-using previous steps to arrive at

$$I(t) = I(0)\,\frac{P_I(0,t)}{P_n(0,t)}\,e^{-V(0,t)+H_I(t)\,z_I(t)-\int_0^t H_I(s)\,\alpha_I(s)\,dW_I(s)}.$$

The Ito integral on the right-hand side is driven by the same Wiener process as $z_I(t)$, but due to the additional factor $H_I(s)$ in the integral, this integral represents an additional random variable y_I,

$$y_I(t) = \int_0^t H_I(s)\,\alpha_I(s)\,dW_I(s)$$

which is not perfectly correlated with $z_I(t)$ because H_I is inevitably time-dependent.[5]

[5] One finds a similar result when computing the bank account $B(t) = \exp(\int_0^t r(s)\,ds)$ in the one-factor Hull-White model in the risk-neutral measure. $B(t)$ turns out to be driven by two state variables rather than one as one might initially expect.

To complete this section, we can now summarize the Dodgson-Kainth model in the LGM measure as follows:

$$dz_n(t) = \alpha_n(t)\, dW_n(t) \tag{13.26}$$

$$dz_I(t) = \alpha_I(t)\, dW_I(t) \tag{13.27}$$

$$dy_I(t) = H_I(t)\,\alpha_I(t)\, dW_I(t) \tag{13.28}$$

$$dW_n(t)\, dW_I(t) = \rho^{nI}\, dt \tag{13.29}$$

with spot index $I(t)$, forward index $\hat{I}(t,T) = P_I(t,T)/P_n(t,T)$

$$\hat{I}(t,T) = \frac{\hat{I}(0,T)}{\hat{I}(0,t)}\, e^{+(H_I(T)-H_I(t))\,z_I(t)+\widetilde{V}(t,T)} \tag{13.30}$$

$$I(t) = I(0)\,\hat{I}(0,t)\, e^{+H_I(t)\,z_I(t)-y_I(t)-V(0,t)} \tag{13.31}$$

and covariances

$$\begin{aligned} V(t,T) &= \frac{1}{2}\int_t^T (H_I(T)-H_I(s))^2\,\alpha_I^2(s)\,ds \\ &\quad - \rho^{nI}\, H_n(T)\int_t^T (H_I(T)-H_I(s))\,\alpha_n(s)\,\alpha_I(s)\,ds \end{aligned} \tag{13.32}$$

$$\widetilde{V}(t,T) = V(t,T) - V(0,T) + V(0,t) \tag{13.33}$$

$$\begin{aligned} &= -\frac{1}{2}\left(H_I^2(T)-H_I^2(t)\right)\zeta_I(t,0) \\ &\quad + (H_I(T)-H_I(t))\,\zeta_I(t,1) \\ &\quad + (H_n(T)\,H_I(T)-H_n(t)\,H_I(t))\,\zeta_{nI}(t,0) \\ &\quad - (H_n(T)-H_n(t))\,\zeta_{nI}(t,1) \end{aligned}$$

$$\begin{aligned} V(0,t) &= \frac{1}{2}H_I^2(t)\,\zeta_I(t,0) - H_I(t)\,\zeta_I(t,1) + \frac{1}{2}\zeta_I(t,2) \\ &\quad - H_n(t)\,H_I(t)\,\zeta_{nI}(t,0) + H_n(t)\,\zeta_{nI}(t,1) \end{aligned}$$

$$\zeta_I(t,k) = \int_0^t H_I^k(s)\,\alpha_I^2(s)\,ds$$

$$\zeta_{nI}(t,k) = \rho^{nI}\int_0^t H_I^k(t)\,\alpha_n(s)\,\alpha_I(s)\,ds$$

It turns out that the DK model is – like JY – driven by three state variables in total if we take the auxiliary state variable y_I into account which is necessary to evolve the inflation index. State variable $z_I(t)$ alone drives $P_I(t,T)/P_n(t,T)$ which determines the stochastic ZCII swap rate

$$r(t) = \left(\frac{P_I(t,T)}{P_n(t,T)} \right)^{\frac{1}{T-t}} - 1.$$

Finally we note that in analogy to the JY model we have

$$\mathbb{E}^N \left[\frac{I(t)}{N(t)} P_I(t,T) \right] = \mathbb{E}^N \left[\mathbb{E}_t^N \left[\frac{I(T)}{N(T)} \right] \right] = \mathbb{E}^N \left[\frac{I(T)}{N(T)} \right] = I(0)\, P_I(0,T) \quad (13.34)$$

where we have used the definition of $P_I(t,T)$,

$$P_I(t,T) = \frac{N(t)}{I(t)} \mathbb{E}_t^N \left[\frac{I(T)}{N(T)} \right],$$

and the tower law of iterated expectations. We checked that the analytical solutions summarized above satisfy property (13.34).

To calibrate the DK model, we need to work out, as in the JY case, analytical expressions for ZCII Swap, YoYII Swap, ZCII Cap/Floor and YOYII Caplet/Floorlet. This is done in the following section using the "building" blocks $P_I(t,T)$ and $I(t)$.

ZCII swap

We repeat the result from the beginning of the previous section (inflation leg only):

$$\text{ZCIIS}(t) = \frac{I(t)}{I(T_0)} P_I(t,T) - P_n(t,T)$$

The fair ZCII swap rate $r(t)$ at time t (fixing $T_0 = t$) satisfies

$$P_I(t,T) - P_n(t,T) = \left((1 + r(t,T))^{T-t} - 1 \right) P_n(t,T)$$

or

$$r(t,T) = \left(\frac{P_I(t,T)}{P_n(t,T)} \right)^{\frac{1}{T-t}} - 1 = \left(\hat{I}(t,T) \right)^{\frac{1}{T-t}} - 1.$$

ZCII Swaps with maturities T quoted today ($t = 0$) therefore allow the direct calibration of the forward inflation index

$$\hat{I}(t,T) = (1 + r(t,T))^{T-t}.$$

YoYII swaplet

Here we compute the value of a YoYII Swaplet's inflation leg for start time S and end time $T > S$. As in the JY section we have

$$
\begin{aligned}
\mathrm{YoYIIS}(t) &= \mathbb{E}^N\left[\frac{N(t)}{N(T)}\left(\frac{I(T)}{I(S)}-1\right)\Big|\mathcal{F}_t\right] \\
&= \mathbb{E}^N\left[\frac{N(t)}{N(S)}P_I(S,T)\Big|\mathcal{F}_t\right] - P_n(t,T)
\end{aligned}
$$

For simplicity we consider $t=0$ and compute the relevant expectation $\mathbb{E}^N\left(P_I(S,T)/N(S)\right)$ by inserting (13.25)

$$
\mathbb{E}^N\left[\frac{P_I(S,T)}{N(S)}\right] = \frac{P_I(0,T)}{P_I(0,S)}\,P_n(0,S)\,e^{\widetilde{C}(S,T)}
$$

where

$$
\begin{aligned}
e^{\widetilde{C}(S,T)} &= \mathbb{E}^N\left[e^{+(H_I(T)-H_I(S))\,z_I(S)-(H_n(T)-H_n(S))\,z_n(S)+\widetilde{V}(S,T)-H_n(S)z_n(S)-\frac{1}{2}H_n^2(S)\zeta_n(S)}\right] \\
&= e^{\widetilde{V}(S,T)-\frac{1}{2}H_n^2(S)\zeta_n(S)}\,\mathbb{E}^N\left[e^{+(H_I(T)-H_I(S))\,z_I(S)-H_n(T)\,z_n(S)}\right] \\
&= e^{\widetilde{V}(S,T)-\frac{1}{2}H_n^2(S)\zeta_n(S)+\frac{1}{2}(H_I(T)-H_I(S))^2\zeta_I(S)+\frac{1}{2}H_n^2(T)\zeta_n(S)} \\
&\quad\times e^{-\rho^{nI}\,(H_I(T)-H_I(S))\,H_n(T)\int_0^S\alpha_I(s)\alpha_n(s)\,ds} \\
&= e^{\widetilde{V}(S,T)+\frac{1}{2}(H_n^2(T)-H_n^2(S))\zeta_n(S)+\frac{1}{2}(H_I(T)-H_I(S))^2\zeta_I(S)} \\
&\quad\times e^{-\rho^{nI}\,(H_I(T)-H_I(S))\,H_n(T)\int_0^S\alpha_I(s)\alpha_n(s)\,ds} \\
&= e^{V(S,T)-V(0,T)+V(0,S)+\frac{1}{2}(H_I(T)-H_I(S))^2\zeta_I(S)} \\
&\quad\times e^{-\rho^{nI}\,(H_I(T)-H_I(S))\,H_n(T)\int_0^S\alpha_I(s)\alpha_n(s)\,ds}.
\end{aligned}
$$

In summary, we have

$$
\begin{aligned}
\widetilde{C}(S,T) &= V(S,T)-V(0,T)+V(0,S)+\frac{1}{2}(H_I(T)-H_I(S))^2\,\zeta_I(S) \\
&\quad-\rho^{nI}\,(H_I(T)-H_I(S))\,H_n(T)\int_0^S\alpha_I(s)\,\alpha_n(s)\,ds \qquad (13.35)
\end{aligned}
$$

which yields, after inserting $V(\cdot)$ and rearranging terms,

$$
\begin{aligned}
&= -\left(H_I(T) - H_I(S)\right) \int_0^S \left(H_I(S) - H_I(t)\right) \alpha_I^2(t)\, dt \\
&\quad + \rho^{nI} \left(H_n(T) - H_n(S)\right) \int_0^S \left(H_I(S) - H_I(t)\right) \alpha_n(t)\, \alpha_I(t)\, dt \qquad (13.36)
\end{aligned}
$$

For constant Hull-White parameters, that is $H_{I,n}(t) = (1 - \exp(-\lambda_{I,n} t)/\lambda_{I,n}$ and $\alpha_{I,n}(t) = \sigma_{I,n} \exp(\lambda_{I,n} t)$, this agrees with Equation (37) in [58]. Note that the sign of the second term in (13.36) is positive (as opposed to the comment following Equation (37) in [58]. We checked

$$
\mathbb{E}^N \left[\frac{1}{N(T)} \frac{I(T)}{I(S)} \right] = \frac{P_I(0,T)}{P_I(0,S)}\, P_n(0,S)\, e^{\widetilde{C}(S,T)}
$$

by Monte Carlo sampling based on (13.26–13.32).

ZCII Cap/Floor

Recall the payoff

$$
\mathrm{ZCIICF}(T) = N \left[\omega \left(\frac{I(T)}{I(T_0)} - K \right) \right]^+ = \widetilde{N} \left[\omega \left(I(T) - \widetilde{K} \right) \right]^+
$$

where $\widetilde{N} = N/I(T_0)$ and $\widetilde{K} = K \cdot I(T_0)$, so that the caplet/floorlet price for $t = 0$ is

$$
\mathrm{ZCIICF} = \widetilde{N}\, \mathbb{E}^N \left[\frac{1}{N(T)} \left[\omega (I(T) - \widetilde{K}) \right]^+ \right].
$$

Moving to the T-forward measure, we can apply the standard Black76 formula with non-zero mean (see Appendix C):

$$
\begin{aligned}
\mathrm{ZCIICF} &= \widetilde{N}\, P_n(0,T)\, \mathbb{E}^T \left[\left[\omega (I(T) - \widetilde{K}) \right]^+ \right] \\
&= \widetilde{N}\, P_n(0,T)\, \omega \left(m\, \Phi(\omega\, d_+) - \widetilde{K}\, \Phi(\omega\, d_-) \right) \qquad (13.37)
\end{aligned}
$$

with

$$
d_\pm = \frac{1}{\sqrt{v}} \ln \frac{m}{\widetilde{K}} \pm \frac{1}{2} \sqrt{v}
$$

and

$$m = \mathbb{E}^T[I(T)] = \frac{1}{P_n(0,T)} \mathbb{E}^N\left[\frac{I(T)}{N(T)}\right] = I(0)\,\frac{P_I(0,T)}{P_n(0,T)}$$

$$\begin{aligned} v &= Var(\ln I(T)) = Var(H_I(T)\, z_I(T) - y_I(T)) \\ &= H_I^2(T)\,\zeta_I(T) + \int_0^T H_I^2(s)\,\alpha_I^2(s)\,ds - 2H_I(T)\int_0^T H_I(s)\,\alpha_I^2(s)\,ds \\ &= \int_0^T (H_I(T) - H_I(s))^2\,\alpha_I^2(s)\,ds. \end{aligned} \tag{13.38}$$

YoYII Caplet/Floorlet

Recall the price of a YoYII Caplet/Floorlet with unit notional for period $[S, T]$

$$\text{YoYIICF} = \mathbb{E}^N\left[\frac{1}{N(T)}\left(\omega\left(\frac{I(T)}{I(S)} - K\right)\right)^+\right],$$

or, after changing to the T-forward measure

$$= P_n(0,T)\,\mathbb{E}^T\left[\left(\omega\left(\frac{I(T)}{I(S)} - K\right)\right)^+\right]$$

As in the JY model, $\ln I(T)/I(S)$ has a normal distribution so that the expectation above will lead to a Black76 formula with key inputs mean m and variance v,

$$m = \mathbb{E}^T\left[\frac{I(T)}{I(S)}\right], \qquad v = \text{Var}\left[\ln\frac{I(T)}{I(S)}\right]$$

so that

$$\text{YoYIICF} = P_n(0,T)\,\omega\,[m\,\Phi(\omega\, d_+) - K\,\Phi(\omega\, d_-)]\,. \tag{13.39}$$

with

$$d_\pm = \frac{1}{\sqrt{v}}\ln\frac{m}{K} \pm \frac{1}{2}\sqrt{v}.$$

We have computed mean m already in the previous section, which is essentially the first term of the YoYII Swaplet, as in the analogous JY case,

$$m = E^T\left[\frac{I(T)}{I(S)}\right] = \frac{1}{P_n(0,T)}\,E^N\left[\frac{P_I(S,T)}{N(S)}\right] = \frac{P_n(0,S)}{P_n(0,T)}\,\frac{P_I(0,T)}{P_I(0,S)}\,e^{\tilde{C}(S,T)}. \tag{13.40}$$

We finally need to determine variance v by inserting the expression for $I(t)$ and computing the expectation,

$$
\begin{aligned}
v &= \mathrm{Var}\left[\ln\frac{I(T)}{I(S)}\right] \\
&= \mathrm{Var}\left[H_I(T)\,z_I(T) - H_I(S)\,z_I(S) - y_I(T) + y_I(S)\right] \\
&= \mathrm{Var}\left[(H_I(T) - H_I(S))\,z_I(S) + H_I(T)\,(z_I(T) - z_I(S)) - (y_I(T) - y_I(S))\right] \\
&= (H_I(T) - H_I(S))^2\,\zeta_I(S) + H_I^2(T)\,(\zeta_I(T) - \zeta_I(S)) \\
&\quad + \int_S^T H_I^2(s)\,\alpha_I^2(s)\,ds - 2H_I(T)\int_S^T \alpha_I^2\,H_I(s)\,ds \\
&= (H_I(T) - H_I(S))^2\,\zeta_I(S) + \int_S^T (H_I(T) - H_I(s))^2\,\alpha_I^2(s)\,ds,
\end{aligned}
\tag{13.41}
$$

which completes the YoYII Caplet pricing. We checked the analytical pricing formula (13.39) with Monte Carlo simulation.

Direct comparison of the YoYII Caplet variance (13.41) to the ZCII Cap with the same expiry (13.38) shows that the former is systematically larger.

13.3.1 Calibration

Assuming that the nominal model is calibrated already, one simple way of calibrating the inflation model involves the following three steps:

1. Calibrate function $P_I(0,t)$ to the term structure of ZCII Swaps
2. Calibrate $H_I(t)$ and $\alpha_I(t)$ to match quoted CPI Caps/Floors; Figure 13.1 shows e.g. a calibration to CPI Floors at three different strike levels, the parametrization here is minimal – assuming volatility functions $H_I(t) = (1 - \exp(-\lambda_I t))/\lambda_I$ and $\alpha_I(t) = \sigma_I \exp(\lambda_I t)$. The match can be made perfect by choosing a piecewise volatility function $\alpha_I(t)$ with nodes at expiry dates. Note that the CPI Cap/Floor model price/volatility is independent of the model's correlation between the nominal and inflation short rate process, see Equation (13.38). This means one can choose ρ arbitrarily at this stage without affecting the CPI Cap/Floor calibration.
3. On the other hand, ρ does affect the YoY Cap/Floor price via the convexity adjustment in (13.40). In this third step one can therefore use ρ to attempt a fit to relevant YoY Caps or Floors, keeping $H_I(t)$ and $\alpha_I(t)$ unchanged.

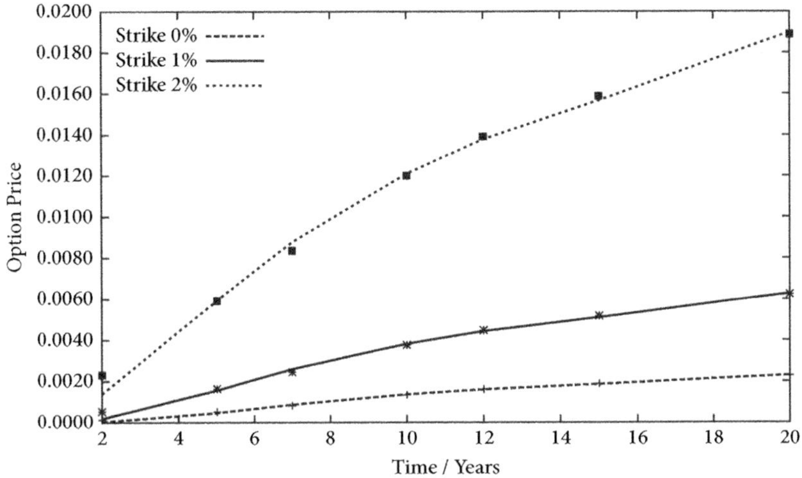

Figure 13.1 Dodgson-Kainth model calibrated to CPI floors (at strikes 0%, 1% and 2%, respectively), market data as of 30 September 2014. Symbols denote market prices; the lines model prices

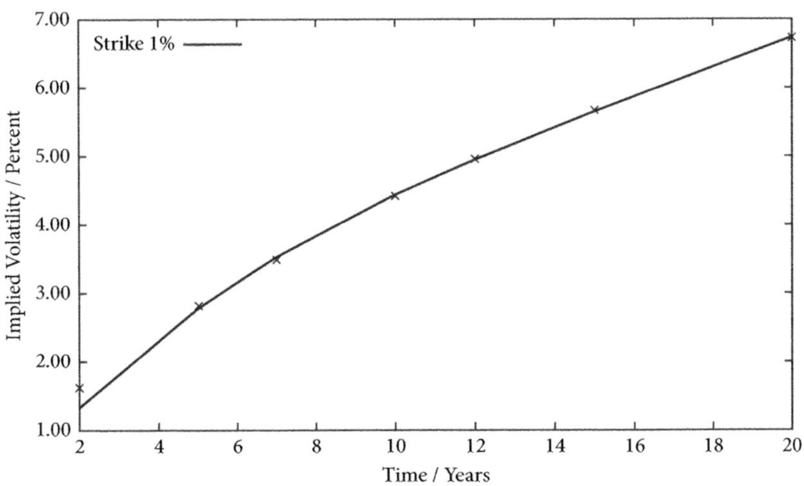

Figure 13.2 Dodgson-Kainth model calibrated to CPI floors (at strike 1%), market data as of 30 September 2014. Symbols denote volatilities implied from market prices; lines are volatilities implied from model prices

13.3.2 Foreign currency inflation

To integrate an inflation component modelled á la DK into the cross-currency setup, we need – as in the JY case – to finally consider a case where the numeraire is a *domestic* (e.g. Euro) LGM numeraire while the inflation component considered is e.g. UK or US inflation. We know the change of measure drift $\gamma_f(t)$ for the foreign nominal rate component from the IR/FX section already, and we expect – at first glance – additional drift terms $\delta(t)$ for the processes $z_I(t)$ and accordingly $y_I(t)$, respectively, when we choose the domestic LGM measure:

$$dz_f(t) = \gamma_f(t)\,dt + \alpha_f(t)\,dW_f(t) \tag{13.42}$$

$$dz_I(t) = \delta(t)\,dt + \alpha_I(t)\,dW_I(t) \tag{13.43}$$

$$dy_I(t) = H_I(t)\,\delta(t)\,dt + H_I(t)\,\alpha_I(t)\,dW_I(t) \tag{13.44}$$

$$dW_f(t)\,dW_I(t) = \rho_{fI}\,dt \tag{13.45}$$

However, to start, we compute directly the stochastic foreign currency inflation-linked bond converted into domestic currency

$$P_I(t,T) = \frac{N_d(t)}{I(t)\,x(t)}\,\mathbb{E}_t^{N_d}\left[\frac{x(T)\,I(T)}{N_d(T)}\right]$$

building on Appendix F.1 and results from Section 12.1. A straightforward but lengthy calculation (for details see Appendix F.2) yields the same form for the forward inflation index $\hat{I}(t,T) = P_I(t,T)/P_n(t,T)$ and the spot inflation index $I(t)$ as in the domestic inflation case (13.30, 13.31)

$$\hat{I}(t,T) = \frac{\hat{I}(0,T)}{\hat{I}(0,t)}\,e^{+(H_I(T)-H_I(t))\,z_I(t)+\widetilde{V}(t,T)} \tag{13.46}$$

$$I(t) = I(0)\,\hat{I}(0,t)\,e^{H_I(t)\,z_I(t)-y_I(t)-V(0,t)} \tag{13.47}$$

with

$$\widetilde{V}(t,T) = V(t,T) - V(0,T) + V(0,t)$$

and

$$\begin{aligned} V(t,T) = {} & \frac{1}{2}\int_t^T (H_I(T)-H_I(s))^2\,\alpha_I^2(s)\,ds \\ & - \rho_{dI}\int_t^T H_d(s)\,\alpha_d(s)\,(H_I(T)-H_I(s))\,\alpha_I(s)\,ds \\ & - \rho_{fI}\int_t^T (H_f(T)-H_f(s))\,\alpha_f(s)\,(H_I(T)-H_I(s))\,\alpha_I(s)\,ds \\ & + \rho_{xI}\int_t^T \sigma_x(s)\,(H_I(T)-H_I(s))\,\alpha_I(s)\,ds \end{aligned} \tag{13.48}$$

Note that $V(t,T)$ now differs from (13.22). For vanishing FX volatility $\sigma_x \equiv 0$ and identical (i.e. perfectly correlated) domestic and foreign interest rates ($H_d(t) \equiv H_f(t), \alpha_d(t) \equiv \alpha_f(t)$), the new variance (13.48) collapses to (13.22), as expected.

To determine the change of measure drift $\delta(t)$ we now analyse the foreign inflation-linked bond converted into domestic currency in units of the domestic LGM numeraire which is a martingale under the domestic LGM measure

$$M(t) = \frac{I(t)\, P_I(t,T)\, x(t)}{N_d(t)} = \underbrace{I(t)\,\frac{P_I(t,T)}{P_f(t,T)}}_{:=X(t)}\,\underbrace{\frac{P_f(t,T)\, x(t)}{N_d(t)}}_{=U(t)}$$

We know the martingale $U(t)$ and its differential $dU(t)$ already from Section 12.1, Equation (12.9). Moreover it is convenient to work with the product

$$X(t) = I(t)\,\frac{P_I(t,T)}{P_f(t,T)} = I(0)\,\hat{I}(0,T)\, e^{H_I(T)\, z_I(t) - y_I(t) + V(t,T) - V(0,T)}$$

with $\hat{I}(0,T) = P_I(0,T)/P_f(0,T)$. The program is again to compute the SDE for $M(t)$ and then claim that its drift term vanishes.

$$\begin{aligned}
\frac{dM(t)}{M(t)} &= \frac{dX}{X} + \frac{dU}{U} + \frac{1}{2}\frac{dX}{X}\frac{dU}{U} \\
&= \underbrace{m(t)}_{=0}\, dt + (\ldots)\, dW_I(t) + (\ldots)\, dW_x(t) + (\ldots)\, dW_d(t) + (\ldots)\, dW_f(t)
\end{aligned}$$

The missing bit here is the differential of $X(t)$. Applying the Ito Formula we find

$$\begin{aligned}
\frac{dX(t)}{X(t)} &= \left[\partial_t V(t,T) + [H_I(T) - H_I(t)]\,\delta(t) + \frac{1}{2}(H_I(T) - H_I(t))^2 \alpha_I^2(t)\right] dt \\
&\quad + (H_I(T) - H_I(t))\,\alpha_I(t)\, dW_I(t)
\end{aligned}$$

Moreover recall from (12.9)

$$\frac{dU(t)}{U(t)} = -H_d(t)\,\alpha_d(t)\, dW_d(t) - (H_f(T) - H_f(t))\,\alpha_f(t)\, dW_f(t) + \sigma_x(t)\, dW_x.$$

These two inputs allow collecting the drift terms in $dM(t)/M(t)$:

$$\begin{aligned}
m(t) &= \partial_t V(t,T) + \frac{1}{2}(H_I(T) - H_I(t))^2 \alpha_I^2(t) \\
&\quad + [H_I(T) - H_I(t)] \times (\delta(t) - \rho_{dI}\, H_d(t)\alpha_d(t)\alpha_I(t) + \rho_{xI}\, \sigma_x(t)\, \alpha_I(t) \\
&\quad - \rho_{fI}\left[H_f(T) - H_f(t)\right] \alpha_f(t)\, \alpha_I(t)).
\end{aligned}$$

The first term on the right-hand side is obtained by differentiating (13.48), which yields

$$\partial_t V(t,T) = [H_I(T) - H_I(t)] \times \Big(-\frac{1}{2}(H_I(T) - H_I(t))\,\alpha_I^2(t) + \rho_{dI} H_d(t)\,\alpha_d(t)\,\alpha_I(t) + \rho_{fI}(H_f(T) - H_f(t))\alpha_f(t)\,\alpha_I(t) - \rho_{xI}\sigma_x(t)\,\alpha_I(t) \Big)$$

so that all terms in $m(t)$ cancel out and we are left with

$$m(t) = [H_I(T) - H_I(t)] \times \delta(t).$$

Vanishing martingale drift $m(t) \equiv 0$ therefore implies

$$\delta(t) \equiv 0. \tag{13.49}$$

There is no need to adjust the SDE, the change of measure is fully taken into account already in the new variance expression $V(t,T)$. We could have expected this result, as we started with zero-drift SDEs for $z_I(t)$ and $y_I(t)$ and incorporated the change of measure effect into the shift function $\mu(t)$ which was then eliminated using initial conditions.

13.4 Seasonality

It is well known that the evolution of inflation indices is modulated by significant seasonal patterns. For example, December inflation tends to be higher than the annual average, or inflation during the (northern hemisphere) spring period from March to May tends to be higher than in summer from June to August [108], due to the seasonal variation of prices of goods that are constituents of the index's basket. Therefore seasonality varies between inflation indices (i.e. by region, country, basket composition) and has to be estimated from historical data for each index.

If one builds an inflation term structure (e.g. from zero coupon inflation swaps), then the available quotes are of course only given for maturities which are at least a year apart: 1Y, 2Y, 3Y, 5Y, 7Y, 10Y, etc. This curve can then be used to accurately "project" the CPI index to these annual maturities as we have discussed at the beginning of this chapter. If we need maturities in between such grid dates for pricing an inflation derivative during its life, then one has to interpolate between adjacent grid points as in the case of interest rate curves. In the case of inflation one also has to take seasonality into account, that is in addition to the usual interpolation one should superimpose a seasonality pattern to the interpolated inflation zero rates. For example, we can write the projected inflation index in terms of the continuously compounded inflation forward rate $f(t)$ as

$$I(T) = I(T_0) \exp\left(\int_{T_0}^{T} (f(u) + s(u))\, du\right), \quad s(u) = \begin{cases} s_1, & u \text{ in January} \\ \vdots & \vdots \\ s_{12}, & u \text{ in December} \end{cases}$$

where $s(t)$ is the seasonality adjustment, a piecewise constant function within a given month. This also shows that the integral over one year of adjustments should be equal to zero so that the effect for full-year swaps vanishes.

What does that mean for the simulation of inflation in the JY and DK models we discussed above? In both models we generate realizations of the future CPI index $I(t)$ as well as realizations of the forward index $\hat{I}(t,T)$. For accurate pricing under different scenarios we should therefore adjust both CPI and inflation forwards by the seasonality pattern. Assuming that this pattern is deterministic, this is a straightforward modification of the scheme.

13.5 Exposure evolution examples

We finish the chapter on inflation, as we did in the preceding ones, with typical exposure evolutions, here for a zero coupon inflation index swap in Figure 13.3 which is – not surprisingly – qualitatively similar to an FX Forward exposure evolution, due to the ZCII Swap payoff with a single index-linked payment at the end swapped for a fixed payment, where the index is driven by Geometric Brownian motion. For the next two examples, we first need to introduce another inflation index.

The LPI index

The Limited Price Indexation (LPI) is a UK specialty. It is the index used to calculate increases of components of scheme pension payments in the UK. It is based on the UK Retail Price Index (RPI), the standard inflation index that is published monthly by the Office for National Statistics, but typically capped and floored each year. The most common floor is 0%, the most common cap 5%, but there are other values possible as well. The market quotes rates for LPI swaps directly.

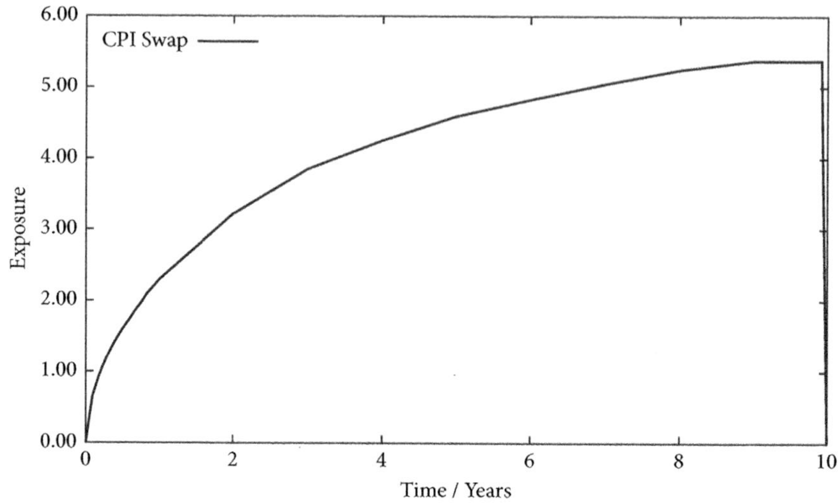

Figure 13.3 Exposure evolution for an at-the-money ZCII Swap with fixed rate 3%. Market data is as of end of March 2015; risk factor evolution model is Jarrow-Yildirim with parameters as in Table 13.6

The LPI rate for a future point in time t as of today (time 0) is defined as

$$\begin{aligned} LPI_0 &= RPI_0 \\ LPI_t &= LPI_{t-1} \cdot \min\left(\max\left(1+F, \frac{RPI_t}{RPI_{t-1}}\right), 1+C\right) \\ &= LPI_{t-1} \cdot \left[1 + \min\left(\max\left(F, \frac{RPI_t}{RPI_{t-1}} - 1\right), C\right)\right] \end{aligned}$$

where F and C are the floor and cap levels, respectively. Both the JY and the DK model, after calibration to the relevant inflation cap/floor products, can be used to price an LPI by Monte Carlo simulation.

If one is interested in the future exposure of an LPI product, that is not the best way to go because it means having to do simulations within a simulation. In the struggle between accuracy and speed it is therefore necessary to find a faster approach to LPI pricing. Such an approach was introduced by Greenwood & Svoboda [73]. It gives an analytic approximation of LPI_t using a SABR model. The SABR model was introduced by Hagan et al. in their seminal paper [80]. It is employed in [73] in the following fashion. Model the RPI forward year-on-year rate

Y_t as a normal model (i.e. $\beta = 0$), so that

$$dY_t = \alpha_t \, dW_t^1, \qquad Y_0 = y$$
$$d\alpha_t = \nu \, \alpha_t \, dW_t^2, \qquad \alpha_0 = \alpha$$

with constant correlation

$$dW_t^1 \, dW_t^2 = \rho \, dt$$

Because the YOY rate is supposed to be normal, we need the implied normal volatility for the normal Black76 Formula (C.5). It is approximated by

$$\sigma(K, y) = \alpha \, \frac{z}{\chi(z)} \left(1 + \frac{2 - 3\rho^2}{24} \, \nu^2 \, T\right)$$

with

$$z := \frac{\nu}{\alpha} \, (y - K), \quad \chi(z) := \ln\left(\frac{\sqrt{1 - 2\rho \, z + z^2} + z - \rho}{1 - \rho}\right).$$

The three parameters α_i, ν_i, ρ_i are fitted for each maturity i such that quoted YOY Caps and Floors are priced correctly. Then the caps C_i and floors F_i appearing in the payoff

$$LPI_t = LPI_0 \cdot \prod_{i=1}^{t} \left(\frac{RPI_i}{RPI_{i-1}} + F_i - C_i\right)$$

are priced individually (without taking correlations between the different RPI quotients into account).

The approximation is actually quite good; certainly good enough to use in an exposure simulation. The approach is to fit the parameters to today's market data and to keep them constant throughout the simulation.

Let us compare now the exposure evolution of a standard LPI Swap (with single LPI-linked payment at maturity swapped for a fixed payment) and compare it to a simple ZCII (CPI) Swap. Recall that LPI agrees with CPI when the cap strike is sufficiently high and the floor strike is sufficiently low (negative). Such a comparison is shown in Figure 13.4 (top) for receiver LPI Swaps with caps and floors as noted in the figure. Since these swaps receive the inflation linked payments, the introduction of caps in the LPI index lowers the exposure profile whereas a floor increases exposure (at least for short times), as expected.

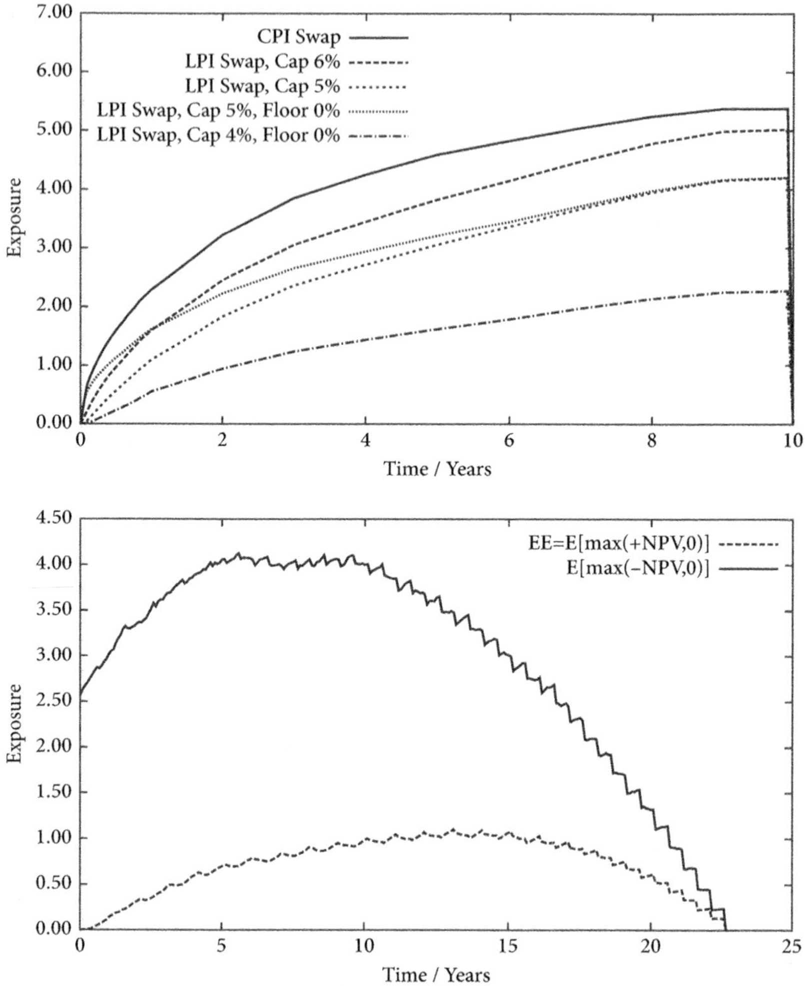

Figure 13.4 Top: comparison of exposure evolutions of a Receiver CPI Swap to Receiver LPI Swap with varying cap strike, without floor or zero floor. Bottom: exposure evolution for a bespoke inflation-linked swap, exchanging a series of LPI-linked payments $N \times LPI(t)/LPI(t_0)$ for a series of fixed payments $N \times (1+r)^{t-t_0}$, time to maturity about 22 years, annual payment amounts are broken into semi-annual payments on both legs. This can be decomposed into a series of LPI Swaps with increasing maturities. Risk factor evolution: Jarrow-Yildirim model with parameters as in Table 13.6

Finally, the bottom graph in Figure 13.4 shows the exposure evolution of a bespoke inflation-linked swap which exchanges LPI for fixed payments on a semi-annual basis rather than just at final maturity, an exposure profile that could be due to an interest rate swap at first glance.

14 Equity and Commodity

14.1 Equity

We next show how to extend the IR/FX setup to include multiple equity processes in order to cover equity derivatives. We make the simplest possible choice here and model each equity with *Geometric Brownian Motion* driven by the short rate-dividend yield differential, in analogy to the FX model of the previous section. The starting point is the equity process S_k, expressed in units of a foreign (nominal) bank account Q^{B_i}, where i denotes the currency of equity S_k:

$$dS_k(t)/S_k(t) = [n_i(t) - q_k(t)]dt + \sigma_k^S(t)\, dW_{S_k}^{B_i}(t) \tag{14.1}$$

As a first step, our aim is to derive the dynamics of S_k under the LGM numeraire Q^{N_i} by finding the drift adjustment $\phi_{S_k}^{N_i}(t)$ such that

$$dW_{S_k}^{N_i}(t) = dW_{S_k}^{B_i}(t) - \phi_{S_k}^{N_i}(t)\, dt \tag{14.2}$$

Consider the equity asset $\hat{S}_k$ (i.e. the sum of the equity price process S_k and the dividend process $q_k\, S_k$) expressed in units of foreign LGM numeraire. This is a tradable asset and as such is a martingale under the foreign LGM measure when expressed in units of the foreign LGM numeraire. Therefore the SDE given by

$$d\left(\frac{\hat{S}_k(t)}{N_i(t)}\right) = \frac{\hat{S}_k(t)}{N_i(t)}\left(\left[n_i(t) + \phi_{S_k}^{N_i}(t)\,\sigma_k^S(t) - n_i(t) + \rho_{il}^{zs}\, H_i^z(t)\,\alpha_i^z(t)\,\sigma_k^S(t)\right] dt \right.$$
$$\left. + \sigma_k^S(t)\, dW_{S_k}^{N_i}(t) - H_i^z(t)\,\alpha_i^z(t)\, dW_{z_i}^{N_{i_j}}(t)\right)$$

must have zero drift. Solving for $\phi_{S_k}^{N_i}(t)$ yields

$$\phi_{S_k}^{N_i}(t) = \rho_{il}^{zs}\, H_i^z(t)\,\alpha_i^z(t) \tag{14.3}$$

Next we derive the dynamics of S_k under the domestic LGM measure Q^{N_0} by finding the drift adjustment $\phi_{S_k}^{N_0}(t)$ such that

$$dW_{S_k}^{N_0}(t) = dW_{S_k}^{N_i}(t) - \phi_{S_k}^{N_0}(t)\,dt. \tag{14.4}$$

Firstly, inserting (14.2) and (14.3) into (14.4) yields

$$dW_{S_k}^{N_0}(t) = dW_{S_k}^{B_i}(t) - (\rho_{il}^{zs}\,H_i^z(t)\,\alpha_i^z(t) + \phi_{S_k}^{N_0}(t))dt. \tag{14.5}$$

Now, the equity asset $\hat{S}_k$, converted into *domestic* currency and expressed in units of *domestic* numeraire must be a martingale under the *domestic* LGM numeraire. Therefore the SDE given by

$$\begin{aligned}
\frac{d\left(\frac{\hat{S}_k(t)\,x_i(t)}{N_0(t)}\right)}{\frac{\hat{S}_k(t)\,x_i(t)}{N_0(t)}} &= \Big[n_i(t) + \phi_{S_k}^{N_0}(t)\,\sigma_k^S(t) + \rho_{il}^{zs}\,H_i^z(t)\,\alpha_i^z(t)\,\sigma_k^S(t) \\
&\quad + n_0(t) - n_i(t) + \rho_{0i}^{zx}\,H_0^z(t)\,\alpha_0^z(t)\,\sigma_i^x(t) \\
&\quad - n_0(t) + \rho_{il}^{xs}\,\sigma_i^x(t)\,\sigma_k^S(t) - \rho_{0l}^{zs}\,H_0^z(t)\,\alpha_0^z(t)\,\sigma_k^S(t) \\
&\quad - \rho_{0i}^{zx}\,H_0^z(t)\,\alpha_0^z(t)\,\sigma_i^x(t)\Big]dt \\
&\quad + \sigma_k^S(t)\,dW_{S_k}^{N_0}(t) + \sigma_i^x(t)\,dW_{x_i}^{N_0}(t) \\
&\quad - H_0^z(t)\,\alpha_0^z(t)\,dW_{z_0}^{N_0}(t) \\
&= \Big[\phi_{S_k}^{N_0}(t)\,\sigma_k^S(t) + \rho_{il}^{zs}\,H_i^z(t)\,\alpha_i^z(t)\,\sigma_k^S(t) \\
&\quad + \rho_{il}^{xs}\,\sigma_i^x(t)\,\sigma_k^S(t) - \rho_{0l}^{zs}\,H_0^z(t)\,\alpha_0^z(t)\,\sigma_k^S(t)\Big]dt \\
&\quad + \sigma_k^S(t)\,dW_{S_k}^{N_0}(t) + \sigma_i^x(t)\,dW_{x_i}^{N_0}(t) - H_0^z(t)\,\alpha_0^z(t)\,dW_{z_0}^{N_0}(t)
\end{aligned}$$

must be driftless. Solving for $\phi_{S_k}^{N_0}(t)$ yields

$$\phi_{S_k}^{N_0}(t) = \rho_{0l}^{zs}\,H_0^z(t)\,\alpha_0^z(t) - \rho_{il}^{zs}\,H_i^z(t)\,\alpha_i^z(t) - \rho_{il}^{xs}\,\sigma_i^x(t) \tag{14.6}$$

and inserting (14.6) and (14.5) into (14.1) gives the dynamics of S_k under the domestic LGM measure:

$$\begin{aligned}
dS_k(t)/S_k(t) &= [n_i(t) - q_k(t) + \rho_{0l}^{zs}\,H_0^z(t)\,\alpha_0^z(t)\,\sigma_k^S(t) - \epsilon_i\,\rho_{il}^{xs}\,\sigma_i^x(t)\,\sigma_k^S(t)]dt \\
&\quad + \sigma_k^S(t)\,dW_{S_k}^{N_0}(t)
\end{aligned} \tag{14.7}$$

This equity evolution model can be calibrated to the "risk-free" yield curve, the dividend yield term structure for the given equity and a selection of European equity options (such as a series of at-the-money options – using a procedure that is similar to the calibration of FX options in Section 12. The exposure evolution of a basic Equity Forward is therefore also (qualitatively) similar to that of an FX Forward which we have seen already in Section 12.5.

14.2 Commodity

In this section we explore simple modelling approaches to cover commodity derivatives. The simplest possibility is again to model spot commodity prices using *Geometric Brownian Motion (GBM)* which we have seen applied to precious metals (gold, silver, platinum, palladium, including copper) with drift determined by appropriate *lease rate curves*. For other commodities, modelling the futures/forward price instead seems to be the more common approach. Particularly popular in this context is the *Gabillon model* [67]. See also [7] where Andersen develops a framework for construction of Markov models for commodity derivatives which also covers a Markov diffusion model corresponding to Gabillon's approach.

The two-factor model and its calibration

Gabillon used the following model for the futures price $F(t,T)$ observed at time time t with delivery in T:

$$\frac{dF(t,T)}{F(t,T)} = g(T)\left(\sigma_S\, e^{-\kappa\,(T-t)}\, dW_t^S + \sigma_L\left(1 - e^{-\kappa\,(T-t)}\right) dW_t^L\right). \tag{14.8}$$

The futures price curve is driven by two factors representing shocks to the short and far long end of the curve, respectively. For $t \to T$, close to futures expiry, only the short term $\sigma_S\, dW_t^S$ is left, while for very long terms $T - t \to \infty$, long before futures expiry, only $\sigma_L\, dW_t^L$ drives $F(t,T)$, that is in fact a mix of both terms drives $F(t,T)$ for any finite time to expiry $T-t$. Parameter κ controls the "decay" of the short term factor and the "switching over" to the long term factor. The time-dependent parameter $g(T)$ that we added here to Gabillon's original model, which has constant parameters only, allows extra flexibility in calibrating the model. Overall, the dynamics are log-normal with instantaneous volatility σ_{tT}

$$\sigma_{tT}^2 = g^2(T)\left[\sigma_L^2 + (\sigma_S^2 + \sigma_L^2 - 2\,\rho\,\sigma_s\sigma_L)e^{-2\kappa(T-t)} - 2\,(\sigma_L^2 - \rho\,\sigma_S\sigma_L)\,e^{-\kappa(T-t)}\right]$$

and Black volatility Σ_{tT}

$$\Sigma_{tT}^2 = \frac{1}{T-t}\int_t^T \sigma_{sT}^2\, ds. \tag{14.9}$$

The model is typically calibrated to the futures price curve as initial values $F(0,T)$. Parameter $g(T)$ can be used to achieve a perfect match with at-the-money futures options. This leaves the constant parameters $(\sigma_S, \sigma_L, \kappa, \rho)$ to be determined by either matching selected exotics (such as Asian options or commodity swaptions) or by fitting empirical covariances of futures prices with different expiries. We will explore the latter possibility now.

Historical commodity price data is available for long periods. For example, the UBS Constant Maturity Commodity Index (CMCI) family covers 28 commodity futures contracts representing the energy, precious metals, industrial metals, agricultural and livestock sectors [140]. It provides daily futures price fixings back to 1997 for expiries from three months up to three years (e.g. 3M, 6M, 1Y, 2Y, 3Y) from each date in the time series. This allows constructing an empirical covariance matrix for each sector by computing

$$V_{ij}^* = \frac{1}{\tau}\sum_{k=1}^{m} \ln\frac{F(t_k, t_k+\tau_i)}{F(t_{k-1}, t_{k-1}+\tau_i)}\,\ln\frac{F(t_k, t_k+\tau_j)}{F(t_{k-1}, t_{k-1}+\tau_j)}, \qquad \tau = t_m - t_0,$$

where indices $i, j = 1, \ldots, 5$ label the available contract expiries. On the other hand one can compute the corresponding model-implied covariance matrix (setting $g(T) = 1$)

$$\begin{aligned}
V_{ij} &= \frac{1}{\tau}\int_t^{t+\tau} \frac{dF(s,s+\tau_i)\, dF(s,s+\tau_j)}{F(s,s+\tau_i)\, F(s,s+\tau_j)} \\
&= \frac{1}{\tau}\int_t^{t+\tau} \left(\sigma_S\, e^{-\kappa\,\tau_i}\, dW_s^S + \sigma_L\left(1-e^{-\kappa\,\tau_i}\right) dW_s^L\right) \\
&\quad \times \left(\sigma_S\, e^{-\kappa\,\tau_j}\, dW_s^S + \sigma_L\left(1-e^{-\kappa\,\tau_j}\right) dW_s^L\right) ds \\
&= \sigma_S^2\, e^{-\kappa(\tau_i+\tau_j)} + \sigma_L^2\left(1-e^{-\kappa\,\tau_i}\right)\left(1-e^{-\kappa\,\tau_j}\right) \\
&\quad + \rho\,\sigma_S\sigma_L\left(e^{-\kappa\tau_i} + e^{-\kappa\tau_j} - 2\,e^{-\kappa(\tau_i+\tau_j)}\right)
\end{aligned}$$

The model parameters $(\sigma_S, \sigma_L, \kappa, \rho)$ can then be chosen such that the square deviation $\sum_{i,j}(V_{ij} - V_{ij}^*)^2$ between empirical and model-implied covariances is minimized.

To tailor the model then to a particular commodity in the sector, one can adjust $g(T)$ for each available futures option contract expiry T so that model Black volatility Σ_T (which contains $g(T)$ as a multiplicative factor) matches the market quoted volatilities of futures options for this commodity.

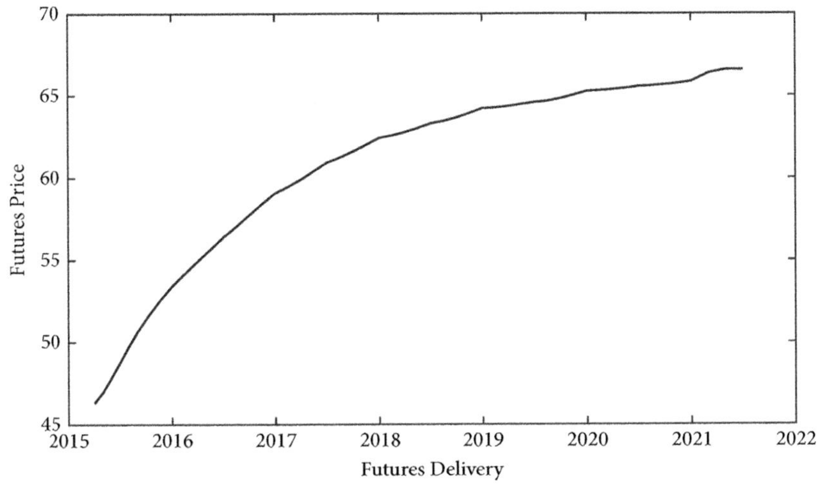

Figure 14.1 Crude Oil WTI futures prices as of 22 January 2015

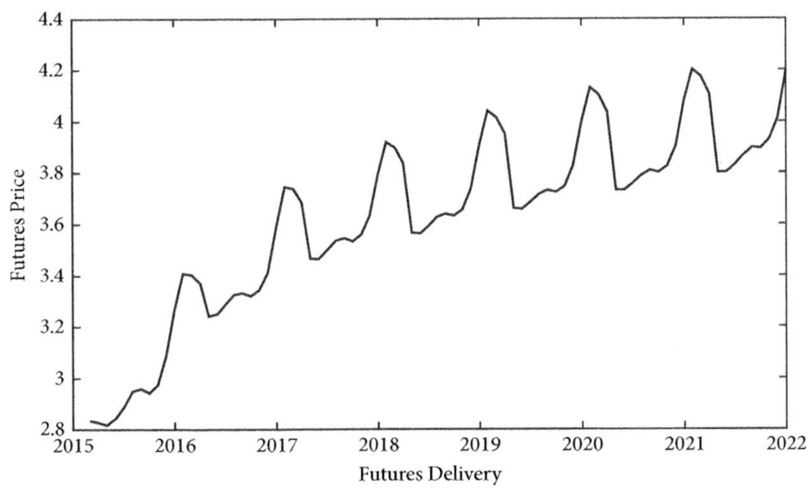

Figure 14.2 Natural Gas futures prices as of 22 January 2015

Figures 14.1 and 14.2 show typical commodity futures curves with less (oil) or more (gas) pronounced seasonality impact. Futures options implied volatilities are quoted by multiplicative strike (0.2–0.4 times ATM strike) and by option expiry (monthly). The underlying future contract is assumed to mature at expiry, that is $T_1 = T_2$.

Propagation

In order to propagate a particular futures price $F(t,T)$, it is convenient to express the futures curve dynamics in terms of an artificial 2-d spot price process

$$S_t = A(t)\exp\left(B(t)\left(X_1(t)+X_2(t)\right)\right), \qquad F(t,T) = \mathbb{E}_t[S(T)]$$

where $X_i(t)$ follow Ornstein-Uhlenbeck processes starting at $X_i(0)=0$

$$\begin{aligned} dX_1(t) &= -\kappa\, X_1(t)\, dt + \sigma_1(t)\, dW_1(t) \\ dX_2(t) &= \sigma_2(t)\, dW_2(t) \\ dW_1(t)\, dW_2(t) &= \rho_{12}\, dt \end{aligned} \tag{14.10}$$

in the risk-neutral measure of the commodity currency with

$$\begin{aligned} \sigma_1^2(t) &= \alpha^2(t)\left(\sigma_S^2+\sigma_L^2-2\rho\,\sigma_S\sigma_L\right) \\ \sigma_2^2(t) &= \alpha^2(t)\,\sigma_L^2 \\ \rho_{12} &= \frac{\sigma_S\,\rho-\sigma_L}{\sigma_1(t)/\alpha(t)} \end{aligned}$$

The conditional futures curve in terms of variables $X_{1,2}(t)$ then reads

$$\begin{aligned} F(t,T) = F(0,T)\exp\Big[g(T)\left(X_1(t)\,e^{-\kappa(T-t)}+X_2(t)\right) \\ -\frac{1}{2}\,g^2(T)\left(V(0,T)-V(t,T)\right)\Big] \end{aligned}$$

with the variance of log-returns of futures prices

$$\begin{aligned} V(t,T) &= \int_t^T \sigma_2^2\, ds + e^{-2\kappa T}\int_t^T \sigma_1^2\, e^{2\kappa s}\, ds + 2\rho_{12}\, e^{-\kappa T}\int_t^T \sigma_1\sigma_2\, e^{\kappa s}\, ds \\ &= \sigma_2^2\,(T-t) + \sigma_1^2\,\frac{1-e^{-2\kappa(T-t)}}{2\kappa} + 2\rho_{12}\sigma_1\sigma_2\,\frac{1-e^{-\kappa(T-t)}}{\kappa} \end{aligned}$$

This matches with the Black variance $(T-t)\cdot\Sigma_{tT}^2$ in (14.9) for $g(T)=1$, ensures $F(t,T)$ is a martingale, and satisfies the initial condition $F(0,T)$. The Ornstein-Uhlenbeck processes are propagated as usual using

$$X_1(t)-X_1(s) = -X_1(s)\left(1-e^{-\kappa(t-s)}\right) + \int_s^t \sigma_1(\tau)\, e^{-\kappa(t-\tau)}\, dW_1(\tau)$$

$$X_2(t)-X_2(s) = \int_s^t \sigma_2(\tau)\, dW_2(\tau)$$

15 Credit

To cover CVA calculations for netting sets including credit derivatives as well as to deal with wrong-way risk or the full bilateral CVA/DVA formula (8.4), we have to model "credit worthiness" as we model other market factors such as interest, foreign exchange or inflation rates. Our aim in this section is to analyse a few model candidates that allow evolving stochastic "creditworthiness" through time and to evaluate credit-linked products (such as Credit Default Swaps) under such scenarios, so that we can build consistent exposure profiles through time for such products and net them with the remainder of the netting set.

This text is not meant as a thorough introduction into modelling and pricing credit risk. For such an introduction refer for example to the text books by Schönbucher [131] or Brigo and Mercurio [33]. Nevertheless, we introduce a few fundamental terms before we start exploring a selection of models. Creditworthiness is typically expressed by means of the *probability of default (PD)* and the *loss given default (LGD)*, the latter being the complement of the *recovery rate (RR = 1 − LGD)*. The *expected loss (EL)* is the product of the two. The complement of PD is the *survival probability (SP)*, i.e. PD = 1 − SP. We will use both terms in parallel, but more often SP which will be labelled $S(t)$ in formulas. Both PD/SP and LGD can be assumed stochastic, but the approaches we will present in this section will only treat PD/SP as stochastic while LGD is kept deterministic, being a constant or – at best – a deterministic function of time. PDs can be expressed in terms of various "helpers" such as *hazard rates (HR)*, also called default intensities and labelled $\lambda(t)$, or *default densities (DD)*, labelled $\rho(t)$ in the following. The relation between SP and HR/DD is

$$S(t) = e^{-\int_0^t \lambda(s)\,ds} = 1 - \int_0^t \rho(s)\,ds.$$

In the expression for $S(t)$ above, $\lambda(t)$ is a deterministic function of time. The key generalization is now to assume that $\lambda(t)$ is a stochastic process instead, that is default intensity is a random number at any point in time. First, this means that $S(t)$ above is now a random variable as well – it is the survival probability up to time t on a given path/realization of $\lambda(\cdot)$ up to time t. Its expectation (average over many scenarios) has to be matched with the market's view on what the survival probability up to time t is for a given name or entity. Let us refer to this market survival probability as $S^M(t)$. Then we claim that

$$S^M(t) = \mathbb{E}\left[e^{-\int_0^t \lambda(s)\,ds}\right]$$

where the expectation is taken under the *standard market filtration* excluding information on defaults, see Section 8.1, that is assuming survival up to today $(t=0)$. We can generalize a bit further and define the *conditional survival probability*

$$S(t,T) = \mathbb{E}_t\left[e^{-\int_t^T \lambda(s)\,ds}\right], \qquad S(0,T) = S^M(T), \tag{15.1}$$

conditional on survival up to time t in the future, that is using the standard market filtration up to time t. The expression looks just like the conditional zero bond price for maturity T computed in the bank account measure

$$P(t,T) = \mathbb{E}_t\left[e^{-\int_t^T r(s)\,ds}\right], \tag{15.2}$$

where we swapped the short rate $r(t)$ with $\lambda(t)$, a fact that will allow us to employ short rate models for the hazard rate. Note that $S(t,T)$ is a random variable for $t > 0$.

In the models that we will consider, the randomness will enter into $S(t,T)$ at the level of the hazard rate λ at time t, that is (15.1) will have the form $S(t,T,\lambda)$. Moreover, $S(t,T,\lambda)$ will be a monotonically decreasing function of λ.

The equivalence between (15.1) and (15.2) can be explored, that is one can pick short rate models developed for the interest rate space to apply them to credit "space". This is the reason why numerous practitioners and academics have used the hazard rate as a starting point for *dynamic* credit modelling, and we will follow this approach for now.

For the purpose of CVA/DVA calculation we are looking for a model that

- easily integrates with the models chosen so far for interest rate, foreign exchange and inflation asset classes;
- can be calibrated quickly to market quoted instruments, see next section;
- is – preferably – as analytically tractable as the models we have seen so far.

15.1 Market

Any of the models we shall consider will have to be calibrated to market-quoted instruments. The analogous instruments to interest rate swaps and European swaptions we used in Section 11.1 are *Credit Default Swaps (CDS)* and *Credit Default Swap Options (CDSO)*.[1] Let us introduce some notation for these two products which will be applied across all subsequent sections.

A *Credit Default Swap* is an insurance contract: the protection buyer pays a premium cash flow – a constant so-called spread K on the notional – to the protection seller until contract maturity or until the default event happens. Conversely, the protection buyer receives a single loss amount when the default event happens. The premium cash flows span a time grid of premium periods. To value a CDS (at time t), it is common to assume that the default – if it happens – occurs in the middle of such a premium period. In this *mid-point approximation* we can write the value of the CDS at time t as follows (unit notional, protection seller perspective):

$$
\begin{aligned}
\mathrm{CDS}(t) = \mathbb{1}_{\{\tau>t\}} \Bigg\{ & \sum_{i=1}^{n} K\,\delta_i\, S(t,t_i)\, P(t,t_i) \\
& - \sum_{i=1}^{n} \left(LGD - K\frac{\delta_i}{2} \right) \left(S(t,t_{i-1}) - S(t,t_i) \right) P\left(t, \frac{t_{i-1}+t_i}{2} \right) \Bigg\}
\end{aligned} \tag{15.3}
$$

What does this mean? The first line is the premium leg value where K is the premium rate, δ_i is the year fraction of period i, $S(t,t_i)$ is the survival probability up to cash flow time t_i as seen at valuation time t, and $P(t,t_i)$ is the discount factor (zero bond price) for cash flow time t_i as seen at valuation time t. The overall indicator factor $\mathbb{1}_{\{\tau>t\}}$ means that the CDS value is zero if the default occurred at default time τ before valuation time t.[2] The second line reflects the protection leg value as an aggregation over potential defaults in each interest period: if default happens, the protection seller pays the LGD (times notional), but receives half of the premium (the accrued spread for the time up to default in the middle of the period); the cash flow is discounted back from the middle of the period where the default occurs, and each flow is weighted with the probability of default in this period $PD(t_{i-1},t_i) = S(t_{i-1}) - S(t_i)$. We can now rearrange the terms and write the CDS value as a sum over survival probabilities $S(t_i)$:

$$
\begin{aligned}
\mathrm{CDS}(t) &= \mathbb{1}_{\{\tau>t\}} \sum_{i=1}^{n} \left\{ (C_i + D_i)\, S(t,t_i) - C_i\, S(t,t_{i-1}) \right\} \\
&= \mathbb{1}_{\{\tau>t\}} \sum_{i=0}^{n} G_i\, S(t,t_i)
\end{aligned}
$$

[1] Note, however, that the CDSO market is by no means as liquid as the European Swaption market.

[2] We have to explicitly multiply by the default indicator because the standard market filtration does not include the default information, and $S(t,T)$ assumes survival up to time t.

where

$$C_i = \left(LGD - K\frac{\delta_i}{2}\right) P\left(t, \frac{t_{i-1}+t_i}{2}\right) > 0, \qquad i = 1, ..., n$$

$$D_i = K\,\delta_i\, P(t,t_i) > 0, \qquad i = 1, ..., n$$

$$G_0 = -C_1 < 0$$

$$G_i = C_i + D_i - C_{i+1} > 0, \qquad i = 1, ..., n-1$$

$$G_n = C_n + D_n > 0$$

This compact bond-like representation will be convenient in what follows.

A *Credit Default Swap Option* is a European option on a CDS. Traded CDS options are typically limited to index underlyings such as the CDS indices iTraxx/ CDX investment grade and high yield. The underlying term is then 5Y only, and option expiries are short term, typically less than a year. The CDS option "market" therefore only gives a limited view at market-implied credit spread volatility so far. A CDS option payoff at expiry t is the positive part of the underlying CDS price at expiry, so that we can write a CDSO value – in the t-forward measure – as follows

$$\begin{aligned}\mathrm{CDSO} &= \mathbb{E}\left[(\mathrm{CDS}(t))^+\right] \\ &= \mathbb{E}\left[e^{-\int_0^t \lambda_s\, ds}\left[\omega \sum_{i=0}^{n} G_i\, S(t,t_i,\lambda_t)\right]^+\right],\end{aligned}$$

where $\omega = \pm 1$ switches between protection seller and buyer CDS underylings.

Since $S(t,t_i,\lambda_t)$ is a monotonic function of λ_t, we can apply – as in the analogous interest rate cases – the Jamshidian decomposition here: Compute the root λ_t^* of the term in brackets:

$$\sum_{i=0}^{n} G_i\, S(t,t_i;\lambda_t^*) = 0 \quad \Leftrightarrow \quad G_0 = -\sum_{i=1}^{n} G_i \frac{S(t,t_i;\lambda_t^*)}{S(t,t_0;\lambda_t^*)}$$

This root is unique because $S(t,T,\lambda)$ is a monotonic function of λ, G_0 is negative, and all other coefficients G_i are positive. Then eliminate G_0 and assume that expiry

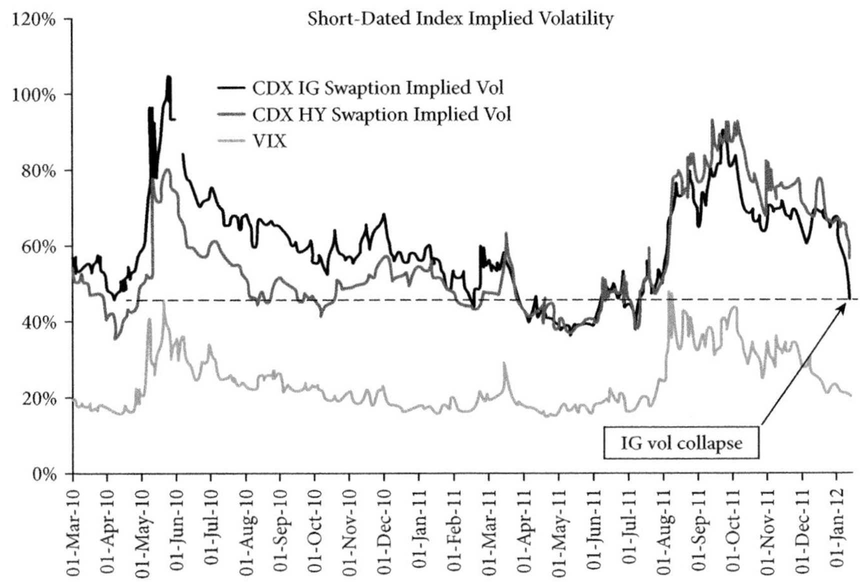

Figure 15.1 History of short-dated index implied volatility since 2010 for options on CDX IG and HY, in comparison to VIX. Source: Credit Suisse, http://soberlook.com/2012/01/cdx-ig-swaption-vol-finally-followed.html

coincides with the first period's start, $t = t_0$, so that $S(t, t_0, \lambda) = 1$:

$$
\begin{aligned}
\text{CDSO} &= \mathbb{E}\left[e^{-\int_0^t \lambda_s ds}\left[\omega \sum_{i=1}^{n} G_i\left(S(t, t_i; \lambda_t) - S(t, t_i; \lambda_t^*)\right)\right]^+\right] \\
&= \mathbb{E}\left[e^{-\int_0^t \lambda_s ds} \sum_{i=1}^{n} G_i\left[\omega\left(S(t, t_i; \lambda_t) - S(t, t_i; \lambda_t^*)\right)\right]^+\right] \\
&= \sum_{i=1}^{n} G_i \underbrace{\mathbb{E}\left[e^{-\int_0^t \lambda_s ds}\left[\omega\left(S(t, t_i; \lambda_t) - S(t, t_i; \lambda_t^*)\right)\right]^+\right]}_{=:E_i}
\end{aligned}
\qquad (15.4)
$$

where the last step – swapping sum and expectation (Jamshidian decomposition) – is permissible again because of the monotonicity of $S(t, T; \lambda_t)$: the terms in the sum are all either zero, positive or negative. This shows that in order to value a CDSO we need to tackle expectations E_i only, each of which is the equivalent of a zero bond option price in the interest rate space. If this is available in closed form, the CDSO pricing is almost analytic (except for searching the root λ_t^*), a fact which facilitates model calibration significantly.

To state more precisely the requirement for the chosen model, let us have a brief look at the market history in terms of implied CDS option volatilities. Figure 15.1 shows an evolution of implied volatilities for at-the-money index CDS options with 6M expiry and 5Y term for a two-year period from early 2010. The implied volatilities σ in the latter figure are Black volatilities, that is related at-the-money CDS option prices (for unit notional and time to expiry t, six months) are computed using the Black76 formula (C.3) as

$$NPV = \bar{A}(t,T)\,\text{Black}(\omega, F, F, \sigma\sqrt{t}), \tag{15.5}$$

$$\bar{A}(t,T) = \sum_{i=1}^{n} \delta_i\, P(0,t_i)\, S(0,t_i), \quad t = t_0, \quad T = t_n,$$

where again $\omega = \pm 1$ (which sign is irrelevant here as the option is at-the-money) and F is the fair CDS premium for a 5Y-CDS starting at time t_e (see also Brigo & Mercurio [33]). Because of its similarity to the annuity factor for interest rate swaps $\bar{A}$ is sometimes called the *risky annuity*. If it is chosen as numeraire, a Black76 formula for the CDS option price (15.5) can be derived using the change of numeraire toolkit from Appendix A. Conversely, when we compute model-implied black volatilities, we will use this Black pricing formula to back out σ associated with a model NPV.

In particular the options on investment grade CDS (with relatively low spreads up to around 200 bp) but high implied volatilities (above 100% in crisis times) can turn out to be challenging to calibrate to, for different reasons we will discuss in the following sections.

We now switch to the consideration of a number of model candidates, starting with the simplest possible choice.

15.2 Gaussian model

To start, let us assume that

- the hazard rate follows a Hull-White process in the bank account measure

$$d\lambda(t) = a(\theta(t) - \lambda(t))\,dt + \sigma_v(t)\,dW^Q(t) \tag{15.6}$$

- interest rates are deterministic.

Copying from Appendix D, we immediately get the result for the conditional survival probability

$$
\begin{aligned}
S(t,T) &= \mathbb{E}^Q\left[e^{-\int_t^T \lambda(s)\,ds}\right] \\
&= \frac{S(0,T)}{S(0,t)} e^{-H_a(T-t)\,v(t)-\frac{1}{2}\int_0^t \left[H_a^2(T-s)-H_a^2(t-s)\right]\sigma_v^2(s)\,ds}
\end{aligned}
$$

where $H_a(t) = (1 - \exp(-at))/a$, and v is a Gaussian random variable with zero mean and variance $\int_0^t e^{-2a(t-s)}\sigma_v^2(s)\,ds$.

This model is calibrated to the term structure of survival probabilities (e.g. implied from CDS) by construction, and we could go ahead and compute CDS option prices in this model in order to calibrate the model's volatility parameters a and σ_v. But that is inconvenient for the same reasons we have seen in the interest rate section – it amounts to solving a two-dimensional option pricing problem.

Alternatively, we may apply the LGM machinery from Section 11.1 to model $\lambda(t)$. We can then re-use previous results of Section 11.1, including option prices without the need to derive anything from scratch. In summary, this means

$$
\begin{aligned}
\lambda_t &= \lambda_t^M + \dot{H}_t\, z_t + \dot{H}_t\, H_t\, \zeta_t \\
dz_t &= \alpha_t\, dW_t, \qquad z_0 = 0 \qquad\qquad (15.7) \\
S(t,T,z_t) &= \frac{S(0,T)}{S(0,t)} \exp\left(-(H_T - H_t)\, z_t - \frac{1}{2}(H_T^2 - H_t^2)\zeta_t\right) \\
N(t) &= \frac{1}{S(0,t)} \exp\left(H_t\, z_t + \frac{1}{2} H_t^2 \zeta_t\right)
\end{aligned}
$$

where we have switched to using z_t rather than λ_t as a random factor. λ_t^M is the market hazard rate, the equivalent of the instantaneous forward rate in interest rate space. It is connected to the market survival probability curve via

$$
\lambda_t^M = -\frac{\partial \ln S(0,t)}{\partial t}.
$$

The expectation E_i in (15.4) is then computed in the $N(t)$-measure rather than the measure associated with numeraire $\exp(-\int_0^t \lambda_s ds)$, and we can copy the result from

Section 11.2.1:

$$\begin{aligned} E_i &= \mathbb{E}^N\left[\left[\omega\,\frac{S(t,t_i,z)-K_i}{N(t)}\right]^+\right], \qquad K_i = S(t,t_i,z_t^*) \\ &= S(0,t)\,\Phi(d_+) - S(0,t)\,K\,\Phi(d_-) \\ d_\pm &= \frac{1}{\Sigma}\left(\ln\frac{S(0,T)}{K_i\,S(0,t)} \pm \frac{1}{2}\Sigma^2\right), \qquad \Sigma^2 = (H_T - H_t)^2\,\zeta_t \end{aligned}$$

This is all we need in order to calibrate the model to the market survival probability curve $S(0,t)$ and quoted CDS options. But note again that in copying the results above we have made the assumption that interest rates are *deterministic*. Otherwise, taking the expectation above would still be a two-dimensional task. Assuming deterministic rates *for the purpose of calibrating the hazard rate model* is quite common to our knowledge, as the stochastic interest rate only has a minor impact on CDS option prices, see for example the analysis in [33].

Domestic currency credit: interest rate–credit correlation

To fit credit spread dynamics into the cross-currency setting for exposure simulation, we have to face the fact that interest rates are stochastic and that there may be a non-zero correlation between interest rate and hazard rate moves. We will start with the single currency case and, similar to Schönbucher [131], we will start with a two-factor Gaussian model. For the interest rate part we will use the domestic LGM, and for the hazard rate part we first use the Hull-White model

$$dz_n = \alpha_n(t)\,dW_n^N(t) \tag{15.8}$$

$$d\lambda(t) = a\,(\theta(t) - \lambda(t))\,dt + \sigma_\lambda(t)\,dW_\lambda^N(t) + \gamma\,(t)\,dt, \tag{15.9}$$

where we have chosen the domestic (interest rate) LGM measure, hence the change of measure drift $\gamma\,(t)$ in the second equation.

The simplest credit-linked interest rate product is a defaultable zero bond which pays 1 at maturity T if no default occurs before T, and zero otherwise (zero recovery). This product combines interest rate and credit dynamics. In the two-factor Gaussian case we can compute its future value in closed form which makes it a useful tool for exploring interest rate–credit modelling.

The defaultable bond price at time t can be written

$$P^{def}(t,T) = \mathbb{E}_t^N\left[e^{-\int_t^T \lambda_s\,ds}\,\frac{N(t)}{N(T)}\right]. \tag{15.10}$$

where $N(t)$ is the LGM numeraire of the interest rate process. Now note that the SDE (15.8,15.9) has just the same form of the Dodgson-Kainth model

(13.18,13.19), and the defaultable bond above has the same form as the inflation-indexed zero bond (13.20) except for the sign in front of the integral. We can therefore copy from the Dodgson-Kainth section to state the result[3] in terms of the ratio of defaultable to credit-risk-free zero bond

$$\widetilde{S}(t,T) = \frac{P^{def}(t,T)}{P_n(t,T)} = \frac{\widetilde{S}(0,T)}{\widetilde{S}(0,t)}\, e^{-(H_\lambda(T)-H_\lambda(t))\, z_\lambda(t)+\widetilde{V}(t,T)} \tag{15.11}$$

$$S(t) = S(0)\,\widetilde{S}(0,t)\, e^{-H_\lambda(t)\, z_\lambda(t)+y_\lambda(t)+V(0,t)} \tag{15.12}$$

with

$$z_\lambda(t) = \int_0^t \alpha_\lambda(s)\, dW_\lambda(s)$$

$$y_\lambda(t) = \int_0^t H_\lambda(s)\, \alpha_\lambda(s)\, dW_\lambda(s)$$

and

$$\begin{aligned}
\widetilde{V}(t,T) =& -\frac{1}{2}\left(H_\lambda^2(T) - H_\lambda^2(t)\right) \zeta_\lambda(t,0) \\
& + (H_\lambda(T) - H_\lambda(t))\, \zeta_\lambda(t,1) \\
& - (H_n(T)\, H_\lambda(T) - H_n(t)\, H_\lambda(t))\, \zeta_{n\lambda}(t,0) \\
& + (H_n(T) - H_n(t))\, \zeta_{n\lambda}(t,1) \\
V(0,t) =& \frac{1}{2} H_\lambda^2(t)\, \zeta_\lambda(t,0) - H_\lambda(t)\, \zeta_\lambda(t,1) + \frac{1}{2}\zeta_\lambda(t,2) \\
& - H_n(t)\, H_\lambda(t)\, \zeta_{n\lambda}(t,0) + H_n(t)\, \zeta_{n\lambda}(t,1) \\
\zeta_\lambda(t,k) =& \int_0^t H_\lambda^k(s)\, \alpha_\lambda^2(s)\, ds \\
\zeta_{n\lambda}(t,k) =& \rho^{n\lambda} \int_0^t H_\lambda^k(s)\, \alpha_n(s)\, \alpha_\lambda(s)\, ds.
\end{aligned}$$

Foreign currency credit

To fit foreign currency credit-linked assets into the Monte Carlo framework, the credit processes will get adjusted for credit-FX and credit-domestic interest rate correlation. This follows because we now have to consider a defaultable bond

[3] Compare to the inflation-linked zero bond in (13.23) and its derivation. To state the result for the defaultable bond price we have switched signs in front of z_λ and in $\widetilde{V}(t,T)$ appropriately.

denominated in a foreign currency, converted into domestic currency:

$$P_f^{def}(t,T) = \mathbb{E}_t^{N_d}\left[\exp\left(-\int_t^T \lambda_s\,ds\right)\frac{x(T)}{x(t)}\frac{N_d(t)}{N_d(T)}\right], \tag{15.13}$$

so that

$$M(t) = \frac{S(t)\,P_f^{def}(t,T)\,x(t)}{N_d(t)}$$

is a martingale in the domestic LGM measure. If we compute (15.13) directly, then the martingale property above is ensured by construction, since

$$\begin{aligned}
\mathbb{E}^{N_d}[M(t)] &= \mathbb{E}^{N_d}\left[\frac{S(t)\,P_f^{def}(t,T)\,x(t)}{N_d(t)}\right]\\
&= \mathbb{E}^{N_d}\left[S(t)\,\mathbb{E}_t^{N_d}\left[\exp\left(-\int_t^T \lambda_s\,ds\right)\frac{x(T)}{N_d(T)}\right]\right]\\
&= \mathbb{E}^{N_d}\left[\exp\left(-\int_0^T \lambda_s\,ds\right)\frac{x(T)}{N_d(T)}\right]\\
&= x(0)\,P_f^{def}(0,T)\\
&= M(0)
\end{aligned}$$

As in the domestic currency credit case we can copy results from the Dodgson-Kainth model Section 13.3.2, Equations (13.46–13.48) while switching labels and signs appropriately:

$$\widetilde{S}(t,T) = \frac{P^{def}(t,T)}{P_n(t,T)} = \frac{\widetilde{S}(0,T)}{\widetilde{S}(0,t)}\,e^{-(H_\lambda(T)-H_\lambda(t))\,z_\lambda(t)+\widetilde{V}(t,T)} \tag{15.14}$$

$$S(t) = S(0)\,\widetilde{S}(0,t)\,e^{-H_\lambda(t)\,z_\lambda(t)+y_\lambda(t)-V(0,t)} \tag{15.15}$$

with

$$\widetilde{V}(t,T) = V(t,T) - V(0,T) + V(0,t)$$

and

$$\begin{aligned}
V(t,T) &= \frac{1}{2}\int_t^T (H_\lambda(T)-H_\lambda(s))^2\,\alpha_\lambda^2(s)\,ds \\
&\quad + \rho_{d\lambda}\int_t^T H_d(s)\,\alpha_d(s)\,(H_\lambda(T)-H_\lambda(s))\,\alpha_\lambda(s)\,ds
\end{aligned} \tag{15.16}$$

$$+\rho_{f\lambda}\int_t^T (H_f(T)-H_f(s))\,\alpha_f(s)\,(H_\lambda(T)-H_\lambda(s))\,\alpha_\lambda(s)\,ds$$
$$-\rho_{x\lambda}\int_t^T \sigma_x(s)\,(H_\lambda(T)-H_\lambda(s))\,\alpha_\lambda(s)\,ds$$

The change of measure to the domestic LGM affects the variance function $V(t,T)$ only, and the SDEs remain drift-free, that is

$$z_\lambda(t)=\int_0^t \alpha_\lambda(s)\,dW_\lambda(s)$$
$$y_\lambda(t)=\int_0^t H_\lambda(s)\,\alpha_\lambda(s)\,dW_\lambda(s).$$

Moving the change of measure effect into variance $V(t,T)$ and keeping the SDE drift-free is handy in the credit case: it is quite common that companies issue bonds in more than one "home" currency. Accordingly, one finds CDS in for example EUR and USD referencing the same entity. With our approach above it is sufficient to propagate only *a single* pair $(z_\lambda(t),y_\lambda(t))$ per credit entity and use these paths with different $\widetilde{S}(t,T)$ and $S(t)$ depending on currency.

15.2.1 Conclusion

The Gaussian credit model is attractive because it integrates seamlessly into the Monte Carlo framework and yields an entirely analytically tractable cross-asset risk factor evolution model. It allows closed form pricing of CDS, semi-analytical pricing of CDS options with non-zero correlation between interest rates and credit spreads. Unfortunately it allows for negative future hazard rates and negative future fair CDS spreads, and mean reversion provides only limited control over this undesirable feature. Therefore we inevitably have to explore models that avoid negative spreads or allow better control over these.

15.3 Cox-Ingersoll-Ross model

The Gaussian modelling approach of the previous section is analytically tractable and fits well into the framework developed so far. However, it suffers from the general drawback that hazard rates can become negative in the model, although this is not possible in reality.[4] When credit spread volatility is high and spread levels are low – as happened in particular for investment grade CDS during the financial

[4] In contrast to interest rates where negative rates are possible and "normal" rate models are now even required for some currencies such as CHF or EUR in the current low interest rate environment.

crisis following the Lehman shock in 2008 – then the probability of hazard rates assuming negative values can become significant. Therefore one should – in our opinion – at least consider alternative models for comparison which do not allow negative hazard rates, or where it is possible to control the probability of negative hazard rates in some way. The models of this section and the following Sections 15.4 and 15.5 have this property. In the following we will explore these credit models "in isolation", that is *assuming zero correlation with the domestic interest rate process.* This does not exclude the possibility of non-zero correlation to any other process such as non-domestic interest rates, foreign exchange rates, inflation rates, equity and commodity prices.

We start this tour with the Cox-Ingersoll-Ross model (CIR) and its jump extension, because it has the additional advantage of being analytically tractable.

15.3.1 CIR without jumps

Let us ignore jumps initially and review what is well known [33, 54, 65, 66]. The *Extended Cox-Ingersoll-Ross model (CIR++)* for the hazard rate λ can be formulated as follows:

$$\lambda(t) = y(t) + \psi(t)$$
$$dy(t) = a(\theta - y(t))\,dt + \sigma_\lambda\,\sqrt{y(t)}\,dW^Q(t),$$

where $y(t)$ follows a standard CIR process and the deterministic function $\psi(t)$ allows calibration to the current hazard rate curve as for example implied from CDS. From the literature, we see that

- Square root process y does not "touch" the origin if $\epsilon = 2a\theta/\sigma^2 > 1$ (Feller constraint)[5]
- Hazard rate $\lambda(t)$ remains positive with additional constraints for the model parameters
- There are closed-form expressions for the probability density $p(t,\lambda)$ and the stochastic survival probability $S(t,T)$, conditional on survival up to time t, in affine form.

The *probability density* of y in the measure associated with numeraire $N(t) = \exp\left(\int_0^t y(s)\,ds\right)$ is given by a non-central chi-square distribution with ν degrees of

[5] If the Feller constraint is satisfied, density at the origin remains finite. Otherwise density diverges, and finite cumulative probability "piles up" close to the origin such that $\mathbb{P}[y(t) < \bar{y}]$ does not vanish for any $\bar{y} > 0$.

freedom and non-centrality parameter n:

$$\rho(y,t|y_0) = c \cdot \rho_{\chi^2}(c \cdot y; \nu, n)$$

with

$$c = \frac{4a}{\sigma^2\,(1-e^{-at})}, \qquad \nu = \frac{4\,a\theta}{\sigma^2}, \qquad n = c\,y_0\,e^{-at}$$

The expected value of $y(t)$ reverts to θ in the long-term limit:

$$\mathbb{E}[y(t)] = y_0\,e^{-at} + \theta\left(1-e^{-at}\right) \longrightarrow \theta$$

and the mean reversion moreover causes a stable long-term hazard rate variance rather than unlimited growth:

$$\mathbb{V}[y(t)] = y_0\,\frac{\sigma^2}{\theta}\left(e^{-at}-e^{-2at}\right) + \frac{\theta\sigma^2}{2\,a}\left(1-e^{-2at}\right)^2 \longrightarrow \frac{\theta\sigma^2}{2\,a} = \frac{\theta^2}{\epsilon}$$

Note that the relative variance of the hazard rate distribution scales – in the long-term limit – like

$$\frac{\mathbb{V}[y(t)]}{\mathbb{E}^2[y(t)]} \to \frac{1}{\epsilon}.$$

This shows that the constraint $\epsilon > 1$ leads to a limited "relative variance" of the hazard rate distribution. Figure 15.2 shows an example CIR density.

Figure 15.3 compares the densities for different "distances" from the Feller constraint $\epsilon = 2\,a\theta/\sigma^2 = 1$. We see that the densities' variance grows when we lower ϵ, and for $\epsilon < 1$ the plots indicate that the density diverges at the origin $\lambda = 0$. This is analysed in Section 15.3.4 and the associated Appendix G for the more general case with jumps. The density divergence at the origin is associated with non-zero cumulative probability at the origin which means that probability mass gets "stuck" there over time, and the process cannot escape any more. Whether this is problematic from a practical point of view depends on the size of the probability mass. For the two cases with $\epsilon < 1$ in Figure 15.2, we compute the following cumulative probabilities

$$\mathbb{P}\{\lambda(t) < 0.0001\} = \begin{cases} 0.016 & \text{for} \quad \epsilon = 1.5 \\ 0.019 & \text{for} \quad \epsilon = 1.0 \\ 0.011 & \text{for} \quad \epsilon = 0.5 \\ 0.005 & \text{for} \quad \epsilon = 0.25 \end{cases}$$

so that the divergence in the latter two cases actually has a smaller effect on the cumulative probability at the origin than in the former two cases where the density

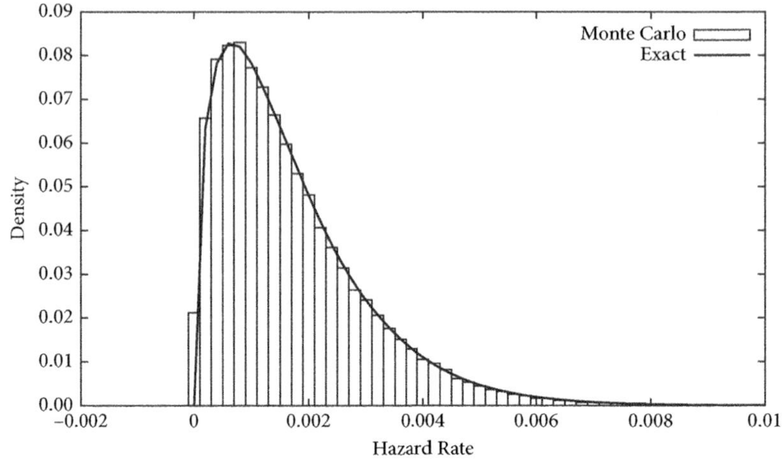

Figure 15.2 CIR density for model parameters in [33], p. 795 ($a = 0.354201$, $\theta = 0.00121853$, $\sigma = 0.0238186$, $y_0 = 0.0181$ so that $2a\theta/\sigma^2 = 1.52154$) at time $t = 10$, comparison between analytical density and histogram from Monte Carlo propagation using (15.17)

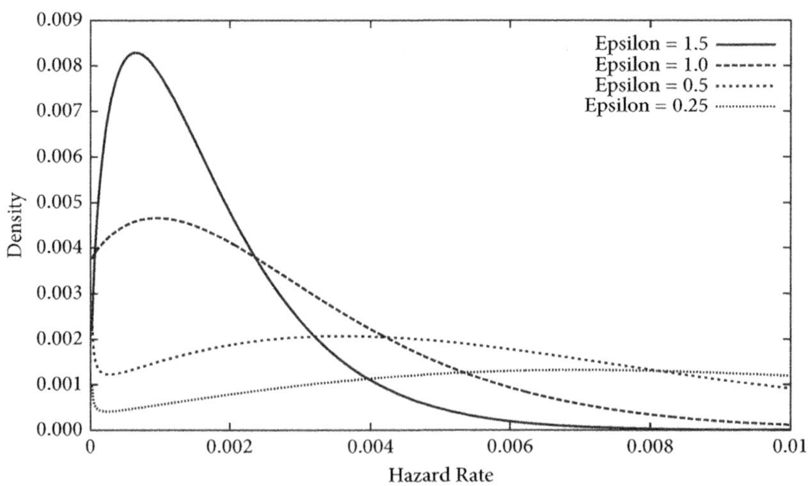

Figure 15.3 CIR density at time $t = 10$ for model parameters as in Figure 15.2 but varying a such that $\epsilon = 2a\theta/\sigma^2$ takes values 1.52, 1.01, 0.51, 0.25

remains finite (at least for this parameter set). This shows that one should not a priori exclude the parameter range $\epsilon < 1$. However, in Section 15.3.2 we will see relevant cases – with high associated implied CDS option volatility – where the cumulative probability of hazard rates piling up at the origin is significant for ϵ well below 1.

The closed-form density leads to a closed-form option pricing formula as we will see shortly. An important building block is the *CIR Zero Bond* price (with $\psi(t) \equiv 0$) which has the form

$$
\begin{aligned}
P^{CIR}(t,T;y) &= \mathbb{E}\left[e^{-\int_t^T y(s)\,ds}\right] \\
&= \mathcal{A}(t,T)\, e^{-\mathcal{B}(t,T)\,y(t)} \\
\mathcal{A}(t,T) &= \left[\frac{2h\, e^{(a+h)(T-t)/2}}{2h+(a+h)(e^{(T-t)h}-1)}\right]^{2a\theta/\sigma^2} \\
\mathcal{B}(t,T) &= \frac{2(e^{(T-t)h}-1)}{2h+(a+h)(e^{(T-t)h}-1)} \\
h &= \sqrt{a^2+2\sigma^2},
\end{aligned}
$$

where we now regard $P^{CIR}(t,T;y)$ as the survival probability to time T conditional on survival up to time t. In this raw version of the model one can try to fit the initial term structure of bond prices (resp. survival probabilities). An exact match is achieved by adding the shift extension $\psi(t)$ which yields the CIR++ survival probability

$$
\begin{aligned}
S(t,T;y) &= \mathbb{E}\left[e^{-\int_t^T \lambda(s)\,ds}\right] \\
&= e^{-\int_t^T \psi(s)\,ds} \cdot P^{CIR}(t,T;y), \qquad y(t) = \lambda(t) - \psi(t)
\end{aligned}
$$

We identify $\psi(t)$ by setting

$$
S(0,T;y_0) = e^{-\int_0^T \psi(s)\,ds} \cdot P^{CIR}(0,T;y_0) = S^M(T)
$$

where $S^M(T)$ are today's market-implied survival probabilities, and substitute $\psi(t)$:

$$
\begin{aligned}
S(t,T;y) &= \bar{A}(t,T) \cdot P^{CIR}(t,T;y(t)), \\
\bar{A}(t,T) &= \frac{S^M(T)}{S^M(t)} \frac{P^{CIR}(0,t;y_0)}{P^{CIR}(0,T;y_0)}
\end{aligned}
$$

After matching today's survival probability term structure we have four constant parameters a, σ, θ and y_0 left which can be used to match quoted option prices.

Propagation

The closed-form expression for density $\rho(y,t)$ allows in principle large step simulations of the hazard rate process. In contrast to all Gaussian models we have considered so far, this nice property breaks down as soon as one considers multiple correlated CIR processes. Therefore any realistic implementation in a CVA context will require a numerical scheme for propagating CIR hazard rate processes such as the following scheme from [32] which is also recommended in [33]:

$$y_{i+1} = \left(\left(1 - \frac{a}{2}(t_{i+1} - t_i)\right) \sqrt{y_i} + \frac{\sigma\,(W_{i+1} - W_i)}{2(1 - \frac{a}{2}(t_{i+1} - t_i))} \right)^2 \\ + (a\theta - \sigma^2/4)(t_{i+1} - t_i) \tag{15.17}$$

This scheme ensures non-negative values under the condition $\sigma^2 \leq 4\,a\theta$ which is satisfied as long as the standard Feller constraint $\sigma^2 \leq 2\,a\theta$ is satisfied. Conversely, it is interesting to note that the numerical scheme allows violating the Feller constraint somewhat without loss of probability at or through the boundary. We come back to this extra flexibility in our CDS option calibration experiments below.

In addition to y (resp. λ) we need to propagate the stochastic survival probability

$$S(0,t) = \exp\left(-\int_0^t \lambda(s)\,ds\right) = \frac{S^M(t)}{P^{CIR}(0,t)} \cdot \exp\left(-\int_0^t y(s)\,ds\right) \tag{15.18}$$

along each hazard rate path in order to determine expected future CDS prices. Simple Euler discretization for the path of $S(0,t)$ would mean

$$\begin{aligned} S(0,t_{i+1}) &= \frac{S^M(t)}{P^{CIR}(0,t)} \cdot \exp\left(-\sum_{j=0}^{i} y_j\,(t_{j+1} - t_j)\right) \\ &= S(0,t_i) \cdot \frac{S^M(t_{i+1})}{S^M(t_i)} \cdot \frac{P^{CIR}(0,t_i)}{P^{CIR}(0,t_{i+1})} \cdot e^{-y_i \cdot (t_{i+1} - t_i)}. \end{aligned}$$

which – in our opinion – is sufficiently accurate when used with weekly time steps. For a more accurate sampling of S_{i+1} given S_i – as developed in the context of Heston model simulations – refer for example to [51]. Figure 15.4 shows the survival probability distribution at time $t = 10$, MC with monthly time steps, for parameters calibrated as above.

Constraints

The CIR model process y cannot become negative by construction. The Feller constraint $2\,a\theta > \sigma^2$ moreover ensures that $y(t)$ remains strictly positive for all times without "getting stuck" at the origin. However, this is not sufficient to keep the hazard rate $\lambda(t) = y(t) + \psi(t)$ positive for all times. An additional constraint $\psi(t) > 0$ is required to ensure this. Recall the calibration of $\psi(t)$ via

$$e^{-\int_0^T \psi(s)\,ds} \cdot P^{CIR}(0,T) = S^M(T) = e^{-\int_0^T \lambda^M(s)\,ds}$$

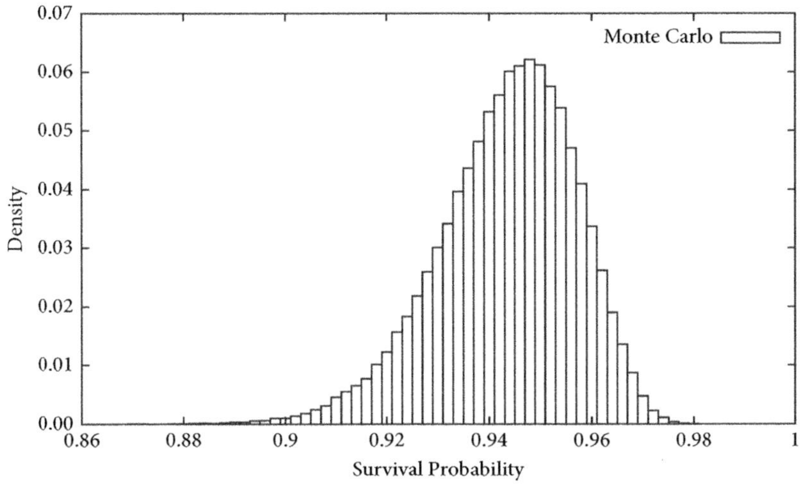

Figure 15.4 CIR survival probability density at time $t = 10$ for the same parameters as in Figure 15.2

Solve this to

$$\psi(t) = \lambda^M(t) + \frac{\partial}{\partial t} \ln P^{CIR}(0,t)$$

The constraint $\psi(t) > 0$ therefore means

$$f(t; a, \theta, \sigma, y_0) = -\frac{\partial}{\partial t} \ln P^{CIR}(0, t; a, \theta, \sigma, y_0) < \lambda^M(t) \qquad \forall t$$

As the analysis in [33] and our own experiments show, this can be hard to achieve when short term hazard rates are low. Conversely, if enforced, this constraint can turn out to be so tight that it prevents achieving high enough implied CDS option volatility. However, if this constraint is violated, the one reason for choosing CIR over for example a fully tractable Gaussian model is lost. One way out at this point may be dropping the shift extension and working with the raw CIR model instead. In doing so, one loses the ability to perfectly match the initial survival probability term structure, yet avoids the rigid additional constraint that disturbs option calibration.

CIR calibration to CDS options

We refer to the general CDS option pricing formula (15.4) and the essential expectation E_i at the beginning of this section. In the CIR model it is convenient to change measure to the CIR Zero Bond numeraire (see below) such that

$$\begin{aligned} E_i(t) &= S^M(t)\,\widetilde{\mathbb{E}}\left\{\left[\omega\left(S(t,t_i;y_t) - S(t,t_i;y_t^*)\right)\right]^+\right\} \\ &= S^M(t)\int_0^\infty \left[\omega\left(S(t,t_i;y_t) - S(t,t_i;y_t^*)\right)\right]^+ \widetilde{p}(y_t)\,dy_t \end{aligned}$$

This can be computed by one-dimensional numerical integration or using the closed-form expression for the CIR++ Zero Bond Option [33], p. 103. Glassermann [70] discusses on page 131 the change to the T-forward measure and shows how the CIR SDE is affected by this change:

- Use CIR model discount bond with maturity T

$$P^{CIR}(t,T) = \mathbb{E}\left[e^{-\int_t^T y(s)\,ds}\right]$$

  as new numeraire;
- The bond SDE is

$$\frac{dP^{CIR}(t,T)}{P^{CIR}(t,T)} = y(t)\,dt - \mathcal{B}(t,T)\,\sigma\,\sqrt{y(t)}\,dW^Q(t);$$

- The relation between Wiener processes in old and new measure is

$$dW^T(t) = dW^Q(t) + \sigma\,\sqrt{y(t)}\,\mathcal{B}(t,T)\,dt;$$

- This leads to the resulting drift change in the SDE for y

$$\begin{aligned} dy(t) &= a(\theta - y(t))\,dt + \sigma\,\sqrt{y(t)}\,dW^Q(t) \\ &= a(\theta - y(t))\,dt + \sigma\,\sqrt{y(t)}\,dW^T(t) - \sigma^2\,y(t)\,\mathcal{B}(t,T)\,dt \\ &= (a\theta - (a+\sigma^2\,\mathcal{B}(t,T))\,y(t))\,dt + \sigma\,\sqrt{y(t)}\,dW^T(t) \\ &= (a+\sigma^2\,\mathcal{B}(t,T))\left(\frac{a\theta}{a+\sigma^2\,\mathcal{B}(t,T)} - y(t)\right)dt + \sigma\,\sqrt{y(t)}\,dW^T(t); \end{aligned}$$

- The CIR density of y in the T-forward measure associated with numeraire $P^{CIR}(t,T)$ is

$$\begin{aligned}
p(y,t|y_0) &= c \cdot p_{\chi^2}(c \cdot y; \nu, n) \\
c &= 2\left[\frac{2h}{\sigma^2(e^{ht}-1)} + \frac{a+h}{\sigma^2} + \mathcal{B}(t,T)\right], \qquad h = \sqrt{a^2 + 2\sigma^2} \\
\nu &= \frac{4a\theta}{\sigma^2} \\
n &= \frac{4[2h/(\sigma^2(e^{ht}-1))]^2\, y_0\, e^{ht}}{c}.
\end{aligned}$$

For the purpose of pricing CDS options we need to evaluate the density at $t = T$, that is $\mathcal{B}(t,T) = 0$. The change of measure has almost no effect on the distribution at expiry $t = 10$ for the chosen model calibration.

To complete this section, let us have a look at a typical CDS exposure evolution graph in Figure 15.5, generated using a CIR++ model with shift extension to ensure a flat model-implied hazard rate curve at 4% with 40% recovery. Note that the protection seller and buyer exposures match at period start dates and that the seller's

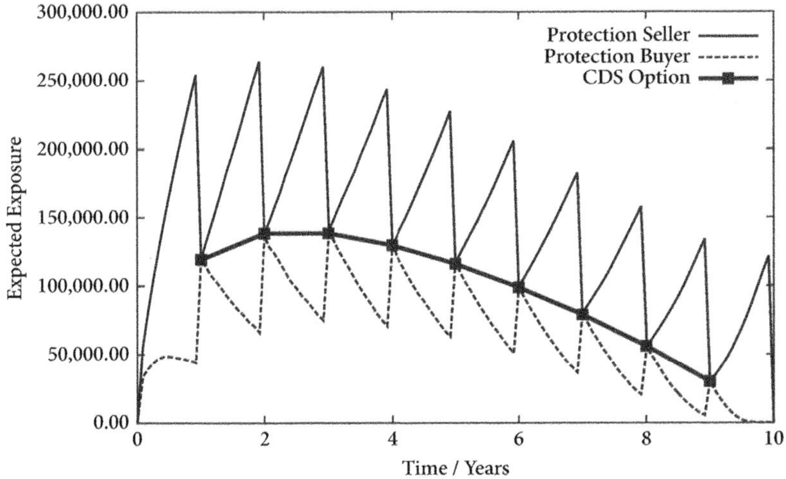

Figure 15.5 Expected exposure evolution for protection seller and buyer CDS, with notional 10m EUR and 10Y maturity, both at-the-money (premium approx. 2.4%) in a flat hazard rate curve environment (hazard rate 0.04, 0.4 recovery), compared to analytical exposure calculations (CDS option prices) at premium period start dates. The credit model used is CIR++ with shift extension, $a = 0.2$, $\theta = y_0 = 0.04$ and σ chosen such that $\epsilon = 2a\theta/\sigma^2 = 2$ well above the Feller constraint $\epsilon > 1$. The implied option volatilities are about 19%, highest at the shortest expiry. The simulation used 10k samples

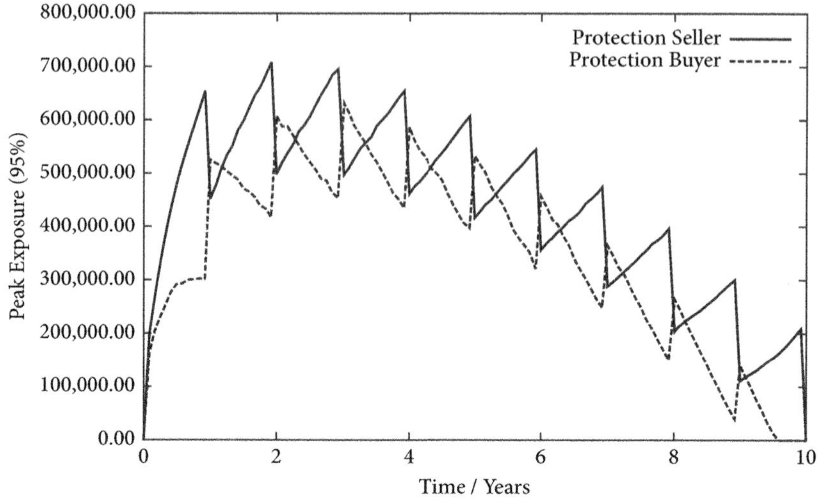

Figure 15.6 95% quantile exposure evolution for the instruments and model in Figure 15.5

expected exposure otherwise systematically exceeds the buyer's expected exposure. For a higher quantile of 95% we see in Figure 15.6 that this relation does not hold any more, and the buyer's exposure occasionally exceeds the seller's. This gets more pronounced as we increase the quantile, as expected, since in extreme hazard rate scenarios – when the reference entity is close to default – the buyer might almost be owed the large LGD amount.

15.3.2 Relaxed feller constraint

Let us come back to the observation that the numerical propagation scheme requires $\sigma^2 \leq 4\,a\theta$ rather than the analytical Feller constraint $\sigma^2 \leq 2\,a\theta$. If we use the former, we can obviously attain higher model σ and higher implied CDS option volatilities. To illustrate the effect, we repeat the exposure calculation shown in Figure 15.5 with a single amendment – setting σ such that $\epsilon = 2\,a\theta/\sigma^2 = 0.51$ close to the lower limit of the numerical scheme. The result is shown in Figure 15.7. Comparison to the exposure level in Figure 15.5 shows a significant increase, and the implied volatilities associated with the ATM option prices are now significantly higher at 33% rather than 19%. Choosing minimal ϵ is clearly necessary to attain high implied volatilities, but not sufficient – the remaining parameters a, θ, y_0 are important, and implied CDS volatility for a given expiry and term is a non-linear function of these.

So which implied volatility levels are attainable at best in CIR? To get an idea, let us simplify and use the unshifted CIR model with an approximately flat hazard rate curve at level λ_0. We achieve an approximately flat model-implied hazard

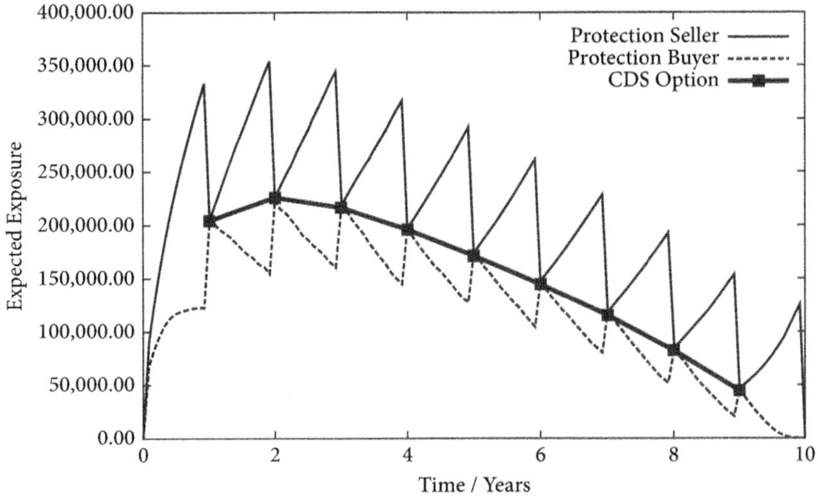

Figure 15.7 Expected exposures for the same parameters as in Figure 15.5, except for $\epsilon = 2a\theta/\sigma^2 = 0.51$. The implied option volatilities are about 33% rather than 19% with $\epsilon = 2$

rate curve if we fix two parameters y_0 and θ at $y_0 = \theta = \lambda_0$. We next focus on a typical index CDS option with expiry 6M and CDS term 5Y – this is where we can realistically hope to find market quotes. Moreover, it is plausible that minimal ϵ is required for maximum volatility. We then evaluate numerically the implied volatility σ_M of the 6Mx5Y CDS option as a function of reversion speed a for a few choices of λ_0 and three cases $\epsilon \approx 1$ and the "forbidden" values $\epsilon = 0.5$ and $\epsilon = 0.25$. It turns out that σ_M is a non-linear function of a (given the other parameters) with a local maximum. Table 15.1 shows the attainable maximum implied volatilities $\hat{\sigma}_M$, and for which reversion speed ($a \approx 0.2$ in all cases) the optimum was reached. The optimum reversion speed $\hat{a}$ and the attainable volatility $\hat{\sigma}_M$ seem almost independent of the flat hazard rate level we choose, and the smaller ϵ gets, the larger $\hat{\sigma}_M$ gets, as expected. The last column of Table 15.1 shows the price for violating Feller's constraint – a significant cumulative probability of hazard rates below 1 basis point at the underlying CDS maturity (five years and six months) which – as expected – grows with increasing time, decreasing ϵ and decreasing hazard rate level.

If one additionally relaxes $y_0 = \theta$ and allows $y_0 < \theta$, then one finds slightly higher $\hat{\sigma}^M$ just above 40% and close to 60% for $\epsilon = 1$ and $\epsilon = 0.5$, respectively. So these are the limits of CDS option volatilities (6M $\times$ 5Y) to which we can calibrate the plain CIR model. As market CDS option volatilities can be significantly higher, in particular in times of stress, we are motivated to explore extensions of the model.

Table 15.1 Maximum implied volatility $\hat{\sigma}_M$ for a 6M expiry 5Y term CDS option for three choices of $\epsilon = 1.0, 0.5, 0.25$ and five choices of $y_0 = \theta = 0.01, ..., 0.05$. $\hat{a}$ is the mean reversion speed for which $\sigma_M = \hat{\sigma}_M$, s is the fair spread of the underlying 5Y CDS with 6M forward start. The rightmost column contains the cumulative probability for hazard rates up to 1bp at maturity of the underlying CDS, five years plus six months

ϵ	λ_0	s	$\hat{a}$	$\hat{\sigma}_M$	$\mathbb{P}\{\lambda(t) < 1bp)\}$
1.00	0.01	0.0060	0.234	0.382	0.009
1.00	0.02	0.0118	0.207	0.384	0.005
1.00	0.03	0.0175	0.214	0.385	0.003
1.00	0.04	0.0232	0.206	0.386	0.002
1.00	0.05	0.0287	0.206	0.388	0.002
0.50	0.01	0.0059	0.207	0.538	0.076
0.50	0.02	0.0116	0.206	0.539	0.054
0.50	0.03	0.0170	0.209	0.540	0.044
0.50	0.04	0.0223	0.205	0.541	0.038
0.50	0.05	0.0274	0.203	0.542	0.034
0.25	0.01	0.0058	0.206	0.752	0.241
0.25	0.02	0.0112	0.205	0.751	0.202
0.25	0.03	0.0162	0.199	0.751	0.183
0.25	0.04	0.0209	0.193	0.750	0.170
0.25	0.05	0.0254	0.183	0.750	0.160

15.3.3 CDS spread distribution

So far we have considered hazard rate distributions, though only the CDS spread distribution[6] which is connected to the CDS option's market price expressed as a Black volatility. That motivates a brief detour here to look at the shape of CDS spread distributions in CIR.

Recall the CDS pricing formula in the mid-point approximation (15.3). Simplifying this by setting the discount factors to 1 and ignoring the rebate term we get the future CDS price

$$\Pi(t) = \mathbb{1}_{\{\tau > t\}} \left\{ K \sum_{i=1}^{n} \delta_i \, S(t, t_i) - LGD \times (1 - S(t, t_n)) \right\}$$

and the fair spread

$$K(t) = LGD \frac{1 - S(t, t_n)}{\sum_{i=1}^{n} \delta_i \, S(t, t_i)}, \tag{15.19}$$

[6] More precisely, the variance of the distribution of the natural logarithm of the CDS spread.

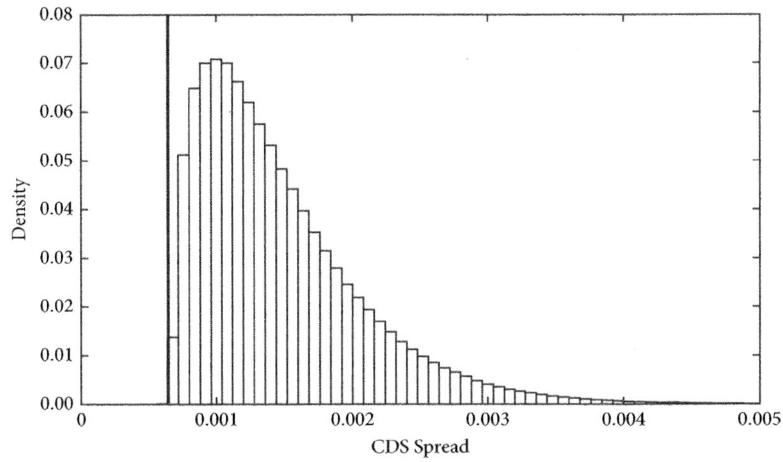

Figure 15.8 Distribution of fair 5Y-CDS spreads in ten years time for the parameters in Figure 15.3, $\epsilon = 1.52$. The position of the lower cutoff is computed as described in the text and indicated by a vertical line

which up to the LGD is precisely the same as formula (1.7) under LIBOR discounting for the par swap rate where discount factors are replaced by survival probabilities. Each term $S(t,T)$ has the affine form

$$S(t,T) = A(t,T)\, e^{-B(t,T)\, y(t)}$$

with $0 \leq A(t,T) < 1$ for $T > t$ and $B(t,T) > 0$. Since $y(t) > 0$ by construction in CIR, $S(t,T)$ assumes its maximum possible value for $y = 0$, and the maximum of $S(t,T)$ is less than 1. This shows – at first glance surprisingly – that the CDS spread distribution cannot "reach" spread values close to $K = 0$, as the enumerator above is always positive. We can compute the *lower cutoff* of the CDS spread distribution by evaluating the fair spread K in (15.19) or its accurate version (15.3) at the minimum hazard rate $y = 0$.

When the spread level is high, this lower cutoff can exclude a significant region of unattainable CDS spreads. Figures 15.8 and 15.9 show distributions of fair 5Y CDS spreads in ten years time for parameters as in Figure 15.3. We have used the unshifted CIR model here. One possible way to work around the cutoff is using the shift extension to move the hazard rate distribution into the negative direction (allowing some $\lambda(t) < 0$) in order to close the CDS spread cutoff. Choosing a shift function $\psi(t)$ such that $A(t,T)\exp(-B(t,T)\,\psi(t)) = 1$ would achieve that; however, this would only work for a single CDS tenor T. Moreover, such a shift

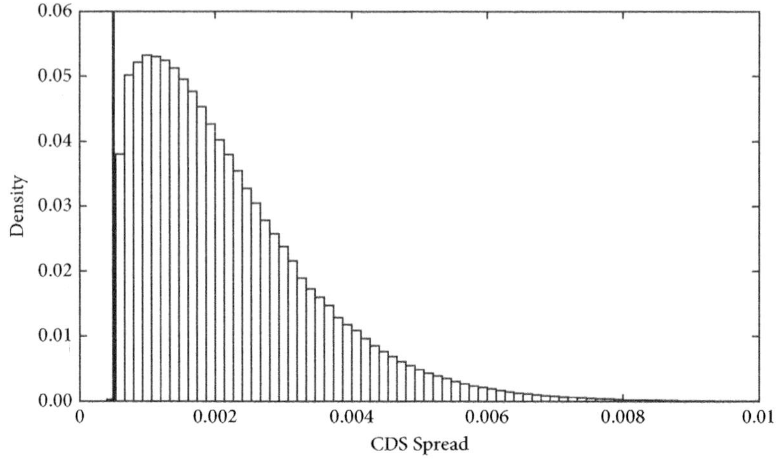

Figure 15.9 Distribution of fair 5Y-CDS spreads in ten years time for the parameters in Figure 15.3, $\epsilon = 1.01$. The position of the lower cutoff is computed as described in the text and indicated by a vertical line

does not make sense for small values of T when the spread distribution is naturally peaked around the starting point.

This finishes the detour, and we continue with an alternative approach which is closely related to CIR.

15.3.4 CIR with jumps: JCIR

As we have seen, the attainable CDS option prices and implied volatilities are constrained in the "plain" CIR model, the origin of this being the Feller constraint $\sigma^2 < 2a\theta$ [65]. To extend the model's option calibration capability, in particular Brigo and El Bachir [34] have studied a jump extension of the model which we will explore now. The extended CIR model, further enhanced by a jump process, is

$$\lambda(t) = y(t) + \psi(t)$$
$$dy(t) = a(\theta - y(t))\,dt + \sigma_\lambda \sqrt{y(t)}\,dW^Q(t) + dJ_{\alpha,\gamma}(t)$$

$J(t)$ is a compound Poisson process

$$J(t) = \sum_{i=1}^{N(t)} S_i$$

where the number of jumps n in any time interval $(t, t+\tau)$ follows a Poisson distribution with intensity α

$$PDF(n) = \frac{e^{-\alpha\tau}\,(\alpha\tau)^n}{n!},$$

and the jump sizes s have exponential distribution with mean γ,

$$PDF(s) = \frac{1}{\gamma}\,e^{-s/\gamma}$$

so that $\mathbb{E}[J(t)] = \alpha\gamma\, t$. This leaves us with six constant model parameters, as opposed to four in the CIR model – a, σ, θ, y_0, α, γ. If we rewrite the process SDE with a zero-expectation jump component $dJ(t) - \alpha\gamma\, dt$, we get

$$dy(t) = a(\theta + \alpha\gamma/a - y(t))\,dt + \sigma_\lambda\sqrt{y(t)}\,dW^Q(t) + (dJ_{\alpha,\gamma}(t) - \alpha\gamma\, dt),$$

and we see that the jumps shift the long term expectation of the hazard rate from θ to $\theta + \alpha\gamma/a$, cf. [34]. Increasing the distribution's variance by adding jumps hence also shifts the implied hazard rate curve (i.e. implied CDS spreads) up. Also note that the standard Feller constraint $2a\theta/\sigma^2 > 1$ still applies in order to prevent the hazard rate process from touching zero and "piling up" probability mass at the origin. This is carefully checked in Appendix G. Figure 15.10 shows typical JCIR hazard rate densities for varying jump intensity/sizes $\alpha = \gamma$ and for two different values of ϵ.

Let us summarize the key results. The JCIR zero bond is

$$\begin{aligned}
p^{JCIR}(t,T;y) &= \mathbb{E}\left[e^{-\int_t^T y(s)\,ds}\right] \\
&= \mathcal{A}^{JCIR}(t,T)\,e^{-\mathcal{B}(t,T)\,y(t)} \\
\mathcal{A}^{JCIR}(t,T) &= \mathcal{A}^{CIR}(t,T)\left[\frac{2h\,e^{(a+h+2\gamma)(T-t)/2}}{2h + (a+h+2\gamma)(e^{(T-t)h} - 1)}\right]^{\frac{2\alpha\gamma}{\sigma^2 - 2a\gamma - 2\gamma^2}} \\
\mathcal{B}(t,T) &= \frac{2(e^{(T-t)h} - 1)}{2h + (a+h)(e^{(T-t)h} - 1)} \\
h &= \sqrt{a^2 + 2\sigma^2}
\end{aligned}$$

To match the market-implied survival probability curve we utilize the shift function as in the CIR++ case. This yields the JCIR++ stochastic survival probability

$$S(t,T;y) = \frac{S^M(T)}{S^M(t)}\,\frac{p^{JCIR}(0,t;y_0)}{p^{JCIR}(0,T;y_0)} \cdot p^{JCIR}(t,T;y(t))$$

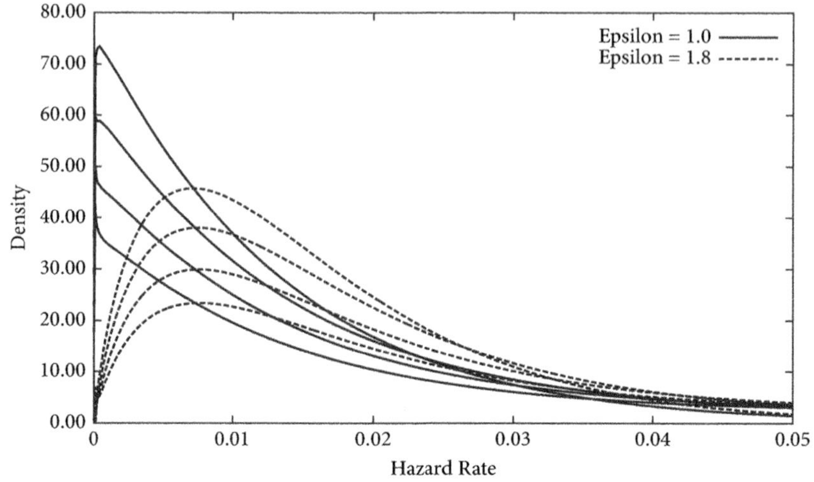

Figure 15.10 Hazard densities at time $t = 5$ in the JCIR model for parameters $a = 0.1125$ (resp. $a = 0.2$), $\theta = 0.022$, $\sigma = 0.07$, $y_0 = 0.005$, i.e. $\epsilon \approx 1.01$ (resp. $\epsilon \approx 1.8$) and $\alpha = \gamma = 0.00, 0.05, 0.10, 0.15$. The parameters result in the following fair spreads of a 5Y CDS with forward start in 6M: 58bp, 90bp, 171bp, 286bp (resp. 73bp, 101bp, 175bp, 280bp)

The hazard rate *propagation* using a generalized numerical scheme is amended as follows:

- Set up the discretization scheme as for CIR++ with small (e.g. weekly) time steps τ
- For each time interval τ determine the number of jumps using the inverse cumulative distribution function of the compound Poisson process
- If $n \geq 1$, determine n jump times uniformly distributed in time interval τ
- For each jump, determine jump size s using the inverse cumulative distribution function of the exponential distribution: $s = -\gamma \ln(1-u)$ where u is a random number uniform in $(0,1)$
- Subdivide the time interval τ into segments separated by jump times
- Propagate y as in CIR++ between jump times, adding jumps when they occur.

JCIR++ calibration to CDS options

Recall the general CDS Option pricing formula (15.4) with essential expectation E_i, which we now enhance for the JCIR++ case:

$$E_i(t) = e^{-\int_0^{t_i} \psi_s\, ds} \cdot A^{JCIR}(t, t_i) \cdot \underbrace{\mathbb{E}\left[e^{-\int_0^t y_s\, ds} \left(\omega \left[e^{-B(t,t_i)\, y_t} - e^{-B(t,t_i)\, y_t^*} \right] \right)^+ \right]}_{E_\omega, \omega \in \{-1,+1\}}$$

$$E_+ = \mathbb{E}\left[e^{-\int_0^t y_s\,ds - B(t,t_i)y_t}\,\mathbb{1}_{\{y_t<y_t^*\}}\right] - e^{-B(t,t_i)y_t^*}\,\mathbb{E}\left[e^{-\int_0^t y_s\,ds}\,\mathbb{1}_{\{y_t<y_t^*\}}\right]$$

$$E_- = -\mathbb{E}\left[e^{-\int_0^t y_s\,ds - B(t,t_i)y_t}\,\mathbb{1}_{\{y_t>y_t^*\}}\right] + e^{-B(t,t_i)y_t^*}\,\mathbb{E}\left[e^{-\int_0^t y_s\,ds}\,\mathbb{1}_{\{y_t>y_t^*\}}\right]$$

$$= E_+ - \mathbb{E}\left[e^{-\int_0^t y_s\,ds - B(t,t_i)y_t}\right] + e^{-B(t,t_i)y_t^*}\,\mathbb{E}\left[e^{-\int_0^t y_s\,ds}\right]$$

Lando [110] with reference to Christensen [52] gives a semi-analytic solution for expectations in JCIR of the form

$$G_{u,b}(t,y_0,\rho,\bar{y}) = \mathbb{E}\left[\exp\left(u y_t - \rho\int_0^t y\,ds\right)\mathbb{1}_{\{b y_t<\bar{y}\}}\right] \tag{15.20}$$

which can be used to determine any of the expectations above. The result, shown in Appendix G, is also given in Brigo and El-Bachir [34].

Impact of jumps on implied volatility: skew

Figure 15.11 shows typical JCIR implied volatilities as a function of strike. The impact of jumps in the model shows up as a strong skew, but with little impact on ATM options.

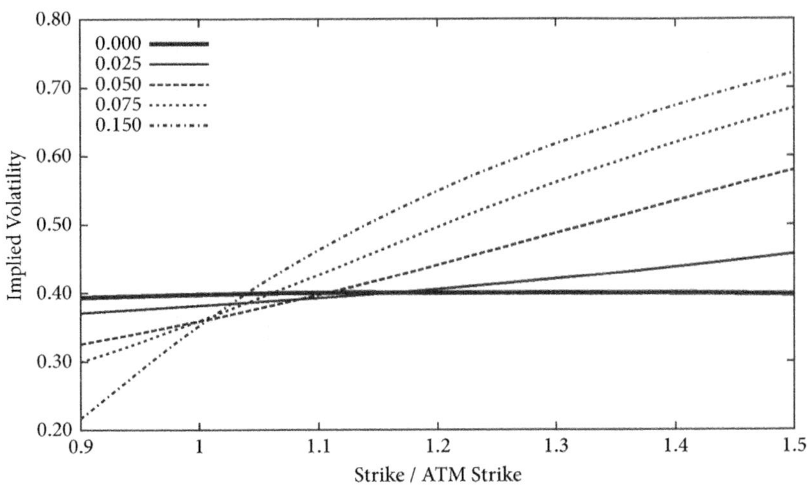

Figure 15.11 Parameters $a = 0.1125$, $\theta = 0.022$, $\sigma = 0.07$, $y_0 = 0.005$ (so that $\epsilon \approx 1.01$) and varying $\alpha = \gamma = 0.00, 0.025, 0.05, 0.075, 0.15$. Option expiry 6M, CDS term 5Y. The fair spread of the underlying CDS associated with the jump parameters is 58bp, 66bp, 89bp, 125bp and 285bp

15.3.5 JCIR extension

Brigo and El-Bachir [64] explored an additional extension of the JCIR model which

- involves a logarithmic time change
- dispenses with mean-reversion.

The model, which the authors label θ-SRJD for *Time-changed Square Root Jump Diffusion*, obeys the following SDE

$$\lambda(t) = X_{\theta(t)}$$
$$\theta(t) = \ln(1 + \nu t), \qquad t \geq 0$$
$$dX(t) = \kappa\,(\mu + X(t))\,dt + \sigma\,\sqrt{X(t)}\,dW(t) + dJ(t)$$

The model parameters still need to satisfy the Feller constraint $\sigma^2 < 2\kappa\,\mu$ so as to avoid probability piling up at the boundary $X(t) = 0$. Because of the positive sign of $X(t)$ and the absence of mean reversion, the expected value of $X(t)$ will grow exponentially. By adding the time change, this growth is turned into a milder polynomial growth of $\lambda(t)$ which can be controlled with parameter ν to be moderate up to the relevant simulation horizon. The model is still analytically tractable with a semi-analytical expression for the conditional survival probability.

The authors show an example of implied volatilities up to about 85% (about 70% at-the-money) for an option with expiry in 1Y and underlying CDS term 5Y and 205 bp forward CDS rate (see their Figure 6) in a θ-SRJD without jumps. This is indeed an improvement compared to CIR and JCIR. However, varying the remaining model parameters we can confirm that implied volatilities (for 1Y expiry and 5Y term at 200bp fair spread) remain limited at about the 90% level.

15.3.6 Examples: CDS CVA and wrong-way risk

As an application of the credit modelling introduced so far, we briefly discuss its application to the calculation of CVA on CDS. In this case we cannot safely assume that the factors which drive the CDS exposure (mainly the reference entity's credit spread) are independent of the counterparty's default risk. It is a classical example of wrong-way risk[7] – if the counterparty tends to default when the reference entity defaults, then the protection tends to be worthless, so we expect a significant

[7] More generally, wrong-way risk describes the dependence of counterparty default on the portfolio exposure. The opposite phenomenon – a decrease of counterparty default probability with increases in exposure – is called *right-way risk*.

Table 15.2 CIR++ model parameters for reference entity and counterparty processes. Parameters $\theta = y_0$ are chosen to match the hazard rate level, and the shift extension is used to ensure that the curve is strictly flat

Parameter	Reference Entity	Counterparty
Hazard rate	0.02	0.03
Recovery rate	0.40	0.40
Reversion Speed	0.20	0.20
$\epsilon = 2a\theta/\sigma^2$	0.51	0.51

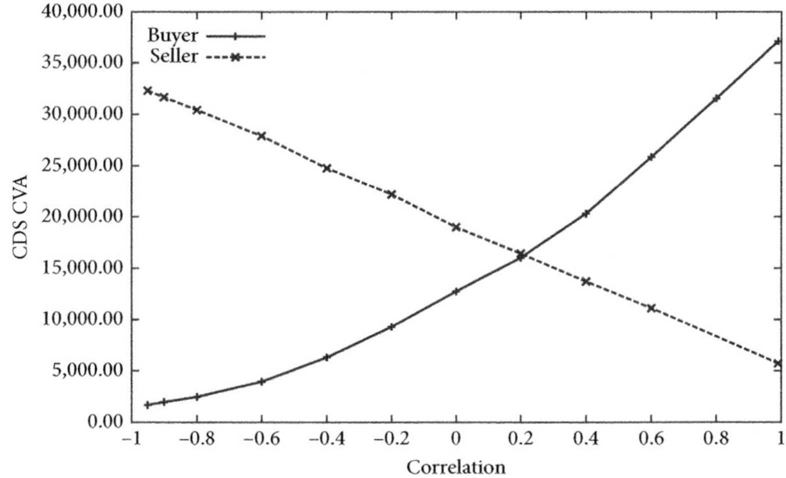

Figure 15.12 Unilateral CVA of a CDS as a function of the correlation between the hazard rate processes for counterparty and reference entity. The underlying CDS is at-the-money, has 10 Mio. notional and maturity in ten years. The process parameters are given in Table 15.2. The Monte Carlo evaluation used 1,000 samples per CVA calculation

impact of the correlation between the respective hazard rate processes on the CDS CVA. The unilateral CVA calculation needs to be based on Equation (8.2) with stochastic counterparty probability of default "within the expectation". We choose CIR++ for both hazard rate processes, and Table 15.2 summarizes the parameter choices. Figure 15.12 then shows an analysis of the dependence of the CVA amount on the correlation between the involved hazard rate processes for an underlying at-the-money CDS with maturity in ten years.

The impact of correlation on CVA is significant, covering a range of up to 40 bp of notional. For example, the CVA increases by a factor of about three for a protection buyer CDS if we increase correlation from 0 up to 1. The direction is plausible: higher correlation means higher likelihood of the protection seller to default when the buyer needs the protection, so the CDS value has to decrease and CVA has to increase (CVA is subtracted from the risk-free NPV). Likewise, when the correlation tends to -1, the protection buyer CDS CVA (almost) vanishes. This result is also plausible since, in that case, the counterparty does not default whenever the reference entity defaults, hence there is no need to correct the risk-free CDS NPV.

Now one may wonder, what about the impact on the CVA of a protection buyer CDS where correlation is high? Does the CIR model yield a sufficient range here, or is a significantly higher impact attainable if we choose a different model?

Without analysing the alternatives, we cannot decide this question. However, we get an indication by considering

$$\rho_{AB} = \frac{p_{AB} - p_A p_B}{\sqrt{p_A(1-p_A)\,p_B(1-p_B)}}$$

as discussed by Schönbucher [129]. The linear default correlation relates the defaults of party A and B, with p_A and p_B denoting the respective marginal cumulative probabilities of default up to some time horizon, and p_{AB} denoting the joint probability of default. In our two-process CIR++ example we can evaluate the joint probability of default and linear default correlation. In Figure 15.13 we show the linear default correlation as a function of time (up to ten years) for hazard rate correlation set to 0.8.

Linear default correlation remains low throughout the life of the ten-year CDS in our example. This is a limitation not only of CIR but of hazard rate models in general, as for example discussed by Peng & Kou in [122]. The approach introduced in [122] to model default clustering in the valuation of CDOs – which is explored in Section 15.5 below – will be analysed with respect to its impact on CDS CVA and wrong-way risk. This is work in progress at the time of writing.

15.3.7 Conclusion

Feller's constraint $2\,a\theta/\sigma^2 > 1$ on the model parameters in CIR and JCIR leads to upper limits (in the area of 40%) in implied volatilities for CDS options (volatilities of CDS spreads) with short time to expiry such as six months. The Feller constraint can be violated somewhat at the price of diverging probability density at the origin and hence finite probability mass "piling up" close to the origin. This allows extending attainable implied volatility to levels around 75% if one accepts significant probability mass such as 20% close to the origin.

However, the observed volatility limits, as well as the lower cutoff in CDS spread distributions, motivate the exploration of alternative models beyond CIR, JCIR and θ-SRJD which have the capability of attaining implied volatilities beyond the 100% level as observed in the market.

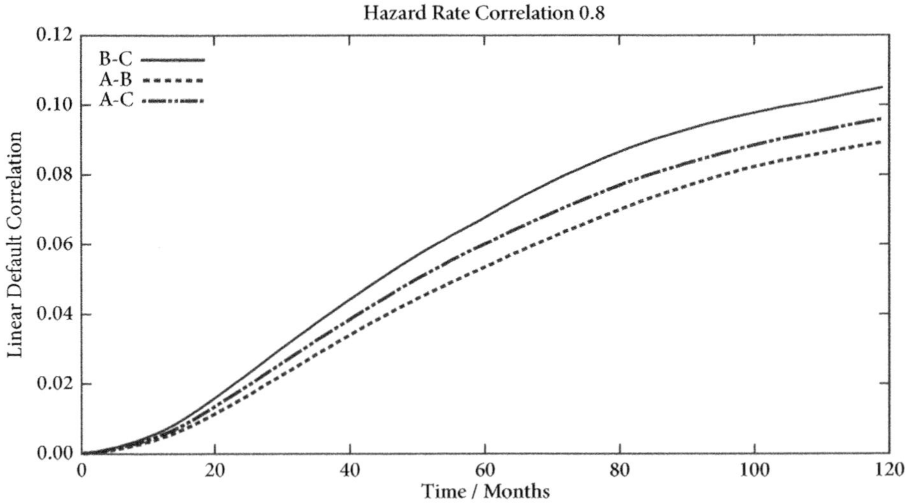

Figure 15.13 Linear default correlation as a function of time between three names (A, B, C) with flat hazard rate levels 0.02, 0.03 and 0.04, respectively, CIR++ model for all three processes with reversion speed 0.2 and high volatility $\epsilon = 0.51$. The hazard rate correlations are 0.8

15.4 Black-Karasinski model

The Black-Karasinski (BK) model [26] is another classical term structure model from interest rate space. Translating short rate into hazard rate, we can write the model

$$\lambda(t) = \exp(x(t) + \varphi(t))$$
$$dx(t) = -a\,x(t)\,dt + \sigma\,dW(t)$$

which shows why it is also called the exponential Vasicek model. It ensures positive rates by construction, but has the disadvantage that it does not have closed-form solutions for the stochastic survival probability

$$S(t,T,\lambda) = \mathbb{E}_t\left[\exp\left(-\int_t^T \lambda(s)\,ds\right)\right],$$

in contrast to the models we have explored before. The shift function $\varphi(t)$ nevertheless allows a perfect match with the term structure of market survival probabilities $S^M(t)$ (without touching the positivity of $\lambda(t)$, also in contrast to the extended CIR model). But $\varphi(t)$ as well as $S(t,T,\lambda)$ and credit derivatives such as CDS options need to be evaluated numerically, usually on a trinomial tree using

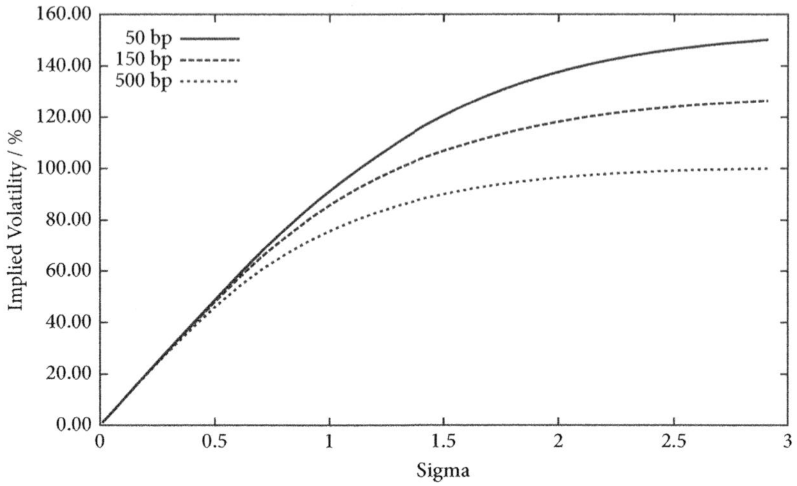

Figure 15.14 CDS option implied volatilities as a function of model σ in the BK model for flat hazard rate curves at 50, 150 and 500 bp, respectively. Mean reversion speed $\alpha = 0.01$. The option is struck at-the-money, it has 6M expiry, and the underlying CDS term is 5Y

a backward induction approach. This complicates model calibration. Moreover, maintaining the tree means significantly higher computer memory requirement for the model than for an analytically tractable model. This can become an issue when a large number of credit names need to be modelled simultaneously.

However, the model has a significant advantage: it turns out that it can be calibrated to market situations with low spread and high implied CDS option volatility levels (the investment grade case shown at the end of Section 15.1). Figure 15.14 shows implied CDS option volatilities as a function of model parameter σ for several flat CDS spread curve scenarios. In our view, this makes the BK model a reasonable candidate for modelling hazard rates in our Monte Carlo framework.

At first glance it seems surprising that the initial linear slope of the curves in Figure 15.14 does not persist, but that we rather see some "saturation" of the attained implied volatility level attained for high model σ (fortunately at quite a high level of implied volatility). To see why this is happening, consider the logarithm of $\lambda(t)$, driven by a Hull-White process. We can therefore use the results from Appendix D to see that

$$\mathbb{V}[\ln \lambda(t)] = \int_0^t e^{-2\alpha(t-s)} \sigma^2(s)\, ds = \sigma^2 \frac{1 - e^{-2\alpha t}}{2\alpha}$$

for constant model parameters α and σ. If the standard deviation of $\ln \lambda(t)$, that is $\sqrt{\mathbb{V}[\ln \lambda(t)]}$ determined the implied CDS option volatility, it would be right to expect a linear dependence on σ without any levelling off. However, it is the

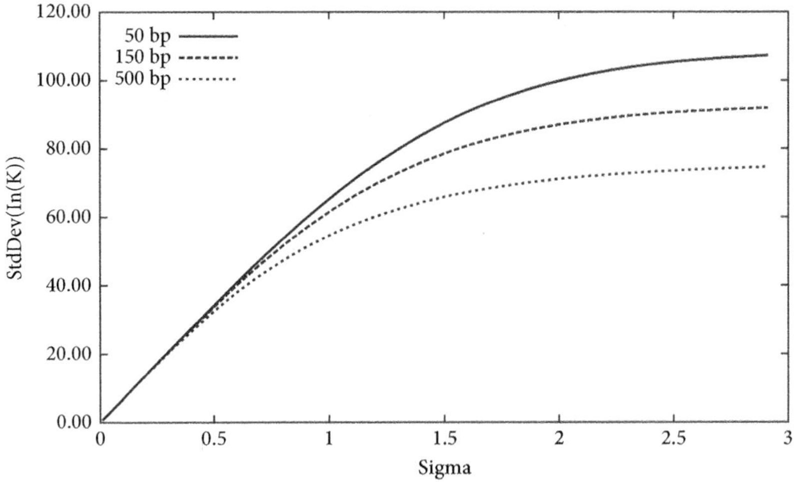

Figure 15.15 Standard deviation of the distribution of fair CDS spread ($\ln K(t)$) as a function of model σ in the BK model for flat hazard rate curves at 50, 150 and 500 bp flat, respectively. Mean reversion speed $\alpha = 0.01$. The CDS is forward starting in six months and has a five-year term

variance of the CDS spread distribution which determines a CDS option price (and hence implied volatility). Recalling the detour in Section 15.3.3 and the stochastic fair CDS spread $K(t)$ in (15.19), we can numerically evaluate the CDS spread distribution and the variance of $\ln K(t)$ which allows plotting $\sqrt{\mathbb{V}[\ln K(t)]}$ vs model σ, see Figure 15.15. This looks qualitatively very much like the plot in Figure 15.14, that is the standard deviation relevant for CDS option pricing shows a similar linear start and "levelling off" for large σ, which makes the previous finding plausible. If we then plot the implied volatility of the CDS option vs standard deviation of the distribution, we find a linear relation which is independent of the hazard rate level, see Figure 15.16.

Calibration and propagation

The BK model calibration to the term structure of CDS fixes the shift function $\varphi(t)$. This requires the calculation of model implied survival probabilities $S(0,T) = \mathbb{E}\left[\exp\left(-\int_0^T \lambda(s)\,ds\right)\right]$ numerically. It seems common to use trinomial trees for this purpose, refer for example to [33] for the tree construction procedure. The remaining parameters (α and σ) are then determined by calibrating to CDS options, though we have also seen α fixed (not calibrated, but exogenous). With time-dependent $\sigma(t)$ the model allows calibration to a term structure of options with varying expiry dates. However, the sparseness of market quoted index CDS options (short expiries less than one year only, if at all) may justify using the

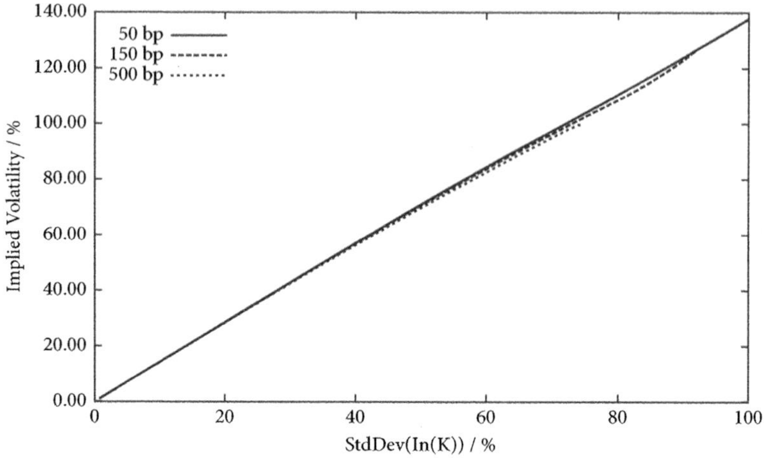

Figure 15.16 CDS Option implied volatilities as a function of standard deviation of the distribution of the fair CDS spread ($\ln K(t)$) in the BK model for flat hazard rate curves at 50, 150 and 500 bp flat, respectively. Mean reversion speed $\alpha = 0.01$

constant σ version of the model, calibrated to a single ATM CDS option to capture the level of volatility.

Once calibrated, the propagation of hazard rates in the BK model is straightforward as we need to propagate the underlying Ornstein-Uhlenbeck process $x(t)$. The path of $x(t)$ yields the path of $\lambda(t)$ by applying the shift $\varphi(t)$. This also yields the cumulative probability of default up to time t on the path

$$S(t) = \exp(-\sum_i \lambda(t_i)\,(t_i - t_{i-1}).$$

If we then want to evaluate payoffs on the path using the conditional survival probability function $S(t,T)$, we are struggling again with the limited analytical tractability of the BK model. Conditional on time t and the hazard rate level $\lambda(t)$ reached by time t, we need to compute $S(t,T,\lambda(t)) = \mathbb{E}_t\left[\exp\left(-\int_t^T \lambda(s)\,ds\right)\right]$ numerically by rolling back on a tree or embedding another Monte Carlo simulation. The latter is inefficient, and we rather pre-compute a cube of $S(t,T,\lambda(t))$ with appropriate discretization of times t and T and hazard rate level $\lambda(t)$, and then interpolate on this cube to find the conditional survival probability that is required on the path.

This Monte Carlo simulation can for example be used to produce the CDS spread distribution histograms in Figure 15.17 which are taken at the typical option expiry time in six months.

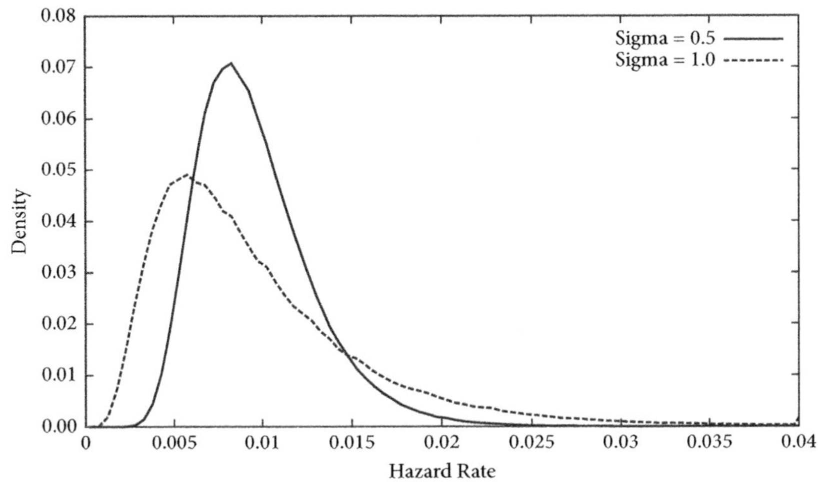

Figure 15.17 CDS spread distributions at time $t = 0.5$ for hazard rate level 150 bp, $\alpha = 0.01$ and $\sigma = 0.5$ and $\sigma = 1.0$, respectively

15.5 Peng-Kou model

All approaches we have presented so far model the hazard rate and apply "classical" techniques borrowed from the history of modelling (short) interest rates. In this last part of the credit model section we want to explore a different route.

The model we are referring to in this section is described in the 2009 working paper by Peng and Kou (PK) [122]. It was originally developed to model default clustering in the valuation of CDOs. In this section we apply a simplified version of the PK model to the valuation of CDS options, in particular to explore whether (for our purpose) sufficiently high implied CDS option volatilities are attainable in the model. The key idea of PK's approach is to model the *cumulative intensity* process $\Lambda(t)$ of a single name and assume that $\Lambda(t)$ (rather than hazard rate $\lambda(t)$) follows a one factor process with a deterministic shift $X(t)$:

$$\Lambda(t) = \int_0^t \lambda(s)\,ds = M(t) + X(t).$$

$M(t)$ is some stochastic process and $X(t)$ is a deterministic shift to match the market CDS term structure. The building blocks of the PK model are the conditional survival probability $q^c(t)$ and the marginal survival probability $q(t)$:

$$q^c(t) = \mathbb{P}(\tau > t|M(t)) = e^{-(M(t)+X(t))}$$

$$q(t) = \mathbb{P}(\tau > t) = e^{-X(t)}\mathbb{E}\left[e^{-M(t)}\right]$$

where

$$X(t) = -\ln\left(\frac{q^{Mkt}(t)}{\mathbb{E}\left[e^{-M(t)}\right]}\right)$$

$$q^c(t) = q^{Mkt}(t)\,\frac{e^{-M(t)}}{\mathbb{E}\left[e^{-M(t)}\right]}.$$

The variable τ denotes the time of default, and $q^{Mkt}(t)$ is the market-implied or otherwise observed probability of default.

15.5.1 Review CDS and CDS option

Before we start specifying $M(t)$, we review the CDS and CDS option pricing formulas from Section 15.1 and express them in terms of cumulative intensity $\Lambda(t)$. A careful check including filtration switching is provided in Appendix H. The results for CDS at time t and CDS option as of today with expiry at time t are as expected

$$\Pi_{CDS}(t) = \mathbb{1}_{\{\tau>t\}} \sum_{i=0}^{n} G_i\, q(t,t_i)$$

$$\begin{aligned}\Pi_{CDSO}(0) &= P(0,t)\,\mathbb{E}\left[e^{-\Lambda(t)}\left[\omega \sum_{i=0}^{n} G_i\, q(t,t_i)\right]^+\right] \\ &= P(0,t)\,\mathbb{E}\left[e^{-M(t)}\left[\omega \sum_{i=0}^{n} G_i\,\frac{q^{Mkt}(t_i)}{\mathbb{E}(e^{M(t_i)})}\,\mathbb{E}_t\left(e^{-(M(t_i)-M(t))}\right)\right]^+\right]\end{aligned} \tag{15.21}$$

with

$$q(t,t_i) = \mathbb{E}\left[e^{-(\Lambda(t_i)-\Lambda(t))}|\mathcal{F}_t\right]$$

and G_i defined as in Section 15.1 assuming deterministic interest rates, and $\omega = \pm 1$ switches between options on protection seller and buyer CDS.

15.5.2 Compound Poisson process

To start, let us check the CDS option price (15.21) if we model $M(t)$ as a pure *Compound Poisson process*, that is M is composed of a series of jumps

$$M(t) = \sum_{i=1}^{N(t)} S_i$$

where the number of jumps n in any time interval $(t, t+\tau)$ follows a Poisson distribution with intensity ψ

$$PDF(n) = \frac{e^{-\psi\tau}(\psi\tau)^n}{n!}$$

and the jump sizes s have an exponential distribution with mean γ:

$$PDF(s) = \frac{1}{\gamma}e^{-s/\gamma}.$$

Note that this is exactly the jump component J used in the JCIR model of Section 15.3.4 which is now driving the *cumulative* hazard rate process. Expectations of the type that appear in (15.21) can be easily computed using the Laplace transform of the compound Poisson process, that is

$$\mathbb{E}\left[e^{-uM(t)}\right] = e^{-\psi\, t(1-\phi_S(u))}$$

where $\phi_S(u)$ is the Laplace transform of exponentially distributed jump sizes

$$\phi_S(u) = \frac{1}{1+u\gamma}.$$

This shows that the conditional expectations in (15.21) are deterministic and of the form

$$\mathbb{E}_t\left[e^{-(M(t_i)-M(t))}\right] = e^{-\psi\,(t_i-t)\gamma/(1+\gamma)}.$$

Hence a CDS option in this "model" would have zero time value. If we model the cumulative hazard rate process directly we thus need a more general process beyond compound Poisson.

15.5.3 Compound Polya process

The alternative discussed in [122] – which also gives rise to default clustering in their context – is a *Compound Polya* process. We still have

$$M(t) = \sum_{i=1}^{N(t)} S_i$$

but the number of jumps n in any time interval $(t, t+\tau)$ is Poisson distributed with a *random* intensity $\psi\tau$, where ψ is *gamma* distributed with density

$$f_\psi(x;\alpha,\beta) = \frac{\beta^{-\alpha}x^{\alpha-1}e^{-x/\beta}}{\Gamma(\alpha)}$$

The gamma distribution is controlled by two parameters, *shape* α and *scale* β. The expectation of x is given by the product $\alpha\,\beta$, and the variance of x is $\alpha\,\beta^2$. As in the Compound Poisson case, the distribution of jump sizes is exponential with parameter γ. One can show that the gamma distributed jump intensity then leads to a *Negative Binomial* distribution of the number of jumps up to time t:

$$\begin{aligned}\mathbb{P}(N(t)=n) &= \int_0^\infty \mathbb{P}(N(t)=n|\psi=x)\,f_\psi(x)\,dx \\ &= \frac{(\alpha+n-1)!}{(\alpha-1)!\,n!}\left(\frac{1}{1+\beta t}\right)^\alpha\left(\frac{\beta t}{1+\beta t}\right)^n, t>0,\, n\geq 0, \\ &= \mathcal{NB}(n;\alpha,p), \text{ with } p=\frac{1}{1+\beta\,t}\end{aligned}$$

as opposed to a binomial distribution in case of the Compound Poisson process. Let us summarize a few essential facts:

- The number of jumps $N(t)$ up to time t is negatively binomially distributed.
- Conditional on ψ, $N(t)$ is a Poisson process with intensity $\psi\,t$.
- The Polya process has positively correlated increments

$$Cov\,(N(t), N(t+h)-N(t)) = h\,t\,\alpha\,\beta^2$$

- The Laplace transform of the Compound Polya process $M(t)$ is

$$\mathbb{E}\left[e^{-uM(t)}\right] = \left(\frac{p}{1-(1-p)\phi_S(u)}\right)^\alpha, \quad p=\frac{1}{1+\beta\,t} \tag{15.22}$$

  where $\phi_S(u)$ is the Laplace transform of exponentially distributed jump sizes,

$$\phi_S(u) = \frac{1}{1+u\,\gamma}$$

- Expectation and variance of $N(t)$ are given by

$$\mathbb{E}[N(t)] = \frac{(1-p)\,\alpha}{p} = \alpha\,\beta\,t, \qquad \mathbb{V}[N(t)] = \frac{(1-p)\,\alpha}{p^2} = \alpha\,\beta\,t\,(1+\beta\,t).$$

Conditional survival probability

To compute the *conditional* survival probability $S(t,T) = \mathbb{E}_t[\exp(-(\Lambda(T)-\Lambda(t)))]$ we need one more ingredient: the *conditional* Polya distribution of the number of jumps in the time interval $T-t$ conditional on the number of jumps $N(t)$ up to time t. This is given in [63]:

$$\begin{aligned}\mathbb{P}\{N(T)-N(t)=n\,|\,N(t)=k\} &= \mathcal{NB}(n;\alpha+k,p_{tT})\\ &= \binom{\alpha+k+n-1}{n} p_{tT}^n\,(1-p_{tT})^{\alpha+k}\end{aligned}$$

where

$$\begin{aligned}p_{tT} &= \frac{p_T-p_t}{1-p_t} \qquad p_t=\frac{\beta\, t}{1+\beta_t}\\ &= \frac{\beta\,(T-t)}{1+\beta\, T}\end{aligned}$$

which has the form of an unconditional Polya distribution with modified parameters.

Equipped with the Laplace transform of the Compound Polya process (15.22) and the conditional Polya distribution above we can now determine the conditional survival probability $S(t,T)$ implied by the Compound Polya process:

$$\begin{aligned}S(t,T,N_t) &= \mathbb{E}_t\left[e^{-(\Lambda(T)-\Lambda(t))}\right]\\ &= e^{-X_T+X_t}\,\mathbb{E}\left[e^{-(M_T-M_t)}\right]\\ &= e^{-X_T+X_t}\left(\frac{1-p_{tT}}{1-\frac{p_{tT}}{1+\gamma}}\right)^{\alpha+N_t}\\ &= \frac{S^M(T)}{S^M(t)}\left(\frac{1-p_T}{1-\frac{p_T}{1+\gamma}}\right)^{-\alpha}\left(\frac{1-p_t}{1-\frac{p_t}{1+\gamma}}\right)^{\alpha}\left(\frac{1-p_{tT}}{1-\frac{p_{tT}}{1+\gamma}}\right)^{\alpha+N_t}\\ &:= A(t,T)\,e^{-B(t,T)N_t}\end{aligned}\tag{15.23}$$

where

$$\begin{aligned}A(t,T) &= \frac{S^M(T)}{S^M(t)}\left(\frac{1-p_T}{1-\frac{p_T}{1+\gamma}}\right)^{-\alpha}\left(\frac{1-p_t}{1-\frac{p_t}{1+\gamma}}\right)^{\alpha}\left(\frac{1-p_{tT}}{1-\frac{p_{tT}}{1+\gamma}}\right)^{\alpha}\\ B(t,T) &= \ln\left(\frac{1-\frac{p_{tT}}{1+\gamma}}{1-p_{tT}}\right)>0\\ p_{tT} &= \frac{p_T-p_t}{1-p_t}, \qquad p_t=\frac{\beta t}{1+\beta t}\end{aligned}\tag{15.24}$$

with expectation

$$\mathbb{E}[S(t,T,N_t)] = A(t,T)\left(\frac{1-p_t}{1-p_t\, e^{-B(t,T)}}\right)^{\alpha} \tag{15.25}$$

and variance

$$\mathbb{V}[S(t,T,N_t)] = A^2(t,T)\left\{\left(\frac{1-p_t}{1-p_t\, e^{-2B(t,T)}}\right)^{\alpha} - \left(\frac{1-p_t}{1-p_t\, e^{-B(t,T)}}\right)^{2\alpha}\right\}.$$

In summary, this yields a model which

- matches the initial term structure of default probabilities
- has a simple closed-form expression for the conditional survival probability which is determined by three model parameters α, β and γ
- lacks an obvious constraint (such as Feller's in CIR) that limits the model parameters
- is discrete in the sense that conditional survival probability is a function of the discrete number of jumps $N(t)$ up to time t.

In the following we investigate four questions which determine whether this modelling approach is promising before we finish this chapter with preliminary conclusions.

1. Is $S(t,T,N_t)$ a monotonously decreasing function of T?
2. Can we attain sufficiently high implied volatilities of 6Mx5Y CDS options under realistic market conditions (spread levels)?
3. Is there a non-zero probability of negative implied CDS spreads at future times? If so, can this be controlled or even avoided by appropriate additional constraints?
4. Does the discrete nature of $S(t,T)$ – which is driven by the discrete number $N(t)$ of jumps up to time t – cause problems?

Monotonicity of conditional survival probability

The survival probability $S(t,T,N_t)$ is a monotonically decreasing function of T if and only if the following condition is satisfied:

$$\begin{aligned}
0 &\geq \frac{\partial S(t,T,N_t)}{\partial T} \\
&= \frac{S^{M\prime}(T)}{S^M(T)} + \frac{\alpha\beta\gamma}{1+\gamma\,(1+\beta T)} - \frac{(\alpha+N_t)\beta\gamma}{1+\beta t+\gamma\,(1+\beta T)} \\
&= \frac{S^{M\prime}(T)}{S^M(T)} + \frac{\alpha\beta^2\gamma\, t - \beta\gamma\,(1+\gamma\,(1+\beta T))N_t}{(1+\gamma\,(1+\beta T))^2 + (1+\gamma\,(1+\beta T))\beta t}.
\end{aligned}$$

This condition will surely hold if it is valid in cases where $N_t = 0$, because larger values of N_t further reduce the right-hand side. A sufficient condition is that

$$-\frac{S^{M\prime}(T)}{S^M(T)} \geq \frac{\alpha\beta^2\gamma\, t}{(1+\gamma\,(1+\beta T))^2 + (1+\gamma\,(1+\beta T))\beta t}$$

for any $t \leq T$. Now note that the right-hand side's derivative by t is

$$\frac{\alpha\beta^2\gamma}{(1+\gamma\,(1+\beta T)+\beta\, t)^2} > 0,$$

which means that the right-hand side takes its maximum at $t = T$. Therefore, a sufficient condition for monotonically decreasing survival probabilities is given by

$$\frac{\alpha\beta^2\gamma\, T}{(1+\gamma\,(1+\beta T))^2 + (1+\gamma\,(1+\beta T))\beta T} \leq \frac{S^{M\prime}(T)}{S^M(T)} = \frac{\partial \ln S^M(T)}{\partial T} = \lambda^M(T),$$

where $\lambda^M(T)$ is the market-implied hazard rate.

15.5.4 Examples

We continue the analysis with the central question of which implied volatilities (again for six months expiry option on a five-year at-the-money CDS) can be

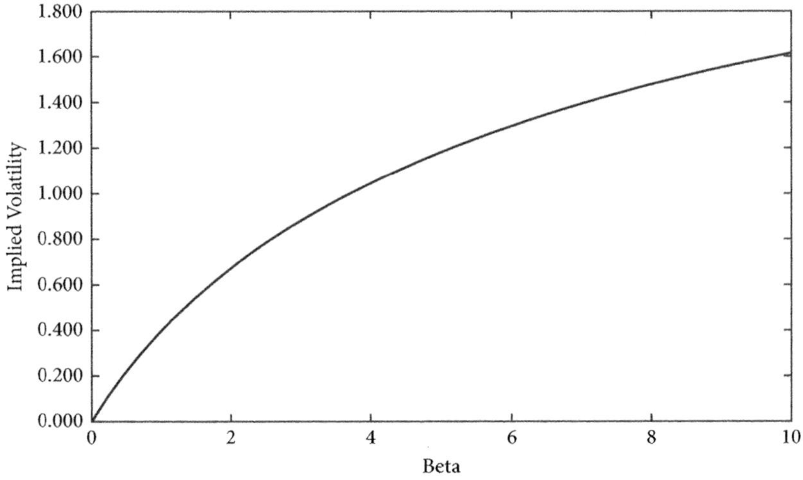

Figure 15.18 Attainable implied volatility in the Peng-Kou model for flat hazard rate at 200bp, mean jump size $\gamma = 0.0045$ and mean jump intensity $\alpha\beta = 5$. Parameter β is varied while mean jump intensity is kept constant, i.e. α is varied accordingly. As β increases, we hence increase the variance of the jump intensity distribution. The implied volatility refers to a CDS option with expiry in six months and a five-year term

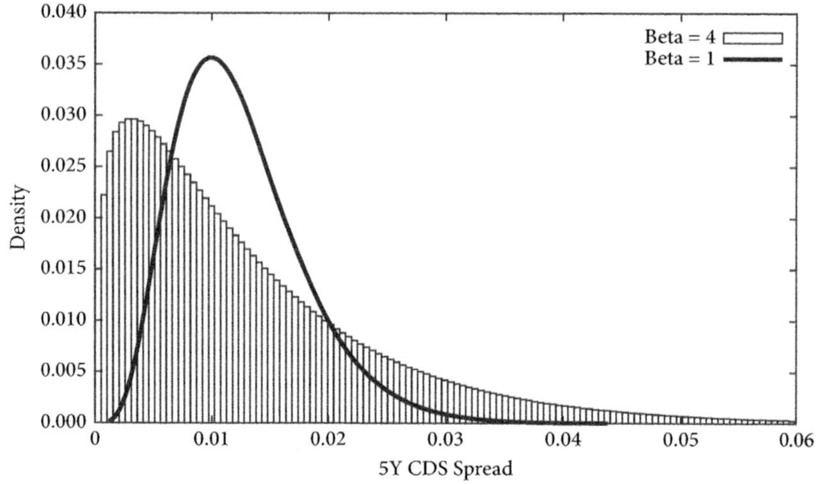

Figure 15.19 Distributions of fair 5y CDS at time $t=5$ for the parameters in Figure 15.18 with $\beta=1$ and $\beta=4$, respectively. The case $\beta=1$ is associated with 40% implied volatility for a six-months expiry option on a five-year at-the-money CDS, $\beta=4$ is associated with 105% implied volatility

Table 15.3 Attainable implied volatilities (six months expiry, five years at-the-money CDS term) in the Peng-Kou model for several choices of market hazard rate levels, mean jump size γ, mean jump intensity $\alpha\beta$ and scale parameter β

#	λ^M	γ	$\alpha\beta$	β	implied vol
1	0.01	0.0021	5.0	1.0	0.38
2	0.01	0.0021	5.0	4.0	1.01
3	0.02	0.0045	5.0	1.0	0.40
4	0.02	0.0045	5.0	4.0	1.05
5	0.03	0.0070	5.0	1.0	0.41
6	0.03	0.0070	5.0	4.0	1.05
7	0.05	0.0130	5.0	1.0	0.44
8	0.05	0.0130	5.0	4.0	1.08

attained with this model. We did this analysis initially in a brute force way by simply varying model parameters in a wide range, excluding parameter combinations that violate the monotonicity constraint above for times up to five years, and evaluating the model implied CDS option prices and related implied volatilities. We did this for a number of flat market hazard curve scenarios (0.01, 0.02, 0.03, 0.05). In our data we moreover observed cases for which the resulting CDS spread distribution seemed "realistic" in the sense that it did not show a significant lower

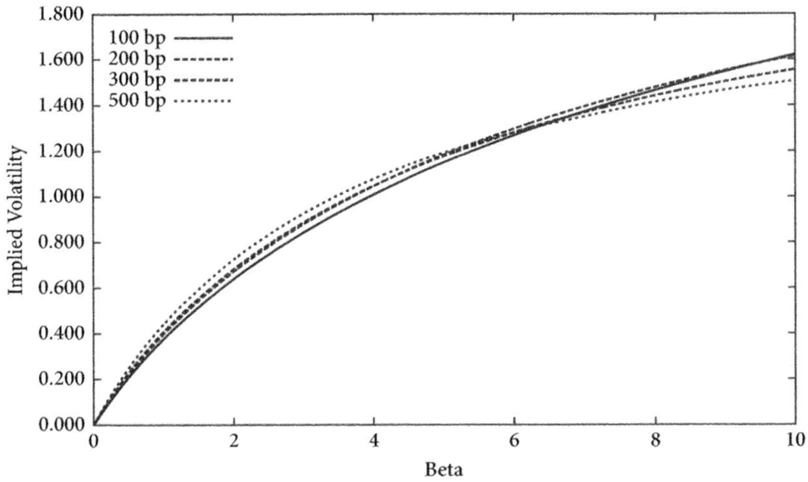

Figure 15.20 Attainable implied volatility in the Peng-Kou model as a function of β for the cases summarized in Table 15.3

cutoff (as observed with CIR). The occurrence of negative CDS spreads is ruled out by enforcing monotonicity of $S(t, T)$ already.

One typical result of this search is shown in Figure 15.18. By varying the jump intensity's scale parameter β – while keeping the mean jump intensity fixed – we tune the jump intensity's variance with a strong impact on the implied volatility of a six-month expiry, five-year term CDS option, towards well above the 100% level. We now pick two parameter sets from Figure 15.18 ($\beta = 1$ and $\beta = 4$) to evaluate the distributions of fair 5y CDS at future time $t = 5$. These are shown in Figure 15.19.

The results for all hazard rate levels considered are summarized in Table 15.3.

The attainable implied volatilities across all cases in Table 15.3 as a function of β are illustrated in Figure 15.20, the distributions of fair CDS spreads at time $t = 5$ for case 1/2 and 7/8 in Figure 15.21.

15.5.5 Conclusion

From the examples above we conclude that the Peng-Kou model combines a number of desirable features – it is analytically tractable, sufficiently high implied CDS option volatilities seem attainable across various relevant market hazard rate levels, the shape of implied distributions of CDS spreads is realistic, and negative CDS spreads and significant lower cutoffs in spread distributions can be avoided. The discrete nature of the spread distribution does not seem to be an issue when the mean jump size is chosen significantly smaller than the market hazard rate

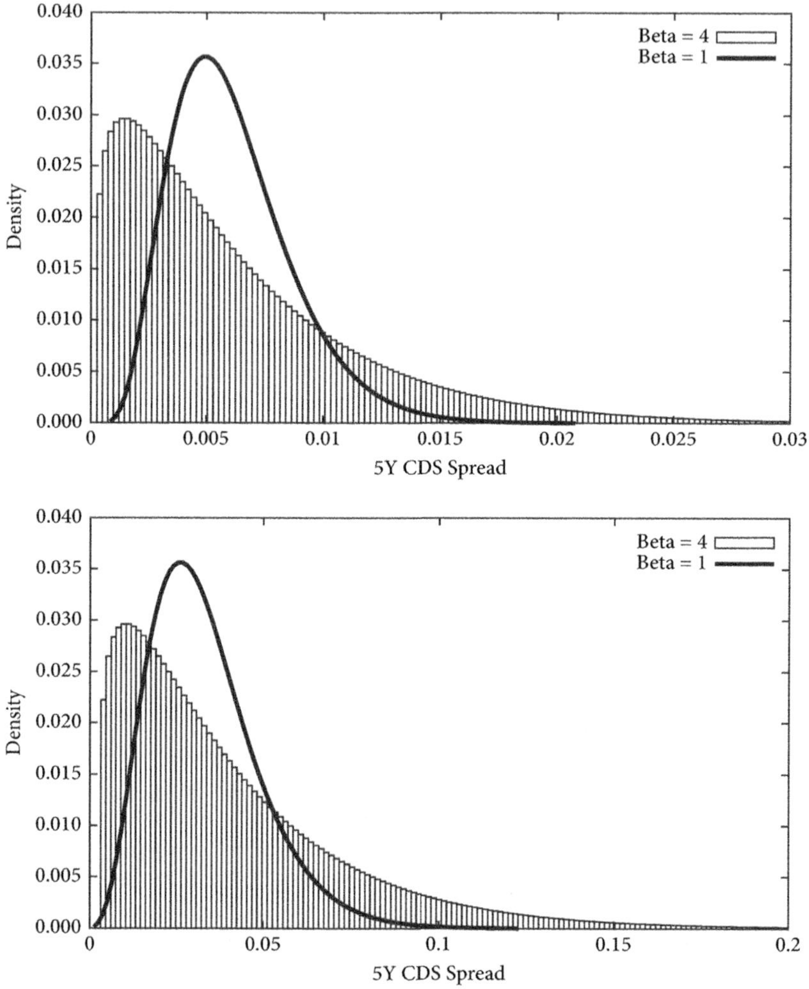

Figure 15.21 Distributions of fair 5y CDS at time $t = 5$ for cases 1/2 (top) and 7/8 (bottom) in Table 15.3

level, as we did in the examples. In our opinion, the model therefore deserves further investigation and integration for multiple credit names into the risk factor simulation framework presented in this part of the book.

A further generalization of the Peng-Kou model using *Dirac processes* – which integrate jumps in the cumulative default intensity process – is presented by Kenyon & Green in [105].

IV | XVA

Introduction

The calculation of CVA is relatively straightforward for simple, single trades. After we have defined what to compute in Part II, and how to model the risk factors of complex derivatives or of portfolios of derivatives, it is time to move on to the computation of CVA on the portfolio level. This requires plugging the models for individual asset classes together into a unified simulation framework that can value the future exposures of portfolios under netting and collateralization.

Theoretical modelling is one thing, but the complexity of exposure simulation requires the efficient usage of existing (computational) resources. Therefore, it is important to solve the problem that arises when computing future exposures of trades that require simulations or other time-consuming pricing algorithms, like multi-callables. Pricing has to be optimized in such a fashion that the exposure calculation does not become prohibitively slow. A way around that is an algorithm that is commonly known as *American Monte Carlo.*

Another requirement that uses up a lot of performance is the computation of sensitivities of CVA numbers (CVA risk). If a single calculation run already requires hours of computation time, it is not possible to use brute force by bumping all the relevant risk factors and recalculating CVA for the whole portfolio. Fortunately, the financial industry has realized that an old numerical method for calculating derivatives of implemented functions called *algorithmic differentiation* can be employed to tackle this problem.

We saw in the previous chapters that the calculation of realistic credit and debit value adjustments is a complex task that requires highly sophisticated hybrid models for risk factor evolution. Up until the mid-2000s, the topic was dealt with only by a small number of banks, typically with unilateral CVA numbers, and even fewer institutions performed active CVA management. Only with the beginning of the credit crisis in 2007 did it become clear that the counterparty credit risk of derivatives as part of the pricing was not negligible. For the lending business, credit risk has always been a component in pricing. However, the simplified approach of taking the outstanding notional of a loan as the exposure at default makes the quantification of the expected loss quite simple, provided that the default probability term structure of the borrower is known.

What else can we learn from the loan business? A lender has to cover its costs by including them in the loan pricing. Most prominently, those are credit risk provisions, funding costs and capital costs. One reason that this was not done for derivatives in the past is that the future exposure is difficult to determine unless one is dealing with very simple trades, in which case it is possible to employ analytic formulas for exposure calculations, as we showed in Chapter 9. Another reason is that the contributions from derivatives to these costs were small before the crisis: funding in terms of spread over the risk-free rate – LIBOR at the time – was cheap, capital requirements were lower and less costly, and product designers in banks were more interested in making the derivatives more and more complex while pricing them with relatively simple models. Note that in the current state of the financial world where central banks flood the markets with cheap funding, the unwary might fall back into thinking that funding is immaterial.

As we have already mentioned in Chapter 3, the regulators' reaction to the banking crisis was to strongly encourage central clearing wherever possible, or by requiring an initial margin reflecting the market risk of a non-cleared transaction between banks. Clearing and initial margin mean higher funding requirements for derivatives transactions because initial margins have to be posted on top of current exposure.

Furthermore, a new capital charge was introduced with Basel III that penalizes the CVA volatility, see BCBS 189 [18]. Furthermore, the old standard approach for computing regulatory exposure (in order to determine the required capital due to credit risk from derivatives), the Current Exposure Method (CEM), will change to the new Standard Approach for Counterparty Credit Risk (SA-CCR) in 2017, see BCBS 279 [22].

In all, we see that the new regulations try to make the derivatives markets more transparent by moving as much business as possible to clearing houses, and to reduce default risk because central counterparties are viewed as being virtually free of default risk. On the other hand, the increased margin requirements mean a higher liquidity drain especially in crisis situations, so it is fair to say that credit risk is transformed into liquidity risk.

Banks have to find the balance between capital and liquidity consumption; large international banks even have several different regulatory environments to cope with, each with its own requirements. The message is that there is no sweet spot for anyone anymore where derivatives can be done at zero cost. In order to optimize their cost structure, banks will have to use a machinery that allows them to decide which hedge will lead to the lowest cost impact. Given that there is a multitude of CSAs to consider, certainly several different clearing houses worldwide, and the problem of many regulatory jurisdictions, it should be clear that this task is extremely complex.

This part of the book starts with the generation of cross-asset scenarios for the exposure evolution in Chapter 16. Chapter 17 then describes how to include the features of a CSA in the CVA calculation. In the next Chapter 18, we show an application of American Monte Carlo for the exposure calculation of complex trades. Following that, Chapter 19 introduces the method of algorithmic differentiation. The last two chapters give an overview of the additional important value adjustments – usually summarized under the acronym XVA – that are in the process of becoming new market standards: the Funding Value Adjustment (FVA), comprising the Funding Benefit Adjustment (FBA), the Funding Cost Adjustment (FCA) and the Margin Value Adjustment (MVA), which we cover in Chapter 20, and the Capital Value adjustment (KVA) which is the subject of Chapter 21. As we shall see, both concepts further erode the paradigm of a single fair market value for a derivative because they are idiosyncratic by their very nature. FVA, like CVA, depends on the CSA (or clearing regime) under which the transaction is done. KVA actually depends on the entire portfolio of the organization.

16 Cross-Asset Scenario Generation

In Sections 11.4, 12.5, 13.5 and 15.3.6 we have seen already a number of exposure evolution examples for basic vanilla products across asset classes. These were in fact produced by a joint evolution model which we have developed in Part III step by step. In some of the asset classes (such as inflation and credit) we have seen alternatives we can choose from.

It is time to show at least one integrated version of the joint model with a particular model choice. In the following we present a combined model for IR, FX, INF and CR which uses the Jarrow-Yildirim model for inflation and LGM for credit. This yields a joint model specified by the SDE

Interest rates

$$dz_0 = \alpha_0^z \, dW_0^z \tag{16.1}$$

$$dz_i = \gamma_i \, dt + \alpha_i^z \, dW_i^z \tag{16.2}$$

Foreign exchange

$$dx_i/x_i = \mu_i^x \, dt + \sigma_i^x \, dW_i^x \tag{16.3}$$

Inflation

$$dy_j = \theta_j \, dt + \alpha_j^y \, dW_j^y \tag{16.4}$$

$$dc_j/c_j = \mu_j^c \, dt + \sigma_j^c \, dW_j^c \tag{16.5}$$

Credit

$$dz_k^\lambda = \alpha_k^\lambda \, dW_k^\lambda, \tag{16.6}$$

$$dy_k^\lambda = H_k^\lambda \, \alpha_k^\lambda \, dW_k^\lambda \tag{16.7}$$

where we have dropped time-dependencies to lighten notation, and indices run from $i = 0, \ldots, n-1$, $j = 1, \ldots, m$, $k = 1, \ldots, o$. The no-arbitrage drift terms are

$$
\begin{aligned}
\gamma_i &= -H_i^z\,(\alpha_i^z)^2 + H_0^z\,\alpha_0^z\,\alpha_i^z\,\rho_{0i}^{zz} - \sigma_i^x\,\alpha_i^z\,\rho_{ii}^{zx} \\
\mu_i^x &= n_0 - n_i + H_0^z\,\alpha_0^z\,\sigma_i^x\,\rho_{0i}^{zx} \\
\theta_j &= -H_j^y\,(\alpha_j^y)^2 + H_0^z\,\alpha_0^z\,\alpha_j^y\,\rho_{0j}^{zy} - \alpha_j^y\,\sigma_j^c\,\rho_{jj}^{yc} - \epsilon_{i_j}\,\alpha_j^y\,\sigma_{i_j}^x\,\rho_{ji_j}^{yx} \\
\mu_j^c &= n_{i_j} - r_j + H_0^z\,\alpha_0^z\,\sigma_j^c\,\rho_{0j}^{zc} - \epsilon_{i_j}\,\sigma_j^c\,\sigma_{i_j}^x\,\rho_{ji_j}^{cx} \\
\epsilon_i &= \begin{cases} 0 & \text{if } i = 0 \text{ (domestic)} \\ 1 & \text{if } i \neq 0 \text{ (foreign)} \end{cases}
\end{aligned}
$$

Indices i_j in the inflation drift terms refer to the foreign currency interest rate process and the corresponding exchange rate process for the inflation index's currency. The system is completed by closed form expressions for

- domestic numeraire (11.1) under the LGM measure
- stochastic zero bond (11.4) for both domestic and foreign currencies,
- short interest rate expressed in terms of LGM variables (11.6) for both domestic and foreign currencies,
- stochastic real rate zero bond (13.9) for domestic and foreign currency inflation indices,
- stochastic (conditional) survival probability (15.11) and (15.14) for domestic and foreign currency context
- stochastic survival probability up to time t (15.14) and (15.15) for domestic and foreign currency context

The extension to equity and commodity based on Section 14 is straightforward. This setup is entirely analytically tractable because we know the joint distribution of the model factors

$$z_0, z_i, \ln x_i, y_j, \ln c_j, z_k^\lambda, y_k^\lambda$$

analytically – it is multivariate normal and hence fully specified by expectations and covariances of the model factors. We summarize these in Section 16.1 for completeness.

16.1 Expectations and covariances

This section documents the expectations and covariances of changes of the joint IR/FX/INF/CR model factors over time intervals $[s, t]$. These quantities determine the joint distribution of factor moves and are the key inputs for generating multi-dimensional model paths. All moments are given by one-dimensional time integrals over model parameters. Throughout this section we use the notation $\Delta\phi(t) := \phi(t) - \phi(s)$ where $s < t$ to denote the change in the stochastic process ϕ over the time interval $[s, t]$. Moreover we omit time-dependencies where possible to lighten the notation.

Interest rates

Since z_i obeys

$$dz_i = \epsilon_i \gamma_i \, dt + \alpha_i^z \, dW_i^z,$$

we have

$$\begin{aligned}\Delta z_i = & -\int_s^t H_i^z \, (\alpha_i^z)^2 \, du + \rho_{0i}^{zz} \int_s^t H_0^z \, \alpha_0^z \, \alpha_i^z \, du \\ & - \epsilon_i \rho_{ii}^{zx} \int_s^t \sigma_i^x \, \alpha_i^z \, du + \int_s^t \alpha_i^z \, dW_i^z.\end{aligned}$$

Thus,

$$\begin{aligned}\mathbb{E}[\Delta z_i] = & -\int_s^t H_i^z \, (\alpha_i^z)^2 \, du + \rho_{0i}^{zz} \int_s^t H_0^z \, \alpha_0^z \, \alpha_i^z \, du - \epsilon_i \rho_{ii}^{zx} \int_s^t \sigma_i^x \, \alpha_i^z \, du \\ \mathrm{Cov}[\Delta z_a, \Delta z_b] = & \rho_{ab}^{zz} \int_s^t \alpha_a^z \, \alpha_b^z \, du\end{aligned}$$

Foreign exchange

Since x_i obeys

$$dx_i / x_i = \mu_i^x \, dt + \sigma_i^x \, dW_i^x,$$

we have

$$\begin{aligned}\Delta \ln x_i = & \ln\left(\frac{P_0^n(0,s)}{P_0^n(0,t)} \frac{P_i^n(0,t)}{P_i^n(0,s)}\right) - \frac{1}{2}\int_s^t (\sigma_i^x)^2 \, du + \rho_{0i}^{zx} \int_s^t H_0^z \, \alpha_0^z \, \sigma_i^x \, du \\ & + \int_s^t \zeta_0^z \, H_0^z \, (H_0^z)' \, du - \int_s^t \zeta_i^z \, H_i^z \, (H_i^z)' \, du \\ & + \int_s^t \left(H_0^z(t) - H_0^z\right) \alpha_0^z \, dW_0^z + \left(H_0^z(t) - H_0^z(s)\right) z_0(s) \\ & - \int_s^t \left(H_i^z(t) - H_i^z\right) \alpha_i^z \, dW_i^z - \left(H_i^z(t) - H_i^z(s)\right) z_i(s) \\ & - \int_s^t \left(H_i^z(t) - H_i^z\right) \gamma_i \, du + \int_s^t \sigma_i^x dW_i^x\end{aligned}$$

Integration by parts yields

$$
\begin{aligned}
&\int_s^t \zeta_0^z\, H_0^z\, (H_0^z)'\, du - \int_s^t \zeta_i^z\, H_i^z\, (H_i^z)'\, du \\
&= \frac{1}{2}\left((H_0^z(t))^2\zeta_0^z(t) - (H_0^z(s))^2\zeta_0^z(s) - \int_s^t (H_0^z)^2(\alpha_0^z)^2\, du\right) \\
&\quad - \frac{1}{2}\left((H_i^z(t))^2\zeta_i^z(t) - (H_i^z(s))^2\zeta_i^z(s) - \int_s^t (H_i^z)^2(\alpha_i^z)^2\, du\right)
\end{aligned}
$$

so that the expectation is

$$
\begin{aligned}
\mathbb{E}[\Delta \ln x_i] =& \ln\left(\frac{P_0^n(0,s)}{P_0^n(0,t)}\,\frac{P_i^n(0,t)}{P_i^n(0,s)}\right) - \frac{1}{2}\int_s^t (\sigma_i^x)^2\, du + \rho_{0i}^{zx}\int_s^t H_0^z\,\alpha_0^z\,\sigma_i^x\, du \\
&+ \frac{1}{2}\left((H_0^z(t))^2\zeta_0^z(t) - (H_0^z(s))^2\zeta_0^z(s) - \int_s^t (H_0^z)^2(\alpha_0^z)^2\, du\right) \\
&- \frac{1}{2}\left((H_i^z(t))^2\zeta_i^z(t) - (H_i^z(s))^2\zeta_i^z(s) - \int_s^t (H_i^z)^2(\alpha_i^z)^2\, du\right) \\
&+ \left(H_0^z(t) - H_0^z(s)\right) z_0(s) - \left(H_i^z(t) - H_i^z(s)\right) z_i(s) \\
&- \int_s^t \left(H_i^z(t) - H_i^z\right) \gamma_i\, du,
\end{aligned} \tag{16.8}
$$

and IR-FX and FX-FX covariances are

$$
\begin{aligned}
\mathrm{Cov}[\Delta \ln x_a, \Delta \ln x_b] =& \int_s^t \left(H_0^z(t) - H_0^z\right)^2 (\alpha_0^z)^2\, du \\
&- \rho_{0b}^{zz}\int_s^t \left(H_0^z(t) - H_0^z\right)\alpha_0^z\left(H_b^z(t) - H_b^z\right)\alpha_b^z\, du \\
&+ \rho_{0b}^{zx}\int_s^t \left(H_0^z(t) - H_0^z\right)\alpha_0^z\sigma_b^x\, du \\
&- \rho_{0a}^{zz}\int_s^t \left(H_a^z(t) - H_a^z\right)\alpha_a^z\left(H_0^z(t) - H_0^z\right)\alpha_0^z\, du \\
&+ \rho_{ab}^{zz}\int_s^t \left(H_a^z(t) - H_a^z\right)\alpha_a^z\left(H_b^z(t) - H_b^z\right)\alpha_b^z\, du \\
&- \rho_{ab}^{zx}\int_s^t \left(H_a^z(t) - H_a^z\right)\alpha_a^z\sigma_b^x,\, du \\
&+ \rho_{0a}^{zx}\int_s^t \left(H_0^z(t) - H_0^z\right)\alpha_0^z\,\sigma_a^x\, du \\
&- \rho_{ba}^{zx}\int_s^t \left(H_b^z(t) - H_b^z\right)\alpha_b^z\,\sigma_a^x\, du + \rho_{ab}^{xx}\int_s^t \sigma_a^x\,\sigma_b^x\, du
\end{aligned} \tag{16.9}
$$

$$\begin{aligned}\mathrm{Cov}[\Delta z_a, \Delta \ln x_b]) = &\rho^{zz}_{0a} \int_s^t \left(H^z_0(t) - H^z_0\right) \alpha^z_0 \alpha^z_a \, du \\ &- \rho^{zz}_{ab} \int_s^t \alpha^z_a \left(H^z_b(t) - H^z_b\right) \alpha^z_b \, du \\ &+ \rho^{zx}_{ab} \int_s^t \alpha^z_a \sigma^x_b \, du. \end{aligned} \tag{16.10}$$

Inflation

Since y_j and c_j obey

$$\begin{aligned} dy_j &= \theta_j \, dt + \alpha^y_j \, dW^y_j, \\ dc_j/c_j &= \mu^c_j \, dt + \sigma^c_j \, dW^c_j, \end{aligned}$$

we have

$$\begin{aligned} \Delta y_j = &- \int_s^t H^y_j (\alpha^y_j)^2 \, du + \rho^{zy}_{0j} \int_s^t H^z_0 \alpha^z_0 \alpha^y_j \, du \\ &- \rho^{yc}_{jj} \int_s^t \alpha^y_j \sigma^c_j \, du - \epsilon_{i_j} \rho^{xy}_{i_j j} \int_s^t \alpha^y_j \sigma^x_{i_j} \, du + \int_s^t \alpha^y_j \, dW^y_j \\ \Delta \ln c_j = &\ln \left(\frac{P^n_{i_j}(0,s)}{P^n_{i_j}(0,t)} \frac{P^r_j(0,t)}{P^r_j(0,s)} \right) - \frac{1}{2} \int_s^t (\sigma^c_j)^2 \, du + \rho^{zc}_{0j} \int_s^t H^z_0 \alpha^z_0 \sigma^c_j \, du \\ &- \epsilon_{i_j} \rho^{xc}_{i_j j} \int_s^t \sigma^x_{i_j} \sigma^c_j \, du \\ &+ \int_s^t \zeta^z_{i_j} H^z_{i_j} (H^z_{i_j})' \, du - \int_s^t \zeta^y_j H^y_j (H^y_j)' \, du \\ &+ \int_s^t \left(H^z_{i_j}(t) - H^z_{i_j}\right) \alpha^z_{i_j} \, dW^z_{i_j} + \left(H^z_{i_j}(t) - H^z_{i_j}(s)\right) z_{i_j}(s) \\ &+ \int_s^t \left(H^z_{i_j}(t) - H^z_{i_j}\right) \gamma_{i_j} \, du - \int_s^t \left(H^y_j(t) - H^y_j\right) \alpha^y_j \, dW^y_j \\ &- \left(H^y_j(t) - H^y_j(s)\right) y_j(s) - \int_s^t \left(H^y_j(t) - H^y_j\right) \theta_j \, du \\ &+ \int_s^t \sigma^c_j dW^c_j \end{aligned}$$

Integration by parts again yields

$$
\begin{aligned}
&\int_s^t \zeta_{i_j}^z H_{i_j}^z (H_{i_j}^z)' \, du - \int_s^t \zeta_j^y H_j^y (H_j^y)' \, du \\
&= \frac{1}{2}\left((H_{i_j}^z(t))^2 \zeta_{i_j}^z(t) - (H_{i_j}^z(s))^2 \zeta_{i_j}^z(s) - \int_s^t (H_{i_j}^z)^2 (\alpha_{i_j}^z)^2 \, du \right) \\
&- \frac{1}{2}\left((H_j^y(t))^2 \zeta_j^y(t) - (H_j^y(s))^2 \zeta_j^y(s) - \int_s^t (H_j^y)^2 (\alpha_j^y)^2 \, du \right)
\end{aligned}
$$

Therefore the expectations are

$$
\begin{aligned}
\mathbb{E}[\Delta y_j] = &- \int_s^t H_j^y (\alpha_j^y)^2 \, du + \rho_{0j}^{zy} \int_s^t H_0^z \alpha_0^z \alpha_j^y \, du \\
&- \rho_{jj}^{yc} \int_s^t \alpha_j^y(t) \sigma_j^c(t) \, du - \epsilon_{i_j} \rho_{i_j j}^{xy} \int_s^t \alpha_j^y \sigma_{i_j}^x \, du
\end{aligned}
\tag{16.11}
$$

$$
\begin{aligned}
\mathbb{E}\left(\Delta \ln c_j\right) = &\ln\left(\frac{P_{i_j}^n(0,s)}{P_{i_j}^n(0,t)} \frac{P_j^r(0,t)}{P_j^r(0,s)} \right) - \frac{1}{2} \int_s^t (\sigma_j^c)^2 \, du \\
&+ \rho_{0j}^{zc} \int_s^t H_0^z \alpha_0^z \sigma_j^c \, du - \epsilon_{i_j} \rho_{i_j j}^{xc} \int_s^t \sigma_i^x \sigma_i^c \, du \\
&+ \frac{1}{2}\left((H_{i_j}^z(t))^2 \zeta_{i_j}^z(t) - (H_{i_j}^z(s))^2 \zeta_{i_j}^z(s) - \int_s^t (H_{i_j}^z)^2 (\alpha_{i_j}^z)^2 \, du \right) \\
&- \frac{1}{2}\left((H_j^y(t))^2 \zeta_j^y(t) - (H_j^y(s))^2 \zeta_j^y(s) - \int_s^t (H_j^y)^2 (\alpha_j^y)^2 \, du \right) \\
&+ \left(H_{i_j}^z(t) - H_{i_j}^z(s) \right) z_{i_j}(s) - \left(H_j^y(t) - H_j^y(s) \right) y_j(s) \\
&+ \int_s^t \left(H_{i_j}^z(t) - H_{i_j}^z \right) \gamma_{i_j} \, du - \int_s^t \left(H_j^y(t) - H_j^y \right) \theta_j \, du
\end{aligned}
\tag{16.12}
$$

and covariances are

$$\mathrm{Cov}[\Delta y_a, \Delta z_b] = \rho^{zy}_{ba} \int_s^t \alpha^z_b \alpha^y_a \, du \tag{16.13}$$

$$\begin{aligned}\mathrm{Cov}[\Delta y_a, \Delta \ln x_b] =& \rho^{zy}_{0j} \int_s^t \alpha^z_0 \left(H^z_0(t) - H^z_0\right) \alpha^y_a \, du \\ & - \rho^{zy}_{ba} \int_s^t \left(H^z_b(t) - H^z_b\right) \alpha^z_j \alpha^y_a \, du + \rho^{xy}_{ba} \int_s^t \alpha^y_a \sigma^x_b \, du\end{aligned} \tag{16.14}$$

$$\mathrm{Cov}[\Delta y_a, \Delta y_b] = \rho^{yy}_{ab} \int_s^t \alpha^y_a \alpha^y_b \, du \tag{16.15}$$

$$\begin{aligned}\mathrm{Cov}[\Delta y_a, \Delta \ln c_b] =& \rho^{zy}_{i_b a} \int_s^t \alpha^z_{i_b} \left(H^z_{i_b}(t) - H^z_{i_b}\right) \alpha^y_a \, du \\ & - \rho^{yy}_{ab} \int_s^t \alpha^y_b \left(H^y_b(t) - H^y_b\right) \alpha^y_a \, du + \rho^{yc}_{ab} \int_s^t \alpha^y_a \sigma^c_b \, du\end{aligned} \tag{16.16}$$

$$\begin{aligned}\mathrm{Cov}[\Delta \ln c_a, \Delta z_b] =& \rho^{zz}_{i_a b} \int_s^t \alpha^z_{i_a} \left(H^z_{i_a}(t) - H^z_{i_a}\right) \alpha^z_b \, du \\ & - \rho^{zy}_{ba} \int_s^t \alpha^y_a \left(H^y_a(t) - H^y_a\right) \alpha^z_b \, du + \rho^{zc}_{ba} \int_s^t \sigma^c_a \alpha^z_b \, du\end{aligned} \tag{16.17}$$

$$\begin{aligned}\mathrm{Cov}[\Delta \ln c_a, \Delta \ln x_b] =& \rho^{zz}_{0 i_a} \int_s^t \left(H^z_{i_a}(t) - H^z_{i_a}\right) \alpha^z_{i_a} \left(H^z_0(t) - H^z_0\right) \alpha^z_0 \, du \\ & - \rho^{zz}_{i_a b} \int_s^t \left(H^z_{i_a}(t) - H^z_{i_a}\right) \alpha^z_{i_a} \left(H^z_b(t) - H^z_b\right) \alpha^z_b \, du \\ & + \rho^{zx}_{i_a b} \int_s^t \left(H^z_{i_a}(t) - H^z_{i_a}\right) \alpha^z_{i_a} \sigma^x_b \, du \\ & - \rho^{zy}_{0a} \int_s^t \left(H^y_a(t) - H^y_a\right) \alpha^y_a \left(H^z_0(t) - H^z_0\right) \alpha^z_0 \, du \\ & + \rho^{zy}_{ba} \int_s^t \left(H^y_a(t) - H^y_a\right) \alpha^y_a \left(H^z_b(t) - H^z_b\right) \alpha^z_b \, du \\ & - \rho^{xy}_{ba} \int_s^t \left(H^y_a(t) - H^y_a\right) \alpha^y_a \sigma^x_b \, du \\ & + \rho^{zc}_{0a} \int_s^t \sigma^c_a \left(H^z_0(t) - H^z_0\right) \alpha^z_0 \, du \\ & - \rho^{zc}_{ba} \int_s^t \sigma^c_a \left(H^z_b(t) - H^z_b\right) \alpha^z_b \, du + \rho^{xc}_{ba} \int_s^t \sigma^c_a \sigma^x_b \, du\end{aligned} \tag{16.18}$$

$$\begin{aligned}
\mathrm{Cov}[\Delta \ln c_a, \Delta \ln c_b] = {} & \rho^{zz}_{i_a i_b} \int_s^t \left(H^z_{i_a}(t) - H^z_{i_a}\right) \alpha^z_{i_a} \left(H^z_{i_b}(t) - H^z_{i_b}\right) \alpha^z_{i_b}\, du \\
& - \rho^{zy}_{i_a b} \int_s^t \left(H^z_{i_a}(t) - H^z_{i_a}\right) \alpha^z_{i_a} \left(H^y_b(t) - H^y_b\right) \alpha^y_b\, du \\
& + \rho^{zc}_{i_a b} \int_s^t \left(H^z_{i_a}(t) - H^z_{i_a}\right) \alpha^z_{i_a} \sigma^c_b\, du \\
& - \rho^{zy}_{i_b a} \int_s^t \left(H^z_{i_b}(t) - H^z_{i_b}\right) \alpha^z_{i_b} \left(H^y_a(t) - H^y_a\right) \alpha^y_a\, du \\
& + \rho^{yy}_{ab} \int_s^t \left(H^y_a(t) - H^y_a\right) \alpha^y_a \left(H^y_b(t) - H^y_b\right) \alpha^y_b\, du \\
& - \rho^{yc}_{ab} \int_s^t \left(H^y_a(t) - H^y_a\right) \alpha^y_a \sigma^c_b\, du \\
& + \rho^{zc}_{i_b a} \int_s^t \left(H^z_{i_b}(t) - H^z_{i_b}\right) \alpha^z_{i_b} \sigma^c_a\, du \\
& - \rho^{yc}_{ba} \int_s^t \left(H^y_b(t) - H^y_b\right) \alpha^b_a \sigma^c_a\, du \\
& + \rho^{cc}_{ab} \int_s^t \sigma^c_a \sigma^c_b\, du
\end{aligned} \tag{16.19}$$

Credit: update the y^λ covariances

Since z^λ_k and y^λ_k obey

$$\begin{aligned}
dz^\lambda_k &= \alpha^\lambda_k\, dW^\lambda_k, \\
dy^\lambda_k &= H^\lambda_k\, \alpha^\lambda_k\, dW^\lambda_k
\end{aligned}$$

we have

$$\begin{aligned}
\Delta z^\lambda_k &= \int_s^t \alpha^\lambda_k\, dW^\lambda_k \\
\Delta z^\lambda_k &= \int_s^t H^\lambda_k\, \alpha^\lambda_k\, dW^\lambda_k
\end{aligned}$$

Thus

$$\mathbb{E}[\Delta z^\lambda_k] = 0 \tag{16.20}$$

$$\mathbb{E}[\Delta y^\lambda_k] = 0 \tag{16.21}$$

and

$$\mathrm{Cov}[\Delta z_a^\lambda, \Delta z_b] = \rho_{ba}^{z\lambda} \int_s^t \alpha_a^\lambda \alpha_b^z \, du \tag{16.22}$$

$$\begin{aligned}\mathrm{Cov}[\Delta z_a^\lambda, \Delta \ln x_b] = & \rho_{0a}^{z\lambda} \int_s^t \alpha_0^z \left(H_0^z(t) - H_0^z\right) \alpha_a^\lambda \, du \\ & - \rho_{ba}^{z\lambda} \int_s^t \alpha_b^z \left(H_b^z(t) - H_b^z\right) \alpha_a^\lambda \, du \\ & + \rho_{ba}^{x\lambda} \int_s^t \sigma_b^x \alpha_a^\lambda \, du \end{aligned} \tag{16.23}$$

$$\mathrm{Cov}[\Delta z_a^\lambda, \Delta y_b] = \rho_{ba}^{y\lambda} \int_s^t \alpha_b^y \alpha_a^\lambda \, du \tag{16.24}$$

$$\begin{aligned}\mathrm{Cov}[\Delta z_a^\lambda, \Delta \ln c_b] = & \rho_{i_b a}^{z\lambda} \int_s^t \alpha_{i_b}^z \left(H_{i_b}^z(t) - H_{i_b}^z\right) \alpha_a^\lambda \, du \\ & - \rho_{ba}^{y\lambda} \int_s^t \alpha_b^y \left(H_b^y(t) - H_b^y\right) \alpha_a^\lambda \, du \\ & + \rho_{ba}^{c\lambda} \int_s^t \sigma_b^c \alpha_a^\lambda \, du \end{aligned} \tag{16.25}$$

$$\mathrm{Cov}[\Delta z_a^\lambda, \Delta z_b^\lambda] = \rho_{ab}^{\nu\lambda} \int_s^t \alpha_a^\lambda \alpha_b^\lambda \, du \tag{16.26}$$

$$\mathrm{Cov}[\Delta y_a^\lambda, \Delta z_b] = \rho_{ba}^{z\lambda} \int_s^t \alpha_a^\lambda \alpha_b^z \, du \tag{16.27}$$

$$\begin{aligned}\mathrm{Cov}[\Delta y_a^\lambda, \Delta \ln x_b] = & \rho_{0a}^{z\lambda} \int_s^t \alpha_0^z \left(H_0^z(t) - H_0^z\right) \alpha_a^\lambda \, du \\ & - \rho_{ba}^{z\lambda} \int_s^t \alpha_b^z \left(H_b^z(t) - H_b^z\right) \alpha_a^\lambda \, du \\ & + \rho_{ba}^{x\lambda} \int_s^t \sigma_b^x \alpha_a^\lambda \, du \end{aligned} \tag{16.28}$$

$$\mathrm{Cov}[\Delta y_a^\lambda, \Delta y_b] = \rho_{ba}^{y\lambda} \int_s^t \alpha_b^y \alpha_a^\lambda \, du \tag{16.29}$$

$$\begin{aligned}\mathrm{Cov}[\Delta y_a^\lambda, \Delta \ln c_b] = & \rho_{i_b a}^{z\lambda} \int_s^t \alpha_{i_b}^z \left(H_{i_b}^z(t) - H_{i_b}^z\right) \alpha_a^\lambda \, du \\ & - \rho_{ba}^{y\lambda} \int_s^t \alpha_b^y \left(H_b^y(t) - H_b^y\right) \alpha_a^\lambda \, du \\ & + \rho_{ba}^{c\lambda} \int_s^t \sigma_b^c \alpha_a^\lambda \, du \end{aligned} \tag{16.30}$$

$$\mathrm{Cov}[\Delta y_a^\lambda, \Delta y_b^\lambda] = \rho_{ab}^{\nu\lambda} \int_s^t \alpha_a^\lambda \alpha_b^\lambda \, du \tag{16.31}$$

16.2 Path generation

The system of SDE (16.1–16.7) can be evolved in *arbitrarily large time steps* without a time discretization error, because we know the multivariate normal joint distribution of factor moves analytically, and we can "draw" factor moves from the joint distribution. To illustrate the algorithm, let us label the key quantities as follows:

- model factors f_i, or $\mathbf{F}$ in vector notation with vector size d
- expected change of model factor f_i over time period $[t_{k-1}, t_k]$: $e_i(t_k)$, or $\mathbf{E}(t_k)$ in vector notation
- covariance between changes of f_i and f_j over time period $[t_{k-1}, t_k]$: $c_{ij}(t_k)$, or $\mathbf{C}(t_k)$ in matrix notation
- correlations between changes of f_i and f_j over time period $[t_{k-1}, t_k]$: $r_{ij}(t_k) = c_{ij}(t_k)/\sqrt{c_{ii}(t_k)\, c_{jj}(t_k)}$, or $\mathbf{R}(t_k)$; note that these terminal correlations are different from the instantaneous correlations between the Wiener processes involved.

We then generate a multi-dimensional path of the model parameters $\mathbf{F}$ by iterating the following steps:

1. Draw d *independent uniform pseudo-random* numbers[1] $\mathbf{U}$ in $[0,1]$, also independent of the sample drawn in the previous iteration for the previous time step;
2. Turn these into *independent standard-normal* random numbers $\mathbf{G}$, e.g. by evaluating the inverse cumulative normal distribution,[2] $g_i = N^{-1}(u_i)$;
3. Turn these into *correlated standard-normal* random variables $\mathbf{W}$ by multiplying $\mathbf{G}$ with a *pseudo-square root*[3] $\mathbf{A}$ of the correlation matrix which satisfies $\mathbf{C}(t_k) = \mathbf{A} \cdot \mathbf{A}^{\mathrm{T}}$, i.e. $\mathbf{W} = \mathbf{A} \cdot \mathbf{G}$;
4. Advance all factors

$$f_i(t_k) = f_i(t_{k-1}) + e_i(t_k) + \sqrt{c_{ii}(t_k)} \cdot w_i.$$

[1] *Pseudo*-random stresses the fact the random numbers are not truly random but generated by deterministic algorithms. We do not want to delve here into alternative algorithms for generating uniform pseudo-random numbers and refer to the specialized literature. Our usual choice, however, is Mersenne Twister 19937 (with period length $2^{19937} - 1$).

[2] Another popular alternative is the Box-Muller method.

[3] The pseudo-root is defined for symmetric matrices (such as correlation matrices), and it is not unique. Common methods for computing pseudo-square roots are Cholesky decomposition or spectral decomposition [95, 70]. Cholesky decomposition of $\mathbf{R}$ yields a lower triangular matrix $\mathbf{A}$ as square root. The standard two-dimensional Cholesky decomposition example is

$$\mathbf{R} = \begin{pmatrix} \rho & 1 \\ 1 & \rho \end{pmatrix} \quad \Rightarrow \quad \mathbf{A} = \begin{pmatrix} 1 & 0 \\ \rho & \sqrt{1-\rho^2} \end{pmatrix}$$

Though this approach is free of any time-discretization error, we are still exposed to the usual statistical error when we try to estimate for example an expected exposure using a finite number n of Monte Carlo paths. It is well known that the error of the estimate decreases (slowly) with the number of paths/samples as $\propto 1/\sqrt{n}$. A natural extension that reduces the error level (but does not change the convergence speed $\propto 1/\sqrt{n}$) is *antithetic sampling*. How does it work? Let us consider an entire path of length n and dimension d which requires $n \cdot d$ uniform random numbers $u_1, u_2, u_3, \ldots, u_{n \cdot d}$. With antithetic sampling one generates a second path by "inverting" the original one, that is by using $1 - u_1, 1 - u_2, 1 - u_3, \ldots, 1 - u_{n \cdot d}$, which is also a valid path, instead of calling the random number generator again. The reduced statistical error means one can use fewer paths with antithetic sampling to reach a similar accuracy of the estimate.

In Section 16.3 we will see how *quasi-random numbers* [95] speed up convergence (error reduction as a function of number of samples) compared to pseudo-random numbers.

Before we continue, let us briefly discuss how the scenario generation changes when we use Black-Karasinski or Cox-Ingersoll-Ross models for the credit component.

Cox-Ingersoll-Ross hazard rates

As soon as we have to deal with multiple correlated hazard rate processes, the joint density of hazard rate moves is not available in analytical form any more, and we need to propagate hazard rates using a numerical scheme, see Section 15.3. This means we have to amend the propagation step 4 above for the credit process according to this scheme. Moreover, this introduces a time-discretization error. To keep this error small for the hazard rate component, we are forced to simulate small time steps such as weeks or at best months. And this in turn forces the time grid for the entire set of model factors (interest rates, foreign exchange, inflation, etc.) down to the same time-step size, because we need to correlate the Wiener process increments across all processes. This seems to be a severe constraint at first glance. However, when we deal with realistic situations – where collateral is posted, see Chapter 17 – we have to choose small time steps anyway, so that this restriction hardly matters in practice.

Black-Karasinski hazard rates

Since the Black-Karasinski model is driven by an Ornstein-Uhlenbeck process again, it is integrated into the joint model without limiting the simulation time step. As explained in Section 15.4, the more severe constraint is now the fact that the conditional survival probability $S(t, T, \lambda(t))$ is not available in closed form, but needs to be computed numerically, for example on a trinomial tree. Doing this naively within the simulation (on each Monte Carlo path, for each hazard rate level $\lambda(t)$ and each required maturity T) would be a major performance issue. Therefore,

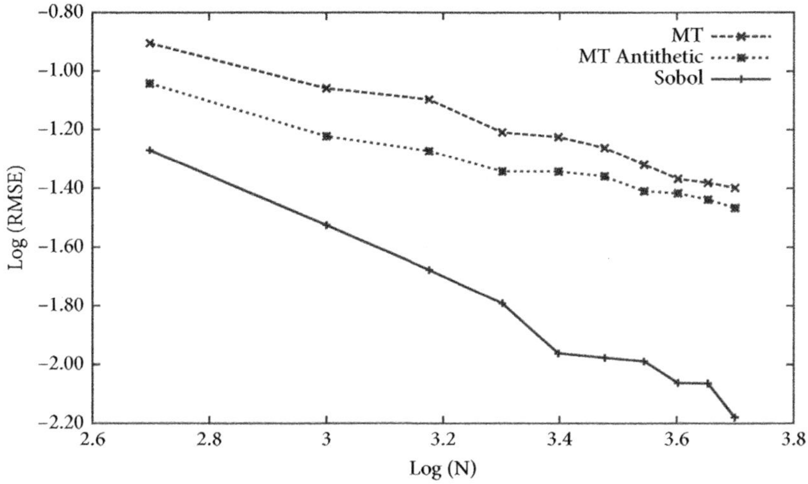

Figure 16.1 Convergence comparison for the expected exposure of 30Y maturity interest rate swap (slightly out-of-the-money) at horizon 10Y. We compare the reduction of root mean square error of the estimate vs number of paths on log-log scale (base 10) with maximum number of samples $N = 5000$. The slope of the regressions is -0.50 for Monte Carlo with pseudo-random numbers (labelled MT), -0.39 for antithetic sampling and -0.88 for the quasi-Monte Carlo simulation using Sobol sequences

one would rather tabulate $S(t, T, \lambda)$ once after the hazard model is calibrated, and then interpolate on the tabulated data to locate $S(t, T, \lambda)$ as required during the Monte Carlo simulation.

16.3 Pseudo-random vs low discrepancy sequences

In this section we briefly discuss an alternative to "ordinary" Monte Carlo simulation (using pseudo-random numbers) which uses *quasi-random numbers* or *low-discrepancy* sequences instead. For an introduction into this subject see for example Glasserman [70]. Rather than trying to "mimic randomness", as Glasserman says, quasi-random numbers seek to increase accuracy by a more evenly filling of the state space. This leads to the astonishing potential of quasi-Monte Carlo methods to increase the convergence rate to nearly $\propto 1/N$ as opposed to $\propto 1/\sqrt{N}$ achieved by Monte Carlo methods based on pseudo-random numbers. Famous algorithms for generating quasi-random numbers are those introduced by Halton, Faure or Sobol. However, the examples we will show below will be based on Sobol sequences only. Figure 16.1 shows a first comparison between convergence speeds. In this example, we compute the expected exposure of a 30Y

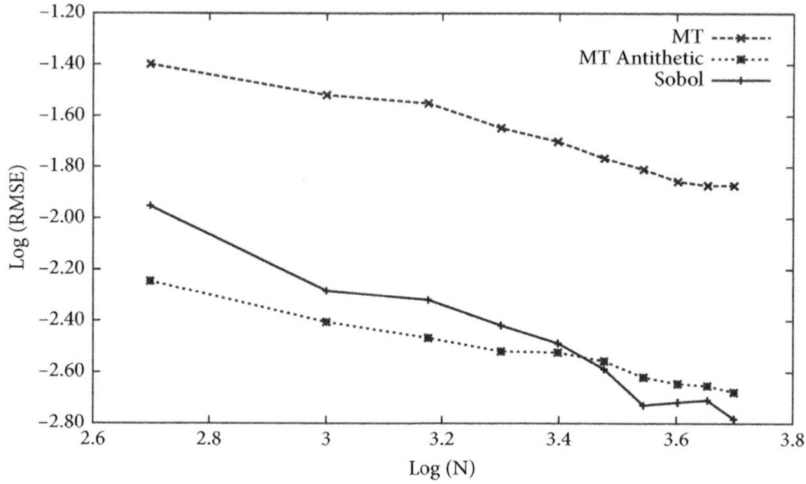

Figure 16.2 Convergence comparison for the expected exposure of 30Y maturity interest rate swap as in Figure 16.1 but with switched pay and receive leg (slightly in-the-money). The exposure is again estimated at the 10Y horizon. Regression line slopes are in this example −0.51, −0.42 and −0.81, respectively

maturity interest rate swap, which is slightly out-of-the-money, at the 10Y horizon. The double-logarithmic (base 10) plot shows the root mean square error (relative to the "exact" expected exposure) vs number of samples/paths used to compute it. The exact exposure is determined numerically using a large number of paths (250k), and the root mean square error is computed from 50 estimates using the same number of samples N. The slope of the regression line for the pseudo-Monte Carlo simulation matches the theoretical value of −0.5 while the quasi-Monte Carlo slope is significantly better at −0.83, but still larger than the optimal slope −1 we can expect at best. The slope for pseudo-Monte Carlo with antithetic sampling is similar to the case without antithetic sampling. Antithetic sampling yields an offset in the root mean square error, but hardly affects convergence speed. In this example, quasi-Monte Carlo seems clearly preferable to pseudo-Monte Carlo.

However, when we look at the example in Figure 16.2, which is the exposure convergence analysis for a swap which is slightly in-the-money (we have switched the pay and receive legs), then we see that the Monte Carlo simulation with pseudo-random numbers and antithetic sampling yields even lower errors for small numbers of paths. Nevertheless, Sobol is beyond about 3000 samples because of its higher convergence rate. These two examples indicate that quasi-Monte Carlo simulation is advantageous in a CVA context, as expected. It yields consistently lower errors than pseudo-Monte Carlo across in-the-money, at-the-money and out-of-the-money swap exposures with moderate numbers of samples around 5000

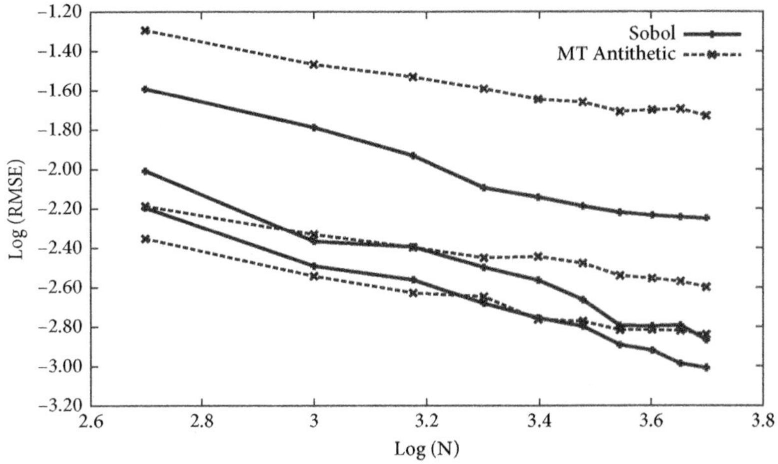

Figure 16.3 Convergence comparison for the expected exposure of 15Y maturity interest rate swaps of varying moneyness. The exposure is again estimated at the 10Y horizon

and error levels well below 1%.[4] This is a pattern that we see across various interest swaps and FX forwards with maturities up to 30Y observed around the middle of their life. Figure 16.3 shows another convergence comparison for 15Y maturity swaps with varying moneyness which confirms the statement above.

16.4 Long-term interest rate simulation

In this section we show that the estimation of exposures at long horizons (say beyond 20 years) deserves attention, since long horizons potentially introduce an additional error of the Monte Carlo exposure estimate which cannot be overcome by quasi-Monte Carlo methods or realistic numbers of samples N.

To use a simple example of applying the joint evolution model and the path generation above, we focus in this section on the single factor that drives the domestic numeraire and zero bond prices. We investigate the accuracy of a basic expectation estimate for which we know the exact result – the expected value of the inverse numeraire at time t. The relevant subset of model and path generation is then:

1. Calibrate the LGM model for instance to yield curve and swaption data.
2. Evolve factor $z(t)$ according to $z(t) = \int_0^t \alpha(t)\, dW(t)$ which is normally distributed with zero mean and variance $\zeta(t) = \int_0^t \alpha^2(s)\, ds$. We can generate

[4] Which we tend to regard as sufficient in CVA computations, given the uncertainty around PD/LGD and correlation estimates that enter into the CVA calculation.

Monte Carlo samples of $z(t)$ by drawing random numbers from the normal distribution for horizon t without intermediate time steps. Alternatively, we can choose a time grid $t_0, t_1, \ldots, t_n$ and draw increments $\Delta z = z(t_i) - z(t_{i-1}) = \int_{t_{i-1}}^{t_i} \alpha(s)\, dW(s)$ from normal distributions with zero mean and variance $\zeta(t_i) - \zeta(t_{i-1})$.

3. On each grid point t_i (or just at the end point t_n), we then compute the numeraire $N(t_i)$ and stochastic discount bond price $P(t_i, T)$ as functions of the random variable $z(t_i)$ and the model parameters.
4. This allows e.g. computing sample values of cash flows at time t_i (dividing by the numeraire), cash flows at times $T > t_i$ (multiplying with $P(t_i, T)$ and then dividing by $N(t_i)$), or functions of stochastic zero bond prices such as zero bond option payoffs $[P(t_i, T) - K]^+/N(t_i)$.
5. Averaging over many Monte Carlo paths of z then yields the desired price.

The price of a fixed unit cash flow at time t is given by

$$\Pi = \mathbb{E}\left[\frac{1}{N(t)}\right]. \tag{16.32}$$

Recall the numeraire in LGM:

$$N(t) = \frac{1}{P(0,t)} \exp\left(X + \frac{1}{2}\mathbb{V}[X]\right)$$

with

$$X = H(t)\, z(t), \quad \mathbb{V}[X] = H^2(t)\, \zeta(t), \quad \mathbb{E}[X] = 0.$$

Analytically, the expectation therefore yields

$$\begin{aligned}\Pi = \mathbb{E}\left[\frac{1}{N(t)}\right] &= P(0,t) \exp\left(-\frac{1}{2}\mathbb{V}[X]\right) \mathbb{E}[\exp(-X)] \\ &= P(0,t) \exp\left(-\frac{1}{2}\mathbb{V}[X]\right) \exp\left(-\mathbb{E}[X] + \frac{1}{2}\mathbb{V}[X]\right) \\ &= P(0,t),\end{aligned}$$

as expected. Now we look at what we get from Monte Carlo sampling. We calibrate our model to market data as of 30 September 2015 (6M tenor swap curve, a “column” of swaptions with fixed swap term 5Y complemented with a single

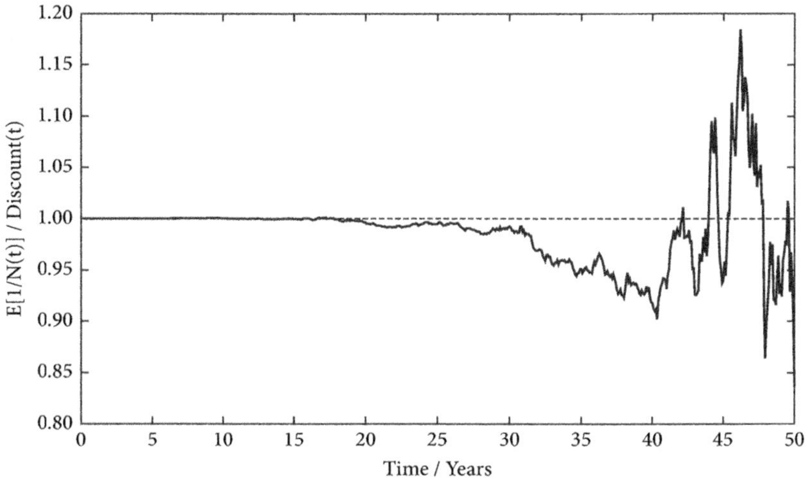

Figure 16.4 Monte Carlo estimate of (16.32) divided by the expected value $P(0,t)$ as a function of time

swaption with 20Y expiry and longer term of 10Y). We choose an LGM model with $H(t)$ parameterized by "Hull-White" mean reversion speed λ, that is

$$H(t) = \frac{1 - e^{-\lambda t}}{\lambda},$$

and piecewise linear $\zeta(t)$ given at unique expiry times of the calibration options. The model matches the quoted option prices perfectly. Using this calibration we propagate $z(t)$ in monthly time steps out to 50Y and estimate (16.32) using 10,000 Monte Carlo paths.[5] Figure 16.4 shows the estimate $\Pi/P(0,t)$ at each time step t which should equal unity for the majority of the paths. For moderate horizons we get the expected outcome. But apparently the deviation of the Monte Carlo estimate from the expected value increases with time, reaches unacceptable levels (beyond 1%) for times beyond the 20Y horizon and renders the simulated paths useless towards the long-time end.[6] One can check that the error decreases with increasing number of Monte Carlo paths; however, the number of paths is limited in real applications – with 10,000 being a typical upper limit in a CVA context – in order to control computation time. So, what is the root of this error?

[5] Using pseudo-random numbers with antithetic sampling.
[6] Note that we get similar results with quasi-Monte Carlo simulation.

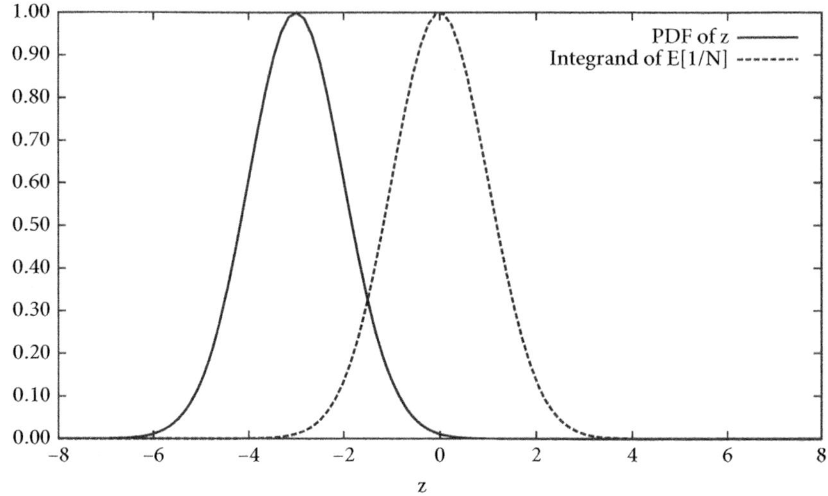

Figure 16.5 Comparison of sampling region to the region of essential contributions to (16.32

To shed some light on this, we reformulate the expectation (16.32) divided by $P(0,t)$ in terms of the random variable's probability density

$$
\begin{aligned}
\frac{1}{P(0,t)}\mathbb{E}\left[\frac{1}{N(t)}\right] &= \mathbb{E}\left[\exp\left(-H_t z_t - \frac{1}{2}H_t^2\zeta_t\right)\right] \\
&= \frac{1}{\sqrt{2\pi\zeta_t}}\int_{-\infty}^{\infty}\exp\left(-H_t z - \frac{1}{2}H_t^2\zeta_t - \frac{z^2}{2\zeta_t}\right)dz \\
&= \frac{1}{\sqrt{2\pi\zeta}}\int_{-\infty}^{\infty}\exp\left(-\frac{(z+H_t\zeta_t)^2}{2\zeta_t}\right)dz \\
&= \frac{1}{\sqrt{2\pi}}\int_{-\infty}^{\infty}\exp\left(-\frac{(x+H_t\sqrt{\zeta_t})^2}{2}\right)dx \\
&= 1 \qquad \text{(analytically)}
\end{aligned}
$$

where we have introduced a standard normal random variable $x = z/\sqrt{\zeta}$ in the last step. When we generate our Monte Carlo paths as described at the beginning of this section, we approximate the latter integral using standard normal variates x concentrated around the origin. However, the *essential* contributions to the expectation come from a region of width 1 around $x = -H_t\sqrt{\zeta_t}$. The difference is illustrated in Figure 16.5.

This shows that large values $H_t\sqrt{\zeta_t}$ move the bulk of the sampling away from the relevant region. Can we reduce this term? With our chosen parametrization, $H(t)$ is non-negative and monotonically increasing with time, likewise $\zeta(t)$. Fortunately,

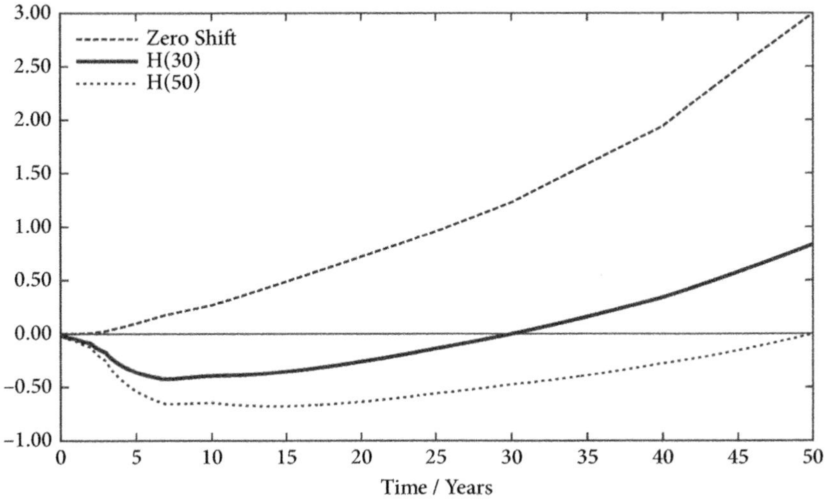

Figure 16.6 $(H(t) - C)\sqrt{\zeta(t)}$ with different shifts applied, $C = 0$, $C = H(30)$, $C = H(50)$

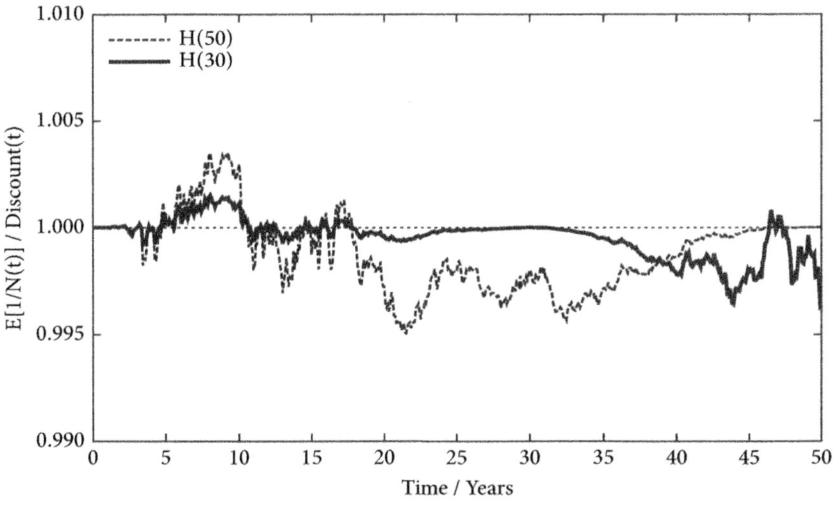

Figure 16.7 Monte Carlo estimate of (16.32) divided by the expected value $P(0,t)$ as a function of time for $H(t)$ shifts by $-H(T)$ with $T = 50$ and $T = 30$, respectively

we can apply the LGM model's "shift invariance" (see Section 11.1.2): after the model is calibrated, we are free to add resp. subtract any constant shift to resp. from $H(t)$. In particular, we can choose a shift $-H(T)$ with T somewhere in the simulation grid. Time T at the beginning yields the unshifted LGM, T close to the middle or at the end of the simulation horizon has the effect on $H(t)\sqrt{\zeta(t)}$

shown in Figure 16.6. The shift close to the middle of the simulation horizon keeps $(H(t) - C)\sqrt{\zeta(t)}$ particularly well within the range $[-1,1]$ in this example. These shifts reduce the Monte Carlo estimate's "error" observed above significantly, as shown in Figure 16.7.

The choice of whether a shift should be applied at all and its size depends on market data, the required simulation horizon and the maturity structure of the portfolio. Simulations up to 10Y do not require shifts in normal market situations, while long-term simulations as shown here generally deserve – in our opinion – a shift with T around the middle of the simulation grid.

17 Netting and Collateral

As already explained in Section 5.5, many of the features of a CSA cannot be priced by adjusting the discount curve but have to be included in a simulation which is capable of computing path-wise future exposures. We saw in Chapter 5 and Section 12.4 that one exception is the option to switch the currency of the posted collateral.[1] When estimating counterparty exposure, the following use-cases can be distinguished:

- A counterparty portfolio which is not covered by any ISDA or similar[2] netting agreement; i.e. no netting of trade exposures is possible.
- A counterparty portfolio which is fully covered by an ISDA or similar netting agreement; i.e. netting of trade-level exposures is valid.
- A counterparty portfolio covered by an ISDA agreement containing a *Credit Support Annex* (CSA); in this instance the aggregate portfolio exposure may be mitigated via the exchange of collateral. A CSA always comes together with a netting agreement.
- A counterparty portfolio which is only partially covered by an ISDA agreement; in such a case only a subset of the portfolio is eligible for netting and collateralization.

All these cases are covered by the methodology described below. The definition of ISDA master agreement and CSA was given in Chapter 5.

Since the exchange of collateral acts to reduce counterparty credit exposure, it is necessary to account for the existence of a CSA when calculating CVA. Conversely, the CSA features which deviate from perfect collateralization, like a threshold amount, can change the resulting CVA amount significantly.

[1] Under US law only.
[2] Like the German "Deutscher Rahmenvertrag"(DRV).

17.1 Netting

This section outlines the methodology for calculating netted counterparty exposures, but does not take collateral into account.

17.1.1 Non-netted counterparty exposures

We first consider the case of a counterparty with whom no ISDA netting agreement has been signed. If no netting agreement exists, the exposure from each OTC derivative contract must be considered individually, as it may be possible for the counterparty to "cherry-pick", that is to default on only a subset of the outstanding portfolio while still demanding that obligations be met upon other transactions which are favourable to the counterparty. Therefore, the non-netted counterparty replacement cost at a time t, denoted $U_{ctp}(t)$ is expressed as

$$U_{ctp}(t) = \sum_i \max(0, V_i(t)), \tag{17.1}$$

where $V_i(t)$ is the value of the i_{th} trade as of time t.

17.1.2 Netting set exposures

We next consider the case of a counterparty with whom an ISDA netting agreement has been signed. The existence of a netting agreement removes the possibility of "cherry-picking" of obligations among those trades covered by the agreement. In other words, for a set of trades covered by a single ISDA netting agreement, the net replacement cost at time t, denoted $V_{set}(t)$ is expressed as

$$V_{set}(t) = \max\left(0, \sum_i V_i(t)\right), \tag{17.2}$$

where the sum runs over all trades contained in the netting set and, again, $V_i(t)$ is the value of the i_{th} trade as of time t.

17.1.3 Generalized counterparty exposures

We now generalize to the case of a counterparty portfolio which is only partially covered by netting agreements. In many cases, an ISDA netting agreement will specify a list of trade types which are eligible for netting, or in some cases might even explicitly list some trade types which are *not covered* by the netting agreement.

Consider the case of a counterparty portfolio containing N trades, of which only n are covered by an ISDA agreement (for avoidance of doubt, $n < N$). We begin by grouping the trades into separate "netting sets". The n trades covered by the ISDA agreement get grouped into one single netting set, while the remaining non-nettable trades each get assigned their own unique netting set. Once this grouping has been completed, the counterparty replacement cost at time t, denoted $V_{ctp}(t)$ is calculated as

$$V_{ctp}(t) = \sum_{j=1}^{m} \max(0, V_{set_j}(t)) \tag{17.3}$$

where

- m is the number of unique netting sets which combined comprise the counterparty portfolio[3]
- $V_{set_j}(t)$ is the value of the j_{th} netting set as of time t (calculated via Equation 17.2)

17.2 Collateralization

In this section we extend the methodology outlined in Section 17.1 to account for the benefits of collateralization. To do this accurately, the precise details of the underlying CSA need to be considered (e.g. marginmargining frequency, minimum transfer amount, threshold).

It is important to note at this point that not all ISDA agreements include a CSA. Therefore, not all netting sets are collateralized. The methodology outlined in this section allows for the possibility that only a subset of the counterparty portfolio is covered by a CSA.

17.2.1 Collateralized netting set exposure

The collateral-adjusted value of a netting set j at time t, denoted $V^C_{set_j}(t)$ is expressed as

$$V^C_{set_j}(t) = V_{set_j}(t) - C_j(t) \tag{17.4}$$

where

- $V_{set_j}(t)$ is the uncollateralized value of a netting set j at time t, calculated via Equation 17.2
- $C_j(t)$ is the value at time t of the collateral being held against netting set j.

[3] Note that for the normal case of a single ISDA agreement having been signed with the counterparty, $m = N - n + 1$. It is straightforward to generalize to the case of multiple ISDA agreements covering separate sections of the portfolio. This is also observed in practice, albeit rarely.

The collateral-adjusted exposure of a counterparty, denoted $V^C_{ctp}(t)$, is thus calculated as follows:

$$V^C_{ctp}(t) = \sum_j^m \max(0, V^C_{set_j}(t)) \tag{17.5}$$

Therefore, if we can estimate the value of $C_j(t)$ we can calculate the collateral-adjusted exposure of each netting set j and hence the counterparty.

17.2.2 CSA margining

As discussed above, the terms of a Credit Support Annex usually allow for a periodic re-margining of the collateral account to reflect changes in the value of the underlying portfolio. The margin frequency is usually either daily or weekly, although other frequencies are also possible.

At a margining date t_m we know the uncollateralized value of our netting set, $V_{set}(t_m)$ and the value of the corresponding collateral, $C(t_m)$. We also know the values of the following:

- T_{hold}, the threshold exposure below which no collateral is required[4]
- MTA, the minimum transfer amount for collateral margin flow requests[5]
- I_A, the sum of all collateral independent amounts attached to the underlying portfolio of trades (positive amounts imply that the bank has received a net inflow of independent amounts from the counterparty), assumed here to be cash.[6]

With this information, collateral requirement (aka the *Credit Support Amount*) at t_m, denoted $CSA(t_m)$ is calculated as:[7]

$$CSA(t_m) = \begin{cases} \max(0, V_{set}(t_m) - I_A - T_{hold}), & V_{set}(t_m) - I_A \geq 0 \\ \min(0, V_{set}(t_m) - I_A + T_{hold}), & V_{set}(t_m) - I_A < 0 \end{cases} \tag{17.6}$$

As the collateral account already has a value of $C(t_m)$ at time t_m, the collateral shortfall is simply the difference between $C(t_m)$ and $CSA(t_m)$. However, we also need to account for the possibility that margin calls issued in the past have not

[4] Note that separate threshold amounts can be specified for each party to the CSA, depending on the direction of the exposure. Furthermore, thresholds can be changing according to rating triggers, which then either have to be simulated separately or linked to the hazard rate level of the counterparty.

[5] Similar to the threshold, separate minimum transfer amounts can be specified, depending on which party is issuing the margin request.

[6] Note that independent amounts can be time-dependent, for instance on some number related to the position's market risk.

[7] Note the possibility of a negative collateral requirement (i.e. the obligation to post collateral to a counterparty). However, in some cases the governing CSA may be "unilateral" in nature (i.e. only one of the parties is entitled to receive collateral for the purposes of default risk mitigation).

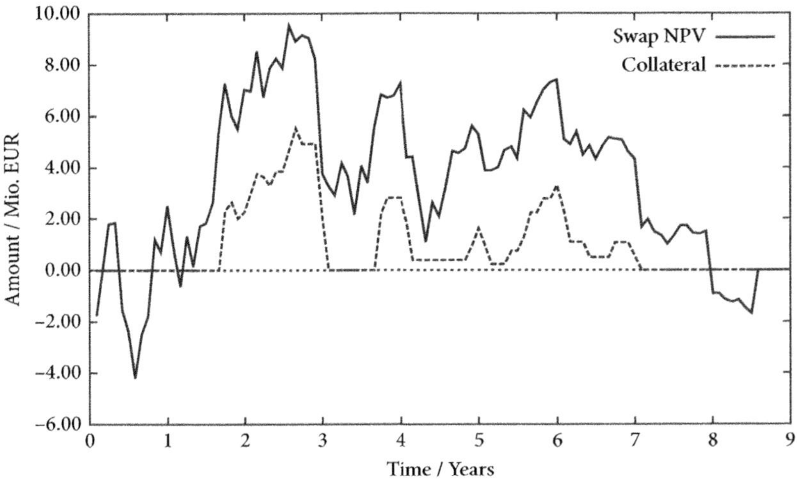

Figure 17.1 Interest rate swap NPV and collateral evolution for threshold 4 Mio. EUR, minimum transfer amount 0.5 Mio. EUR and margin period of risk two weeks

yet been settled (for instance, because of disputes). If $M(t_m)$ denotes the net value of all outstanding margin calls at t_m, and $\Delta(t)$ is the difference $\Delta(t) = CSA(t_m) - C(t_m) - M(t_m)$ between the *Credit Support Amount* and the current and outstanding collateral, then the actual margin *Delivery Amount* $D(t_m)$ is calculated as follows:

$$D(t_m) = \begin{cases} \Delta(t), & |\Delta(t)| \geq MTA \\ 0, & |\Delta(t)| < MTA \end{cases} \tag{17.7}$$

This is illustrated in Figure 17.1 which shows the evolution of the PV of a single-trade netting set consisting of one interest rate swap in comparison to the related collateral account value $C(t)$.

17.2.3 Margin settlement

Once a margin request has been issued, the value of the collateral account is not adjusted until the amount $D(t_m)$ has been delivered. If we consider the trivial case of continuous margining and instantaneous settlement of margin calls, as well as zero thresholds, minimum transfer amounts and independent amounts, it should be clear from Equation 17.4 that the collateral-adjusted netting set value $V^C_{set}(t)$ is always zero. However, this is not a realistic case, for the following reasons:

- Many CSAs contain non-zero thresholds, MTA and independent amounts. In particular MTA is often in the range of 500,000 to 2 million for practical reasons.

- Parties to the CSA usually have the right to dispute margin calls if they do not agree with the requested delivery amount. In such a case a reconciliation process is initiated, which depending upon the circumstances may last for a not insignificant period of time.
- If a counterparty defaults, it may take some time to "close out" the underlying portfolio and find appropriate replacement trades.[8] During this interval the non-defaulting party is still exposed to shifts in the value of both the underlying portfolio and the collateral itself.

Therefore, there is still residual counterparty credit exposure in the case of collateralization, even if the threshold and MTA vanish. To account for this exposure in the CVA context, the concept of a *Margin Period of Risk* is introduced. It is assumed that any margin calls will not be settled until after the specified MPR has elapsed. Depending upon the size and content of a netting set, typical values for the MPR range between one week and two months. A standard assumption for derivative portfolios is ten business days.[9] Figure 17.2 compares the exposure evolution of the uncollateralized swap to the collaterized swap for varying thresholds. In the case of zero threshold and zero minimum transfer amount it is just the margin period of risk which causes the remaining exposure.

Finally note that in the Monte Carlo simulation framework it is easy to model the margin period of risk symmetrically or asymmetrically:

- *Symmetric*: all margin calls only settle after the specified margin period of risk has elapsed.
- *Asymmetric CVA*: if we request margin from the counterparty, the request only settles after the MPR; if the counterparty requests margin from us, the margin is settled immediately.
- *Asymmetric DVA*: if the counterparty requests margin from us, the request only settles after the MPR; if we request margin from the counterparty, the margin is settled immediately.

17.2.4 Interest accrual

As with all cash accounts, interest usually accrues on the balance of the collateral account over time. These interest accruals must be taken into account when calculating $C(t)$ and the margin Delivery Amounts $D(t)$. For PFE and CVA

[8] This close-out time can be particularly important for less liquid bespoke OTC trades, as the default of Lehman Brothers in 2008 painfully showed.

[9] The Basel II guidelines suggest an MPR of five business days for REPO portfolios, ten business days for small liquid OTC portfolios, and 20 business days for large OTC portfolios or portfolios containing bespoke/illiquid OTC trades. The Basel guidelines also recommend doubling the MPR if there is a history of collateral disputes.

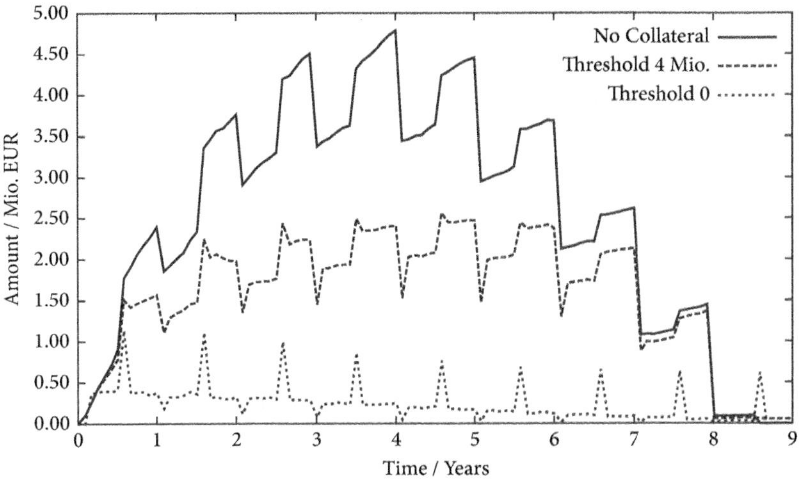

Figure 17.2 Uncollateralized vs collateralized swap exposure with threshold 4 Mio. EUR and minimum transfer amount is 0.5 Mio. EUR (middle), zero threshold and minimum transfer amount (bottom). In both collateralized cases the margin period of risk is two weeks

calculations, the projected interest accruals are calculated using *simulated* interest rates.[10] Typically, interest on cash collateral is accrued at the overnight rate, sometimes with a negative spread.

17.2.5 FX risk

In general, uncollateralized trade and portfolio exposures are denominated in a single reporting currency, regardless of the contractual currencies of the underlying trades. If an active CSA specifies for example its thresholds and minimum transfer amounts in a currency other than the reporting currency, an additional FX risk must be accounted for in the calculations. The same holds if the collateral currency is different from the reporting currency.

This risk is built into the PFE/CVA calculations by means of converting the thresholds and MTA resp. the collateral amounts into the reporting currency at each margining date t_m using *simulated* FX rates.[11]

17.2.6 Collateral choice

As outlined in Chapter 5, many CSAs specify multiple currencies (or even securities) which are eligible for delivery as collateral.

[10] That is the rates implied at each time point t by the IR model used in the Monte-Carlo process

[11] That is those rates implied at each margining date t_m by the FX model used in the Monte-Carlo process.

Currency options under American law which allow the complete move of collateral from one currency to another by the party owing collateral can be priced using the curve-building approach outlined in Section 12.4. The path-dependency of the British variation has to be taken care of by checking which currency is advantageous on each simulated path at each margining date t_m.

If other assets than cash are eligible as collateral, the cheapest-to-deliver optimization described in Section 5.4 has to be done on each margining date t_m.

18 Early Exercise and American Monte Carlo

When we talk about portfolio CVA with collateral – processing large numbers of trades on many paths in small time steps – it is necessary to consider the computational effort involved: CVA analysis is a computationally intensive task. Let us do a simple back-of-the-envelope calculation to give an idea of this. Consider a CVA calculation for

- a moderate portfolio of 10,000 vanilla swap trades
- 10,000 Monte Carlo scenarios
- 120 future evaluation dates, i.e. ten years in monthly steps for (crude) collateral tracking

Given an average pricing time of about 30 microseconds per NPV[1] for ten-year term swaps with semi-annual fixing this takes about 1.5 hours processing time on a 64 core machine which is still a significant piece of hardware (as of 2015). This ignores any administrative overhead in the computation, time for scenario generation and post processing of the NPV "cube" data, but gives an idea. So this calculation would fit into an overnight batch.

What about structured products? Let us consider Bermudan swaptions here as an example. If we use the LGM model of Section 11.1 to price a Bermudan with nine exercise dates and an underlying swap with a 10Y term, then we find typical pricing times of about 3 milliseconds[2] instead of 30 micro-seconds for the vanilla swap considered before, a factor of 100. For a single-trade pricing this is fast, but considering a portfolio with 1000 structured products like this Bermudan, then this part of the portfolio alone would require about 15 hours CVA processing time – a challenge for the overnight batch.

This consideration may be over-simplified, but it shows that millisecond pricing times cause a performance issue in the CVA context and should be avoided for any significant part of the portfolio. But structured products do exist. So what is the way to get CVA calculated in finite time?

[1] Using QuantLib [2] on a single core of an Intel Core i7 CPU
[2] This excludes the time required for model calibration.

18.1 American Monte Carlo

The *American Monte Carlo (AMC)* or *Least Square (LS) Monte Carlo* method was introduced by Longstaff and Schwartz in 2001 [114] and provides a relatively simple approach for handling early exercise features (which require backward induction) in a Monte Carlo simulation framework (which generates paths in the forward direction).

Before we summarize the LS algorithm, let us recall how we price a Bermudan swaption on the LGM grid, see Section 11.1:

1. Denote the underlying price at final expiry by $u(t_n, z_n)$, where z_n is stochastic. Conditional on z_n (located on the LGM grid) we can determine $u(\cdot)$. The derivative price at final expiry is then

$$v(t_n, z_n) = \max(u(t_n, z_n), 0).$$

2. At an earlier time we can compute continuation values as conditional expectations of the future derivative value,

$$c(t_i, z_i) = N(t_i, z_i)\, \mathbb{E}_i^N \left[\frac{v(t_{i+1}, z_{i+1})}{N(t_{i+1}, z_{i+1})} \right]$$

by numerical convolution on the LGM grid. We can determine underlying values $u(t_i, z_i)$ at the final expiry date. The derivative value is then the greater of continuation value (positive by construction) and the underlying value:

$$v(t_i, z_i) = \max(u(t_i, z_i), c(t_i, z_i)).$$

if time t_i is an exercise time. Otherwise, $v(t_i, z_i) = c(t_i, z_i)$.

3. Iterating back to t_0 then yields the derivative price $v(t_0)$. Note that this requires stepping over exercise times only in Hagan's approach.

We can compute the conditional expectations in step 2 above because we are using an orderly grid in z-direction with known transition probabilities between states z_i and z_{i+1}, as illustrated in Figure 18.1

If we simulate paths $z_1, z_2, \ldots, z_n$, then we are lacking these (transition probability) links between all states at t_i and all states at t_{i+1} which we need at first glance to allow backward induction. Longstaff and Schwartz's idea was to use *regression analysis across paths* to gather the information for computing the conditional expectations and continuation values. The LS algorithm for pricing the Bermudan swaption has two passes.

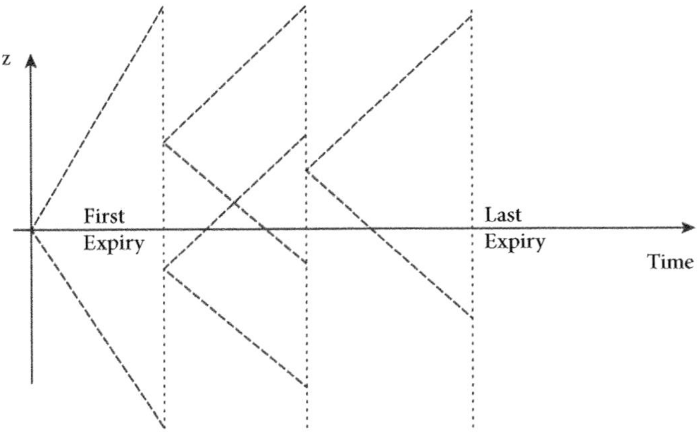

Figure 18.1 Bermudan Swaption with three exercise dates on the LGM grid: conditional expectations of future values by convolution

The first *rollback* pass can be summarized as follows:

1. Generate N paths of LGM factor z from today to final expiry; these paths must contain the exercise times; for the Bermudan swaption pricing we limit the time grid to exercise times only.
2. Price the underlying swap (outstanding cash flows) at each point of each path. This yields a matrix of underlying values $u_j(t_i, z_i) := u_{ji}$ where $j = 1, \ldots, N$ labels the path. Then determine associated exercise values as the intrinsic values of the option $e_j(t_i, z_i) = \max(u_{ji}, 0) := e_{ji}$ across all paths and all times.
3. At an interim exercise point in time t_i, compute the continuation values on all paths as follows:
   a. Consider the vectors of underlying prices $x_j = u_{ji}$ and discounted payoffs $y_j = e_{j,k_j} \cdot N_{j,i}/N_{j,k_j}$ where k_j is initially set to the final expiry, i.e. y_j may be zero;
   b. exclude all paths j with $y_j = 0$, i.e. which are out-of-the-money at time t_i;
   c. compute a regression curve $f_i(x)$ on the remaining points (x_j, y_j) which minimizes $\sum_j (y_j - f_i(x_j))^2$;
   d. use $f_i(x_j)$ as the conditional expectation $\mathbb{E}[y_j|x_j]$, i.e. the continuation values are

$$c_{ji} = \mathbb{E}[y_j|x_j] = f(x_j).$$

   This regression step incorporates information from paths in the "neighbourhood" of x_j, that is the regression effectively averages over y_j values for similar x_j values.[3] This is illustrated in Figure 18.2.

[3] The simplest approach is linear regression. However, this usually does not perform well across the entire range of points (x_j, y_j). Higher order polynomials are the obvious extension (we have used orders 3 and 4).

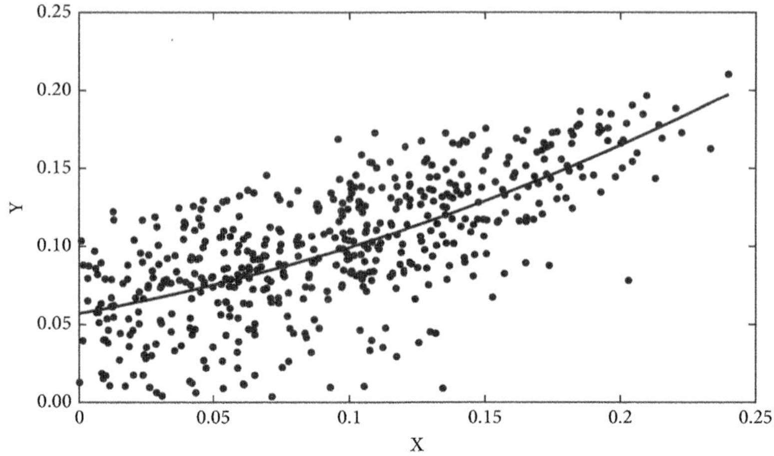

Figure 18.2 Regression at the second exercise of a Bermudan swaption with underlying swap start in 5Y, term 10Y, annual exercise dates. The AMC simulation used 1000 paths only (for presentation purposes), out of which about 50% are in-the-money at the second exercise time. The resulting quadratic regression polynomial we have fitted here is $f(x) = 0.05697 + 0.3081 \cdot x + 1.1578 \cdot x^2$

4. If the exercise value exceeds the continuation value, $e_{ji} > c_{ji}$, we update the "exercise index" for path j to $k_j = i$ and continue to the previous exercise time to repeat the regression procedure.
5. Iterating back to the first expiry t_1 we thus obtain as a result of the first pass the (parameters of) regression functions $f_i(x)$, associated with each expiry time t_i.

The second *pricing* pass then uses the regression functions of the first pass to make actual exercise decisions and to price the swaption:

1. Generate a new set of N paths[4] of LGM factor z from today to final expiry (again assuming we are stepping over exercise times only);
2. Price the underlying swap (outstanding cash flows) on each point of the paths. This yields a matrix of underlying values $u_j(t_i, z_i) := u_{ji}$ where $j = 1, \ldots, N$ labels the path, as well as exercise values $e_{ji} = \max(u_{ji}, 0)$.
3. Compute continuation values $c_{ji} = f_i(x_{ji})$
4. For each path j: exercise at the earliest time t_i where $e_{ji} > c_{ji}$ and add the discounted payoff e_{ji}/N_{ji} to the swaption's value; a path's contribution may be zero if all exercise values are zero along the path.

[4] Some people use different numbers of paths in the first and second pass, e.g. fewer "trigger" paths in the first pass. Others use the same number of paths or even identical sets of paths, although LS recommend using independent sets.

To save computational effort in this second pass, one can evaluate the paths in the forward direction, that is compute underlying, exercise and continuation values only up to the positive exercise decision.

Pricing example

Let us consider a concrete case now, a Bermudan swaption with underlying swap terms

- notional: 100 EUR
- maturity: 30 September 2039
- fixed leg: pay 3%, 30/360, annual
- floating leg: receive Euribor-6M without spread, semi-annual

and 20 annual exercise dates between 30 September 2019 and 30 September 2038.

Pricing this trade as of 30 September 2014 with market data as of this date on the **LGM grid**[5] yields the swaption NPV 10.634 EUR. The **AMC pricing**[6] yields almost the same NPV 10.636 EUR (just 0.2 basis points of notional upfront difference to the grid price).

The pricing times[7] differ significantly – LGM grid pricing in about **20 milliseconds** vs AMC pricing in about **2 seconds**, so AMC is slower by a factor of 100, as expected. One would not use AMC for pricing this product in a single-factor model, single pass setting. But the point is that the single AMC pricing generates the entire exposure evolution for the (cash-settled) Bermudan swaption (for 10,000 scenarios and a monthly grid) as a by-product. This in turn is very fast compared to the "brute-force" alternative: grid pricing of the Bermudan swaption under scenarios through time – $10,000 \times 300$ monthly evaluations in about three milliseconds to price the average Bermudan, that is about **2.5 hours**, or about 20 minutes if we restrict the exposure analysis to annual time steps only.[8]

18.2 Utilizing American Monte Carlo for CVA

First note that we get the cash-settled Bermudan swaption exposure *at any desired point in time* by just evaluating the remaining underlying swap on exercise dates.

5 The model is calibrated to co-terminal at-the-money swaptions, and we use a grid with discretization as recommended by Hagan [77, 78, 79], i.e. $s_y = 4, n_y = 10, s_x = 4, n_x = 18$.

6 Using the same calibrated LGM model as in the grid pricing, with 10,000 pseudo-random paths each for the rollback and pricing phases, 300 monthly time steps, regression with fourth order polynomials.

7 On a single core of an Intel Core i7 CPU.

8 And these times do not even factor in the time for recalibrating the model under each scenario and for each future evaluation date. This would significantly increase the "brute-force" calculation effort and time.

Therefore we should compare to the brute-force calculation time above with repricing on exercise dates only (which would take about 17 minutes in our example). Brute-force exposure calculation would reprice *Bermudan swaptions* under different scenarios, whereas AMC just reprices *underlying swaps* under different scenarios. The source of the speed-up is hence the pricing speed difference between swaption pricing and swap pricing which is of the order of 100 (or more) as we saw earlier.

Cash settlement

Consider the second pass of the pricing algorithm where we use the regression functions to make exercise decisions. We are considering each path separately in this phase as the regression functions incorporate all "lateral" information already. We determine an exercise time per path and add the discounted payoff (say Y) as of this exercise time to the instrument's price (weighted with $1/N$, the inverse of the number of paths). Therefore, it is clear that this discounted payoff Y is also the path's contribution to the swaption's expected exposure (discounted to today) for any time *before* the path's exercise time. And the exposure contribution to any time *beyond* exercise is zero because of cash settlement. This shows why no additional underlying swap evaluation is required to construct the exposure contribution of each path. The contribution of each single path to the overall exposure profile is hence a step function which drops to zero at exercise time.

Physical settlement

Physical settlement is a slight variation of the algorithm just described. Exposure contributions for times before the path's exercise time are the same as for cash settlement. Beyond exercise, the swaption turns into the underlying swap. Therefore future exposure contributions of the path are discounted swap values along the path. To construct the exposure for physical settlement, we therefore spend additional time on pricing swaps which is not needed for plain pricing. In terms of the Bermudan swaption pricing example above this means that we need about **seven seconds** rather than two seconds to build the physical settlement exposure.

Figure 18.3 shows the resulting exposure graphs for the Bermudan swaption example with cash and physical settlement.

In summary, the computational effort for the Bermudan option exposure calculation is of the same order as the effort for exposure calculation for the underlying swap itself, roughly twice as high because of the two passes of the LS algorithm and the time spent on regression analysis.

Finally note that the AMC method, illustrated here using the Bermudan swaption example, is of course more generally applicable to exposure generation

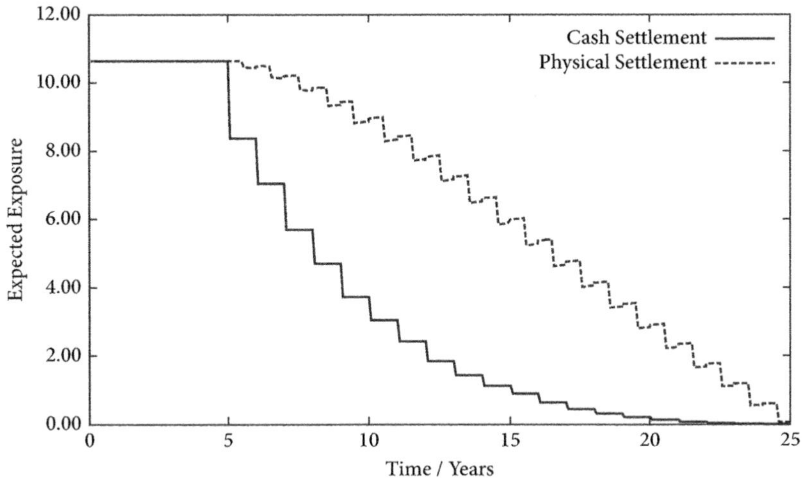

Figure 18.3 Bermudan swaption exposure evolution for the example described in the text, cash vs physical settlement

for structured products which may include path dependence and early exercise features – such as *Power Reverse Dual Currency* swaps or *Target Redemption* derivatives to name just a few. In that case we feed the multi-dimensional paths generated by the procedure in Section 16.2 into the LS algorithm.

19 CVA Risk and Algorithmic Differentiation

As CVA/DVA is a derivative value component, it is natural to include it in market risk analysis in order to monitor CVA management. Given the computational effort for coming up with the "plain" CVA by using a netting set across a realistic portfolio, this is a frightening task from an IT person's perspective as market risk conventionally requires repeated evaluation of the underlying (here including CVA) under many market scenarios, historical or hypothetical. Even a simple parametric Value-at-Risk (VaR) calculation would require calculating sensitivities to all kinds (dozens or hundreds) of risk factors driving the valuation, including CVA.

The issue is real though, and not only for CVA management, trading and hedging: it is key to include CVA into market risk analysis. With its focus on counterparty credit risk (CCR), the Basel Committee of Banking Supervision has introduced CVA with Basel III into the calculation of CCR capital, in particular banks are required to include a separate CVA capital charge which accounts for losses resulting from an increase of CVA.

Under Basel III there are two available approaches, the *standardized* and the *advanced* approach, the latter being available to banks with an approved internal model method (IMM). Under the advanced approach banks would compute a ten-day VaR as well as a stressed VaR at the 99% confidence level for the unilateral[1] CVA for each counterparty which then enters into a prescribed formula; see Section 24.7 for details. But note that the *expected exposure profiles can be kept fixed* for the purpose of the VaR calculation so that only credit spread factors are relevant for the advanced CVA VaR and resulting capital calculation. This is a significant simplification from a practical point of view, since the VaR calculation can reuse the time-consuming part of the CVA calculation. Furthermore, as the bilateral CVA affects the P&L, a bank would want to know the actual market risk to which CVA is exposed.

[1] The reason being that DVA cannot be used to reduce the capital charge. This is in stark contrast with the accounting standard IFRS which makes the computation of DVA mandatory.

Under the standardized approach this is further simplified, since the capital charge is then calculated according to a formula specified in the Basel Committee of Banking Supervision published in 2010.

We elaborate further on these approaches in Section 24.7. For the remaining part of this chapter we will assume that we *cannot* make the Basel III simplifying assumption that CVA risk is due to credit spread variability only, but take all other market risk factors affecting the exposure profiles into account. This means recalculation of exposure profiles under market risk scenarios and the IT person's "horror" scenario mentioned at the beginning of the chapter. How can this be tackled? The brute force approach of recalculating CVA under different scenarios takes at least two orders of magnitude of CPU time longer than "plain" CVA which demands significant hardware already. If hardware budget and availability is limited, this means that a full CVA risk calculation may be beyond the feasibility of an overnight batch and daily reporting.

19.1 Algorithmic differentiation

Automatic differentiation (AD), also called algorithmic differentiation or computational differentiation, is a set of techniques for automatically augmenting computer programs with statements/code for the computation of derivatives (sensitivities) [1]. AD is hence an alternative approach to

- numerical differentiation using finite difference expressions

$$\frac{df(x)}{dx} \approx \lim_{h \to 0} \frac{f(x+h) - f(x)}{h},$$

- symbolic differentiation as implemented in computer algebra packages such as Mathematica, Maple, Maxima, etc.,
- symbolic differentiation "by hand", subsequently turned into computer code.

AD has been well known in computer science since the 1980s with applications in for example computational fluid dynamics, meteorology and engineering design optimization. It has gained attention in the quantitative finance community more recently [69, 112, 101, 48, 46, 47, 49], to name a few, where the seminal paper by Giles and Glasserman [69] addresses the problem of fast Greeks computation in a Libor Market Model setting. In January 2015 AD has even made it to the front page of RISK [134]. For a problem like CVA risk, where the underlying CVA numbers are computed by Monte Carlo techniques, "fast Greeks" are not only nice to have but a hard requirement, which explains the recently raised attention.

In summary, it can be shown [75] that the overall complexity of sensitivity calculation using adjoint AD is no more than four times greater than the complexity (number of operations) of the original valuation, an astonishing reduction in complexity compared to the conventional bump/revalue approach to sensitivity calculation.

19.2 AD basics

Consider the evaluation of some function $y = f(x_1, ..., x_n)$ of n input variables (e.g. an instrument value as a function of many market data points). Any such function evaluation can be expressed in terms of m intermediate variables to which we apply simple unary built-in functions (such as $\exp(x)$, $\log(x)$, $\sin(x)$, ...) and binary operations (addition, subtraction, multiplication, division).

AD is a "mechanical" application of the chain rule of differentiation to the series of intermediate results. The sequence can be evaluated in two ways, forward and backward direction, as well as combinations of both. The following sections sketch these procedures.

Forward mode

The concept of this mode is the one that is easier to understand. We assume that our functions do not operate on real numbers but on *dual numbers* $x + \epsilon x'$ with an arithmetic defined by $\epsilon^2 = 0$. Basic operations – addition, subtraction, multiplication, division of dual numbers – follow from this definition as

$$
\begin{aligned}
(x+\epsilon x') \pm (y+\epsilon y') &= x \pm y + \epsilon(x' \pm y') \\
(x+\epsilon x') \times (y+\epsilon y') &= xy + \epsilon(xy' + x'y) \\
(x+\epsilon x')/(y+\epsilon y') &= \frac{(x+\epsilon x') \times (y-\epsilon y')}{(y+\epsilon y') \times (y-\epsilon y')} = \frac{xy+\epsilon(x'y-y'x)}{y^2} \\
&= x/y + \epsilon(x'/y - y'x/y^2)
\end{aligned}
$$

Function evaluations of dual arguments follow from their truncated Taylor expansion[2] (as all powers $\epsilon^2, \epsilon^3, \ldots$ vanish):

$$f(x+\epsilon x') = f(x) + \epsilon f'(x)\, x'$$

[2] Assuming that the derivative $f'(x)$ exists.

which also yields the chain rule

$$\begin{aligned} f(g(x+\epsilon x')) &= f(g(x)+\epsilon\, g'(x)\, x') \\ &= f(g(x))+\epsilon\, f'(g(x))\, g'(x)\, x' \end{aligned}$$

by iterated application of the first truncated Taylor series. For $x' = 1$ the right-hand side of the latter is just the derivative of $f(\cdot)$ with respect to x. All we need to do is generalize all operations to *dual numbers* and evaluate $f(g(x+\epsilon))$. This yields mechanically the usual "primal" valuation $f(g(x))$ and the function's derivative by looking up the ϵ coefficient (second component) of the resulting dual number.

Generalizing to functions of n variables $x_1, ..., x_n$, and their dual generalization $(x_i + \epsilon x_i')$, the difference is in the truncated Taylor expansion for the function evaluations

$$f(x_1+\epsilon x_1', \ldots, x_n+\epsilon x_n') = f(x_1, \ldots, x_n) + \epsilon \sum_{i=1}^{n} \frac{\partial f}{\partial x_i} x_i'.$$

This shows that we get any first order partial derivative by setting its *seed* x_i' to one and all others to zero. Hence this forward mode requires n passes/valuations to get all n partial derivatives. The forward mode is efficient if we need to evaluate many functions f of few variables.

In finance it is often the other way around, few functions need sensitivity calculation with respect to many input variables. The *backward* mode, sketched in the following, is suited for this situation.

Backward mode, adjoint algorithmic differentiation (AAD)

The backward mode evaluates the chain rule along intermediate calculation steps in *reverse* order. Consider a sequence of evaluations [49]

$$X \to \ldots \to U \to V \to \ldots \to Y$$

which transforms the input X (of dimension n) to the output Y (of dimension m) using basic arithmetic operations and simple built-in function calls for which the derivative is built-in as well. We are interested in all partial derivatives

$$\frac{\partial Y_i}{\partial X_j}.$$

The derivative of the function $Y:\mathbb{R}^n \to \mathbb{R}^m, X \mapsto Y(X)$ in $\xi \in \mathbb{R}^n$ is a linear operator $DY(\xi):\mathbb{R}^n \to \mathbb{R}^m$ which maps

$$\begin{pmatrix} x_1 \\ \vdots \\ x_n \end{pmatrix} \mapsto \begin{pmatrix} \frac{\partial Y_1}{\partial X_1}(\xi) & \cdots & \frac{\partial Y_1}{\partial X_n}(\xi) \\ \vdots & \ddots & \vdots \\ \frac{\partial Y_m}{\partial X_1}(\xi) & \cdots & \frac{\partial Y_m}{\partial X_n}(\xi) \end{pmatrix} \begin{pmatrix} x_1 \\ \vdots \\ x_n \end{pmatrix} = \begin{pmatrix} \sum_{i=1}^n \frac{\partial Y_1}{\partial X_i}(\xi)\, x_i \\ \vdots \\ \sum_{i=1}^n \frac{\partial Y_m}{\partial X_i}(\xi)\, x_i \end{pmatrix}.$$

Because all variables are real, the adjoint operator of $DY(\xi)$ is

$$(DY(\xi)^* = \begin{pmatrix} \frac{\partial Y_1}{\partial X_1}(\xi) & \cdots & \frac{\partial Y_1}{\partial X_n}(\xi) \\ \vdots & \ddots & \vdots \\ \frac{\partial Y_m}{\partial X_1}(\xi) & \cdots & \frac{\partial Y_m}{\partial X_n}(\xi) \end{pmatrix}^{\top} = \begin{pmatrix} \frac{\partial Y_1}{\partial X_1}(\xi) & \cdots & \frac{\partial Y_m}{\partial X_1}(\xi) \\ \vdots & \ddots & \vdots \\ \frac{\partial Y_1}{\partial X_n}(\xi) & \cdots & \frac{\partial Y_m}{\partial X_n}(\xi) \end{pmatrix}.$$

For intermediate functions, the chain rule in conjunction with the multiplication rule for transposed matrices yields:

$$\begin{aligned} Y(X) &= Y(V(X)) \Rightarrow \\ (DY(\xi))^* &= (DY(V(\xi))\, DV(\xi))^* \\ &= (DV(\xi))^*\, (DY(V(\xi)))^* \end{aligned}$$

which allows us to compute the derivatives backwards, provided we can compute the adjoint operators. Hence, the backward mode considers *adjoint* variables

$$\bar{V}_k = \sum_{j=1}^{m} \bar{Y}_j \frac{\partial Y_j}{\partial V_k}$$

which collect the sensitivity of the result with respect to intermediate variable V_k. Likewise

$$\bar{U}_i = \sum_{j=1}^{m} \bar{Y}_j \frac{\partial Y_j}{\partial U_i} = \sum_{j=1}^{m} \bar{Y}_j \sum_{k} \frac{\partial Y_j}{\partial V_k} \frac{\partial V_k}{\partial U_i} = \sum_{k} \bar{V}_k \frac{\partial V_k}{\partial U_i}$$

Starting from the adjoint of the output we can eventually generate the adjoint of the input variables

$$\bar{X}_i = \sum_{j=1}^{m} \bar{Y}_j \frac{\partial Y_j}{\partial X_i} \tag{19.1}$$

by applying the chain rule to all intermediate results in reverse order

$$\bar{X} \leftarrow \cdots \leftarrow \bar{U} \leftarrow \bar{V} \leftarrow \cdots \leftarrow \bar{Y}.$$

Initializing the output adjoint for index j with one (and all other with zero) in (19.1) therefore yields the entire set of sensitivities of Y_i to all n input variables. Due to the formulation in terms of adjoint variables, AD in backward mode is also referred to as *Adjoint Algorithmic Differentiation (AAD)* [76]. Recall that the overall complexity of sensitivity calculation using AAD is no more than four times greater than the complexity (in terms of number of operations) of the original valuation. The general rule is: the adjoint method should be used in case there are many inputs (curve points, volatilities, credit spreads, etc.) but few outputs (prices, value adjustments). If there are few inputs but many outputs, the forward method is better.

Note that the reverse procedure uses partial derivatives of internal variables V_k with respect to internal variables U_i which are generally dependent on the values of internal variables. This means they need to be computed in a first forward *sweep* and then stored for usage in the backward sweep. This memory impact is different from the pure forward sweep which does not require storing intermediate results.

AD Tools

Forward and backward mode processing can be automated. The community website for AD [1] provides a long list of software tools which implement AAD in various languages, the majority in C/C++. As stated in [47] and [134], various investment banks are in progress of upgrading their quant libraries to support AD or have done so already. OpenGamma claim on their web site (www.opengamma.com) to have implemented AAD in their analytics library. Finally, projects aiming at enabling AAD in QuantLib, the free open-source library for quantitative finance [2], were initiated at the end of 2014 and are well advanced at the time of writing.

19.3 AD examples

In this section we apply AD to the sensitivity calculation for a number of simple illustrative cases.

19.3.1 Vanilla swap and interest rate sensitivities

Let us check the principle with a stylized vanilla swap portfolio with 10,000 trades, unit notional, 20–30 years to maturity, annual interest periods on the fixed and floating legs, fixed coupon rate 2% (actual/actual) and zero floating rate margin. The swaps are priced on a flat swap curve at 2% (annual, actual/actual) [3] with 30

[3] A single curve for forwarding and discounting

grid points. We price a portfolio of trades here in order to get portfolio pricing times on the order of 10 milliseconds. Each pricing includes bootstrapping the discount/zero curve. In our swap pricing we use zero rates implied from the bootstrapped discount factors so that we are forced to use the exponential function which adds some complexity beyond basic arithmetic operations (+, -, *, /). This is implemented in C++ for the purpose of this experiment. For AAD we use the software package CppAD (http://www.coin-or.org/CppAD) which uses operator overloading to track the operations. Essentially this means

1. we add #include <cppad/cppad.hpp> at the top of the source file
2. we use the data type CppAD::AD<double> instead of double, for simplicity we introduce typedef CppAD::AD<double> Real;
3. we store all independent variables in a vector (vector<Real> x), these are the market rates which constitute the swap curve;
4. start the "tape recording" by calling CppAD::Independent(x); on this vector;
5. call the bootstrap and price the portfolio once; this returns a vector of results (vector<Real> y = price(...);), possibly one-dimensional, i.e. a single price for the entire portfolio;
6. we stop the tape recording by calling CppAD::ADFun<double> f(x, y);
7. and finally we kick off the reverse computation of derivatives with respect to the independent variable in vector x by calling dw = f.Reverse(1, w); where w is a one-dimensional vector initialized with 1.0, and dw is the n-dimensional vector containing the AAD partial derivatives with respect to the independent variables;

The AAD derivatives are close to the sensitivities we get by traditional bump/revalue with shift size of one basis point. The following Table 19.1 shows the comparison for the relevant part of the interest rate sensitivities around swap maturities.

The computation times (in milliseconds) are shown in Table 19.2. This indicates a significant overhead in using AD<double> as opposed to simple double, so that the overall speedup for 30 Greeks with AAD for this type of product is almost negligible.

19.3.2 European swaptions with deltas and vega cube

The methodology pays off when a large number of Greeks is computed – for example when vegas for swaption cubes need to be analysed. A swap CVA is essentially the pricing of large numbers of European swaptions with Monte Carlo, which is particularly relevant here. Our second example therefore shows timings for AAD pricing of a European swaption portfolio with 30 interest rate deltas as before and 1260 vegas for a volatility cube with 15 expiry dates, 12 swap terms and seven

Table 19.1 Comparison of interest rate sensitivity results, bump/revalue vs AAD for the stylized vanilla swap portfolio described in the text

Bucket	1bp sensitivity	AAD $\times 10^{-4}$	Difference
...	...	...	...
19y	−0.001008	−0.001008	−0.000000
20y	1.175403	1.174969	−0.000434
25y	3.250128	3.249373	−0.000755
30y	3.730946	3.729581	−0.001365
35y	4.165842	4.163699	−0.002143
40y	4.560392	4.557296	−0.003097
45y	4.918725	4.914491	−0.004235
50y	3.101113	3.098638	−0.002474

Table 19.2 Comparison of computation times for a vanilla swap portfolio. The "unrecorded" pricing slows down by a factor of about 2.8, and the total time for 30 AD Greeks is only faster than the traditional approach of bumping and repricing by a factor 1.3

	double	AD<double>
Unrecorded price	**13.15**	**36.28**
Recorded price		127.82
ADFun<double>		82.73
Backward mode Greeks		86.99
Total AD Greeks		**297.54**
Bumped Greeks	**400.09**	1085.26

strikes. Again we see that the deltas and vegas under AAD are close to the traditional bump/revalue sensitivities. Table 19.3 shows a comparison of timings for European Swaption pricing using

- analytical Black Scholes (10,000 trades), and
- Monte Carlo simulation of the forward swap rate in the Black-Scholes model (ten trades, 1000 Monte Carlo samples each with a single step to expiry).

Due to the large number of computed Greeks we find a significant advantage of using AAD here with overall speedup by a factor of around 40. On the other hand, the AD run takes up to about 30 times the effort for a single pricing with built-in

Table 19.3 Comparison of computation times for vanilla swaption portfolios priced with analytical Black-Scholes and Monte Carlo. The overall speedup of using AAD ("Total AD Greeks") vs the traditional bump/revalue approach ("Bumped Greeks") is about 40 in both cases. In the latter Monte Carlo valuation, we moreover find that the "Total AD Greeks" takes only about 4.7 times the computation time for unrecorded pricing with AD<double>

	Analytical (10,000)		Monte Carlo (10)	
	double	AD<double>	double	AD<double>
Unrecorded price	**7.69**	**26.15**	**7.09**	**39.11**
Recorded price		105.36		97.53
ADFun<double>		66.50		44.18
Backward mode Greeks		69.69		42.63
Total AD Greeks		**241.55**		**184.34**
Bumped Greeks	**9,785.76**	33,226.73	**6,866.78**	48,035.92

double variables, so it is not for free. But this limited extra effort yields access to an almost unlimited number of Greeks that are otherwise hardly accessible at all.

19.4 Further applications of AD

Apart from CVA risk, the obvious application of AAD is using the fast Greeks for timely enterprise-wide risk analysis, real-time or near time where it may have been feasible overnight only with a conventional "bump and reprice" approach to sensitivity calculation. This is particularly important because the financial crisis pushed the growth of risk factor volume even in vanilla instruments – OIS curves, tenor basis curves, cross-currency basis, as discussed extensively in Part I. Even computing option and structured product sensitivity to many points on the swaption volatility matrix or cube becomes feasible with AAD.

Moreover, we are going to see two more potential applications of AAD:

MVA The computation of the initial margin value adjustment (MVA) requires a simulation of the future market risk of the position. This can be solved by using algorithmic differentiation on the future exposure calculation. This is described in Section 20.7.

KVA Likewise, the capital value adjustment (KVA) depends on knowing the future market risk of the position, because the market risk capital charge and the CVA capital charge both depend on the regular VaR and the stressed VaR (at least for IMM banks), see Chapter 21.

20 FVA

FVA has seen a long discussion as to its right to live, see Hull and White [88], [89], Burgard & Kjaer [39], Carver [50] and Laughton & Vaisbrot [111]; so far, it seems it will stay around. While the FVA debate trundled on, many large international banks started reporting FVA numbers in their quarterly results, creating facts for the market which will – in our opinion – eventually lead to the requirement to report it under IFRS and other similar GAAPs.

At the heart of the debate is the following question. If a bank does an uncollateralized derivative with some client and hedges it with an offsetting derivative which is fully collateralized, do the funding costs or benefits of the collateral amount reflect on the price of the original derivative?

Hull and White [88] originally categorically said no. They argue that the cost (or benefit) of the hedge were every bank's own problem, and the fact that every bank would apply its own funding spreads to compute the cost showed that risk-neutral pricing would break down. If one looks at a liquid bond, a potential buyer certainly has to consider whether she can fund the amount such that she creates excess income. And she certainly will not be able to argue that in addition to the funding cost of the notional amount she will also have to fund the collateral for the hedge. No seller will accept a lower price if the buyer's funding costs are too high. The source and the cost of the money should not make a difference to the *market price*, only its risk. In the loan business, banks will certainly try to get their cost components back, including funding costs. But the loan market is a lot less liquid and transparent than the bond market, and business is often local, so banks may succeed in charging most of their funding costs. Since all banks are trying to do it, it makes sense to allow the minimum funding spread in the market to be incorporated in loan pricing, and therefore in derivatives pricing as well. This view is shared for instance by the Dutch bank ING according to an interview in RISK magazine, see [45]. "By adding those [FVA] costs the bank is not coming up with a market price but an internal costbase-derived price", the bank's global head of credit exposure management is quoted there.

The advocates of FVA argued that the existence of a bank-specific price component showed that the assumptions behind risk-neutral pricing are not satisfied in reality, because markets are not complete, and not all risks can be perfectly hedged. In their paper [37], Burgard & Kjaer show that FVA is indeed zero if banks can fund themselves at the risk-free rate – everything falls back onto the Black-Scholes-Merton scenario. In reality, banks cannot do that even when investing the money in seemingly risk-free activities like collateralized derivatives, because the market ignores the usage of the money lent, see Laughton & Vaisbrot [111]. It gets even worse. In their later paper [40], Burgard & Kjaer show that different funding strategies will lead to different FVA numbers. That should not really be surprising; the consequence is that not only does the funding cost for a bank depend on its exogenously given capability of raising funds, but also on how it chooses to do so.

Burgard & Kjaer state themselves in [37]: "In this context, 'price' does not mean clearing or mark-to-market price but the economic value of the derivative to the issuer including counterparty risk and funding cost. The counterparty would clear the derivative with the issuer that has the best funding position."

So, is it all a misunderstanding? Hull & White do not deny that a hedge creates the costs that are labelled FVA, they only argue that these costs should not be incorporated in the market value. Burgard & Kjaer seem to say the same. Kenyon & Green [104] show that a single risk-neutral measure that can be applied by the whole market is an illusion not only because of the differences in funding costs and strategies but also due to the different regulatory regimes across the globe. This triggered another brief debate with Hull and White, see [82, 102].

Meanwhile, what is the market doing? The website *risk.net* reported FVA-related results from banks, see Table 20.1.

Also according to *risk.net*, Barclays, Goldman Sachs and Deutsche Bank have also included FVA numbers in their quarterly reports, starting as early as 2011 in Goldman's case. As of April 2015, Risk magazine reported that 20 banks had so far reported FVA numbers, see [25]. So all these global players obviously consider FVA a real contribution to their derivatives' fair market values. In addition, the BCBS has started an FVA project [23]. It looks like FVA is going to stay, even if it is not exactly clear yet in what shape.

Note that an adjustment that depends very much on the individual features of the bank – the funding spread, the funding strategy, the way derivatives are used – renders moot the original argument for including a DVA for symmetry reasons: symmetry is broken anyway.

20.1 A simple definition of FVA

FVA in its original form is only attributed to uncollateralized derivatives. The reasoning is that the derivative is usually hedged by an offsetting derivative, which

Table 20.1 Quarterly FVA results as reported by *risk.net*

Date	Bank	FVA Amount
28/03/2013	RBS[1]	−475 mn GBP
28/03/2013	Lloyds	−143 mn GBP
14/01/2014	JP Morgan	−1,500 mn USD
06/02/2014	Nomura	−10,000 mn JPY
15/10/2014	Citi Bank	−474 mn USD
30/10/2014	UBS	−267 mn CHF
15/01/2015	BAML[2]	−497 mn USD
22/01/2015	Morgan Stanley	−468 mn USD
12/02/2015	Credit Suisse	−279 mn CHF

[1] Royal Bank of Scotland
[2] Bank of America Merrill Lynch

will be done under an CSA. If the uncollateralized derivative has a positive value for the bank, the offsetting trade will require collateral; if the value is negative, collateral will be received. Posted collateral only accrues interest at the collateral rate, while it is usually funded via unsecured borrowing in the money market, and so will create a cost of the funding spread. The opposite is true for any received collateral: if it is rehypothecable, it saves the bank the funding spread or can be invested, generating a funding benefit of the lending spread. If the uncollateralized counterparty defaults, the offsetting trade is closed, so it is only necessary to take cash flows into account while both parties are still alive.

Based on this argument, a simple definition of FVA can be given in a very similar fashion as the sum of unilateral CVA and DVA which we defined by (8.2), namely as an expectation of exposure times funding spreads, see for example Chapter 14 in Gregory [74]:

$$FVA(t) = \underbrace{\sum_{i=1}^{n} f_b(t,t_{i-1},t_i)\,\delta_i\,\mathbb{E}_t^{\mathbb{Q}}(S_C(t,t_{i-1})\,S_B(t,t_{i-1})\,PV(t_i)^+\,D(t,t_i))}_{\text{Funding Benefit Adjustment (FBA)}}$$
$$+\underbrace{\sum_{i=1}^{n} f_l(t,t_{i-1},t_i)\,\delta_i\,\mathbb{E}_t^{\mathbb{Q}}(S_C(t,t_{i-1})\,S_B(t,t_{i-1})\,PV(t_i)^-\,D(t,t_i))}_{\text{Funding Cost Adjustment (FCA)}} \quad (20.1)$$

where

$D(t,t_i)$ stochastic discount factor

$PV(t_i)^+$ positive portfolio value (after potential collateralization)

$PV(t_i)^-$ negative portfolio value (after potential collateralization)

$S_C(t, t_j)$ survival probability of the counterparty;

$S_B(t, t_j)$ survival probability of the bank;

$f_b(t, t_j)$ borrowing spread for the bank;

$f_l(t, t_j)$ lending spread for the bank.

The interpretation of this formula is that if the current exposure of the uncollateralized derivative at some future point in time is positive, the bank will pay collateral on the offsetting trade, which costs an equal amount of funding at the bank's borrowing rate. Likewise, a negative current exposure creates a funding benefit which can be invested at the lending rate.

The major difference between Gregory's equation (14.1) and our Equation (20.1) is that we allow dependencies between the default times and the risk factors of the exposure because all are within the expectation.

Writing (20.1) for FVA only makes two assumptions: that default times of both the bank and the counterparty as well as the exposure and its value drivers are independent of the lending and borrowing spreads, and that collateral can be rehypothecated (otherwise, the FBA part collapses to zero).

If we assume deterministic borrowing and lending spreads, implementing formula (20.1) requires no extra work on top of our existing CVA/DVA framework as all the ingredients are already accounted for. However, determining these spreads is actually the difficult bit, see Section 20.3.

With the advent of OIS discounting, many banks only switched their collateralized portfolios to discounting with OIS and kept the uncollateralized ones on LIBOR curves, or added their funding spread to the LIBOR curve. This approach amounts to using a simplified version of (20.1) by ignoring default, setting $f_l = f_b$ and keeping that constant, and approximating the sum of the future exposures by the average future value of the trade, compare Gregory [74]. Given that one of the most important realizations of the crisis was that borrowing and lending rates are *not* the same (and neither equals the risk-free rate in general), assuming $f_l = f_b$ is certainly questionable. In addition, the approach only works if there is no collateralization at all and not just some asymmetric or high threshold CSA. As we already mentioned in Section 5.5, these can only be handled by properly simulating the exposure due to their path-dependent nature.

20.2 DVA = FBA?

In the public discussions about FVA, one often reads that FVA as defined above makes a double counting error in that DVA is the same as (or at least contained in) the FBA component, see for instance Gregory [74] or Cameron [44]. Why should that be the case? Let us use the simple approximation to bilateral CVA given by the sum of unilateral CVA and DVA:

$$\begin{aligned} BCVA(t) = & \underbrace{(1-R_C)\sum_{i=1}^{n}\mathbb{E}_t^{\mathbb{Q}}[S_B(t,t_i)(S_C(t,t_{i-1})-S_C(t,t_i))\,PV(t_i)^+\,D(t,t_i)]}_{\text{CVA}} \\ & \underbrace{+\,(1-R_B)\sum_{i=1}^{n}\mathbb{E}_t^{\mathbb{Q}}[S_C(t,t_i)(S_B(t,t_{i-1})-S_B(t,t_i))\,PV(t_i)^-\,D(t,t_i)]}_{\text{DVA}} \end{aligned} \tag{20.2}$$

where R_C resp. R_B is the (constant) recovery rate of the counterparty resp. the bank, and we have written the probability of either counterparty defaulting in period i as the difference of the survival probabilities for the start and end of that period. If we now assume a constant hazard rate λ_B and CDS spread s_B for the bank, we can use the following well-known approximative relationship between s_B, λ_B and recovery rate R_B (see, for instance, (3.10) in Kenyon & Stamm [107]):

$$\lambda_B \approx \frac{s_B}{1-R_B}. \tag{20.3}$$

Then we can write the probability of default in the ith period, that is the difference of the survival probabilities, as follows:

$$\begin{aligned} (1-R_B)\,[S_B(t,t_{i-1})-S_B(t,t_i)] &= S_B(t,t_{i-1})\,(1-R_B)\left[1-\frac{S_B(t,t_i)}{S_B(t,t_{i-1})}\right] \\ &= S_B(t,t_{i-1})\,(1-R_B)\,[1-e^{-\lambda_B\delta_i}] \\ &\approx S_B(t,t_{i-1})\,(1-R_B)\,\lambda_B\,\delta_i \\ &\approx S_B(t,t_{i-1})\,s_B\,\delta_i. \end{aligned}$$

We see that under these approximations, the only difference between the FBA and the DVA term is the difference between the lending spread f_l and the CDS spread s_B. If the CDS spread is part of the funding spread, double counting actually happens. This can only be circumvented by carefully looking at all the cash flows, which we will do in Sections 20.4 and 20.5.

It should also be noted that contrary to the DVA, which was only introduced to make pricing symmetric again and which cannot be hedged or even realized before default, FBA is an actual gain accruing into the P&L. We now discuss the problem of the right spreads and the question of whether to use FBA instead of or together with DVA in the next section.

20.3 The role of the spreads

The fair value of a derivative has to be an exit price – a value which a market participant would agree to pay/receive in an arm's length transaction. Even when transferring something as simple as a loan, valuations between banks may differ. The selling bank has no way of knowing which funding cost term structure a hypothetical buyer may have. A common approach to this problem is to assume that the buyer will be a peer and therefore has the same spreads as the seller. This is also widely accepted by auditors.

Derivatives are different from loans in that the latter very rarely have to be valued at market value, while the former – at least under IFRS and similar GAAPs – must be shown at market value, that is the exit price. While the market for new derivatives is very liquid, transfers of running trades are few and far between. One activity that currently gives many banks a reason to novate derivatives is the backloading of clearable trades which are transferred to a CCP. However, the closing values of such novations are usually not public. Furthermore, during a novation whole parts of a portfolio between two counterparties are transferred *en bloc* at one price. It is one of the many mysteries of the accounting rules that a derivative transaction has to have an individual price even if it is clear that it is only one piece of a large portfolio whose value depends on portfolio-related topics: is it centrally cleared, what are the features of the CSA, etc.

To cut a long story short, it is also common practice to use one's own funding cost term structure to compute the FCA, see for instance the reports "The black art of FVA" by Cameron [44] and Becker & Sherif[25].

It seems obvious that one should use the own funding (borrowing) spread when computing FBA because that is the benefit one has from rehypothecable collateral, and it is reasonable to assume that a buyer of the derivative (portfolio) would have a similar credit rating and hence funding cost structure. However, as we saw in Section 20.1 above, it won't do for simple formulas like (20.1) to just use the full funding spread. A simple solution seems to be to use the bond-CDS basis instead, the difference between the zero or yield spread of a risky (i.e. unsecured) bond and the CDS spread on the same issuer. Before the beginning of the credit crisis in 2007, this basis was very small, see for instance Bai & Collin-Dufresne [15]. With the credit and liquidity crunch came the realization that even a significant basis was not easy to arbitrage anymore, and the basis reached average levels of 200 basis points in 2009 for investment grade names, and more than 650 basis points for high yield names, according to the research in [15]. The basis can become negative, which would lead to new problems; since the crisis, however, this scenario is less likely. A positive basis clearly shows the difference between a fully funded instrument – the bond – and the collateralized derivative. The basis should therefore contain the funding cost of the issuer. Unfortunately, the basis cannot be set equal to the funding costs because

- the bond credit spread contains other elements such as liquidity premia (or discounts), depending on issue size, maturity, issuer, market segment, structure, etc., which are notoriously difficult to extract;
- CDS are not as liquid as one might hope, and usually only a few maturities (like five years) are liquid at all;
- the CDS spread may contain a premium due to the capital relief a CDS offers for CVA hedging, see Green & Kenyon [103], which is not induced by credit risk.

It seems that FBA is more "real" than DVA, and, under normal circumstances, contains it; unfortunately, it is unclear to what extent. As long as IFRS prescribe the reporting of DVA (and do not enforce the reporting of FVA), users computing FVA with a simple expectation formula like (20.1) should compute a full FBA based on the funding spread over the risk-free rate, compute DVA as well, and report both DVA and the difference of FBA and DVA.

20.4 The expectation approach

As we have seen, the simple formula (20.1) does not seem to fully consider the connection between CVA, DVA and FVA, even though it is in some sense a complement of them – while CVA and DVA deal with the situation where one of the parties defaults, FVA in this definition looks at what happens for as long as both parties are still alive. In [120], Pallavicini et al. derive an approach which includes bilateral credit risk as well as all funding costs in an expectation expression, which we present here.

The risk and cost-adjusted value is given by

$$\begin{aligned}\bar{V}(C,F) = &\, \mathbb{E}(\Pi(t,T\wedge\tau)+\gamma(t,T\wedge\tau,C)+\varphi(t,T\wedge\tau,F)\,|\,\mathcal{G}_t)\\ &+\mathbb{E}(\mathbb{1}_{\{\}}\{\tau<T\}D(t,\tau)\theta_\tau(C,\varepsilon)\,|\,\mathcal{G}_t),\end{aligned} \tag{20.4}$$

where

$\mathcal{G}_t$	is the filtration containing the information on exposure risk factors and both parties' defaults;
C	is the collateral cash account;
F	is the cash account for trading and funding;
$\tau=\tau_B\wedge\tau_C$	is the first default time of either bank or counterparty;
$\Pi(t,T\wedge\tau)$	is the risk-free value of all cash flows between t and $T\wedge\tau$;
$\gamma(t,T\wedge\tau,C)$	are the collateral margining costs/benefits between t and $T\wedge\tau$;
$\varphi(t,T\wedge\tau,F)$	are the funding costs/investment benefits between t and $T\wedge\tau$;
$\theta_\tau(C,\varepsilon)$	is the cash flow at default, ε the close-out amount.

Assume that the interest on a positive collateral cash amount accrues at rate c_p, and at rate c_n for a negative one. Likewise, keep the notation f_b resp. f_l for the borrowing resp. lending funding rate. The risk-free rate (not necessarily the collateral rate!) is denoted by r. Then define the zero coupon bond

$$P_x(t,T) := \frac{1}{1+\delta(t,T)\,x(t,T)}$$

for any rate

$$x = r, c_p, c_n, f_l, f_b.$$

It can be shown (for details, see in [120]) that the expression for $\varphi(t, T\wedge\tau, F)$ is given by:

$$\varphi(t,T\wedge\tau,F) = \sum_{i=1}^{n-1} \mathbb{1}_{\{\}}\{t_i < T\wedge\tau\} D(t,t_i)\left(F(t_i) - F(t_i)^- \frac{P_r(t_i,t_{i+1})}{P_{f_b}(t_i,t_{i+1})} - F(t_i)^+ \frac{P_r(t_i,t_{i+1})}{P_{f_l}(t_i,t_{i+1})}\right),$$

and likewise

$$\gamma(t,T\wedge\tau,C) = \sum_{i=1}^{n-1} \mathbb{1}_{\{\}}\{t_i < T\wedge\tau\} D(t,t_i)\left(C(t_i) - C(t_i)^- \frac{P_r(t_i,t_{i+1})}{P_{c_n}(t_i,t_{i+1})} - C(t_i)^+ \frac{P_r(t_i,t_{i+1})}{P_{c_p}(t_i,t_{i+1})}\right).$$

These two components together represent the funding requirements. The F-terms in φ are (in first order approximation)

$$-F(t_i)^-\,(f_b - r) - F(t_i)^+\,(f_l - r),$$

so we see that they represent the funding costs and benefits from the trading cash account. The same applies to the C-terms in γ, which represent the funding costs and benefits from the collateral cash account.

The credit component is captured in the default cash flow $\theta_\tau(C,\varepsilon)$. To fully understand it, we must look at the close-out amount ε. There are two possible default scenarios: either counterparty C defaults ($\tau = \tau_C$), or the bank B ($\tau = \tau_B$). In each case, the surviving party will compute the close-out amount, so we write

$$\varepsilon_\tau = \mathbb{1}_{\{\}}\{\tau = \tau_C < \tau_B\}\varepsilon_{B,\tau} + \mathbb{1}_{\{\}}\{\tau = \tau_B < \tau_C\}\varepsilon_{C,\tau}.$$

Before we go further into the details of the default payment θ, a word on rehypothecation. If the received collateral can be reused (either by lending it at the lending rate f_l or by using it as collateral, thus accruing the collateral rate c_n), the posting party will, upon default of the receiving party, only get back some fraction of any excess collateral. This fraction can be different from the recovery rate of the receiving party, so we denote it by R'.

Now following Pallavicini et al. [120], we distinguish four cash flow scenarios from the bank's perspective in case of C's default:

1. B sees a positive exposure, and C has posted some collateral: $\tau = \tau_C, \varepsilon_{B,\tau} > 0, C_\tau > 0$: only $R_C\,(\varepsilon_\tau - C_\tau)^+$ of any under-collateralized exposure is paid back. Any over-collateralization has to be paid back in full: $(\varepsilon_\tau - C_\tau)^-$;
2. B sees a positive exposure, and B has posted some collateral: $\tau = \tau_C, \varepsilon_{B,\tau} > 0, C_\tau < 0$: exposure comes back at recovery R_C, posted collateral at rehypothecated recovery R'_C: $R_C\,\varepsilon_\tau - R'_C\,C_\tau$;
3. B sees a negative exposure, and C has posted some collateral: $\tau = \tau_C, \varepsilon_{B,\tau} < 0, C_\tau > 0$: both amounts have to be paid back in full, $(\varepsilon_\tau - C_\tau)$;
4. B sees a negative exposure, and B has posted some collateral: $\tau = \tau_C, \varepsilon_{B,\tau} < 0, C_\tau < 0$: any under-collateralized exposure $(\varepsilon_\tau - C_\tau)^-$ is paid to C, any over-collateralized amount is paid back with recovery R'_C: $R'_C\,(\varepsilon_\tau - C_\tau)^+$.

The same kind of analysis is done for the case where party B defaults. This leads to the definition of (using $LGD_X = 1 - R_X$)

$$\theta_\tau(C,\varepsilon) = \mathbb{1}_{\{\}}\{\tau = \tau_C < \tau_B\}\Big(\varepsilon_{B,\tau} - LGD_C(\varepsilon^+_{B,\tau} - C^+_\tau)^+ - LGD'_C(\varepsilon^-_{B,\tau} - C^-_\tau)^+\Big)$$
$$+\mathbb{1}_{\{\}}\{\tau = \tau_B < \tau_C\}\Big(\varepsilon_{C,\tau} - LGD_B(\varepsilon^-_{C,\tau} - C^-_\tau)^- - LGD'_B(\varepsilon^+_{C,\tau} - C^+_\tau)^-\Big).$$

Unfortunately, Equation (20.4) does not allow writing the adjusted value of the derivative/portfolio in the form

$$\bar{V} = V - CVA + DVA - FVA$$

anymore, because it is recursive in nature: the funding, collateral and the close-out amount depend on each other's values. This problem can only be dispensed with if one assumes that $c_p = c_n$ and $f_l = f_b$, because then the funding and collateral adjustments become agnostic as to the sign of the cash accounts. The former equality can be assumed to hold in CSA portfolios, that is derivatives portfolios between two banks which are not done via a CCP. The latter equation is not true – certainly not after 2007, as we've reiterated several times in this text. It is nevertheless an assumption often made in practice. See also the discussion in Section 20.3.

20.5 The semi-replication approach

The approach for pricing the value adjustments we present here was published by Burgard & Kjaer [37, 38, 40]; see a summary in Kenyon & Stamm [107]. It was later extended by Green et al. [72] and Green & Kenyon [71, 106] in order to take KVA and other value adjustments into account as well. The name semi-replication is chosen because not all risks are (nor can be) hedged, namely the default of the bank itself. This is further extended to the risk warehousing in [106], where the authors acknowledge the fact that even CDS on counterparties may be illiquid or not exist at all, so the counterparty credit risk is left unhedged by choice or necessity as well.

The basic assumption underlying this approach is that the investor or bank B can issue *two bonds* with different recovery rates $R_1 < R_2$; both bonds are supposed to be unsecured. Furthermore, there is a zero recovery, zero coupon bond issued by the counterparty C. The bond-CDS basis is assumed to be zero for all bonds. The bonds' prices are denoted by P_i and P_C, and their rates by r_i and r_c, respectively. Finally, there is an underlying S on which the two parties trade a derivative. The underlying pays a continuous yield γ_S. The counterparty bond and the underlying may be repo-able and can thus be used for funding purposes as well; the respective repo cash accounts are denoted by β_S and β_C and accrue the repo rates q_S and q_C, respectively. The unadjusted value of the derivative at time t is denoted by $V(t,S)$ and is assumed to be valued by classic Black-Scholes pricing. In order to compute the overall value adjustment $U(t,S)$, which will later be broken down into several components, a replicating portfolio Π is defined, which uses the available assets in the market: $S, P_C, P_1, P_2, \beta_S, \beta_C$ and the collateral cash account X, which accrues interest at rate r_X. The adjusted value of the derivative is denoted by $\hat{V}(t,S) = V(t,S) - U(t,S)$, and the risk-free rate by r.

Because of the assumption of no bond-CDS basis, we must have

$$r_i - r = (1 - R_i)\lambda_B,$$

where λ_B is B's hazard rate, because the right-hand side is just the CDS spread by (20.3) which equals the yield spread on the left-hand side. Likewise, we have (recall the zero recovery assumption for P_C)

$$r_C - q_C = \lambda_C.$$

The bonds and stock evolve according to the SDE

$$\begin{aligned} dS &= \mu\, S\, dt + \sigma\, S\, dW \\ dP_C &= r_C\, P_C\, dt - P_C\, dJ_C \\ dP_i &= r_i\, P_i\, dt - (1 - R_i) P_i\, dJ_B, \end{aligned} \tag{20.5}$$

where J_C and J_B are jump processes representing the default of C resp. B. On default of either party, the derivative takes the value

$$\begin{aligned} \hat{V}(t,S,1,0) &= g_B(M_B,X) \quad \text{(bank defaults)} \\ \hat{V}(t,S,0,1) &= g_C(M_C,X) \quad \text{(counterparty defaults)} \end{aligned}$$

where M_Y is the close-out value upon default of party Y; remember that X is the collateral posted for the derivative. The most common assumption for the functions g_Y is that the close-out value is the risk-free derivative value V and hence

$$\begin{aligned} g_B(M_B,X) &= (V - X)^+ + R_B(V - X)^- + X \\ g_C(M_C,X) &= R_C(V - X)^+ + (V - X)^- + X \end{aligned} \tag{20.6}$$

for some (derivative-related) recovery rates R_Y. Note that the close-out uses the risk-free value of the derivative, as is customary.

By assumption, the two bonds P_1 and P_2 are used for funding any cash requirements that are not covered by collateral, so we have the condition

$$\hat{V}(t,S) - X(t) + \alpha_1(t)\, P_1(t) + \alpha_2(t)\, P_2(t) = 0. \tag{20.7}$$

Note that this also means that any over-collateralization will be *invested* in bonds P_i – in other words, is used to buy them back. We use the shorthand notation $P(t) := \alpha_1(t)\, P_1(t) + \alpha_2(t)\, P_2(t)$ for the value of the bank bond portfolio before B's default, and $P_D(t) = \alpha_1(t)\, R_1\, P_1(t) + \alpha_2(t)\, R_2\, P_2(t)$ for the value after B's default. By definition, the accounts β are used to fund their respective positions in S and P_C, in other words,

$$\delta(t)\, S(t) - \beta_S(t) = 0 = \alpha_C(t)\, P_C(t) - \beta_C(t).$$

Now the hedging portfolio is defined as

$$\begin{aligned} \Pi(t) = {} & \delta(t)\, S(t) + \alpha_1(t)\, P_1(t) + \alpha_2(t)\, P_2(t) + \alpha_C(t)\, P_C(t) \\ & + \beta_S(t) + \beta_C(t) - X(t), \end{aligned}$$

with differential (dropping the ts)

$$\begin{aligned} d\Pi &= \delta\, dS + \delta\,(\gamma_S - q_S)\, S\, dt + \alpha_1\, dP_1 + \alpha_2\, dP_2 \\ &\quad + \alpha_C\, dP_C - \alpha_C\, q_C\, P_C\, dt - r_X\, X\, dt \\ &= \delta\, dS + \delta\,(\gamma_S - q_S)\, S\, dt + \alpha_1\, r_1\, P_1\, dt - \alpha_1\,(1-R_1) P_1\, dJ_B \\ &\quad + \alpha_2\, r_2\, P_2\, dt - \alpha_2\,(1-R_2) P_2\, dJ_B + \alpha_C\, r_C\, P_C\, dt \\ &\quad - \alpha_C\, P_C\, dJ_C - \alpha_C\, q_C\, P_C\, dt - r_X\, X\, dt. \end{aligned}$$

By Ito's formula for jump processes, the differential of $\hat{V}$ is given by

$$d\hat{V} = \frac{\partial \hat{V}}{\partial t}\, dt + \frac{1}{2}\sigma^2 S^2 \frac{\partial^2 \hat{V}}{\partial S^2}\, dt + \frac{\partial \hat{V}}{\partial S}\, dS + \Delta\hat{V}_B\, dJ_B + \Delta\hat{V}_C\, dJ_C,$$

where $\Delta\hat{V}_Y = g_Y - \hat{V}$ is the value change associated with default of party Y, by definition of the g-functions in Equation (20.6). Upon B's default, the unhedged value is

$$\varepsilon_h := \Delta\hat{V}_B - (P - P_D),$$

namely the recovered value of the derivative minus the LGD of the bond portfolio. This definition of the hedging error ε_h looks different from the one defined in [40]. However, if we look at the definitions and bear in mind Equation (20.7), we see that

$$\begin{aligned} \varepsilon_h &= \Delta\hat{V} - (P - P_D) \\ &= g_B - \hat{V} - P + P_D \\ &= g_B - (\hat{V} + \alpha_1\, P_1 + \alpha_2\, P_2) + P_D \\ &= g_B - X + P_D, \end{aligned}$$

the value from [40].

We then compute[1]

$$\begin{aligned} \alpha_1\, r_1\, P_1 + \alpha_2\, r_2\, P_2 &= \alpha_1\, P_1\,(r + (1-R_2)\,\lambda_B) + \alpha_2\, P_2\,(r + (1-R_2)\,\lambda_B) \\ &= r\,P + \lambda_B\, P - \lambda_B\, P_D \\ &= r(X - \hat{V}) + \lambda_B\, P - \lambda_B\, P_D \\ &= r\,X - (r + \lambda_B)\,\hat{V} + \lambda_B\,\hat{V} + \lambda_B\, P - \lambda_B\, P_D \\ &= r\,X - (r + \lambda_B)\,\hat{V} + \lambda_B\, g_B - \lambda_B\, g_B + \lambda_B\,\hat{V} + \lambda_B\, P - \lambda_B\, P_D \\ &= r\,X - (r + \lambda_B)\,\hat{V} - \lambda_B\,(\varepsilon_h - g_B). \end{aligned} \tag{20.8}$$

[1] Thanks to Chris Kenyon for his useful presentation on XVA.

We can thus write

$$d\Pi = \Big\{\delta\, dS + \delta\,(\gamma_S - q_S)\, S - (r + \lambda_B)\, \hat{V} - \lambda_B\,(\varepsilon_h - g_B) \\ + \lambda_C\, \alpha_C\, P_C - (r_X - r)\, X\Big\}\, dt - (P - P_D)\, dJ_B - \alpha_C\, P_C\, dJ_C.$$

Summing the differentials of Π and $\hat{V}$, we get using (20.5) and (20.8):

$$d\hat{V} + d\Pi = \left\{\frac{\partial \hat{V}}{\partial t} + \frac{1}{2}\sigma^2 S^2 \frac{\partial^2 \hat{V}}{\partial S^2} + \delta\,(\gamma_S - q_S)\, S - (r + \lambda_B)\, \hat{V} \right. \\ \left. - \lambda_B\,(\varepsilon_h - g_B) + \lambda_C\, \alpha_C\, P_C - (r_X - r)\, X\right\} dt \\ + \varepsilon_h\, dJ_B + \left\{\delta + \frac{\partial \hat{V}}{\partial S}\right\} dS + \{\Delta \hat{V}_C - \alpha_C\, P_C\} dJ_C. \tag{20.9}$$

If all risks except own default are hedged, we must have

$$\delta = -\frac{\partial \hat{V}}{\partial S}$$

$$\alpha_C\, P_C = \Delta\, \hat{V}_C = g_C - \hat{V},$$

and the diffusion term must be zero as well:

$$\begin{aligned} 0 &= \frac{\partial \hat{V}}{\partial t} + \frac{1}{2}\sigma^2 S^2 \frac{\partial^2 \hat{V}}{\partial S^2} + \delta\,(\gamma_S - q_S)\, S \\ &\quad - (r + \lambda_B)\, \hat{V} - \lambda_B\,(\varepsilon_h - g_B) + \lambda_C\, \alpha_C\, P_C - (r_X - r)\, X \\ &= \frac{\partial \hat{V}}{\partial t} + \frac{1}{2}\sigma^2 S^2 \frac{\partial^2 \hat{V}}{\partial S^2} - (\gamma_S - q_S)\, S \frac{\partial \hat{V}}{\partial S} \\ &\quad - (r + \lambda_B)\, \hat{V} - \lambda_B\,(\varepsilon_h - g_B) + \lambda_C\,(g_C - \hat{V}) - (r_X - r)\, X \\ &= \frac{\partial \hat{V}}{\partial t} + \frac{1}{2}\sigma^2 S^2 \frac{\partial^2 \hat{V}}{\partial S^2} - (\gamma_S - q_S)\, S \frac{\partial \hat{V}}{\partial S} \\ &\quad - (r + \lambda_B + \lambda_C)\hat{V} + g_C\, \lambda_C + g_B\, \lambda_B - \varepsilon_h\, \lambda_B - (r_X - r)\, X. \end{aligned} \tag{20.10}$$

Since, by assumption, the risk-free value of the derivative satisfies the Black-Scholes PDE

$$0 = \frac{\partial V}{\partial t} + \frac{1}{2}\sigma^2 S^2 \frac{\partial^2 V}{\partial S^2} - (\gamma_S - q_S)\, S \frac{\partial V}{\partial S}, \qquad V(T, S) = 0,$$

the value adjustment $U = \hat{V} - V$ satisfies

$$\begin{aligned} \frac{\partial U}{\partial t} + \frac{1}{2}\sigma^2 S^2 \frac{\partial^2 U}{\partial S^2} - (\gamma_S - q_S)\, S \frac{\partial U}{\partial S} - (r + \lambda_B + \lambda_C)\, U \\ = -(g_C - V)\,\lambda_C - (g_B - V)\,\lambda_B + \varepsilon_h \lambda_B + (r_X - r)\, X, \\ U(T,S) = 0. \end{aligned} \tag{20.11}$$

Now we can use the Feynman-Kac Theorem from Appendix B to get for $y := r + \lambda_B + \lambda_C$

$$\begin{aligned} U = & -\underbrace{\int_t^T \lambda_C(u)\, \mathbb{E}_t\left[e^{-\int_t^u y(s)\,ds}\,(V(u) - g_C(V(u),X(u)))\right] du}_{CVA} \\ & -\underbrace{\int_t^T \lambda_B(u)\, \mathbb{E}_t\left[e^{-\int_t^u y(s)\,ds}\,(V(u) - g_B(V(u),X(u)))\right] du}_{DVA} \\ & -\underbrace{\int_t^T \lambda_B(u)\, \mathbb{E}_t\left[e^{-\int_t^u y(s)\,ds}\,\varepsilon_h(u)\right] du}_{FCA} \\ & -\underbrace{\int_t^T (r_X(u) - r(u))\, \mathbb{E}_t\left[e^{-\int_t^u y(s)\,ds}\,X(u)\right] du}_{COLVA} \end{aligned} \tag{20.12}$$

under some appropriate measure (which is the measure that makes S grow with a drift rate of $q_S - \gamma_S$). The labels for the individual adjustment components are as in [40]. The following points are noteworthy:

- Contrary to [37] and following papers, we have kept $\exp(-\int_t^u y(s)\,ds)$ within the expectation so as to reduce the number of independence assumptions.
- We see that there is no term called funding benefit adjustment; under the assumptions in our derivation, it is identical to the DVA and cannot be double-counted because of how we derived the adjustment.
- The discount factors in formula (20.12) all contain the risk-free rate as well as the hazard rates (which are the funding rates under the assumptions of the derivation) of *both* parties. This is perfectly reasonable because

$$e^{-\int_t^u \lambda_Y(s)\,ds} = S_Y(t,u)$$

is the survival probability and

$$\lambda_Y(u)\, e^{-\int_t^u \lambda_Y(s)\, ds} =: \rho_Y(u)$$

is the probability density of the default time of party Y, so integrating terms like $f(u)\,\rho_Y(u)$ amounts to computing the expectation of f under the default probability. With the definition of g_C in (20.6), $V - g_C(V,X) = (1-R_C)\,(V - X)^+$, so the term dubbed CVA is really

$$-\int_t^T \lambda_C(u)\,(1-R_C)\,\mathbb{E}_t\left[e^{-\int_t^u y(s)\, ds}\,(V(u) - X(u))^+\right] du,$$

which is just the CVA term from formula (8.4), although computed under a different measure, and the same holds for the DVA term.

- All terms but the one called FCA are the same (with opposite signs) for both parties. The hedging error, which is idiosyncratic, introduces the pricing asymmetry.
- We see that under the assumptions of this section, the FCA and the DVA=FBA use the same spread. See the discussions in Section 20.3.
- It is worth discussing whether it is possible for a bank to issue two (unsecured) bonds with different recovery levels. This will not be the case in general, and certainly not for unlimited amounts. However, the contingent capital (CoCo) instrument, which is a bond which turns into equity when the bank gets into trouble, in conjunction with normal unsecured bonds, might do the trick.

We now look at the funding strategy that is suggested as Strategy I in [40]. It makes more concrete assumptions about the recovery rates and usage of the two bonds issued by the bank, namely that $R_1 = 0$, $R_2 = R_B$, and

$$\begin{aligned}
\alpha_1\, P_1 &= -(\hat{V} - V) = -U,\\
\alpha_2\, P_2 &= -\alpha_1\, P_1 - \hat{V} + X = -(V - X).
\end{aligned}$$

In other words, the zero recovery bond is used to fund (or invest) the value adjustment, and the second bond is used to fund (or invest) the uncollateralized (over-collateralized) risk-free value. Under this strategy, we see that the hedging error can be computed as

$$\begin{aligned}
\varepsilon_h &= g_B - X + P_D\\
&= (V - X)^+ + R_B\,(V - X)^- + X - X + P_D
\end{aligned}$$

$$
\begin{aligned}
&= (V-X)^+ + R_B(V-X)^- - R_B(V-X) \\
&= (V-X)^+ - R_B(V-X)^+ \\
&= LGD_B(V-X)^+.
\end{aligned}
$$

Also, note that

$$V - g_B = V - ((V-X)^+ + R_B(V-X)^- + X) = LGD_B(V-X)^-$$

and likewise

$$V - g_C = V - (R_C(V-X)^+ + (V-X)^- + X) = LGD_C(V-X)^+.$$

The adjustments are thus simply computed as

$$
\begin{aligned}
CVA &= -LGD_C \int_t^T \lambda_C(u)\,\mathbb{E}_t\left[e^{-\int_t^u y(s)\,ds}(V(u)-X(u))^+\right] du \\
DVA &= -LGD_B \int_t^T \lambda_B(u)\,\mathbb{E}_t\left[e^{-\int_t^u y(s)\,ds}(V(u)-X(u))^-\right] du \\
FCA &= -LGD_B \int_t^T \lambda_B(u)\,\mathbb{E}_t\left[e^{-\int_t^u y(s)\,ds}(V(u)-X(u))^+\right] du \qquad (20.13)\\
COLVA &= -\int_t^T (r_X(u)-r(u))\,\mathbb{E}_t\left[e^{-\int_t^u y(s)\,ds}X(u)\right] du.
\end{aligned}
$$

Note that the DVA and FCA terms are identical up to the positive/negative operator in the expectation, so they sum to

$$FVA = -LGD_B \int_t^T \lambda_B(u)\,\mathbb{E}_t\left[e^{-\int_t^u y(s)\,ds}(V(u)-X(u))\right] du.$$

In particular, FVA only uses one funding spread, namely that of the bank.

Bearing in mind that the adjustment thus computed gives us the hedging cost for a derivative, that is the sum of the values of the original derivative plus that of a hedging derivative, we first look at an uncollateralized derivative. In this case, $X \equiv 0$, and hence $COLVA = 0$ as well. For the other adjustments, we get

$$
\begin{aligned}
CVA_C &= -LGD_C \int_t^T \lambda_C(u)\,\mathbb{E}_t\left[D_C(t,u)\,V(u)^+\right] du \\
FVA_C &= -LGD_B \int_t^T \lambda_B(u)\,\mathbb{E}_t[D_C(t,u)\,V(u)]\,du
\end{aligned}
\qquad (20.14)
$$

This is the cost of a CDS to hedge the credit risk, plus the funding cost/benefit of a fully collateralized (i.e. for which collateral $X = V$!) market risk hedge, which makes perfect sense.

If, in another example, we are looking at the adjustment of a fully collateralized derivative, we have $X \equiv V$, so the hedging cost reduces to

$$COLVA_D = \int_t^T (r_X(u) - r(u))\,\mathbb{E}_t\,[D_D(t,u)\,V(u)]\,du. \tag{20.15}$$

If the collateral rate is assumed to be the risk-free rate, then this term vanishes as well, so a fully collateralized trade is hedged by an opposite, fully collateralized trade at no extra cost – any cash flows can be passed from the one where they are received to the one where they are owed. So again, this result makes sense.

In [40], Burgard & Kjaer also investigate what happens if only one bond is (or can be) used for funding, which they call Strategy II. This amounts to setting $\alpha_1\,P_1 \equiv 0$. This leads to a recursive formula for the adjustment U because it turns out that we have to set

$$\alpha_2\,P_2 = -(V + U - X)$$

in this case, which contains the term U we want to determine. So we are in a similar situation to the expectation approach then. Without going into the details, the situation can be healed by carefully inspecting the PDE (20.10) and changing it to

$$\frac{\partial \hat{V}}{\partial t} + \frac{1}{2}\sigma^2 S^2\,\frac{\partial^2 \hat{V}}{\partial S^2} - (\gamma_S - q_S)\,S\,\frac{\partial \hat{V}}{\partial S} = -g_C\,\lambda_C - (r_2 - r_X)\,X$$

which leads to the following adjustments:

$$CVA = -(1 - R_C)\int_t^T \lambda_C(u)\,\mathbb{E}_t\left[e^{-\int_t^u z(s)\,ds}\,(V(u) - X(u))^+\right]du$$

$$DVA = -\int_t^T (r_2(u) - r(u))\,\mathbb{E}_t\left[e^{-\int_t^u z(s)\,ds}\,(V(u) - X(u))^-\right]du$$

$$FCA = -\int_t^T (r_2(u) - r(u))\,\mathbb{E}_t\left[e^{-\int_t^u z(s)\,ds}\,(V(u) - X(u))^+\right]du$$

$$COLVA = -\int_t^T (r_X(u) - r(u))\,\mathbb{E}_t\left[e^{-\int_t^u z(s)\,ds}\,X(u)\right]du,$$

where $z = r_2 + \lambda_C$ in this case.

When we analyse the total adjustment for the portfolio of an uncollateralized and a fully collateralized derivative whose risk-free cash flows offset each other under this funding strategy, we get similar formulas as (20.14) and (20.15), we only have to use the discount factors

$$D'_Y(t,u) := \exp\left(-\int_t^u r_2(s) + \lambda_Y(s)\,ds\right)$$

for $Y = C, D$ instead. This means there are two changes to the situation under Strategy I: the LGD is dropped from the equation, and instead of the hazard rate, the actual unsecured funding spread is used in the calculation of FVA.

In [41], Burgard & Kjaer present a funding strategy which reproduces the FVA calculation suggested in Albanese et al. [3]. The FVA is there based on the assumption that any over-collateralization cannot be invested at a rate that is higher than the risk-free rate r, while fresh collateral that is owed has to be borrowed at the unsecured funding rate r_2.

These results show that the semi-replication approach is more general than the expectation approach in that it allows different funding strategies, and can reproduce the common formulas for CVA/DVA/FVA by choosing the right combination of funding instruments. It is also cleaner in that it uses hedging (as far as possible) for deriving the results, which is exactly what the market does. It furthermore shows that the value adjustments are not only dependent on the bank and its funding costs, but also on the funding strategy that the bank employs. In other words, asymmetry has two sources: the bank-specific funding parameters of the bank, and its choice of funding strategy. We shall see in Chapter 21 that more sources of asymmetry are added with the introduction of KVA.

This approach is used to derive one formula for the funding costs associated with a derivative. In reality, this "standard" cost will be charged to the client derivatives desk by the funding desk (which would nowadays be a desk managing all XVAs). The funding desk will then generate its P&L by optimizing the actual funding (and other) cost. For instance, a hedge with counterparty D may attract less funding cost than with counterparty E because of the different CSAs. The same holds for the adjustments we shall meet next.

20.6 CSA pricing revisited

In Sections 5.3 and 11.3 we discussed the phenomenon of negative overnight rates and the impact of a specific CSA feature ("OIS Floor") – to truncate the rate paid or received on posted collateral at zero, that is to ensure that no interest has to be paid by the party that posts collateral when rates are negative. In Section 11.3 we investigated in particular the impact of the OIS Floor feature on a single interest rate swap's valuation. The CSA applies to a netting set, in general a portfolio of trades, and the portfolio's valuation is affected.

In this section, however, we want to consider the value of the OIS Floor as a financial instrument, that is the value of the OIS Floor feature that originates directly from the interest paid or received on posted collateral. For that purpose, let us consider the value of collateral interest rate cash flows, initially assuming no CSA Floor:

$$\Pi_{NotFloored} = \mathbb{E}\left[\sum_i C(t_i) \cdot r(t_i) \cdot \delta_i \cdot D(t_{i+1})\right],$$

where the sum is taken over the time grid which is in line with the (daily) margining frequency, $C(t)$ is the collateral balance at time t, $r(t)$ is the overnight rate at time t which compounds the collateral balance, and $D(t)$ is the stochastic discount factor. This means we assume here for simplicity that the interest is paid daily rather than compounded over longer periods and paid with a lower frequency. The collateral balance C is driven by the netting set's valuation, but also depending on CSA details such as thresholds and minimum transfer amounts. If we now introduce the OIS Floor feature, the value of collateral interest cash flows changes to

$$\Pi_{Floored} = \mathbb{E}\left[\sum_i \widetilde{C}(t_i) \cdot r^+(t_i) \cdot \delta_i \cdot \widetilde{D}(t_{i+1})\right],$$

that is no interest is accrued when overnight rates are negative. Note that portfolio valuation, collateral balance and discounting are all modified in this case as discussed above. We indicate this by introducing $\widetilde{C}(t) \neq C(t)$ and $\widetilde{D}(t) \neq D(t)$. The value of the OIS Floor feature in the CSA is therefore the difference between these two values,

$$\Pi_{Floor} = \Pi_{Floored} - \Pi_{NotFloored} \tag{20.16}$$

Recalling that the impact of the OIS Floor feature on trade pricing is noticeable but small (in the ballpark of 1% of the instrument price in case of the interest rate swaps considered in Section 11.3), we make the simplifying assumption $\widetilde{C}(t) = C(t)$ and $\widetilde{D}(t) = D(t)$ to arrive at

$$\Pi_{Floor} \approx \mathbb{E}\left[\sum_i C(t_i) \cdot (-r(t_i))^+ \cdot \delta_i \cdot D(t_{i+1})\right] \tag{20.17}$$

since $r^+ - r = (-r)^+$. This corresponds to the *COLVA* adjustment introduced in Section 20.5.

To illustrate the quality of this approximation from (20.16) to (20.17), we investigate the "exact" and approximate floor values for single-trade netting sets – containing vanilla payer interest swaps of various terms and fixed rates – under an otherwise ideal CSA (zero threshold and minimum transfer amount). The posted

Table 20.2 "Exact" vs. approximate floor value and relative error for various EUR payer swaps (fixed vs. 6M Euribor, 10 Mio. EUR nominal) in single-trade netting sets. Interest rates are modelled using Hull-White with constant model parameters $\lambda = \sigma = 0.01$ and yield curve data as of 30 June 2015. Both floor values are computed via Monte Carlo simulation using 10,000 identical short rate paths

Term	Rate	Floor	Approximation	Rel. Error
5	2%	19,779	19,803	0.12%
5	3%	26,790	26,842	0.19%
5	4%	33,802	33,882	0.24%
5	5%	40,814	40,921	0.26%
10	2%	71,197	71,053	−0.20%
10	3%	96,698	96,958	0.27%
10	4%	122,199	122,862	0.54%
10	5%	147,700	148,767	0.72%
20	2%	185,575	184,060	−0.82%
20	3%	256,561	256,577	0.01%
20	4%	327,548	329,095	0.47%
20	5%	398,534	401,612	0.77%
30	2%	308,060	305,879	−0.71%
30	3%	428,731	428,881	0.03%
30	4%	549,403	551,883	0.45%
30	5%	670,074	674,885	0.72%

collateral C and $\widetilde{C}$, respectively, is then just the negative swap value, and we assume that the collateral rate differs from the plain overnight rate only up to the end of year ten from today. The results in Table 20.2 indicate that the relative approximation error (here in the $\pm$ 1% range) is quite small, in particular less than typical Monte Carlo error. Results do not change significantly when we shift the yield curve environments (-20 basis points, +100 basis points). To evaluate the OIS Floor, it is therefore – in our opinion – sufficient to apply the approximate COLVA formula (20.17), that is we can evolve the netting set values for example using the risk factor evolution models introduced in Part III of this text.

Finally note that the OIS Floor's "nominal" is the posted collateral (negative netting set value) associated with negative rate scenarios, that is the nominal is significantly different from the expected posted collateral amount. This is illustrated in Figure 20.1.

20.7 MVA

One particular funding cost component for derivatives has not been included in the FVA derivation so far: the posting of an initial margin which causes

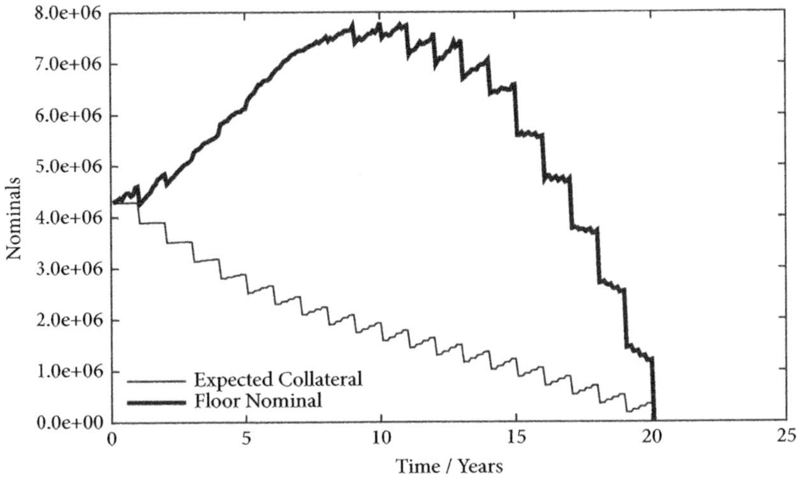

Figure 20.1 Expected posted collateral compared to the relevant collateral ("Floor Nominal"), the average over negative rate scenarios. The example considered here is a 20Y Swap with 10 Mio. EUR nominal which pays 4% fixed and receives 6M Euribor. The model is calibrated to market data as of 30 June 2015

the *(initial) margin value adjustment* (MVA). Basel III penalizes non-centrally cleared standardized derivatives by the CVA capital charge. Furthermore, the Basel Committee has made initial margin mandatory for these non-centrally cleared transactions[2] in [21], with the declared goal of promoting central clearing. It published, among others, the following key principles (p. 4 in [21]):

2. All financial firms and systemically important non-financial entities ("covered entities") that engage in non-centrally cleared derivatives must exchange initial and variation margin as appropriate to the counterparty risks posed by such transactions.

3. The methodologies for calculating initial and variation margin that serve as the baseline for margin collected from a counterparty should (i) be consistent across entities covered by the requirements and reflect the potential future exposure (initial margin) and current exposure (variation margin) associated with the portfolio of non-centrally cleared derivatives in question and (ii) ensure that all counterparty risk exposures are fully covered with a high degree of confidence.

5. Initial margin should be exchanged by both parties, without netting of amounts collected by each party (i.e. on a gross basis), and held in such a

[2] That is such transactions that cannot be centrally cleared. The transactions that can but are not centrally cleared are penalized by the CVA capital charge.

> way as to ensure that (i) the margin collected is immediately available to the collecting party in the event of the counterparty's default; and (ii) the collected margin must be subject to arrangements that fully protect the posting party to the extent possible under applicable law in the event that the collecting party enters bankruptcy.

Covered entities are allowed to set thresholds and minimum transfer amounts (MTA), but these may not exceed 50 million EUR and 500,000 EUR, respectively. It is further specified (p. 11) that the potential future exposure (PFE) which is the basis for computing the required initial margin

> should reflect an extreme but plausible estimate of an increase in the value of the instrument that is consistent with a one-tailed 99 per cent confidence interval over a 10-day horizon,[3] based on historical data that incorporates a period of significant financial stress. The initial margin amount must be calibrated to a period that includes financial stress ... The required amount of initial margin may be calculated by reference to either (i) a quantitative portfolio margin model or (ii) a standardised margin schedule. ... the identified period must include a period of financial stress and should cover a historical period not to exceed five years. Additionally, the data within the identified period should be equally weighted for calibration purposes.

The standardized margin schedule is given in Appendix A of [21] and assigns percentages of the notional amount of a contract, depending on asset class and maturity, which lie between 1% and 15%. The approach is similar to the current exposure method (CEM) for add-on calculations, see Section 24.4.

The requirement of initial margin on top of variation margin is therefore a funding cost that any bank will have to bear – unless it decides not to clear, even though it could, and instead shoulders the additional capital cost.

The standardized calculation can be used with our existing future exposure calculation framework to compute actual margin requirements for the non-centrally cleared part of the portfolio. The centrally cleared part, however, definitely needs a more sophisticated computation, because in that case, initial margin is for sure computed as some risk measure (99% VaR or expected shortfall). This means that it only makes sense for a bank to opt for the standardized method in the unlikely event that it only has non-clearable derivatives in its portfolio. Otherwise, we need to estimate the future VaR in addition to the future exposure. Since it is not practical to do a historical simulation at each exposure calculation, it will be necessary to calculate the VaR differently. We suggest using the sensitivities that are computed

[3] "The 10-day requirement should apply in the case that variation margin is exchanged daily. If variation margin is exchanged at less than daily frequency then the minimum horizon should be set equal to 10 days plus the number of days in between variation margin exchanges."

via algorithmic differentiation as presented in Chapter 19. That way, the sensitivities of the whole portfolio can be computed within reasonable additional time, and then be used to compute a parametric VaR. Using parametric VaR seems acceptable in this case given the performance restraints as well as the other model uncertainties that are inherent in the exposure modelling.

Other approaches are possible, for example imitating the Longstaff-Schwartz approach used in American Monte Carlo simulations as discussed by Green & Kenyon in [71]. There, the authors also derive a formula for MVA, which reads

$$MVA = -\int_t^T ((1 - R_B)\,\lambda_B(u) - s_I(u))\,\mathbb{E}_t\left[e^{-\int_t^u y(s)\,ds} I(u)\right] du,$$

where $s_I = r_I - r$ is the spread received on initial margin, $I(u)$ is the initial margin cash account, and $y = r + \lambda_C + \lambda_B$ as in Equation (20.12). All the other parameters are defined as before. The derivation of the MVA formula follows exactly the same steps as the ones we took in Section 20.5, so we do not present it here.

20.8 Outlook

The question of how to handle FVA is far from being definitively answered. Besides generating a different FVA number, Albanese et al. [3] also suggest that the way FVA should be accounted for should be different from the current practice. They estimate that this could lead to a reduction of FVA numbers reported so far by two-thirds or even more, see [25]. Some banks are following their approach or other approaches now. One way is certainly to look at the actual funding cost by calculating it where it truly appears, namely on the side of the collateralized derivative.[4] That way offsetting portfolio effects and rehypothecation can be taken into account which leads to a reduction almost naturally. Albanese et al. also suggest that some parts of the FVA number should not go through the P&L but rather into the equity of the bank (Common Equity Tier I capital or CET1). It is yet unclear what the regulators' view is, but the BCBS has launched an FVA project [23].

Interested readers should try to keep up to date with the development of the topic, both from an accounting and from a regulatory perspective.

[4] This is a view that the authors also strongly support.

21 KVA

As mentioned in the introduction, the cost of required capital for derivatives transactions should be priced – at least as an internal cost if not as a part of the market value – in parallel to the practice for loans. Contrary to the loan business, where capital is based on exposure which is simply the outstanding notional, however, regulators require capital for derivatives for several reasons:

1. Counterparty credit risk (CCR) – depending on the level of sophistication of the bank, it has to hold a capital amount computed by standard formulae (CEM until end of 2016, thereafter SA-CCR), or by internal models;
2. CVA risk – again, either a standardized formula is used, or a VaR based on regulatory CVA or the credit spread sensitivity, see Section 24.7;
3. Market risk – again, standardized formula vs VaR.

However, in order to calculate the *future* capital requirement of a derivatives portfolio, it is necessary to project all three types of capital charges for the whole lifetime of the portfolio under investigation. Given the fact that the capital calculations are often only performed on a monthly basis in mid-sized or small banks, it should be clear that this exercise generates a significant effort if it is to be executed daily or even near-time. Furthermore, while the CVA capital charge and the CCR charge can be computed along netting sets and then aggregated, the market risk charge depends on the entire portfolio of the bank.

21.1 KVA by semi-replication

The semi-replication approach by Burgard & Kjaer that we presented in Section 20.5 was expanded by Green et al. [72] to incorporate the capital value adjustment, and later by Green & Kenyon [106] to take tax (via the so-called tax value adjustment (TVA)) into account as well as the fact that, besides own default, there may be other risks that are not hedged, either by choice or necessity. We present the results from [72] here and discuss the extended version from [106] afterwards. The extended equations are so similar to those from Section 20.5 that we go through them in much less detail here.

The hedging relationship (20.7) is expanded by one more component. The capital requirement K is a function of the current exposure of the derivative (portfolio), its market risk, the counterparty (via its rating and credit spread), and the collateral account. Furthermore, the hedging trades contribute to the capital requirements as well, namely the stock and the C-bond positions. It does not make sense to try to break these connections apart; the KVA number will be an honest portfolio number, even if it only refers to a single derivatives trade.

If ϕ is a fraction of capital that can potentially close a funding gap, (20.7) becomes

$$\hat{V}(t,S) - X(t) + \alpha_1(t)\,P_1(t) + \alpha_2(t)\,P_2(t) - \phi K = 0. \tag{21.1}$$

Associated with the capital K is a cash account β_K which accrues interest at rate γ_K:

$$d\beta_K = -\gamma_K\, K\, dt,$$

reflecting the fact that capital has to be borrowed from the shareholders. Jump to default does not contribute to the capital cash account as the effects of default on capital are already intrinsic in the recovery rate R_B. By following the steps taken in Section 20.5, we get a hedging error

$$\varepsilon_h = g_B + X - P_D - \phi K = \varepsilon_{h_0} + \varepsilon_{h_K},$$

where ε_{h_0} is the hedging error that does not depend on K. It is not the ε_h from the semi-replication for FVA because of the dependence of (21.1) on K. The PDE (20.11) for the adjustment U becomes

$$\begin{aligned}
&\frac{\partial U}{\partial t} + \frac{1}{2}\sigma^2 S^2 \frac{\partial^2 U}{\partial S^2} - (\gamma_S - q_S)\, S\frac{\partial U}{\partial S} - (r + \lambda_B + \lambda_C)\, U \\
&\quad = -(g_C - V)\,\lambda_C - (g_B - V)\,\lambda_B + \varepsilon_h \lambda_B + (r_X - r)\, X + \gamma_K K - r\phi K, \\
&\qquad\qquad\qquad\qquad\qquad\qquad U(T,S) = 0. \qquad (21.2)
\end{aligned}$$

The Feynman-Kac Theorem yields the same expressions for CVA, DVA, FCA[1] and COLVA as in Equation (20.12). The KVA term is given by

$$KVA = -\int_t^T \mathbb{E}_t \left\{ e^{-\int_t^u \gamma(s)\, ds} \left[(\gamma_K(u) - \phi\, r(u))\, K(u) + \lambda_B \varepsilon_{h_K}(u) \right] \right\} du. \tag{21.3}$$

[1] We only have to replace ε_h with ε_{h_0}.

21.2 Calculation of KVA

As in the case of MVA, the proper handling of the market risk capital charge requires a projection of VaR numbers over the lifetime of the portfolio. For the same reasons, we again suggest that the sensitivities be computed using algorithmic differentiation. The standardized formulae can then be evaluated on the exposures generated by the risk factor evolution methods we have presented so far. For internal model banks, the CVA risk also needs to be computed properly – since we suggest computing CVA risk using algorithmic differentiation anyway (see Chapter 19), it only makes sense to use the same methodology for other risk numbers as well.

One big problem for banks is the role of changes in regulation. As an important example, take the exemptions on the CVA capital charge (see Section 24.7). A large number of derivatives is excluded from the charge in the EU, but not in other countries like Japan, Switzerland or the US. Recently, the European Banking Authority (EBA) has recommended that these exemptions be discontinued. The estimated impact would be an increase of the CVA capital charge by 100% to 200%, in absolute numbers by 23.5 billion EUR to 47 billion EUR. It is obviously important to know in the KVA calculations if the exemptions are applicable or not, and for how long.

Another source of uncertainty is the leverage ratio which prescribes how much equity per exposure has to be held, see [135]. Basel III sets this to a minimum of 3%, but the US have implemented a range of 4%–6%. The UK is considering a minimum 3% level with two additional leverage buffers that would be set at the discretion of the Bank of England's macroprudential regulatory committee.

Finally, the Basel Committee wants to introduce a floor on capital requirements for banks with an internal model, which would be a percentage of the standardized approach's result. It is yet unclear what that floor is going to be.

We see that KVA is a number which comes with a lot of uncertainties. It is also clear that the regulatory regime has a very individual impact on every bank, and that international banks may have many ways to optimize their capital consumption.

21.3 Risk-warehousing and TVA

In [106], Green & Kenyon further generalize the semi-replication approach by introducing the possibility that the counterparty risk be hedged by a fraction ψ which can lie between 0 and 1. Keeping parts or all of the CCR open is dubbed *risk-warehousing*. Furthermore, they recognize the fact that a successful CCR hedge produces a capital relief because it mitigates the CVA capital charge. Therefore, they split up the capital requirement $K = K^U - \psi K^R$, the capital for the situation where no hedging happens at all minus the capital relief due to the (partial) hedging. The case where $\psi = 1$ falls back onto the standard semi-replication case if $\psi < 1$, the formulae have to be adjusted by using a slightly different λ_C as a result of the (partially) open credit position. Namely, if $\lambda_C^{\mathbb{P}}$ is the hazard rate under the real-world measure, then define $\tilde{\lambda}_C := \psi \lambda_C + (1 - \psi) \lambda_C^{\mathbb{P}}$. Then the formulae for CVA, DVA, FVA[2] and COLVA are the same as in Equation (20.12), with λ_C replaced by $\tilde{\lambda}_C$, and KVA is the same with K replaced by $K^U - \psi K^R$.

A consequence of the risk-warehousing is that the P&L of the total portfolio – derivative and (partial) hedges – shows volatility now, which will have an impact on tax. The replication machine produces an additional Tax Value Adjustment (TVA). In the numerical examples in [106], the contribution of TVA to the overall value adjustment is so small as to be negligible in most cases; it never grows above 10% of the overall adjustment. Given the uncertainties in the production of the XVA numbers, this can be considered noise.

2 Again, using ε_{h_0} instead of ε_h.

V | Credit Risk

22 Introduction

The primary aim of this final part of the book is to provide an overview of the methodologies nowadays applied to derivative products in credit risk monitoring and credit capital allocation. This chapter is therefore not a thorough introduction into the wide area of credit risk modelling, for which we refer the reader for example to the text books by Schönbucher [129] or Bluhm, Wagner and Overbeck [29]. Due to the focus of this text, we will, for example, not cover rating models, the estimation of probabilities of default (PD) and losses given default (LGD) for individual credit entities, to name just a few gaps.

We will start, nevertheless, in Section 22.1 with a brief summary of basic concepts in credit risk – some of which we have come across already in the credit risk factor evolution for XVA in Section 15.

Section 22.2 is then a tour around conventional ways of modelling *portfolio* default risk assuming *marginal*, that is single entity/name, probabilities of default (PD), losses given default (LGD) and exposures at default (EAD) for all portfolio constituents given.

In Chapter 23 we take a brief detour exploring a facet of portfolio default in the context of the pricing of portfolio credit products which are enjoying greater popularity again after an extended pause following the 2008 events.

Chapter 24 then shows how the exposure at default is determined if a credit entity represents a portfolio of derivatives rather than loans. This subject has a lot in common with the exposure measurements for XVA if we apply the "advanced" approaches required by the regulators for internal credit risk model approval since Basel II.

Finally, Chapter 25 touches on an important part of the justification to the regulator of the models used in the advanced approaches for derivative EAD computation, the backtesting of projected exposures against the realized ones.

22.1 Fundamentals

This section briefly lists the basic concepts or notions that appear in credit risk modelling, starting with the *Expected Loss (EL)* for a single entity defined as

$$EL = EAD \times LGD \times PD$$

with *Exposure at Default (EAD)*, *Loss Given Default (LGD)* and *Probability of Default (PD)* which is equal to the expectation $\mathbb{E}[\mathbb{1}_D]$. This equation assumes a fixed time horizon (typically one year) which affects in particular the PD. $\mathbb{1}_D$ is the default indicator function for the given entity which assumes value 1 if default occurs up to the end of the time horizon, and 0 otherwise. As mentioned in the introduction, the estimation of LGDs and PDs[1] and their assignment to individual credit entities is beyond the scope of this book.

For loans, the EAD is usually modelled as outstanding nominal amount N plus a fraction γ of outstanding commitment volumes C:

$$EAD = N + \gamma \times C,$$

where the expected value of drawdown ratio γ dependent on creditworthiness and type of loan, calibrated to historical data on drawdown behaviour.[2] In Section 24 we will come back to the determination of EAD for derivative portfolios, which is much more complicated due to the randomness of exposure evolution.

The LGD, also expressed in terms of recovery rate R in $LGD = 1 - R$, depends on the quality and valuation of possible collateral (bonds, guarantees, liens, assets), as well as seniority of debt. The LGD is regarded as a deterministic quantity, that is as an expectation of the underlying stochastic *Loss Severity (SEV)*, $\mathbb{E}[SEV] = LGD$.

While the expected loss is the *expectation* of $EAD \times SEV \times \mathbb{1}_D$ (which yields $EAD \times LGD \times PD$ if the default time and loss severity are independent random variables), the *Unexpected Loss (UL)* is the standard deviation of $EAD \times SEV \times \mathbb{1}_D$. For independent default time and loss severity, as well as deterministic EAD, we can write

$$\begin{aligned} UL &= \sqrt{\mathbb{V}(EAD \times SEV \times \mathbb{1}_D)} \\ &= EAD\sqrt{\mathbb{E}[SEV^2] \times \mathbb{E}[\mathbb{1}_D^2] - \mathbb{E}^2[SEV] \times \mathbb{E}^2[\mathbb{1}_D]} \end{aligned}$$

[1] Apart from implying them from quoted CDS spreads

[2] For example, the Basel *foundation approach* assumes $\gamma = 0.75$.

$$= EAD\sqrt{E[SEV^2] \times PD - \mathbb{E}^2[SEV] \times PD^2}$$
$$= EAD\sqrt{\mathbb{V}(SEV) \times PD + \mathbb{E}^2[SEV] \times PD \times (1 - PD)}$$
$$= EAD\sqrt{\mathbb{V}(SEV) \times PD + LGD^2 \times PD \times (1 - PD)}.$$

Let us move on to a portfolio with n constituents now. We can write the portfolio loss as a random variable

$$L_{PF} = \sum_{i=1}^{n} EAD_i \times SEV_i \times \mathbb{1}_{D_i}.$$

The *Expected Portfolio Loss* (EL_{PF}) is just the sum of individual expected losses of the constituents (with same independence assumption between each constituent's default time and loss severity as above)

$$EL_{PF} = \mathbb{E}[L_{PF}] = \sum_{i=1}^{n} \underbrace{EAD_i \times LGD_i \times PD_i}_{EL_i}.$$

The *Unexpected Portfolio Loss* (UL_{PF}), however, is in general *not* the sum of the constituent unexpected losses because of the correlation between defaults of individual names:

$$UL_{PF}^2 = \mathbb{V}(L_{PF}) = \sum_{i=1}^{n}\sum_{j=1}^{n} EAD_i \times EAD_j \times \mathrm{Cov}[SEV_i \times \mathbb{1}_{D_i}, SEV_j \times \mathbb{1}_{D_j}],$$

which is strongly dependent on the correlation/covariances between *loss severities* and default events. For deterministic SEV_i we can write this as:

$$= \sum_{i=1}^{n}\sum_{j=1}^{n} EAD_i \times EAD_j \times LGD_i \times LGD_j \times \rho_{ij} \times \sqrt{DP_i(1 - DP_i)DP_j(1 - DP_j)},$$

with

$$\rho_{ij} = \mathrm{Corr}[\mathbb{1}_{D_i}, \mathbb{1}_{D_j}].$$

Consider a simple example of two loans with $LGD_{1,2} = 1$, $EAD_{i,2} = 1$,

$$UL_{PF}^2 = PD_1(1 - PD_1) + PD_2(1 - PD_2) + 2\rho_{12}\sqrt{PD_1(1 - PD_1)}\sqrt{PD_2(1 - PD_2)}$$

and distinguish the following cases:

1. Perfect correlation $\rho_{12} = 1$ yields the maximum unexpected loss:

$$UL_{PF} = \sqrt{(PD_1(1 - PD_1)} + \sqrt{PD_2(1 - PD_2)}.$$

2. Independence, $\rho_{ij} = 0$, leads to

$$UL_{PF} = \sqrt{PD_1(1 - PD_1) + PD_2(1 - PD_2)}.$$

3. The perfect "hedge" with $PD_1 = PD_2$ and $\rho_{12} = -1$ yields

$$UL_{PF} = 0.$$

In order to define *Risk Capital (RC)*, the unexpected loss associated with the standard deviation of the portfolio loss is not a good, that is conservative, choice since the probability of losses beyond EL+UL is still significant. One usually defines *RC* via a sufficiently high *quantile* of the loss distribution

$$\begin{aligned} RC_\alpha &= L_\alpha - EL_{PF}, \\ L_\alpha &= \min\{L > 0 \,|\, \mathbb{P}[L_{PF} \leq L] \geq \alpha\}. \end{aligned}$$

or alternatively in terms of an expected shortfall, that is the average over losses beyond some quantile. The key object for this is the loss distribution as shown for an example (large) portfolio in Figure 22.1.

The following Section 22.2 deals with ways as to how such a portfolio loss distribution can be determined if EAD, PDs and LGDs for the constituents of the portfolio are given.

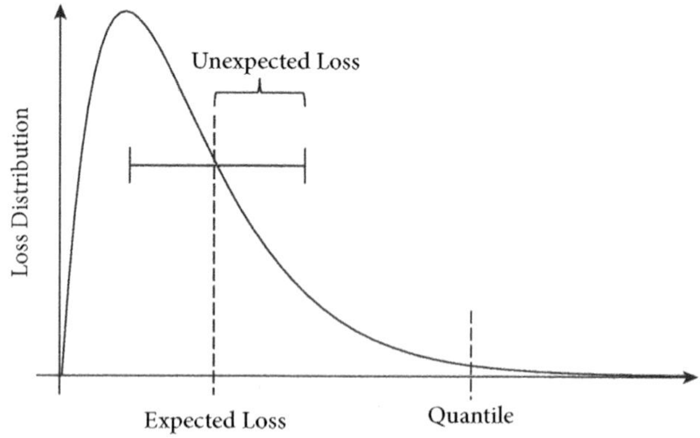

Figure 22.1 Example of a portfolio loss distribution illustrating expected loss, unexpected loss and risk capital associated with a high quantile of the loss distribution

22.2 Portfolio credit models

22.2.1 Independent defaults

If the correlations of defaults between any two names in the basket are zero, the assets can be analysed individually, and the basket loss distribution can be built from the individual assets' loss distributions using a combinatoric approach,

$$P(L,t) = \sum_{L=l_1+\cdots+l_n} \prod_{j=1}^{n} p_j(l_j,t)$$

where l_j is the binary outcome for asset j (zero loss or full loss of amount L_j), $p_j(l_j,t)$ is the probability for asset j of losing l_j until time t, the sum is taken over all combinations $(l_1,\ldots,l_n)$ that add up to L, and the product $\prod$ is taken over all assets and their probabilities of default or no-default until time t. Note that $p_j(L_j,t) = 1 - p_j(0,t)$. Computing this sum is generally a complicated task that needs to be performed numerically. Simple exact solutions are available when

- all $L_j = l$ and $p_j(L_j,t) = p$ are identical (binomial case), or
- all $L_j = l$ are identical, while $p_j(l,t)$ vary (homogeneous case)

In the former case, the solution is analytical and given by a binomial distribution

$$\mathbb{P}(L = k \cdot l,\, t) = \binom{n}{k} p^k (1-p)^{n-k}, \qquad 0 \le k \le n.$$

In the latter case, the solution can be obtained numerically via recursion, see Section 22.2.1. Moreover, three numerical methods are presented below that allow approximating the true basket loss distribution in the general case of varying L_j and $p_j(L_j)$, a probability bucketing algorithm in Section 22.2.1, a Fourier transform approach in Section 22.2.1, and Monte Carlo simulation in Section 22.2.1.

In general, the portfolio loss distribution can be constructed iteratively, by adding assets step by step to the portfolio. In each step, this requires computing the convolution of the new asset's loss distribution with the portfolio loss distribution of the previous step. As this iterative approach is the basis for the procedures in Sections 22.2.1 and 22.2.1, the basic formulae are presented in the following section.

Convolution

Consider loss distributions

$$\mathbb{P}\{L_i > z\} = \int_0^\infty \Theta(x-z)\,\rho_i(x)\,dx, \qquad i = 1,2,\ldots$$

The joint excess loss probability distribution for total loss $L = L_1 + L_2$ is then given by the convolution

$$\mathbb{P}\{L > z\} = \int_0^\infty \int_0^\infty \Theta(x+y-z)\,\rho_1(x)\,\rho_2(y)\,dy\,dx,$$

$$\rho(z) = \int_0^\infty \rho_1(x)\,\rho_2(z-x)\,dx. \tag{22.1}$$

Let ρ_2 denote the loss density for a single asset with volume L_2,

$$\rho_2(y) = (1-p_2)\,\delta(y) + p_2\,\delta(y-L_2), \tag{22.2}$$

then the convolution (22.1) reads

$$\begin{aligned}\rho(z) &= \int_0^\infty \rho_1(x)\,\big\{(1-p_2)\,\delta(z-x) + p_2\,\delta(z-x-L_2)\big\}\,dx\\ &= (1-p_2)\,\rho_1(z) + p_2\,\rho_1(z-L_2).\end{aligned} \tag{22.3}$$

Recursion for the homogeneous case

This section shows how to construct the exact loss distribution for a homogeneous portfolio where possible loss amounts are integer multiples of a base loss quantity $(0,\ 1\cdot L, 2\cdot L, \ldots, N\cdot L)$. Note that loss probabilities can vary, as opposed to the binomial case.

The portfolio loss distributions can be worked out iteratively by computing the convolution of the loss density of one additional contract $\rho_1(x) = p_k\,\delta(x-L) + (1-p)\delta(x)$ with the total loss density of the previous iteration step. Due to the discrete equidistant loss outcomes the iteration can be written as follows.

Initialize:

$$P_0^{(0)} = 1,$$

$$P_i^{(0)} = 0. \qquad (i = 1, \ldots, N)$$

Iteration step $(n \to n+1)$:

$$P_0^{(n+1)} = (1-p^{(n+1)})\,P_0^{(n)},$$

$$P_i^{(n+1)} = p^{(n+1)}\,P_{i-1}^{(n)} + (1-p^{(n+1)})\,P_i^{(n)}, \qquad (i = 1, \ldots, N-1)$$

$$P_N^{(n+1)} = p^{(n+1)}\,P_{N-1}^{(n)},$$

where $p^{(n)}$ is the loss probability of the nth asset $(n = 1, \ldots, N)$, and $P_i^{(n)}$ is the probability of portfolio loss $i \cdot L$ after adding n assets to the portfolio. As shown in [115], this procedure yields numerically stable results.

Probability bucketing

In general, when the loss amounts per asset are not integer multiples of a base quantity L, determination of the exact loss distribution becomes a complicated task, as the grid of possible loss outcomes is generally irregular and the number of exact grid points can grow quickly with portfolio size.

The probability bucketing method constructs an approximate distribution iteratively, again adding contracts one after another to the portfolio and deforming the loss distribution gradually [6, 87]. It is a generalization of the iteration in Section 22.2.1 as it allows for varying loss amounts.

Possible losses are discretized in buckets b_i $(i = 0, \ldots, B)$. Bucket b_0 represents zero loss, the following buckets b_i span ranges $]x_{i-1}, x_i]$, where $x_0 = 0$. Each bucket is associated with the probability density P_i and mean loss A_i given the loss is in bucket b_i. The iteration starts with an empty portfolio: $P_0 = 1$, $P_i = 0$ for $i > 0$, $A_i = (x_i - x_{i-1})/2$. Adding a contract with volume v and loss probability p then leads to the following updates for buckets b_k, $k = 0, ..., B$: Let

$$\begin{aligned} \Delta P &= P_k^* \cdot p, \\ u(k) &= \text{index of the bucket that contains the loss } A_k + v. \end{aligned}$$

If $u(k) = k$, only the average loss in bucket k is increased, $A_k = A_k^* + p \cdot v$. Otherwise the update procedure is:

$$\begin{aligned} P_u &= P_u^* + \Delta P, \\ P_k &= P_k^* - \Delta P, \\ A_u &= \frac{P_u^* \cdot A_u^* + \Delta P \cdot (A_k^* + v)}{P_u^* + \Delta P}. \end{aligned}$$

Values marked with an asterisk (*) are values before adding the current contract. Note that the outcome of the iteration can depend on the order of assets being added to the portfolio; the loss distribution is path-dependent.

Fourier transform

Taking the Fourier transform of (22.1) yields the simple relation

$$\tilde{\rho}(k) = \int_{-\infty}^{\infty} \rho(z)\, e^{ikz}\, dz = \tilde{\rho}_1(k)\, \tilde{\rho}_2(k). \tag{22.4}$$

One can therefore construct the Fourier transform of the portfolio loss density iteratively by taking the scalar product of the Fourier transforms of sub-portfolio loss densities, for example of single-asset loss densities.

The Fourier transform of the single-asset loss density (22.2) is

$$\tilde{\rho}_2(k) = 1 - p_2 + p_2\, e^{ikL_2},$$

so that the portfolio loss density's Fourier transform is given by

$$\tilde{\rho}_P(k) = \prod_{j=1}^{N} \left\{1 - p_j + p_j\, e^{ikL_j}\right\} := \prod_{j=1}^{N} a_j e^{i\varphi_j}, \tag{22.5}$$

and transformed back into configuration space

$$\rho_P(z) = \frac{1}{2\pi} \int_{-\infty}^{\infty} \tilde{\rho}_P(k)\, e^{-ikz}\, dk = \frac{1}{\pi} \int_0^{\infty} \Re\left\{\tilde{\rho}_P(k)\, e^{-ikz}\right\} dk, \tag{22.6}$$

where

$$\begin{aligned}
\Re\left\{\tilde{\rho}_P(k)\, e^{-ikz}\right\} &= \cos(\phi - kz) \prod_{j=1}^{N} a_j, \\
\phi &= \varphi_1 + \varphi_2 + \cdots + \varphi_N, \\
\tan\varphi_j &= \frac{p_j \sin(kL_j)}{1 - p_j + p_j \cos(kL_j)}, \\
a_j^2 &= (1 - p_j)^2 + p_j^2 + 2p_j(1 - p_j)\cos(kL_j), \\
&= 1 - 4p_j(1 - p_j)\sin^2(kL_j/2).
\end{aligned} \tag{22.7}$$

The cumulative portfolio loss probability is

$$\begin{aligned}
\mathbb{P}(L < z) &= \int_0^z \rho_P(z')\, dz' \\
&= \frac{1}{\pi} \int_0^{\infty} \prod_{j=1}^{N} a_j \frac{1}{k} (\sin\phi - \sin(\phi - kz))\, dk \\
&= \frac{2}{\pi} \int_0^{\infty} \prod_{j=1}^{N} a_j \frac{1}{k} \sin(kz/2) \cos(\phi - kz/2)\, dk.
\end{aligned} \tag{22.8}$$

Note that the integrand of (22.8) has roots at

$k = (2n+1)\,\pi/L_j$	for all j with $p_j = 1/2$ due to the cos term in (22.7)
$k = 2n\pi/z$	due to the sin term in (22.8)
$kz/2 - \phi = (2n+1)\pi/2$	due to the cos term (22.8)

An approximate solution to (22.8) is obtained when k-space is discretized in order to compute the Fourier integral numerically. The grid is chosen such that it contains the roots listed above as grid points. Accuracy is then controlled via the number of grid points chosen between these roots and the cutoff k_{max}. Reproducing simple binomial cases (e.g. $n = 20$, $p = 0.3$) requires cutoff $k_{max} \sim 100$ (to reproduce steps with negligible oscillation) and fine discretization $dk \sim 0.001$ up to $k \sim 3$ (to ensure normalization).

Monte Carlo simulation

A systematic numerical way of evaluating the loss distribution is Monte Carlo simulation: the simulation generates a large number K of random samples. Each sample contains a decision on draw/no-draw for each contract, so that for each sample a total draw amount can be computed. From the K realizations of portfolio draw amounts one can then compute the draw amount distribution, average and amounts at confidence levels. The draw/no-draw decision per contract is made as follows:

- draw a random number r, equally distributed in $[0, 1]$
- if $r \leq p_i$, the amount v_i is added to the portfolio draw amount V of this sample, else V remains unchanged

Note that this procedure can be generalized by using correlated random numbers. Monte Carlo simulation allows for varying loss amounts and loss probabilities.

Tranching

In a CDO, losses of the underlying basket are "filtered" by a tranche with attachment point A and detachment point D. This means when basket losses are less than A, these are not filtered through and effectively treated as zero losses of the tranche; similarly, if losses are larger than D, these are treated as losses $D - A$ of the tranche; basket losses L between A and D appear as losses $L - A$.

The following is expressed in terms of the excess loss probability $\mathbb{P}\{L > x\}$ introduced in Section 23.2.2 as this is the quantity relevant for the computation of expected CDO tranche losses. The excess *tranche* loss probability is, according to the reasoning above, given by

$$\mathbb{P}\{L_T(t) \geq x\} = \begin{cases} 1, & x = 0 \\ \mathbb{P}\{L(t) > x + A\}, & 0 < x \leq D - A \\ 0, & x > D - A \end{cases} \tag{22.9}$$

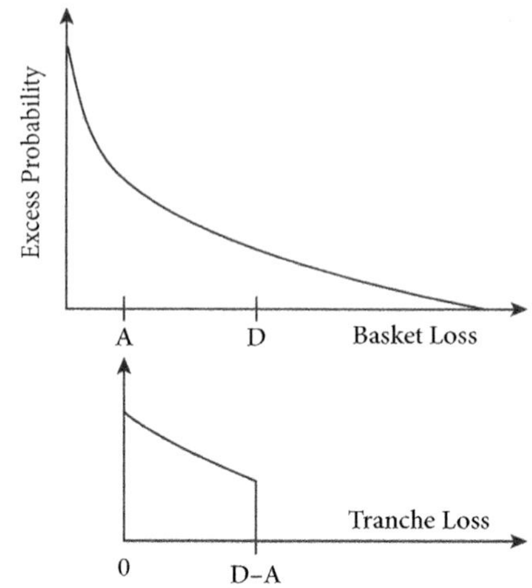

Figure 22.2 Relation between basket and tranche excess loss distributions, Equation (22.9)

Note the discontinuity at $x = 0$, since $\mathbb{P}\{L(t) > A\} < 1$ for $A > 0$. The expected tranche loss (23.2) can now also be written as

$$\mathbb{E}[L_T(t)] = \int_0^\infty \mathbb{P}\{L_T(t) \geq x\}\, dx. \tag{22.10}$$

The relation between basket and tranche excess loss distributions is illustrated in Figure 22.2. Note that we can derive the loss density from (22.9) via

$$\rho(x)\,\delta x = \mathbb{P}\{x \leq L < x + \delta x\} = \mathbb{P}\{L \geq x\} - \mathbb{P}\{L \geq x + \delta x\}. \tag{22.11}$$

22.2.2 Static default correlation modelling

So far, default events were assumed to be independent. The following sections show how correlation can be introduced, but making use of the previous results for independent defaults.

Copula approach

In the copula approach, the individual assets' probability distributions are glued together into a multivariate distribution that introduces correlated default events. The copula approach ensures by construction that the marginal distributions recover each asset's probability of default.

Let $Q_i(t)$ be the cumulative probability that asset i will default before time t, that is the time of draw $t_i < t$. Evaluated at the horizon T, $Q_i(T) = p_i$. In a one-factor copula model, consider random variables

$$Y_i = a_i M + \sqrt{1 - a_i^2}\, Z_i, \tag{22.12}$$

where M and Z_i have independent zero-mean unit-variance distributions and $-1 \le a_i \le 1$. The correlation between Y_i and Y_j is then $a_i a_j$. Let $F_i(y)$ be the cumulative distribution function of Y_i. y is mapped to t such that percentiles match, that is $F_i(y) = Q_i(t)$ or $y = F_i^{-1}(Q_i(t))$. Now let $H_i(z)$ be the cumulated distribution function of Z_i. For a given realization of M, this determines the distribution of y:

$$\mathbb{P}(y_i < y|M) = H\left(\frac{y - a_i M}{\sqrt{1 - a_i^2}}\right),$$

or

$$\mathbb{P}(t_i < t|M) = H\left(\frac{F_i^{-1}(Q_i(t)) - a_i M}{\sqrt{1 - a_i^2}}\right). \tag{22.13}$$

Let $G(m)$ be the cumulative distribution function of M, so that $g(m) = -\partial_m G(m)$ is its density: integrating (22.13) over the density $g(m)$ yields the marginal probability of default for asset i

$$Q_i(t) = \int_{-\infty}^{\infty} \mathbb{P}(t_i < t|M)\, g(m)\, dm = \int H\left(\frac{F_i^{-1}(Q_i(t)) - a_i m}{\sqrt{1 - a_i^2}}\right) g(m)\, dm.$$

The loss distribution is now evaluated as follows:

- For each realization m of M: evaluate the probability $p_i = Q_i(T)$ of default for each contract using (22.13) and determine the loss distribution with these probabilities p_i, e.g. using the bucketing algorithm in Section 22.2.1 – this yields $P_k(m)$ for all buckets k
- Average the outcomes $P_k(m)$ for each bucket k over the distribution of M:

$$P_k = \int_{-\infty}^{\infty} P_k(m)\, g(m)\, dm. \tag{22.14}$$

Gaussian copula

In the popular Gaussian copula model as introduced by David Li [113], G and H are set to the cumulative standard normal distribution. The integral (22.14) is evaluated numerically, realizations of M need not be generated with Monte Carlo simulation.

Note that the Gaussian distribution is stable under convolution, that is the distribution F of Y is again Gaussian.

Student t copula

This copula is based on the Student t distribution,

$$f(t) = \frac{\Gamma((n+1)/2)}{\sqrt{n\pi}\,\Gamma(n/2)}\left(1+\frac{t^2}{n}\right)^{-(n+1)/2},$$

that has heavier tails than the Gaussian (and converges to a Gaussian in the limit of $n \to \infty$). Its disadvantage is that the distribution of Y does not have an analytical expression even if the distributions of M and Z are Student t distributions with identical degrees of freedom n – unlike the Gaussian, the Student t distribution is not stable under convolution. The distribution of Y needs to be computed numerically for each choice of the correlation parameter.

Large homogeneous pool (LHP)

For the special case of

- a large homogeneous pool (the number of names in the pool is infinite while the total pool notional is finite, all names have identical probability of default),
- Gaussian one-factor copula

one can find a closed form expression for the pool loss distribution [142, 141].

Recall the conditional probability of default of issuer i up to time t (22.13) for $F = G = H = \Phi$ cumulative Gaussians, identical correlations $a_i \equiv a$ for all names, as well as identical marginal probabilities of default, $\Phi^{-1}(Q_i(t)) \equiv C$:

$$\mathbb{P}(t_i < t|M) = \Phi\left(\frac{C - aM}{\sqrt{1-a^2}}\right) =: p.$$

In a finite homogeneous pool of N names, the probability of the percentage portfolio loss L being $L_k = k/N$ (zero recovery) up to time t is then the binomial probability

$$\mathbb{P}(L = L_k|M) = \binom{N}{k} p^k (1-p)^{N-k}.$$

Integration over the distribution of factors yields

$$\mathbb{P}(L = L_k) = \binom{N}{k} \int_{-\infty}^{\infty} \Phi\left(\frac{C - a\,u}{\sqrt{1-a^2}}\right)^k \left(1 - \Phi\left(\frac{C - a\,u}{\sqrt{1-a^2}}\right)\right)^{N-k} d\Phi(u),$$

and

$$
\begin{aligned}
\mathbb{P}(L \leq \theta) &= \sum_{k=0}^{[N\theta]} \mathbb{P}(L = L_k) \\
&= \sum_{k=0}^{[N\theta]} \binom{N}{k} \int_{-\infty}^{\infty} \Phi\left(\frac{C - a\,u}{\sqrt{1-a^2}}\right)^k \left(1 - \Phi\left(\frac{C - a\,u}{\sqrt{1-a^2}}\right)\right)^{N-k} d\Phi(u) \\
&= \sum_{k=0}^{[N\theta]} \binom{N}{k} \int_0^1 s^k (1-s)^{N-k}\, d\Phi\left(\frac{\sqrt{1-a^2}\,\Phi^{-1}(s) - C}{a}\right),
\end{aligned}
$$

with $s = (C - a\,u)/\sqrt{1-a^2}$. Since

$$
\lim_{N\to\infty} \sum_{k=0}^{[N\theta]} \binom{N}{k} s^k (1-s)^{N-k} = \begin{cases} 0, & \theta < s \\ 1, & \theta > s \end{cases}
$$

we get

$$
\lim_{N\to\infty} \mathbb{P}(L \leq \theta) = \Phi\left(\frac{\sqrt{1-a^2}\,\Phi^{-1}(\theta) - C}{a}\right), \tag{22.15}
$$

for the infinitely large homogeneous pool. With this closed form solution one also obtains a closed form expression for the expected tranche loss (22.9, 22.10).

Figure 22.3 shows the loss probability density in the LHP model with Gaussian copula for varying correlation. Figure 22.4 shows the related excess basket loss probability $\mathbb{P}\{L(t) \geq x\}$ which yields after tranching the excess tranche loss probability $\mathbb{P}\{L_T(t) \geq x\}$ and after integration the expected tranche loss $\mathbb{E}[L_T(t)]$ (22.9), the key quantity in valuing a CDO tranche; see following section.

22.2.3 Dynamic default correlation modelling

Dynamic models for default correlation are usually intensity-based. This means that the default time of a single name is modelled as the first jump time of a doubly stochastic Poisson process that is specified by its default intensity or hazard rate process with default times given by

$$
\tau_i = \inf\left\{ t \geq 0 : \int_0^t \lambda_i(s)\, ds \geq E_i \right\}, \quad i = 1, \ldots, n \tag{22.16}
$$

where $\lambda_i(t)$ is the default intensity of name i and E_i are independent exponential random variables with unit mean. Single-name intensity models were introduced

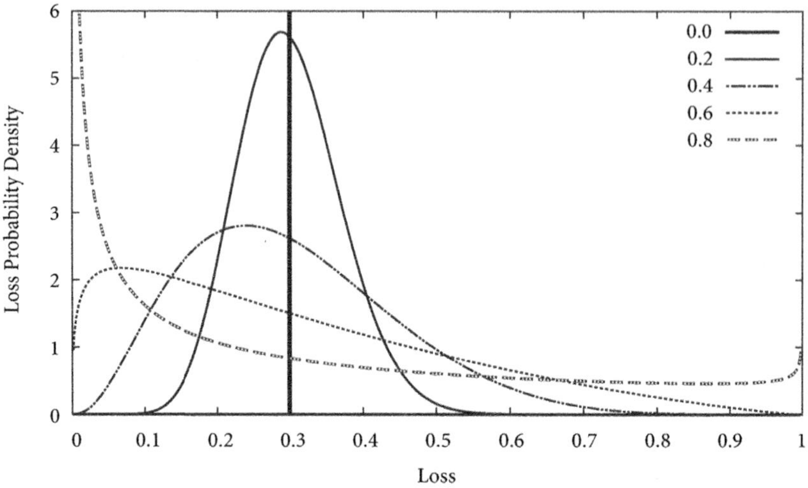

Figure 22.3 LHP loss probability density for $Q_i(t) = 0.3$ and correlations between 0 and 0.8

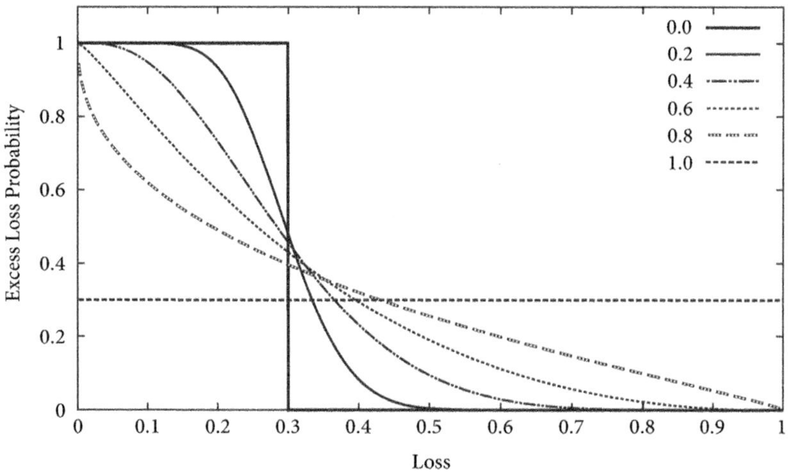

Figure 22.4 LHP excess basket loss probability for $Q_i(t) = 0.3$ and correlations between 0 and 1

in the 1990s [98, 109, 130, 62], and we have seen concrete examples in Section 15. Multi-name intensity models have originally [60] also been based on intensities, where individual names' intensities $\lambda_i(t)$ are coupled via a common *market factor* intensity $\lambda^m(t)$,

$$\lambda_i(t) = a_i \lambda^m(t) + \lambda_i^{id}(t). \tag{22.17}$$

The second components are λ_i^{id} independent idiosyncratic intensities, and all intensities are modelled as *basic affine jump diffusion processes* [60]. The coupling a_i introduces default correlation as in the single-factor copula models discussed above.

Even if the default intensity has a jump component, cumulative intensity

$$\Lambda_i(t) = \int_0^t \lambda_i(s)\,ds, \tag{22.18}$$

is still continuous, and the random barriers E_i in (22.16) will not be crossed simultaneously by several names. Though such default clustering is observed in crisis times, a multi-name model based on intensities cannot describe it.

Default clustering

Motivated by the observation of simultaneous defaults of many names (default clustering) and evidence of serial correlation between number of defaults in successive time intervals, Peng and Kou [122] introduced their *Conditional Survival Model* in 2009 – shortly after the financial turmoil following the collapse of Lehman Brothers and others – for the purpose of CDO pricing. We have presented their model already in Section 15.5 for the evolution of hazard rates and pricing of CDS options. Thus we just recall the model's key ingredients here:

- modelling of the cumulative intensity (22.18) rather than hazard rates using a jump process, where
- the arrival of jumps follows a *Polya* process (loosely speaking a Poisson process with random, gamma distributed, jump intensity).

The second property generates serial correlation of the number of jumps in successive periods (*default clustering in time*). The first property allows for simultaneous defaults of several names (*cross-sectional default clustering*), as the authors couple cumulative intensities $\Lambda_i(t)$ of single names using J market cumulative intensity processes $M_j(t)$ via

$$\Lambda_i(t) = \sum_{j=1}^{J} a_{ij}\,M_j(t) + X_i(t),$$

extending the model (22.17). Peng and Kou show that one can eliminate the idiosyncratic factors $X_i(t)$ by means of the single name marginal probabilities of default, and their modelling focuses on the dynamics of the market factors $M_j(t)$ using compound Polya processes for crisis times and integrated CIR process (see Section 15.3) for "normal" times with less volatile market fluctuations. As in the copula models discussed above, default events are conditionally independent given these market factors.

A portfolio's loss distribution (cumulative up to time t) in Peng and Kou's model can be computed by Monte Carlo simulation of the market factors $M_j(t)$ or semi-analytically, for example using Laplace transform methods. However, the latter has no computational advantage when $M(t)$ is multi-dimensional. Note that Peng and Kou's aproach is closely related to the CreditRisk$^+$ model sketched in the following section.

22.3 Industry portfolio credit models

The approaches to building portfolio loss distributions discussed in the previous section are typical examples of credit modelling for the purpose of valuing basket credit products such as synthetic CDOs. The approach taken by the industry for the purpose of credit risk measurement has (even pre-crisis) been typically based on multiple "factors" rather than a single factor. In the following we will briefly sketch two such approaches, CreditRisk$^+$ and KMV.

CreditRisk$^+$

CreditRisk$^+$ was developed and published by Credit Suisse First Boston in 1997 [31]. Credit risk is modelled under this approach using multiple factors, each of them representing a *sector* which may stand for an industry, a country, a region, etc. Each sector is associated with a default rate process Λ_s (a single factor for each sector s, $s = 1, \ldots, S$). The default rate processes of any two sectors, Λ_{s_1} and Λ_{s_2}, are independent. The key feature is now the assumption that the annual default rate Λ_s is Gamma-distributed with probability density function

$$PDF_{\alpha_s,\beta_s}(x) = \frac{1}{\beta_s^{\alpha_s}\,\Gamma(\alpha_s)}\, e^{-x/\beta_s}\, x^{\alpha_s - 1},$$

expectation and variance

$$\mathbb{E}[\Lambda_s] = \alpha_s \beta_s, \qquad \mathbb{V}[\Lambda_s] = \alpha_s \beta_s^2,$$

and *relative default variance* $\sigma_s^2 = \mathbb{V}[\Lambda_s]/\mathbb{E}^2[\Lambda_s] = \beta_s/\mathbb{E}[\Lambda_s]$. Non-zero correlation between obligors/names is modelled in the original CreditRisk$^+$ by mapping each obligor i to more than one sector, that is by assigning obligor i a weight ω_{is} in sector s such that total weight across all sectors adds up to one for each obligor, $\sum_{s=1}^{S} \omega_{is} = 1$. Finally, sector exposures are grouped into bands, each band representing an integer multiple of a fundamental exposure unit L (a simplifying approximation).

This leads to a closed form of the *probability density for n defaults in sector k up to time t* which is given by a negative binomial distribution with density

$$PDF(n) = \binom{\alpha+n-1}{n}\left(\frac{1}{1+\beta t}\right)^{\alpha}\left(\frac{\beta t}{1+\beta t}\right)^{n}, \qquad t>0, \quad n\geq 0$$

where the binomial coefficient for non-integer $x > y-1, y \geq 0$ is

$$\binom{x}{y} = \frac{\Gamma(x+1)}{\Gamma(y+1)\,\Gamma(x-y+1)}.$$

Moreover, the *overall portfolio loss distribution is a convolution of sector loss distributions* in closed form.

CreditRisk$^+$ is therefore a simple, entirely analytic portfolio credit model which allows rapid risk analysis without Monte Carlo simulation.

One of the shortcomings of the model is the assumption of independent sectors. This forces the user to assign each obligor to a mixture of independent sectors (*sector analysis*) in order to model default correlation, which turns out to be difficult to achieve in practice. Therefore this original model was extended subsequently by several authors. Bürgisser et al. [42], for example, introduce explicit default correlations ρ_{s_1,s_2} between any two sectors s_1, s_2. This leads to an expression for the relative default variance of the entire portfolio in terms of sector expected losses, sector default variances and the correlation structure, that is independent of the precise form of the joint distribution of default rates. This portfolio default variance is then used to build a full portfolio loss distribution *assuming it has the form of Gamma distribution* as for a single sector.

Default intensity based modelling approaches appear to be appropriate for SME and retail portfolios with significant numbers of observed defaults.

The following model is asset-return based and hence more suited for corporate portfolios with readily available equity returns.

KMV

KMV is a software tool originally developed by San Francisco-based quantitative risk management firm KMV (named after Kealhofer, McQuown and Vasicek) that was acquired by Moody's in 2002, which merged the KMV software with its Risk Management Service to form Moody's KMV.

The KMV methodology is inspired by Merton's model. Consider asset value log-returns r_i, that is the asset value at horizon T is

$$A_i(T) = A_i(0)\exp(r_i).$$

Assume further that asset value returns are driven by composite *systemic* factors Φ_i and *specific* factors ϵ_i.

$$r_i = \beta_i \Phi_i + \epsilon_i, \qquad i = 1, \ldots, n.$$

Finally, one assumes that default occurs if $A_i(T)$ is below some critical threshold C_i

$$L_i = \mathbb{1}_{A_i(T) < C_i} = \mathbb{1}_{r_i < c_i}.$$

The correlations between the returns of different assets r_i and r_j is induced by composite systemic factors $\Phi_{i,j}$. One further assumes that the specific (or idiosyncratic) *residuals* ϵ_i *are independent*, and that the distribution of returns $(r_1, \ldots, r_n)$ is *multi-variate normal.*

The KMV model can be written more concisely in normalized form, that is by normalizing each asset value log-return with respect to its volatility and by shifting it such that the scaled return $\tilde{r}_i$ has zero mean:

$$\tilde{r}_i = \frac{r_i - \mathbb{E}[r_i]}{\sigma_i}, \qquad \sigma_i = \mathbb{V}[r_i], \qquad r_i \sim N(0,1).$$

The normalized return is then decomposed as follows

$$\tilde{r}_i = \frac{\beta_i}{\sigma_i}(\Phi_i - \mathbb{E}[\Phi_i]) + \frac{\epsilon_i - \mathbb{E}[\epsilon_i]}{\sigma_i} = R_i \tilde{\Phi}_i + \tilde{\epsilon}_i,$$

where

$$R_i = \frac{\beta_i}{\sigma_i}\sqrt{\mathbb{V}[\Phi_i]}, \quad \tilde{\Phi}_i = \frac{\Phi_i - \mathbb{E}[\Phi_i]}{\sqrt{\mathbb{V}[\Phi_i]}}, \quad \tilde{\epsilon}_i = \frac{\epsilon_i - \mathbb{E}[\epsilon_i]}{\sigma_i},$$

with unit variance

$$\mathbb{V}(\tilde{r}_i) = R_i^2 + \mathbb{V}(\tilde{\epsilon}_i) = 1.$$

In terms of the *coefficients of determination* R_i we can therefore write the returns

$$\tilde{r}_i = R_i \tilde{\Phi}_i + \tilde{\epsilon}_i.$$

The normalized return r_i, the normalized composite factor $\tilde{\Phi}_i$ and the normalized residual $\tilde{\epsilon}_i$ are normally distributed with zero mean and unit variance, with the exception of $\tilde{\epsilon}_i$ which has variance $1 - R_i^2$. The correlation between normalized log-returns follows as

$$Corr[\tilde{r}_i, \tilde{r}_j] = R_i R_j Corr[\tilde{\Phi}_i, \tilde{\Phi}_j].$$

Key now is the interpretation of the composite factors which is done in two steps. First (KMV level II), each composite factor Φ_i is decomposed into industry indices $\Psi_1,\ldots,\Psi_{K_0}$ and country indices $\Psi_{K_0+1},\ldots,\Psi_K$:

$$\Phi_i = \sum_{k=1}^{K} \omega_{ik}\Psi_k, \qquad i = 1,\ldots,n.$$

The weights in this decomposition satisfy

$$\omega_{i,k} > 0, \qquad \sum_{k=1}^{K_0} \omega_{ik} = \sum_{k=K_0+1}^{K} \omega_{ik} = 1.$$

Second (KMV level III), industry and country indices are further decomposed into *independent* global factors, typically by principal component analysis:

$$\Psi_k = \sum_{n=1}^{N} b_{kn}\Gamma_n + \delta_k.$$

Once this decomposition is done and all weights are determined, one can calibrate the KMV model to *marginal probabilities of default*: recall that default of entity i occurs when its asset log-return is less than some critical threshold c_i:

$$\tilde{r}_i = R_i\tilde{\Phi}_i + \tilde{\epsilon}_i < \tilde{c}_i$$

or – solving for the residual – when

$$\tilde{\epsilon}_i < \tilde{c}_i - R_i\tilde{\Phi}_i.$$

The marginal probability of default is therefore

$$p_i = \mathbb{P}[\tilde{r}_i < \tilde{c}_i] = N(\tilde{c}_i),$$

so that we can express the threshold c_i in terms of the marginal p_i, that is $c_i = N^{-1}(\tilde{p}_i)$. One then is ready to determine the probability of default *conditional* on the composite systemic factor $\tilde{\Phi}_i$:

$$p_i(\tilde{\Phi}_i) = \mathbb{P}[\tilde{\epsilon}_i < \tilde{c}_i - R_i\tilde{\Phi}_i] = N\left(\frac{N^{-1}(p_i) - R_i\tilde{\Phi}_i}{\sqrt{1-R_i^2}}\right).$$

Conditional on the realization of systemic factors $(\Phi_1, \ldots, \Phi_n)$, the individual loss variables are independent. The overall portfolio loss distribution can then be determined by Monte Carlo simulation as follows:

- "toss coins" to generate a realization of composite factors $(\Phi_1, \ldots, \Phi_n)$
- "toss coins" again to decide for each name whether default happens or not, based on $p_i(\tilde{\Phi}_i)$ above (and to determine each loss severity)
- this yields one realization of portfolio loss to the chosen horizon (taking into account all exposures at default and loss severities)
- iterate until the statistic is sufficient for determining the desired quantile of the portfolio loss distribution

When multiple factors drive the composite Φ_i, Monte Carlo sampling is the only feasible approach for building the portfolio loss distribution. For a small number of factors (e.g. one), there are more efficient alternatives, as we have seen in Section 22.2.2. While one factor is generally insufficient for credit risk modelling, one factor models have (or had) applications for example in CDO pricing.

23 Pricing Portfolio Credit Products

23.1 Introduction

Portfolio credit products have a long history in the financial markets, stretching back to the German (Prussian) Pfandbrief (Covered Bond) with its origins in the late 1700s' reconstruction following the Seven Years War. There are many names for and structural features of portfolio credit instruments but they all share the common feature of having a claim secured on a portfolio of single credit instruments (typically loans, bonds, credit derivatives, etc.) with additional structural features to enhance the credit quality. While portfolio credit products in general have a long and successful history as financial instruments, many having performed well even throughout the credit crisis of 2007–2009, it is also true to say that some areas of the securitization market, in particular subprime RMBS and much of the synthetic securitization market, were the proximate cause of the financial crisis. In these cases the poor quality of the underlying assets (subprime mortgages) together with the leverage enhancing effect of synthetic structures created widespread and largely unforeseen losses on assets that were highly rated by the Rating Agencies which precipitated the global financial markets into the credit crisis. The accompanying freezing of the interbank market required large scale government interventions to prevent an even worse crisis than ultimately transpired.

Since the financial crisis the process of natural selection has taken its course with many of the failed structures being consigned to history. Structures and instruments that fared well through the crisis ultimately retained their former value and have become the basis for a renewed securitization market. In particular asset backed cashflow securitizations based on good quality underlying assets and the transparent forms of synthetic products form the basis for portfolio credit products following the financial crisis. The market for synthetic CDOs, for instance, is picking up again. According to Risk magazine [53], new issuances for 2014 are estimated to be of the order of $20 billion, with Citibank alone issuing $10 billion. This is clearly far from the levels seen before the crisis, yet with the advent of central bank funding initiatives and the need for alternative sources of secured term funding for financial institutions, it is clear that there is a strong future for portfolio credit products. An exhaustive description of all of the varieties and flavours of instruments is beyond the scope of this chapter, but we focus on two main categories, namely synthetic and cashflow structures. Synthetic products (funded or unfunded) are portfolio credit derivatives where the losses on the underlying reference assets are transformed through a prescribed derivative payoff to losses on the portfolio product. Synthetic products include index CDS, Synthetic Collateralized Debt Obligations (CDOs), and so-called CDO squared. Cashflow products (generally funded) derive their interest income and credit losses directly from the underlying assets without an intervening credit derivative. Cashflow products include among others Asset Backed Securities (ABS), Residential Mortgage Backed Securities (RMBS), Cashflow CDO, Commercial Mortgage Backed Securities (CMBS) and Collateralized Loan Obligations (CLO).

Cashflow structures form the backbone of the modern securitization market; however, the structural credit enhancement features make their pricing a more complex affair. We start first with their synthetic cousins whose pricing is more straightforward and intuitive.

23.2 Synthetic portfolio credit derivatives

23.2.1 Nth-to-default basket

In an Nth-To-Default the protection seller receives a premium cash flow in exchange for providing (notional) protection against the n-th default in a basket of underlyings. Premium is paid until the relevant credit event occurs or until maturity of the contract otherwise. The relevant probability in this case is the probability of at least n default events up to time t, $P_n(t)$. The NTD can be priced technically like a CDS if the probability of default $P_d(t) = 1 - P_s(t)$ up to time t in the CDS pricing formula is replaced by $P_n(t)$.

A First-to-Default Basket is the special case for $n = 1$.

23.2.2 Synthetic collateralized debt obligation

In a Collateralized Debt Obligation, the protection seller receives a premium cash flow in exchange for providing (notional) protection against portfolio losses due to defaults in a specific tranche characterized by the attachment point A and detachment point D. Attachment point A is the fraction of the portfolio loss-given-default (LGD) where the protection starts, and the detachment point is the corresponding fraction where protection stops. The LGD is given by the sum of defaulted asset notional amounts N_i, reduced by their respective recovery rate R_i, that is $LGD_i = (1 - R_i)\,N_i$.

The total loss given default of the basket up to time t is hence given by

$$L(t) = \sum_{i=1}^{N} L^i(t), \qquad L^i(t) = (1 - R_i)\, N_i\, 1_{\tau_i < t}, \tag{23.1}$$

where N is the number of assets, and $1_{\tau_i<t}$ is the indicator function that is equal to one if the time to default τ_i for asset number i is less than t. $L(t)$ is a random variable at the default times τ_i. The tranche loss is then given by

$$L_T(t) = \min(L(t), D) - \min(L(t), A) = \begin{cases} 0, & L(t) \leq A \\ L(t) - A, & A < L(t) < D \\ D - A, & L(t) \geq D \end{cases}$$

The expected tranche loss is calculated by integrating the tranche loss $L_T(t)$ over the probability density function $\rho(x)$ for loss $L_T(t) = x$,

$$\begin{aligned} \mathbb{E}[L_T(t)] &= \int_0^\infty (\min(x, D) - \min(x, A))\, \rho(x)\, dx \\ &= \int_A^D (x - A)\, \rho(x)\, dx + (D - A) \int_D^\infty \rho(x)\, dx \\ &= (D - A) \int_A^D \rho(x)\, dx - \int_A^D \int_A^x \rho(x')\, dx'\, dx + (D - A) \int_D^\infty \rho(x)\, dx \\ &= (D - A) \int_A^\infty \rho(x)\, dx - \int_A^D \int_A^x \rho(x')\, dx'\, dx \\ &= (D - A)\, \mathbb{P}\{L > A\} - \int_A^D \mathbb{P}\{A < L < x\}\, dx \\ &= (D - A)\, \mathbb{P}\{L > A\} - \int_A^D (1 - \mathbb{P}\{L < A\} - \mathbb{P}\{L > x\})\, dx \\ &= \int_A^D \mathbb{P}\{L_T(t) > x\}\, dx, \end{aligned} \tag{23.2}$$

which shows that only the the excess loss probability $\mathbb{P}\{L_T(t) > x\}$ is required to evaluate expected losses. This is for example computed using one of the methods introduced in Section 22.2.2.

The present value PV of the expected payoff in time interval $[t_1, t_2]$ is then given by

$$PV = \{\mathbb{E}[L_T(t_2)] - \mathbb{E}[L_T(t_1)]\}\; P((t_1 + t_2)/2),$$

and the present value of the entire protection leg by

$$V_1 = \sum_{i=1}^{N} \{\mathbb{E}[L_T(t_i)] - \mathbb{E}[L_T(t_{i-1})]\} \, P((t_i + t_{i-1})/2),$$

where $P(t)$ is the discount factor for maturity t. Note that we assume that losses occur uniformly throughout the period so that discounting at the mid-point is justified.

The premium is paid on the protected notional amount, initially $D - A$. This notional is reduced by the expected protection payments E_i at times t_i, so the premium value is calculated as

$$V_2 = m \cdot \sum_{i=1}^{N} (D - A - \mathbb{E}[L_T(t_i)]) \cdot \Delta_{i-1,i} \cdot P(t_i),$$

where m is the premium rate, $\Delta_{i-1,i}$ is the day count fraction between date/time t_{i-1} and t_i. The total CDO price for the protection seller is therefore $V = V_2 - V_1$.

A mezzanine CDO tranche with attachment point A and detachment point D can be represented as the spread of the two equity tranches with detachment points D and A, respectively,

$$CDO(A, D, p) = CDO(0, D, p) - CDO(0, A, p),$$

where both CDOs pay the same premium p, see Figure 23.1. The market tends to price mezzanine CDO tranches as spreads of such equity tranches. In the single-factor Gaussian copula model (see Section 22.2.2), each of the equity tranches is assigned a so-called *base correlation* so that any mezzanine tranche is priced in general using two different base correlations. Given a series of fair tranche premiums for the same underlying reference basket, a related series of base correlations can be implied in an iterative manner.

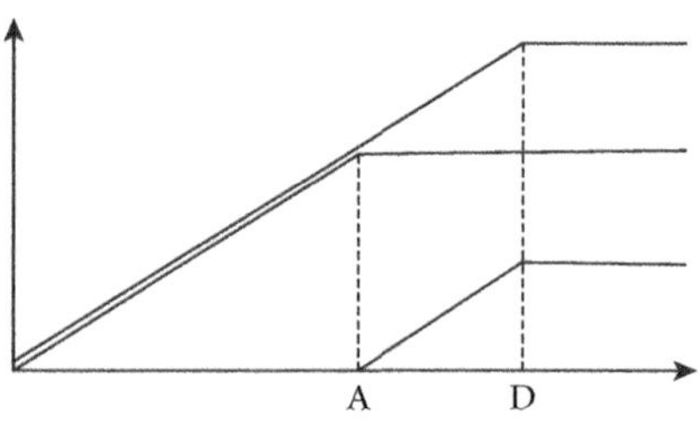

Figure 23.1 Mezzanine CDO tranche payoff as difference between two equity tranches

Let $0 < D_1 < D_2 < \cdots < D_n \leq 1$ denote the detachment points, p_i the fair premiums for the tranches with detachment points D_i. This means that the following CDO tranches have zero value:

$$\begin{aligned}
\mathrm{CDO}(0, D_1, p_1, \rho_1) &= 0 \\
\mathrm{CDO}(D_1, D_2, p_2) &= 0 = \mathrm{CDO}(0, D_2, p_2, \rho_2) - \mathrm{CDO}(0, D_1, p_2, \rho_1) \\
&\vdots \\
\mathrm{CDO}(D_{n-1}, D_n, p_n) &= 0 = \mathrm{CDO}(0, D_n, p_n, \rho_n) - \mathrm{CDO}(0, D_{n-1}, p_n, \rho_{n-1}).
\end{aligned}$$

This shows that the value of subsequent equity tranches is given by :

$$\begin{aligned}
(1) \qquad & \mathrm{CDO}(0, D_1, p_1, \rho_1) = 0 \\
(2) \qquad & \mathrm{CDO}(0, D_2, p_2, \rho_2) = \mathrm{CDO}(0, D_1, p_2, \rho_1) \\
& \vdots \\
(n) \qquad & \mathrm{CDO}(0, D_n, p_n, \rho_n) = \mathrm{CDO}(0, D_{n-1}, p_n, \rho_{n-1}).
\end{aligned}$$

After solving line 1, ρ_1 is fixed. Then the right-hand side of line 2 can be computed and line 2 solved for ρ_2 etc. up to line n and ρ_n. To calibrate the correlations for a bespoke CDO tranche one typically uses index CDS tranches, such as the investment grade, high yield or emerging market flavours of CDX or iTraxx with similar maturity as the bespoke CDO to be priced. For each index/maturity we can derive base correlation curves as sketched above. In order to price a bespoke CDO, one needs to determine the relevant base correlations from the base correlation curve $\rho_r(x_r)$ determined from tranches on a reference basket. It is market practice to "scale" the x-axis in looking up correlation, as follows. Looking for a base correlation $\rho_b(x_b)$ one assigns

$$\rho_b(x_b) = \rho_r\left(x_r \cdot \frac{EL_b}{EL_r}\right),$$

where EL_b and EL_r are the expected losses of the 0–100% tranche of the bespoke and reference CDO, respectively. This assignment aligns detachment points roughly according to associated expected loss. Note that this recipe does not accurately align expected tranche losses: while these could be computed for the reference tranches (as their spreads are quoted), these losses can only be computed for the bespoke tranches *after* the base correlations are assigned. Look-up will generally require interpolation and may also require extrapolation. We choose to fit a cubic polynomial to the raw curve $\rho_r(x_r)$ to facilitate both interpolation and extrapolation.

The Gaussian copula model was – at least up to the financial crisis following the 2007 and 2008 events – a popular and predominant model for the pricing of CDOs, and it continues to be used as a quoting device like the Black model is used for quoting European option prices. However, the Gaussian copula model's weaknesses have been pointed out by various authors [122, 59, 100, 36, 118] even before the crisis started:

- Quoted base correlations for index equity tranches for different detachment points but same underlying basket typically differ (*correlation smile/skew*); this indicates an inconsistency of the model – meaningful correlation should be connected with the default correlation of names involved and not vary with tranche details;
- The reduction of hundreds or even thousands of correlations (for larger pools of underlying assets) to a single correlation number oversimplifies the pricing model;
- The Gaussian copula model does not show *tail dependence*: conditioning on the rare default event of one name, the probability of default for other names should increase in a model that can handle crisis times. However, this conditional probability of default vanishes in the Gaussian copula model;
- Delta hedging of CDO tranches based on the Gaussian copula model was reported to be ineffective during the crisis.

Post-crisis dynamic intensity models as for example introduced in [122] and sketched in Section 22.2.3 address these weaknesses.

As mentioned in the introduction, the market for these products is picking up again, see [53].

23.2.3 Synthetic CDO^2

The payoff (23.1) can be generalized to cases where any of the L^is in (23.1) are tranched payoffs of CDOs rather than single name related payoffs. This is achieved by replacing

$$L^i(t) \to L^i_T(t) = \min(\mathcal{L}^i(t), D^i) - \min(\mathcal{L}^i(t), A^i),$$

where

$$\mathcal{L}^i(t) = \sum_{j=1}^{N^i} (1 - R^i_j)\, N^i_j\, 1_{\tau^i_j < t},$$

is the loss given default of another basket of underlying names rather than a single name. Note that there may be overlap, that is names may appear as single names and as part of baskets.

23.3 Cashflow structures

23.3.1 Introduction

Cashflow CDO and CLO structures are the subject of considerable interest in light of the role of securitization in the credit crisis which started in 2007. We introduce a new framework for the pricing of Cashflow CLO and CDO structures based on the Synthetic CDO loss-bucketing framework introduced by Hull and White [87], offering the advantages of tractability, speed and stability over existing Monte Carlo methods. In addition we introduce an analytical understanding of the payoff structure and the factors influencing the pricing.This new method may be of interest to practitioners and academics alike in seeking to better understand the internal dynamics of these transactions and to improve methods for their pricing.

The semi-analytical loss bucketing method of Hull and White [87] has been widely adopted for the pricing of synthetic tranched CDOs where the straightforward payoff structure on the loss distribution lends itself to analytical calculation once the loss distribution of the underlying basket of names is known. In short, a tranche of a synthetic CDO can be viewed as an option on the loss distribution of the underlying assets. Loss distributions are typically calculated using copula models, either the analytical Homogeneous Pool model or the numerical loss-bucketing algorithm introduced by Hull and White in [87]. Many alternatives to the standard Gaussian Copula have been proposed for the generation of more realistic loss distributions, for example [4].

Cashflow CDO and CLO structures have a more complex cashflow distribution structure in which the principal and interest flows from the basket of underlying assets are distributed to the tranches of the CDO in order of seniority with additional credit enhancement features, such as interest coverage (IC) and over-collateralization (OC) tests in place to divert cashflows to the senior note holder under distressed circumstances. The IC and OC tests together with the deferred payment of unpaid interest add an element of path dependence in the payoff. The payoff structure of cashflow transactions has been thought to be too complex for analytical approaches and is generally treated using Monte Carlo simulation of joint default times in the basket of underlying assets.

We first introduce the Cashflow CDO and then set out the analytical pricing framework and an analytical approximation that reduces the order of the problem. We illustrate the nature and errors associated with the approximation using an analytical approach. Finally we show some results from an implementation of the model and discuss details such as the implementation of over-collateralization and interest coverage tests.

23.3.2 Cashflow CDO structures

We consider an n tranche cashflow CDO. The underlying assets consist of a portfolio of bonds or loans assumed to be bullet structures for clarity of exposition, although the framework allows for amortizing profiles. The portfolio can contain fixed or floating rate obligations. Maturities cover a range and need not coincide. We assume that hazard rate data is available, either provided externally or implied from asset prices.

The deal is assumed to be structured as a cashflow securitization. Interest and principal repayments are directed in an order of priority first to the senior note holder. We assume the available pool for notional repayments consists of scheduled bond notional repayments and recovery amounts. The pool available for interest payments consists of coupons received on the portfolio during the payment period in question.

The most junior or equity tranche receives the excess pool coupon available after other items in the interest waterfall are discharged.

A typical interest and notional waterfall is given by:

Interest waterfall:

1. Taxes
2. Trustee fees and expenses subject to cap
3. Administration fees and expenses subject to cap
4. Payments for hedge transactions other than early termination
5. interest and fees under the liquidity facility
6. Senior servicing fee
7. Interest due on senior notes
8. Redemption of senior notes if over-collateralization or interest coverage tests not met (sufficient to ensure tests are met)
9. Interest due on next most senior notes
10. Redemption of next most senior notes if over-collateralization or interest coverage tests not met (sufficient to ensure tests are met)
11. ⋮
12. Interest deflection test
13. Ratings-based deflection test
14. Trustee fees in excess of the cap
15. Administration fees
16. Payments of hedge termination fees for early termination
17. Subordinated servicing fee
18. Excess to equity notes up to an IRR hurdle
19. Management incentive fee
20. Excess to the equity notes.

Principal waterfall:

1. Unpaid items in the first six items of the interest waterfall
2. Unpaid Interest on the senior notes

3. Redemption of the senior notes if OC and IC tests not met (sufficient to ensure tests are met)
4. Purchase of additional securities during the reinvestment period
5. Redemption of the senior notes
6. Redemption of the next most senior notes
7. ⋮
8. Unpaid subordinated portfolio servicing fees
9. Redemption of the equity notes

In summary, interest after tax and expenses goes first to the senior note holders and then on down the order of priority and finally to the equity noteholder after ensuring that any tests are satisfied. Notional repayments after expenses go to redemption of the senior notes and finally to the equity note holder.

23.3.3 Overall pricing framework

We explicitly write down the pricing formula for each of the notes. First some notation:

- t_i are the scheduled payment dates of the trade,
- $C_k(t_i)$ are the coupons paid on the class k notes on the ith payment date,
- $N_k(t_i)$ are the outstanding notionals,
- $R_k(t_i)$ are the notional redemptions payable on the ith payment date. Note $N_k(t_i) = N_k(t_{i-1}) - R_k(t_i)$,
- Π_k is the present value of the notes which we seek.

When we take expectations we assume that time to default and interest rates are independent and so all payments are multiplied by the bank's risk-free discount factor to the payment date, and the symbol $\mathbb{E}$ is reserved for expectations under the credit measure.

Using these conventions we can write the present values as

$$\Pi_k = \sum_{i=1}^{n} \mathbb{E}(C_k(t_i))D(t,t_i) + \sum_{i=1}^{n} \mathbb{E}(R_k(t_i))D(t,t_i), \tag{23.3}$$

We will assume in the following that we know the marginal probability of default of each underlying asset to any desired date and that we use a standard copula framework to compute expectations in the presence of joint defaults as described in Hull and White [87].

We seek formulas for the expected tranche coupons and expected principal repayments in the remainder of this section.

We work with a one-factor copula model with systematic risk factor M and idiosyncratic risk factor Z_j for each of the m names in the basket, that is

$$Y_j = \sqrt{\rho}\, M + \sqrt{1-\rho}\, Z_j, \tag{23.4}$$

where M and Z_j have independent zero-mean unit-variance distributions and $0 \leq \rho \leq 1$. The correlation between Y_j and Y_k is then ρ.

Given a portfolio variable with a distribution $P(x)$ that can be calculated conditional on M, we can integrate with respect to M to compute the unconditional distribution. In other words

$$P(x) = \int_{-\infty}^{\infty} P(x|m) g(m) dm,$$

where $g(m)$ is the density function of the systematic risk factor M. Thus when we require the distribution of losses, coupons and repayments, we only need to compute it conditional on M and then integrate. However conditional on M, all assets are independent, and so the computation of the conditional distributions is reduced to simple convolutions which are easily implemented.

23.3.4 Pricing formulas

The complexity in this trade type (as opposed to a standard tranched synthetic CDO) comes from the conditional dependence between the interest available for payment and the outstanding notional on which it is to be paid.

For clarity of exposition we assume that interest unpaid in a period on a class of notes is not made up in subsequent periods. In the same spirit we omit fees, and IC and OC tests. These features are important for pricing, can be built into the implementation of this approach and are discussed later.

First we calculate the tranche notionals, $N_k(t)$. To do this we need the distributions of the redemptions on a single asset of notional N^j, which is given by

$$Red^j(t) = \begin{cases} R^j N^j \mathbb{1}_{\{\tau^j < t\}}, & t < T^j, \\ R^j N^j \mathbb{1}_{\{\tau^j < T^j\}} + N^j \mathbb{1}_{\{\tau^j \geq T^j\}}, & t \geq T^j, \end{cases}$$

where τ^j is the default time, R^j the recovery rate, and T^j the maturity date, all of the jth asset. Redemptions are any scheduled principal repayments or recovery amounts in the event of defaults. This can be expressed using indicator functions as

$$Red^j(t) = R^j N^j \mathbb{1}_{\{\tau^j < t\}} \mathbb{1}_{\{t < T^j\}} + N^j \left[R^j \mathbb{1}_{\{\tau^j < T^j\}} + \mathbb{1}_{\{\tau^j \geq T^j\}} \right] \mathbb{1}_{\{t \geq T^j\}},$$

The distribution of the portfolio redemption to time t is the sum over all assets:

$$Red(t) = \sum_j Red^j(t).$$

This distribution can be calculated used the Hull-White loss bucketing algorithm conditional on M using the usual conditional independence property.

Once this distribution is known we can calculate the tranche notionals as follows:

$$N_1(t) = \max(N_1(0) - Red(t), 0),$$

$$\vdots$$

$$N_k(t) = \max\left(N_k(0) + \min\left(\sum_{j=1}^{k-1} N_j(0) - Red(t), 0\right), 0\right),$$

$$\vdots$$

$$N_n(t) = \max\left(N_n(0) + \min\left(\sum_{j=1}^{n-1} N_j(0) - Red(t), 0\right), 0\right).$$

Expectations of these notionals are calculated in a straightforward way once the distribution of $Red(t)$ is known and so the terms in the second sum of the NPV formula (23.3) are known.

We now turn to the expected interest payments. The interest due on the senior note at time t_i is given by

$$K_i^1 N_1(t_{i-1}),$$

where K_i^1 is the coupon rate on the senior note in the ith period. The available interest at time t_i is

$$\sum_j C^j(t_i)\mathbb{1}_{\{\tau^j \geq t_i\}},$$

where $C^j(t_i)$ is the total coupon paid on the jth bond in the ith payment period of the trade. The interest payment to the senior note holder is thus the lower of the interest claim or the available interest collection for the note. In other words

$$\begin{aligned} C_1(t_i) &= \min(K_i^1 N_1(t_{i-1}), \sum_j C^j(t_i)\mathbb{1}_{\{\tau^j \geq t_i\}}) \\ &= \min(K_i^1 \max(N_1(0) - Red(t_{i-1}), 0), \sum_j C^j(t_i)\mathbb{1}_{\{\tau^j \geq t_i\}}). \end{aligned}$$

Likewise, for the kth tranche the interest paid is given by

$$
\begin{aligned}
C_k(t_i) &= \min(K_i^k N_k(t_{i-1}), \max(\sum_j C^j(t_i)\mathbb{1}_{\{\tau^j \geq t_i\}} - \sum_{l=1}^{k-1} K_i^l N_l(t_{i-1}), 0)) \\
&= \min\left\{ K_i^k \max\left[N_k(0) + \min\left(\sum_{j=1}^{k-1} N_j(0) - Red(t_{i-1}), 0 \right), 0 \right], \right. \\
&\quad \left. \max\left[\sum_j C^j(t_i)\mathbb{1}_{\{\tau^j \geq t_i\}} - \sum_{l=1}^{k-1} K_i^l N_l(t_{i-1}), 0 \right] \right\},
\end{aligned} \tag{23.5}
$$

where K_i^k is the coupon rate on the kth tranche in the ith period.

The calculation of expectations of $C_k(t_i)$ unfortunately requires the joint distribution of portfolio redemption and coupons available as it is a function of both these quantities. The expectation is therefore a two-dimensional integral over the joint distribution of these quantities. This difficulty combined with additional features such as IC and OC tests have led practitioners to resort to Monte Carlo simulation for the pricing of cashflow CDO.

However, we notice that there is a strong structure in the joint distribution of portfolio redemption and coupons available, and we propose a novel approach to reduce the two-dimensional distribution to a univariate distribution which renders the problem suitable for a conventional loss bucketing approach. This assumption has a strong analytical underpinning and is found to produce excellent agreement with Monte Carlo simulation under a wide range of portfolio parameters.

We proceed by introducing two random variables, X resp. Y, which are the portfolio redemption resp. portfolio interest distributions at times t_{i-1} and t_i as follows:

$$
\begin{aligned}
X &= Red(t_{i-1}), \\
Y &= \sum_j C^j(t_i)\mathbb{1}_{\{\tau^j \geq t_i\}}.
\end{aligned}
$$

The expected coupon on the kth tranche, $\mathbb{E}(C_k(t_i))$, can be written as

$$
\mathbb{E}(C_k(t_i)) = \int\int g_k(x,y) f_{XY}(x,y)\, dx\, dy, \tag{23.6}
$$

where $f_{XY}(x,y)$ is the joint distribution of X and Y, and $g_k(x,y)$ is the function representing Equation (23.5) expressed in terms of X, Y and known quantities:

$$g_k(x,y) = \min\left\{K_i^k \max\left[N_k(0) + \min\left(\sum_{j=1}^{k-1} N_j(0) - x, 0\right), 0\right],\right. \tag{23.7}$$

$$\left.\max\left[y - \sum_{l=1}^{k-1} K_i^l \max(N_l(0) + \min\left(\sum_{j=1}^{l-1} N_j(0) - x, 0\right), 0), 0\right]\right\}.$$

Simplifying approximation: dimension reduction

We believe that the distributions of X and Y are heavily dependent in that they are both linearly linked to the number of defaults up to time t_{i-1} and t_i. This hypothesis can be further motivated by looking at the joint distribution of X and Y obtained from Monte Carlo simulation, see Figure 23.2, which is derived from a strongly heterogeneous portfolio with varying coupons, notionals, maturities and recovery rates. Motivated by the consideration that few defaults in the portfolio give rise to high interest available and redemptions close to the scheduled ones, and that many defaults give rise to low interest available and redemptions close to the sum of

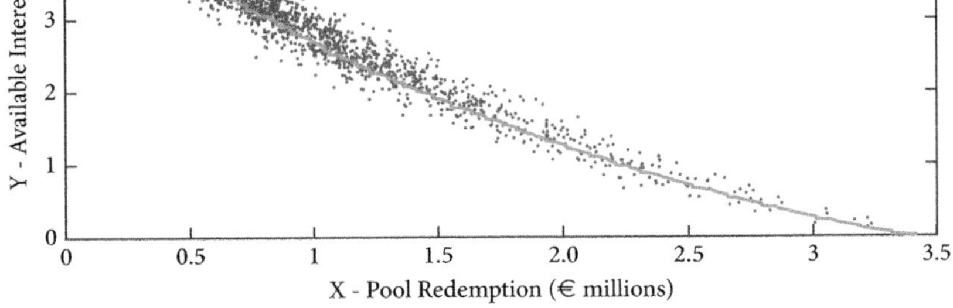

Figure 23.2 Available Interest at t_2 versus Pool Redemption at t_1 for a portfolio, and the Q-Q approximation curve. The point $(x = 0, y = 5.14M)$ corresponds to the case where none of the companies default and so there is available interest from every company but no redemptions (note there are no scheduled repayments from any of the bonds at or before t_2). The point $(x = 3.43M, y = 0)$ corresponds to the situation where every company has defaulted and so there is no interest available but there is an amount of redemption equal to the sum of all the recovery amounts: a recovery rate of $R^j = 0.01$ is assumed for all assets

recovery amounts, we associate a given portfolio interest amount and redemption amount if their cumulative probabilities of materializing are equal. This is known as the q-q plot in the statistics literature. More formally we look at the deviation of X and Y from their values in the absence of defaults, say X_{rf}, Y_{rf}, which are given by

$$X_{rf} = \sum_j N^j \mathbb{1}_{\{t > T^j\}},$$

$$Y_{rf} = \sum_j C_j(t_i).$$

We note that

$$\begin{aligned}\hat{X}(t) &= X_{rf} - X \\ &= \sum_j N^j(1 - R^j)\mathbb{1}_{\{\tau^j < T^j\}}\mathbb{1}_{\{t > T^j\}} - \sum_j R^j N^j \mathbb{1}_{\{\tau^j \le t\}}\mathbb{1}_{\{t \le T^j\}} \\ \hat{Y}(t) &= Y_{rf} - Y \\ &= \sum_j C^j(t_i)\mathbb{1}_{\{\tau^j \le t\}}\end{aligned}$$

The proposed approximation is to reduce the two-dimensional joint distribution of X and Y to a univariate distribution using a certain curve in the x-y plane. We associate $\hat{x}^*$ and $\hat{y}^*$ if

$$F_{\hat{X}}(\hat{x}^*) = F_{\hat{Y}}(\hat{y}^*), \tag{23.8}$$

where $F(.)$ represents the cumulative probability distribution. At these values we get

$$\begin{aligned}x^* &= X_{rf} - \hat{x}^* \\ y^* &= Y_{rf} - \hat{y}^*\end{aligned}$$

implicitly defining a relationship $x^*(y^*)$. Along this curve the joint distribution reduces to

$$f_{XY}(x, y) = f_X(x^*)\delta(y - y^*) = f_Y(y^*)\delta(x - x^*)$$

so our two dimensional integral for the expected coupon on tranche k reduces to

$$\mathbb{E}(C_k(t_i)) = \int g_k(x^*, y^*) f_X(x^*) dx^* = \int g_k(x^*, y^*) f_Y(y^*) dy^*. \tag{23.9}$$

Using known quantities, such one-dimensional integrals can easily and efficiently be computed.

23.4 Example results

We have two goals in this section. We wish to confirm the result that, in the absence of IC and OC tests, the semi-analytical method gives equivalent prices to a fully converged Monte Carlo simulation. Secondly we wish to demonstrate the magnitude of the error in the presence of IC and OC in order to test the usability of the method in practice. In all cases we wish to show results that could be reproduced by a third party. We will thus set out a test portfolio and market conditions that are reproducible and as a result somewhat idealized. We first define the test deal and market conditions that we use. Next we describe the details of the one factor copula model used for test comparison. We then present the results and comment on them in some detail with reference to the credit spread sensitivities (CS01) of the portfolio.

23.4.1 Test deal

We separate between the trade details and the market scenario on which we price the trade. We choose the initial deal and market data so that the tranches of the deal are close to par at inception.

The deal is a three-tranche structure with a maturity of five years, quarterly fixed coupon payments and total notional of 100 million units. The size, fixed coupon rates, interest coverage and over-collateralization ratios are set out in Table 23.1 below.

The underlying portfolio is a pool of 100 non-amortizing bonds, each of notional 1 million units with quarterly fixed rate payments of 3% and five-year maturity. Each bond has a probability of default derived from a flat hazard rate curve and a deterministic recovery rate associated with it. These probabilities of default (PD) and recovery rates are varied in each of the scenarios set out in Table 23.2. The yield curve used is a 2% flat forward curve.

In order to model the joint probability of default we must choose a distribution. In our case we use a one-factor Gaussian copula model with a single correlation parameter, ρ, which is an input. We present semi-analytical results based on the loss bucketing algorithm with 400 uniform loss buckets and 150 Euler integral steps from -6 standard deviations to 6 standard deviations in the systematic risk

Table 23.1 Test deal characteristics

Tranche	Notional	Coupon Rate	IC Ratio	OC Ratio
A (Senior)	80M	3% fixed	1.1	1.1
B (Mezzanine)	10M	8% fixed	1.05	1.05
C (Equity)	10M	Excess Interest	N/A	N/A

Table 23.2 Market data scenario

Scenario	Hazard Rate (bp)	R	ρ
1 (Base)	500	0.4	0.6

Table 23.3 Price results and differences in basis points without IC and OC

Tranche	Q-Q	MC	Δ (bp)
	Scenario 1		
Portfolio	99.78	99.81	−3
A	99.83	99.88	−5
B	96.55	96.58	−3
C	102.59	102.53	6

factor. We compare two separate Monte Carlo random number generators, one using Sobol generated random numbers and one using a standard Mersenne twister algorithm without antithetic sampling. We find that Sobol random numbers are required to get reasonably well converged results, and we use 100,000 Sobol random numbers.

The market data for this trade consists of default probabilities for each bond, recovery rates, correlation parameters and a yield curve. The base case that we apply is set out in Table 23.2.

23.4.2 Test results

In Tables 23.3 and 23.4 we set out the tabular results. In each case we give the price in percent of notional of the overall portfolio (sum of tranches) and the individual tranches together with the differences (Δ) between the Q-Q approximation and Monte Carlo results in basis points of notional upfront. The results of these scenarios in the absence of IC and OC tests (where we expect that the semi-analytical Q-Q method should reproduce the true price to within numerical error) are set out in Table 23.3. The results with IC and OC tests switched on, where we expect there to be some difference in the Q-Q approximation due to non-linearity, are shown in Table 23.4.

23.4.3 Discussion of results

Any discussion of the results requires an objective measure of errors and differences. In our case we are comparing two numerical methods, both of which are subject to discretization error. We will discuss the efforts used to control the discretization

Table 23.4 Price results with IC and OC

Tranche	Q-Q	MC	Δ (bp)
	Scenario 1		
Portfolio	99.75	99.81	−7
A	100.83	100.86	−3
B	95.40	95.58	−18
C	95.46	95.65	−19

Table 23.5 Credit spread sensitivity in scenario 1

Tranche	CS01 (bp) without IC/OC	CS01 (bp) with IC/OC
Portfolio	4	4
A	2	2
B	10	11
C	14	14

error in each case. We also need an *objective* measure of error, and in this case we use the credit spread sensitivity of the deals (CS01), that is, the sensitivity of the price to a 1 basis point change in the credit spread of the underlying portfolio. The CS01 measures the error on the tranches as a function of changes in the input spreads. We know in practice that there is considerable uncertainty around credit spreads, particularly for illiquid bonds and in light of the uncertainty in the presence or absence of capital relief in CDS spreads, and so it is only reasonable to measure errors in the context of uncertainty in the input data. The CS01 for the base case is set out in Table 23.5.

As we are comparing two numerical methods it is important to ensure both are well converged. In the case of the Monte Carlo results we chose to show results based on 100,000 Sobol random samples having also tested the convergence of a standard Mersenne twister approach. Running 100,000 Monte Carlo samples takes 23 minutes of processor time on a single core of a 1.8 GHz Intel Core i5 processor; for modern risk analysis requiring multiple revaluations this would in fact be impractical. Using a standard Mersenne twister, the standard error at 100,000 samples was found to be in the order of the CS01, which is still considerable for the purposes of comparison. With 100,000 Sobol random numbers we believe the error to be in the order of 1 basis point. In the case of the Q-Q approximation, we use a loss bucketing approach and present results based on 400 uniform buckets and 150 Euler integral steps which reduces the numerical error to less than the CS01. We note that there is still some residual numerical error at this resolution but further increasing the resolution did not reduce the error. This may be due to a small inherent residual error in the implementation of the method. With this level of resolution the loss bucketing method takes 30 seconds to produce a price.

In the absence of IC and OC tests the Q-Q approach should give the true answer, and we can see from Table 23.3 that the results are within a single CS01 and consistent with the overall level of numerical error inherent in the loss bucketing algorithm (which has been reduced to the level of the CS01).

In the presence of IC and OC tests we know that there may be some additional error due to non-linearity in the pay-off (cure payments), and our objective is to quantify these errors and determine if the method is useful in practice given the inherent benefits of speed associated with a semi-analytical method. We see from Table 23.4 that the base case results have errors less than twice the CS01.

24 Credit Risk and Basel Capital for Derivatives

24.1 Introduction

Credit risk for derivatives is a subject that is in many ways catching up with credit risk for longer standing funded instruments, for example loans, bonds and guarantees. That there can be considerable counterparty risk in a portfolio of derivatives is clear, that is, a counterparty can default at a time when the mark to market of the bank's derivatives portfolio is significantly positive (constituting an asset to the bank). The fact that a derivative portfolio can constitute both an asset and a liability at different times has caused considerable confusion, and CVA and DVA are nothing but the equivalent of credit spread-based discounting (in the derivatives setting) that has been applied for many years for cash instruments. The counterpart of lending limits and risk capital for lending portfolios applied to derivatives is the subject of this chapter.

Unlike conventional loans and bonds, derivative exposures are highly volatile and can be an asset at one time (positive mark to market) and a liability at another (negative mark to market). The estimation of derivative exposures is required for two primary purposes in a financial institution. In the first instance for the prudent monitoring of current and potential future exposure (PFE). In the second instance in order to determine the required capital for regulatory purposes. The evolution of a derivative exposure into the future is dependent on the evolution of the underlying risk factors driving the price of the derivative and the pricing model used to mark the derivative to market. Thus credit exposure in this setting is inherently model-dependent; it is influenced by both the risk factor evolution equations (RFE) and the derivative pricing model.

This observation – that credit exposure in derivatives is highly model-dependent – brings to the fore the model risk inherent in both prudent credit limit monitoring and the computation of risk capital associated with derivatives. This model risk highlights the need for strong model governance processes as well as a robust internal and regulatory challenge as to the limitations and assumptions used for derivative exposure calculation.

We start by discussing potential future exposure and its calculation, and we introduce the real-world measure. We move to counterparty credit risk capital calculation, starting with the standard approaches of Basel for completeness and moving on to the advanced Internal Model Method (IMM).

24.2 Potential future exposure

We start with potential future exposure, that is the estimation of the possible exposure that one party in a derivative contract may have to the other over the life of the derivative. To compare with pricing and CVA applications, we start by noting that the current exposure (CE) at time t of one counterparty to the other is the positive part of the net present value of the derivatives in a legally enforceable netting set, that is

$$CE = (PV(t))^{+}.$$

This current exposure is deterministic[1] and is known assuming that we have a pricing model for the derivatives in question and the necessary market data. The evolution of the derivative price (and therefore exposure in the future) is intrinsically stochastic: we do not know in advance how the market will evolve and what the PV of the derivative will be. As seen today there is a distribution of possible outcomes for the derivative at any time horizon up to maturity. The potential future exposure is generally defined as a high quantile (typically 95% or 99%) of the present value distribution to the desired time horizon, assuming such a value is positive. For example, the PFE at the 95th percentile for time horizon t_i in the future is given by

$$PFE_{95} = \left[\sup\{X \,|\, \mathbb{P}(X) \leq 0.95\}\right]^{+}$$

where $\mathbb{P}(X)$ denotes the cumulative probability distribution of $PV(t_i)$. In order to compute such a quantile, we need two ingredients, firstly a stochastic model (risk factor evolution equation) for the market data that determines the price of the derivative, and secondly a pricing model for the derivative. In credit risk applications the RFE model is typically calibrated to the real-world (historical) measure; the pricing model, on the other hand, is calibrated to the risk-neutral measure, although this has its limitations. We introduce the real-world measure in the next section.

The identification of the risk factors and the evolution models that appropriately capture the dynamics of these risk factors are essential for robust credit monitoring

[1] In the sense that it is a deterministic function of the pricing algorithm. This assumption ignores issues like convergence of Monte Carlo simulation or other factors that may make the unique market value an interval of plausible values.

of derivative portfolios. For example, the exposure of a simple vanilla interest rate swap is sensitive to the yield curve in its currency, but also to the foreign exchange rate that converts the exposure into the reporting currency. Likewise, a vanilla swaption is sensitive to the yield curve and foreign exchange rate, but also to the swaption volatility surface.

The next section discusses risk factor evolution for derivative credit risk monitoring and capital purposes.

24.3 Real-world measure

In Part III we developed a Monte Carlo simulation framework for evolving risk factors across several asset classes which is risk-neutral in the sense that it is based on models whose drift terms are calibrated to market yield curves, and volatilities are implied from quoted option prices.[2] When the simulation is used to compute value components (XVA), then a risk-neutral approach is clearly sensible.

Turning to risk analysis (market risk or credit risk) in a Monte Carlo simulation framework, we need to revisit this methodology of risk factor evolution, because regulators require that risk models are backtested. For a credit exposure simulation framework this means that we need to show that the model's projection is consistent with realized risk factor moves in history. We come back to this in more detail in Section 25.3. If we used a risk-neutral setup, then it would be a rather surprising coincidence if the model withstood backtesting: historical volatility is different from market (option) implied volatility, historical interest rate drifts are different from the risk-neutral drifts along the forward curve. This is why one rather looks for alternative models (or alternative calibration approaches) which a priori have better chances of performing well under backtesting.

It seems obvious that such models would involve calibration to historical data of some kind. In the following we discuss three approaches which differ in "proximity" to the risk-neutral machinery of Part III.

24.3.1 Traditional approach

The traditional approach in risk – be it market or credit risk – was the following, where we restrict ourselves to interest rates in a single currency.

The basic model typically considers a series of tenor points τ_i on the zero curve $Z_i(t) = Z_{T_i}(t)$, each of which is modelled using Geometric Brownian Motion with

[2] One should note that many *correlations* in a cross-asset model cannot be implied from the market and have to be estimated from historical data

a drift:

$$d \ln Z_i(t) = \left(\mu_i(t) - \frac{1}{2}\sigma_i^2(t) \right) dt - \sigma_i(t)\, dW_i(t),$$

with correlation ρ_{ij} between the Wiener processes driving Z_i and Z_j. We have seen applications of such a model with different approaches to set the drift – zero drift as well as a mean-reverting drift – to a historical average a_h of Z_i with

$$\mu_i(t) = a \ln \frac{a_h}{Z_i(t)} = a\,(\ln a_h - \ln Z_i(t)),$$

where a is the mean reversion speed, all parameters being calibrated to historical data. Rebonato et al. [128] follow an alternative approach – similar to historical simulation – where they pick sequences of actual past rate changes and apply them to evolve the current yield curve into the future,

$$\ln Z_i(t_{n+m}) = \ln Z_i(t_n) + \sum_{r=1}^{m} \Delta \ln Z_i(t_r),$$

where the rate changes t_r are picked arbitrarily from the past before starting point t_n. The authors show, however, that this method – if applied naively over long time horizons – can lead to unrealistic shapes of the future yield curve with extreme curvature, "kinks" and pronounced changes in the yield curve slope for long maturities. Their semi-parametric approach avoids such shortcomings and ensures realistic yield curve shapes in long-term simulations, in particular by adding terms to the body of the yield curve which tend to decrease its curvature, and by adding mean reverting terms to the yield curve's short and long end.

24.3.2 Adjusted risk-neutral approach

In this section we present an alternative approach to "real-world" risk factor evolution which tries to stay as close to the risk-neutral setup as possible. Our aim is to show how to reuse this setup while eliminating its most undesirable feature, that is the "unrealistic" interest rate drift along the forward curve. Let us recall the general property of the risk-neutral approach without considering any particular model choice. This makes the adjustment we work out below quite generic and applicable to any model.

Let us define the time points t (today) $< S < T$. Given a numeraire N, today's N-discounted price of a zero bond starting at time S and paying at time T is given as

$$\mathbb{E}_t^N \left(P(S,T) \frac{N(t)}{N(T)} \right) = P(t,T).$$

The expected exposure of a bond at time S, seen from time t, is its price compounded to time S

$$EE(t,S,T) = \frac{1}{P(t,S)} \mathbb{E}_t^N \left(P(S,T) \frac{N(t)}{N(S)} \right),$$

from arbitrage-free modelling, which is equal to

$$= \frac{P(t,T)}{P(t,S)} =: P(t,S,T).$$

That is, in a no-arbitrage model, the expected exposure of a bond is *always* given by its forward price. This is true for any numeraire choice – be it bank account, zero bond, LGM or any other. For instance, under the S-forward measure (with numeraire $P(t,S)$), the expectation is particularly simple:

$$EE(t,S,T) = \mathbb{E}_t^S \left(P(S,T) \right) = \frac{P(t,T)}{P(t,S)},$$

while it looks more complicated under the bank account measure: (Q)

$$EE(t,S,T) = \frac{1}{P(t,S)} \mathbb{E}_t^Q \left[P(S,T)\, e^{-\int_t^S r(u)\, du} \right] = \frac{P(t,T)}{P(t,S)},$$

where

$$P(S,T) = \mathbb{E}_S^Q \left[e^{-\int_S^T r(u)\, du} \right],$$

but the result is always the same – the forward bond price. Historical analyses show that the forward price is not, however, a good estimator in hindsight.
Our goal is now to modify the exposure definition such that

$$\widetilde{EE}(t,S,T) = P(t, t+T-S). \tag{24.1}$$

This means that the expected future bond price for tenor $\tau = T - S$ equals today's bond price for the same tenor. Note that original and new exposures agree when the yield curve is flat. When the yield curve is normal, the risk-neutral expected exposure exceeds the new one; if the yield curve is inverse then the risk-neutral exposure undershoots the new definition. The expected exposure as defined in (24.1) expresses that we do *not* expect that forward rates will be realized in the future, rather it takes the neutral view that rates will neither go up nor down.

This is achieved by introducing a deterministic factor $X(t,S,T)$ that modifies the zero bond price $P(S,T)$ in the exposure calculation such that

$$\begin{aligned}\widetilde{EE}(t,S,T) &= \frac{1}{P(t,S)}\mathbb{E}^N_t\left[\underbrace{P(S,T)\,X(t,S,T)}_{\widetilde{P}(S,T)}\frac{N(t)}{N(S)}\right]\\ &= X(t,S,T)\cdot\frac{P(t,T)}{P(t,S)}\\ &:= P(t,t+T-S),\end{aligned}$$

Solving this for X yields the adjustment factor

$$X(t,S,T) = P(t,t+T-S)\,\frac{P(t,S)}{P(t,T)}, \tag{24.2}$$

or in terms of zero rates

$$X(t,S,T) = \exp\left\{-z_{T-S}(t)\cdot(T-S) - z_{S-t}(t)\cdot(S-t) + z_{T-t}(t)\cdot(T-t)\right\}.$$

This is a horizon (S) and tenor-dependent modification for each stochastic zero bond, entirely determined by the current yield curve (at time t). It has the desired effect on zero bond exposure and any instrument that is a linear combination of those (such as swaps in a single-curve setting). Note

- for a flat yield curve, $P(t,T) = \exp(-z(T-t))$, the adjustment is equal to one;
- for a yield curve with linear slope, i.e. zero rate $z = z_0 + m(T-t)$, $P(t,T) = \exp(-(z_0 + m(T-t))\cdot(T-t))$, the adjustment is

$$X(t,S,T) = \exp\left(2\,m\,(S-t)\,(T-S)\right),$$

  i.e. $X > 1$ for $m > 1$ and $X < 1$ otherwise.

Market price of risk

Let us view the adjusted conditional zero bond $\widetilde{P}(S,T)$ as a random variable that is evolved under the *real-world measure* up to time S. Its connection to the zero bond under the risk-neutral measure is given by factor $X(t,S,T)$:

$$\widetilde{P}(S,T) = P(S,T)\cdot X(t,S,T).$$

The real-world measure is usually introduced at the SDE level. In the Hull-White model – which is at the heart of LGM which we use throughout this text – this would mean the additional term $\lambda_t \sigma_t \, dt$ related to the market price of risk λ_t in

$$dr = a(\theta_t - r)\, dt + \sigma_t \, dW^Q + \lambda_t \sigma_t \, dt, \tag{24.3}$$

where we now label the mean reversion speed a in order to keep λ_t for the market price of risk. This drift change propagates to the representation of the conditional zero bond in the Hull-White (and likewise in the LGM) model:

$$\widetilde{P}(S,T) = P(S,T) \exp\left(-H_{T-S} \int_0^S \lambda_t \sigma_t \, e^{-a(S-t)} \, dt - \int_S^T H_{T-t} \lambda_t \sigma_t \, dt \right), \tag{24.4}$$

where H is the LGM model's H function connected with mean reversion speed a, that is $H(t) = (1 - \exp(-a\,t))/a$. For the market price of risk λ_t to "generate" the adjustment $X(0,S,T)$ we therefore need to match $X(0,S,T)$ with the exponential on the right-hand side of (24.4). Since $X(0,0,T) = 1$, we see that we have to define $\lambda_t \equiv 0$ for $t \geq S$, and we are left with

$$\frac{\widetilde{P}(S,T)}{P(S,T)} = \exp\left(-H_{T-S} \int_0^S \lambda_t \sigma_t \, e^{-a(S-t)} \, dt \right) = X(0,S,T). \tag{24.5}$$

The adjustment for exposure time S is hence connected with a non-zero market price of risk for the period up to time S only. Assuming a constant market price of risk λ and constant volatility σ, we solve (24.5) for

$$\lambda\sigma = -\frac{\ln X(0,S,T)}{H_{T-S} \cdot H_S} = \frac{z_{T-S} \cdot (T-S) - (z_T \cdot T - z_S \cdot S)}{H_{T-S} \cdot H_S},$$

since $H_S = \int_0^S e^{-a(S-t)} \, dt$.

Let us finally consider the change in the expected value of $r(S)$ due to the additional market price of risk drift $\lambda_t \sigma_t dt$. This change is according to Appendix D given by

$$\Delta\mathbb{E}[r(S)] = \int_0^S \lambda_t \sigma_t \, e^{-a(S-t)} \, dt,$$

using (24.5) this is

$$= -\frac{\ln X(0,S,T)}{H_{T-S}} = \frac{z_{T-S} \cdot (T-S) - (z_T \cdot T - z_S \cdot S)}{H_{T-S}},$$

and with $H_{T-S} \approx (T-S)$ for $a \ll 1$ it simplifies to

$$\approx z_{T-S} - \frac{z_T T - z_S S}{T-S}.$$

The expected value of $r(S)$ in the real-world measure is therefore the sum of (D.4) and the terms above,

$$\widetilde{\mathbb{E}}[r(S)] \approx f(0,S) + \text{convexity} + z_{T-S} - \frac{z_T T - z_S S}{T-S}$$
$$= f(0,S) + \text{convexity} + \frac{1}{T-S}\int_0^{T-S} f(0,t)\,dt - \frac{1}{T-S}\int_S^T f(0,t)\,dt.$$

The market price of risk and the adjusted expectation is clearly tailored to the exposure horizon S but moreover dependent on bond maturity T. For an infinitesimally small time difference $T-S>0$, the term on the right-hand side is just the negative of the instantaneous forward rate at time S, so that this compensates the risk-neutral expectation (D.4) except for a usually small convexity term. The remaining term z_{T-S} converges to the current short rate r_0 for $T \to S$. This shows that the expectation of $r(S)$ with the market price of risk above is essentially reduced to its current value, that is the short rate drift over the period up to time S is eliminated. Similarly, if we set T to $S+\Delta$ for small Δ, then we see that the real-world expectation of the short rate beyond S is approximately given by

$$\widetilde{\mathbb{E}}[r(S+\Delta)] \approx f(0,\Delta) + \text{convexity},$$

that is the real-world short rate drift is reset at time S to that of time zero.

Here we have been working backwards from a desired adjustment to the corresponding market price of risk drift in the original short rate's SDE and change in the short rate expectations. The next section takes the opposite approach of trying to derive the market price of risk from historical data.

Note:

1. Adjustment $X(t,S,T)$ is *model-independent*, but its "translation" into a market price of risk is model-dependent.
2. To improve RFE backtesting performance via zero bond adjustments $X(t,S,T)$ one sacrifices the no-arbitrage paradigm. Exposure concepts in CVA management and credit exposure monitoring diverge, but are still based on the same underlying Monte Carlo simulation framework.
3. Adjustments $X(t,S,T)$ are determined by the yield curve shape at time t. Therefore one cannot expect that $X(t,S,T)$ remains stable through time; it varies from day to day. However, this is true for all model parameters when the model is recalibrated.
4. For each time t, $X(t,S,T)$ is a multiplicative deterministic adjustment to $P(S,T)$ so that model-implied covariances of zero/forward rates (based on $\ln P(S,T)$ by definition) are not affected by the adjustment.

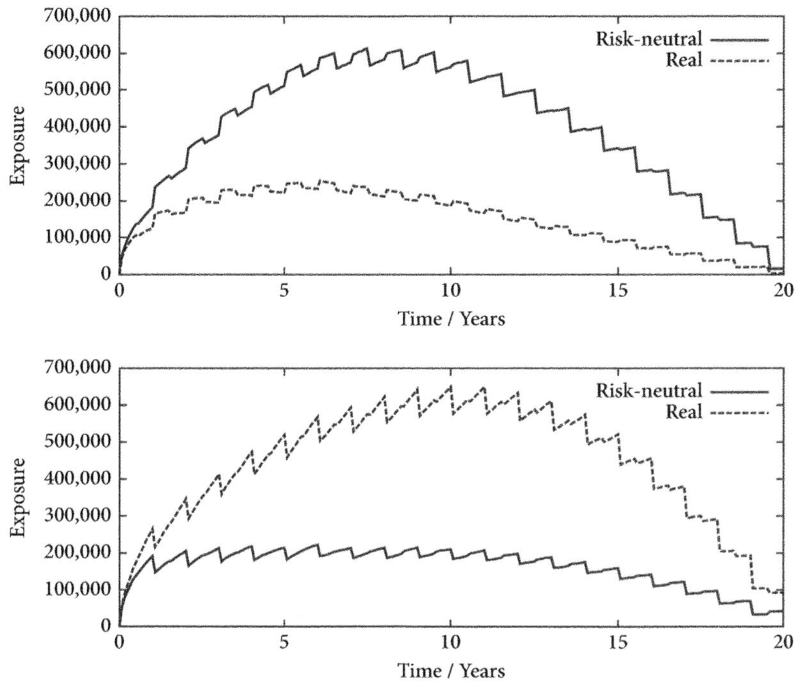

Figure 24.1 Exposure evolution for a vanilla fixed payer swap (top) and receiver swap (bottom) in EUR in the risk-neutral and real-world measure. The real-world measure evolution is generated from the risk-neutral evolution by means of the drift adjustment in Section 24.3.2

To illustrate the effect of the drift adjustment, Figures 24.1 and 24.2 show exposure graphs for vanilla interest rate swaps in EUR and USD in both measures, risk-neutral (LGM) and real-world.

Market data for these graphs are as taken from 30 January 2015. In both currencies, EUR and USD, the yield curves are upward sloping, hence the fixed payer swap moves deeper into-the-money over time in the risk-neutral measure, whereas in the real-world measure – which eliminates the risk-neural drift – the moneyness does not change through time. Therefore the risk-neutral exposure for the payer swaps is higher than the real-world exposure. For the receiver swap it is vice versa.

Taking the *neutral view* above may seem plausible but it is clearly ad hoc. We may improve on that subjective choice by calibrating $X(t, S, T)$ to historical data, that is incorporate observed moves. But note that this calibration has subjective elements as well, such as the choice of the time window from which we pick our observations, or the weighting of the individual moves. The approach described in the following section is an attempt in that direction.

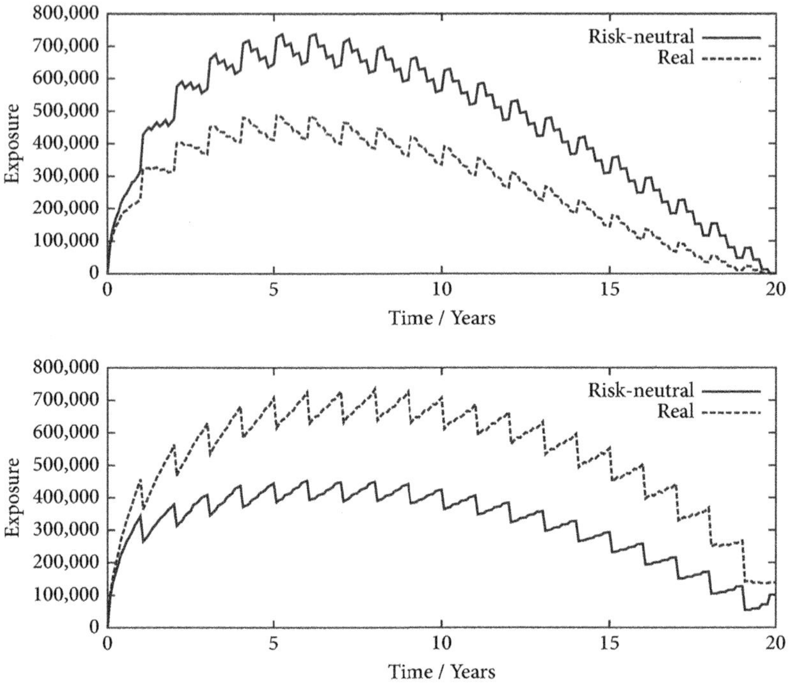

Figure 24.2 Exposure evolution for a vanilla fixed payer swap (top) and receiver swap (bottom) in USD in the risk-neutral and real-world measure. The real-world measure evolution is generated from the risk-neutral evolution by means of the drift adjustment in Section 24.3.2

24.3.3 Joint measure model approach

Hull et al. advocate in [84] using "short-rate joint-measure models" to allow risk-neutral and real-world scenario generation for XVA and credit exposure measurement, respectively, in a single model framework.

Their key idea is illustrated with a single-factor Markov model for the short rate r which has – under the risk-neutral measure – the SDE

$$dr = \mu(t,r)\,dt + \sigma(t,r)\,dW,$$

with deterministic drift and volatility functions. The corresponding real-world model differs by the market price of risk $\lambda(t,r,\ldots)$ which may depend on time, the short rate r and generally on other market variables:

$$dr = (\mu(t,r) + \lambda(t,r,...)\,\sigma(t,r))\,dt + \sigma(t,r)\,dW.$$

In the real-world measure, bond prices are higher than in the risk-neutral world, and correspondingly interest rate drifts are lower, which means that the market price of risk should be negative. To ensure that the model remains a single-factor model, the authors assume that λ is a function of time and short rate r only. If one estimates the market price of risk using a single-factor short rate model from historical data for rates of varying maturity T, Hull et al. find a strong dependence on maturity with $\lambda \approx -1.0$ for short rates such as six months (consistent with previous research on market price of risk) and $\lambda \approx -0.2$ for long rates with maturity 20 to 30 years. They interpret the strong maturity dependence as (yet another) indication that rates are effectively driven by multiple factors. Hull et al. suggest using a time-dependent market price of risk in a short rate model context. To illustrate their approach, the authors apply a simple local volatility model introduced by Deguillaume et al. [56] which is an extension of the Hull-White short rate model:

$$dr = [\theta(t) - a\,r]\,dt + \sigma(r)\,dW, \tag{24.6}$$

where volatility switches between normal and log-normal regimes

$$\sigma(r) = \begin{cases} s\,r/r_d, & r \le r_d \\ s, & r_d < r < r_u \\ s\,r/r_u, & t \ge r_u \end{cases} \tag{24.7}$$

with $r_d = 0.015$, $r_u = 0.06$ and fixed mean reversion speed $a = 0.05$.

The joint measure model construction proposed by Hull et al. is then done in two stages:

1. Determine market prices of risk consistent with historical data: compute long-run historical average of the yield curve and the volatility s of rate changes (Hull et al. use data back to 1982); construct a tree [83] for the model above (24.6), calibrated to the average historical yield term structure and with volatility structure (24.7); the market prices of risk[3] λ_i in each time step i of the tree are then chosen such that *the expected future short rate is equal to the long-run historical average short rate* r_0 which is also the root of the tree. Note that λ is chosen to be a function of time only, not a function of the short rate level.
2. Build a new risk-neutral tree calibrated to current yield curve and option data (which also leads to a different value of model volatility s). The market prices of risk $\lambda(t)$ determined in the previous step are then applied to each node of the tree to reduce the drift at each node.

[3] Hull et al. label these local prices of risk.

If one rather wants to fix model-implied expectations of particular long-term rates to their long-run averages, Hull et al. suggest scaling the market prices of risk found in stage one of the procedure above accordingly.

Hull et al. finally claim [84] that their concept of local price of risk can be similarly applied to multi-factor short rate models, Libor market models and SABR models with each factor in a multi-factor model associated with its own local price of risk function, "to be derived econometrically".

Let us consider how this approach would be applied to the LGM model framework of Section 11, which is in fact a single-factor Hull-White model expressed under a convenient measure. We proceed again in two stages as above:

1. We first determine an average historical yield curve $P_h(0,T)$, fix mean reversion speed λ_h , estimate short rate volatility σ_h from historical data,[4] reversion speed and volatility, then determine the LGM model functions $H_h(t) = (1 - \exp(-\lambda_h t))/\lambda_h$ and $\zeta_h(t) = \sigma_h^2/2\lambda_h(\exp(2\lambda_h t) - 1)$. The expectation of the model-implied future short rate (11.6) is $\mathbb{E}[r(t)] = f_h(0,t) + \zeta_h(t)\, H_h'(t) H_h(t)$, that is given by the instantaneous forward curve plus some convexity adjustment. The additional drift $\bar{\lambda}(t)\sigma_h\, dt$ due to the market market price of risk $\bar{\lambda}(t)$ in the original Hull-White SDE (24.3) leads to[5] the real-world expectation

$$\widetilde{\mathbb{E}}[r(t)] = f_h(0,t) + \zeta_h(t)\, H_h'(t) H_h(t) + \sigma_h \int_0^t \bar{\lambda}(s)\, e^{-\lambda_h(t-s)}\, ds.$$

The local price of risk function $\bar{\lambda}(t)$ is then chosen such that $\widetilde{\mathbb{E}}[r(t)] = f_h(0,0)$, or

$$\sigma_h \int_0^t \bar{\lambda}(s)\, e^{-\lambda_h(t-s)}\, ds = -\left(f_h(0,t) - f_h(0,0)\right) + \zeta_h(t)\, H_h'(t) H_h(t)\big).$$

2. We then calibrate the LGM model as usual to market data (yield curve and options) and adjust the model's risk-neutral short rate $r(t)$ by adding $\bar{\lambda}(t)\,\sigma(t)\, dt$ to the short rate drift or correspondingly by adjusting the stochastic zero bond $P(t,T)$ as in Equation (24.5).

Note that this drift adjustment leaves all rate distributions' variances unchanged, in contrast to the simple local volatility model discussed in [84] where lower rate levels also induce lower short rate variance.

Although more sophisticated than the simple drift adjustment approach in the previous section, the approach by Hull et al. summarized here also has subjective

4 Either directly from time series data or as an average of market implied model volatility

5 See appendix D and equation (24.5).

elements (setting short rate expectations to long-run average short rates, or the suggested scaling to fix the expectation of another desired rate). Whether these approaches are sound and acceptable will eventually have to be confirmed by backtesting the risk factor evolution model, see Section 25.3.

24.4 Standardized approach, CEM and SA-CCR

Financial institutions either apply a *standardized* or an *advanced* approach for determining the regulatory capital amounts to be assigned to their derivative activity. The advanced approach is accessible to institutions with an internal model method (IMM) for credit risk capital which is approved by the regulator. This method involves sophisticated analysis of future exposures by Monte Carlo simulation methods using real-world measure risk factor evolutions as sketched in Section 24.3. We elaborate on this method below in Section 24.5. Institutions without approved IMM have to apply a standardized approach instead, which is simplified in that it does not require Monte Carlo exposure simulation but resorts to formulas suggested by the Basel Committee for Banking Supervision and enforced by the respective regulator. These formulas attempt to conservatively approximate the credit exposures which would have been obtained by more sophisticated IMM approaches. The current standardized approach (Current Exposure Method, CEM) as published by the (BCBS) in 2006 [17] is summarized in Section 24.4.1. A revised standardized approach for counterparty credit risk from derivative activity (SA-CCR) as published in 2014 [22] will be in effect from the beginning of 2017. This revised method is summarized in Section 24.4.2.

24.4.1 Current standardized approach: CEM

The key quantity in the current standardized approach (or current exposure method, CEM) is the exposure at default (EaD) or *credit equivalent amount* which consists of two additive terms, current replacement cost and potential future exposure add-on,

$$\mathrm{EaD} = \mathrm{RC} + \mathrm{Notional} \times \mathrm{NettingFactor} \times \mathrm{AddOn}.$$

The replacement cost RC is simply given by the current exposure which is the current positive value of the netting set after subtracting collateral (C)

$$\mathrm{RC} = \max(0, \mathrm{PV} - \mathrm{C}).$$

Replacement cost is aggregated over all derivative contracts and netting sets.

The second term is supposed to approximately reflect the potential future exposure over the remaining life of the contract. It depends on the (fairly rough)

Table 24.1 Add-on factor by product and time to maturity. Single currency interest rate swaps are assigned a zero add-on, i.e. judged on replacement cost basis only, if their maturity is less than one year. Forwards, swaps, purchased options and derivative contracts not covered in the columns above shall be treated as "Other Commodities". Credit derivatives (total return swaps and credit default swaps) are treated separately with 5% and 10% add-ons depending on whether the reference obligation is regarded as "qualifying" (public sector entities (!), rated investment grade or approved by the regulator). Nth to default basket transactions are assigned an add-on based on the credit quality of nth lowest credit quality in the basket

Residual Maturity	Interest Rates	FX Gold	Equity	Precious Metals	Other Commodities
$\leq$ 1 Year	0.0%	1%	6%	7%	10%
1-5 Years	0.5%	5%	8%	7%	12%
> 5 Years	1.5%	7.5%	10%	8%	15%

product type classification and on time to maturity in three bands as shown in Table 24.1 which is in use in this form since 1988.

The netting factor acknowledges netting also in the potential future exposure estimate of the netting set. If there is no netting as of today, that is net NPV equals gross NPV, the netting factor is equal to 1, otherwise it can be as low as 0.4. Additional netting benefit results from using a central clearing counterpary :

$$\text{NettingFactor} = \begin{cases} 0.4 + 0.6 \times \dfrac{\max\left(\sum_i PV_i, 0\right)}{\sum_i \max(PV_i, 0)} & \text{bilateral netting,} \\[2ex] 0.15 + 0.85 \times \dfrac{\max\left(\sum_i PV_i, 0\right)}{\sum_i \max(PV_i, 0)} & \text{central clearing.} \end{cases}$$

Finally, the notional amounts that enter into the potential future exposure term are understood as effective notional amounts which for example take into account leverage which may be expressed through factors in structured product payoff formulas.

Note that this current (old) standard approach is valid until the end of 2016.

24.4.2 New standardized approach: SA-CCR

With its 2014 publication [22], the Basel Committee for Banking Supervision has revised the standardized approach. The new method takes collateralization into account in a more detailed way than before which has the potential to reduce the credit equivalent amounts. On the other hand, the new method attempts to mimic a more conservative potential exposure, the *effective expected positive exposure* (EEPE, see below) which tends to increase the resulting credit equivalent amounts. In summary, only a detailed impact analysis for specific portfolios will be able to tell whether the overall impact of the new method results in an increase or in a decrease of derivative capital charges. In the following we summarize the ingredients of the new methodology.

The exposure at default is still composed of a replacement cost and a potential future exposure term

$$\text{EAD} = 1.4 \times (\text{RC} + \text{PFE}),$$

but scaled up by a factor of 1.4 which is motivated by the committee's attempt to mimic a different (higher) exposure measure (see below). On the other hand, the replacement cost per netting set takes into account more details of the collateral agreement:

$$\text{RC} = \max(\text{PV} - \text{C}; \text{TH} + \text{MTA} - \text{NICA}; 0),$$

where TH is the CSA's threshold amount, MTA the CSA's minimum transfer amount, and NICA is the net independent collateral amount if posted. So even if the posted collateral C matches the PV so that the first term on the right-hand side vanishes, the various CSA slippage terms can cause a positive replacement cost contribution here. This supposedly imitates CVA behaviour.

The potential future exposure term has two drivers

$$\text{PFE} = \text{Multiplier} \times \text{AddOn},$$

with an add-on factor that is significantly more complex than in the current standardized approach's definition. The multiplier's purpose is to reward excess collateral:

$$\begin{aligned}\text{Multiplier} &= \min\left(1; 0.05 + 0.95 \times \exp\left(\frac{\text{PV} - \text{C}}{1.9 \times \text{AddOn}}\right)\right) \\ &= 1 \quad \text{if } PV \geq C \\ &< 1 \quad \text{if } PV < C \text{ (excess collateral).}\end{aligned}$$

The add-on is a composite

$$\text{AddOn} = \sum_a \text{AddOn}_a,$$

where the sum is taken over various *asset classes* in the netting set, and AddO_a denotes the add-on factor for each asset class. The add-on factor within each asset class

$$\text{AddOn}_a = \sum_i \text{SupervisoryFactor}_i \times \text{EffectiveNotional}_i, \tag{24.8}$$

is a sum over contributions from various *hedging sets* for asset class a, for example currencies for interest rate derivatives. The asset class assignment follows *primary risk drivers*, but split assignment may be required for complex trades.

As mentioned above, the potential future exposure term aims to mimic a particularly conservative exposure measure. This choice is built into the definition of the supervisory factors, quoting [22]:

> A factor or factors specific to each asset class is used to **convert the effective notional amount into Effective EPE** based on the measured volatility of the asset class. Each factor has been calibrated to reflect the Effective EPE of a single at-the-money linear trade of unit notional and one-year maturity. This includes the estimate of realised volatilities assumed by supervisors for each underlying asset class.

The supervisory factors are displayed in Table 24.2.

Let us briefly list here the various exposure definitions used in Basel III documentation:

Expected Exposure

$$EE(t) = \mathbb{E}[\max(PV(t) - C(t), 0)]. \tag{24.9}$$

Expected Positive Exposure

$$EPE(T) = \frac{1}{T} \sum_{t<T} EE(t) \cdot \Delta t. \tag{24.10}$$

Effective Expected Exposure

$$EEE(t) = \max(EEE(t - \Delta t), EE(t)). \tag{24.11}$$

Effective Expected Positive Exposure

$$EEPE(T) = \frac{1}{T} \sum_{t<T} EEE(t) \cdot \Delta t, \tag{24.12}$$

which shows how EPE, EEE and EEPE are “derivatives” of the expected exposure evolution EE(t). The last one, Effective EPE, is targeted by the Basel Committee for EAD and capital calculation since Basel II [16]. The time average in the EEPE calculation is taken over *the first year* of the exposure evolution (or until maturity if all positions of the netting set mature before one year).

These exposures and their relations are illustrated in Figures 24.3 and 24.4. Figure 24.4 illustrates the fact that EEE and EEPE are particularly conservative exposure definitions derived from the expected exposure evolution EE(t).

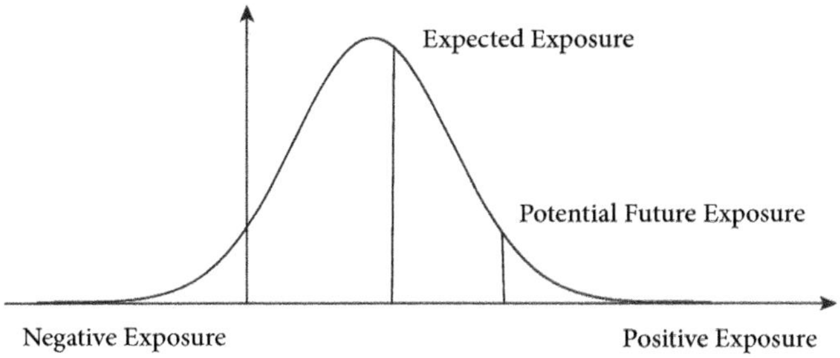

Figure 24.3 NPV distribution and the location of expected exposure EE and potential future exposure (peak exposure) PFE

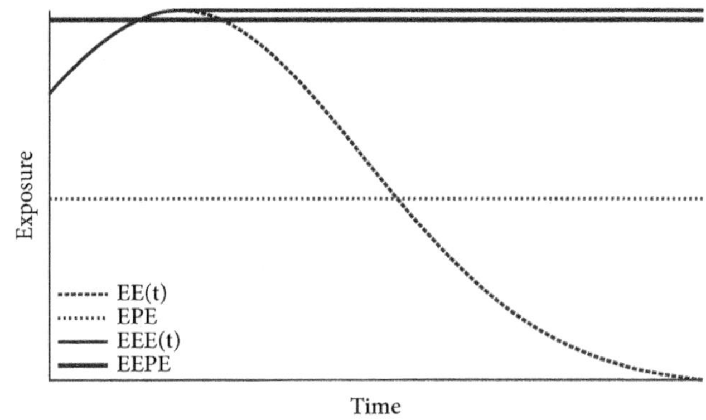

Figure 24.4 Evolution of the expected exposure through time, EE(t), and corresponding EPE(t), EEE(t) and EEPE(t)

Let us continue with sketching the hedging set **EffectiveNotional** in (24.8). This is computed using contributions $D_{1,2,3}$ from trades allocated to three time buckets

- D_1: < 1 year
- D_2: 1–5 years
- D_3: > 5 years

Each contribution is a sum over all trades in the hedging set and maturity bucket:

$$D_{1,2,3} = \sum_i \delta_i \times d_i \times MF_i,$$

with trade specific parameters δ_i, d_i, MF_i explained below. These time bucket contributions $D_{1,2,3}$ are aggregated as follows

$$\text{EffectiveNotional} = \sqrt{D_1^2 + D_2^2 + D_3^2 + 1.4 \cdot (D_1 \cdot D_2 + D_2 \cdot D_3) + 0.6 \cdot D_1 \cdot D_3}.$$

The trade specific parameters δ_i, d_i and MF_i in $D_{1,2,3}$, finally, have the following origins:

1. *d* **(position size and maturity)**
   - Interest and credit derivatives: Notional times duration
   - FX derivatives: Maximum foreign currency notional in domestic currency
2. *MF* **(maturity factor)**
   - For uncollateralized positions computed from the time to maturity M in years: $\sqrt{\min(M,1)}$
   - For collateralized positions computed from the margin period of risk MPR (in years) used: $1.5 \cdot \sqrt{MPR}$
3. δ **(adjustment for direction and non-linearity)**
   - Options: In this case δ is an option delta (derived from the Black76 formula),

$$\delta_i = \omega\, \Phi\left(\frac{\ln(P_i/K_i) + 0.5\,\sigma_i^2\, T_i}{\sigma_i \sqrt{T_i}} \right),$$

     where P_i is the price of the underlying (typically the forward price), K_i is the strike price of the option, T_i is the expiry date of the option, ω is a sign (+ for long calls and short puts, − for short calls and long puts) and σ_i is given as defined in Table 24.2.
   - CDO tranches: $\pm\frac{15}{(1+14A)(1+14D)}$ for purchased (sold) protection, where A and D denote the attachment and detachment point of the tranche, respectively
   - Others: ± 1 depending on whether long or short in the primary risk factor

24.5 Basel internal model approach

With the introduction of Basel II [16, 17] in 2004, the Basel Committee for Banking Supervision (BCBS) recommended that banks with permission to use the internal models method (IMM) to calculate counterparty credit risk regulatory capital (IMM banks) should measure derivative exposure at default (EAD) based on the *Effective Expected Positive Exposure (EEPE)* which we introduced in the previous section, Equation (24.12). The netting set's EEPE is based on a time-average of the evolution of expected exposure up to the one-year horizon (or the maturity of the

Table 24.2 Supervisory factors and option volatilities from [22]

Asset Class	Subclass	Supervisory Factor	Correlation	Supervisory Option Volatility
Interest rate		0.5%	N/A	50%
Foreign exchange		4.0%	N/A	15%
Credit, Single Name	AAA	0.38%	50%	100%
	AA	0.38%	50%	100%
	A	0.42%	50%	100%
	BBB	0.54%	50%	100%
	BB	1.06%	50%	100%
	B	1.6%	50%	100%
	CCC	6.0%	50%	100%
Credit, Index	IG	0.38%	80%	80%
	SG	1.06%	80%	80%
Equity, Single Name		32%	50%	120%
Equity, Index		20%	80%	75%
Commodity	Electricity	40%	40%	150%
	Oil/Gas	18%	40%	70%
	Metals	18%	40%	70%
	Agricultural	18%	40%	70%
	Other	18%	40%	70%

netting set if all positions in the netting set mature before the one-year horizon); see the definition in Equation (24.9). EEPE is generally determined by Monte Carlo simulation of the market drivers (interest rates, foreign exchange rates, etc.) and by evaluating the netting set's positions including collateral under many Monte Carlo market scenarios through time. A footnote in [16] comments on the market evolution:

> In theory, the expectations should be taken with respect to the actual probability distribution of future exposure and not the risk-neutral one. Supervisors recognise that practical considerations may make it more feasible to use the risk-neutral one. As a result, supervisors will not mandate which kind of forecasting distribution to employ.

In Part III we elaborated risk-neutral risk factor evolutions, and we showed in Section 24.3 how to propagate market factors under the real-world measure, in particular how to modify and re-use the risk-neutral machinery for this purpose.

Once EEPE is computed, the derivative exposure at default is computed using

$$\mathrm{EaD} = \alpha \times \mathrm{EEPE},$$

where $\alpha = 1.4$ by default. This scaling factor is a conservative 40% "add-on" to account for imperfect modelling of the risk factor evolution, in particular to account for shortcomings in the modelling of correlations between default of credit names or the correlation between interest and hazard rates. The regulator may allow own estimates performed by the institution (with a floor of 1.2 though), or may require higher $\alpha > 1.4$ in certain situations (low granularity of counterparties, significant wrong-way risk, high correlation of exposures across counterparties, etc.).

It is not sufficient to run EEPE simulations for capital calculations in isolation. Rather, the bank has to convince its supervisor that this kind of capital calculation is embedded into the organization's application of sound practices for day-to-day counterparty credit risk (CCR) management.

Models and estimates designed and implemented exclusively to qualify for the internal models method are not acceptable.

The Basel Committee for Banking Supervision has formulated various operational requirements that need to be met [16]. We briefly summarize and excerpt from these requirements here:

- Use peak exposures from the same exposure simulation that feeds EEPE for capital calculation for counterparty credit limits; use EEPE for internal capital allocation
- Demonstrate credible track record of applying exposure simulation for at least a year before applying for IMM treatment
- Independent control unit responsible for design and implementation of the CCR system, with direct reporting to senior management
- Systems capability for daily exposure estimation on a time grid appropriate for adequately reflecting the structure of future cash flows and maturity of contracts; for example: daily up to ten days, weekly up to one month, monthly up to 18 months, quarterly up to five years, etc.
- Exposure measurement over the entire life of the portfolio (rather than just the one-year horizon for capital calculation)
- Sound stress testing processes
- Awareness of significant general and specific wrong-way risk
- Integrity of the modelling process and security of the trade and market data inputs
- Usage of current market data for computing current exposures
- Usage of at least three years of historical data for model calibration, e.g. where historical data is used to estimate volatilities and correlations
- Sound validation process for the exposure model, identification of "*conditions under which assumptions are violated and may result in an understatement of EPE*".
- Internal procedures to verify that collateral meets appropriate legal certainty standards

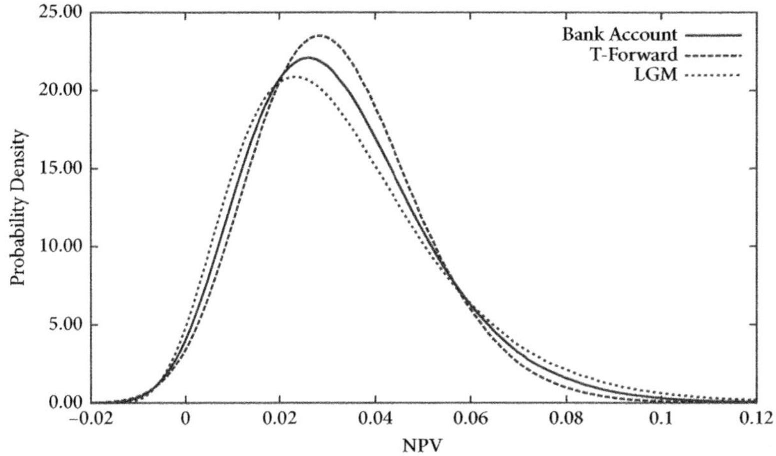

Figure 24.5 NPV distribution at time $t = 5$ for an in-the-money forward starting single-period swap with start in $t = 9$ and maturity in $t = 10$. The distributions are computed in three different risk-neutral measures – the bank account measure, the T-forward measure with $T = 10$ and the LGM measure. Due to calibration to the same market data, all three distributions agree on the expected NPV and expected $\max(NPV, 0)$. However, quantile values clearly differ and are measure dependent

Measure-dependent peak exposures

Basel II recommends combining Monte Carlo based EEPE simulations for credit capital calculation with peak exposure evaluations under the same method for counterparty credit risk management and limit setting. As we elaborated above, one might use "drift-adjusted" versions of risk-neutral market scenario generators to produce real-world scenarios. While risk-neutral scenario generators – if calibrated to the same market data – will agree on expected exposures, this is generally not the case for any quantile or other tail risk measure such as expected shortfall. This is illustrated for a particularly simple case in Figure 24.5. This measure-dependence "of the tails" should therefore be taken into account when choosing a measure for credit risk management purposes.

Basel III

Reacting to the financial crisis following Lehman's default in 2008, the Basel Committee for Banking Supervision finally issued "Basel III" in 2010 [18]. Basel III introduces additional capital requirements and a minimum leverage ratio. The new liquidity requirements (Liquidity Coverage Ratio and Net Stable Funding Ratio) were added to ensure liquidity over the next 30 days and stable funding over a one-year period of extended stress, respectively. These measures are phased in over a transition period between 2014 and 2019. Basel III moreover extended the risk coverage in particular by

- stronger focus on wrong-way risk,
- an increased margin period of risk,
- a revised short-cut method for estimating Effective EPE if collateral cannot be accurately modelled,
- enforcing exposure calculation under stress calibrations, see 24.5,
- adding a capital charge for CVA, see Section 24.7.

Finally, the exposure system's integrity and consistency is further strengthened by requiring *"a regular programme of backtesting, i.e. an ex-post comparison of the risk measures generated by the model against realised risk measures, as well as comparing hypothetical changes based on static positions with realised measures."*. We will return to backtesting in detail in Section 25.3.

Stressed parameters for counterparty risk

Prior to the crisis banks could calibrate their risk factors to a wide range of possibilities. These did not, however, have to include a crisis. Thus, if the bank did not include a business cycle within its calibration and, more to the point, have a model that was capable of including all parts of the business cycle, then it might have insufficient capital to meet a crisis. Creating regime dependent models was significantly more sophisticated than most banks were willing to pay for — at least this is the authors' conjecture. Hence the regulators have decided to impose something simple and effective: calculate under normal and crisis conditions and take the worst result as your capital requirement.

- Banks must calculate the default risk capital charge under current market conditions and under stressed market conditions and take the worst at a total portfolio level. That is, across all netting sets and all counterparties.
- The stressed calibration must be a single consistent stress for all counterparties.
- If calibration is historical, then three years of data must be used. If not, market-implied parameters must be updated at least quarterly (or more if conditions indicate).
- Stress is defined as a period when the CDS spreads of a representative selection of the bank's counterparties are elevated.
- This does not include the CVA risk capital charge (Section 24.7).

Will this recipe produce a good outcome in the next crisis? The problem is that this depends on exactly what the next crisis is. However, it will have done its job well if it prevents a repeat of the previous crisis. Preventing all possible crises, whilst permitting banking to continue as a profitable activity, is too much to ask for.

There is one point to note with respect to this recipe – it will probably only be applied to the previous crisis. This is reasonable in that this crisis was the worst since the Great Depression. However, the crisis was a credit crisis, not an inflation crisis like that of the oil shocks in the 1970s. Thus the interest rates that will appear in the recipe will not control interest rate induced capital volatility because the interest rates during the crisis were very low compared to historical highs.

24.6 Capital requirements for centrally cleared derivatives

Central counterparties (CCPs) are viewed as a means for reducing counterparty credit risk in the derivatives business. They are subject to strong regulation and have a default fund which makes them near risk-free. Nevertheless, as we already mentioned in Chapter 3, the power of the CCP to call upon surviving direct members to replenish the default fund exposes them to their fellow members' potential bankruptcy. Furthermore, there is a residual credit exposure[6] to the CCP for direct members and their clients alike. These two remaining sources of CCR are recognized by the Basel Committee for Banking Supervision (BCBS) in its publication [19], later clarified by an FAQ document [20]. The paper specifies the risk weights for such exposures.

According to [19], the risk weight for any exposure of a member to a CCP[7] gets a risk weight of 2%. Likewise, the exposure of a client to either the intermediary member or the CCP directly (where a member guarantees the performance) gets a risk weight of 2%. The exposure of a clearing member to one of its clients is treated as for a normal OTC trade; the only difference is that the margin period of risk (MPR) may be shorter, thus reducing the EAD by up to 29%, depending on the method used for measuring exposure.

If a direct member is acting as intermediary between the CCP and one of its clients, the member does not have to hold capital against the CCP unless it guarantees the CCP's performance to the client. In this case, the 2% risk weight applies as well.

The exposure of a direct member to the default fund (and hence its fellow members) can be calculated by one of two methods. The simpler method just adds the member's default fund contribution, multiplied by 12.5, to the capital

[6] The exposure is calculated according to the bank's chosen method, that is, either IMM, CEM or SA-CCR.

[7] More precisely, a *qualifying* CCP, but we do not go into details here. See [19].

requirement of the trades (2% of the exposure). The result is capped at 20% of the trade exposure.

The second, more complicated method requires information on the default fund contribution and exposures of the other members.[8] This data is used to compute the losses to the default fund due to the default of two average members; the losses are then distributed to the surviving members according to their participation in the fund. For details, see [19] and [20].

Derivatives with CCPs are exempt from the CVA capital charge which is meant to give a further incentive to use central clearing.

24.7 CVA capital charge

We saw in Chapter 21 that Basel III [18] requires a CVA capital charge that covers the risk associated with CVA moves. The Basel Committee on Banking Supervision (BCBS) wrote in [18]:

> "during the financial crisis [CVA risk] was a greater source of losses than those arising from outright defaults".

Alas, the source of this wisdom is not handed down. Pykhtin [126] even claims (without giving a concrete source) that

> "the Basel Committee noted that CVA losses accounted for two-thirds of CCR losses during the 2007–2009 financial crisis."

The method to compute the CVA charge is prescribed by the regulator; a bank can only choose between a standard approach or an internal model method (IMM) approach. The charge can be mitigated by hedging with CDS where possible. CDS can be done on individual names or on indices. Centrally cleared trades are exempt from the CVA charge.

24.7.1 The standard approach

First of all, each counterparty gets a weight depending on its rating; the weights range from 0.7% for AAA-rated counterparties to 10% for CCC-rated counterparties. If an index x is used for hedging, it also has to be assigned a weight

[8] One requirement for a CCP to be considered a qualifying CCP is to be able to provide this information to its direct members.

w^x. The charge K is then given by

$$K = 2.33 \cdot \left(\left[\frac{1}{2} \sum_i w_i \left(M_i \, EAD_i - M_i^h \, B_i \right) - \sum_j w_j^x \, M_j^x \, B_j^x \right]^2 + \frac{3}{4} \sum_i w_i^2 \left(M_i \, EAD_i - M_i^h \, B_i \right)^2 \right)^{\frac{1}{2}}, \tag{24.13}$$

where

w_i	weight of counterparty i
w_j^x	weight of index j
M_i	effective maturity of portfolio with CP i
M_i^h	effective maturity of CDS hedge(s) on CP i
M_j^x	effective maturity of CDS index hedge(s)
B_i	notional of portfolio with CP i
B_i^h	notional of CDS hedge(s) on CP i
B_j^x	notional of CDS index hedge(s)
EAD_i	exposure at default for CP i, computed including collateral as described in Section 24.4.

If counterparty i is a constituent of an index j, the notional B_j^h may be reduced by the amount attributable to CP i, and B_i^h may be increased by that amount instead, if the regulator approves.

Pykhtin [126] shows that Formula (24.13) is a conservative estimate of CVA VaR under the assumption that CVA is only driven by one systematic (credit) risk factor. Pykhtin's paper has become an official source for the derivation of the standard formula, see EBA [13].

24.7.2 The IMM approach

Here we assume that banks with IMM approval also have Specific Interest Rate Risk VaR model approval. This is called the Advanced CVA risk capital charge. Both approvals are required because machinery from both areas is used. The pieces are put into the bank's VaR model for bonds but only considering changes in credit spreads. This VaR model restriction means that wrong-way risk will not be included in the calculation. Equally, right-way risk will also be excluded.

The following formula must be used as part of the calculation of the charge; it is defined in [18] proscriptively.

$$
\begin{aligned}
CVA &= LGD \sum_{i=1}^{N} \max\left(0, \exp\left(-\frac{s_{i-1}\, t_{i-1}}{LGD}\right) - \exp\left(-\frac{s_i\, t_i}{LGD}\right)\right) \\
&\quad \times \left(\frac{EE_{i-1}\, D_{i-1} + EE_i\, D_i}{2}\right) \qquad (24.14) \\
&= LGD \sum_{i=1}^{N} \max(0, \text{PD in interval } i) \times \left(\text{average exposure in interval } i\right),
\end{aligned}
$$

where

$[t_{i-1}, t_i]$	i^{th} period, $t_0 = 0$
t_N	longest contractual maturity with the counterparty
EE_i	regulatory expected exposure
s_i	CDS spread of the CP at t_i; if this is not available then any proxy must be based on rating, industry and region
LGD	market assessment of LGD loss given default, *not* an internal assessment
D_i	default risk-free discount factor at time t_i.

How Equation (24.14) is used depends on the bank's VaR engine as follows:

- Full revaluation: Use Equation (24.14) as it is within the calculation.
- Sensitivities per tenor: Use the sensitivity approximation

$$0.0001 \cdot t_i \cdot \exp\left(-\frac{s_i\, t_i}{LGD}\right)\left(\frac{EE_{i-1}\, D_{i-1} - EE_{i+1}\, D_{i+1}}{2}\right).$$

- Parallel shifts: Use the sensitivity approximation

$$
\begin{aligned}
&LGD \sum_{i=1}^{N} \left(t_i \cdot \exp\left(-\frac{s_i\, t_i}{LGD}\right) - t_{i-1} \cdot \exp\left(-\frac{s_{i-1}\, t_{i-1}}{LGD}\right)\right) \\
&\quad \times \left(\frac{EE_{i-1}\, D_{i-1} + EE_i\, D_i}{2}\right).
\end{aligned}
$$

- Second-order: As parallel but with additional second-order terms.

The VaR engine has to be used twice in the capital calculation because stressed VaR is part of capital calculations, too. Thus the result is the sum of the stressed and non-stressed VaR. For the stressed VaR, the stressed *EE* profiles must be used together with a VaR calibration to the worst one-year period within the three-year stressed period chosen for counterparty credit risk.

24.7.3 Mitigation of the CVA capital charge

[18] clarifies which types of mitigation are allowed. Furthermore, certain mitigation strategies are explicitly forbidden.

- Only hedges expressly targeted for CVA risk and managed as such may be included in the VaR model used to calculate the CVA capital charge. Using existing CDS trades from other portfolios in the bank is not sufficient.
- The only eligible hedges, which have to be removed from the bank's market risk capital calculation, are:
  - Single-name CDSs
  - Single-name contingent CDSs[9]
  - Equivalent hedging instruments referencing the counterparty directly
  - Index CDSs where the basis between the counterparty and the index is included in the VaR model. The same applies if a CDS on a proxy for the counterparty is used. When no spread is available, a representative basket of similar names may be used.
- The following trades are not eligible for mitigation:
  - n-th to default CDSs
  - Tranched structures.

24.7.4 Exemptions

While the Basel III CVA capital charge has in principle been adopted in European legislation, there are many exemptions from the CVA capital charge in Europe (see the Capital Requirements Regulation (CRR)[121]): By Article 382(3), any derivatives with a CCP are exempt. Furthermore, Article 382(4) specifies that

> The following transactions shall be excluded from the own funds requirements for CVA risk:
>
> (a) transactions with non-financial counterparties as defined in point (9) of Article 2 of Regulation (EU) No 648/2012, or with non-financial counterparties established in a third country, [...]
>
> (b) intragroup transactions [...]

[9] CDS on a changing value, e.g. the market value of a derivatives portfolio

> (c) transactions with counterparties referred to in point (10) of Article 2 of Regulation (EU) No 648/2012 and subject to the transitional provisions set out in Article 89(1) of that Regulation until those transitional provisions cease to apply;[10]
>
> (d) transactions with counterparties referred to in Article 1(4)(a) and (b) and Article 1(5)(a), (b) and (c) of Regulation (EU) No 648/2012 and transactions with counterparties for which Article 115 of this Regulation specifies a risk weight of 0% for exposures to those counterparties.[11]
>
> The exemption from the CVA charge for those transactions referred to in point (c) of this paragraph) which are entered into during the transitional period laid down in Article 89(1) of Regulation (EU) No 648/2012 shall apply for the length of the contract of that transaction.

That actually does not leave much for which the charge has to be applied. The official reason for these exemptions is that the CVA charge would entice banks to buy protection against credit defaults on those kinds of entities, which would increase demand for CDS. This in turn would lead to higher CDS spreads and market-implied default probabilities, and hence the CVA value itself would increase, leading to an even higher demand for CDS protection. Exempting the above-mentioned entities from the CVA capital charge would prevent such an upward spiral. Cynics say that the European governments do not want to pay the banks' capital cost when doing derivatives with them. It is a fact that the CDS market is drying up rather than growing.

Other countries such as Switzerland, Japan or the USA do not have these exemptions. Local European regulators like the Bundesanstalt für Finanzdienstleistungsaufsicht (BaFin) in Germany consider making this charge mandatory for such deals anyway (see [43]) – local regulators are allowed to use more conservative rules than Basel III. As a result, regulation is getting more fragmented rather than unified across the globe.

In a recent opinion paper, the European Banking Authority (EBA) has performed an investigation [12] of the impact that reneging on the exemption would have. The result is described as follows on p. 54:

> The total own funds requirements for CVA risks of the 26 participating banks that provided the impacts were EUR 12.4 billion as of 31 March 2014. After removing the EU exemptions from the CVA risk charge (i.e. using the Basel scope), this figure would rise to EUR 31.1 billion (increase of more than 150%).
>
> To give an order of magnitude of this impact, the total aggregated own funds requirements for CVA risks of 192 European banks, for which the EBA receives

[10] These are transactions with pension funds.

[11] These refer to supra-national entities, sovereigns and such sub-sovereigns that have a risk-weighting of 0.

> the COREP submissions, amounted to EUR 23.5 billion as of 31 March 2014. Assuming that the impact of removing the EU exemptions from the CVA risk charge would fall within the range of +100% to +200% (large extrapolation from the actual impacts calculated for 26 banks), the total aggregated own funds requirements for CVA risks after removing the EU exemptions would be comprised between EUR 47 billion and EUR 70 billion (in absolute values of additional own funds requirements, between EUR 23.5 billion and EUR 46.5 billion).

In an accompanying opinion paper [13], the EBA recommends dispensing with the exemptions from the Basel III standard. Apparently such an action would not be so simple, see p. 58 in [12]:

> As specified in CRR Article 456(2), redefining or removing EU exemptions is outside the scope of the provisions that the Commission is empowered to amend via delegated act. Only the clients' trade exemption set out under CRR Article 382(3) could be amended via delegated act.
>
> Therefore, regardless of any action that could be undertaken in the short-term to monitor or partially mitigate excessive risks generated by EU exemptions, only a full legislative process will be able to address the issues raised by EU exemptions in a consistent manner across the EU.

Further recommendations include:

- CVA should be moved to the market risk framework and treated as a fair value adjustment subject to prudent valuation requirements;
- Market risk hedges of CVA (interest rate, FX hedges, etc.) should be recognized as eligible hedges;
- Subject to conditions, advanced institutions should be allowed to use their internal CVA pricing models (without reference to the regulatory formula) for the purposes of computing the own funds requirement for CVA risks.

25 Backtesting

25.1 Introduction

Backtesting arises in several contexts in financial applications, for example as the need to test the effectiveness of a particular trading strategy by performing a backtest over a significant period, or the need to backtest a VaR model by comparing the distribution of realized profit and loss (PnL) to the values predicted by the VaR model.

In this chapter we look at backtesting in the context of the regulatory requirement to backtest models used for capital requirement calculations. We look at the specific example of the current Basel Committee regulations (Basel III), though the framework has wider applicability beyond this.

We will first review the theory and background to a consistent approach for backtesting. Then we will go on to discuss the application to Risk Factor Evolution (RFE) backtesting in Section 25.3 and portfolio backtesting in Section 25.4 with concrete examples.

25.2 Backtest model framework

The model framework that we discuss in this chapter was first introduced by Kenyon and Stamm [107] and later extended by Anfuso et al. [10]. At the high level we have the following setup. We are equipped with a model, complete with calibration procedure, which we will use to make assertions about the future conditional on today's information (for example the expected exposure (EE) of a derivative portfolio or the future value of a particular swap rate). This model is one of those we have discussed earlier in this book, that is an SDE for the evolution of a set of market variables and an associated calibration procedure (risk-neutral or real world).

We wish to have a rational basis for deciding whether that model makes acceptable predictions about the future, and we wish to decide this on the basis of the model's performance in making such predictions in the past, that is a backtest. We will formulate this decision (accept or reject the model) as a classical hypothesis test. We will look to reduce the performance measure for the model to a single statistic (or set of statistics), that is a number with a sampling distribution. Armed with such a distribution we can then accept (or reject) the hypothesis that the model is consistent with the observed history at our desired confidence level.

Our models, whether for RFE or portfolios, make forecasts about the distribution of future values based on today's and past information; that is, for any variable, we have the distribution of that variable at a future time conditional on today's value. This distribution may be available analytically or only numerically, but let us assume we can evaluate it in some form. Then we can use the standard machinery of the probability integral transform (PIT) to determine whether the observed realizations of the variable are consistent with the forecast distribution using the procedure set out below. First, however, an observation that forms the basis of the PIT. Assume we have a continuous random variable X and the associated cumulative density function (CDF), $F(X)$. Then the new variable $Y = F(X)$ is uniformly distributed. This is briefly shown as follows:

$$\begin{aligned}\mathbb{P}(Y \leq k) &= \mathbb{P}(F(X) \leq k)\\ &= \mathbb{P}(X \leq F^{-1}(k))\\ &= F(F^{-1}(k))\\ &= k,\end{aligned}$$

where $k \in [0, 1]$, which is the definition of a uniformly distributed random variable.

Armed with the PIT we can proceed as follows. We have a time series of historical data available to us, say on n dates in the past, t_i, $i = 1 \ldots n$. For each past date t_i we can calibrate our model and extract the CDF $F_i(\delta)$ for a financial variable's evolution δ over a horizon h, that is the subsequent time interval of length h. The variable may be for example a five-year swap rate, an FX rate, an equity price, etc. The time horizon h does not necessarily agree with the time interval $t_{i+1} - t_i$ between observations. For each of the n past intervals we also have the realized change of the financial variable's value over the horizon h, $\delta_i = x(t_i + h) - x(t_i)$, and we can determine $y_i = F_i(\delta_i)$. Clearly, all y_i are confined to the $[0, 1]$ range by construction. If, moreover, the model's CDF $F_i(\cdot)$ is perfectly consistent with the distribution of realized moves δ_i, then the sample of n values y_i should be a sample from the uniform distribution. Thus, we have reduced the problem to testing whether the sample $\{y_i\}$, $i = 1 \ldots n$ *is* a sample from the uniform distribution. We can pose this question in the form of a hypothesis test, that is we hypothesize that $\{y_i\}$, $i = 1 \ldots n$ is indeed a sample from the uniform distribution at our desired confidence interval (say 95% or 99%). We now set about framing that hypothesis test.

Let us reduce the question of uniformity of a sample of numbers to a single distance metric. That is, for every sample $\{y_i\} = F_i(\delta_i)$ we will compute a distance number d as follows:

$$d = \int_{-\infty}^{\infty} (F_n(x) - F(x))^2 \, w(x) \, dF(x), \tag{25.1}$$

where $F_n(x)$ is the empirical (sample) cumulative distribution function (CDF) of the sequence of values y_i, $F(x)$ is the desired model's CDF, and $w(x)$ is a weighting function that weights the squared distance from the sample distribution to the desired distribution. With various choices of the weighting function $w(x)$ we can place emphasis on different parts of the distribution. Common choices or named tests are

$$w(x) = \begin{cases} 1 & \text{Cramer-von-Mises} \\ (1 - F(x))/F(x) & \text{Anderson-Darling} \\ H(F(x) - a)/a & \text{one-sided tail test} \\ H(F(x) - a)/a + H(b - F(x))/b & \text{two-sided tail test} \end{cases}$$

where $H(z)$ is the heavyside function with $H(z) = 1$ for $z > 0$ and $H(z) = 0$ otherwise. We note that these tests check the distance from uniformity of the sample across the entire distribution. The Cramer-von-Mises test applies no particular weighting, the Anderson-Darling function weights the regions around the ends of the distribution more heavily than the central part, whereas the tail tests pick out the behaviours in one or both tails of the distribution.

Thus armed with a distance metric, d, we can now proceed to generate a sampling distribution of d from within our calibrated model. That can sometimes be done analytically (in the case of non-overlapping time periods), but generally needs to be done numerically. If being done numerically, we proceed to generate a large number of sample model paths, $j = 1 \ldots m$, and on each path we compute d_j using Equation (25.1). The distribution of d_j is the numerically generated sampling distribution of d. We then produce the distance for the realized path in history d_{real}. We can produce a p value for d_{real} depending on where it sits in the sampling distribution, and so we are able to accept or reject the hypothesis that the realized path is consistent with the model at our desired confidence level.

For a small number of cases (e.g. the Anderson-Darling test with non-overlapping sampling time periods) it is possible to produce the sampling distribution analytically (at least asymptotically), and we will consider that case in the next section. In general, when we are dealing with overlapping time periods (i.e. results from adjacent time periods that cannot be considered independent as they share common information) or when we are dealing with models that are not analytically tractable, we will use numerical methods (Monte-Carlo simulation) to produce the sampling distributions for our distance statistic.

25.2.1 Example: Anderson-Darling test

In this section we will give one of the few examples where this procedure can be implemented analytically. Let us consider one of the simplest models possible for the evolution of a single interest rate, say the one-month money market rate, and that we look at its evolution over a time horizon of one month. In this way, a history of ten years' worth of data would give us 120 independent monthly observations of the realized change in this interest rate. We will model the rate as being normally distributed with zero drift (that is, the expected rate in the future is todays rate) and a fixed volatility, σ. If $x(t)$ is our interest rate at time t, then our simple model says that the rate change δ_i over the horizon h is

$$\delta_i = x(t_i + h) - x(t_i) \simeq N(0;\sigma).$$

So the function $F_n(X)$ is the cumulative normal distribution with mean zero and standard deviation σ, $\Phi(x;\sigma)$, in this example. For each δ_i we can compute $y_i = \Phi(\delta_i;\sigma)$ and we can compute the Anderson-Darling distance using 25.1. However, it turns out that this integral representation has a more convenient finite sum representation (see e.g. [9]) as

$$d = -n - \frac{1}{n}\sum_{j=1}^{n}(2j-1)\left[\ln y_j + \ln(1 - y_{n-j+1})\right]. \tag{25.2}$$

In the case where the y_i can be assumed to be independent and identically distributed, as they are in this case, the large n asymptotic form of the sampling distribution of d is known analytically, see for example [9], and, for example, the 95% confidence level value of d is 2.492, meaning that 95% of random samples of 120 observations of a normal variable will have an Anderson-Darling distance less than 2.492. Figure 25.1 shows the statistical distribution for the Anderson-Darling test with 120 non-overlapping observations.

25.3 RFE backtesting

The first plank of a backtesting approach is to ensure that the evolution models for the underlying risk factors driving the future exposure of the portfolio pass a backtest. In any future exposure framework, we will have calibrated models that evolve the key interest rates, FX rates, credit spreads and other economically relevant drivers of the portfolio value. In practice we do not have an infinite history from which to choose, for example the CDS spread market did not even exist before the early years of the millennium, and thus there is no more than a decade of

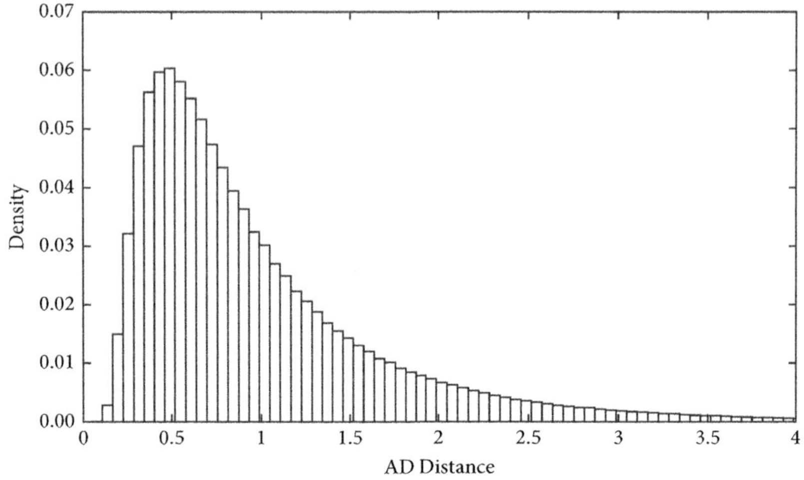

Figure 25.1 Statistical distribution for the Anderson-Darling distance *d* with 120 non-overlapping observations with 95% quantile at 2.49 and 99% quantile at 3.89, as computed using the asymptotic approximation from [9]

history available. Further, we are obliged to deal with time horizons which are relevant for the exposures of the portfolio, which may mean that we care about time horizons of five years or beyond. These dual constraints of availability of history and long time horizons mean that we inevitably have to deal with overlapping time periods or autocorrelation in the data. In the example of Section 25.2.1 we had the luxury of dealing with a short horizon and thus could consider the observations as identically independently distributed, allowing us to use analytical results for the sampling distribution. For any longer time horizon we have to deal with the autocorrelation. The change that this brings is that we must numerically generate the sampling distribution of distances. Without access to analytical results, the sampling distribution of distances must be produced numerically using Monte Carlo simulation.

25.3.1 Creating the sample distance and sampling distribution

Calculating the distance for the realized values is a straightforward matter of (a) selecting the distance metric (Anderson-Darling, Cramer-von-Mises, etc.) and (b) calculating the distance using the formula (25.1).

The calculation of the sampling distribution of distances is more involved. We must create a large number of consistent paths through history for the risk drivers in our portfolio according to our evolution model, then calculate the distance along each path using (25.1). We know that – if time periods are non-overlapping –

the resulting sampling distribution is independent of the evolution model, so the purpose of numerically constructing the sampling distribution is to capture the degree of autocorrelation inherent in our evolution model.

Finally, once we have the sampling distribution of distances, our remaining task is to determine the p value for our realized history and accept or reject the hypothesis at the desired confidence level.

25.3.2 Example I: Risk-neutral LGM

In this section we consider an LGM short rate model for the evolution of the euro yield curve and use it to backtest the realized rates against the forecast distributions. In particular, we will backtest a market-implied model that is calibrated to the yield curve and market quoted swaptions. This example will be illustrative of the diagnostic strengths of the PIT approach. Let us start with a look at interest rate evolution from 1999 to 2015 as shown in Figure 25.2. Note that the rates of all tenors generally declined from the 5%–6% peak levels in 2000/2001 down to 0%–1% levels by Q1 2015 with relatively short interim periods of rate increases, and with particularly steep declines in at least four periods since Lehman's default in 2008. On the other hand, the euro yield curve was usually normal, that is upward sloping, for most of the time (except around 2008), implying a positive short rate drift throughout the entire period of declining rates. Running the backtest machinery on the full period (1999–2015) with monthly observations and a one-month horizon yields the corresponding PIT graph as shown in Figure 25.3. We have picked here only the ten-year zero rate tenor; shorter tenors yield similar results. In case of a

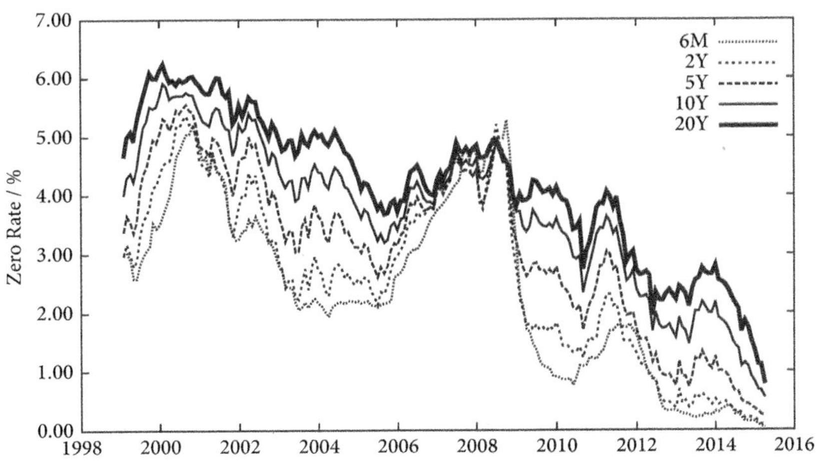

Figure 25.2 Evolution of euro interest rates (continuously compounded zero rates with tenors between 6M and 20Y, derived from EUR Sswap curves) in the period from 1999 to 2015

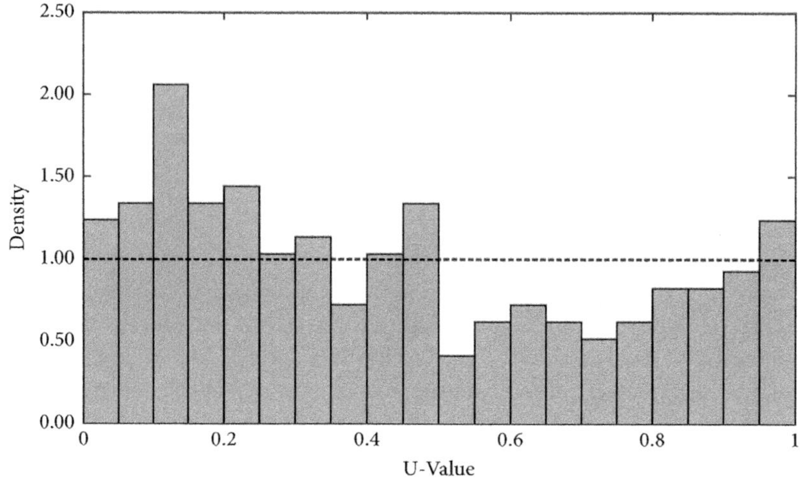

Figure 25.3 PIT for the backtest of 10Y zero rates with monthly observations (1999–2015) of moves over a one-month horizon

good fit between model and real evolution, we would expect to see a histogram that approximates a uniform distribution. However, in this case we see a pronounced bias towards the left side of the PIT which means that quite often we experience rate moves which are lower than the model predicts. The reason is obvious from the rate evolution as mentioned above – model drift is positive whereas real drift is negative on average in the period considered. The PIT can be turned into an Anderson-Darling distance measure, and we find $d \approx 6.4$ which corresponds to the 99.96% quantile of the Anderson-Darling statistic in Figure 25.1, or a *p-value* of 0.04% (the complement of the quantile). Table 25.1 shows that the p-values are similarly low across various zero rate tenors and horizons. A p-value of less than 5% would usually be considered critical, p-values less than 1% for a significant part of the backtests as in Table 25.1 would suggest rejecting the initial hypothesis that the model is consistent with reality. The last two columns in Table 25.1 list the number of "exceptions" (counts) of u-values below 5% and above 95%, respectively. One would expect less than ten exceptions on each side for the 183–194 observations used. The excessive counts at the lower end confirm our previous comments and the low p-values below 1% across all tenors and horizons. Note that the number of available observations reduces with increasing horizon given a limited time series of 194 monthly data points.

To illustrate the sensitivity of the backtest approach and narrow down the "problem period" which causes the test to fail, let us proceed by cutting the available history into two parts of similar length, one from 1999 to the end of 2006, the second from 2007 to today, where the former is clearly the more "normal" period

Table 25.1 Anderson-Darling statistics for various horizons and zero rate tenors using a risk-neutral LGM calibration and 1999–2015 history

Horizon	Tenor	Observations	*d*	p-value	Ex < 5%	Ex > 95%
1M	3Y	194	6.0119	0.0006	11	11
1M	5Y	194	8.0867	0.0000	13	13
1M	7Y	194	7.8554	0.0000	14	12
1M	10Y	194	6.3976	0.0004	12	12
3M	3Y	192	14.7900	0.0008	24	8
3M	5Y	192	19.1908	0.0000	19	8
3M	7Y	192	19.2282	0.0006	21	9
3M	10Y	192	16.6399	0.0000	22	11
6M	3Y	189	24.4498	0.0040	22	8
6M	5Y	189	29.8554	0.0012	30	8
6M	7Y	189	28.9830	0.0018	34	11
6M	10Y	189	24.6337	0.0044	32	10
1Y	3Y	183	44.4968	0.0070	32	6
1Y	5Y	183	52.5185	0.0032	35	6
1Y	7Y	183	49.7923	0.0036	39	5
1Y	10Y	183	42.6875	0.0074	31	5

with fewer and less steep rate drops, that is less stress. If we perform the same analysis now for these two periods we find the PITs shown in Figure 25.4. None of the PITs is close to uniform, but the 1999–2006 is clearly more balanced, and the 2007–2015 PIT seems even more biased to the left than the full-period PIT in Figure 25.3. Correspondingly, the Anderson-Darling p-values for the latter are worse (lower) than the ones for the full period PIT. On the other hand, the Anderson-Darling test for the early period is all "green", with p-values well above 5% across all horizons and tenors we have inspected, leading to an acceptance of the hypothesis. The results are displayed in Table 25.2. This shows, as expected, that the crisis years following events in 2008, with several periods of steeply decreasing rates, cause the test to fail. We could continue narrowing down the stress period, but let us stop here. Our conclusion is that the risk-neutral LGM model clearly does not pass the Anderson-Darling test when the backtest time window contains the Lehman stress period. We need to explore alternatives which can cope with such periods. Let us have a look at one alternative in the following section.

25.3.3 Example II: Risk-neutral LGM with drift adjustment

In Section 24.3.2 we had a look at a simple approach which uses – as a starting point – an interest rate model, calibrated to yield curve and quoted option prices. The model's risk-neutral (short rate) drift is thereafter adjusted to zero up to the backtest horizon to generate an entirely unprejudiced forecast to the backtest horizon. Rather than trying to calibrate accurately to the past "drift" in order to

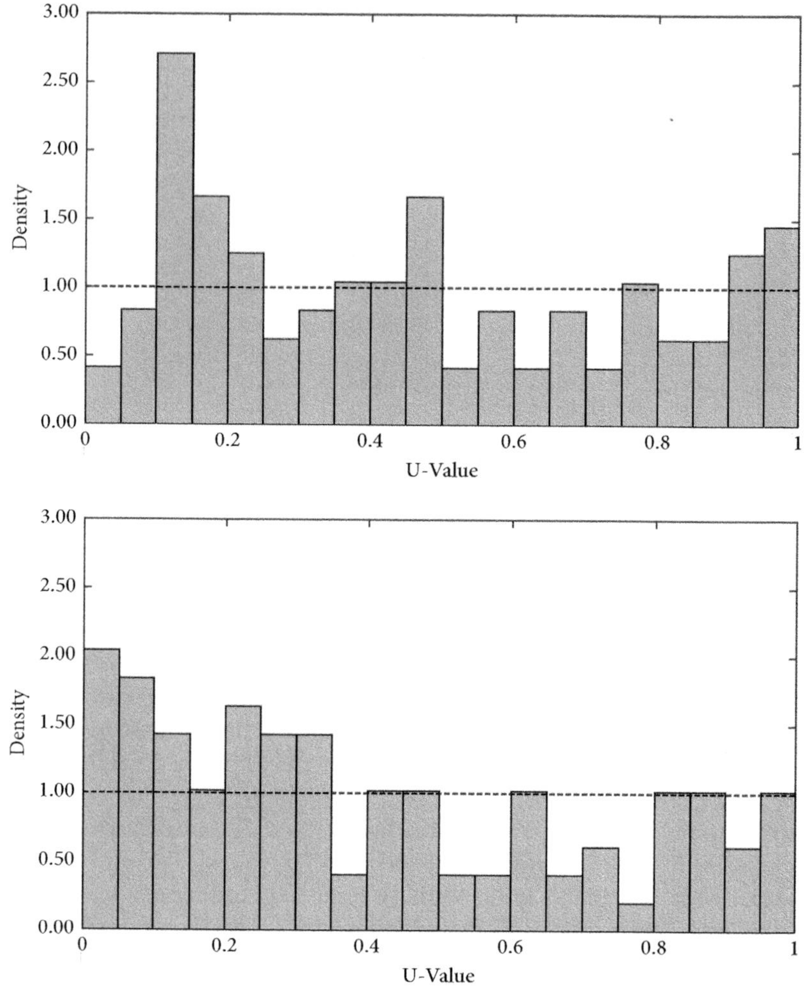

Figure 25.4 PIT for the backtest of 10Y zero rates as in Figure 25.3. Top: Period 1999–2006. Bottom: Period 2007–2015

increase our chances to pass a backtest, we assume indifferent zero "drift" since past evolution is not necessarily a reliable indicator for future evolution either.

In the following we show the backtesting performance of such a drift-adjusted LGM model against the full 1999–2015 interest rate history including the stress periods. The usual PIT is shown in Figure 25.5, and the Anderson-Darling p-values for a range of zero rate tenors and backtest horizons are shown in Table 25.3. This model is under pressure as well over the full period with some p-values in the

Table 25.2 Anderson-Darling statistics for the early period 1999–2006. The number of 96 observations is constant here as we can use 2007 data for evaluating the realized moves over all horizons shown here

Horizon	Tenor	Observations	*d*	p-value	Ex < 5%	Ex > 95%
1M	3Y	96	1.9226	0.0982	7	7
1M	5Y	96	2.1762	0.0684	5	8
1M	7Y	96	1.8094	0.1106	5	8
1M	10Y	96	1.6383	0.1400	2	7
3M	3Y	96	3.8060	0.1482	15	4
3M	5Y	96	3.6554	0.1601	12	3
3M	7Y	96	3.1991	0.2042	8	5
3M	10Y	96	2.8057	0.2510	6	6
6M	3Y	96	6.4275	0.1778	12	6
6M	5Y	96	6.4587	0.1812	13	7
6M	7Y	96	6.0301	0.1966	14	9
6M	10Y	96	5.8319	0.2206	10	8
1Y	3Y	96	10.8856	0.2071	15	6
1Y	5Y	96	11.7951	0.1924	16	6
1Y	7Y	96	11.2741	0.2087	15	5
1Y	10Y	96	10.2114	0.2424	13	5

3%–4% range for the short one-month horizon, but clearly a vast improvement compared to the plain risk-neutral model of the previous example.

25.4 Portfolio backtesting

Portfolio backtesting proceeds in theory in a very similar manner to RFE backtesting, with one important modification and one additional problem that requires solution. The modification is with respect to directionality. With an RFE backtest, we are concerned about over or under-estimation of the value of the risk factor. However, in portfolio backtesting, if our estimate of the value of the portfolio is conservative, that is, if we overestimate the value of the portfolio, we do not have an issue. The additional problem relates to the practicalities of portfolio selection.

If one is only concerned about the instances where the observed portfolio value is less than the predicted value, we can introduce a modified distance that only penalizes such instances. Following Anfuso et al. we can introduce a modified distance d_{cons} given by

$$d_{cons} = \int_{-\infty}^{\infty} (\max(F_n(x) - F(x), 0))^2 \, w(x) \, dF(x), \tag{25.3}$$

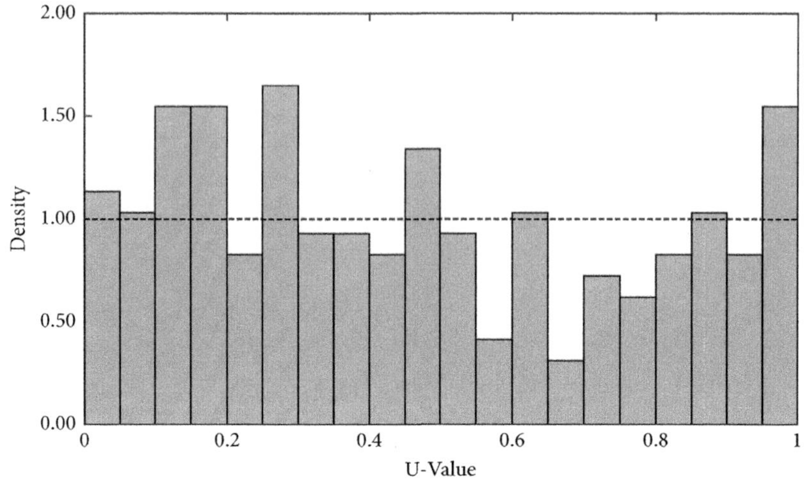

Figure 25.5 PIT for the backtest of 10Y zero rates for the full period 1999–2015 using an LGM model with drift adjustment as described in Section 24.3.2

where $F(n)$ is the sample distribution of the portfolio MtM distribution. With this modification the procedure goes through as before.

The remaining problem of portfolio selection can be tackled in two ways. The obvious choice is to select real and material counterparty portfolios and their evolutions through time. However, practical challenges of data collection and in particular long histories of trade evolution often militate against this approach. In addition changing portfolio composition through time makes it more challenging to pinpoint systematic weaknesses with specific trade types. The alternative approach is to construct synthetic portfolios, that is portfolios whose composition is chosen to test a specific aspect of the model, for example a portfolio containing in-the-money options where the strike is modified through time to keep the options at a predefined level of moneyness. In reality both approaches complement each other and are useful.

25.5 Outlook

The modelling approaches sketched in this book, in particular risk factor evolution models presented in Part III combined with "real-world" adjustments such as those in Sections 24.3.2 and 24.3.3, reflect the recent advances in the investment banking industry with respect to XVA and credit exposure simulation. The relatively basic RFE models of Part III seem acceptable in that they allow for computationally efficient calibration and simulation while keeping a relatively high level of accuracy.

Table 25.3 Anderson-Darling statistics for the full period 1999–2015 using an LGM model with drift adjustment as described in Section 24.3.2

Horizon	Tenor	Observations	*d*	p-value	Ex<5%	Ex>95%
1M	3Y	194	1.2377	0.2559	8	16
1M	5Y	194	2.6347	0.0436	9	16
1M	7Y	194	2.8720	0.0292	8	14
1M	10Y	194	2.7758	0.0374	11	15
3M	3Y	192	2.6084	0.2652	14	12
3M	5Y	192	4.7129	0.1048	12	14
3M	7Y	192	5.8430	0.0596	10	14
3M	10Y	192	6.2326	0.0550	15	13
6M	3Y	189	4.3717	0.3076	19	15
6M	5Y	189	6.3198	0.1786	16	14
6M	7Y	189	7.4351	0.1490	18	13
6M	10Y	189	8.2232	0.1248	21	13
9M	3Y	186	5.2743	0.3692	20	12
9M	5Y	186	8.4103	0.2413	14	11
9M	7Y	186	10.1129	0.1652	14	10
9M	10Y	186	11.1350	0.1388	14	9
1Y	3Y	183	8.4249	0.3084	23	14
1Y	5Y	183	10.3155	0.2426	20	10
1Y	7Y	183	12.1993	0.1990	19	7
1Y	10Y	183	13.5753	0.1644	16	6
2Y	3Y	171	27.9508	0.1438	35	9
2Y	5Y	171	32.3705	0.1222	26	6
2Y	7Y	171	36.9291	0.0906	21	6
2Y	10Y	171	42.0916	0.0648	10	1

This is key against the background of the complex task of computing the overall XVA and exposure numbers for all netting sets in a large portfolio of hundreds of thousands of derivative transactions. The complexity is still growing with the increasing need for XVA risk analysis or the need for taking "Dynamic Initial Margin" into account in MVA and credit exposure to CCPs.

In addition, the pressure from regulators is also rising with respect to the underlying RFE which have to become more realistic, at least under the following two aspects:

- The factor distributions across all asset classes as presented in Part III are either normal or log-normal thus far. It is well-known that this is unrealistic, and one has to consider local or stochastic volatility models that lead to richer distributions with fatter tails, as is done in accurate derivatives pricing (mark-to-market). For example, in equity space the Heston model would be a natural extension which still has a decent degree of analytical tractability; in

interest rate/FX space one should move to models that are consistent with the skew and smile observed in the swaption and FX option markets. Hagan's and Woodward's "β-η" model [81, 8] seems to be a natural extension of the interest rate modelling used in this text to capture the skew part of the volatility smile.
- The stochastic nature of volatility surfaces has not been addressed in Part III. We assumed there that today's volatility structure is static or moves forward through time without variation; when analysing the future exposure distribution of option products, this clearly tends to under-estimate the distribution's variance.

Such "enhanced" RFEs across asset classes as well as RFEs making use of stochastic volatility are an important area of extension which we are currently investigating and are hence beyond the scope of this text.

VI | Appendix

A The Change of Numeraire Toolkit

This appendix gives a short review of the change of numeraire toolkit as described in Brigo & Mercurio [33].

When pricing derivatives it is necessary to calculate expectations of future payoffs, usually discounted to the time of pricing. In many models, the discount factor is given as a function of the short rate which is defined in more detail in the text. We need the following definitions:

- The (stochastic) risk-free short rate r_t for $t >= 0$,
- The *bank account* $B_t = B(t) = \exp(\int_0^t r_s\, ds)$,
- The *stochastic discount factor*

$$D(t,T) = \frac{B_t}{B_T} = \exp\left(-\int_t^T r_s\, ds\right),$$

- The *zero bond prices* $P(t,T) = \mathbb{E}(D(t,T) \mid \mathcal{F}_t)$.

Pricing derivatives seems a hopeless task because we do not know the real probabilities of future events that drive market values. One can try to use historical data to glean information about this *real-world measure*, but from past shocks to the system it seems to be impossible to fully understand this measure. Yet we shall see below that prices can still be calculated, albeit under a different measure.

To explain this, we have to introduce two notions: arbitrage and completeness. A market is said to be *arbitrage-free* if it is not possible to produce a portfolio with zero investment that has a positive future value with positive probability. This is usually summarized by the saying "There is no such thing as a free lunch".

A market is said to be *complete* if every attainable claim can be replicated by a self-financing trading strategy. This means intuitively that a future payoff that is not too weird can be replicated by the basic instruments in the market.

If a market is arbitrage-free and complete, then there is a unique measure $\mathbb{Q}$ which is equivalent to the real-world measure (i.e. they have exactly the same null sets) such that the time-t value of any attainable claim H at time T is given by

$$\pi_t = \mathbb{E}(D(t,T)\cdot H \mid \mathcal{F}_t) = \mathbb{E}\left(\frac{B_t}{B_T} H \,\middle|\, \mathcal{F}_t\right) = B_t \cdot \mathbb{E}\left(\frac{H}{B_T} \,\middle|\, \mathcal{F}_t\right),$$

for any $0 \leq t \leq T$, and the process π_t is a martingale. The measure $\mathbb{Q}$ is called the risk-neutral measure.

When calculating π_t as above, we compare the development of an investment against the development of the (risk-free) bank account. We normalize the cash flow with the risk-free rate. We could use other positive price processes to normalize our cash flow. Such a positive price process of an asset that does not pay any dividends is called a *numeraire.*

Proposition

Assume that there is a numeraire process N_t and a probability measure $\mathbb{Q}^N$ which is equivalent to the real-world measure such that the time-t price H_t for any traded asset H without payments before time T, normalized by N_t, is a martingale:

$$\frac{H_t}{N_t} = \mathbb{E}^N\left(\frac{H_T}{N_T} \,\middle|\, \mathcal{F}_t\right), \quad 0 \leq t \leq T.$$

We know that in a complete, arbitrage-free market, $B(t)$ is such a numeraire.

(a) Assume we have another numeraire M_t. Then there is a measure $\mathbb{Q}^M$, equivalent to $\mathbb{Q}^N$, such that any traded asset H without payments before time T, normalized by M_t, is a martingale.

(b) The Radon-Nikodym derivative to change between the two measures is given by

$$\frac{d\mathbb{Q}^M}{d\mathbb{Q}^N} = \frac{M_T \cdot N_0}{M_0 \cdot N_T}.$$

This proposition has two important consequences, as described in [33]:

FACT 1: For any numeraire N_t, the time-t price π_t of any attainable claim H is a martingale. This follows from part (a) of the proposition.

FACT 2: For any numeraire N_t, the time-t price π_t of any attainable claim H is given by

$$\begin{aligned}\pi_t &= B_t \cdot \mathbb{E}\left(\frac{H}{B_T} \,\middle|\, \mathcal{F}_t\right)\\ &= N_t \cdot \mathbb{E}^N\left(\frac{H}{N_T} \,\middle|\, \mathcal{F}_t\right).\end{aligned}$$

This follows from part (b) of the proposition.

The art in derivatives pricing is very often to find the right numeraire which makes the computation of $\mathbb{E}^N(H/N_T \mid \mathcal{F}_t)$ easy. We give many examples for good choices in the text.

B | The Feynman-Kac Connection

The Feynman-Kac theorem allows us to make a connection between stochastic differential equations (SDE) and (non-stochastic) partial differential equations (PDE). We present it in the form of Shreve [136], Theorem 6.4.3 ("Discounted Feynman-Kac").

Consider the SDE

$$dX(t) = \mu(t,X)dt + \sigma(t,X)dW(t) \tag{B.1}$$

where W is a Brownian motion. For some Borel-measurable function h, let

$$f(t,x) := -\mathbb{E}^{t,x}\left(e^{-r(T-t)}h(X(T))\right) \tag{B.2}$$

be the expectation where X solves (B.1) satisfying the boundary condition $X(t) = x$. Assume that $\mathbb{E}^{t,x}(|h(X(T)|) < \infty$ for all t, x. Then f satisfies the PDE

$$\frac{\partial f}{\partial t} + \mu(t,x)\frac{\partial f}{\partial x} + \frac{1}{2}\sigma^2(t,y)\frac{\partial^2 f}{\partial x} - rf = 0, \qquad f(T,x) = g(x). \tag{B.3}$$

Conversely, if f is a function satisfying (B.3), then f can be represented in the form (B.2), see for example Theorem 8.2.1 in Øksendal [119]. More generally, and adapted to our financial applications, if f satisfies

$$\frac{\partial f}{\partial t} + \mu(t,x)\frac{\partial f}{\partial x} + \frac{1}{2}\sigma^2(t,y)\frac{\partial^2 f}{\partial x} - rf = h(t,x), \qquad f(T,x) = g(x) \tag{B.4}$$

where $r(x,t)$ is also a function of x and t, then f can be written as

$$f(t,x) = -\mathbb{E}^{t,x}\left[\int_t^T e^{-\int_t^u r(X(s),s)\,ds} h(u,X(u))\,du - e^{-\int_t^T r(X(s),s)\,ds} g(X(T))\right], \tag{B.5}$$

given that

$$\int_t^T \mathbb{E}_t\left\{\left[\sigma(t,X)\frac{\partial}{\partial x}Y(s,X)\right]^2\right\} < \infty.$$

C The Black76 Formula

C.1 The standard Black76 formula

In Black's model [27] it is assumed that variable F for future times t follows a Geometric Brownian Motion (GBM):

$$\frac{dF}{F} = \mu(t)\,dt + \sigma(t)\,dW(t).$$

This SDE has the solution

$$F(t) = F(0)\exp\left\{\int_0^t \left(\mu(s) - \frac{1}{2}\sigma^2(s)\right) ds + \int_0^t \sigma(s)\,dW(s)\right\} \tag{C.1}$$

so that log-returns $\ln(F/F_0)$ are normally distributed with variance and mean

$$v(t) = \int_0^t \sigma^2(s)\,ds$$

$$m(t) = \int_0^t \left(\mu(s) - \frac{1}{2}\sigma^2(s)\right) ds$$

The density of $\ln F$ is hence given by

$$p(\ln x, t) = \frac{1}{\sqrt{2\pi\,v(t)}}\exp\left(-\frac{(\ln(x/x_0) - m(t))^2}{2\,v(t)}\right) \tag{C.2}$$

The price of a European call option on F with expiry T and strike K is thus computed as

$$\begin{aligned}\Pi &= P(T)\,\mathbb{E}^T\left\{(F(T)-K)^+\right\}\\ &= P(T)\int_0^\infty [x-K]^+\, p(\ln x, T)\, d\ln x\\ &= P(T)\,\{F_0\,\Phi(d_+) - K\,\Phi(d_-)\}\end{aligned}$$

where $\Phi(\cdot)$ is the cumulative standard normal distribution and

$$d_+ = \frac{\ln F_0/K - m(T)}{\sqrt{v(T)}}, \qquad d_- = d_+ - v(T)$$

The price of a European put option is computed analogously. In summary one obtains the *Black76 formula*

$$\begin{aligned}\Pi &= P(T)\cdot \text{Black}(\omega, F_0, K, v(T), m(T))\\ \text{Black}(\omega, F, K, v) &= \omega\,\{F\,\Phi(\omega\, d_+) - K\,\Phi(\omega\, d_-)\}\end{aligned} \tag{C.3}$$

with $\omega = \pm 1$ for call and put, respectively. If F is a forward price or yield, and the Wiener process is assumed in the T-forward measure, then the Geometric Brownian Motion is drift free, $\mu(t) \equiv 0$, and $m(t) = -v(t)/2$ is redundant.

C.2 The normal Black76 formula

For items such as spreads or other processes that may become negative, it is more natural to assume that the drift-free stochastic process for the object is a standard martingale rather than a geometric Brownian Motion. In that case, the SDE for F has the form

$$dF = \sigma(t)\, dW^T(t),$$

which has the solution

$$F(t) = F(0) + \int_0^t \sigma(s)\, dW^T(s). \tag{C.4}$$

Then $F(t)$ is normally distributed with mean $F_0 = F(0)$ and variance $v^2 = \int_0^t \sigma^2(s)\, ds$. Hence, if we denote the standard normal distribution function by $\phi(x)$, we get

$$\begin{aligned}
&\mathbb{E}^T\left\{(F(T)-K)^+\right\}\\
&=\frac{1}{v}\int_{-\infty}^{\infty}(x-K)^+\cdot\phi\left(\frac{x-F(T)}{v}\right)dx\\
&=v\left(\phi\left(\frac{K-F(T)}{v}\right)+\frac{F(T)-K}{v}\left(1-\Phi\left(\frac{K-F(T)}{v}\right)\right)\right),
\end{aligned}$$

which, because of

$$\Phi(x)=1-\Phi(-x)$$

and

$$\phi(x)=\phi(-x)$$

gives us for $d=\frac{F(T)-K}{v}$:

$$\mathbb{E}^T\left\{(F(T)-K)^+\right\}=v\cdot(\phi(d)+d\cdot\Phi(d)).$$

The same calculation for a put option leads us to the *normal Black76 formula*

$$\begin{aligned}
\Pi &= P(T)\cdot\text{N-Black}(\omega,F(T),K,v(T))\\
\text{N-Black}(\omega,F,K,v) &= \{v\cdot\phi(d)+\omega\cdot(F(T)-K)\cdot\Phi(\omega\cdot d)\}.
\end{aligned}\tag{C.5}$$

with $\omega=\pm1$ for call and put, respectively.

D Hull-White Model

D.1 Summary

Hull and White's model is a one-factor model of the short rate $r(t)$, first published in [85] and generalized later [86]. Throughout this appendix, we use the following notation for the model:

$$dr(t) = \lambda\,(\theta(t) - r(t))\,dt + \sigma(t)\,dW(t), \tag{D.1}$$

with time-dependent volatility $\sigma(t)$ and mean reversion $\theta(t)$ and constant reversion speed λ. This model has the solution

$$\begin{aligned} r(t) &= \mu(t) + x(t) \\ \mu(t) &= r_0\,e^{-\lambda t} + \lambda \int_0^t e^{-\lambda(t-s)}\,\theta(s)\,ds \\ x(t) &= \int_0^t e^{-\lambda(t-s)}\,\sigma(s)\,dW(s) \end{aligned}$$

with mean

$$\mathbb{E}[r(t)] = \mu(t)$$

and variance

$$\mathbb{V}[r(t)] = \mathbb{V}[x(t)] = \int_0^t e^{-2\lambda(t-s)}\,\sigma^2(s)\,ds$$

Note that $r(t)$ has a normal distribution, fully specified by mean and variance above.

Zero bonds

The value at future time t of a zero bond with maturity T has a closed-form expression in the Hull-White model:

$$P(t,T) = \mathbb{E}^Q\left[e^{-\int_t^T r(s)\,ds}\right] = A(t,T)\,e^{-H(T-t)\,x(t)} \tag{D.2}$$

where

$$A(t,T) = \frac{P(0,T)}{P(0,t)}\exp\left\{-\frac{1}{2}\int_0^t \left[H^2(T-s) - H^2(t-s)\right]\sigma^2(s)\,ds\right\} \tag{D.3}$$

$$H(t) = \frac{1}{\lambda}\left(1 - e^{-\lambda t}\right)$$

Note that $P(t,T)$ has a log-normal distribution.

In the process of deriving (D.2) one eliminates drift $\mu(t)$ by claiming that $P(0,T)$ is consistent with today's yield term structure. The form of $\mu(t)$ which ensures consistency with today's yield term structure, is

$$\mu(t) = f(0,t) + \frac{1}{2}\frac{\partial}{\partial t}\int_0^t H^2(t-s)\,\sigma^2(s)ds. \tag{D.4}$$

where $f(0,t)$ is the instantaneous forward curve, $f(0,t) = -\partial_t \ln P(0,t)$. For constant volatility $\sigma(t) = \sigma$, the integral term simplifies to

$$\frac{1}{2}\frac{\partial}{\partial T}\int_0^T H^2(T-s)\,\sigma^2(s)ds = \frac{\sigma^2}{2\lambda^2}\left(1 - e^{-\lambda T}\right)^2.$$

If we integrate the drift (D.4), we can also write

$$\begin{aligned} e^{-\int_0^T \mu(t)\,dt} &= P(0,T)\times\exp\left(-\frac{1}{2}\int_0^T H^2(T-s)\,\sigma^2(s)ds\right) \\ &= P(0,T)\times\exp\left(-\frac{1}{2}\int_0^T (H(T)-H(s))^2\,\alpha^2(s)\,ds\right) \end{aligned} \tag{D.5}$$

where $\alpha(s) = e^{\lambda s}\sigma(s)$. Note that we get the same results (D.2-D.5) for time-dependent mean reversion speed $\lambda(t)$ with

$$H(t) = \int_0^t e^{-\beta(s)}ds, \qquad \beta(t) = \int_0^t \lambda(s)\,ds.$$

Zero bond options

The pricing formula of a zero bond option with expiry S, bond maturity $T > S$ and strike price K under the (convenient) S-forward measure is given by

$$\Pi(t) = N\, P(t,S)\mathbb{E}^S\left[(P(S,T) - K)^+\right]. \tag{D.6}$$

$P(S,T)$ has a log-normal distribution and no drift term under the S-forward measure, so that we can apply the Black76 formula (C.3). The outstanding piece of information is the variance Σ^2 which can be computed from the closed-form expression for $P(t,T) = A(t,T)\exp(-h_\lambda(T-t)\,r(t))$, using the mean and variance of $r(t)$:

$$\begin{aligned}\Sigma^2 &= \mathbb{E}[\ln^2 P(S,T)] - \mathbb{E}^2[\ln P(S,T)]\\ &= H_\lambda^2(T-S)\left(\mathbb{E}[r^2(S)] - \mathbb{E}^2[r(S)]\right) \;=\; H_\lambda^2(T-S)\,\mathbb{V}[r(S)]\\ &= H_\lambda^2(T-S)\int_0^S e^{-2\lambda(T-s)}\sigma^2(s)ds\end{aligned}$$

so that

$$\begin{aligned}\Pi(t) &= w\left\{P(t,T)\,\Phi(w\,d_+) - K\,P(t,S)\,\Phi(w\,d_-)\right\}\\ d_\pm &= \frac{1}{\Sigma}\ln\frac{P(t,T)}{K\,P(t,S)} \pm \frac{\Sigma}{2}\end{aligned}$$

Caps/Floors

A zero bond put/call is related to a caplet/floorlet price via the following correspondence between bond strike price K and caplet/floorlet strike k:

$$K = \frac{1}{1+\delta(S,T)\,k}$$

and

$$\Pi_{Caplet} = \frac{1}{K}\Pi_{Put}, \qquad \Pi_{Floorlet} = \frac{1}{K}\Pi_{Call}. \tag{D.7}$$

Coupon bond options

Recall that the price of a coupon bond at time t is

$$\Pi_{CB}(t) = N\sum_{i=1}^{n} c_i\delta_i P(t,t_i) + N\,P(t,t_n) = \sum_{i=1}^{n}\widetilde{c}_i P(t,t_i),$$

with

$$\widetilde{c}_i := \begin{cases} N\,c_i\delta_i & \text{for } i < n \\ N\,(1 + c_n\delta_n) & \text{for } i = n \end{cases}$$

The price of a coupon bond call option with expiry S under the risk-neutral measure is hence given by

$$CBCO(t,S,T) = \mathbb{E}^Q\left[e^{-\int_t^S r(s)ds}[\Pi_{CB}(S) - K]^+\right].$$

Note that in the HW model, $\Pi_{CB}(t)$ is a function of t and $r(t)$, because the same is true for each zero bond price. We therefore write

$$\Pi_{CB}(t,r) = \sum_{i=1}^{n}\widetilde{c}_i P(t,t_i,r).$$

Jamshidian introduced the following trick to make the positive part operator $[\cdot]^+$ more tractable:

1. Find r^* such that $K = \Pi_{CB}(S,r^*) = \sum_{i=1}^{n}\widetilde{c}_i P(t,t_i,r^*)$ and rewrite the argument within the positive part operator:

$$[\Pi_{CB}(S,r) - K]^+ = \left[\sum_{i=1}^{n}\widetilde{c}_i\,(P(S,t_i,r) - P(S,t_i,r^*))\right]^+$$

2. Since $\partial_r P(s,t,r) < 0$ for all $0 < s < t$, we have $\Pi_{CB}(S,r) < K$ for $r > r^*$ (don't exercise the call!), and $\Pi_{CB}(S,r) > K$ for $r < r^*$ (exercise the call!). This is true for each difference $P(S,t_i,r) - P(S,t_i,r^*)$ in the disassembled argument of the positive part operator above. In other words, the differences are either all positive or non-positive.
3. Therefore we can exchange the positive part operator with the sum:

$$[\Pi_{CB}(S,r) - K]^+ = \sum_{i=1}^{n}\widetilde{c}_i\,[P(S,t_i,r) - P(S,t_i,r^*)]^+,$$

so that the coupon bond option can be divided into a series of zero bond call options (with respective strikes $P(S, t_i, r^*)$) for which we have found a closed form solution already.

European swaptions

In the single-curve world, a European swaption can be viewed as an option on a coupon bond with notional N and strike price N: If we artificially introduce a notional repayment at maturity on both the floating and the fixed leg, the floating leg is (at least on each fixing date) worth par. A European option on a receiver swap is therefore associated with a coupon bond call option; an option on a payer swap associated with a coupon bond put option.

D.2 Bank account and forward measure

One usually starts formulating the Hull-White model in a particular risk-neutral measure, the bank account measure. We have come across a different measure, the T-forward measure, in the previous section as well when deriving the zero bond option price. In this section, we want to compare the expressions for the numeraire and stochastic discount bond in these two measures, starting with the bank account measure.

One can express the bank account in terms of model parameters as follows:[1]

$$\begin{aligned} B(t) &= \exp\left(\int_0^t r(s)\,ds\right) \qquad \Leftrightarrow \qquad dB(t) = B(t)\,r(t)\,dt \\ &= \exp\left(\int_0^t x(s)\,ds + \int_0^t \mu(s)\,ds\right) \\ &= \frac{1}{P(0,t)} \exp\left(\int_0^t (H_t - H_s)\,\alpha_s\,dW_s + \frac{1}{2}\int_0^t (H_t - H_s)^2\,\alpha_s^2\,ds\right) \end{aligned} \tag{D.8}$$

where

$$H(t) = \frac{1 - e^{-\lambda t}}{\lambda} \qquad \text{and} \qquad \alpha(t) = \sigma\, e^{\lambda t}$$

The first term in the exponent of (D.8) is an Ito integral with Gaussian distribution, expectation zero and variance equal to twice the second term in the exponent, that

[1] Skipping all intermediate steps, which are left as an exercise for the reader.

is the numeraire is of the form

$$B(t) = \frac{1}{P(0,t)}\, e^{X+\frac{1}{2}\mathbb{V}[X]}$$

so that

$$\mathbb{E}\left[\frac{1}{B(t)}\right] = P(0,t)\, e^{-\frac{1}{2}\mathbb{V}[X]}\, \mathbb{E}\left[e^{-X}\right].$$

Since $\mathbb{E}[e^X] = e^{\mathbb{E}[X]+\frac{1}{2}\mathbb{V}[X]}$ for a normal random variable X, it follows that

$$\mathbb{E}\left[\frac{1}{B(t)}\right] = P(0,t),$$

as it should. It is also instructive to compute the "reduced" stochastic discount bond $P(t,T)/B(t)$ from (D.2) and (D.8) as this ratio appears in the expectations that needs to be computed for pricing. Skipping intermediate steps again, one arrives at

$$\frac{P(t,T)}{B(t)} = P(0,T)\, \exp\left(-\int_0^t (H_T - H_s)\,\alpha_s\, dW_s - \frac{1}{2}\int_0^t (H_T - H_s)^2 \alpha_s^2\, ds\right) \quad \text{(D.9)}$$

As above we conclude that $\mathbb{E}[P(t,T)/B(t)] = P(0,T)$, as expected. Note the similarity of (D.8) and (D.9), driven by the same Wiener process $W(t)$ of course, but via different Ito integrals

$$\int_0^t (H_t - H_s)\,\alpha_s\, dW_s \qquad \text{and} \qquad \int_0^t (H_T - H_s)\,\alpha_s\, dW_s.$$

Alternatively, we can say that both the numeraire and reduced discount bond are driven by a single Wiener process, but two random variables

$$x_1 = \int_0^t \alpha_s\, dW_s \qquad \text{and} \qquad x_2 = \int_0^t H_s\,\alpha_s\, dW_s$$

which are not perfectly correlated as one might think at first glance. In analytical and numerical calculations in the bank account measure, this is a complication as it requires in fact tracking a two-dimensional stochastic process (x_1, x_2), see for example [70]. This is the reason why one usually switches to a different measure, especially for analytical calculations.

We now want to switch to the T-forward measure. We use the change of numeraire toolkit from Appendix A which we summarize as follows:

1. We denote the Wiener process under the new measure $\widetilde{W}(t)$ which is related to the old measure via drift $\theta(t)$ as $\widetilde{W}(t) = W(t) + \int_0^t \theta(s)\, ds$
2. Given the drift $\theta(t)$, the Radon-Nikodym derivative is given by

$$Z(t) = \exp\left(-\int_0^t \theta(s)\, dW(s) - \frac{1}{2}\int_0^t \theta^2(s)\, ds\right)$$

   with $\mathbb{E}[Z] = 1$.
3. Expectations under the old resp. new measure are then computed as $\mathbb{E}[V] = \widetilde{\mathbb{E}}[V/Z]$.
4. In other words, the new numeraire $\widetilde{N}(t)$ is computed from the old numeraire $N(t)$ and Radon-Nicodym derivative $Z(t)$ via
   $\widetilde{N}(t)/\widetilde{N}(0) = Z(t) \cdot N(t)/N(0)$ so that $\mathbb{E}[V/N] = \widetilde{\mathbb{E}}[V/\widetilde{N}]$.

This toolkit can be used in different ways:

- If the new numeraire $\widetilde{N}(t)$ is known, one can compute the Radon-Nicodym derivative $Z(t) = \widetilde{N}(t)/N(t) \cdot N(0)/\widetilde{N}(0)$ from step 4, expressed in terms of the Wiener process $W(t)$ under the old measure. From this expression of $Z(t)$ one then determines the drift $\theta(t)$ by comparing with the definition of $Z(t)$ above. Using the drift $\theta(t)$, one then substitutes $W(t)$ by $\widetilde{W}(t) - \int_0^t \theta(s)\, ds$ in the expression for $\widetilde{N}(t)$.
- If the change of measure drift $\theta(t)$ is known, we can conversely compute $Z(t)$ directly using its definition in step 2, expressed in terms of the Wiener process $W(t)$ in the old measure. We then get the new numeraire $\widetilde{N}(t)$ from step 4. Finally, we then substitute $W(t)$ by $\widetilde{W}(t) - \int_0^t \theta(s)\, ds$ in the expression for $\widetilde{N}(t)$.

Let us apply this program to move to the T-forward measure. We know the new numeraire, it is the zero bond with maturity T, that is the product of (D.8) and (D.9):

$$\begin{aligned}
\widetilde{N}(t) &= P(t,T) \\
&= \frac{P(0,T)}{P(0,t)} \exp\left(-(H_T - H_t)\int_0^t \alpha_s\, dW_s - \frac{1}{2}\int_0^t (H_T - H_s)^2 \alpha_s^2\, ds\right) \\
&\qquad \times \exp\left(\frac{1}{2}\int_0^t (H_t - H_s)^2 \alpha_s^2\, ds\right) \\
&= \frac{P(0,T)}{P(0,t)} \exp\left(-(H_T - H_t)\int_0^t \alpha_s\, dW_s\right) \\
&\qquad \times \exp\left(-\frac{1}{2}\int_0^t (H_T^2 - H_t^2 - 2(H_T - H_t)H_s)\, \alpha_s^2\, ds\right)
\end{aligned}$$

$$= \frac{P(0,T)}{P(0,t)} \exp\left(-(H_T - H_t)\left(\int_0^t \alpha_s \, dW_s - \int_0^t H_s \alpha_s^2 \, ds\right)\right)$$
$$\times \exp\left(-\frac{1}{2}(H_T^2 - H_t^2)\int_0^t \alpha_s^2 \, ds\right)$$

still expressed in the old measure $W(t)$. The Radon-Nikodym derivative $Z(t) = \widetilde{N}(t)/\widetilde{N}(0) \cdot N(0)/N(t)$ is hence (using old numeraire $N(t) = B(t)$ in (D.8), with $N(0) = 1$, $\widetilde{N}(0) = P(0,T)$ and skipping all intermediate steps)

$$Z(t) = \exp\left(-\int_0^t \underbrace{(H_T - H_s)\alpha_s}_{=\theta(s)} \, dW_s - \frac{1}{2}\int_0^t \underbrace{(H_T - H_s)^2 \alpha_s^2}_{=\theta^2(s)} \, ds\right).$$

This shows – comparing to the definition of $Z(t)$ – that the change of measure drift is $\theta(t) = (H_T - H_t)\alpha(t)$, and substituting $dW(t) = d\widetilde{W}(t) - \theta(t)\,dt$ in $\widetilde{N}(t)$ then yields

$$\widetilde{N}(t) = P(t,T) \tag{D.10}$$
$$= \frac{P(0,T)}{P(0,t)} \exp\left(-(H_T - H_t)\int_0^t \alpha_s \, d\widetilde{W}_s + \frac{1}{2}(H_T - H_t)^2 \int_0^t \alpha_s^2 ds\right)$$
$$= \frac{P(0,T)}{P(0,t)} \exp\left(-(H_T - H_t)\widetilde{z}_t + \frac{1}{2}(H_T - H_t)^2 \zeta_t\right) \tag{D.11}$$

with

$$\widetilde{z} = \int_0^t \alpha_s \, d\widetilde{W}_s \quad \text{and} \quad \zeta_t = \int_0^t \alpha_s^2 \, ds$$

in agreement with [91], Section 17.3.2.

The zero bond for any other maturity $S \neq T$ has the same form as (D.11). In contrast to the bank account measure, we have a situation where both numeraire and stochastic zero bond are not only driven by the same Wiener process $\widetilde{W}(t)$, but even by the same random variable $\widetilde{z}(t)$. This significantly simplifies analytical as well as numerical calculations.

D.3 Cross-currency Hull-White model

The *Cross-Currency Hull-White* model discussed here can be traced back to work by Babbs in 1994 [14, 57, 123, 124].

We are going to use the following form of the model's SDE

$$
\begin{aligned}
\frac{dx}{x} &= \left[r_d(t) - r_f(t)\right] dt + \sigma_x \, dW_x \\
dr_d &= \lambda_d \left[\theta_d(t) - r_d(t)\right] dt + \sigma_d \, dW_d \\
dr_f &= \lambda_f \left[\theta_f(t) - r_f(t)\right] dt - \rho_{xf}\sigma_x\sigma_f \, dt + \sigma_f \, dW_f \\
dW_x \, dW_d &= \rho_{xd} \, dt \\
dW_x \, dW_f &= \rho_{xf} \, dt \\
dW_d \, dW_f &= \rho_{df} \, dt.
\end{aligned}
$$

Domestic short rate process

We are working in the domestic risk-neutral measure, hence there is no change to the usual calibration procedure:

- The domestic drift is calibrated to match the domestic zero bond prices

$$
\begin{aligned}
\mathbb{E}\{r_d(t)\} = \mu_d(t) &= r_0 \, e^{-\lambda_d t} + \lambda_d \int_0^t e^{-\lambda_d(t-s)} \, \theta_d(s) \, ds \\
&= f_d(0,t) + \frac{1}{2}\frac{\partial}{\partial t} \int_0^t h^2_{\lambda_d}(t-s) \, \sigma^2_d(s) \, ds \\
&= f_d(0,t) + \frac{\sigma^2_d}{2} \, h^2_{\lambda_d}(t)
\end{aligned}
$$

  where $f_d(0,t)$ is the domestic instantaneous forward curve and the latter follows for constant $\sigma_d(t) \equiv \sigma_d$.
- The domestic volatility structure (λ_d and σ_d) is calibrated as usual, for example to European swaptions

Foreign short rate process

We first state the formal solution of the SDE for r_f

$$
\begin{aligned}
r_f(t) &= \mu_f(t) + \int_0^t e^{-\lambda_f(t-s)} \, \sigma_f \, dW_f \\
\mu(t) &= r_f(0) \, e^{-\lambda_f t} + \lambda_f \int_0^t e^{-\lambda_f(t-s)} \, \theta_f(s) \, ds - \int_0^t e^{-\lambda_f(t-s)} \rho_{xf} \, \sigma_x \, \sigma_f \, ds
\end{aligned}
$$

with

$$\mathbb{E}[r_f(t)] = \mu(t)$$
$$\mathbb{V}[r_f(t)] = \int_0^t e^{-2\lambda_f(t-s)}\,\sigma_f^2\,ds.$$

The derivation follows the procedure of the domestic case (e.g. variation of constants).

Note that $\mu(t)$ differs from the drift $\bar{\mu}(t)$ of the foreign process under its own foreign risk-neutral measure by

$$\mu(t) - \bar{\mu}(t) = -\int_0^t e^{-\lambda_f(t-s)}\,\rho_{xf}\,\sigma_x\,\sigma_f\,ds.$$

Moreover we will need the formal solution of the FX rate process.

The SDE can be rewritten (Ito) as

$$d\ln x = \left[r_d(t) - r_f(t) - \frac{1}{2}\sigma_x^2\right] dt + \sigma_x\,dW_x$$

It is formally solved by

$$\ln(x(t)/x_0) = \int_0^t \left[r_d(t) - r_f(t) - \frac{1}{2}\sigma_x^2\right] dt + \int_0^t \sigma_x\,dW_x.$$

To match the current foreign yield curve, we need to compute the foreign zero bond price in the domestic measure:

- payoff 1 in foreign currency at maturity T
- convert into domestic currency (using the forward FX rate $x(T)$)
- discount to time t using domestic rates
- convert back into foreign currency (using the FX rate $1/x(t)$).

That means that we can write

$$P_f(t,T) = \mathbb{E}_t\left\{\exp\left(-\int_t^T r_d(s)\,ds\right)\cdot\frac{x(T)}{x(t)}\right\}$$

As we are working in a measure different from the foreign spot measure, we carefully review the computation of $P_f(0,T)$ as a function of model parameters $\theta_f, \sigma_f, \lambda_f$ and "solve" for function $\theta_f(t)$ to match the current foreign yield curve.

To be computed:

$$P_f(t,T) = \mathbb{E}_t\left\{\exp\left(-\int_t^T r_d(s)\,ds + \ln\frac{x(T)}{x(t)}\right)\right\}.$$

Insert the formal solution of $\ln x$:

$$P_f(t,T) = \mathbb{E}_t\left\{\exp\left(-\int_t^T r_f(s)\,ds - \frac{1}{2}\int_t^T \sigma_x^2\,ds + \int_t^T \sigma_x\,dW_x\right)\right\}$$

Compare this to the domestic zero bond in the domestic risk-neutral measure

$$P_d(t,T) = \mathbb{E}_t\left\{\exp\left(-\int_t^T r_d(s)\,ds\right)\right\}$$

Note that both exponents are Gaussian random variables.

We want to"take what is known out of the expectation", that is the time t-measurable parts, and for that purpose we rewrite ($t < s$)

$$r_f(s) = g(s,t) + \int_t^s e^{-\lambda_f(s-\tau)}\sigma_f\,dW_f(\tau)$$
$$g(s,t) := \mu_f(s) + e^{-\lambda_f(s-t)}(r_f(t) - \mu_f(t))$$

as in the domestic case. Note that all terms in $g(s,t)$ are either known at time τ or deterministic. We insert this expression for $r_f(s)$ into $P_f(t,T)$ and obtain:

$$\begin{aligned}P_f(t,T) &= e^{\int_t^T\left(-g(s,t)-\frac{1}{2}\sigma_x^2\right)ds}\,\mathbb{E}_t\left[e^{-\int_t^T\left(\int_t^s e^{-\lambda_f(s-\tau)}\sigma_f\,dW_f(\tau)d\tau\right)ds+\int_t^T\sigma_x dW_x}\right]\\ &= e^{\int_t^T\left(-g(s,t)-\frac{1}{2}\sigma_x^2\right)ds}\,\mathbb{E}_t\left[e^{-\int_t^T h_{\lambda_f}(T-s)\sigma_f\,dW_f(s)+\int_t^T\sigma_x dW_x(s)}\right]\end{aligned}$$

where we have used the usual integration by parts in the last step.

The exponent inside the expectation

$$Y = -\int_t^T h_{\lambda_f}(T-s)\sigma_f\,dW_f(s) + \int_t^T \sigma_x dW_x(s)$$

is a Gaussian random variable so that $\mathbb{E}[e^Y] = e^{\mathbb{E}[Y]+\frac{1}{2}\mathbb{V}[Y]}$. Since $\mathbb{E}[Y]=0$ (because it is the sum of Ito integrals), we have

$$\mathbb{E}\left[e^Y\right] = e^{\frac{1}{2}\mathbb{V}[Y]} = e^{\frac{1}{2}\int_t^T\left(h_{\lambda_f}^2(T-s)\sigma_f^2+\sigma_x^2\right)ds-\int_t^T h_{\lambda_f}(T-s)\sigma_f\sigma_x\rho_{fx}\,ds}$$

Inserting $g(s,t)$ and rearranging terms we therefore get

$$P_f(t,T) = e^{-h_{\lambda_f}(T-t)[r_f(t)-\mu_f(t)]+\int_t^T \left(-\mu_f(s)+\frac{1}{2}h^2_{\lambda_f}(T-s)\sigma_f^2 - h_{\lambda_f}(T-s)\sigma_f\sigma_x\rho_{fx}\right) ds}$$

We now substitute $\mu(t) = \bar{\mu}(t) - \int_0^t e^{-\lambda_f(t-s)}\rho_{xf}\,\sigma_x\sigma_f\, ds$ and note that

$$\int_t^T \int_0^s e^{-\lambda(s-\tau)} f(\tau) d\tau\, ds = \int_t^T h_\lambda(T-s) f(s) ds + h_\lambda(T-t) \int_0^t e^{-\lambda(t-s)} f(s) ds$$

(which follows from integration by parts). This yields the result

$$P_f(t,T) = A(t,T)\, e^{-h_{\lambda_f}(T-t)\, r_f(t)}$$

$$A(t,T) = \exp\left\{+h_{\lambda_f}(T-t)\,\bar{\mu}_f(t) + \int_t^T \left(-\bar{\mu}_f(s) + \frac{1}{2} h^2_{\lambda_f}(T-s)\sigma_f^2\right) ds\right\}.$$

This is the same result that we would have obtained in the foreign risk-neutral measure.

Despite working in the domestic risk-neutral measure, the foreign rate process calibration does not have to be amended and works as if we only had a single (foreign) currency:

- The foreign drift is calibrated as usual to match the foreign zero bond prices

$$\bar{\mu}_f(t) = f_f(0,t) + \frac{1}{2}\frac{\partial}{\partial t} \int_0^t h^2_{\lambda_f}(t-s)\,\sigma_f^2(s)\, ds = f_f(0,t) + \frac{\sigma_f^2}{2}\, h^2_{\lambda_f}(t)$$

  where $f_f(0,t)$ is the foreign instantaneous forward curve and the latter follows for constant $\sigma_f(t) \equiv \sigma_f$.
- The foreign volatility structure (λ_f and σ_f) is calibrated as usual, e.g. to European swaptions; this part is anyway not affected by the change of measure.

FX process

Recall the formal solutions (after $r_{d,f}$ calibration)

$$x(t) = x_0 \exp\left(\int_0^t \left[r_d(t) - r_f(t) - \frac{1}{2}\sigma_x^2\right] dt + \int_0^t \sigma_x\, dW_x\right)$$

$$
\begin{aligned}
r_{f,d}(t) &= \mu_{f,d}(t) + \int_0^t e^{-\lambda_{f,d}(t-s)}\,\sigma_{f,d}\,dW_{f,d} \\
\mu_d(t) &= f_d(0,t) + \frac{1}{2}\frac{\partial}{\partial t}\int_0^t h^2_{\lambda_d}(t-s)\,\sigma_d^2(s)\,ds \\
&= f_d(0,t) + \frac{\sigma_d^2}{2}\,h^2_{\lambda_d}(t) \qquad \text{(if parameters are constant)} \\
\mu_f(t) &= f_f(0,t) + \frac{1}{2}\frac{\partial}{\partial t}\int_0^t h^2_{\lambda_f}(t-s)\,\sigma_f^2(s)\,ds - \int_0^t e^{-\lambda_f(t-s)}\rho_{xf}\,\sigma_x\sigma_f\,ds \\
&= f_f(0,t) + \frac{\sigma_f^2}{2}\,h^2_{\lambda_f}(t) - \rho_{xf}\,\sigma_x\sigma_f\,h_{\lambda_f}(t) \qquad \text{(if parameters are constant)}
\end{aligned}
$$

Since the short rates $r_{d,f}(t)$ are normally distributed, $x(t)$ is log-normal and fully determined by mean and variance of log-returns.

Expected log-return

$$
\begin{aligned}
\mathbb{E}\{\ln x(t)\} &= \ln x_0 + \mathbb{E}\left\{\int_0^t \left(r_d(s) - r_f(s) - \frac{1}{2}\sigma_x^2(s)\right) ds\right\} \\
&= \ln x_0 + \int_0^t \left(\mathbb{E}\{r_d(s)\} - \mathbb{E}\{r_f(s)\} - \frac{1}{2}\sigma_x^2(s)\right) ds \\
&= \ln x_0 + \int_0^t \left(\mu_d(s) - \mu_f(s) - \frac{1}{2}\sigma_x^2(s)\right) ds \\
&= \ln x_0 + \ln\frac{P_f(t)}{P_d(t)} - \frac{1}{2}\int_0^t \sigma_x^2(s)\,ds \\
&\quad + \frac{1}{2}\int_0^t h^2_{\lambda_d}(t-s)\,\sigma_d^2(s)\,ds - \frac{1}{2}\int_0^t h^2_{\lambda_f}(t-s)\,\sigma_f^2(s)\,ds \\
&\quad + \int_0^t h_{\lambda_f}(t-s)\,\sigma_f(s)\,\sigma_x(s)\,\rho_{xf}\,ds \\
&:= \mu_x(t)
\end{aligned}
$$

For constant volatilities $\sigma_{d,f}$ the integrals simplify to

$$
\begin{aligned}
\mathbb{E}\{\ln x\} = \ln x_0 + \ln\frac{P_f(t)}{P_d(t)} - \frac{1}{2}\sigma_x^2\,t + \frac{1}{2}\left(\frac{\sigma_d}{\lambda_d}\right)^2 \cdot \left(t - 2\,h_{\lambda_d}(t) + h_{2\lambda_d}(t)\right) \\
- \frac{1}{2}\left(\frac{\sigma_f}{\lambda_f}\right)^2 \cdot \left(t - 2\,h_{\lambda_f}(t) + h_{2\lambda_f}(t)\right) + \frac{\rho_{xf}\,\sigma_x\sigma_f}{\lambda_f}\left(t - h_{\lambda_f}(t)\right)
\end{aligned}
$$

Note that

$$
h_\lambda(t) = \frac{1 - e^{-\lambda t}}{\lambda} \longrightarrow \begin{cases} t & \text{for } \lambda \to 0, \quad t \to 0 \\ 1/\lambda & \text{for } t \to \infty \end{cases}
$$

Variance of log-returns

$$
\begin{aligned}
\mathbb{V}\{\ln x(t)\} &= \mathbb{V}\left\{+\int_0^t h_{\lambda_d}(t-s)\,\sigma_d\,dW_d(s) - \int_0^t h_{\lambda_f}(t-s)\,\sigma_f\,dW_f(s) + \int_0^t \sigma_x\,dW_x(s)\right\}\\
&= \int_0^t \left(\sigma_x^2 + h_{\lambda_d}^2(t-s)\,\sigma_d^2 + h_{\lambda_f}^2(t-s)\,\sigma_f^2\right) ds\\
&\quad - 2\int_0^t h_{\lambda_d}(t-s)\,h_{\lambda_f}(t-s)\,\sigma_d\,\sigma_f\,\rho_{df}\,ds\\
&\quad + 2\int_0^t h_{\lambda_d}(t-s)\,\sigma_d\,\sigma_x\,\rho_{xd}\,ds\\
&\quad - 2\int_0^t h_{\lambda_f}(t-s)\,\sigma_f\,\sigma_x\,\rho_{xf}\,ds\\
&:= \Sigma^2(t)
\end{aligned}
$$

For constant parameters, the integrals simplify to

$$
\begin{aligned}
\int_0^t h_{\lambda_i}(t-s)\,ds &= \frac{1}{\lambda_i}\left(t - h_{\lambda_i}(t)\right)\\
\int_0^t h_{\lambda_i}^2(t-s)\,ds &= \frac{1}{\lambda_i^2}\left(t - 2\,h_{\lambda_i}(t) + h_{2\lambda_i}(t)\right)\\
\int_0^t h_{\lambda_d}(t-s)\,h_{\lambda_f}(t-s)\,ds &= \frac{1}{\lambda_d\lambda_f}\left(t - h_{\lambda_d}(t) - h_{\lambda_f}(t) + h_{\lambda_d+\lambda_f}(t)\right)
\end{aligned}
$$

so that

$$
\begin{aligned}
\mathbb{V}\{\ln x(t)\} &= \sigma_x^2\,t + \frac{\sigma_d^2}{\lambda_d^2}\left(t - 2h_{\lambda_d}(t) + h_{2\lambda_d}(t)\right)\frac{\sigma_f^2}{\lambda_f^2}\left(t - 2h_{\lambda_f}(t) + h_{2\lambda_f}(t)\right)\\
&\quad - 2\,\rho_{df}\,\frac{\sigma_d\,\sigma_f}{\lambda_d\lambda_f}\left(t - h_{\lambda_d}(t) - h_{\lambda_f}(t) + h_{\lambda_d+\lambda_f}(t)\right)\\
&\quad + 2\,\rho_{xd}\,\frac{\sigma_d\,\sigma_x}{\lambda_d}\left(t - h_{\lambda_d}(t)\right) - 2\,\rho_{xf}\,\frac{\sigma_f\,\sigma_x}{\lambda_f}\left(t - h_{\lambda_f}(t)\right)
\end{aligned}
$$

Covariance

To fully specify the cross-currency process, we list in the following the covariances $Cov(\ln x(t), r_d(t))$, $Cov(\ln x(t), r_f(t))$ and $Cov(r_d(t), r_f(t))$.

$$
\begin{aligned}
Cov(\ln x, r_d) &= \mathbb{E}[\ln x \cdot r_d] - \mu_x\,\mu_d\\
&= \mathbb{E}\left[\ln x(t)\cdot\int_0^t e^{-\lambda_d(t-s)}\,\sigma_d\,dW_d(s)\right]
\end{aligned}
$$

$$
\begin{aligned}
&= \mathbb{E}\left[\left(\int_0^t (r_d(s) - r_f(s))\, ds + \int_0^t \sigma_x\, dW_x(s)\right) \cdot \int_0^t e^{-\lambda_d(t-s)}\, \sigma_d\, dW_d(s)\right] \\
&= \mathbb{E}\left[\left(\int_0^t h_{\lambda_d}(t-s)\, \sigma_d\, dW_d(s) - \int_0^t h_{\lambda_f}(t-s)\, \sigma_f\, dW_f(s)\right.\right. \\
&\qquad \left.\left. + \int_0^t \sigma_x\, dW_x(s)\right) \cdot \int_0^t e^{-\lambda_d(t-s)}\, \sigma_d\, dW_d(s)\right] \\
&= \int_0^t h_{\lambda_d}(t-s)\, e^{-\lambda_d(t-s)}\, \sigma_d^2\, ds - \rho_{df} \int_0^t h_{\lambda_f}(t-s)\, e^{-\lambda_d(t-s)}\, \sigma_d \sigma_f\, ds \\
&\qquad\qquad + \rho_{xd} \int_0^t e^{-\lambda_d(t-s)}\, \sigma_x \sigma_d\, ds \\
&= \frac{\sigma_d^2}{\lambda_d}\left(h_{\lambda_d}(t) - h_{2\lambda_d}(t)\right) - \rho_{df} \frac{\sigma_d \sigma_f}{\lambda_f}\left(h_{\lambda_d}(t) - h_{\lambda_d+\lambda_f}(t)\right) \\
&\qquad + \rho_{xd}\, \sigma_x \sigma_d\, h_{\lambda_d}(t)
\end{aligned}
$$

assuming constant parameters in the last step. Likewise

$$
\begin{aligned}
Cov(\ln x, r_f) &= -\frac{\sigma_f^2}{\lambda_f}\left(h_{\lambda_f}(t) - h_{2\lambda_f}(t)\right) + \rho_{df} \frac{\sigma_d \sigma_f}{\lambda_d}\left(h_{\lambda_f}(t) - h_{\lambda_d+\lambda_f}(t)\right) \\
&\qquad + \rho_{xf}\, \sigma_x \sigma_f\, h_{\lambda_f}(t) \\
Cov(r_d, r_f) &= \rho_{df}\, \sigma_d \sigma_f\, h_{\lambda_d+\lambda_f}(t)
\end{aligned}
$$

Terminal correlations

Correlations are defined in terms of variances/covariances of the random variables $Z = (z_1, z_2, z_3) = (\ln x(t), r_d(t), r_f(t))$ as usual:

$$
\rho_{ij} = \frac{Cov(z_i, z_j)}{\sqrt{\mathbb{V}(z_i)\, \mathbb{V}(z_j)}}.
$$

These terminal correlations differ from the *instantaneous* correlations $\rho_{xf}, \rho_{xd}, \rho_{df}$ (which drive the short interest and FX rates) significantly, with the exception of

$$
\rho_{23} = \rho_{df} \frac{h_{\lambda_d+\lambda_f}(t)}{\sqrt{h_{2\lambda_d}(t)\, h_{2\lambda_f}(t)}}
$$

which stays close to ρ_{df} for all times. ρ_{12} and ρ_{13} vanish for $t \to \infty$, as the variance of $\ln(x)$ grows without limits.

Figure D.1 shows the evolution of terminal correlations for typical model parameters.

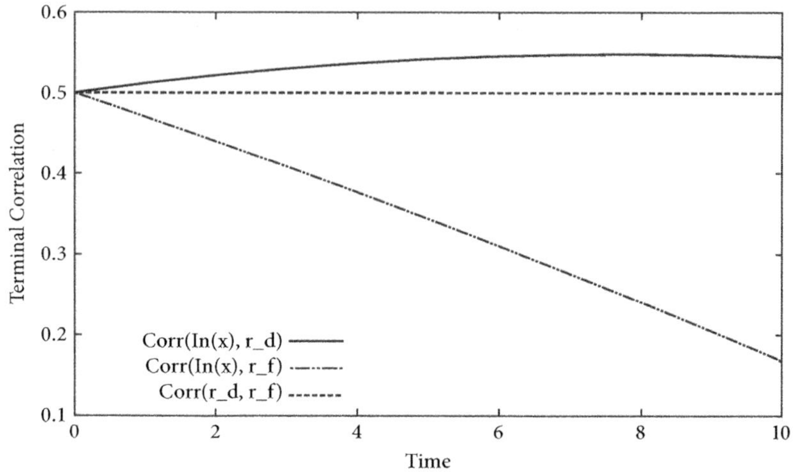

Figure D.1 Evolution of terminal correlations in the cross-currency Hull-White model with parameters $\lambda_d = 0.03$, $\sigma_d = 0.01$, $\lambda_f = 0.015$, $\sigma_f = 0.015$, $\rho_{xd} = \rho_{xf} = \rho_{df} = 0.5$

Joint density

$\ln x(t)$, $r_d(t)$ and $r_f(t)$ are joint-normal with means and variances/covariances as computed before. We can write the joint density of the process for any given time t in terms of the three-dimensional random variable $z = (z_1, z_2, z_3) = (\ln x(t), r_d(t), r_f(t))$ and mean $\mu = (\mu_1, \mu_2, \mu_3) = (\mu_x(t), \mu_d(t), \mu_f(t))$

$$\Phi(z) = \frac{1}{(2\pi)^{3/2}\sqrt{det(C)}} \exp\left(-\frac{1}{2}(z-\mu)^T C^{-1}(z-\mu)\right)$$

where C is the covariance matrix defined as $C_{11} = \mathbb{V}(\ln x(t))$, $C_{22} = \mathbb{V}(r_d(t))$, $C_{33} = \mathbb{V}(r_f(t))$, $C_{12} = Cov(\ln x(t), r_d(t)) = \rho_{12}\sqrt{\mathbb{V}(z_i)\,\mathbb{V}(z_j)}$, etc., as computed in the previous section. We also define the standard deviations $\Sigma_i = \sqrt{C_{ii}}$.

Conditioning on two variables

In the following we will make use of the "factorization" of the joint density $\Phi(z_1, z_2, z_3)$ into conditional and marginal densities

$$\Phi(z_1, z_2, z_3) = \Phi_{z_2,z_3}(z_1) \cdot \Phi(z_2, z_3)$$

where the (bivariate-normal) marginal density is

$$\begin{aligned}\Phi(z_2,z_3) &= \int_{-\infty}^{\infty} \Phi(z_1,z_2,z_3)\,dz_1\\ &= \frac{1}{2\pi\sqrt{1-\rho_{23}^2}\,\Sigma_2\,\Sigma_3}\exp\left(-\frac{(y_2^2+y_3^2-2\rho_{23}\,y_2\,y_3)^2}{2(1-\rho_{23}^2)}\right),\\ y_i &= \frac{z_i-\mu_i}{\Sigma_i}\end{aligned}$$

and the (normal) conditional density in z_1 given z_2 and z_3 is

$$\Phi_{z_2,z_3}(z_1) \sim N\left(\mu_1', \Sigma_1'^2\right)$$

with mean

$$\begin{aligned}\mu_1' = \mu_1 + \frac{1}{1-\rho_{23}^2}\Bigg\{&\frac{\Sigma_1}{\Sigma_2}(z_2-\mu_2)(\rho_{12}-\rho_{13}\,\rho_{23})\\ &+\frac{\Sigma_1}{\Sigma_3}(z_3-\mu_3)(\rho_{13}-\rho_{12}\,\rho_{23})\Bigg\}\end{aligned}$$

and variance

$$\Sigma_1'^2 = \Sigma_1^2\left(1-\frac{\rho_{12}^2+\rho_{13}^2-2\,\rho_{12}\,\rho_{13}\,\rho_{23}}{1-\rho_{23}^2}\right).$$

Conditioning on one variable

Occasionally the relevant joint density collapses down to the bivariate normal

$$\begin{aligned}\Phi(z_2,z_3) &= \int_{-\infty}^{\infty} \Phi(z_1,z_2,z_3)\,dz_1\\ &= \frac{1}{2\pi\sqrt{1-\rho_{23}^2}\,\Sigma_2\,\Sigma_3}\exp\left(-\frac{(y_2^2+y_3^2-2\rho_{23}\,y_2\,y_3)^2}{2(1-\rho_{23}^2)}\right),\\ y_i &= \frac{z_i-\mu_i}{\Sigma_i}\end{aligned}$$

which is represented in terms of marginal and conditional density as

$$\Phi(z_2, z_3) = \Phi_{z_3}(z_2)\,\Phi(z_3)$$
$$\Phi(z_3) = \int_{-\infty}^{\infty} \Phi(z_2, z_3)\,dz_2 \sim N(\mu_3, \Sigma_3^2)$$
$$\Phi_{z_3}(z_2) \sim N\left(\mu_2 + \frac{\Sigma_2}{\Sigma_3}\rho_{23}(z_3 - \mu_3), (1-\rho_{23}^2)\,\Sigma_2^2\right)$$

Domestic *T*-forward measure

We have seen in the previous sections how to calibrate all model parameters (except for correlations). The program of this section is to describe the change from the domestic spot to the domestic T-forward measure and computing the amended means of x, r_d and r_f. Recall that variances/covariances remain unchanged.

In the domestic T-forward measure the SDE is amended as follows:

$$d\ln x = \left(r_d(t) - r_f(t) - \frac{1}{2}\sigma_x^2 - \rho_{xd}\sigma_x\sigma_d\, h_{\lambda_d}(T-t)\right) dt + \sigma_x\, d\widetilde{W}_x$$
$$dr_d = \left(\lambda_d\left[\theta_d(t) - r_d(t)\right] - \sigma_d^2\, h_{\lambda_d}(T-t)\right) dt + \sigma_d\, d\widetilde{W}_d$$
$$dr_f = \left(\lambda_f\left[\theta_f(t) - r_f(t)\right] - \rho_{xf}\sigma_x\sigma_f - \rho_{df}\sigma_d\sigma_f\, h_{\lambda_d}(T-t)\right) dt + \sigma_f\, d\widetilde{W}_f$$
$$d\widetilde{W}_x\, d\widetilde{W}_d = \rho_{xd}\, dt$$
$$d\widetilde{W}_x\, d\widetilde{W}_f = \rho_{xf}\, dt$$
$$d\widetilde{W}_d\, d\widetilde{W}_f = \rho_{df}\, dt$$

The following integrals are calculated assuming constant model parameters. We denote the drift terms as determined before in the domestic spot measure as $\bar{\mu}_x(t)$, $\bar{\mu}_d(t)$ and $\bar{\mu}_f(t)$.

Domestic drift

The new domestic drift is given by

$$\mu_d(t) = \bar{\mu}_d(t) - \int_0^t \sigma_d^2\, h_{\lambda_d}(T-s)\, e^{-\lambda_d(t-s)}\, ds$$
$$= \bar{\mu}(t) - \frac{\sigma_d^2}{\lambda_d}\left(h_{\lambda_d}(t) - e^{-\lambda_d(T-t)}\, h_{2\lambda_d}(t)\right)$$

Foreign drift

Likewise, the new domestic drift is given by

$$\begin{aligned}\mu_f(t) &= \bar{\mu}_f(t) - \int_0^t \rho_{df}\sigma_d\sigma_f\, h_{\lambda_d}(T-s)\, e^{-\lambda_f(t-s)}\, ds \\ &= \bar{\mu}_f(t) - \rho_{df}\frac{\sigma_d\sigma_f}{\lambda_d}\left(h_{\lambda_f}(t) - e^{-\lambda_d(T-t)}\, h_{\lambda_d+\lambda_f}(t)\right)\end{aligned}$$

FX drift

The FX drift calculation is again more involved

$$\begin{aligned}\mu_x(t) - \bar{\mu}_x(t) &= \int_0^t \left\{\mu_d(s) - \bar{\mu}_d(s) - (\mu_f(s) - \bar{\mu}_f(s)) - \rho_{xd}\sigma_x\sigma_d\, h_{\lambda_d}(T-s)\right\} ds \\ &= -\frac{\sigma_d^2}{\lambda_d}\left\{\frac{t - h_{\lambda_d}(t)}{\lambda_d} - \frac{1}{2}e^{-\lambda_d(T-t)}\, h_{\lambda_d}^2(t)\right\} \\ &\quad + \rho_{df}\frac{\sigma_d\sigma_f}{\lambda_d}\left\{\frac{t - h_{\lambda_f}(t)}{\lambda_f} - \frac{e^{-\lambda_d(T-t)}h_{\lambda_d}(t) - e^{-\lambda_d T}h_{\lambda_f}(t)}{\lambda_d + \lambda_f}\right\} \\ &\quad - \rho_{xd}\frac{\sigma_x\sigma_d}{\lambda_d}\left\{t - e^{-\lambda_d(T-t)}\, h_{\lambda_d}(t)\right\}\end{aligned}$$

For $t = T$, this simplifies to

$$\begin{aligned}\mu_x(T) - \bar{\mu}_x(T) &= -\frac{\sigma_d^2}{\lambda_d}\left\{\frac{T - h_{\lambda_d}(T)}{\lambda_d} - \frac{1}{2}h_{\lambda_d}^2(T)\right\} \\ &\quad + \rho_{df}\frac{\sigma_d\sigma_f}{\lambda_d}\left\{\frac{T - h_{\lambda_f}(T)}{\lambda_f} - \frac{h_{\lambda_d}(T) - e^{-\lambda_d T}h_{\lambda_f}(T)}{\lambda_d + \lambda_f}\right\} \\ &\quad - \rho_{xd}\frac{\sigma_x\sigma_d}{\lambda_d}\left\{T - h_{\lambda_d}(T)\right\} \\ &= -\frac{\sigma_d^2}{\lambda_d^2}\left\{T - 2\,h_{\lambda_d}(T) + h_{2\lambda_d}(T)\right\} \\ &\quad + \rho_{df}\frac{\sigma_d\sigma_f}{\lambda_d\lambda_f}\left\{T - h_{\lambda_f}(T) - h_{\lambda_d}(T) + h_{\lambda_d+\lambda_f}(T)\right\} \\ &\quad - \rho_{xd}\frac{\sigma_x\sigma_d}{\lambda_d}\left\{T - h_{\lambda_d}(T)\right\}\end{aligned}$$

so that

$$
\begin{aligned}
\mu_x(T) = \ln x_0 + \ln \frac{P_f(T)}{P_d(T)} - \frac{1}{2}\sigma_x^2 T + \frac{1}{2}\frac{\sigma_d^2}{\lambda_d^2}\{T - 2h_{\lambda_d}(T) + h_{2\lambda_d}(T)\} \\
- \frac{1}{2}\frac{\sigma_f^2}{\lambda_f^2}\left\{T - 2h_{\lambda_f}(T) + h_{2\lambda_f}(T)\right\} \\
+ \rho_{xf}\frac{\sigma_x\sigma_f}{\lambda_f}\left\{T - h_{\lambda_f}(T)\right\} - \frac{\sigma_d^2}{\lambda_d^2}\{T - 2h_{\lambda_d}(T) + h_{2\lambda_d}(T)\} \\
+ \rho_{df}\frac{\sigma_d\sigma_f}{\lambda_d\lambda_f}\left\{T - h_{\lambda_f}(T) - h_{\lambda_d}(T) + h_{\lambda_d+\lambda_f}(T)\right\} \\
- \rho_{xd}\frac{\sigma_x\sigma_d}{\lambda_d}\{T - h_{\lambda_d}(T)\}
\end{aligned}
$$

which collapses to

$$
\begin{aligned}
\mu_x(T) &= \ln\left(x_0\frac{P_f(T)}{P_d(T)}\right) - \frac{1}{2}\sigma_x^2 T - \frac{1}{2}\frac{\sigma_d^2}{\lambda_d^2}\{T - 2h_{\lambda_d}(T) + h_{2\lambda_d}(T)\} \\
&\quad - \frac{1}{2}\frac{\sigma_f^2}{\lambda_f^2}\left\{T - 2h_{\lambda_f}(T) + h_{2\lambda_f}(T)\right\} + \rho_{xf}\frac{\sigma_x\sigma_f}{\lambda_f}\left\{T - h_{\lambda_f}(T)\right\} \\
&\quad - \rho_{xd}\frac{\sigma_x\sigma_d}{\lambda_d}\{T - h_{\lambda_d}(T)\} + \rho_{df}\frac{\sigma_d\sigma_f}{\lambda_d\lambda_f}\left\{T - h_{\lambda_f}(T) - h_{\lambda_d}(T) + h_{\lambda_d+\lambda_f}(T)\right\} \\
&= \ln F(0,T) - \frac{1}{2}\Sigma_x^2(T)
\end{aligned}
$$

as expected, since the forward FX rate $F(t,T) = x(t)\,P_f(t,T)/P_d(t,T)$ is a martingale under the T-forward measure.

E Linear Gauss Markov Model

E.1 One factor

The starting point is the Hull-White model with time-dependent parameters in the bank account measure

$$dr_t = (\theta_t - \lambda_t r_t)\, dt + \sigma_t\, dW_t.$$

This can be written

$$\begin{aligned} r_t &= \mu_t + x_t \\ d\mu_t &= (\theta_t - \lambda_t \mu_t)\, dt \\ dx_t &= -\lambda_t x_t\, dt + \sigma_t\, dW_t \end{aligned}$$

with solution

$$\begin{aligned} \mu_t &= r_0\, e^{-\beta_t} + e^{-\beta_t} \int_0^t e^{+\beta_s} \theta_s\, ds \\ x_t &= e^{-\beta_t} \int_0^t e^{\beta_s} \sigma_s\, dW_s \\ \beta_t &= \int_0^t \lambda_s\, ds \end{aligned}$$

and short rate variance

$$\mathbb{V}[r_t] = \mathbb{V}[x_t] = e^{-2\beta_t} \int_0^t \alpha_s^2\, ds, \qquad \alpha_t = e^{\beta_t} \sigma_t.$$

It can be shown that the drift term is specified by the initial term structure as follows

$$\int_0^t \mu(s)\,ds = -\ln P(0,t) + \frac{1}{2}\int_0^t (H_t - H_s)^2 \alpha_s^2\,ds, \qquad H(t) = \int_0^t e^{-\beta(s)}\,ds.$$

The stochastic zero bond price is then given by

$$\begin{aligned}
P(t,T) &= \mathbb{E}_t\left[e^{-\int_t^T r(s)\,ds}\right]\\
&= \frac{P(0,T)}{P(0,t)} \exp\left\{-(H_T - H_t)\,e^{\beta_t}\,x_t - \frac{1}{2}\int_0^t \left[(H_T - H_s)^2 - (H_t - H_s)^2\right]\alpha_s^2\,ds\right\}\\
&= \frac{P(0,T)}{P(0,t)} \exp\left\{-(H_T - H_t)\,(y_t - \Psi_t) - \frac{1}{2}(H_T^2 - H_t^2)\,\zeta_t\right\} \qquad \text{(E.1)}
\end{aligned}$$

with

$$y_t = e^{\beta_t}\,x_t = \int_0^t \alpha_s\,dW(s), \qquad \zeta_t = \int_0^t \alpha_s^2\,ds, \qquad \Psi_t = \int_0^t H_s \alpha_s^2\,ds.$$

Before we continue with the transition to the LGM formulation, note that the current numeraire – the bank account – can be expressed in terms of model parameters as follows:

$$\begin{aligned}
B(t) &= e^{\int_0^t r(s)\,ds}\\
&= \frac{1}{P(0,t)} \exp\left(\int_0^t (H_t - H_s)\,\alpha_s\,dW_s + \frac{1}{2}\int_0^t (H_t - H_s)^2\,\alpha_s^2\,ds\right). \qquad \text{(E.2)}
\end{aligned}$$

Dividing (E.1) by (E.2) we obtain the *reduced* zero bond in the bank account measure,

$$\frac{P(t,T)}{B(t)} = P(0,T)\,\exp\left\{-\int_0^t (H_T - H_s)\,\alpha_s\,dW_s - \frac{1}{2}\int_0^t (H_T - H_s)^2 \alpha_s^2\,ds\right\}. \qquad \text{(E.3)}$$

Comparing (E.2) with (E.3), we see that they are driven by different random variables, namely

$$\int_0^t (H_t - H_s)\,\alpha_s\,dW_s \qquad \text{resp.} \qquad \int_0^t (H_T - H_s)\,\alpha_s\,dW_s,$$

which makes (not only) analytical calculations in the bank account measure inconvenient.

The zero bond representation in (E.1) suggests introducing yet another variable

$$z(t) = y(t) - \Psi(t). \tag{E.4}$$

However, this process has a drift term:

$$dz = dy - d\Psi(t) = \alpha(t)\,dW(t) - H(t)\,\alpha^2(t)\,dt$$

but it can be made drift-free with the following change of measure:

$$dz = \alpha(t)\,d\widetilde{W}(t), \qquad \widetilde{W}(t) = W(t) - \int_0^t H(s)\,\alpha(s)\,ds,$$

such that z is Gaussian with zero mean and variance $\zeta(t)$ under the new measure.

The Radon-Nikodym derivative for the change of measure is

$$Z(t) = \exp\left\{\int_0^t H_s\,\alpha_s\,dW_s - \frac{1}{2}\int_0^t H_s^2\,\alpha_s^2\,ds\right\}$$

so that the new numeraire $N(t) = B(t)\,Z(t)$ (choosing $N(0) = 1$) is

$$\begin{aligned}
N(t) &= B(t)\exp\left\{\int_0^t H_s\,\alpha_s\,dW_s - \frac{1}{2}\int_0^t H_s^2\,\alpha_s^2\,ds\right\} \\
&= \frac{1}{P(0,t)}\exp\left\{\int_0^t H_s\,\alpha_s\,dW_s - \frac{1}{2}\int_0^t H_s^2\,\alpha_s^2\,ds \right. \\
&\quad \left. +\frac{1}{2}\int_0^t (H_t - H_s)^2\,\alpha_s^2\,ds + \int_0^t (H_t - H_s)\,\alpha_s\,dW_s\right\} \\
&= \frac{1}{P(0,t)}\exp\left\{H_t\int_0^t \alpha_s\,dW_s + \frac{1}{2}H_t^2\int_0^t \alpha_s^2\,ds - H_t\int_0^t H_s\alpha_s^2\,ds\right\} \\
&= \frac{1}{P(0,t)}\exp\left\{H_t\,z_t + \frac{1}{2}H_t^2\,\zeta_t\right\}.
\end{aligned} \tag{E.5}$$

The zero bond price (E.1) in terms of the new random variable z and normalized with the LGM numeraire (E.5) is

$$\begin{aligned}
\frac{P(t,T)}{N(t)} &= \frac{\frac{P(0,T)}{P(0,t)}\exp\left\{-(H_T - H_t)\,z_t - \frac{1}{2}(H_T^2 - H_t^2)\,\zeta_t\right\}}{\frac{1}{P(0,t)}\exp\left\{H_t\,z_t + \frac{1}{2}H_t^2\,\zeta_t\right\}} \\
&= P(0,T)\exp\left\{-H_T\,z_t - \frac{1}{2}H_T^2\zeta_t\right\}.
\end{aligned} \tag{E.6}$$

Note that under the new LGM measure, both reduced zero bond price and numeraire (E.5) are functions of the single Gaussian random variable z_t, in contrast to the price under the bank account measure (which involves two variables), yet similar to that under the T-forward measure.

Moreover, the zero bond price (E.1) in terms of the new random variable z,

$$P(t,T) = \frac{P(0,T)}{P(0,t)} \exp\left\{-(H(T)-H(t))\,z(t) - \frac{1}{2}(H^2(T)-H^2(t))\,\zeta(t)\right\},$$

directly implies the following forms of forward and short rate:

$$\begin{aligned} f(t,T) &= f(0,T) + z(t)\,H'(T) + \zeta(t)\,H'(T)H(T) \\ r(t) = f(t,t) &= f(0,t) + z(t)\,H'(t) + \zeta(t)\,H'(t)H(t). \end{aligned}$$

E.2 Two factors

The one-factor LGM can be extended to two factors, as follows:

$$N(t) = \frac{1}{P(0,t)} \times \exp\left\{H_t^\top z_t + \frac{1}{2} H_t^\top\, C_t\, H_t\right\} \tag{E.7}$$

$$\frac{P(t,T)}{N(t)} = P(0,T) \times \exp\left\{-H_T^\top z_t - \frac{1}{2} H_T^\top\, C_t\, H_T\right\} \tag{E.8}$$

where

$$H_t = \begin{pmatrix} H_1(t) \\ H_2(t) \end{pmatrix}, \qquad z_t = \begin{pmatrix} z_1(t) \\ z_2(t) \end{pmatrix},$$

$$C_t = \begin{pmatrix} \zeta_{11}(t) & \zeta_{12}(t) \\ \zeta_{12}(t) & \zeta_{22}(t) \end{pmatrix}, \qquad \zeta_{ij}(t) = \rho_{ij} \int_0^t \alpha_i(s)\,\alpha_j(s)\,ds.$$

The generalization to more than two factors is straightforward. In the following we derive the two-factor version.

The starting point is the G2++ model (equivalent to the two-factor Hull-White model) [33]:

$$\begin{aligned} r(t) &= \varphi(t) + x_1(t) + x_2(t) \\ dx_1 &= -a_1\,x_1\,dt + \sigma_1\,dW_1 \end{aligned}$$

$$
\begin{aligned}
dx_2 &= -a_2\, x_2\, dt + \sigma_2\, dW_2 \\
dW_1\, dW_2 &= \rho_{12}\, dt
\end{aligned}
$$

We introduce new variables

$$
\begin{aligned}
x_i' &= x_i\, e^{\beta_i} = \int_0^t \alpha_i\, dW_i, & \alpha_i &= \sigma_i\, e^{\beta_i}, \\
\beta_i &= \int_0^t a_i\, ds, & H_i &= \int_0^t e^{-\beta_i} ds
\end{aligned}
$$

and express the bank account in terms of new model variables

$$
\begin{aligned}
B(t) &= \exp\left\{\int_0^t \varphi(s)\, ds + \int_0^t (x_1(s) + x_2(s))\, ds\right\} \\
&= \exp\left\{\int_0^t \varphi(s)\, ds + \int_0^t (H_1(t) - H_1(s))\, \alpha_1\, dW_1\right. \\
&\quad \left. + \int_0^t (H_2(t) - H_2(s))\, \alpha_2\, dW_2\right\}.
\end{aligned}
$$

We then perform the same change of measure for each variable as in the one-factor LGM,

$$
dz_i = \alpha_i\, d\widetilde{W}_i = \alpha_i\, (dW_i - \alpha_i\, H_i\, dt)
$$

both with zero mean under the new measure. The Radon-Nikodym derivative for this change of measure is

$$
\ln Z(t) = \sum_{i=1}^{2} \left(\int_0^t \alpha_i\, H_i\, dW_i - \frac{1}{2}\int_0^t \alpha_i^2\, H_i^2\, ds \right) - \sum_{i<j} \rho_{ij} \int_0^t \alpha_i \alpha_j\, H_i\, H_j\, ds
$$

so that $\mathbb{E}[Z(t)] = 1$. We then compute the new numeraire $N(t) = B(t)\, Z(t)$ (assuming $N(0) = 1$):

$$
\begin{aligned}
\ln N(t) &= \ln B(t) + \ln Z(t) \\
&= \int_0^t \varphi(s)\, ds + \int_0^t (H_1(t) - H_1(s))\, \alpha_1\, dW_1 + \int_0^t \alpha_1\, H_1\, dW_1 \\
&\quad + \int_0^t (H_2(t) - H_2(s))\, \alpha_2\, dW_2 + \int_0^t \alpha_2\, H_2\, dW_2 \\
&\quad - \frac{1}{2}\int_0^t \alpha_1^2\, H_1^2\, ds - \frac{1}{2}\int_0^t \alpha_2^2\, H_2^2\, ds - \rho \int_0^t \alpha_1\, \alpha_2\, H_1\, H_2\, ds \\
&= \int_0^t \varphi(s)\, ds + H_1(t)\, z_1(t) + H_2(t)\, z_2(t) + H_1(t) \int_0^t \alpha_1^2\, H_1\, ds \\
&\quad + H_2(t) \int_0^t \alpha_2^2\, H_2\, ds - \frac{1}{2}\int_0^t \alpha_1^2\, H_1^2\, ds - \frac{1}{2}\int_0^t \alpha_2^2\, H_2^2\, ds \\
&\quad - \rho \int_0^t \alpha_1\, \alpha_2\, H_1\, H_2\, ds
\end{aligned}
$$

We eliminate $\varphi(t)$ by matching the initial term structure, that is we compute the current zero bond price for some maturity t,

$$
\begin{aligned}
P(0,t) &= \mathbb{E}_0^N\left[\frac{1}{N(t)}\right] \\
&= \exp\left\{ -\int_0^t \varphi(s)\, ds - H_1(t) \int_0^t \alpha_1^2\, H_1\, ds - H_2(t) \int_0^t \alpha_2^2\, H_2\, ds \right. \\
&\qquad \left. + \frac{1}{2}\int_0^t \alpha_1^2\, H_1^2\, ds + \frac{1}{2}\int_0^t \alpha_2^2\, H_2^2\, ds + \rho \int_0^t \alpha_1\, \alpha_2\, H_1\, H_2\, ds \right\} \\
&\qquad \times \mathbb{E}_0^N\left[e^{-H_1(t)\, z_1(t) - H_2(t)\, z_2(t)} \right] \\
&= \exp\left\{ -\int_0^t \varphi(s)\, ds - H_1(t) \int_0^t \alpha_1^2\, H_1\, ds - H_2(t) \int_0^t \alpha_2^2\, H_2\, ds \right. \\
&\qquad + \frac{1}{2}\int_0^t \alpha_1^2\, H_1^2\, ds + \frac{1}{2}\int_0^t \alpha_2^2\, H_2^2\, ds + \rho \int_0^t \alpha_1\, \alpha_2\, H_1\, H_2\, ds \\
&\qquad + \frac{1}{2} H_1^2(t)\, \zeta_1(t) + \frac{1}{2} H_2^2(t)\, \zeta_2(t) \\
&\qquad \left. + \rho\, H_1(t)\, H_2(t) \int_0^t \alpha_1\, \alpha_2\, ds \right\}.
\end{aligned}
$$

Then we solve this for $\int_0^t \varphi(s)\,ds$ and substitute $\int_0^t \varphi(s)\,ds$ in $N(t)$:

$$\begin{aligned}
\ln(N(t)\,P(0,t)) &= -H_1(t)\int_0^t \alpha_1^2\,H_1\,ds - H_2(t)\int_0^t \alpha_2^2\,H_2\,ds\\
&\quad + \frac{1}{2}\int_0^t \alpha_1^2\,H_1^2\,ds + \frac{1}{2}\int_0^t \alpha_2^2\,H_2^2\,ds\\
&\quad + \rho\int_0^t \alpha_1\,\alpha_2\,H_1\,H_2\,ds + \frac{1}{2}\,H_1^2(t)\,\zeta_1(t) + \frac{1}{2}\,H_2^2(t)\,\zeta_2(t)\\
&\quad + \rho\,H_1(t)\,H_2(t)\int_0^t \alpha_1\,\alpha_2\,ds + H_1(t)\,z_1(t) + H_2(t)\,z_2(t)\\
&\quad + H_1(t)\int_0^t \alpha_1^2\,H_1\,ds + H_2(t)\int_0^t \alpha_2^2\,H_2\,ds\\
&\quad - \frac{1}{2}\int_0^t \alpha_1^2\,H_1^2\,ds - \frac{1}{2}\int_0^t \alpha_2^2\,H_2^2\,ds - \rho\int_0^t \alpha_1\,\alpha_2\,H_1\,H_2\,ds\\
&= H_1(t)\,z_1(t) + H_2(t)\,z_2(t) + \frac{1}{2}\,H_1^2(t)\,\zeta_1(t)\\
&\quad + \frac{1}{2}\,H_2^2(t)\,\zeta_2(t) + \rho\,H_1(t)\,H_2(t)\,\zeta_{12}(t)
\end{aligned}$$

which is the numeraire (E.7). Finally, we compute the reduced zero bond price:

$$\begin{aligned}
\widetilde{P}(t,T) &= \frac{P(t,T)}{N(t)}\\
&= E_t^N\left[\frac{1}{N(T)}\right]\\
&= P(0,T)\times e^{-\frac{1}{2}H_1^2(T)\zeta_1(T)-\frac{1}{2}H_2^2(T)\zeta_2(T)-\rho\,H_1(T)\,H_2(T)\zeta_{12}(T)}\\
&\qquad\times \mathbb{E}_t\left[e^{-H_1(T)\,z_1(T)-H_2(T)\,z_2(T)}\right]\\
&= P(0,T)\times e^{-H_1(T)\,z_1(t)-H_2(T)\,z_2(t)-\frac{1}{2}H_1^2(T)\zeta_1(t)}\\
&\qquad\times e^{-\frac{1}{2}H_2^2(T)\zeta_2(t)-\rho\,H_1(T)\,H_2(T)\zeta_{12}(t)}
\end{aligned}$$

which is the reduced zero bond (E.8).

E.3 Cross-currency LGM

This section is an extension of Section 12.1 to demonstrate that the expression for the *foreign zero bond under the domestic LGM measure* is

$$P_f(t,T) = \frac{P_f(0,T)}{P_f(0,t)} \exp\left\{-\left(H_f(t) - H_f(t)\right) z_f(t) - \frac{1}{2}\left(H_f^2(t) - H_f^2(t)\right)\zeta_f(t)\right\}$$

that is that it has the same form as under the foreign LGM measure.

Recall Equations (12.2) and (12.3), the dynamics of the domestic and foreign numeraire process under the domestic LGM measure:

$$\begin{aligned} dN_d(t) &= N_f(t)\left[\left(r_d(t) + H_d^2(t)\alpha_d^2(t)\right)dt + H_d(t)\alpha_d(t)\,dW_d(t)\right] \\ dN_f(t) &= N_f(t)\left[\left(r_f(t) + H_f^2(t)\alpha_f^2(t) + H_f(t)\gamma_f(t)\right)dt + H_f(t)\alpha_f(t)\,dW_f(t)\right] \end{aligned}$$

whose solutions are given by

$$\begin{aligned} N_d(t) = N_d(0)\exp&\left\{\int_0^t r_d(u)\,du + \frac{1}{2}\int_0^t H_d^2(u)\,\alpha_d^2(u)\,du \right. \\ &\left. + \int_0^t H_d(u)\alpha_d(u)\,dW_d(u)\right\} \end{aligned} \tag{E.9}$$

$$\begin{aligned} N_f(t) = N_f(0)\exp&\left\{\int_0^t r_f(u)\,du + \frac{1}{2}\int_0^t H_f^2(u)\,\alpha_f^2(u)\,du \right. \\ &\left. + \int_0^t H_f(u)\gamma(u)\,du + \int_0^t H_f(u)\alpha_f(u)\,dW_f(u)\right\} \end{aligned} \tag{E.10}$$

By substituting the short rates $r_d(t)$ and $r_f(t)$ in the above equations

$$r_i(t) = f(0,t) + z_i(t)\,H_i'(t) + \zeta_i(t)\,H_i'(t)H_i(t),\ i = \{d,f\}$$

we get, as expected

$$N_d(t) = \frac{1}{P_d(0,t)}\exp\left\{H_d(t)\int_0^t \alpha_d(u)dW_d(u) + \frac{1}{2}H_f^2(t)\,\zeta_f(t)\right\} \tag{E.11}$$

$$N_f(t) = \frac{1}{P_f(0,t)} \exp\left\{ H_f(t) \int_0^t \alpha_f(u) dW_f(u) + H_f(t) \int_0^t \gamma(u) du + \frac{1}{2} H_f^2(t) \zeta_f(t) \right\}. \tag{E.12}$$

We want to compute the foreign zero bond price in the domestic measure. To do so, we consider a payoff of 1 in foreign currency at maturity T, convert it into domestic currency (by factor $x(T)$), then discount back to time t using domestic rates ($N_d(t)/N_d(T)$). Finally convert the amount back into foreign currency (by factor $1/x(t)$).

$$P_f(t,T) = E_d\left(\frac{x(T)}{x(t)} \frac{N_d(t)}{N_d(T)} \right)$$

which, by substituting $N_d(\cdot)$ by Equation (E.9) and inserting the solution of $x(t)$, can be written as

$$\begin{aligned} = \mathbb{E}_d\Bigg(\exp\Bigg\{ & \int_t^T r_f(u) du + \rho_{xd}\sigma_x \int_t^T H_d(u)\alpha_d(u) du \\ & - \frac{1}{2}\int_t^T \sigma_x^2 dt + \int_t^T \sigma_x dW_x(u) \\ & - \frac{1}{2}\int_t^T H_d^2(u)\alpha_d^2(u) du - \int_t^T H_d(u)\alpha_d(u) dW_d(u) \Bigg\}\Bigg) \end{aligned} \tag{E.13}$$

then using Equation (E.10),

$$\begin{aligned} = \mathbb{E}_d\Bigg(\exp\Bigg\{ & \frac{N_f(t)}{N_f(T)} + \frac{1}{2}\int_t^T H_f^2(u)\alpha_f^2(u) du \\ & + \int_t^T H_f(u)\alpha_f(u) dW_f(u) + \int_t^T \gamma(u) H_f(u) du \\ & + \rho_{xd}\sigma_x \int_t^T H_d(u)\alpha_d(u) du - \frac{1}{2}\int_t^T \sigma_x^2 dt \\ & + \int_t^T \sigma_x dW_x(u) - \frac{1}{2}\int_t^T H_d^2(u)\alpha_d^2(u) du \\ & - \int_t^T H_d(u)\alpha_d(u) dW_d(u) \Bigg\}\Bigg) \end{aligned}$$

$$
\begin{aligned}
= \frac{P_f(0,T)}{P_f(0,t)} \mathbb{E}_d \Bigg(\exp \Bigg\{ & - H_f(T) \int_0^T \alpha_f(u) dW_f(u) \\
& + H_f(t) \int_0^t \alpha_f(u) dW_f(u) \\
& - H_f(T) \int_0^T \gamma(u) du + H_f(t) \int_0^t \gamma(u) du \\
& - \frac{1}{2} H_f^2(T) \zeta_f(T) + \frac{1}{2} H_f^2(t) \zeta_f(t) \\
& + \frac{1}{2} \int_t^T H_f^2(u) \alpha_f^2(u) du + \int_t^T \gamma(u) H_f(u) du \\
& + \int_t^T H_f(u) \alpha_f(u) dW_f(u) - \frac{1}{2} \int_t^T \sigma_x^2 dt \\
& + \rho_{xd} \sigma_x \int_t^T H_d(u) \alpha_d(u) du + \int_t^T \sigma_x dW_x(u) \\
& - \frac{1}{2} \int_t^T H_d^2(u) \alpha_d^2(u) du) - \int_t^T H_d(u) \alpha_d(u) dW_d(u) \Bigg\} \Bigg)
\end{aligned}
$$

where we substituted $N_f(\cdot)$ by Equation (E.12). After further lengthy calculations, we obtain

$$
\begin{aligned}
P_f(t,T) = & \frac{P_f(0,T)}{P_f(0,t)} \exp \Bigg\{ - \left(H_f(t) - H_f(t) \right) \left(\int_0^t \alpha_f(u) dW_f(u) + \int_0^t \gamma(u) d(u) \right) \\
& - \frac{1}{2} \left(H_f^2(t) - H_f^2(t) \right) \zeta_f(t) \Bigg\} \\
= & \frac{P_f(0,T)}{P_f(0,t)} \exp \Bigg\{ - \left(H_f(t) - H_f(t) \right) z_f(t) - \frac{1}{2} \left(H_f^2(t) - H_f^2(t) \right) \zeta_f(t) \Bigg\}.
\end{aligned}
$$

F Dodgson-Kainth Model

F.1 Domestic currency inflation

In this section we provide some more detail on the derivation of the stochastic inflation-indexed bond price in the Dodgson-Kainth model under the LGM measure:

$$P_I(t,T) = \frac{N(t)}{I(t)}\,\mathbb{E}_t^N\left[\frac{I(T)}{N(T)}\right] = N(t)\,\mathbb{E}_t^N\left[\frac{1}{N(T)}\,e^{\int_t^T i(s)\,ds}\right]. \tag{13.20'}$$

We start by considering the inflation short rate integral:

$$\begin{aligned}
\int_t^T i(s)\,ds &= \int_t^T \mu(s)\,ds + \int_t^T x(s)\,ds \\
&= \int_t^T \mu(s)\,ds + x(t)\,e^{\lambda_I t}\int_t^T e^{-\lambda_I s}\,ds \\
&\quad + \int_t^T \left(e^{-\lambda_I s}\int_t^s \alpha_I(u)\,dW_I(u)\right)ds \\
&= \int_t^T \mu(s)\,ds + (H_I(T) - H_I(t))\,z_I(t) \\
&\quad + \int_t^T (H_I(T) - H_I(s))\,\alpha_I(s)\,dW_I(s)
\end{aligned}$$

where

$$H_I(t) = \int_0^t e^{-\lambda_I s} ds = \frac{1-e^{-\lambda_I t}}{\lambda_I}.$$

We now insert this, together with the explicit expression for the LGM numeraire,

$$N(t) = \frac{1}{P_n(0,t)}\exp\left\{H_n(t)\,z_n(t) + \frac{1}{2}H_n^2(t)\,\zeta_n(t)\right\}, \tag{11.1'}$$

into (13.20') and compute the expectation:

$$
\begin{aligned}
P_I(t,T) &= N(t)\,\mathbb{E}_t^N\Big[e^{\int_t^T \mu(s)\,ds+(H_I(T)-H_I(t))\,z_I(t)+\int_t^T (H_I(T)-H_I(s))\,\alpha_I(s)\,dW_I(s)} \\
&\qquad \times P_n(0,T)\,e^{-H_n(T)z_n(T)-\frac{1}{2}H_n^2(T)\zeta_n(T)}\Big] \\
&= N(t)\,P_n(0,T)\,e^{\int_t^T \mu(s)\,ds+(H_I(T)-H_I(t))\,z_I(t)-\frac{1}{2}H_n^2(T)\zeta_n(T)} \\
&\quad \times \mathbb{E}_t^N\Big[e^{-H_n(T)z_n(T)+\int_t^T (H_I(T)-H_I(s))\,\alpha_I(s)\,dW_I(s)}\Big] \\
&= N(t)\,P_n(0,T)\,e^{\int_t^T \mu(s)\,ds+(H_I(T)-H_I(t))\,z_I(t)-\frac{1}{2}H_n^2(T)\zeta_n(T)} \\
&\qquad \times e^{-H_n(T)z_n(t)+\frac{1}{2}H_n^2(T)(\zeta_n(T)-\zeta_n(t))+\frac{1}{2}\int_t^T (H_I(T)-H_I(s))^2\,\alpha_I^2(s)\,ds} \\
&\qquad \times e^{-\rho^{nI}H_n(T)\int_t^T (H_I(T)-H_I(s))\,\alpha_I(s)\,\alpha_n(s)\,ds} \\
&= N(t)\,P_n(0,T)\,e^{\int_t^T \mu(s)\,ds+(H_I(T)-H_I(t))\,z_I(t)} \\
&\qquad \times e^{-H_n(T)z_n(t)-\frac{1}{2}H_n^2(T)\zeta_n(t)+\frac{1}{2}\int_t^T (H_I(T)-H_I(s))^2\,\alpha_I^2(s)\,ds} \\
&\qquad \times e^{-\rho^{nI}H_n(T)\int_t^T (H_I(T)-H_I(s))\,\alpha_I(s)\,\alpha_n(s)\,ds} \\
&= \frac{P_n(0,T)}{P_n(0,t)}\,e^{H_n(t)\,z_n(t)+\frac{1}{2}H_n^2(t)\zeta_n(t)} \\
&\qquad \times e^{\int_t^T \mu(s)\,ds+(H_I(T)-H_I(t))\,z_I(t)} \\
&\qquad \times e^{-H_n(T)z_n(t)-\frac{1}{2}H_n^2(T)\zeta_n(t)+\frac{1}{2}\int_t^T (H_I(T)-H_I(s))^2\,\alpha_I^2(s)\,ds} \\
&\qquad \times e^{-\rho^{nI}H_n(T)\int_t^T (H_I(T)-H_I(s))\,\alpha_I(s)\,\alpha_n(s)\,ds} \\
&= \frac{P_n(0,T)}{P_n(0,t)}\,e^{-(H_n(T)-H_n(t))\,z_n(t)-\frac{1}{2}(H_n^2(T)-H_n^2(t))\zeta_n(t)} \\
&\qquad \times e^{\int_t^T \mu(s)\,ds+(H_I(T)-H_I(t))\,z_I(t)} \\
&\qquad \times e^{+\frac{1}{2}\int_t^T (H_I(T)-H_I(s))^2\,\alpha_I^2(s)\,ds} \\
&\qquad \times e^{-\rho^{nI}H_n(T)\int_t^T (H_I(T)-H_I(s))\,\alpha_I(s)\,\alpha_n(s)\,ds}
\end{aligned}
$$

With the LGM zero bond

$$
P_n(t,T) = \frac{P_n(0,T)}{P_n(0,t)}\,e^{-(H_n(T)-H_n(t))\,z_n(t)-\frac{1}{2}(H_n^2(T)-H_n^2(t))\zeta_n(t)} \qquad (11.4')
$$

and defining the abbreviation

$$V(t,T) = \frac{1}{2}\int_t^T (H_I(T) - H_I(s))^2\,\alpha_I^2(s)\,ds$$
$$-\rho^{nI}\,H_n(T)\int_t^T (H_I(T) - H_I(s))\,\alpha_n(s)\,\alpha_I(s)\,ds \qquad (13.22')$$

we arrive at

$$P_I(t,T) = P_n(t,T)\exp\left((H_I(T) - H_I(t))\,z_I(t) + V(t,T) + \int_t^T \mu(s)\,ds\right). \qquad (13.21')$$

F.2 Foreign currency inflation

In this section, we explicitly derive the price of the foreign currency inflation-linked bond in the DK model under the domestic LGM measure. Again, we start with

$$\begin{aligned} i(t) &= \mu(t) + x(t) \\ x(t) &= x(t_0)\,e^{-\lambda_i(t-t_0)} + e^{-\lambda_i t\int_{t_0}^t \alpha_I(s)\,dW_I(s)} \\ P_I(t,T) &= \frac{N_0(t)}{I(t)\,FX(t)}\,\mathbb{E}_t^{N_0}\left[\frac{I(T)\,FX(T)}{N_0(T)}\right] \\ &= \frac{N_0(t)}{FX(t)}\,\mathbb{E}_t^{N_0}\left[\frac{FX(T)}{N_0(T)}\,e^{\int_t^T i(s)\,ds}\right]. \end{aligned} \qquad (F.1)$$

Note that μ will be different from its single-currency counterpart, but we do not really care about that because as before we will be able to eliminate it later. We also make use of the result in (11.1):

$$N_0(t) = \frac{1}{P(0,t)}\exp\left\{H_0(t)\,z_0(t) + \frac{1}{2}H_0^2(t)\,\zeta_0(t)\right\}, \qquad (11.1')$$

and the same for index i instead of 0. For the log-difference of FX rates, recall Equation (12.13):

$$\ln\frac{FX_i(T)}{FX_i(t)} = \mathbb{E}_t\left(\ln\frac{FX_i(T)}{FX_i(t)}\right) + \int_t^T \sigma_i(s)\,dW_i^x(s)$$
$$+ \int_t^T (H_0(T) - H_0(s))\,\alpha_0(s)\,dW_0^z(s)$$
$$- \int_t^T (H_i(T) - H_i(s))\,\alpha_i(s)\,dW_i^z(s), \qquad (12.13')$$

where, according to (12.14):

$$\mathbb{E}_t\left(\ln\frac{FX_i(T)}{FX_i(t)}\right) = \ln\frac{P_i(0,T)}{P_i(0,t)}\frac{P_0(0,t)}{P_0(0,T)} - \frac{1}{2}\int_t^T \sigma_i^2(s)\,ds$$
$$+ \frac{1}{2}\left(H_0^2(T)\zeta_0(T) - H_0^2(t)\,\zeta_0(t) - \int_t^T H_0^2(s)\,\alpha_0^2(s)\,ds\right)$$
$$- \frac{1}{2}\left(H_i^2(T)\zeta_i(T) - H_i^2(t)\,\zeta_i(t) - \int_t^T H_i^2(s)\,\alpha_i^2(s)\,ds\right)$$
$$+ \rho_{0i}^{zx}\int_t^T \alpha_0(s)\,H_0(s)\,\sigma_i(s)\,ds$$
$$+ \int_t^T (H_i(T) - H_i(s))\left(\alpha_i^2(s)\,H_i(s) + \rho_{ii}^{zx}\,\sigma_i(s)\,\alpha_i(s)\right) ds$$
$$- \int_t^T (H_i(T) - H_i(s))\,\rho_{i0}^{zz}\,\alpha_i(s)\,\alpha_0(s)\,H_0(s)\,ds$$
$$+ (H_0(T) - H_0(t))\,z_0(t) - (H_i(T) - H_i(t))\,z_i(t). \qquad (12.14')$$

Now we compute

$$P_I(t,T) = \frac{N_0(t)}{FX(t)}\,\mathbb{E}_t^{N_0}\left[\frac{FX(T)}{N_0(T)}\,e^{\int_t^T i(s)\,ds}\right]$$
$$= N_0(t)\,\mathbb{E}_t^{N_0}\left[\frac{1}{N_0(T)}\exp\left(\int_t^T i(s)\,ds + \ln\frac{FX(T)}{FX(t)}\right)\right]$$
$$= \frac{P(0,T)}{P(0,t)}\,\mathbb{E}_t^{N_0}\left[\exp\left(\int_t^T i(s)\,ds + \ln\frac{FX(T)}{FX(t)}\right)\right.$$
$$\times \exp\left(H_0(t)\,z_0(t) + \frac{1}{2}H_0^2(t)\,\zeta_0(t) - H_0(T)\,z_0(T)\right.$$
$$\left.\left. - \frac{1}{2}H_0^2(T)\,\zeta_0(T)\right)\right].$$

We continue to expand the term inside the exponential. To prevent any awkward formulas, we restrict ourselves to the terms in the exponent from now on (which will be awkward enough). Inserting the bits we know, the exponent is

$$\begin{aligned}
&\int_t^T \mu(s)\,ds + (H_I(T) - H_I(t))z_I(t) + \ln \frac{P_i(0,T)}{P_i(0,t)} \frac{P_0(0,t)}{P_0(0,T)} - \frac{1}{2}\int_t^T \sigma_i^2(s)\,ds \\
&\quad + \frac{1}{2}\left(H_0^2(T)\zeta_0(T) - H_0^2(t)\,\zeta_0(t) - \int_t^T H_0^2(s)\,\alpha_0^2(s)\,ds\right) \\
&\quad - \frac{1}{2}\left(H_i^2(T)\zeta_i(T) - H_i^2(t)\,\zeta_i(t) - \int_t^T H_i^2(s)\,\alpha_i^2(s)\,ds\right) \\
&\quad + \rho_{0i}^{zx}\int_t^T \alpha_0(s)\,H_0(s)\,\sigma_i(s)\,ds \\
&\quad + \int_t^T (H_i(T) - H_i(s))\left(\alpha_i^2(s)\,H_i(s) + \rho_{ii}^{zx}\,\sigma_i(s)\,\alpha_i(s)\right) ds \\
&\quad - \int_t^T (H_i(T) - H_i(s))\,\rho_{i0}^{zz}\,\alpha_i(s)\,\alpha_0(s)\,H_0(s)\,ds \\
&\quad + (H_0(T) - H_0(t))\,z_0(t) - (H_i(T) - H_i(t))\,z_i(t) \\
&\quad + H_0(t)\,z_0(t) + \frac{1}{2}H_0^2(t)\,\zeta_0(t) - \frac{1}{2}H_0^2(T)\,\zeta_0(T) \\
&\quad - H_0(T)\,z_0(T) + \int_t^T (H_I(T) - H_I(s))\alpha_I(s)\,dW_I(s) + \int_t^T \sigma_i(s)\,dW_i^x(s) \\
&\quad + \int_t^T (H_0(T) - H_0(s))\,\alpha_0(s)\,dW_0^z(s) - \int_t^T (H_i(T) - H_i(s))\,\alpha_i(s)\,dW_i^z(s).
\end{aligned}$$

Note that

$$H_0(T)z_0(T) = H_0(T)\left(z_0(t) + \int_t^T \alpha_0(s)\,dW_0^z(s)\right),$$

so we can see that

$$H_0(t)z_0(t) - H_0(T)z_0(T) + (H_0(T) - H_0(t))z_0(t) = -H_0(T)\int_t^T \alpha_0(s)\,dW_0^z(s).$$

Furthermore, some of the ζ_0-terms cancel out, so we are left with

$$\begin{aligned}
&\int_t^T \mu(s)\,ds + (H_I(T)-H_I(t))z_I(t) + \ln\frac{P_i(0,T)}{P_i(0,t)}\frac{P_0(0,t)}{P_0(0,T)} - \frac{1}{2}\int_t^T \sigma_i^2(s)\,ds \\
&-\frac{1}{2}\int_t^T H_0^2(s)\,\alpha_0^2(s)\,ds - \frac{1}{2}\left(H_i^2(T)\zeta_i(T) - H_i^2(t)\,\zeta_i(t) - \int_t^T H_i^2(s)\,\alpha_i^2(s)\,ds\right) \\
&+\rho_{0i}^{zx}\int_t^T \alpha_0(s)\,H_0(s)\,\sigma_i(s)\,ds - (H_i(T)-H_i(t))\,z_i(t) \\
&+\int_t^T (H_i(T)-H_i(s))\left(\alpha_i^2(s)\,H_i(s) + \rho_{ii}^{zx}\,\sigma_i(s)\,\alpha_i(s)\right)ds \\
&-\int_t^T (H_i(T)-H_i(s))\,\rho_{i0}^{zz}\,\alpha_i(s)\,\alpha_0(s)\,H_0(s)\,ds \\
&+\int_t^T (H_I(T)-H_I(s))\alpha_I(s)\,dW_I(s) + \int_t^T \sigma_i(s)\,dW_i^x(s) \\
&-\int_t^T H_0(s)\,\alpha_0(s)\,dW_0^z(s) - \int_t^T (H_i(T)-H_i(s))\,\alpha_i(s)\,dW_i^z(s).
\end{aligned}$$

Only the last two lines consist of expressions that are not deterministic or t-measurable. The contribution of the Ito integrals to the time-t expectation is 0. They do, however, contribute to the variance. We next focus on

$$\begin{aligned}
&\frac{1}{2}\mathbb{V}\Bigg(\int_t^T (H_I(T)-H_I(s))\alpha_I(s)\,dW_I(s) + \int_t^T \sigma_i(s)\,dW_i^x(s) \\
&\quad -\int_t^T H_0(s)\,\alpha_0(s)\,dW_0^z(s) - \int_t^T (H_i(T)-H_i(s))\,\alpha_i(s)\,dW_i^z(s)\Bigg) \\
&= \frac{1}{2}\int_t^T (H_I(T)-H_I(s))^2\alpha_I^2(s)\,ds + \frac{1}{2}\int_t^T \sigma_i^2(s)\,ds + \frac{1}{2}\int_t^T H_0^2(s)\alpha_0^2(s)\,ds \\
&\quad +\frac{1}{2}\int_t^T (H_i(T)-H_i(s))^2\alpha_i^2(s)\,ds + \rho_{ii}^{xI}\int_t^T (H_I(T)-H_I(s))\alpha_I(s)\sigma_i(s)\,ds \\
&\quad -\rho_{0i}^{zI}\int_t^T (H_I(T)-H_I(s))\alpha_I(s)H_0(s)\alpha_0(s)\,ds \\
&\quad -\rho_{ii}^{zI}\int_t^T (H_I(T)-H_I(s))\alpha_I(s)(H_i(T)-H_i(s))\,\alpha_i(s)\,ds
\end{aligned}$$

$$
\begin{aligned}
&- \rho_{0i}^{zx} \int_t^T H_0(s)\alpha_0(s)\sigma_i(s)\,ds - \rho_{ii}^{zx} \int_t^T (H_i(T) - H_i(s))\,\alpha_i(s)\sigma_i(s)\,ds \\
&+ \rho_{0i}^{zz} \int_t^T (H_i(T) - H_i(s))\,\alpha_i(s)H_0(s)\alpha_0(s)\,ds.
\end{aligned}
$$

We can simplify

$$
\begin{aligned}
&\frac{1}{2}\int_t^T (H_i(T) - H_i(s))^2\alpha_i^2(s)\,ds + \frac{1}{2}\int_t^T H_i^2(s)\alpha_i^2(s)\,ds \\
&\quad + \int_t^T (H_i(T) - H_i(s))\alpha_i^2(s)\,H_i(s)\,ds \\
&\quad - \frac{1}{2}(H_i^2(T)\zeta_i(T) - H_i^2(t)\,\zeta_i(t)) \\
&= -\frac{1}{2}(H_i^2(T) - H_i^2(t))\zeta_i(t).
\end{aligned}
$$

Now we can compute $\mathbb{E}_t(\exp(\cdot)) = \exp(\mathbb{E}_t(\cdot) + \frac{1}{2}\mathbb{V}_t(\cdot))$ by summing up everything except the Ito integrals:

$$
\begin{aligned}
&\int_t^T \mu(s)\,ds + (H_I(T) - H_I(t))z_I(t) - (H_i(T) - H_i(t))z_i(t) \\
&\quad + \ln\frac{P_i(0,T)}{P_i(0,t)}\frac{P_0(0,t)}{P_0(0,T)} - \frac{1}{2}(H_i^2(T) - H_i^2(t))\zeta_i(t) \\
&\quad + \frac{1}{2}\int_t^T (H_I(T) - H_I(s))^2\alpha_I^2(s)\,ds \\
&\quad + \rho_{ii}^{xI}\int_t^T (H_I(T) - H_I(s))\alpha_I(s)\sigma_i(s)\,ds \\
&\quad - \rho_{0i}^{zI}\int_t^T (H_I(T) - H_I(s))\alpha_I(s)H_0(s)\alpha_0(s)\,ds \\
&\quad - \rho_{ii}^{zI}\int_t^T (H_I(T) - H_I(s))\alpha_I(s)(H_i(T) - H_i(s))\,\alpha_i(s)\,ds.
\end{aligned}
$$

Now

$$
\begin{aligned}
P_i(t,T) = \frac{P(0,T)}{P(0,t)} &\exp\left(\ln\frac{P_i(0,T)}{P_i(0,t)}\frac{P_0(0,t)}{P_0(0,T)} - (H_i(T) - H_i(t))z_i(t)\right) \\
&\times \exp\left(-\frac{1}{2}(H_i^2(T) - H_i^2(t))\zeta_i(t)\right)
\end{aligned}
$$

so we finally get

$$
\begin{aligned}
P_I(t,T) = P_i(t,T)\exp\Bigg(\int_t^T & \mu(s)\,ds + (H_I(T) - H_I(t))z_I(t) \\
& + \frac{1}{2}\int_t^T (H_I(T) - H_I(s))^2 \alpha_I^2(s)\,ds \\
& + \rho_{ii}^{xI}\int_t^T (H_I(T) - H_I(s))\alpha_I(s)\sigma_i(s)\,ds \\
& - \rho_{0i}^{zI}\int_t^T (H_I(T) - H_I(s))\alpha_I(s)H_0(s)\alpha_0(s)\,ds \\
& - \rho_{ii}^{zI}\int_t^T (H_I(T) - H_I(s))\alpha_I(s)(H_i(T) - H_i(s))\,\alpha_i(s)\,ds\Bigg),
\end{aligned}
$$

as claimed.

G | CIR Model with Jumps

In this appendix we summarize a result from Lando [110], Appendix E – a semi-analytical solution for (15.20)

$$G_{u,b}(t,y_0,\rho,\bar{y}) = \mathbb{E}\left\{\exp\left(uy_t - \rho\int_0^t y\,ds\right)\mathbb{1}_{\{by_t<\bar{y}\}}\right\},$$

which is the building block for computing European options in the JCIR model. Moreover we explore some of its properties, for example to see whether the presence of jumps leads to a different constraint than the Feller constraint in the pure CIR case.

Duffie et al. [61] have shown:

$$\begin{aligned} G_{u,b}(t,y_0,\rho,\bar{y}) &= \frac{1}{2}\Psi(u,t,y_0,\rho) \\ &+ \frac{1}{4\pi}\int_{-\infty}^{\infty}\frac{e^{iv\bar{y}}\Psi(u-ivb,t,y_0,\rho)-e^{-iv\bar{y}}\Psi(u+ivb,t,y_0,\rho)}{iv}\,dv \end{aligned} \tag{G.1}$$

where $\Psi(\cdot)$ solves an ODE. For real u one can write (G.1) more compactly as

$$G_{u,b}(t,y_0,\rho,\bar{y}) = \frac{1}{2}\Psi(u,t,y_0,\rho) - \frac{1}{\pi}\int_0^{\infty}\Im\left[e^{-iv\bar{y}}\Psi(u+ivb,t,y_0,\rho)\right]\frac{dv}{v} \tag{G.2}$$

For $b=0$, that is switching off the indicator function, (G.1) reduces to

$$\begin{aligned} G_{u,0}(t,y_0,\rho,\bar{y}) &= \frac{1}{2}\Psi(u,t,y_0,\rho) + \frac{\Psi(u,t,y_0,\rho)}{4\pi}\int_{-\infty}^{\infty}\frac{e^{iv\bar{y}}-e^{-iv\bar{y}}}{iv}\,dv \\ &= \Psi(u,t,y_0,\rho) \end{aligned}$$

Christensen [52] has furthermore shown that $\Psi(\cdot)$ has a closed form solution:

$$\Psi(z,t,y_0,\rho) = \exp\left(\alpha_\Psi + \beta_\Psi\, y_0\right)$$

$$\begin{aligned}
\alpha_\Psi &= \frac{2\kappa\mu}{\sigma^2}\ln\left[\frac{2\gamma\, e^{(\gamma+\kappa)t/2}}{2\gamma + (\gamma+\kappa - z\sigma^2)\left(e^{\gamma t}-1\right)}\right] \\
&\quad + \frac{\lambda\eta\,(2\rho + z(\gamma+\kappa))\, t}{\gamma - \kappa + z\sigma^2 - \eta\,(2\rho + z(\gamma+\kappa))} \\
&\quad - \frac{2\lambda\eta}{\sigma^2 - 2\eta\kappa - 2\rho\eta^2} \\
&\qquad \times \ln\left[1 + \frac{(\gamma+\kappa - z\sigma^2 + \eta(2\rho - z(\gamma-\kappa)))\left(e^{\gamma t}-1\right)}{2\gamma\,(1 - z\eta)}\right] \\
\beta_\Psi &= \frac{-2\rho\left(e^{\gamma t}-1\right) + z e^{\gamma t}(\gamma-\kappa) + z(\gamma+\kappa)}{2\gamma + (\gamma+\kappa - z\sigma^2)\left(e^{\gamma t}-1\right)} \\
\gamma &= \sqrt{\kappa^2 + 2\rho\sigma^2}
\end{aligned}$$

with

$$\kappa = a, \quad \mu = \theta, \quad \gamma = h, \quad \lambda = \alpha, \quad \eta = \gamma_{JCIR}$$

Note that

- G is real when u is real
- $G = \Psi$ for u real and $b = 0$
- $G = \Psi$ is the characteristic function $\widetilde{\phi}(x,t)$ of y_t for imaginary u and $b = \rho = 0$:

$$\widetilde{\phi}(x,t) = G_{ix,0}(t,y_0,0,\bar{y}) = \Psi(ix,t,y_0,0)$$

- Probability density $\phi(y,t)$ given by the inverse Fourier transform

$$\phi(y,t) = \frac{1}{2\pi}\int_{-\infty}^{\infty} e^{-ixy}\,\widetilde{\phi}(x,t)\,dx = \frac{1}{\pi}\int_0^{\infty} \Re\left[\widetilde{\phi}(x,t)\, e^{-ixy}\right] dx$$

  since $\widetilde{\phi}(-x,t) = \widetilde{\phi}^*(x,t)$ by definition as FT of a real density.
- Norm: $\widetilde{\phi}(0,t) = \Psi(0,t,y_0,0) \equiv 1$ for all times, can be shown using L'Hôpital in one of the terms in α_ψ

We now briefly discuss the question whether the usual Feller constraint $2\,a\theta > \sigma^2$ is modified by the jump component in JCIR.

JCIR Constraint

We require that the density at the origin remains finite for $t \to \infty$, that is

$$\lim_{t\to\infty} \phi(0,t) = \lim_{t\to\infty} \frac{1}{\pi} \int_0^{\infty} \Re[\widetilde{\phi}(x,t)]\, dx < \infty$$

Therefore, consider $\widetilde{\phi}(x,t) = \Psi(z = ix, t, y_0, 0)$:

$$\alpha_\Psi = \frac{2\kappa\mu}{\sigma^2} \ln\left[\frac{2\kappa e^{\kappa t}}{2\kappa + (2\kappa - z\sigma^2)\left(e^{\kappa t} - 1\right)}\right] + \frac{2\lambda\eta\kappa\, t}{\sigma^2 - 2\eta\kappa}$$

$$- \frac{2\lambda\eta}{\sigma^2 - 2\eta\kappa} \times \ln\left[1 + \frac{(2\kappa - z\sigma^2)\left(e^{\kappa t} - 1\right)}{2\kappa(1 - z\eta)}\right]$$

$$\beta_\Psi = \frac{2\kappa\, z}{2\kappa + (2\kappa - z\sigma^2)\left(e^{\kappa t} - 1\right)}$$

Consider its limit for $t \to \infty$:

$$\beta_\Psi \to 0, \qquad \alpha_\Psi \to \frac{2\kappa\mu}{\sigma^2} \ln\left[\frac{1}{1 - \frac{\sigma^2}{2\kappa} z}\right] + \frac{2\lambda\eta}{\sigma^2 - 2\eta\kappa} \ln\left[\frac{1 - \eta z}{1 - \frac{\sigma^2}{2\kappa} z}\right]$$

Hence

$$\lim_{t\to\infty} \widetilde{\phi}(x,t) = \lim_{t\to\infty} e^{\alpha_\Psi + \beta_\Psi y_0} = \frac{(1 - \eta\, ix)^{\delta}}{\left(1 - \frac{\sigma^2}{2\kappa}\, ix\right)^{\epsilon+\delta}}$$

where

$$\epsilon = \frac{2\kappa\mu}{\sigma^2}, \qquad \delta = \frac{2\lambda\eta}{\sigma^2 - 2\eta\kappa}$$

The asymptotic characteristic function is stationary (due to mean reversion) and independent of the initial condition y_0. In terms of absolute value and phase:

$$\lim_{t\to\infty} \widetilde{\phi}(x,t) = \frac{(1 + \eta^2 x^2)^{\frac{\delta}{2}}}{\left(1 + \frac{\sigma^4}{4\kappa^2} x^2\right)^{\frac{\epsilon+\delta}{2}}} \times e^{i\varphi},$$

$$\varphi = (\epsilon + \delta) \arctan(\sigma^2 x / 2\kappa) - \delta \arctan(\eta x)$$

For large values of x ($x \gg 1/\eta$ and $x \gg 2\kappa/\sigma^2$), its real part decays as

$$\left(\frac{2\kappa\eta}{\sigma^2}\right)^{\delta} \times \left(\frac{\sigma^2}{2\kappa} x\right)^{-\epsilon} \times \cos(\epsilon\,\pi/2)$$

Its absolute value decays $\propto x^{-\epsilon}$ for $x \to \infty$. For the integral over the characteristic function to converge, we therefore need $\epsilon > 1$: **The Feller constraint still holds, as in the pure CIR case.**

Limiting Cases

We now explore whether special limiting cases of the JCIR model offer further insight and possibly a weaker constraint for convergence.

1. CIR case, $\lambda \to 0$:

$$\lim_{t\to\infty} \Re\widetilde{\phi}(x,t) \sim \left(\frac{\sigma^2}{2\kappa}x\right)^{-\epsilon} \times \cos(\epsilon\,\pi/2)$$

   This requires $\epsilon = 2\kappa\,\mu/\sigma^2 > 1$ for convergence.
2. Poisson case, $\sigma \to 0$, $\delta = -\lambda/\kappa$:

$$\lim_{t\to\infty} \Re\widetilde{\phi}(x,t) \sim (\eta\,x)^{\delta} \cos(\mu\,x - \delta\pi/2)$$

   Due to the oscillatory term, the integral converges for any λ/κ as long as $\mu > 0$. For $\mu = 0$, convergence requires $\lambda > \kappa$.
3. $\sigma^2 = 2\kappa\,\eta$ so that $\delta \to \infty$, $\epsilon = \mu/\eta$ and $\varphi = \epsilon \arctan(\eta\,x)$:

$$\lim_{t\to\infty} \Re\widetilde{\phi}(x,t) \sim (\eta\,x)^{-\epsilon} \cos(\epsilon\,\pi/2)$$

   with $\epsilon = \mu/\eta = 2\kappa\,\mu/\sigma^2 > 1$ again for convergence.
4. $\eta \to 0$ (i.e. $\eta \ll \sigma^2/2\kappa$) and $\lambda \to \infty$ (i.e. $\lambda = \delta\sigma^2/2\eta$) for finite $\delta > 0$:

$$\lim_{t\to\infty} \Re\widetilde{\phi}(x,t) \sim \left(\frac{\sigma^2}{2\kappa}x\right)^{-\epsilon-\delta} \times \cos((\epsilon+\delta)\,\pi/2)$$

   with $\epsilon + \delta > 1$ for convergence.

Let us inspect the characteristic function for case 4 (set $2\lambda\eta = \delta\sigma^2$ and then $\eta = 0$):

$$
\begin{aligned}
\alpha_\Psi &= \epsilon \ln\left[\frac{e^{\kappa t}}{1+\left(1-\frac{\sigma^2}{2\kappa}\right)\left(e^{\kappa t}-1\right)}\right] + \delta\kappa t \\
&\quad - \delta \ln\left[1+\left(1-\frac{\sigma^2}{2\kappa}z\right)\left(e^{\kappa t}-1\right)\right] \\
&= (\epsilon+\delta)\ln\left[\frac{e^{\kappa t}}{1+\left(1-\frac{\sigma^2}{2\kappa}\right)\left(e^{\kappa t}-1\right)}\right] \\
\beta_\Psi &= \frac{z}{1+\left(1-\frac{\sigma^2}{2\kappa}z\right)\left(e^{\kappa t}-1\right)}
\end{aligned}
$$

The characteristic function in case 4 has CIR form with a modified mean reversion level

$$\mu' = \mu + \delta\frac{\sigma^2}{2\kappa}.$$

since the compound Poisson process variance $(2\lambda\eta^2 t)$ vanishes in the limit of case 4. Hence only for finite intensity and jump size, JCIR is an extension of CIR.

JCIR Survival Probability

We obtain the JCIR survival probability from $G_{u,b}(t, y_0, \rho, \bar{y})$ by choosing $u = b = 0$, $\rho = 1$, arbitrary $\bar{y} > 0$:

$$
\begin{aligned}
G_{0,0}(t, y_0, 1, \bar{y}) = \Psi(0, t, y_0, 1) &= \exp\left(\alpha_\Psi + \beta_\Psi\, y_0\right) \\
\alpha_\Psi &= \frac{2\kappa\mu}{\sigma^2}\ln\left[\frac{2\gamma\, e^{(\gamma+\kappa)t/2}}{2\gamma + (\gamma+\kappa)\left(e^{\gamma t}-1\right)}\right] + \frac{2\lambda\eta t}{\gamma-\kappa-2\eta} \\
&\quad - \frac{2\lambda\eta}{\sigma^2 - 2\eta\kappa - 2\eta^2} \times \ln\left[1+\frac{(\gamma+\kappa+2\eta)\left(e^{\gamma t}-1\right)}{2\gamma}\right] \\
\beta_\Psi &= -\frac{2\left(e^{\gamma t}-1\right)}{2\gamma + (\gamma+\kappa)\left(e^{\gamma t}-1\right)} \\
\gamma &= \sqrt{\kappa^2 + 2\sigma^2}
\end{aligned}
$$

with

$$\kappa = a, \quad \mu = \theta, \quad \gamma = h, \quad \lambda = \alpha, \quad \eta = \gamma_{JCIR}$$

H | CDS and CDS Option: Filtration Switching and the PK Model

In this appendix we review the CDS and CDS Option pricing formulas stated in Section 15.1 and express them in terms of the Peng-Kou model's cumulative intensity process in Section 15.5).

Recall the filtration switching formula [33]:

- Let $\mathcal{F}_t$ be the filtration containing the default-free information
- Let $\sigma(\{\tau < u\}, u \leq t)$ be the default monitoring filtration
- $\mathcal{G}_t = \mathcal{F}_t \vee \sigma(\{\tau < u\}, u \leq t)$

Then:

$$
\begin{aligned}
\mathbb{E}(\mathbb{1}_{\{\tau > T\}} X \,|\, \mathcal{G}_t) &= \mathbb{E}(\mathbb{1}_{\{\tau > t\}} \mathbb{1}_{\{\tau > T\}} X \,|\, \mathcal{G}_t) = \mathbb{1}_{\{\tau > t\}} \mathbb{E}(\mathbb{1}_{\{\tau > T\}} X \,|\, \mathcal{G}_t) \\
&= \mathbb{1}_{\{\tau > t\}} \mathbb{E}\left(\mathbb{1}_{\{\tau > T\}} X \,|\, \mathcal{F}_t, \{\tau > t\}\right)
\end{aligned}
$$

Note that the expectation is conditioned on $\tau > t$, since $\tau \leq t$ does not contribute to the expectation calculation

$$
\begin{aligned}
&= \mathbb{1}_{\{\tau > t\}} \frac{\mathbb{E}\left(\mathbb{1}_{\{\tau > t\}} \mathbb{1}_{\{\tau > T\}} X \,|\, \mathcal{F}_t\right)}{P(\tau > t \,|\, \mathcal{F}_t)} \\
&= \frac{\mathbb{1}_{\{\tau > t\}}}{P(\tau > t \,|\, \mathcal{F}_t)} \mathbb{E}\left(\mathbb{1}_{\{\tau > T\}} X \,|\, \mathcal{F}_t\right)
\end{aligned}
$$

We now apply this (carefully) to the pricing of a CDS at future time t in mid-point approximation (protection seller view):

$$
\begin{aligned}
\Pi_{CDS}(t) = \mathbb{E}\Bigg\{ \Bigg[& \sum_{i=1}^{n} K\,\delta_i\,\mathbb{1}_{\{\tau > t_i\}}\,P(t,t_i) \\
& - \sum_{i=1}^{n}\left(LGD - K\frac{\delta_i}{2}\right)\mathbb{1}_{\{t_{i-1}<\tau<t_i\}}\,P\left(t,\frac{t_{i-1}+t_i}{2}\right)\Bigg]\Bigg|\mathcal{G}_t\Bigg\} \\
= \mathbb{1}_{\{\tau>t\}}\,\mathbb{E}\Bigg\{\Bigg[& \sum_{i=1}^{n} K\,\delta_i\,\mathbb{1}_{\{\tau > t_i\}}\,P(t,t_i) \\
& - \sum_{i=1}^{n}\left(LGD - K\frac{\delta_i}{2}\right)\mathbb{1}_{\{t_{i-1}<\tau<t_i\}}\,P\left(t,\frac{t_{i-1}+t_i}{2}\right)\Bigg]\Bigg|\mathcal{G}_t\Bigg\} \\
= \frac{\mathbb{1}_{\{\tau>t\}}}{Q(\tau>t\,|\,\mathcal{F}_t)}\,\mathbb{E}\Bigg\{\mathbb{1}_{\{\tau>t\}}\Bigg[& \sum_{i=1}^{n} K\,\delta_i\,\mathbb{1}_{\{\tau > t_i\}}\,P(t,t_i) \\
& - \sum_{i=1}^{n}\left(LGD - K\frac{\delta_i}{2}\right)\mathbb{1}_{\{t_{i-1}<\tau<t_i\}}\,P\left(t,\frac{t_{i-1}+t_i}{2}\right)\Bigg]\Bigg|\mathcal{F}_t\Bigg\} \\
= \frac{\mathbb{1}_{\{\tau>t\}}}{Q(\tau>t\,|\,\mathcal{F}_t)}\,\mathbb{E}\Bigg\{\Bigg[& \sum_{i=1}^{n} K\,\delta_i\,\mathbb{1}_{\{\tau > t_i\}}\,P(t,t_i) \\
& - \sum_{i=1}^{n}\left(LGD - K\frac{\delta_i}{2}\right)\mathbb{1}_{\{t_{i-1}<\tau<t_i\}}\,P\left(t,\frac{t_{i-1}+t_i}{2}\right)\Bigg]\Bigg|\mathcal{F}_t\Bigg\} \\
= \frac{\mathbb{1}_{\{\tau>t\}}}{Q(\tau>t\,|\,\mathcal{F}_t)}\,\mathbb{E}\Bigg\{\Bigg[& \sum_{i=1}^{n} K\,\delta_i\;P(t,t_i)\,\mathbb{E}\left[\mathbb{1}_{\{\tau > t_i\}}|\mathcal{F}_{t_n}\right] \\
& - \sum_{i=1}^{n}\left(LGD - K\frac{\delta_i}{2}\right)P\left(t,\frac{t_{i-1}+t_i}{2}\right)\times\mathbb{E}\left[\mathbb{1}_{\{t_{i-1}<\tau<t_i\}}|\mathcal{F}_{t_n}\right]\Bigg]\Bigg|\mathcal{F}_t\Bigg\} \\
= \frac{\mathbb{1}_{\{\tau>t\}}}{Q(\tau>t\,|\,\mathcal{F}_t)}\,\mathbb{E}\Bigg\{\Bigg[& \sum_{i=1}^{n} K\,\delta_i\;P(t,t_i)\,Q\left(\tau>t_i|\mathcal{F}_{t_n}\right) \\
& - \sum_{i=1}^{n}\left(LGD - K\frac{\delta_i}{2}\right)P\left(t,\frac{t_{i-1}+t_i}{2}\right) \\
& \times\left[\mathbb{Q}\left(\tau>t_{i-1}|\mathcal{F}_{t_n}\right)-\mathbb{Q}\left(\tau>t_i\,|\,\mathcal{F}_{t_n}\right)\right]\Bigg]\Bigg|\mathcal{F}_t\Bigg\}
\end{aligned}
$$

$$
\begin{aligned}
&= \frac{\mathbb{1}_{\{\tau>t\}}}{e^{-\Lambda(t)}} \mathbb{E}\left\{\left[\sum_{i=1}^{n} K\,\delta_i\, P(t,t_i)\, e^{-\Lambda(t_i)}\right.\right.\\
&\left.\left.\quad - \sum_{i=1}^{n}\left(LGD - K\frac{\delta_i}{2}\right) P\left(t, \frac{t_{i-1}+t_i}{2}\right) \times \left[e^{\Lambda(t_{i-1})} - e^{-\Lambda(t_i)}\right]\right] \middle| \mathcal{F}_t\right\}\\
&= \mathbb{1}_{\{\tau>t\}}\left[\sum_{i=1}^{n} K\,\delta_i\, P(t,t_i)\,\mathbb{E}\left[e^{-(\Lambda(t_i)-\Lambda(t))} \mid \mathcal{F}_t\right]\right.\\
&\quad - \sum_{i=1}^{n}\left(LGD - K\frac{\delta_i}{2}\right) P\left(t, \frac{t_{i-1}+t_i}{2}\right)\\
&\left.\quad \times \left[\mathbb{E}\left[e^{-(\Lambda(t_{i-1})-\Lambda(t))} \mid \mathcal{F}_t\right] - \mathbb{E}\left[e^{-(\Lambda(t_i)-\Lambda(t))} \mid \mathcal{F}_t\right]\right]\right]\\
&= 1_{\tau>t}\left\{\sum_{i=1}^{n} K\,\delta_i\, q(t,t_i)\, P(t,t_i)\right.\\
&\left.\quad - \sum_{i=1}^{n}\left(LGD - K\frac{\delta_i}{2}\right)\left(q(t,t_{i-1}) - q(t,t_i)\right) P\left(t, \frac{t_{i-1}+t_i}{2}\right)\right\}\\
&= 1_{\tau>t}\sum_{i=1}^{n}\left\{(C_i + D_i)\, q(t,t_i) - C_i\, q(t,t_{i-1})\right\}\\
&= 1_{\tau>t}\sum_{i=0}^{n} G_i\, q(t,t_i)
\end{aligned}
$$

with

$$
q(t,t_i) = \mathbb{E}_t\left(e^{-(\Lambda(t_i)-\Lambda(t))}\right) = q^{Mkt}(t)\,\mathbb{E}_t\left(e^{-\Lambda(t_i)}\right)
$$

and the coefficients C_i, D_i, G_i are defined as in Section 15.1.

CDS Option

The price of a CDS Option with expiry at time t, assuming deterministic interest rates, then follows:

$$
\begin{aligned}
\Pi_{CDSO} &= P(0,t)\,\mathbb{E}\left\{\mathbb{1}_{\{\tau>t\}}\,[\Pi_{CDS}(t)]^{+}\,|\,\mathcal{F}_0\right\}\\
&= P(0,t)\,\mathbb{E}\left\{\mathbb{E}\left\{\mathbb{1}_{\{\tau>t\}}\,[\Pi_{CDS}(t)]^{+}\,|\,\mathcal{F}_t\right\}|\,\mathcal{F}_0\right\}\\
&= P(0,t)\,\mathbb{E}\left\{[\Pi_{CDS}(t)]^{+}\,\mathbb{E}\left\{\mathbb{1}_{\{\tau>t\}}\,|\,\mathcal{F}_t\right\}|\,\mathcal{F}_0\right\}\\
&= P(0,t)\,\mathbb{E}\left\{e^{-\Lambda(t)}\,[\Pi_{CDS}(t)]^{+}\,|\,\mathcal{F}_0\right\}\\
&= P(0,t)\,\mathbb{E}\left\{e^{-\Lambda(t)}\left[\omega\sum_{i=0}^{n} G_i\,q(t,t_i,\Lambda(t))\right]^{+}\right\}\\
&= P(0,t)\,\mathbb{E}\left\{e^{-\Lambda(t)}\left[\omega\sum_{i=0}^{n} G_i\,\mathbb{E}_t\left(e^{-(\Lambda(t_i)-\Lambda(t))}\right)\right]^{+}\right\}\\
&= P(0,t)\,\mathbb{E}\left\{e^{-M(t)}\left[\omega\sum_{i=0}^{n} G_i\,\frac{q^{Mrkt}(t_i)}{\mathbb{E}(e^{M(t_i)})}\,\mathbb{E}_t\left(e^{-(M(t_i)-M(t))}\right)\right]^{+}\right\}
\end{aligned}
$$

with $\omega = \pm 1$ switching between options on protection seller and buyer CDS.

Bibliography

[1] Community portal to automatic differentiation (AD). http://www.autodiff.org.

[2] QuantLib, the free/open library for quantitative finance. http://quantlib.org.

[3] Claudio Albanese, Leif Andersen, and Stefano Iabichino. Fva accounting, risk management and collateral trading. *RISK*, February 2015.

[4] H. Albrecher, S. Ladoucette, and W. Schoutens. A generic one-factor Levy model for pricing synthetic CDOs. *in 'Advances in Mathematical Finance' R. J. Elliot et al (eds)*, 2007.

[5] Fernando Ametrano and Marco Bianchetti. Everything you always wanted to know about multiple interest rate curve bootstrapping but were afraid to ask. *http://ssrn.com/abstract=2219548*, 2013.

[6] Leif Andersen, Jakob Sidenius, and Susanta Basu. All Your Hedges in One Basket. *RISK*, November 2003.

[7] Leif B. G. Andersen. Markov Models for Commodity Futures: Theory and Practice. *http://papers.ssrn.com/sol3/papers.cfm?abstract_id=1138782*, 2008.

[8] Leif B.G. Andersen and Vladimir V. Piterbarg. *Interest Rate Modeling. Volumes 1–3.* Atlantic Financial Press, 2010.

[9] T.W. Anderson and D.A. Darling. A Test of Goodness of Fit. *Journal of the American Statistical Association*, 49(268), 1954.

[10] Fabrizio Anfuso, Dimitris Karyampas, and Andreas P. Nawroth. Credit exposure models backtesting for Basel III. RISK, September 2014.

[11] Alexandre Antonov and Vladimir V. Piterbarg. Collateral Choice Option Valuation. *SSRN eLibrary*, 2014.

[12] European Banking Authority. EBA Report on CVA. 2015.

[13] European Banking Authority. Opinion of the European Banking Authority on Credit Valuation Adjustment (CVA). 2015.

[14] S.H. Babbs. The valuation of cross-currency interest-sensitive claims under the cross-currency extended Vasicek model: A PDE approach. *Research Note, First National Bank of Chicago, London*, 1994.

[15] Jennie Bai and Pierre Collin-Dufresne. The CDS-Bond Basis. *SSRN eLibrary*, 2013.

[16] BCBS-118. International Convergence of Capital Measurement and Capital Standards - A Revised Framework. *Basel Committee for Bank Supervision, available online at http://www.bis.org/publ/bcbs118.pdf*, November 2005.

[17] BCBS-128. International Convergence of Capital Measurement and Capital Standards - A Revised Framework. *Basel Committee for Bank Supervision, available online at http://www.bis.org/publ/bcbs128.pdf*, June 2006.

[18] BCBS-189. Basel III: A global regulatory framework for more resilient banks and banking systems. *Basel Committee for Bank Supervision*, 2011.

[19] BCBS-227. Capital requirements for bank exposures to central counterparties. *Basel Committee for Bank Supervision, available online at http://www.bis.org/publ/bcbs227.pdf*, July 2012.
[20] BCBS-237. Capital requirements for bank exposures to central counterparties - Frequently asked questions. *Basel Committee for Bank Supervision, available online at http://www.bis.org/publ/bcbs237.pdf*, December 2012.
[21] BCBS-261. Margin requirements for non-centrally cleared derivatives. *Basel Committee for Bank Supervision*, September 2013.
[22] BCBS-279. The standardised approach for measuring counterparty credit risk exposures. *Basel Committee for Bank Supervision, available online at http://www.bis.org/publ/bcbs279.pdf*, March 2014.
[23] Lukas Becker. Basel Committee launches FVA project. *RISK*, April 2015.
[24] Lukas Becker. CCPs raise alarm on South African OTC reform. *RISK*, March 2015.
[25] Lukas Becker and Nazneen Sherif. The black art of FVA, part III: A $4bn mistake? *RISK*, April 2015.
[26] F. Black and P. Karasinski. Bond and Option pricing when Short rates are Lognormal. *Financial Analysts Journal*, 1991.
[27] Fisher Black. The pricing of commodity contracts. *Journal of Financial Economics, 3*, 167–179, 1976.
[28] Bloomberg. OIS versus Cross Currency Basis Implied Discount Curves. 2011.
[29] C. Bluhm, L. Overbeck, and C. Wagner. *An Introduction to Credit Risk Modelling*. Chapman & Hall, 2003.
[30] Wolfram Boenkost and Wolfgang M. Schmidt. Cross Currency Swap Valuation. *SSRN eLibrary*, 2005.
[31] Credit Suisse First Boston. *CreditRisk+, A Credit Risk Management Framework.*
[32] D. Brigo and A. Alfonsi. Credit default swaps calibration and option pricing with the SSRD stochastic intensity and interest-rate model. *Finance and StochasticsIX(1)*, 2005.
[33] D. Brigo and F. Mercurio. *Interest Rate Models: Theory and Practice, 2nd Edition.* Springer, 2006.
[34] Damiano Brigo and Naoufel El-Bachir. An Exact Formula for Default Swaptions Pricing in the SSRJD Stochastic Intensity Model. *Mathematical Finance*, 20, No. 3:365–382, 2010.
[35] Damiano Brigo, Andrea Pallavicini, and Vasileios Papatheodorou. Bilateral counterparty risk valuation for interest-rate products: impact of volatilities and correlations. *arXiv.org*, 2009.
[36] Damiano Brigo, Andrea Pallavicini, and Roberto Torresetti. *Credit Models and the Crisis.* Wiley, 2010.
[37] Christoph Burgard and Mats Kjaer. In the Balance. *RISK*, November 2011.
[38] Christoph Burgard and Mats Kjaer. PDE Representations of Options with Bilateral Counterparty Risk and Funding Costs. *Journal of Credit Risk*, 7(3), 2011.
[39] Christoph Burgard and Mats Kjaer. The fva debate: In theory and practice. *http://ssrn.com/abstract=2157634*, 2012.
[40] Christoph Burgard and Mats Kjaer. Funding strategies, funding costs. *RISK*, December 2013.
[41] Christoph Burgard and Mats Kjaer. Derivatives Funding, Netting and Accounting. *SSRN*, 2015.

[42] P. Bürgisser, A. Kurth, A. Wagner, and M. Wolf. Integrating Correlations. *RISK*, July 1999.

[43] Matt Cameron. Bafin weighing CVA charge despite European exemptions. *RISK Magazine*, June, 2013.

[44] Matt Cameron. The black art of FVA: Banks spark double-counting fears. *RISK*, April 2013.

[45] Matt Cameron. The black art of FVA, part II: Conditioning chaos. *RISK*, April 2014.

[46] L. Capriotti. Fast Greeks by algorithmic differentiation. *Journal of Computational Finance*, 4:3–35, 2011.

[47] L. Capriotti and M.B. Giles. Algorithmic differentiation: Adjoint Greeks made easy. *http://ssrn.com/paper=1801522*, 2011.

[48] L. Capriotti and M.B. Giles. Fast correlation Greeks by adjoint algorithmic differentiation. *RISK*, March 2010.

[49] L. Capriotti, S. Lee, and M. Peacock. Real time counterparty credit risk management in Monte Carlo. *http://ssrn.com/paper=1824864*, 2011.

[50] Laurie Carver. Traders close ranks against fva critics. *RISK*, September 2012.

[51] Jiun Hong Chan and Mark S. Joshi. Fast and Accurate Long Stepping Simulation of the Heston Stochastic Volatility Model. *http://papers.ssrn.com/sol3/papers.cfm?abstract_id=1617187*, 2010.

[52] J.H. Christensen. Kreditderivater og deres prisfastsaettels. *Thesis, Institute of Economics, University of Copenhagen*, 2004.

[53] Catherine Contiguglia. A structured return. *RISK*, April 2015.

[54] J.C. Cox, J.E. Ingersoll, and S.A. Ross. A Theory of the Term Structure of Interest Rates. *Econometrica*, 53:385–407, 1985.

[55] Duy Minh Danga, Christina C. Christara, Kenneth R. Jackson, and Asif Lakhanyb. A PDE pricing framework for cross-currency interest rate derivatives. *International Conference on Computational Science, ICCS*, 2010.

[56] N. Deguillaume, R. Rebonato, and A. Pogudin. The nature of the dependence of the magnitude of rate moves on the level of rates: a universal relationship. *Quantitative Finance*, 13(3):351–367, 2013.

[57] M.A.H. Dempster and J.P. Hutton. Numerical Valuation of Cross-Currency Swaps and Swaptions. *http://papers.ssrn.com/sol3/papers.cfm?abstract_id=40872*, 1996.

[58] Matthew Dodgson and Dhermider Kainth. *Inflation-linked derivatives*. 2006. Published: QuaRC website.

[59] D. Duffie. Innovations in credit risk transfer: implications for financial stability. *Working paper, Stanford University*, 2007.

[60] D. Duffie and N. Garleanu. Risk and valuation of collateralized debt obligations. *Financial Analysts Journal*, 57:41–59, 2001.

[61] D. Duffie, J. Pan, and K. Singleton. Transform analysis and asset pricing for affine jump diffusions. *Econometrica*, 68:1343–1376, 2000.

[62] D. Duffie and K. Singleton. Modeling term structure of defaultable bonds. *Review of Financial Studies*, 12:687–720, 1999.

[63] James E. Dunne. Characterization of the bivariate negative binomial distribution. *Arkansas Academy of Science Proceedings*, 21, 1967.

[64] Naoufel El-Bachir and Damiano Brigo. An Analytically Tractable Time-changed Jump-Diffusion Default Intensity Model. *ICMA Centre Discussion Papers in Finance DP2008-6*, 2008.

[65] William Feller. Two Singular Diffusion Problems. *The Annals of Mathematics*, 54 No. 1:173–182, 1951.
[66] William Feller. *An Introduction to Probability Theory and its Applications, Volume II.* John Wiley & Sons, 1971.
[67] Jaques Gabillon. The term structures of oil futures prices. *Oxford Institute for Energy Studies, Working Paper WPM 17.*, 1991.
[68] Mark B. Garman and Steven W. Kohlhagen. Foreign currency option values. *Journal of International Money and Finance, 2, 231–237*, 1983.
[69] Michael Giles and Paul Glasserman. Smoking adjoints: fast Monte Carlo Greeks. *RISK*, January 2006.
[70] P. Glasserman. *Monte Carlo methods in Financial Engineering.* 2004. Published: Springer.
[71] Andrew Green and Chris Kenyon. MVA by Replication and Regression. *RISK*, 27, May 2014.
[72] Andrew Green, Chris Kenyon, and Chris Dennis. KVA: Capital Valuation Adjustment by replication. *RISK*, 2014.
[73] Mark Greenwood and Simona Svoboda. LPI swaps – Pricing and Trading. *Risk and Investment Conference 2010 Presentation*, 2010.
[74] Jon Gregory. *Counterparty Credit Risk and Credit Value Adjustment, 2nd Ed.* Wiley Finance, New York, 2012.
[75] A. Griewank. *Evaluating derivatives: principles and techniques of algorithmic differentiation.* Society for Industrial and Applied Mathematics, 2000.
[76] A. Griewank and A. Walther. *Evaluating derivatives: principles and techniques of algorithmic differentiation, 2nd edition.* Society for Industrial and Applied Mathematics, 2008.
[77] Patrick S. Hagan. Evaluating and Hedging Exotic Swap Instruments via LGM. *http://www.researchgate.net/profile/Patrick_Hagan3/publications*, 2002–2005.
[78] Patrick S. Hagan. Methodology for Callable Swaps and Bermudan "Exercise Into" Swaptions. *http://www.researchgate.net/profile/Patrick_Hagan3/publications*, 2002–2005.
[79] Patrick S. Hagan. Bermudan Pricing with a Tobin Tax. *http://www.researchgate.net/profile/Patrick_Hagan3/publications*, 2013–2014.
[80] Patrick S. Hagan, D.S. Kumar, A. Lesniewski, and D.E. Woodward. Managing smile risk. *Wilmott*, pages 83–108, 2002.
[81] Patrick S. Hagan and Diana E. Woodward. Markov Interest Rate Models. *Applied Mathematical Finance 6, 233-260*, 1999.
[82] J. Hull and A. White. Risk neutrality stays. *RISK*, 27:48, October 2014.
[83] John Hull and Alan White. A Generalized procedure for building trees for the short rate and its application to determining market implied volatility functions. *Quantitative Finance*, Forthcoming, 2014.
[84] John C. Hull, Alexander Sokol, and Alan White. Short-rate joint-measure models. *RISK*, October 2014.
[85] John C. Hull and Alan White. Pricing interest-rate derivative securities. *The Review of Financial Studies, Vol 3, No. 4, pp. 573–592*, 1990.
[86] John C. Hull and Alan White. The General Hull-White Model and Super Calibration. *http://papers.ssrn.com/sol3/papers.cfm?abstract_id=1295228*, 2000.

[87] John C. Hull and Alan White. Valuation of a CDO and nth to Default CDO Without Monte Carlo Simulation. *Journal of Derivatives*, 12(2), 2004.

[88] John C. Hull and Alan White. The fva debate. *RISK*, August 2012.

[89] John C. Hull and Alan White. Hull and white respond to their critics. *RISK*, October 2012.

[90] John C. Hull and Alan White. LIBOR vs. OIS: The Derivatives Discounting Dilemma. *http://ssrn.com/abstract=2245821*, 2013.

[91] P.J. Hunt and J.E. Kennedy. Financial Derivatives in Theory and Practice. *John Wiley & Sons Ltd*, 2004.

[92] James M. Hyman. Accurate Monotonicity Preserving Cubic Interpolation. *SIAM Journal on Scientific and Statistical Computing*, 4(4):645–654, 1983.

[93] IASB. International Accounting Standard 39 Financial Instruments: Recognition and Measurement. 2010.

[94] IFRS. IFRS 9 Project Summary. *www.ifrs.org*, 2014.

[95] Peter Jaeckel. *Monte Carlo Methods in Finance*. Whiley, 2002.

[96] Peter Jaeckel. A note on multivariate Gauss-Hermite quadrature. *http://www.jaeckel.org*, 2005.

[97] F. Jamshidian. Libor and swap market model and measures. *Finance and Stochastics*, 1:293–330, 1997.

[98] R. Jarrow and S. Turnbull. Pricing options on financial securities subject to credit risk. *Journal of Finance*, 50:53–85, 1995.

[99] Robert Jarrow and Yildiray Yildirim. Pricing Treasury Inflation Protected Securities and Related Derivatives using an HJM Model. *Journal of Financial and Quantitative Analysis* 38(2):409–430, 2003.

[100] H. Joe. *Multivariate Models and Dependence Concepts*. Chapman & Hall/CRC, New York, 1997.

[101] M. Joshi and C. Yang. Fast Gamma computations for CDO tranches. *http://ssrn.com/paper=1689348*, 2010.

[102] C. Kenyon and A. Green. Regulatory costs remain. *RISK*, 27:49, October 2014.

[103] Chris Kenyon and Andrew Green. Pricing CDS's capital relief. *RISK*, 26(10):62–66, 2014.

[104] Chris Kenyon and Andrew Green. Regulatory costs break risk neutrality. *RISK*, 27:76–80, September 2014.

[105] Chris Kenyon and Andrew Green. Dirac Processes and Default Risk. *SSRN, abstract=2593037*, pages 1–32, 2015.

[106] Chris Kenyon and Andrew Green. Warehousing credit risk: Pricing, capital and tax. *RISK*, 28:70–75, February 2015.

[107] Chris Kenyon and Roland Stamm. *Discounting, LIBOR, CVA and Funding*. PalgraveMacmillan, 2012.

[108] Jeroen Kerkhof. Inflation Derivatives Explained - Markets, Products and Pricing. *Lehman Brothers Quantitative Research, available online at http://www.scribd.com*, July 2005.

[109] David Lando. On Cox processes and credit risky securities. *Review of Derivatives Research*, 2:99–120, 1998.

[110] David Lando. *Credit Risk Modeling: Theory and Applications*. Princeton Series in Finance, 2004.

[111] Stephen Laughton and Aura Vaisbrot. In defence of fva – a response to Hull and White. *RISK*, September, 2012.
[112] M. Leclerc, Q. Liang, and I. Schneider. Fast Monte Carlo Bermudan Greeks. *RISK*, July 2009.
[113] David X. Li. On default correlation: a copula function approach. *Journal of Fixed Income*, 9:43–54, 2000.
[114] Francis A. Longstaff and Eduardo S. Schwartz. Valuing American Options by Simulation: A Simple Least-Squares Approach. *The Review of Financial Studies 38(2), 409–430*, 14, No. 1:113–147, 2001.
[115] Xiaofong Ma. Numerical Methods for the Valuation of Synthetic Collateralized Debt Obligations. *PhD Thesis, Graduate Department of Computer Science, University of Toronto*, 2007.
[116] Fiona Maxwell. South Africa still unsure about onshore CCP. *RISK*, September 2014.
[117] Fabio Mercurio. Interest Rates and The Credit Crunch: New Formulas and Market Models. *Bloomberg Portfolio Research Paper No. 2010-01-FRONTIERS*, 2009.
[118] Massimo Morini. *Understanding and Managing Model Risk*. Wiley, 2011.
[119] Bernt Øksendal. *Stochastic Differential Equations: An Introduction with Applications*. Springer, London, 2002.
[120] A. Pallavicini, D. Perini, and D. Brigo. Funding, Collateral and Hedging: Uncovering the Mechanics and the Subtleties of Funding Valuation Adjustments . *SSRN eLibrary*, 2012.
[121] European Parliament. REGULATION (EU) No 575/2013 OF THE EUROPEAN PARLIAMENT AND OF THE COUNCIL (CRR). *Official Journal of the European Union*, 2013.
[122] Xianhua Peng and Steven Kou. Default Clustering and Valuation of Collateralized Debt Obligations. *Working paper*, 2009.
[123] Vladimir Piterbarg. A Multi-currency Model with FX Volatility Skew. *http://papers.ssrn.com/sol3/papers.cfm?abstract_id=685084*, 2005.
[124] Vladimir V. Piterbarg. Smiling Hybrids. *RISK*, 2005.
[125] Vladimir V. Piterbarg. Cooking With Collateral. *RISK*, 2012.
[126] Michael Pykhtin. Model foundations of the Basel III standardised CVA charge. *RISK*, July 2012.
[127] Juan Ramirez. *Accounting for Derivatives*. John Wiley & Sons, 2007.
[128] Riccardo Rebonato, Sukhdeep Mahal, Mark Joshi, Lars-Dierk Buchholz, and Ken Nyholm. Evolving yield curves in the real-world measures: a semi-parametric approach. *Journal of Risk*, 7 No 3, 2005.
[129] Schonbucher. *Credit derivatives pricing methods*. Wiley, London, 2005.
[130] Philipp J. Schönbucher. Term structure modelling of defaultable bonds. *Review of Derivatives Research*, 2:161–192, 1998.
[131] Philipp J. Schönbucher. *Credit Derivaties Pricing Models*. 2003. Published: Wiley.
[132] Dirk Schubert. *Multi-Curve Valuation Approaches and their Application to Hedge Accounting According to IAS 39*. KPMG, 2012.
[133] Dirk Schubert. Multi-Curve Hedge Accounting Models. *RISK*, 2013.
[134] Nazneen Sherif. AAD vs GPU: banks turn to maths trick as chips lose appeal. *RISK*, January 2015.
[135] Nazneen Sherif. KVA: banks wrestle with the cost of capital. *RISK*, March 2015.
[136] Steven E. Shreve. *Stochastic Calculus for Finance II*. Springer, 2004.

[137] J. Sippel and S. Ohkoshi. All power to PRDC notes. *RISK*, 2002.

[138] E.H. Soerensen and T.F. Bollier. Pricing Swap Default Risk. *Financial Analysts Journal, 50.*, 1994.

[139] Katsumi Takada. Valuation of Arithmetic Average of Fed Funds Rates and Construction of the US dollar Swap Yield Curve. *SSRN eLibrary*, 2011.

[140] UBS. UBS Bloomberg CMCI Index Family. http://www.bloombergindexes.com/ubs-bloomberg-cmci-index-family.

[141] Oldrich Vasicek. Limiting loan loss probability distribution. *Memo, KMV corporation*, August 1987.

[142] Oldrich Vasicek. Probability of loss on a loan portfolio. *Memo, KMV corporation*, February 1987.

[143] Michael Watt. South Africa considers onshore mandate for OTC clearing. *RISK*, March 2013.

[144] Duncan Wood. Negative Eonia splits US and EU banks, traders and lawyers. *RISK*, November 2014.

Index

Printed by Printforce, the Netherlands